S0-FKL-442

Outstanding Studies in

Early American History

EDITED BY
John Murrin
Princeton University

A Garland Series

William Duane, Radical Journalist in the Age of Jefferson

Kim Tousley Phillips

Garland Publishing, Inc.
NEW YORK & LONDON 1989

Library of Congress Cataloging-in-Publication Data

Phillips, Kim Tousley.
William Duane, radical journalist in the age of Jefferson/ Kim Tousley Phillips.
p. cm. — (Outstanding studies in early American history)
Bibliography: p.
ISBN 0-8240-6193-4 (alk. paper)
1. Duane, William, 1760—1835. 2. Journalists—United States—Biography. 3. Journalism—United States—History—19th century. I. Title. II. Series.
PN4874.D8P45 1989
070.92—dc20 89-33878
[B]

Printed on acid-free, 250-year-life paper

MANUFACTURED IN THE UNITED STATES OF AMERICA

TABLE OF CONTENTS

INTRODUCTION

In 1822, the year that William Duane retired from the Aurora, a rival editor half his age admitted that he was weary of defending Duane's enemies against the fierce onslaughts from the maverick journalist. "Duane strikes away, right and left," the President one day, the Secretary of State the next, as prepared for battle as the Irish general who kept his sword in one hand and his pistol in the other. "But after writing for nearly a quarter of a century, and squabbling with almost everybody, does the Editor of the Aurora never suspect that he may be *sometimes* in the wrong?"

Duane did not suspect it very often, and when he did he was more likely to suppress the insight behind a wall of self-confident bluster than to retreat from an argument or to apologize to a wronged person. "I believe Duane to be a very honest man, and sincerely republican," Thomas Jefferson wrote to a doubting Virginian; "but his passions are stronger than his prudence, and his personal as well as general antipathies, render him very intolerant." Jefferson thought that "These traits lead him astray, & require his readers, even those who value him for his steady support of the republican cause, to be on their guard against his occasional aberrations."[1]

---

[1]Philadelphia *Franklin Gazette*, 1 Jan. 1822; Jefferson to William Wirt, 3 May 1811, William Wirt Papers, Maryland Historical Society.

Duane paid heavily for the luxury of his aberrations, in an age when newspaper editors were not expected and could ill afford to be truly independent. Sometimes he brooded on his misfortunes, and blamed his political abandonment upon the cruelty of an ungrateful public. His candor in judging political friends by the same strict principles with which they judged the common enemy was not always considered a welcome quality. But Duane brought many of his troubles upon himself, by the prickly, defensive nature of his personality. He was inclined to turn every disagreement into a quarrel and most quarrels into lasting enmities. With his talents he "might have made twenty fortunes," yet at the end of his career he was "poor and embarrassed." He was "a very foolish and unaccountable fellow," mused his friend Richard Mentor Johnson, who had "always been the worst enemy to himself that lived."[2]

Duane has suffered in historical reputation as well for his pride and independence. To an earlier generation of historians with pro-Federalist assumptions, he was among the worst of a group of "contemporary mercenary libellers," and "one must use rose colored glasses to find in them much that places them above those Lord Macauley called 'the polecats of literature.'"[3] He has been less hated but equally suspect to those succeeding generations who have

---

[2]John Quincy Adams, Memoirs of John Quincy Adams, Comprising Portions of his Diary from 1795 to 1848, Charles Francis Adams, ed., 12 vols. (Philadelphia, 1874-1877), IV (18. Jan. 1820), 507.

[3]Paul Leicester Ford to the Editor of the Nation, draft, n.d., William Duane folder, Miscellaneous Papers, New York Public Library (NYPL).

regarded the election of 1800 as the birth of a glorious age of Republican unity and virtue. Puzzled by any departure from the partyfold, they have generally concluded that he was motivated by greed and personal ambition. A wholly wrong impression persists that Duane was an ingrate and a traitor to Jefferson. The true story should be known in justice to the courageous editor.

But Duane's story has a broader significance for understanding the reality of American politics in the age of Jefferson. As much as any man of his day, Duane both understood and reflected the varied strains of belief and the inevitably rising tensions within the heterogeneous Republican party. He was a lonely prophet to the succeeding generation, for his perceptive criticisms of his times anticipated problems which were not generally comprehended until the 1830s.

It would be easy to elevate Duane to the role of a misunderstood martyr, but a mistake to pity him, for he loved and believed in the life of political involvement. He was an active observer of the American scene during the years of the first seven Presidents of the United States, and although he was accused of "squabbling with almost everybody," he enjoyed the friendship of two Presidents who always respected his integrity and appreciated his public service, Thomas Jefferson and Andrew Jackson.

CHAPTER I

IRELAND AND INDIA

The earliest years of William Duane are mysterious and lost to memory, even to the boy and man who never knew his father and could never discover the exact place of his birth, or recapture his origins except in imagination. His parents John and Anastasia Sarsfield Duane emigrated from Ireland to the northern frontier of America, near Lake Champlain, and their only child was born on May 17, 1760, somewhere in that remote region. John Duane cleared a farm for his family and hired out as a surveyor for the lands of other arriving settlers. The little farming settlements were nestled in a region whose lakes and rivers and thick forests had first been penetrated by French trappers, moving south along the tributaries of the St. Lawrence River. When William was born, the French and British were at war for the area's rich fur trade, and his father went as a soldier on the side of the French and was wounded. The British victories then put upper New York and all Canada into her possession.

In 1765 John Duane died and Anastasia abandoned the little settlement and took her five year old son away from his lonely birthplace. The boy always felt the loss of his father. As he grew up his personality was affected by the lack of any adult in his life with whom he could identify, or who could give him encouragement and approval. At many points one may glimpse his unconscious yearning for a father figure. It had its most satisfactory resolution in his friendship with Thomas Jefferson and in his loving relationship to his own children.

Anastasia took William to Baltimore first and then they moved to Philadelphia, where he could remember being sent to learn his letters from an old woman who kept school in her home. But his mother was lonely or could not manage on her own in a foreign city; she missed Ireland and decided to go back to County Tipperary, to the family village of Clonmel. William was about eleven when they went, old enough to remember his first country with a vague pride and regret. In his mind America became associated with the idealuzed qualities of his pioneer father--vigorous and brave and manly.[1]

In Clonmel the family was part of the small Roman Catholic middle class. As landowners they were far more prosperous than the vast majority of the Catholic population, which two hundred years of English incursions had reduced to semi-slavery, tenant farming on lands confiscated for the ruling Protestant gentry. Anastasia's maiden name, Sarsfield, was a highly respected one in Ireland, and she was said to be a descendant of the Jacobite military hero

---

[1] Claude G. Bowers, "William Duane," Dictionary of American Biography (DAB), Allen Johnson and Dumas Malone, eds., 21 vols. (New York, 1928-1944), V, 467-468; Allen C. Clark, "William Duane," Records of the Columbia Historical Society, IX (1906), 14-62; [William Duane,II], A Biographical Memoir of William J. Duane (Philadelphia, 1868), 1; E[lizabeth] D[uane] Gillespie, A Book of Remembrance (Philadelphia, 1901), 14; Philadelphia North American, 8 Dec. 1907; India Office Records, Home Miscellaneous Series, 537 (Library of the India Office, Commonwealth Relations Office, London), 22, 138; Aurora, 19 May 1801.

Patrick Sarsfield, whom the dethroned King James II had elevated for his valor in the Irish campaigns against King William III. The family of William's father was also from Clonmel, but an elder brother and a sister had escaped the arid, confining life of the village and gone to London. John's sister had married Michael Bray, who came from a prominent family among the Catholic gentry of Clonmel. Matthew Duane made a spectacular rise to prominence in London, as a barrister and specialist in land law, but especially as an expert on ancient coins, becoming a Fellow of the Royal Society and a trustee of the British Museum.[2]

William was sent to a school taught by Franciscan friars during his adolescent years, and it is probably true that his mother meant him to be "bred for a Roman Catholic priest." But he rebelled violently against the narrow piety and inhumane spirit of his teachers, and against his mother's timid and conventional views. He demanded an explanation for the wretched condition of the Irish people, and was not satisfied with the sterile political tradition which took solace in the memory of brave defeat in the cause of the Catholic Stuarts. The rebellious youth concluded from his own observations and instincts that the priesthood kept the people ignorant and passive, and deserved a large share of the blame for their political

---

[2]William P. Burke, History of Clonmel (Waterford, Ireland, 1907), 96, 108, 111, 112-166, 301, 315, 328; [Duane], Biog. Memoir of W.J.Duane, 1-2; Marquis of Ruvigny and Raineval, The Jacobite Peerage (Edinburgh, 1904), 81-82; John Burke and John Bernard Burke, A Genealogical and Heraldic Dictionary of the Landed Gentry of Great Britain and Ireland, 3 vols. (London, 1846), II, 1189-90; Warwick Wroth, "Matthew Duane," Dictionary of National Biography (DNB), Leslie Stephen and Sidney Lee, eds., 66 vols. (London, 1885-1901), XVI, 76.

bondage. In Ireland, he wrote later, the "human mind is besotted and benumbed," and "reformation is likely to spread itself to Siberia, or Constantinople, ere it will arrest the attention of the Irish people." He had a skeptical outlook upon "the character of the people and the unfabled history of the nation" for some time after he escaped his mother's constricted world into a cosmopolitan life of his own choosing. It was only when he returned to the United States that Duane became an Irish nationalist.[3]

The rejection of his early religious training had a lasting effect on Duane's adult character and convictions. It took courage for the strong-willed boy to defy the monks, and the experience undoubtedly gave him some of his instinctive distrust of authority and combative self-confidence. Throughout his life he was hostile to the Roman Catholic church in Europe, but he was also unsympathetic to clergymen generally and distrusted most formal religious expression. He was a child of his generation in the militant secularism of his politics. When he returned to America, he found a congenial spirit in his political companions. But this outspoken secularism was muted in the following generation; it almost seemed to be confined to those who reached adulthood in the 1780s. If he had remained in Ireland, he probably would have joined in the Society of United Irish, a movement dedicated to the notion that the people must renounce the religious prejudices which kept them separated and unite nationalistically to demand their political

---

[3]J.Q. Adams, Memoirs, IV (18 Jan. 1820), 508; William Duane, A Visit to Colombia, in the years 1822 & 1823 . . . (Philadelphia, 1826), 492; The (Calcutta) World, 4 Feb., 14 July 1792.

freedom. Led by members of Duane's own generation, it was the only willfully secular movement in Ireland's bloody political history. Its abortive rebellion of 1798 was ruthlessly suppressed by British forces and most of its leaders were killed or executed.[4]

The conflict between mother and son reached its climax in 1779 when the nineteen year old boy married a Protestant girl. Catharine Corcoran, who was the seventeen year old child of William Corcoran of Clonmel, may already have been pregnant with the son who was born to them in the spring of 1780. His mother refused to receive the girl, and no doubt accused her son of wasting his education and spoiling his opportunities. Her pride met her son's headstrong temper and the two quarreled beyond reconciliation. When Anastasia died her only son was disinherited.

The pattern of Duane's compulsive self-defensiveness, in wrong as in right actions, may have been permanently fixed by this crucial episode ending in estrangement from his mother. In effect he had been twice orphaned, and the loneliness of his early years contributed to his passionate temperament and the intensity of his personal relationships. He was a warm, generous, gregarious person, but quick to anger, who placed a high value on the virtue of loyalty. In later years his political contemporaries understood his emotionalism, and knew that the most effective way to influence him was through expressions of respect and affection.

Duane went to work in Clonmel as an apprentice in a print-

---

[4]Robert R. Palmer, The Age of the Democratic Revolution, A Political History of Europe and America, 1760-1800, 2 vols. (Princeton, 1964), II, 491-505.

ing establishment. He needed to learn a trade in order to support Catharine and the baby, and as a printer he could apply his gentleman's education, and begin to satisfy his curiosity about the world and his awakened interest in politics. Probably his employer was Edward Collins, a Dubliner who had established the village's first newspaper, the Clonmel Gazette or Hibernian Advertiser. Politically the paper denounced Stuartism and extolled English Whiggery. These views were in direct contrast to what Duane had been reared to believe, but they were shared for a number of years by the perversely independent young Irishman.

The young family left Tipperary and went to London when William John was two years old. Duane introduced himself to his rich Uncle Matthew, who suggested that he study the law, according to the younger man's reminiscence. Duane said that he refused the invitation because he disapproved of the class of lawyers as the exploiters of less privileged men. His prejudice against the field of law was a part of his developing political philosophy which grew steadily stronger throughout his lifetime. In February 1785, when he had been working as a journalist in the city for more than two years, Matthew Duane died of a paralytic stroke. He left the bulk of his estate to Michael Bray, William's London-born first cousin. Bray soon after was admitted to membership in Matthew Duane's own Lincoln Inn.[5]

---

[5][Duane], Biog. Memoir of W.J. Duane, 1-3; Burke, Hist. of Clonmel, 346-350; London Gentleman's Magazine, LV, part I (1785), 157; Lincoln's Inn, Records of the Honorable Society of Lincoln's Inn, Admissions, 1420-1893, 2 vols. (London, 1896), I, 521.

During his London years, from 1782 to 1786, Duane was probably employed as a parliamentary reporter on the _General Advertiser_. The journal was among the least prosperous of London's eight daily newspapers. Its owner John Almon had acquired notoriety in the 1760s for his pamphleteering in support of William Pitt and the opposition to the government's repressive policy toward North America. In this period his political loyalty was to Charles James Fox's Whig party.

Parliamentary reporting in the 1780s was an exciting and difficult journalistic assignment, excellent training for a man who aspired to be a newspaper editor. The publication of debates was the only regular source of political news in England. Legally the practice was considered a "breach of privilege," for Parliament had quickly perceived that a verbatim account of debates could be used as indirect criticism of the government. But the rule had not been enforced since Parliament's failure several years earlier to convict some determined journalists who had defied the prohibition. When Duane learned his craft as a shorthand reporter, it was a flourishing and highly competitive profession, requiring quickness, determination and a good deal of stamina.[6]

Duane left the _General Advertiser_ in 1786 for unknown reasons. Perhaps he was discouraged with his prospects for advance-

---

[6] _Aurora_, 9 Aug. 1834; [Duane], _Biog. Memoir of W.J. Duane_, 3; Edward Smith, "John Almon (1737-1805)," _DNB_, I, 340-342; _The History of the Times: 'The Thunderer' in the Making, 1785-1841_ (London, 1935), 21-23; H.R. Fox Bourne, _English Newspapers: Chapters in the History of Journalism_, 2 vols. (London, 1887), I, 249-251; London _General Advertiser_, 21 Oct. 1795 - 28 Feb. 1796, in Burney Collection, British Museum.

ment, or he may have been dismissed by Almon, who was in financial difficulties following a libel suit by the Prime Minister, William Pitt the younger. The publisher testified that he had been away from the city in October when a paragraph was inserted suggesting that Pitt had used privileged information to make ten thousand pounds in the stock market. The jury did not follow the advice of Chief Justice Lord Mansfield to impose a heavy fine in order to discourage future attacks on public figures, but the conviction itself was a disgrace from which the failing newspaper did not recover, and it closed three years later.[7]

II

When he was twenty-six Duane left England and sailed for India, his fourth country of residence within the British empire. He was inspired to go by curiosity and ambition, and perhaps also by the wish to be free of his wife, whom he left behind without regret. She and the three young children, William John, Catharine and Patrick, were sent back to Clonmel to wait until he would send for them. Duane later said that he had first "sought to procure a passage to the United States," his birthplace, but when that was unsuccessful he enlisted as a private in the military service of the East India Company. It was an ignoble position; many of the officers were mere boys in their teens and most of the enlisted

---

[7] Aurora, 19 May 1801; [John Almon], Memoirs of a Late Eminent Bookseller . . . (London, 1790), 236-262; [John Almon], Biographical, Literary and Political Anecdotes of Several of the Most Eminent Persons of the Present Age, 3 vols. (London, 1797), I, 360-364; Fox Bourne, Eng. Newspapers, I, 237-238.

men were native Indians, called sepoys. But as a recruit he received free passage to India and a license to reside in that country from the East India Company. It is unlikely that he ever intended to give up journalism in order to pursue a military career in the tropics. In any case he was summarily dismissed from the Company's service when the Rodney docked in Calcutta in July 1787.[8]

The Company relented after several months and hired him as a clerk in the revenue department. He continued as a civil servant until 1791, earning two hundred rupees a month, which maintained him in modest comfort. He had been in Calcutta about two and a half years when he received the opportunity he wanted. Two owners of the Bengal Journal, Edward Cassan and James Dunkin, approached him late in 1789 and invited him to become the managing editor of their paper. The two were lawyers in Calcutta and their partner Edward Camac was a civil servant. Because they badly needed a trained printer, they offered to sell Duane a two-ninths interest in the journal, to be paid for by deductions from his salary.

In January 1790 Duane took over as editor of the five year old newspaper, which was in financial difficulties, was poorly equipped and had a low circulation. Responding to the situation with eagerness and bold extravagance, a characteristic which was to keep him in trouble most of his life, he borrowed money without consulting his partners and purchased a set of expensive European types. The partners refused to pay when the loan fell due, and Duane had to borrow again at 12 per cent interest in order to meet

---

[8] India Office Records, Home Misc. Series, Vol. 537, 137-138, 222.

the obligation. But gradually he was able to improve the newspaper's standing, and after a year he resigned from the revenue department to work full time as an editor. At thirty he thought that his ambition was realized; then suddenly an incident in Calcutta reversed his prospects and nearly destroyed him.[9]

In May 1791 a rumor circulated in Calcutta that the Governor General of Bengal, Lord Cornwallis, had died on a military expedition in Bangalore. The Bengal Journal of Saturday, May 21, dismissed the story as false and malicious, and commented that it had been traced "to some particular distinguished persons among the renigade French." The gratuitous assault reflected the idealistic young editor's feeling that the French in India were mere adventurers, who were indifferent or opposed to their great national revolution. The British in Bengal are "among the most ardent advocates of freedom themselves," the editorial continued, "yet generously protect those who are not from harm and support them in safety and splendor."[10]

The French commandant in Calcutta, a Colonel Canaple, was an aging monarchist who had not been replaced in office by the new republican government. When he was told of the English newspaper article, he took it as a direct attack on himself since he was the

---

[9]Ibid., 91, 186; Margarita Barns, The Indian Press: A History of the Growth of Public Opinion in India (London, 1940), 63; The World, 29 Sept. 1792.

[10]India Office Records, Home Misc. Series, Vol. 537, 1-111, contains a complete documentary account of the incident; Barns, The Indian Press, 64; John Malcolm, The Political History of India from 1784 to 1823, 2 vols. (London, 1826), II, 293-294.

most "distinguished" Frenchman in the city. He protested immediately to Charles Stuart, the senior member of the British Governor General's Council, who directed the Council's secretary to investigate the incident. Secretary Edward Hay summoned Duane to appear in his office on Monday morning, and requested him to make a "suitable apology" to the Colonel. The inexperienced editor was surprised and rather alarmed that the article had offended his own government, and he readily agreed to retract his statement.

On Tuesday morning he evaded an angry delegation of French residents, bent on violent protest, and went to Canaple's house for his interview. He was kept waiting for an hour while the commandant discussed the incident with two supporters and the English officer, named Conway, who was to speak for him. When Duane was invited into the drawing room, he presented Conway with a copy of Saturday's newspaper and asked him to identify the passages to be retracted. But the Tory officer did not intend to let him go without forcing a confession of guilt from the vulnerable editor. He demanded to know why such articles were ever printed, and told Duane that he should ask permission before publishing any statement about an individual. At first Duane responded politely, asking again for the retraction, but his easily bruised pride could not endure Conway's goading. He lashed out that the Englishman understood nothing about the British press or the British constitution if he thought that newspapers had no right to express political criticism. The disastrous events which followed unfortunately revealed that the officer understood far better than he the nature of British justice as it was practiced in India.

The editor denied that Colonel Canaple had been slandered in the disputed paragraph, since there were several "distinguished" Frenchmen in Calcutta, but Conway replied that it was "evident" who was intended. "You heard the report yourself then," Duane retorted. Finally Conway demanded that he apologize to the commandant. He replied that he would make "reparation for alleged offence" by retracting the article, but he would not apologize because that would be an acknowledgment of guilt. The enraged officer threatened that he would be deported from India for his insolence, but he rejoined that his "language dictated by the heart" would not offend the government, and he left the interview in a spirit of reckless courage. The young man felt sure that he "spoke . . . the sentiments of no Enemy to the British Interests or prosperity."

To Edward Hay he attempted to explain his failure to keep his promise. He and Canaple had quarreled, he admitted, because the Colonel was "despotic" as were "almost all the French of Note in India," whereas "With me it has operated otherwise, born and bred on the bosom of America and confirmed in my love of freedom by a long residence under the British Government." He had been prepared to satisfy the commandant, with dignity, but "upon the whole reparation was not so much sought as humiliation and . . . a sacrifice to pride was required rather than to justice."

The angry Frenchman sent his own account of Duane's conduct in the interview. He said that the editor told him he had been sent to find out if "I was the first author" of the rumor about Lord Cornwallis, and "alsc in a violent manner desired to know if I had not repeated this account to any body." The following day the aggrieved Colonel received a letter of consolation from the British officials, assuring him that they had treated the outrageous statement "against a person of his station and character, with the contempt which it merited."

The Governor General's Council decided at once to punish Duane for the incident to the fullest extent of its power. The members were unfamiliar with the nature of their authority over editors because they had little prior experience with newspaper censorship. The first English newspaper in India, William Hickey's _Bengal Gazette_, had criticized the administration a few year earlier, but the government had successfully forced it out of business by creating a second newspaper. The _Bengal Journal_ survived despite government patronage of the _Calcutta Gazette_, so more drastic action was needed to silence its editor. But Duane was not in the service of the East India Company and therefore had no license to be in the country.

The Council members drafted an inquiry to the Advocate General of Bengal to learn what powers they had over citizens who resided there of sufferance: Did the Governor General have the authority to send William Duane to Europe? If so could the Council keep him imprisoned until the ship sailed, or was it bound to accept security for his appearance? Finally they asked, did the authority to deport him imply authority to use force for this purpose," either because he was unlicensed or because his offense "appears to Government to require such punishment?"

The Council's vindictive spirit toward a completely unknown citizen was rather astounding. Even the home government in London was surprised when it was informed of the incident. The members presumably felt the extreme delicacy at that time of Britain's relations with France, especially in India. Her military and commercial triumph there was still very recent, and the French nationals were potentially dangerous allies of the yet unspecified native states. Moreover the civil government of the colony was in a difficult phase of administering the transition of power from the East India Company to the authority of the crown and parliament. From its viewpoint the Governor General's Council felt fully justified in terminating the civil liberties of a British colonist in Calcutta.[11]

On June 1 Advocate General T. H. Davies gave the opinion that the Council possessed absolute authority over unlicensed British subjects. It was legally free to arrest Duane, to use force if necessary, and to hold him without bond until his departure for Europe. But "it would appear an act of rigour to confine without necessity," he cautioned, and suggested that the offender be allowed to post security unless there was a genuine threat of dangerous behavior.

Duane was arrested at his home on the morning of June 2 by a body of armed sepoys under the command of Lieutenant Cosmo Gordon.

---

[11]H.H. Dodwell, "The Exclusion of the French, 1784-1815," British India, 1497-1858, H.H. Dodwell, ed., Vol. V of The Cambridge History of India (Cambridge, 1929), 323-326; Lilian M. Penson, "The Bengal Administrative System, 1786-1818," ibid., 433-461.

The arresting officer presented him with a statement that he was to be sent to Europe on the first Company ship leaving Calcutta during the autumn season. In the meantime bail had been set at the prohibitive sum of 20,000 rupees. He was imprisoned at Fort William just outside the city, the military and civil headquarters of the British government in Bengal and the site of the famous Black Hole of Calcutta.

From Thursday until Monday he remained in his cell in a kind of dazed apathy, waiting for his partners to free him. In the long silence he began to realize that they had deserted him, but he informed the Council that his friends probably held back from fear of the government's disapproval. Meanwhile someone in Calcutta decided that it was an opportune moment to buy a share in the *Bengal Journal* and sent the prisoner an offer of 6,000 rupees for his interest. Duane asked permission to go into the city to arrange the transaction.

His partners were wholly intent upon saving their property from the consequences of the editor's folly. They invaded his home and office and removed everything belonging to the *Journal*, then sent a representative to see what he had carried with him to prison. Duane tried to prevent John Stapleton from entering his cell when he realized his mission, but the intruder forced his way in and ransacked the editor's few personal belongings. At ten o'clock that evening the prisoner wrote to the Council in desperation to plead for permission to visit Calcutta and save his affairs from ruin.

Under the circumstances the members relented the worst of their harsh measures. They allowed him to enter the city under armed guard, and at the same time reduced his bond to 4,000 rupees, one half to be paid by the prisoner and one quarter by each of two other guarantors. At last he was able to secure a lawyer, Samuel Peat, who filed for a writ of habeas corpus. There was some further delay but his case finally received a hearing before Justice John Hyde of the Supreme Court of Bengal on Thursday, June 16, after he had been in prison for two weeks without charges against him. The attorney for the East India Company, William Jackson, argued that the government had the right to hold Duane without charge pending transportation to England. The Court deliberated at length on the unique situation, then ruled unanimously in favor of the Council and remanded the prisoner to custody in Fort William.

In his cell "a bed, a desk, a rheam of paper, and an old fiddle were the only comforts they left me," he remembered, "except a good stock of animal spirits, which enabled me to scribble care away for two solitary months" of imprisonment.[12] Eventually two Indian citizens of Calcutta, probably professional money lenders, posted security for him. On July 20 he was released on bail and returned to the city.

It appeared that he would go back to his family in disgrace and without a shilling to show for his four years in India. His partners refused to let him sell his share in the Bengal Journal since they had only to wait until his interest would revert to them.

---

[12] The World, 29 Sept. 1792.

They agreed to submit the case to arbitration, after he threatened a lawsuit, but put off the date until late in autumn.[13] In September he petitioned the Council to allow him to remain in Calcutta, since he had been punished enough for his misconduct and could assure the government of his future good behavior. The Council dismissed his plea without consideration, and a month later ordered him to sail for Europe on November 10 aboard the Queen Indiaman.

Suddenly the sentence of exile was lifted just before his departure by a decision as arbitrary as that which imposed it. Colonel Canaple had died during the summer and Duane addressed a last plea for mercy to his successor. The new commandant was an agent of republican France and may have been privately sympathetic to the editor's criticism of his predecessor's royalist predilection. He submitted the view that Duane was an unfortunate man who was sincerely repentant, and that Colonel Canaple would have been satisfied. When the Frenchman interceded the Council reversed its decision without hesitation. Duane regained his freedom as quickly as he had lost it five months earlier.

The British officials in Calcutta had not obtained advice from London during this incident because of the slow transit of mail between India and England. The views of the Court of Directors of the East India Company arrived in April 1792, half a year after the affair was settled. In their opinion the Council had been correct in asking Duane to apologize for the insult to Canaple, since the French were under British protection in India, "and under

---

[13] Ibid.

circumstances which merited the most attentive and liberal conduct toward them." But in future "It will be very desirable and proper that on similar occasions, parties who may find themselves aggrieved should prosecute the offender for the supposed libel in the Supreme Court Judicature." The London officials reminded the Council that this was "the most constitutional mode of proceeding" in such matters. The authorities in Bengal had used arbitrary and excessive force against Duane, for an offense which they knew to be trivial, largely because there was no one to stop them or to protect his civil rights on the occasion.

III

The reprieve opened a new period of prosperity in Duane's life in Calcutta. For a time it appeared that he would succeed in making his fortune as the publisher of the best newspaper in British India. He established a four page weekly called the World soon after his release with 10,000 rupees loaned to him by an unknown benefactor.[14] Duane could not afford to purchase printing equipment, but had the paper published by a local printer in excellent type on fine heavy stock paper. It soon attracted a profitable amount of advertising for public sales of goods arrived from England and for other events and services.

Variety was to be the guiding principle of the new journal which sought to attract a wide readership among the European residents. The coverage of social news was extensive--vital statistics,

---

[14]India Office Records, Home Misc. Series, Vol. 537, 201-202; The World, 15 Oct. 1791.

arrivals and departures, horse races and concerts, meetings of the local freemasons. And it provided the commercial, military and administrative news so important to the life of the colonists.

Politically the chastened editor was highly cautious. "It is the opinion of the _Editor_, that all subjects whatever, ought, _of right_ to be publicly, openly, and unboundedly discussed," he stated at the outset; "but this opinion he urges only as a _Citizen_ of the _World_. The _interests_ of particular communities . . . restrict such discussions."[15] Certainly Bengal was such a community and the _World_ largely avoided editorial comment on colonial matters. It provided straightforward news of Bengal and greater India and occasionally praised the government for its successes, especially Lord Cornwallis who was always treated as a hero.

The paper's outstanding feature was the extensive and intelligent treatment of political news from Europe. The young editor wanted to reform journalism of its "paragraphic plagirism"; he did not publish verbatim accounts but gave his readers a judicious summary of events in Europe. In English politics the paper was biased in favor of Charles James Fox and the Whig party. Probably most of its readers were Englishmen of that persuasion.

Duane created an admirable newspaper in his first endeavor as an independent editor. Journalistically the _World_ was in some ways superior to the less objective Philadelphia _Aurora_. Duane was always a vigorous writer with a gift for lively and forceful expression. As a young man the handsome, vagabond Irishman was amazingly

---

[15]_Ibid_.

gay and cheerful and his high spirits appeared in the pages of his newspaper. In later years he was more opinionated, more embattled, and the *Aurora* lacked some of the charm of his youthful good humor.[16]

Legal entanglements and debts left from the period of political imprisonment retarded his growing prosperity. His former partners in the *Bengal Journal* were reluctant to buy him out, and in the spring of 1792 the case went to arbitration. Duane was awarded 6,643 rupees with costs to be paid by the defendants. This was wholly satisfactory to him but the owners refused to abide by the decision, and after a year of delays succeeded in tricking him out of his money. Edward Camac, the largest shareholder, appealed in the Supreme Court of Bengal, and his attorney James Dunkin, a former partner in the *Journal*, proved that the arbitration award was technically invalid because it deviated from the obligation of the bond filed with the arbiters; hence the judgment was forfeit. This tawdry transaction was the young journalist's first experience with suits at law and it deeply confirmed his instinctive distrust of lawyers.[17]

Duane's respectable role as a rising publisher was compromised slightly in the spring of 1792 by a quarrel over an English actress. He declared that he was the close friend and protector of the lady in question. This woman may have been the mother of the three small children who mysteriously were in Duane's custody at the time that he departed from India. Michael Roworth, the manager of

---

[16]See *The World*, 15 Oct. 1791 - 9 Feb. 1793, Library of the India Office, Commonwealth Relations Office, London.

[17]*The World*, 22, 29 Sept. 1792, 2 Feb. 1793.

the local English theater, had been spurned by the actress and being jealous of Duane he refused to let him eat backstage with the cast before a performance. For a time Duane complied with the interference with his custom, but one night in March there was a special benefit performance given by a friend of his in which the actress was to appear. On this occasion he took his usual seat in the wings and the manager ordered him out of the theater. He yielded his protest when the argument began to disturb the performance. At the end of the evening he returned to "hand the lady to her palanquin," which he considered his duty in order to protect her "from *certain* attacks." Roworth saw him and flew into a rage, but as he called for assistance to throw him out bodily, Duane grabbed him by the nose, gave it two good yanks, "and then returned to avoid the military guard which that instant made its appearance."

As Duane explained later to the judge when he was tried for assault and battery, it was an affair of honor which could not be handled in any other manner. But the judge ruled that the circumstances behind Roworth's behavior were inadmissable as evidence, and thereby "much of that part of the cause which promised to afford amusement was lost to the crowd which attended to hear the trial." The jury decided on a small fine against Duane for the assault on his rival.[18]

IV

In Europe the monarchical powers led by Great Britain were drawing steadily nearer to a war against France by which to turn

---

[1]*Ibid.*, 21 July, 1792.

back the results of her republican Revolution. These international developments had a profound impact on the mind of the young editor in Calcutta and transformed the nature of his political philosophy. He would have liked to remain circumspect in his political comments and stay out of further trouble with the officials in Calcutta. But the evidence that Britain was capable of the ruthless suppression of liberty in another country forced him to abandon his safe liberal sentiments and to speak out for the right of revolution against tyranny.

The World had depicted Great Britain to the homesick colonists as a nation justly "at the height of grandeur and prosperity." "We have lost an Empire, but we have gained one." In America "we have laid the foundation for civilization and the extension of science infallibly in the most extensive region of the earth." And now "on the shores of Asia, we plant science and give peace and prospering security to her long oppressed natives; while we found a new Empire of our own happy and secure to the nations of India and valuable to ourselves."[19]

At home England needed reform of her Parliament, but Duane avowed that extreme measures for change would be as undesirable as the existing corruption. In all political questions "the mediate is preferable to either extremes." A healthy transformation was already taking place, in his opinion, and "the defective or abused parts of her constitution undergoing a temperate and patient cure."[20]

---

[19] Ibid., 30 June 1792. [20] Ibid., 14 July, 6 Oct. 1792.

The *World* acknowledged that "Next to the interest which we feel for home, the situation of France moves our anxiety." Duane openly supported the Revolution in spite of his strictures against extremism. France was exempted from the rule of moderation because her people had been so sunk in misery under the old regime that only radical measures could save them. In 1792 Duane praised France for retaining a formal monarchy, "a singular proof of the prudential sagacity" of her leaders, but he adapted his thinking and excused each new example of radicalism and terror.[21]

Unrealistic optimism pervaded the *World*'s assessment of the political situation in Europe. Duane predicted that France would not be invaded because her strength would intimidate her eastern neighbors and "we cannot suppose the British nation capable of cherishing the despoilers of France or encouraging ignobly the enemies of her liberty." Most English colonists did not share his generous feelings toward their traditional enemy, but he sought to re-educate them. The fear of territorial gains by a rival was founded upon the outmoded principle of the balance of power, he argued, whereas the true protection of a nation's interests was in its thriving trade relations. International political changes could not hurt Great Britain so long as she maintained her commercial greatness. Duane further denied that French terrorism could in any way threaten the domestic harmony of England. Implicit in this alarm was the grave error of "*supposing the people of England on a parallel with those of France*." The crucial difference be-

---

[21]*Ibid.*, 30 June 1792.

tween them was that the English people possessed a large measure of liberty and of property which they would never choose to jeopardize.[22]

As the two countries moved toward war, Duane eventually was forced to declare himself. Without renouncing Britain he unhesitatingly gave his support on the side of liberty and the new order in Europe. The defense of France would plant "the seedlings," he believed, "either of endless glory to this great epoch and happiness to man, or the retrogradation of refined Europe to its prestine [*sic*] Gothic barbarism and brutal servitude." To the idealistic editor it mattered little that his rhetorical division placed his own nation on the side of barbarism. But the British officials took a narrower view and with each Saturday's editorial Duane was helping to write himself a new sentence of exile.[23]

His reflections on liberty in Europe led him unintentionally into criticism of the colonial system abroad. Republican France for example was guilty of "adherence to principles of coercion" in her colonies which at home her people had rejected as "unbearable." But "it is the system of Holland--of England--of all who possess foreign territory," he continued in innocent comment. Duane avoided discussing the situation in India, but condemned the evils of black slavery in Africa. The trouble, he suggested, was that white men's "wants created by artificial means are become necessities thro custom." The simpler values of the new Europe would provide an example for the future.[24]

---

[22] *Ibid.*, 14 July, 18 Aug., 6 Oct. 1792

[23] *Ibid.*, 6 Oct. 1792. [24] *Ibid.*, 14 July, 8 Dec. 1792.

Duane imposed upon the government's tolerance directly when the _World_ became a repository for complaints by the officers of the East India Company Army. The Company men received lower benefits of pay, furlough and promotion than the officers in the King's service, and they pressed for changes in the code of military regulations. Their grievances were well received by the new Governor General of Bengal, Sir John Shore, and by the Board of Control in London, but the long delay in framing a new code created a crisis in military discipline. In 1795 a mutiny was averted by the timely if belated arrival of the new regulations. The _World_ opened its columns to the protesting officers between 1792 and 1794 when the quarrel had not reached dangerous proportions, but the Governor General apparently thought that its role was potentially menacing. The editor's opinions on European politics had convinced him that Duane was an irresponsible agitator and his paper an undesirable influence in the colony.[25]

V

On May 30, 1794, the government of Bengal abruptly decided that William Duane was _persona non grata_ and would be deported

---

[25] _Ibid._, 14 July, 18, 25 Aug., 22 Sept., 10, 24 Nov. 1792; John Shore (Lord Teignmouth), _The Private Record of an Indian Governor-Generalship: The Correspondence of Sir John Shore, Governor-General, with Henry Dundas, President of the Board of Control, 1793-1798_, Holden Furber, ed. (Cambridge, Mass., 1933), 9-16; Sir John Shore to Henry Dundas, Jan. 1794, Charles J. Shore (Second Baron, Lord Teignmouth), _Memoirs of the Life and Correspondence of John Lord Teignmouth_, 2 vols. (London, 1843), I, 275-282; _Calcutta Gazette_, 18 Sept. 1794, W.S. Seton-Kerr, ed., _Selections from the Calcutta Gazette, 1784-1823_, 5 vols. (London, 1864-1869), II, 393-394.

from British India. Governor Shore in a secret meeting of the Council explained that the action was necessary because of the "impropriety and intemperance of various publications" in his newspaper. As before it was legally simple because he was unlicensed and "resides here by sufferance only." The Council, composed of the same men who had punished him three years earlier, swiftly agreed to Shore's request and immediately issued an order for Duane to depart at the beginning of the autumn season and to furnish "good and substantial security" for his compliance.[26]

The stunned editor pleaded for reconsideration of the hasty decision. "Should there be any specific subject which Government may think proper to prohibit the discussion of," he offered, "I shall avoid it in silence." He was naive to imagine that voluntary censorship was still possible, for his political thinking had moved too far distant from acceptable opinion. The Council rejected his appeal but relented on security and allowed him his freedom without bond until his departure.

Duane was unable to sell his newspaper which was entangled in debts and under the blight of government censure. Its good reputation had been steadily dwindling as the English residents grew alarmed by its seeming disloyalty to the mother country. Indeed one colonist had organized his friends into an informal committee to drive the *World* out of business, and its subscriptions and advertising had declined before the official action which destroyed it.

---

[26] India Office Records, Home Misc. Series, Vol. 537, 112-226, contains a complete documentary account of the banishment; Barns, *The Indian Press*, 65-66.

The same colonist supervised a physical attack upon the editor but was later vindicated by a sympathetic jury. The man had sued Duane for recovery of a long-standing debt and suspected that the editor would fail to appear and answer the charges. Consequently he went to Duane's house on the day of the trial with a gang of Indians carrying clubs and chubdar sticks and personally dragged him by the hair to the courtroom. Duane later testified that he had kicked him in the head with iron heeled boots, but by June the editor's standing in Calcutta was so low that a grand jury refused to bring a charge against the assailant. Possibly his enraged creditor was the former benefactor who had loaned him the money to found a Whig newspaper in Calcutta and who felt betrayed by the radical turn of its politics.

In November he was no better prepared to leave than in June and his situation was complicated by the fact that he had three small children. Duane said that he was the guardian of the orphaned boys named Andrews whose father had been an English naval officer killed in the King's service. He appealed to the government for clemency in consideration of the children, but the tactic was useless, and two final petitions for additional time were dismissed with the demand that he be prepared to leave on the date appointed. The destiny of the children is obscure; they returned with Duane to England but did not accompany him to America. Two of them came to the United States as young adults however and he did what he could to help them become established.[27]

---

[27]William Duane to unknown, 14 Aug. 1812, James Wright Brown Collection, New York Historical Society (NYHS).

In the months awaiting exile Duane began to grow bitter toward Great Britain and his thoughts turned nostalgically toward his homeland, America. His only wish was "to proceed and spend my life in my native country," he assured the Council, but was denied his request to await a ship which would take him directly to the United States from India. At some point he applied for help from the American Ambassador in London, John Jay, but was ignored since he had no evidence of United States citizenship.

Several Company ships of the first division were docked in Calcutta at the end of December, preparing their cargoes for the journey to Europe. Duane's departure could be delayed no longer, and on December 26 he published his last edition. "Englishmen," he wrote, "I have experienced the blessings of Liberty in your country and for a time I wished to be as one of you." But now he would return to America where "I shall be received with esteem" by "all who knew me." "I left them without disgrace, I return without disgrace, I trust in God I shall find them free, that I may forget if possible that Slavery exists anywhere."

The same day he wrote to beg an audience with the Governor General, in desperate hope for a delay or a property settlement. "As it is my purpose," he threatened, "to publish tomorrow the state of the Grievances which I have sustained under this Government, an intimation that I shall have the honor of a hearing will prevent it." To be certain that his letter would be seen by Shore, he added a note to Sir John's private secretary: he would wait until nine that evening and if no reply came he would publish his case through Calcutta and the province. The circulars were already printed.

The Governor General read the letter and sent for him to appear at Fort William early the next morning. Duane came in the belief that Shore had consented to listen to his grievances. Instead he was arrested at the entrance to the Governor's apartment by a squad of sepoys with fixed bayonets, conducted to a cell within the Fort and held for immediate transportation to Europe.

That day a copy of the threatened publication was found posted in the barracks of the New Fort. The circular informed the officers that Duane was a martyr in their cause and that "This points out to you the opposition you are to expect by the attack made on him--whose only crime is having spoken your sentiments." But Duane misunderstood or perhaps misrepresented the reasons for his banishment.

The government by this time was certain that the troublesome journalist was a dangerous criminal and took extraordinary precautions to prevent his escape. During the three days until he could be placed on a departing ship, he was kept under the constant watch of an armed guard and could speak to a visitor only with a military officer present. Captain Charles Mitchell of the _William Pitt_ was warned that his prisoner might attempt to escape into the delta while the ship was towed down the Ganges from Calcutta to the ocean. The government charged Mitchell with the responsibility for delivering him safely in Europe.

On New Year's Day, 1795, Duane began a six months journey

from India to England as a prisoner in the hold of an East India Company ship. The children were with him, placed aboard by government order and at government expense, and soon looked like urchins from lack of proper care. Duane himself became sick during the long voyage from "confinement in a wretched dear bought space in the foul air of a close ship." The *William Pitt* reached the Company outpost on St. Helena island in late March and he desperately hoped to go ashore for a rest. He appealed to Governor Robert Brook of St. Helena to intercede with the Captain, but Mitchell persuaded the sympathetic Governor that mercy would be unwise in a case involving "a foreign Incendiary." Duane remained on board for the month that the *William Pitt* stayed at anchor; thirty years later he could still remember the ships he had observed in the harbor at St. Helena.

The ship arrived in England about July 1 and Duane was set free immediately since the East India Company did not intend to press criminal charges against him. Its right to banish an innocent person had been confirmed in 1791 by the Supreme Court of Bengal; Duane's own case had established the precedent and three years later he became the first person expelled under the ruling. The Court of Directors in London "highly approve of your conduct in sending home this turbulent and seditious person," it assured the officials in Calcutta, and promised them support and "particular thanks" for similar cases in the future. A general newspaper censorship was imposed in Bengal a few years later and the Court of Directors defended the policy when the colonists protested by citing the case of William Duane as its principal argument against freedom of the press.

Duane had brooded on his misfortune during the long passage from India. In September he requested reimbursement from the Company for his losses, raising the estimated value of his property from 30,000 to 70,000 rupees. The Court of Directors heard the appeal, then simply ordered it referred to the committee on lawsuits. This closed Duane's relations with the East India Company.

Duane never told the truth about his years in India, even to his own family. He admitted that he had been deported by Sir John Shore, but never revealed the earlier imprisonment under the government of Lord Cornwallis. Understandably he sought to give the impression that he had been prosperous, even rich, until the moment that he incurred disfavor, for his support of the Army officers.[28] The truth was that because of the French Revolution "Our newspapers in Calcutta have . . . assumed a licentiousness too dangerous to be permitted in this Country," and Duane was made the first victim of their suppression.[29]

---

[28]See Nathaniel Burt, The Perennial Philadelphians. The Anatomy of an American Aristocracy (Boston, 1963), 402.

[29]Sir John Shore to Henry Dundas, 31 Dec. 1794, Private Record, Furber, ed., 63.

CHAPTER II

LONDON AND PHILADELPHIA

The French Revolution created a crisis in civil liberties around the world. In 1795 the two rivals for power in Europe, France and Great Britain, had renewed their periodic warfare in the name of their political ideals; they represented their struggle as a fight for the future of republican liberty over tyranny, or for the survival of law and order over anarchy. Other nations, governments and individuals alike, responded emotionally to the international issue, according to their own fears and sympathies. The result was the development of a xenophobic extremism in the domestic politics of several countries. Government authorities tended to regard expressions of support for the revolutionary cause in France as overt threats to the rule of law at home, and to respond with the use of arbitrary force to silence free discussion.

William Duane had the extraordinary fortune during the decade of the 1790s to be a victim of the repression of liberties on three continents. When he was banished from India, he told the British colonists that he would return to America, where "*I trust in God I shall find them free*." But by the time that he arrived in the United States, civil liberties there were falling a victim to the fear of jacobinism.

As Duane travelled from East to West, political censorship appeared to accompany him or follow close behind. When the Revolution broke out, he had had the misfortune to be a liberal journalist in an occupied country administered by a military Governor. As early as 1791 tense British-French relations in India had caused Duane to suffer imprisonment, a sentence of exile, and the incidental loss of his employment and most of his property, for publishing a comment that was mildly libelous at worst. At home in England the authorities had been somewhat shocked by the unconstitutional proceeding, but by 1795 the political climate there had changed drastically. Then the home officials praised the government in Bengal for deporting Duane as an undesirable person, without a hearing and without specific charge, a proceeding more arbitrary than the earlier incident.

When Duane arrived in London in July 1795, after six months' ship's confinement, England was on the verge of a major crisis in civil liberties. Britain's war against the republic of France, to help restore the Bourbon monarchy, was highly unpopular with a large segment of the British people, and the public opposition increased as the commitment and the expense mounted. The Tory government of Prime Minister William Pitt the younger was extremely sensitive to the criticism of its policy and sought means to punish the leading dissenters for disloyalty. In 1794 Pitt's government had actually arrested a number of its most active critics and intended to prosecute them for high treason, but upon trial the first three defendants were acquitted, and the government was forced to drop charges against the remaining prisoners.

The treason trials had been intended to frighten opponents into silence and especially to destroy the political club called the London Corresponding Society, which the government regarded as the most radical and dangerous political organization in England.[1] It was with the Corresponding Society that William Duane associated himself soon after his arrival from India. Duane's political outlook had undergone a sea change. The Whiggish loyalist from County Tipperary, with his faith in British liberties and justice and his confidence in the future reform on the English Parliament, had disappeared and had been replaced by an embittered radical. The person he had been when he went to India was unknown to anyone in his new life, and unself-critical men in authority took him to be an automatic Irish nationalist and a professional troublemaker.

During the ten months in which Duane resided in London, waiting for an opportunity to depart with his family for America, he engaged in political activities which in time surely would have gained him a second banishment. In September Duane was offered temporary employment as the editor of an obscure newspaper called The Telegraph. The year-old journal was one of three small daily newspapers in London which were politically to the left of the Whig party. Each had a circulation of about 350, but about this time Daniel Stuart purchased the two competitors with the intention

---

[1]J. L. LeB. Hammond, Charles James Fox: A Political Study (London, 1903), 100-145; Thomas Erskine May, The Constitutional History of England Since the Accession of George the Third, 1760-1860, 3 vols. (London, 1861-1863, 1912), 44-49; Philip Anthony Brown, The French Revolution in English History (London, 1918), 55-158.

of closing them and enlarging the circulation of the *Morning Post*. In the meantime Duane was hired to conduct the short-lived *Telegraph*. The editorial viewpoint which he inherited and maintained was decidedly anti-war and pro-France. Even the military news was selected and reported in a manner which could give comfort to the enemy and demoralize the British public. Among London newspapers the *Telegraph* alone, the editor boasted, did not abuse the public with "accounts of victories that have not been obtained by the *Imperialists*, and of disasters that have not happened to the French."[2]

The *Telegraph* was also the only London newspaper to promote the work of the London Corresponding Society. In addition the newspaper office served as an unofficial meeting place for the Society's members, along with Lee's bookshop, which sold radical pamphlets, and the lecture room of John Thelwall, a teacher and leader of the Corresponding Society, who had been acquitted of treason in the 1794 trials. Duane recklessly ignored the potential danger to himself in forming leftwing associations in London, while already under informal observation by British officials. Six months after he landed, the Directors of the East India Company informed the government of Bengal that "his subsequent behavior since his arrival justifies your proceedings."[3]

---

[2] *Aurora*, 9 Aug. 1834; Fox Bourne, *English Newspapers*, I, 272-273; London *Telegraph*, 11 Nov. 1795; *ibid*., 3 Aug. -27 Nov. 1795, in Burney Collection, British Museum.

[3] India Office Records, Home Misc. Series, Vol. 537, 225-226; *The History of Two Acts, entitled An act for the safety and preservation of His Majesty's person and government against treasonable*

The London Corresponding Society, viewed from another time and a different angle, was not a seditious or even a terribly radical organization. The members were all republicans, schooled by Thomas Paine and by the American example, but they shunned the idea of revolutionary change for England. The Society advocated an honest, representative Parliament. Its ultimate goal was universal suffrage; rule by the House of Commons was a distant ideal. The great majority of members were gradualists who believed that each stage of reform should be accomplished by consensus.

But to Pitt's nervous government virtually any criticism was seditious. Moreover the London Corresponding Society was especially feared because its membership was almost exclusively working class. At least two thousand men who normally would have been excluded from civic affairs had been introduced to political life through participation in the club. Founded by a journeyman shoemaker in 1792, the Corresponding Society charged dues of just one penny a week; its members met regularly in small groups, called "divisions," which elected delegates to the Society's general committee. Furthermore, since surviving the attempt to convict the leaders of treason, the Society had expanded its appeal to working class men and women by sponsoring mass political rallies where they could express their abhorrence of the war with France.[4]

---

and seditious practices and attempts, and An act for the more effectually preventing seditious meetings and assemblies; . . . (London, 1796), 135-136.

[4]Francis Place Papers, XX, Additional Manuscripts, 27,808, pp. 59-60, 113-117, British Museum; Place Papers, London Corresponding Society, V, Add. MSS, 27,815, p. 18, *ibid*.; "Declaration of the

In October 1795 a tragic incident occurred which demolished the movement for peace and reform. On Monday, October 26, the London Corresponding Society held its second great outdoor rally, attended by more than one hundred thousand persons who wished to vent their opposition to "the present detestable war" and to the "increased corruption" of Parliament. Fearing that paid agitators had been placed in the crowd, the Corresponding Society circulated warning handbills, and the meeting was successfully conducted and dispersed in good order. Three days later King George III was attacked by a mob as he rode forth to the opening of Parliament. As the procession moved through St. James Park a "loud and constant cry was made, of 'Down with Pitt,' 'No War,' 'Give us Bread,' 'No Famine.'" Several stones struck the King's carriage; a window was broken, and a mysterious man in a green coat wrenched open the door and was about to drag the King out into the mob, when the Horse Guard rode down on the crowd and the moment of danger passed.[5]

A royal proclamation of November 4 accused the Corresponding Society's rally of direct responsibility for inciting the outrage. At the meeting "diverse inflammatory Discourses were delivered to the Persons . . . collected, and divers Proceedings were had," the proclamation charged, "tending to create groundless Jealousy and Discontent, and to endanger the Public Peace, and the Quiet and

---

Principles and Views of the London Corresponding Society," _Telegraph_, 26 Nov. 1795, quoted in _Aurora_, 9 Mar. 1796; Brown, _Fr. Revol. in Eng. Hist._, 55-60, 150.

[5]_Hist. of Two Acts_, 6, 98-108; John Binns, _Recollections of the Life of John Binns_ . . . (Philadelphia, 1854), 53-56.

Safety of our faithful subjects." Consequently the King enjoined all magistrates of the realm "to use the utmost Diligence to discourage, prevent, and suppress all Seditious and Unlawful Assemblies."[6]

The King's Ministers introduced two acts into Parliament which would proscribe by law most political dissent. The "treasonable and seditious practices" act would make it treason to threaten the King in any way, by published thoughts as well as by deeds, and would declare it a high misdemeanor "to incite or stir up the people," by speech or writing, "to hatred or contempt of the person of his Majesty, his heirs . . . , or the Government and Constitution of this realm." The second act, introduced by William Pitt into the Commons, was intended to prevent "seditious meetings," through a system of licensing and supervision of political gatherings. In the case of meetings attended by fifty or more persons, local magistrates were given sweeping powers to oversee and judge the proceedings, to arrest individuals and to disperse the meeting if seditious utterances occurred. Failure to disperse upon demand would be a felony punishable by death, and the magistrates were indemnified by the act for the killing, maiming, or hurting of anyone who resisted their authority. The act also provided for the close supervision of smaller political gatherings, in clubs, lectures, or discussions, by the licensing of all indoor and outdoor meeting places. An unapproved meeting place would be classed as a disorderly house and

---

[6] Place Papers, XX, Add. MSS, 27,808, pp. 49-53, Br. Museum; Hist. of Two Acts, 23-24.

fined one hundred pounds per day.[7]

The danger to civil liberties presented by the "Two Acts" was far more serious than had been the threat to the King. For a riot in which perhaps a few hundred persons were guilty, the entire nation was to be punished with the loss of free speech and assembly. While the Tory orators in Parliament depicted a nightmare of anarchy and bloodshed, the Whig party desperately sought to salvage the rights of Englishmen. Charles James Fox, Richard Brinsley Sheridan, Charles Grey, and, in the Peers, Lord Lauderdale and the Duke of Bedford conducted an impassioned appeal to reason, in Parliament and in Westminster, which was to be quickly overwhelmed by the emotional fear of jacobinism. Fox had never associated or sympathized with the republican element in Britain, but on this occasion he thought that the Whig party should unite with every group protesting the infringement of liberties.[8]

The London Corresponding Society, falsely accused of violence, announced a public protest of the Two Acts for Thursday, November 12. "Will you consent that the political improvement of five centuries be at one stroke annihilated," the circular demanded, "and that our laws and constitution should relapse into that state of barbarous ambiguity--that system of constructive treason which prevailed in the tyrannical reign of Edward the Second?" The site of the meeting was Copenhagen Fields, a large open park in Marylebone on the northern outskirts of London.[9]

---

[7] *Ibid.*, 772-780.

[8] Hammond, *Fox*, 124-125.

[9] *Hist. of Two Acts*, 38.

William Duane was invited to be chairman of the meeting. The leaders of the Corresponding Society, who selected a different chairman for each of their public rallies, presumably chose the editor of the *Telegraph* upon this extraordinary occasion because Duane had recently experienced the full eclipse of civil liberties, under a British government in Calcutta. The major speakers were to be John Thelwall, John Ashley and Richard Hodgson, all Corresponding Society leaders. Duane's duty as chairman was to open the meeting with a short speech, to read the resolutions, and to conduct the votes upon them. As chairman he also would sign the record of the proceedings, an action which under the bills moving rapidly toward enactment would have made him liable to a charge of treason.[10]

The meeting was called for eleven o'clock in the morning, but the crowds arriving in Copenhagen Fields were so enormous that the business did not open until half past twelve. Some persons estimated the attendance to be as high as 300,000; this was "no doubt an exaggeration," according to Francis Place, the labor leader, but the gathering was "probably the largest ever assembled." Several Whig Members of Parliament were present, the first time any had appeared at a public assembly not sponsored by the party. Most of the demonstrators were "highly respectable even from their situation in life, and all of them more so from the decency, gravity, and decorum of their demeanour," according to a sympathetic observer, who thought "The philosophical and reflecting mind had never,

---

[10]*Ibid.*, 125-134; *The Life of John Thelwall*, by his widow (London, 1837), 400-403.

perhaps, a finer opportunity of contemplating the mental energies of so vast a number of fellow citizens, as on this memorable day."[11]

In his introductory address as chairman, Duane spoke first of the historic right of petition and free assembly, "the necessity of private and public opinion, and free discussion on all topics which could interest or affect men." He recommended firm and peaceful measures for the redress of grievances, "but he said, it would remain with the people of this country to determine, how long they would bear innovation on their liberties, an unnatural war," and arbitrary usurpation of their rights "in violation of all those dear and sacred principles which the efforts and blood of our ancestors, in a series of ages, had secured to them." Still a Whig in his view of English history, he contrasted former "happy times" with the uncertain present and a bleak future. Finally Duane alluded generally "to the conduct, measure, and opinion of administration, and appeared to feel, that he was embarrassed with a sensibility which we cannot express a sense of in adequate terms."[12]

The resolutions addressed to the King, Lords and Commons founded their appeal upon the liberties won in the Revolution of 1688. The only precedents for the treason and sedition had occurred during the despotic Tudor and Stuart reigns, the petitioners stated, and they ominously recalled the circumstances which placed the House of Brunswick upon the throne. "If the conduct of the

---

[11]Place Papers, XX, Add. MSS, 27,808, p. 54, Br. Museum; Hist. of Two Acts, 125-126.

[12]Ibid., 126-127.

House of Stuart deserves the imitation of this enlightened age, what is the House of Brunswick, whose succession was secured by driving those Stuarts into vagrant exile?" asked the petition to the Lords. "We trust, whatever may be the evil counsels and evil projects of a desperate administration," the petitioners loyally addressed the King, "that the House of Brunswick will not forget the principles, to which they owe their elevation."[13]

When the proceedings ended, the thousands of persons in Copenhagen Fields departed as quietly as they had arrived. "More order than was observed at this meeting was never observed at any meeting either within or without doors," Francis Place averred. The meeting was totally dispersed within half an hour; the speakers and the Corresponding Society leaders gathered for another hour in Copenhagen House, adjoining the fields, before separating to go to their homes. The November 12 rally was a great occasion for those who participated, but on the following day the House of Lords approved the treasonable practices bill with only seven dissenting votes. The increased boldness of the London Corresponding Society, Lord Grenville argued, proved the urgent need to suppress seditious behavior and ensure the public tranquility.[14]

---

[13]Ibid., 128-129. Citizen Lee also published an Account of the proceedings of a meeting of the people . . . Thursday, Nov. 12 . . . with the petitions to the King, Lords, and Commons, of nearly four hundred thousand Britons, inhabitants of London and its environs; assembled . . . to express their free sentiments . . . on the subject of the threatened invasion of their rights by a Convention Bill (London, 1795), pamphlet, NYPL.

[14]Place Papers, XX, Add. MSS, 27-808, pp. 54-55, Br. Museum; Hist. of Two Acts, 177.

In December 1795 the Two Acts became law, with the acquiescence of a vast majority of the British public. The London Corresponding Society was effectively destroyed by the legislation; the moderate members all soon resigned, in view of the high risk associated with the expression of dissent. A remnant of serious radicals and United Irishmen attempted to continue the Society, until it was buried by a bill of attainder in 1799. Fortunately for William Duane, a few months after the enactment of the laws, he was able to leave the country voluntarily.[15]

II

Duane sailed for America in May 1796. He was accompanied by his wife Catharine and his three children, William John, Catharine and Patrick. The family had been separated from Duane for the eight years that he was in India, but they had come from Clonmel to be with him in London. The children forgave him the long separation and the hardship of their early years, for belatedly he became a loving and "a generous parent." William John was already sixteen years old, but he responded to his father's return with a deep attachment and loyalty which made him, Duane admitted, "the dearest of all my affections." His daughter Catharine also was always "much attached to me," and only Patrick, the youngest and perhaps the favorite of his mother, showed any sign of resenting the disappearance and return of his father.[16]

---

[15] Ibid., 772-774; Place Papers, XX, Add. MSS, 27,808, p. 67, Br. Museum; Brown, Fr. Revol. in Eng. Hist., 153-158.

[16] Duane to Caesar A. Rodney, 1 July 1808, Rodney Papers,

A fellow emigre Thomas Lloyd paid for the Duane family's passage. Lloyd was an Irish-born journalist who had recently suffered political imprisonment in Newgate. He and Duane became friends in London during the year of protest, and they remained close during the first difficult years in America.[17]

The party landed in New York on the Fourth of July. Duane's intention was to proceed to Philadelphia, where he had lived as a child, and eventually to move westward and seek his fortune on the frontier, as his own father had done before his birth. Because they lacked money to continue their journey, the Duanes and Lloyd remained in New York for three months seeking employment. Then Duane fortunately secured a contract with the publisher and author John Stewart. "Walking Stewart," as he was known, published travel accounts based on his journeys, and moral philosophy. According to the Federalist _Gazette of the United States_, published in Philadelphia, Stewart was "famous for writing books that few read, and none can understand," and fond of futilely "giving his advice to government."[18]

Stewart hired Duane to compile a history of the French Revolution from 1789 through 1797. The publisher intended to append Duane's anonymous volume to an American edition of the recent three

---

Delaware Historical Society; Duane to Thomas Jefferson, 5 June 1824, Thomas Jefferson Papers, Library of Congress (TJ-LC); [Duane], _Biog. Memoir of W.J. Duane_, 3-4.

17 _The_ (Philadelphia) _Tickler_, 12 Oct. 1807, 10 Oct. 1808; Philadelphia _Gazette of the United States_, 11 July 1800; Philadelphia _Spirit of the Press_, Oct. 1806.

18 _Aurora_, 9 Aug. 1834; Duane to James Monroe, 6 Feb. 1825, Monroe Papers, NYPL; _Gaz. of the U.S._, 6 Dec. 1794.

volume history of France written by an English Tory, John Gifford. Duane worked on the book over the following two years, supplying chapters periodically, and the money he received from Stewart was a major source of his meagre income. The volume Duane produced was a good piece of hack work. Duane did not claim to be author of the history, but its compiler. The work was based upon the most authentic European sources, he maintained, and he cited in the preface a number of contemporary French memoirs. Although Duane did use French accounts for particular episodes and anecdotes, the book in fact was largely plagiarized from an English source, the _Annual Register_.

After the fall of the French monarchy in 1792, his account diverged radically in viewpoint from that of the _Annual Register_, but he continued to use the source while reversing most of its judgments. His version consistently sympathized with the revolutionists, particularly the Girondists and the more moderate Jacobin leader Danton. Duane heaped responsibility for all that was evil in the Revolution upon the name of the dead Robespierre, while he lauded the Constitution establishing the Directory in 1795 as "the most perfect form of republican government yet instituted."

Duane inserted late in the book his own discussion of United States - French relations, which was highly critical of American policy. He condemned George Washington's proclamation of neutrality in the European war as a violation of America's treaty obligations to France and described the Jay Treaty as a virtual alliance with Great Britain. These judgments by the newly arrived

Duane coincided with the opinion of the Republican party in the United States, as expressed especially in its foremost newspaper, the *Aurora*, published in Philadelphia by Benjamin Franklin Bache. However William Duane's six hundred page history of the French Revolution never obtained influence in the United States, and his authorship remained anonymous.[19]

After receiving the contract to write for John Stewart, Duane in October 1796 moved on to Philadelphia. He was "wretchedly poor and friendless" when he first arrived, a Philadelphian recalled long afterward, and "occupied a room, with his family in a small frame house, in an alley" at Fifth and Race streets. The house, which was owned by a "stupid" German woman, stood "abreast of 14 gun batteries or 14 chimnies-." Duane set out immediately to find regular employment as a printer, but he was refused on his first interview because of his wild hair, long beard and fierce expression and because when he was invited to sing, he "bellowed forth tremendously." Duane had no letter of recommendation, only an informal introduction, so Richard Folwell gave that as the reason for his rejection. Years later Folwell claimed that he would have hired him had he known Duane would become a Colonel and "look so pretty about the head" after cropping.[20]

George Washington's farewell address as President appeared

---

[19]John Gifford, *The History of France, from the Earliest Times till the Death of Louis Sixteenth*. . . . *And Continued from the Above Period until the Conclusion of the Present War, by a Citizen of the United States*, 4 vols. (Philadelphia, 1796-1798), IV.

[20]Dairy of William Wood Thackara, Historical Society of Pennsylvania (HSP); *Spirit of the Press*, Aug. 1806.

in September just a few weeks after he arrived, revealing an indifference to civil liberties which he thought that he had escaped. The parallel between its sentiments and Pitt's behavior stimulated him to write an essay in response which became the foundation of his reputation, for good and ill, in Philadelphia. His "Letter to George Washington" was published in the name of "Jasper Dwight," whom he identified as a citizen of Vermont, a reference to his own birth on Lake Champlain. Benjamin Franklin Bache agreed to publish the essay by the unknown immigrant, and advertised it for sale at the _Aurora_ office and all bookstores for twenty-five cents. The excellence of Duane's pamphlet, written under circumstances of unemployment and want, demonstrated to Bache and others his intellectual capacity and outstanding ability as a writer.

George Washington had warned against the dangers to the nation inherent in the "spirit of party," and Duane replied with an eloquent defense of free association. The President depicted the potential threat to the established government through individual disobedience, but Duane observed that there was an equal danger to citizens through aggression by their government. Therefore the people alone, not governments, could judge the safety of civil liberties, for, lamented the late resident of Great Britain, "the declaration of principles is too often the cloak for their violation." In every country, under every ruler "from Augustus to George III the profession of love has been accompanied by the sacrifice of Liberty!" The President deplored political clubs and secret societies, believing their real design was obstruction, but who is to be the judge of their "REAL DESIGN," inquired Duane, the "agents of the powers that be?" The implications of the farewell address, warned the "citizen of Vermont," could be seen in the British treason and sedition laws. Washington's views on political clubs were as harsh as those of William Pitt, and his "doctrines bear a most obstinate resemblance of the measures and language of the British ministry a year ago!"

Duane, having lived in Europe during the Revolution, did not possess the native American's reverent awe of George Washington. He was able to discuss Washington objectively and fairly, within the frame of his own political values. While praising Washington's personal character and his qualities as a military commander, Duane expressed serious misgivings about his achievements as President. The specific acts of his administration--the funding system, the British Treaty, the use of the military against citizens--would be censured by posterity, Duane predicted. More important, Washington was guilty of moral indifference to the social fulfillment of the Revolution: "in vain will [posterity] seek for traces of establishments or institutions calculated to secure the perpetuity of freedom on the strong basis of education and moral equality." Duane sincerely objected that the President had defamed Thomas Paine in order "to defend the religion of Christ," yet Washington himself violated the sacred obligations of morality and liberty "by dealing in HUMAN SLAVES!"

The "Letter to George Washington" was written from a sense of duty, Duane concluded, "to expose the PERSONAL IDOLATRY into which we have been heedlessly running--to awaken my countrymen to a sense of our true situation--and to shew them in the fallibility of the most favored of men, the necessity of thinking for themselves."

The response to the pamphlet verified Duane's warnings. In Philadelphia the Federalists universally read the temperate and restrained criticism as an outrageous assault on General Washington. Although Duane remained obscure for some time thereafter, the notorious "Jasper Dwight" established his lifelong reputation:

> And thou audacious renegadoe,
> With many a libellous bravadoe,
> Assail'dst Columbia's, god-like son.
> The great, th' immortal WASHINGTON.

An English traveller in the United States during this period commented that among the jacobinic faction of French sympathizers, one man alone "was hardy enough to appear the public defamer of Washington; but this man was not an American. His name is Duane,--by birth an Irishman."[21]

During 1797 and early 1798 Duane was employed on two Philadelphia newspapers. Thomas Bradford hired Duane and Thomas Lloyd to edit his <u>Merchants' Daily Advertiser</u>, a predecessor to <u>The True American</u>. "Newgate Lloyd," as he was invariably known, was the senior editor, or so he was considered by William Cobbett of <u>Porcupine's Gazette</u>, who delighted in taunting the pair. "Are not the <u>generous prisons</u>, <u>Newgate</u> and the <u>Jail of Bengal</u>," he asked, "most excellent seminaries for the education of the <u>Conductors</u> of a

---

[21][William Duane], <u>A Letter to George Washington</u> (Philadelphia, 1796), pamphlet, Library of Congress (LC); Charles William Janson, <u>The Stranger in America</u> (London, 1807), 199-201.

patriotic news-paper?" Cobbett considered "the partnership newspaper in Front street" to be a political shadow of B. F. Bache's Aurora, and gibed when Lloyd and Duane differed in opinion from the master. "The upright Conductors of the Merchant's paper say," in denying the authenticity of a letter imputed to Thomas Jefferson, "that there is not the least earthly resemblance between the Federal government and that of Great Britain; but Bache declares, with his friend Tom Paine, that they are alike both in form and substance." The reason for the difference, of course, was that Duane and Lloyd had recently fled from the British treason and sedition laws, while Bache was a native American who sought to shame his country into averting a similar tyranny of opinion. Cobbett declared that the Republican editors should correct the discrepancy: "I think the merchants in partnership with Bradford would do well to appoint a committee (agreeably to the articles) to wait on Bache, and get matters adjusted. The papers must act in concert, or all is ruined."[22]

The Merchants' Advertiser as edited by Duane and Lloyd reported the news from Europe with a slant which greatly annoyed the British propagandist Cobbett. "This paper contains more bloody news from Ireland than all the other papers put together," he complained in July 1797; "I believe the convicts fabricate a good deal of it." If it were true, as they asserted, that the British government was importing 15,000 Hessian mercenaries to defeat the rebellion in Ireland, "the rebel Northern clans," in Cobbett's opinion,

---

[22]Philadelphia Porcupine's Gazette, 20 Apr., 5 May 1797.

"will soon enjoy what they have long been labouring for, ball and bayonet."[23]

Cobbett was merely amused when the foreign radicals extended the principle outlawing titles of nobility in the United States. "In such a republic as this," they had suggested, "men should by every fair means be legally prevented from becoming exorbitantly rich," because rich men as a class form "a separate interest from that of the people, [and] persons of this description are apt to acquire a dangerous influence." To this proposal Porcupine's Gazette commented wryly: "Lloyd's merchants must differ very much from merchants in general, if they would be pleased with a law to prevent them from growing rich." But the majority of the paper's subscribers, Porcupine explained, "is not composed of either Esquires or Merchants." Throughout his life Duane continued to express in some form this early radical ideal for a republican society.[24]

Duane moved from Bradford's paper to the Philadelphia Gazette probably in the fall of 1797. The inexperienced owner Andrew Brown Junior asked Benjamin Franklin Bache to suggest "a person qualified to conduct that paper--and Mr. Bache recommended william Duane, who was engaged and did succeed to the editorship." But for some reason the situation did not last, perhaps because "Mr. Brown was of a temper not well adapted to agree very long with any man."[25]

---

[23] Ibid., 11 July 1797. [24] Ibid., 13 May 1797.

[25] Aurora, 14 Mar. 1812, 9 Aug. 1834; Porcupine's Gaz., 12 Aug., 20 Nov. 1797.

By the spring of 1798 Duane was again unemployed and his wife Catharine was gravely ill. The publisher of his volume on the French Revolution, John Stewart, visited Philadelphia in early June, and Duane hoped to receive money from him in order to pay his rent. His landlady, "an unconscionable foul mouthed Dutch woman," who plagued Duane and abused his wife and children was anxious for the family to leave because she "fears my wife will die in her house!" He told his situation to Stewart, but received no compensation, "and as I am not getting money for my labor," he remarked bitterly, "and there is upwards of 130 dollars due to me," he might as well quit as work. On June 7 when his rent was a week overdue, the landlady "seized on my goods," Duane told James Thackara, in an urgent message to the engraver who was the first good friend he had made in Philadelphia. He had to ask Thackara to ransom his possessions "that I may go to business." Despairing of support from Stewart, Duane determined to resign from the publisher's stable of writers and seek another job. Meanwhile his wife, bedridden in a room next to a hot and smoke-filled alley, was suffering the debilitating effects of cholera. After lingering for several weeks, Catharine Duane died on July 13.[26]

III.

In these circumstances, Duane received employment from Benjamin Franklin Bache on the <u>Aurora</u>. It was an inauspicious moment to begin work as a printer in the city of Philadelphia. The summer

---

[26]Diary of William Wood Thackara, HSP; <u>North American</u>, 8 Dec. 1907.

was intensely hot, and in the increasingly humid and noxious weather of late July, yellow fever appeared. For two months Philadelphia suffered the worst epidemic since 1793. Deaths occurred at the rate of sixty persons a day, but Bache and his staff remained in the city and published the Aurora daily as usual. Moreover in July the Federalist Congress enacted the oppressive alien and sedition laws, intended to silence dissent at home, while preparing to go to war against France for insulting an American diplomatic commission. A journalist could be punished by fine and imprisonment for publishing "any false, scandalous, and malicious writing" against the government of the United States, the Congress or the President; that is, writing "with intent to defame . . . , or to bring them . . . into contempt or disrepute; or to excite against them . . . the hatred of the good people of the United States." Resident aliens were deprived of any protection of their personal liberties, and in the opinion of one Republican Senator, the "political delerium" which had inspired the measures had "not yet got to its highest pitch."[27]

Bache was intended as the first victim of suppression because the hated Aurora was the Republican party's largest and most effective newspaper. He had already been placed under common law indictment for the alleged defamation of government officials and was free on four thousand dollars bond while he awaited trial. But

---

[27]Aurora, 9 Aug. 1834; Porcupine's Gaz., "John Ward Fenno," 9 Aug. 1798; ibid., 7 Aug., 14, 18 Sept. 1798; James Morton Smith, Freedom's Fetters: The Alien and Sedition Laws and American Civil Liberties (Ithaca, 1956), 442; Stevens Thomson Mason to Thomas Jefferson, 6 July 1798, TJ-LC.

before the Federalist courts could prosecute him, Bache died of yellow fever. The courageous and gifted grandson of Benjamin Franklin, only twenty-nine years old, succumbed on September 10 after five days' illness. He left a widow and four small children, the youngest an infant one week old. "In ordinary times, the loss of such a man would be a source of public sorrow," declared the public announcement of his death. "In these times, men who see, and think, and feel for their country and posterity can alone appreciate the loss." But the *Aurora* would continue; "When such arrangements shall have been made as are necessary to ensure its wonted character of intelligence and energy, it will reappear under the direction of HIS WIDOW."[28]

On November 1, 1798, the *Aurora* resumed publication; its editor was William Duane, who pledged himself to conduct the newspaper upon the principles of the late founder. During the next two years, marked in American history by the enforcement and the protest of the alien and sedition laws, Duane as an editor was to become as famous as his predecessor. The names of Bache and Duane gradually became inseparable in the public memory. Consequently historians have inferred that Duane had been Bache's colleague over a long period and was his natural successor. In fact he had been regularly employed on the paper only two months before Bache's death, and his selection as editor was by no means inevitable.[29]

---

[28]Bernard Fay, *The Two Franklins: Fathers of American Democracy* (Boston, 1933), 356-357.

[29]*Aurora*, 11 Aug. 1802, 9 Aug. 1834; *Country Gaz. of the U.S.*, 3 Sept. 1802.

The position, which admittedly offered terrors far greater than its rewards, might for example have been offered to the more infamous Thomas Lloyd, or to James Carey, the brother of Mathew Carey, who was better acquainted among the Republicans. His partisan newspaper, Carey's United States Recorder, which Thomas Jefferson thought the Republicans should support along with the Aurora had been forced to suspend publication just a few days before Bache's death.[30]

The apparent logical choice as editor would have been James Thomson Callender, on the basis of his fame and his prior association with the newspaper as Bache's assistant. The notorious Scottish pamphleteer, whose innuendoes had forced Alexander Hamilton into a confession of private immorality, had wandered drunkenly from "den to den," according to the account of William Cobbett, "till he, at last, took shelter under the disgraceful roof of the abandoned hireling editor of the AURORA." Callender's vituperative writings had earned him the hatred of all Federalists, and he deeply feared their retaliation. In June 1798, when the alien law passed and threatened possible deportation, Callender became a citizen, and on July 13, one day before President John Adams signed the sedition law, he fled the capital and set out on foot toward the Republican state of Virginia.[31] It was then that Bache had hired Duane to replace him.

---

[30] Frank L. Mott, Jefferson and the Press (Baton Rouge, 1943), 28; Porcupine's Gaz., 6 Sept. 1798.

[31] Ibid., 17 Sept. 1798; Worthington Chauncey Ford, ed., Thomas Jefferson and James Thomson Callender, 1798-1802 (Brooklyn, 1897).

Callender was unwilling to return to Philadelphia and the danger of sedition proceedings. "There is . . . no more security in returning than there would have been in Staying," he pleaded in asking the Virginia Republicans for local employment. Moreover "I have not only motives of one kind, but others quite different," he admitted, "for not wishing to revisit that sink of destruction Philadelphia." "I am entirely sick even of the Republicans" there, he confided to Thomas Jefferson. "I have been crushed by the very Gentry whom I was defending." He felt especially aggrieved by the conduct of the late editor of the Aurora. "Bache is buried, and I wish I could bury the consequences of his behaviour to me," Callender lamented. "I know he had many useful and many pleasing qualities; but I was never the better for the one, or the other." During the period of Callender's association with the Aurora, Bache had increasingly censored or rejected the pamphleteer's abusive material. "This was my thanks for the multitudinous columns I have wrote for him." Concluding his catalogue of resentments against the Republicans in Philadelphia, he remarked with contempt, "If they really have [sic] almost any tolerable writers except James Carey I would think less of their treatment of me."[32]

Bache had selected Duane as a writer of superior ability and judgment, and almost certainly before his death he chose him as his preferred successor. Duane himself said, on various occasions, that he had been named editor in Bache's will. A nomination by Bache, according to John Ward Fenno of the Gazette of the United

---

[32]Callender to Jefferson, 22 Sept., 26 Oct. 1798, TJ-LC.

States, "were enough of itself to damn any man to everlasting infamy"; nonetheless he claimed to have information "that it is an utter falsehood and that Wm. Duane is not named nor alluded to." A committee of family friends and Republican leaders offered the position to Duane, on behalf of the heirs. The salary was eight hundred dollars per year, according to Cobbett.[33] A Republican subscription to purchase the Aurora, in order to aid Bache's widow and children, was spoken of but never accomplished.[34] Duane said, at many times during his life, that he "then intended to pass the mountains in the spring of 1799," but that he had agreed to stay and edit the paper for a year. The prosecutions in which he became entangled during that difficult period kept him permanently in Philadelphia.[35]

The spokesman who invited Duane "on behalf of himself and the rest to take charge of the paper" was Senator Stevens Thomson Mason of Virginia, a nephew of George Mason, the famous Anti-Federalist. Duane already knew General Mason, and regarded the planter gratefully as his first patron in America. A political intimate of James Monroe, Mason had succeeded to his Senate seat when Monroe went as minister to France. In 1795 he had initiated the greatest political controversy of the decade when he offered Bache the text

---

[33]Porcupine's Gaz., 8 July 1799; Gaz. of the U.S., 20 May 1799.

[34]Ibid., 16 Jan. 1799; Duane to James Monroe, 6 Feb. 1825, Monroe Papers, NYPL; Duane to Caesar A. Rodney, 1 July 1808, Rodney Papers, Delaware Historical Society.

[35]Aurora, 9 Aug. 1834; Duane to Monroe, 6 Feb. 1825, Monroe Papers, NYPL.

of the Jay Treaty for publication, in violation of the rule of secrecy. George Mason, in the debates on the Constitution, had portrayed the dangers to civil liberties through tyranny by the powerful Congress; his nephew in 1798 to 1800 became the dedicated and generous benefactor of those who suffered persecution under the sedition law.[36]

Long after the Aurora resumed publication, the Federalist press insisted wishfully that the paper was wretched and failing. John Ward Fenno however objected to any offer to Mrs. Bache for purchase by Federalists. "The measure of raising a subscription from the friends of government to prolong the existence of the dying Aurora," he argued, "is too selfish for men of honor to promote." Its writhings are indeed amusing, Fenno agreed, "but in charity we should remember that the Goddess will, after all, have to say, 'this may be sport to you; but it is death to me.'" The Federalist offer, whether real or merely rumored, was no doubt the source of Duane's allegation that Alexander Hamilton had tried to buy off the Aurora. For reprinting the accusation, David Frothingham of the New York Argus was sued by Hamilton and convicted of libel by the state of New York.[37]

For months Fenno and Cobbett pretended that the Aurora had no real editor, but was conducted by an ad hoc committee of incompe-

---

[36]Ibid.; Thomas P. Abernethy, "Stevens Thomson Mason," DAB, XII, 374-375; Porcupine's Gaz., 17 Sept. 1798; Jackson Turner Main, The Antifederalists: Critics of the Constitution, 1781-1788 (Chapel Hill, 1961), 125, 152, 160.

[37]Smith, Freedom's Fetters, 400-414; Gaz. of the U.S., 5 Jan. 1799.

tents, "Mother Bache's gang." They did not know Duane's first name and disdained to call him by his last, addressing him rather as "the Irishman," "Jasper," or "Citizen Dwight." But when a dispute arose "among the writers in the Aurora, on the subject of the merits of their respective essays," Fenno's Gazette reported with malicious pleasure that "upon their appealing to the proprietor, she very modestly decided in favor of the Irishman's performances."[38] Eighteen year old William John Duane, who had recovered from an almost fatal attack of yellow fever, was employed as a clerk in the Aurora office. William Cobbett was amused by the "young foreigner" who "piously imitated" his father.

> Tell of what word young Jacobins are made;
> How the skill'd Gardener grafts with nicest rule
> The slip of Coxcomb on the stock of Fool--
> Forth in bright blossoms bursts the Tender sprig,
> A thing to wonder at--perhaps a Whig.[39]

Porcupine's Gazette was an intelligent and witty newspaper, but Cobbett had at times a sense of humor and of honor that were exceedingly perverse. In Duane's first issue of the Aurora he published a caricature which made Cobbett extremely angry. James Callender, who for a brief time thought that "the Aurora has got into most excellent hands," observed gleefully that Cobbett "looks like a bull frog in the first of Hercules." But Cobbett refused to place the responsibility upon the editor. "I by no means look upon DUANE, or any other vagabond journeyman newsmonger," he explained,

---

[38] Ibid., 5, 10, 16, 28 Jan., 16 May 1799; Porcupine's Gaz., 17 Oct., 3 Nov., 21 Dec. 1798, 19 Jan. 1799.

[39] Ibid., 5 Jan. 1799; [Duane], Biog. Memoir of W.J. Duane, 6.

"as the proper object of attack. The _proprietor_ of the paper, the person _whose name it bears_ . . . is the only one who is _responsible for its contents_." Thereupon he began an editorial assault on Margaret Bache of truly astounding viciousness. When Benjamin Bache died, Cobbett had refused to publish a correspondent's cruel "elegy," because "A _Briton_ scorns to mangle the carcass . . . which has been slain by the Almighty." Yet for half a year he kept up a constant raillery against "Mother Bache," the "Poissarde" who would not "leave talking bawdry." Cobbett ignored the pleas by Americans of both parties that he adopt a more conventional notion of gentlemanly behavior. According to Cobbett, "this _delicate_ dame began her Editorial career by rejoicing at the abolition [by the new Roman legislature] of '_castration in Italy_.'" But a correspondent observed that "the fury of this she citizen, against the _Italian Barbers_, appears very natural, when we recollect the _loss_, she had recently experienced."[40]

IV.

To the Philadelphia Federalists, William Duane was merely an obscure hired journalist, yet a person potentially dangerous because he was Irish. In the opinion of Fenno's and Cobbett's readers, "as well might we attempt to tame the Hyena as to Americanize an Irishman." Consequently a nativist took the occasion, when one of that nationality acceded to the editorship of the

---

[40]Callender to Jefferson, 19 Nov. 1798, TJ-LC; _Porcupine's Gaz._, 19 Sept., 3, 8, 12, 16, 27, 30 Nov., 18 Dec. 1798, 19, 24 Apr., 1, 3 May, 12 July 1799.

Aurora (notwithstanding that the grandson of Benjamin Franklin had been as passionately pro-Irish as any man in America), to warn his countrymen of a vast Irish conspiracy at work in the United States. "We have much to fear from the intrigues and insiduous machinations of France," he agreed, "but we have everything to fear from the horde of traitors within our country."[41]

The source of these exaggerated fears was the Irish Rebellion. Since the emergence abroad of the Society of United Irish, the attitude of American Federalists toward immigration had altered drastically.[42] They resented the crowd of political refugees escaping from British retaliation who brought jacobinical notions into the United States with them. The feeling culminated in the naturalization act and the two alien laws of 1798, all intended to keep strangers out of American politics indefinitely.

The laws were meant as a barrier not only to the intellectual refugees, who wrote and taught French ideas, but also to the mass of Irish newcomers. "A man of known intimacy with the recent motives and measures of administration," Bache revealed in August 1798, "has not scrupled to declare, that the Alien bill was intended to operate against the unfortunate Irish Catholics who have been flying from oppression to the U. S. for four years past." The ulta-Federalists believed that the Irish immigrants would literally furnish the troops for a takeover and enforcement of bloodthirsty

---

[41]Gaz. of the U.S., "3," 7 Mar. 1799; Porcupine's Gaz., "An American," 3 Nov. 1798.

[42]See for example Gaz. of the U.S., 12 Dec. 1794.

French democracy. When William Duane in the summer of 1799 organized a company of volunteer militia, composed of fellow Irishmen, even Secretary of State Timothy Pickering thought that the French symbolism adopted in the insignia was a significant indicator of a hostile purpose. Duane had authorized badges with "a plume of _cock_-neck feathers and a _small_ black cockade with a _large_ eagle. He is doubtless a United Irishman," Pickering concluded, "and the company is probably formed to oppose the authority of the government; and in case of war and invasion by the French, to join them."[43]

The fantasy of danger to America ignored the real circumstances of the United Irish at the end of 1798. In April the rebellion in Ireland had broken out prematurely because of the pressure of British counter measures, and although participation was widespread, the revolt lacked direction. Within a few months it was clear that the rebellion would be crushed; by late in the year the British had 140,000 troops in Ireland engaged in savage reprisals against the rebels. The tiny French expedition of 1,000 men had been quickly forced to surrender. Theobald Wolf Tone, the founder of the United Irish, slit his throat in his prison cell.[44]

The failure of the Irish Rebellion did not diminish the belief in an international conspiracy of jacobinism which threatened to conquer the United States through internal subversion. The French "will excite sedition & rebellion, under pretence of

---

[43] _Aurora_, 14 Aug. 1798; Pickering to John Adams, 24 July 1799, Charles Francis Adams, ed., _The Works of John Adams . . ._, 10 vols. (Boston, 1850-1856), IX, 4.

[44] Palmer, _Age of the Demo. Revol._, II, 491-505.

oppression, as in Ireland," warned one high official, "& when they have inspired a portion of the people with hatred of their own gov.ᵗ they shall kindly offer their aid." An American branch of the United Irish, countless Federalists believed, was secretly and systematically plotting toward this end. Fenno declared that "every United Irishman ought to be hunted from the country, as much as a wolf or a tyger," and Cobbett agreed, because "they possess _here_ infinitely greater advantages than they did" in Ireland.[45]

The _Gazette of the United States_ pledged itself to expose and uproot the conspiracy, and began by publishing a list of the names of suspect persons in Philadelphia. Duane and Lloyd were on the list, along with Mathew and James Carey, and several schoolteachers and instructors at the University. Fenno did not claim that the persons named were members of the Society of United Irish, but identified them as "disaffected Irishmen; Irishmen disaffected to the government of the United States." When Fenno was answered with denials and charges of slander, Cobbett came to his defense and began his own campaign of innuendo against the University of Pennsylvania.[46]

Cobbett had hearsay evidence, which he thought indisputable, in proof of Fenno's accusations against three young teachers on the list, Samuel Wylie and John Black, instructors in the college, and Thomas McAdams, a schoolmaster in Oxford Township. The three had

---

[45]William Loughton Smith to James McHenry, 2 Feb. 1799, James McHenry Papers (photostat, second series), LC; _Porcupine's Gaz._, 27 Nov. 1798.

[46]_Ibid._, 21 Dec. 1798.

resided together in an inn near Oxford during the yellow fever epidemic, and their shocking political conversations had been noted by the offended landlord. Wylie had justified French seizures of American property, had denounced the alien act, and had pronounced that the American government was fit only for Indians and Hottentots. "McAdams behaved with more caution than his mess mates. He was a soft smooth-tongued Teague, always canting about humanity." Black also "was not so unbearably audacious as Wylie," Cobbett was forced to admit. But "They all agreed in their reprobation of the Federal Government and its administration, and were all observed to testify and express great joy at the prospect of the success of the rebels, and their friends the French, in Ireland."

The exposed indifference of the University officials to the presence on the faculty of known political radicals enraged William Cobbett. He charged that "half of the country schools in Pennsylvania" were in the hands of jacobins, and "the learned University herself does not disdain to solicit their assistance." The fact was less astonishing, Cobbett hinted, to those who lived near the University "and who are acquainted with the characters and politics of the persons, who have principally, the direction of its concerns."[47]

In February 1799 an incident occurred which to the nervous Federalists proved their contention of a United Irish conspiracy. "That there is such a banditti, organized for the subversion of government, and the establishment of a system of terror and anar-

---

[47] Ibid., 29 Dec. 1798.

chy," advised one hysterical newspaper correspondent, "cannot longer be doubted by the most incredulous. The '*United Irishmen*' have at length broken out into acts, which render them no longer the objects of uncertain suspicion." For at midday on Sunday, February 10, the peace of Philadelphia was "disturbed by a more daring and flagitious riot," young Fenno's paper reported, "than we remember to have outraged the civil law and the decorum of society for more than forty years."[48]

The scene of the riot was St. Mary's Catholic church. On Sunday morning a group of four Irish Republicans visited St. Mary's to invite the "natives of *Ireland* who worship at this Church . . . to remain in the yard after Divine service until they have affixed their names to a memorial for the *repeal* of the *Alien Bill*." The deputation included William Duane, Samuel Cummings, a journeyman printer, and Robert Moore, who had recently arrived from Ireland.[49] Its leader, the most distinguished and most hated of the group, was Dr. James Reynolds. Reynolds, who had been a close friend of the late Benjamin Franklin Bache, was a physician and a member of the Academy of Medicine in Philadelphia. He was said to be a brother-in-law of the rebel leader Wolf Tone, and among those on Fenno's list of suspicious persons, Reynolds alone had not denied membership in the Society of United Irish.[50]

---

[48] *Gaz. of the U.S.*, 11 Feb. 1799.

[49] *Porcupine's Gaz.*, 12 Feb. 1799.

[50] *Ibid.*, 12 Dec. 1797, 14 Feb. 1799; unidentified newspaper clipping, Duane folder, Misc. Papers, NYPL; *Gaz. of the U.S.*, 18 Jan. 1799.

The four men attempted to post their announcement at the rear of the sanctuary before the service was concluded, but the trustees pulled down their placards and informed the priest, who "gave directions that the congregation should be apprized of [the irreverent act], in order that they might be prepared, should a riot take place." In the churchyard as the worshipers came out, "a man was perceived standing on a tomb stone haranguing some twenty or thirty persons, some of whom had already signed a paper lying on the . . . stone." The trustees arrived to disperse the crowd of listeners, and a fifteen year old boy began to taunt Dr. Reynolds, calling him a traitor to Ireland. "REYNOLDS instantly pulled from his pocket a loaded pistol, and . . . presented it to the breast of the boy"; someone wrenched the pistol away, and the boy "knocked him down, and trampled on him." The others attempted to make a hasty departure, but were pursued by the angry church members who "with one accord . . . seized upon REYNOLDS and his gang, and dragged them forcibly to the Mayor's office," after marching them about the streets and collecting a great crowd of spectators.[51]

While the Federalist Mayor Robert Wharton was examining the prisoners, a more extraordinary disturbance was created by the Chief Justice of the Pennsylvania Supreme Court, who was commonly expected to be the next Republican candidate for Governor. Thomas McKean arrived and pushed through the crowd, demanded admission to to the Mayor and began to denounce the arrest, "abandoning himself

---

[51]<u>Porcupine's Gaz.</u>, 12 Feb. 1799; unidentified newspaper clipping, Duane folder, Misc. Papers, NYPL; Gaz. of the U.S., 11 Feb. 1799.

to paroxisms [*sic*] of convulsive passion." The Chief Justice shouted at the Mayor that his prisoners were the victims not the assailants in the morning's riot, and they "ought to *take up their hats and go away*." The Mayor was firm and the Federalist onlookers insulting, and finally McKean was obliged to withdraw "in a delerium of rage."[52]

Before the afternoon was over all but one of the prisoners was released, on two thousand dollars bond. Duane's friend James Thackara posted bail for the editor, and Dr. Reynold's sureties were two prosperous and distinguished members of the Republican party. The journeyman printer Cummings could not raise the bail. He plaintively asked Reynolds if he was to go to jail alone, and the Doctor replied, "'you'd BETTER GO. I'd rather go than not for my part.' The member of the *Academy of Medecine* took care, however, to let poor *Cummens go by himself*," William Cobbett noted. "This ought to be a warning to Democratic Understrappers."[53]

The four men were indicted and tried on February 21 for riot and assault, and Dr. Reynolds was separately charged with assault with intent to murder the boy, James Gallagher, Jr. Alexander James Dallas, the chief defense counsel, demonstrated that there was no evidence to uphold the charge against Reynold's three companions, and showed that Reynolds himself had acted in self-defense in drawing a pistol. According to Gallagher's own testi-

---

[52]Unidentified newspaper clipping, Duane folder, Misc. Papers, NYPL; *Gaz. of the U.S.*, "Milo," 9 Sept. 1799. See also *ibid.*, 13 Feb., 3, 4 Oct. 1799.

[53]*Ibid.*, 21 Feb. 1799; *Porcupine's Gaz.*, 14 Feb. 1799.

mony, Dr. Reynolds was "keeping at bay five or six persons" when the boy rushed at him, and Gallagher "kicked him three times" after he was knocked to the ground. The trial went on until ten in the evening, when the jury, after deliberating for half an hour, returned a verdict of not guilty on all charges. But to the ultra-Federalists the right of petition exercised by "a set of vagrant scoundrels" was "an open insult to the civil laws and religious institutions" and "a better argument in favor of the Alien Bill, than a thousand pamphlets and speeches."[54]

V.

Duane escaped injury in the incident at St. Mary's, but soon after he was the victim in a disgraceful episode of violent reprisal against his freedom of expression. In March 1799 the nation was alarmed by an incident of armed resistance to the law of Pennsylvania. Citizens in the German-populated, eastern county of Northampton, led by an auctioneer named John Fries, expressed their hatred of the direct tax on property by forcibly rescuing two tax defaultors who were in the custody of the federal marshal. Military preparations to put down Fries Rebellion began at once in Philadelphia, the national capital. President John Adams accepted the proffered services of "McPherson's Blues," a Pennsylvania regiment of volunteer militia commanded by Brigadier-General William McPherson and composed largely of companies of young Philadelphia Federalists.

---

[54]Francis Wharton, State Trials of the United States During the Administrations of Washington and Adams (Philadelphia, 1849), 363-377, 388; unidentified newspaper clipping, Duane folder, Misc. Papers, NYPL.

Following the original outbreak of violence, little occurred in the German counties to justify the belief that an insurrection was in progress. "The Insurgents of Northampton are, it is thought, dispersed by this time," it was reported on March 21, "and ready to submit to the Taxation Law." The first units of militia did not leave Philadelphia until one week later. Porcupine's Gazette expressed annoyance that the crafty rebels, by their peacefulness, sought to evade punishment. They "seem to understand the trim of the times perfectly well. - They calculate to an unit," Cobbett complained. "-Were I their ruler for a little while, their arithmetic would certainly mislead them." On April 6 John Fries and other leaders were imprisoned in Philadelphia. The cavalry units from the city remained in Northampton country for three weeks longer, although the region was quiet except for the minor disturbances caused by the militiamen themselves.[55]

Immediately after the expedition returned, while Fries was awaiting trial for treason, the Aurora began to censure the behavior of the volunteer companies. Duane charged that some units had been guilty of exploitation and mistreatment of the local populace, but he refused to reveal the source of his information. The officers of the city cavalry troops were enraged by the Aurora's insinuations, and on May 15 they organized a private expedition to call on William Duane.

A gang of about thirty young gentlemen gathered in Hardy's Tavern before noon and then marched in a body to the Aurora office

---

[55]Porcupine's Gazette, 21, 23 Mar. 1799.

in Franklin Court, off Market street. The captain of each company was to ask Duane in turn if his troop was intended in the charge of misconduct, and Captain Joseph McKean, the son of the Chief Justice, was to be the first. The officers all crowded into the long printing room on the second floor and stood guard over the pressmen and young William John Duane at work there, while the others waited on the stairs and in the court below.

Peter Meircken and others "shoved forward" Joe McKean to address Duane Senior, seated at his desk. Duane refused to answer whether McKean's company was intended, and he told the son of the Republican candidate for Governor that "he ought to have been the last man to come forward on this occasion, that those who surrounded him had duped him, and made him an instrument to defeat his father's election." Perhaps dimly perceiving the truth of the remark, Joe McKean called Duane "a damned liar" and slapped him across the mouth with the back of his hand. Duane instantly hit back and the "whole gang then rushed on me in a body." Men on each side held Duane fast, with their thumbs between his collar and his throat, "and in this position, nearly throttled, I was dragged down stairs."

When they had Duane in the courtyard, the mob "formed a ring about me as if it had been a cock fight--and in fact," Duane remembered ruefully, "I was knocked down like a cock at the first blow Meircken gave me." Peter Meircken, "their leviathan," superintended the beating, and delivered most of the blows, while others stepped in to hit him a few times, "beside the young cubs who, whenever I was knocked down, came behind, and kicked and struck me, and ran off as I rose." As they beat him methodically, the officers repeatedly asked Duane to tell who was the author of the stories about the cavalry, and Duane continually refused. Each time he was knocked down, Duane staggered to his feet, to attempt to fight back, "but, as I know nothing of boxing, and Meircken had studied under Mendoza, it was not surprising that I could not stand long before him--I believe, however I hurt his feelings occasionally," Duane remembered with satisfaction, "for I recollect perfectly, that having hit him severely, he collected himself, and was about to give me one of his scientific strokes, when I received a blow from behind, under my right ear, which brought me to the ground." Meircken himself boasted that he would have killed Duane with the blow, but Duane was saved by an interloper.

In the confusion William John was able to slip down the staircase and into the yard. The boy "was crying, and pushing his way between the legs of the assailants-," a neighbor recalled; "his father was lying on the ground and he threw himself on his father's body to protect him from the blows," or to see if his father was alive. Someone knocked William John away with a "violent blow" on the side of the head, and others kicked him toward the edge of the ring. The elder Duane struggled up and "made towards him to protect him," but was quickly knocked down again. "My spirits never failed me," Duane remembered, "til I saw my son knocked down--I felt faint, and overpowered by their barbarity then."

When Duane was beaten senseless and could no longer rise, he was whipped with a cowskin as a final discipline. "Mr. Meircken officiated," but each captain, "for his troop, . . . gave him a cut." Some of the officers were discontented and ashamed at the brutality. "Some one . . . said it was too much, and Meircken then desisted." While Duane was still on his feet, the leaders had "several times roared out, carry him to the market house, strip him and flog him." Indeed they had "previously provided a trumpeter for the purpose," but they abandoned the plan, perhaps because "they had beaten me till I had no more feeling or power to move." The officers left Duane where he was, his whole body bruised and lacerated, and returned to Hardy's Tavern to draw up a statement in vindication of their action.[56]

The following day the Gazette of the United States published a defense of the brutal act. Porcupine's Gazette never mentioned the savage incident, for William Cobbett had a sense of decency when his personal emotions were not involved. But John Ward Fenno thought that the officers' aroused feelings were justified, because they had taken two months of trouble and expense for the Northampton expedition and then returned to find themselves called "thieves, ruffians and caitiffs." The would not have been soldiers and men of honor if they had acted otherwise, was Fenno's astounding conclusion, "when they reflected that the same villain and the same paper had called the great and good Washington, a hypocrite, a fool, a liar, a coward, a tyrant and a murderer." (The alleged slanders were pure fabrication by Fenno, but were believed of Duane by the Federalist party.)

---

[56] Minutes of Examination, Taken in Short Notes--on the Trial of the Rioters, for a Riot and Assault on William Duane, on the 15 May, 1799--Trial 28 April, 1801 (Philadelphia, 1801?), pamphlet, LC.

Furthermore the author-victim "was not an American but a foreigner, and not merely a foreigner, but an United Irishman, and not merely an United Irishman, but a public convict and fugitive from justice." Fenno's Gazette depicted "Citizen DWIGHT" as he "received his flagellation" as rather a comic figure.[57]

The outrage upon Duane electrified the Republican party in Philadelphia, and ultimately it proved a major turning point in public opinion of the two parties. Reacting against the militia's behavior, the Republicans decided to organize their own volunteer regiment. The "faction . . . are expressly called upon to associate themselves . . . , not for the purpose of defending their country from foreign invasion," Fenno's Gazette remonstrated, "not for . . . defending their government against . . . domestic traitors, but avowedly in order to act against the Friends of Government." Within a week after the assault on Duane, it was reported that "considerable accessions of strength have already been made to the Militia Companies; and that a band of Jacobins mount guard every evening at his office."[58]

A number of leading Republicans agreed to serve as captains of the several companies which would compose the Philadelphia Militia Legion. One of the first affiliates of the Legion was the cavalry troop of Thomas Leiper, which had served at Northampton and was in fact the Aurora's source of knowledge about the misconduct on the expedition.[59] Leiper was a Scottish-born tobacconist who

---

[57]Gaz. of the U.S., 16 May 1799. [58]Ibid., 23 May 1799.

[59]Minutes of Examination, 20-23.

was a friend of Thomas Jefferson and the Virginian's agent in selling his annual tobacco crop. Duane and Leiper were to enjoy a lifelong friendship and political association, which undoubtedly had strong roots in the editor's courageous silence during the brutal beating of May 15, 1799, when he could have escaped by naming the author of the offending story.

Duane was to be the captain of a new infantry company, "a life guard for his own carcass," the Federalists jibed. "It is said that the French republic are to pay for the uniforms which is [*sic*] to *be green*, with the French Cock feather in their cap. They are to be called the *French Irish Blues*, or the Aurora Life Guard." The Federalists learned of the recruitment to Duane's "Republican Greens" through a circular confiscated from "a young Irishman, of short residence in the country, . . . [who] applied to a gentleman to read it for him." Fenno's *Gazette* thought the details worth publishing because "every thing relating to so dignified a personage as the Aurora-man, must be interesting."[60]

In less than one year as editor of the *Aurora*, Duane had established himself as a man of unusual ability and courage, and was rising to a position of prominence in the Republican party. The Federalists kept up a steady assault upon his past life and associations, inventing wickedly fanciful versions to prove his wretchedness and insignificance. He was "once a Jew Cloathsman in London," they declared, or a "*Peep-o'day* Boy in Ireland," who for gathering arms was transported by the British government "to a

---

[60] *Porcupine's Gaz.*, 9 July 1799; *Gaz. of the U.S.*, 21 June 1799.

colony in the southern Ocean," from where he escaped confinement and fled as a fugitive to the United States. The favorite story about him was that Sir John Shore had allowed Duane to be escorted from Calcutta on a pole, in tar and feathers. "Sir John, however, on the whole, Did wrong to set you on a pole," went the lines of a current poem; "for such a patriot ought to ride/ Suspended from the _under side_." In Philadelphia he bore the nickname "the Calcutta Polerider" the rest of his life.[61]

Yet Duane's enemies had to admit that he was prospering under their treatment. "Whatever declension has been witnessed by the Aurora, Darby the conductor [a new nickname] . . . is certainly in better case," observed Fenno's _Gazette_. "It is said of him that he gets his daily allowance of gin, 'which was not so before.'" The ultra-Federalists sorely resented his notoriety, which they had helped immeasurably to create. Ironically it was they who lifted him permanently out of obscurity by deciding to prosecute him under the sedition law.[62]

In July 1799 the _Aurora_ began to publish a series of extracts from secret documents which threatened to damage the reputation of Secretary of State Timothy Pickering. By misadventure Robert Liston, the British Ambassador, had entrusted his dispatches for Canada to a traveller who was "liable to various prosecutions for criminal acts" and "(on pretence that he was riding a stolen horse)" his goods were seized by "some violent democrats in the

---

[61] _Ibid._, 16, 25 July 1800; Janson, _Stranger in America_, 201.

[62] _Gaz. of the U.S._, 5 Aug. 1799.

Northern parts of Pennsylvania." They forwarded Liston's correspondence to Duane, but Secretary Pickering thought that he would not publish it, "as the views of . . . [the] editor and his patrons will be much better promoted by *misinformation* and *hints*." Ambassador Liston however ruefully acknowledged that the letters would expose his friendly status with the Federalist administration. "They upon the whole shew the existence of a good understanding between the two Countries in so strong a light that their publication" would tend to demonstrate the Republican party's contention that "I am employed . . . to produce a rupture between this Country and France, and to promote such an intimate union between the United States and Great Britain as must end in the total annihilation of American independence." Liston particularly feared the consequences of his statement "that this country had given a degree of *provocation* to France (in the business of St. Domingo) which was likely to lead to a formal rupture." To the Republicans the remark was unquestionable proof that "the members of the present Government are determined at all events, to go to war with the French Republick, and that they are united with the monarchs of Europe in the plan for banishing all genuine liberty from the face of the earth."[63]

Aggrieved by the attack upon his foreign policy, Pickering called upon President John Adams to punish the offending editor.

---

[63]Liston to Lord Grenville, 11 July, 2 Aug., 5 Sept. 1799, British State Papers, Robert Liston Correspondence, LC; Pickering to John Adams, 12 July 1799, Timothy Pickering Papers, Massachusets Historical Society.

"There is in the Aurora of this city an uninterrupted stream of slander on the American government," he wrote to the vacationing President at the end of July. He sent Adams a copy of the *Aurora* for July 24, which asserted that the British government had a direct influence in American affairs and insinuated that it was obtained by the distribution of British secret service money. Pickering said he intended to give the article to the federal District Attorney for Pennsylvania and request him "if he thinks it libellous, . . . to prosecute the editor." Duane "pretends that he is an *American citizen*," the Secretary went on, because he was born in Vermont, but "I understand . . . that he went from America prior to our revolution, remained in the British dominions till after the peace," went to India and got in trouble, and only came to the United States "within three or four years past, . . . to stir up sedition and work other mischief. I presume, therefore, that he is really a British subject," Pickering concluded, "and, as an alien, liable to be banished from the United States."[64]

In reply President Adams agreed that the July 24 edition was "imbued with rather more impudence than is common to that paper. Is there any thing evil in the regions of actuality or possibility," he remarked, "that the Aurora has not suggested of me?" The President was strongly in favor of prosecuting the editor for the article in question. Furthermore he agreed that "The matchless effrontery of this Duane merits the execution of the alien law," and advised

---

[64]Pickering to Adams, 24 July 1799, C.F. Adams, ed., *Works of John Adams*, IX, 4.

the Secretary that "I am very willing to try its strength upon him."[65]

William Rawle, the District Attorney, began proceedings against Duane on July 30 for "the charge of English secret service money distributed in the U. States." At the same time Pickering instructed Rawle "to examine his news-paper and to institute new prosecutions as often as he offends." The Secretary of State's own scrutiny of the *Aurora* led immediately to a decision to prosecute the publishers of two other newspapers, the Baltimore *American* and the New York *Argus*, which Pickering concluded were guilty of calumnies on the government, judging by "passages [from them] which are studiously copied . . . into the Aurora."[66]

Incidentally James Callender at this time was angry with Duane because he declined, from "the meanest personal jealousy of me," to copy articles from Callender's Richmond *Examiner*. "I think some of our columns would have been more to the purpose," he complained, "than his endless trash about Arthur MacConnor and Hindustan, of which I, for one, have never read a Single line." But the British Ambassador read Duane's articles on India with great interest and sent copies to the Foreign Minister and to the Governor General of Bengal, with the advice that "the correspondent at Calcutta . . . be found out and removed" since he "appears to be so

---

[65]Adams to Pickering, 1 Aug. 1799, *ibid.*, 5.

[66]Pickering to Adams, 1 Aug. 1799, Pickering Papers, Mass. Hist. Soc.; Pickering to Richard Harison, U. S. District Attorney for New York, 12 Aug. 1799, *ibid.*; Pickering to Zebulon Hollingsworth, U. S. District Attorney for Maryland, 12 Aug. 1799, *ibid.*; *Gaz. of the U. S.*, 31 July 1799.

strongly disaffected . . . and so zealous in the cause of modern liberty and revolution, that his residence in the British settlements in the East Indies may . . . be attended with some danger."[67]

Duane came to trial upon the charge of seditious libel on October 15, 1799, in the United States Circuit Court sitting at Norristown, Pennsylvania. John Fries and the "Pennsylvania Insurgents" were to be tried for treason in the same session. But after sitting for a week and convicting several persons of misdemeanors, the Court suddenly adjourned and bound over all the witnesses and prisoners, including those "*who had been tried*," to the next circuit at Philadelphia. "The reason for this extraordinary adjournment remains an impenetrable secret excepting with the judges &c.," complained a "Spectator." Robert Liston thought it odd that such important proceedings were to be delayed for six months because "it was found that the Court had not been legally assembled, the writ having been addressed to a Marshall whose time of service had expired."[68]

"We do not say anything about the true Reason of our breaking up," Judge Richard Peters confided to Timothy Pickering. "We are all too much chagrined to say much about the Circumstances or the Consequences." In fact William Duane had closed down the session by announcing that he would use the testimony of President Adams to prove the truth of his alleged libel "that British influ-

---

[67]Callender to Jefferson, 10 Aug. 1799, TJ-LC; Liston to Grenville, 31 Jan. 1799, British State Papers, Liston Corresp., LC.

[68]Liston to Grenville, 5 Nov. 1799, *ibid.*; *Aurora*, 28 Oct. 1799.

ence has been employed, and with effect, in procuring the appointment" of a major government officer. In a letter written in 1792, which Duane had in his possession, Adams had complained that Thomas Pinckney had been appointed Ambassador to England through British influence. According to Liston, Adams' suspicion had "no other ground than that the late Duke of Leeds had asked after that Gentleman and his brother . . . , who had been at school with his Grace at Westminster." But Tench Coxe, a clever political opportunist, had "made it his business for many years" to draw from prominent individuals "avowals of their private sentiments, of which he has regularly taken accurate notes, with a view to make use of them, as future occasion might suggest."[69]

Coxe admitted giving Duane the letter, but "It is singular," he argued, "that Mr. Adams, who has journalized the political, personal and social conversations of men and women in Europe, should complain of the same thing in regard to himself." The President could have been spared the embarrassment if Duane had not been accused of seditious libel. "Had Mr. Pickering used common discretion, and enquired for the authority, it could have been mentioned privately, and the prosecution . . . would have been avoided." In Coxe's opinion, "The whole mischief" had arisen "from the practice of our secretaries and other subordinate officers doing too many things without the knowledge and sanction of the President." The

---

[69]Peters to Pickering, 26 Oct. 1799, quoted in John C. Miller, Crisis in Freedom: The Alien and Sedition Acts (Boston, 1951), 198; Aurora, 24 July 1799, 3 Oct. 1800; Liston to Grenville, 6 Nov. 1800, Br. State Papers, Liston Corresp., LC.

chagrined Adams quietly withdrew the indictment which Pickering had requested.[70]

A few months after the hasty postponement of these proceedings, the Federalists were again to accuse Duane of seditious libel for publishing true statements. In these circumstances the editor naturally grew in stature with the Republicans, and some extremists professed to believe that he was the Jacobins' Eastern commander. A correspondent sent Fenno the "observations of a friend who recently travelled in the stage with two Jacobin foreigners just arrived from Ireland--

> Where are you travelling? said one, I dont [*sic*] know replied the other. If Duane has an opening in his quarter, I shall stop there[,] if not I shall go on either, to Callenders or to [Thomas] Coopers District.

One of them asked the Federalist "how far it was to Callenders quarter," and he replied "he knew of no quarters or Districts bearing the names mentioned." The travellers burst into Gaelic, then turned "and with a sneer said we should all be taught to know things *by their proper names*, within a short time."[71]

Duane's life improved steadily during the two years of legal harrassment. In June 1800 he married the widow of Benjamin Franklin Bache, an enormous step up socially for a man who had married his

---

[70]Tench Coxe to [William Duane], 29 Oct. 1800, *Aurora*, 1 Nov. 1800; Duane to [J.T. Callender], 17 Apr. 1800, *Salem Gazette*, 20 May 1800, extract in Personal Papers Miscellaneous (William Duane), LC. The case is fully discussed in Smith, *Freedom's Fetters*, 285-288. A second indictment was found against Duane for a publication of 3 Aug. 1799, which allegedly slandered the conduct of federal troops, but the case was never tried, *ibid*., 285.

[71]*Gaz. of U.S.*, "A.C.," 15 Aug. 1800.

childhood sweetheart in Clonmel, Ireland. Duane was proud to become the stepfather of the great-grandchildren of Benjamin Franklin, and he was intensely proud of his intelligent and courageous second wife. The former Margaret Hartman Markoe, of Philadelphia and St. Croix, was from a wealthy French family of planters and merchants who considered Bache to be socially beneath them. Margaret had shown her independence and strength in marrying the young radical journalist and in continuing his newspaper after his death. Duane thought after twenty-five years of happy marriage that Margaret had the qualities of a Roman matron.[72]

In early 1800 the *Aurora* revealed a Federalist plan to manipulate the electoral college system so as to capture the presidential contest between Adams and Thomas Jefferson. The Constitution provided that the votes be counted by the Speaker of the House, but Senator James Ross of Pennsylvania proposed the substitution of a special committee of thirteen which would be fully empowered to accept or reject votes. Its secret decision would be final, according to the proposed bill. The committee would have six members each from the Senate and the House, plus the Chief Justice of the Supreme Court. As it happened, the Federalist party had a majority in the House, an overwhelming majority in the Senate, and the sympathies of all the members of the Court. The Ross bill was unquestionably "obnoxious," but the House "will hardly be induced to accede," Senator Mason believed, "to an arrangement which will place the

---

[72]Fay, *The Two Franklins*, 108-109; Duane to Jefferson, 5 June 1824, TJ-LC.

Senate on an equal footing with themselves on a point so important and so contrary the proportionate weight which the Constitution has given the larger States on this subject."[73]

Duane reminisced dramatically at the end of his life that the Ross bill was a scheme for a coup d'etat; "the project was concocted at Mr. Bingham's, now the Mansion House hotel. There _fifteen_ members of the Senate assembled" and drafted the plan for "altering the Constitution." But "One of those who were present related the whole of the occurrences to the editor; his name was never betrayed." Probably it was Charles Pinckney, the Republican Senator from South Carolina, who was a member of the Ross committee. The _Aurora_ exposed the partial caucus, and on February 19 it published the complete text of the bill, which set off a reaction equal to that incited by Bache when he published the Jay Treaty.[74]

The Federalist Senators were enraged by the comment upon their motives, which preceded the text, and decided that the editor should be punished for committing a breach of the Senate's privilege. There was actually no rule which forbade the publication, but the Senate created a committee on privileges and asked it to investigate whether Duane had violated them. Uriah Tracy of Connecticut outlined a grandiose theory of Senatorial prerogative, which asserted that the protection of the members while in the houses of Congress,

---

[73]Andrew Gregg to General William Irvine, 18 Apr. 1800, William Irvine Papers, HSP; Mason to James Madison, 7 Mar. 1800, James Madison Papers, LC.

[74]_Aurora_, 27 Jan., 15, 19 Feb. 1800, 24 Sept. 1834; Smith, _Freedom's Fetters_, 289-290, 292.

granted in the Constitution, was logically self-extensive: "If it is admitted that we have the right of protecting ourselves . . . from attacks made on us in our presence, it follows of course that we are not to be slandered or questioned elsewhere." Tracy insisted that newspapers had no right to publish a bill's contents or to comment critically on an action before it became law.

Republican Senators, speaking in Duane's defense, pointed out that the Constitution did not grant the Senate the right to call individuals into question or to punish them for alleged crimes against the members. If it was intended for the Senate to be the judge, as well as the accuser, what was the purpose of the sedition law of 1798? The Republicans sought to substitute an inquiry into whether the Senate should request that Duane be prosecuted for seditious libel, in the hope of securing for him the normal legal protections of an independent judge and a trial by jury.[75]

However the Senate submitted the matter to the committee on privileges. The committee reported back that the _Aurora_ article of February 19 was false, scandalous and malicious, tending to defame the Senate, to bring it into contempt and disrepute, and (in the language of the sedition law) to excite against it the hatred of the good people of the United States. The Senate in a party vote found Duane guilty of "a daring and high-handed breach of the privileges of this house." They then sent for the editor to appear before them, to speak in excuse or extenuation of his crime, before

---

[75] _Ibid._, 289-294. For a full discussion of the case see _ibid._, 289-306.

the legislative body passed sentence.[76]

Duane received the summons on March 21 and he appeared as ordered on Monday, March 24, "contrary to the general expectation," according to the British Ambassador. He had engaged two prominent Republican lawyers for his defense, Alexander James Dallas, who had represented him before, and Thomas Cooper, the English intellectual who published a newspaper in Northumberland County, Pennsylvania. He requested permission to be represented by counsel and the Senate agreed, but declared that it would only hear arguments in denial or extenuation of the facts. The enjoinder destroyed the basis of Duane's defense, that the Senate possessed no legal jurisdiction in the case since the legislative branch was not free to conduct itself as a judicial body. Duane was ordered to return on March 26.[77]

His attorneys had anticipated this development: They would decline to perform under these conditions, and Duane would consequently refuse further voluntary attendance before the Senate. He addressed Dallas and Cooper formally, requesting them to appear on his behalf. Dallas' refusal was cool and proper, but Cooper replied, "I will not degrade myself by submitting to appear before the senate with _their gag in my mouth_." The letters were published in the _Aurora_ for the edification of the Republican subscribers, and Duane did not go back on Wednesday as directed.[78]

---

[76]"Report of the Committee of Privileges, in Senate of the United States, 14 Mar. 1800," _Aurora_, 17 Mar. 1800.

[77]Liston to Grenville, 7 May 1800, Br. State Papers, Liston Corresp., LC; _Aurora_, 21, 24, 25 Mar. 1800.

[78]_Ibid._, 27 Mar. 1800; Dumas Malone, _The Public Life of Thomas Cooper, 1783-1839_ (New Haven, 1926), 113-114.

The Senate therefore found him guilty of contempt and ordered his arrest by the sergeant at arms. But "It has been impossible to execute this warrant, as the culprit has ever since kept himself concealed." The warrant required that all federal marshals, deputy marshals, civil officers of the government, "and every other person," aid and assist in his capture. Yet the fugitive had remarkably little trouble in evading the law. "You have seen the proceedings in the case of Duane-," a Virginia Congressman wrote to James Madison, "& altho you, & all persons in the U.S. (including, no doubt, army & navy) are called on to assist in apprehending him, he is not yet taken."[79]

Meanwhile Duane advertised in the Aurora that letters delivered "at the office as usual, . . . will be sure to reach him in less than 48 hours." One source claimed that he was hiding at Stenton, George Logan's estate outside the city, but Duane wrote, "I have not been out of town; have lived mostly in my own house, and have been several times on parade with the legion." He admitted that "I keep retired," but only because there was no magistrate in Philadelphia with sufficient knowledge, virtue or courage to grant a writ of habeas corpus. "If there were, I should take care to be arrested immediately." Governor James Monroe of Virginia thought that Duane "ought to have met the censure & judgment of the Senate," in order to gain public sympathy; "as it is they establish the principle and avoid the odium of his [unconstitutional] prosecu-

---

[79]Liston to Grenville, 7 May 1800, Br. State Papers, Liston Corresp., LC; John Dawson to Madison, 30 Mar. 1800, Madison Papers, LC; Smith, Freedom's Fetters, 298.

tion." Perhaps for this reason Senator Mason believed that "those who ordered him to be arrested wish he may not."[80]

When Duane was cited for contempt, a petition of remonstrance to the Senate was circulated in Philadelphia and the vicinity and signed by three or four thousand persons. "It was argued therein," Thomas Cooper recollected in the 1820s, "that the privilege of charging and punishing for contempts, was deduced from the despotic times of the British Parliament." It was "never adopted or practised here; not authorized by any express provision of our constitution, nor in any way implied." The members were actually "enacting by senatorial authority another sedition law, . . . on which the Senate acted arbitrarily as accusers, witnesses, jurymen, judges, and executioners." The petition was presented in the Senate on May 10 and silently dismissed. One Federalist member asked that some of the names of the signers be read, and "on the name of Patrick McCarty being first . . . , a forced smile of contempt was evident on the faces of a few of the phalanx." The complainants were typical partisans of the _Aurora_ in their view: "Fugitives from justice, of all nations, kindreds and language," and "_Brigands_ of all descriptions" who since they disliked the government should "get out of the country as fast as they can."[81]

---

[80]_Ibid_.; Aurora, 28 Mar. 1800; Duane to [J.T. Callender], 17 Apr. 1800, _Salem Gazette_, 20 May 1800, extract in Pers. Papers Misc. (Duane), LC; Monroe to Jefferson, 23 Apr. 1800, TJ-LC; Mason to Madison, 2 Apr. 1800, Madison Papers, LC. See also Jefferson to T[homas] Randolph, 4 Apr. 1800, Jefferson Papers, Mass. Hist. Soc.; Jefferson to Mr. Tasewell, 10 Apr. 1800, _ibid_.

[81]Thomas Cooper, _Two Essays: 1. On the Foundation of Civil Government; 2. On the Constitution of the United States_ (Columbia,

For his notoriety in the Duane defense, Cooper soon suffered the Federalists' revenge. On April 9 he was arrested on a charge of seditious libel for an essay on John Adams written five months before. The trial was set for April 16 before District Judge Richard Peters and Samuel Chase, Associate Justice of the Supreme Court. Cooper was quickly convicted and sentenced to six months in prison and four hundred dollars fine. "The most vigorous and undisguised efforts are making to crush the republican presses, and stifle enquiry as it may respect the ensuing election" for President, Senator Mason observed. As for Cooper's conviction, "a more oppressive and disgusting proceeding I never saw. Chase in his charge to the Jury (in a speech of an hour) shewed all the zeal of a well fee'd Lawyer and the rancour of a vindictive and implacable enemy."[82]

When the Senate was ready to adjourn in the middle of May, William Duane was still at large. The members therefore abandoned the warrant for contempt and requested that he be prosecuted for seditious libel. "Duane the Printer . . . has again appeared in publick, since the adjournment of the Congress, and laughs at the inefficacy of their attempts to punish him," Ambassador Liston reported in his dispatch. "The Senate have expressed a wish that the President would . . . institute a process against this man. But

---

South Carolina, 1826), 40 n.; Aurora, 13 May 1800; unidentified newspaper clipping, Duane folder, Misc. Papers, NYPL.

[82]Mason to Madison, 23 Apr. 1800, William C. Rives Collection, James Madison Papers, LC; Malone, Public Life of Thomas Cooper, 112-119; Smith, Freedom's Fetters, 307-333. See also Mason to Monroe, 29 Apr. 1800, James Monroe Papers, LC.

how far Mr. Adams may think this a regular or an advisable step is not yet determined." In fact the President acted immediately upon the Senate's request and ordered the Attorney General and the District Attorney for Pennsylvania to undertake the prosecution.[83]

While Duane mocked the Federalists for failing to capture him, Cooper defied them from his prison cell. Until his release in October, he sent letters to the Aurora dated at the "Prison of Philadelphia." The Federalists of Northumberland county sought to petition the President to suspend his sentence, but Cooper disavowed the attempt. He would not accept a pardon from John Adams, he said, because forgiveness implied repentance, and because he would not be "the voluntary cats-paw of electioneering clemency."[84]

VII

Duane and Cooper had good cause for their brazen self-confidence, for recent political events had made it unmistakably clear that Thomas Jefferson would defeat Adams in the presidential election in November. The Federalists, by their arrogance and brutality, had exhausted the mandate received in the Congressional elections two years before. In 1798 following the insult from France known as the XYZ Affair, the Secretary of War had been delighted that "The spirit of the people is every where rising, and promises in a short

---

[83] Liston to Grenville, 28 May 1800, Br. State Papers, Liston Corresp., LC; Adams to U.S. Attorney General and U.S. District Attorney of Pa., 16 May 1800, C.F. Adams, ed., Works of John Adams, IX, 56.

[84] Cooper to [Duane], 10 May 1800, Aurora, 17 May 1800; Smith, Freedom's Fetters, 330.

time to be what it always ought to have been." But the Federalists' relentless determination to get the country into a war with France, and their ruthless persecution of those who opposed it, was alienating the persons of moderate views who had given them their former majorities. No party "ever understood so ill the causes of its own power," John Adams later lamented, "or so wantonly destroyed them."[85]

Although the extreme Federalists refused to believe it, the American people did not want to go to war with France. During the autumn of 1798 the tension in foreign affairs had begun to relax; the French Directory was eager to conciliate the offended United States, and Foreign Minister Talleyrand made definite overtures toward peace. In November 1798 the British under Admiral Lord Nelson triumphed overwhelmingly in the Battle of the Niles and destroyed the French fleet. "It is a bone too big for the Democrats to swallow," William Cobbett exulted. "They look like fellows going to the gallows. . . . They now behold the power of France cut off, and with it _their hopes of plunder_."[86]

Yet Cobbett and Fenno continued to demand military preparations and a declaration of war, in spite of the growing reluctance of "the small federalists." "America will . . . remain _firm_," said the lines of a poem by Joseph Hopkinson; "firm as a _post_," mocked Peter Porcupine, thereby launching a newspaper feud with the

---

[85]James McHenry to William L. Smith, 2 Apr. 1798, William Loughton Smith Papers, LC; Adams to Benjamin Stoddert, 31 Mar. 1801, C.F. Adams, ed., _Works of John Adams_, IX, 582.

[86]John C. Miller, _The Federalist Era, 1789-1801_ (New York, 1960), 243; _Porcupine's Gaz._, 27 Nov. 1798.

respected Federalist lawyer. The English journalist was contemptuous of the diffidence upon this subject in more moderate Federalist newspapers, the "trimming, vapid and venal Gazettes," which were continually "feeling the pulse of their patients, their subscribers, to know what to say in future."[87]

President Adams responded to the changing public mood and to the improving foreign situation by announcing in February 1799 that he intended to restore diplomatic relations with France. In the past Adams had been deceived, the Aurora commented in praise of the new policy, by the intrigues of those around him. "There is one man [Alexander Hamilton] whose wily intrigues, whose shocking depravity, are known from one end of the continent to the other," and his ambition "to be the head of a party" was behind all the Federalists' excesses. To this Cobbett responded that praise from William Duane would destroy President Adams.[88]

Porcupine's Gazette insisted that the report of a mission to France was an atrocious lie by the Aurora and explained at length why it was impossible. When the news was verified, Cobbett pointedly refused to apologize, despite "a good deal of grumbling in the gizzard of certain small Federalists respecting my comments." The editor was incensed by their prying: "One of these see-saw creatures had the impertinence to offer his advice on the occasion; and had the unpardonable insolence to tell one of my people that I had abused the President." The moderates' resentment of the English propagandist

---

[87] Ibid., 4, 18, 20 Dec. 1798, 4 Feb. 1799.

[88] Ibid., 21 Feb. 1799.

led to a proposal "for sending me out of the country," Cobbett admitted when the Republicans exposed the dissension. "The tale they tell is very ridiculous to be sure; but nothing they can say is too bad for the base miscreants who made the proposition."[89]

The Hamiltonian wing of the Federalist party was deeply annoyed by the prospect of peace and continued to demand military preparedness against France's unchecked ambition, while its newspapers announced in July 1799 the series of defeats in Italy which "seems to promise a speedy dissolution of the monstrous, bloody, cannibal Republick." The day following the Senate's confirmation of new envoys to France, Cobbett saw "a _tri-colored cockade_" being worn in the street in Philadelphia, "the first I had seen for a long time." He looked upon it as "an early blossom of the returning spring of Sans culottism." The illogical reaction to events disclosed that the real fear of the American Tories was not for the national safety but for their own political principles. "If ever this country is _conquered_ by France," Fenno wrote revealingly, "or, which is the same thing _republicanized_ (according to the meaning attached to this word, by our _exclusive patriots_) and brought under her councils, it will be owing to _indecision_ in its executive."[90]

Consequently the ultra-Federalists grew more extreme in a situation where good sense dictated moderation. They attempted to use the sedition law to force liberal newspaper editors into silence, but "many who have valued themselves as being _friends of order_ and

---

[89] _Ibid._, 27 Feb., 23 July 1799.

[90] _Ibid._, 1 Mar., 20 July 1799; _Gaz. of the U.S._, 20 June 1799.

Supporters of Government admit that this is going too far," Senator Mason observed at the time of Mathew Lyon's conviction; "if to a few such instances of political persecution there should be added just and reasonable overtures of peace on the part of France, . . . the whole bubble of imposition and deception will be blown up at once." Although "the connection between foreign aggression and domestic tyranny is forced and unnatural," he shrewdly commented, "I hope that as the Tories would marry them, they will not be divorced until the peace and liberties of this Country are fully re-established."[91]

The public's reaction against the extremism first became apparent in Pennsylvania. Over all "the republican interest has gain'd rapidly the last 6 months in this State," a Philadelphian exulted to Jefferson in August 1799. "If the Aurora finds its way into your neighbourhood, the whiping [*sic*] business which follow'd the Northampton expedition," when Duane was brutally beaten for revealing misconduct of the militia, and "M[r] Liston's recent dispatches (found on the horse thief)." which showed the administration's cooperation with the British government, "together with many other things of the same stamp must be known to you. those things must have taken place through want of policy," he observed, as they have "very sensibly lessen'd the popularity of the party in Pennsylvania & Newjersey," and "may probably have that effect elsewhere." In his opinion there was "no doubt of M[r] M[c]Kean's being Elected to the Governor's chair by a very respectable majority."[92]

---

[91]Mason to Jefferson, 23 Nov. 1798, TJ-LC.

[92]Elijah Griffiths to Jefferson, 4 Aug. 1799, TJ-LC.

The state's gubernatorial election in October was "an event of some importance in the eyes of the publick in this Country," Ambassador Liston reported to his government. "The powers of both parties were excited and exerted to the utmost," the Federalists admitted, with the result that the Republican Thomas McKean was "carried by a large majority." Their candidate James Ross suffered from being "falsely held up as devoted to Great Britain," Liston complained, which "furnished a pretence for a thousand virulent and declamatory publications" against "His Majestys Government." But the Ambassador acknowledged that "apparently well founded complaints" of British encroachments on the rights of American merchant ships and seamen had helped to produce the victory in Pennsylvania and "have made the most extensive and pernicious impression on all classes of people," including those "most anxious to cultivate a friendly connection with Great Britain" and "the best disposed towards the federal Government." Thomas Jefferson was delighted with the result and encouraged that the middle states seemed "very much regenerated in principles of whiggism."[93]

The following May the state elections of New York were won by the Republican party. Timothy Pickering believed that "This will doubtless turn the scale of the union in favour of M^r^. Jefferson." On the day that President Adams received the news of the New York election, he lost his temper in an interview with Secretary of

[93]Liston to Grenville, 5 Nov. 1799, Br. State Papers, Liston Corresp., LC; James McHenry to William L. Smith, 22 Oct. 1799, William Loughton Smith Papers, LC; Jefferson to S.T. Mason, 27 Oct. 1799, TJ-LC.

War James McHenry and poured out his resentment against the intriguing Hamiltonians in the government. He would rather serve as Vice President under Jefferson, Adams bluntly told McHenry, than owe gratitude "to such a being as Hamilton for the Presidency." Following this interview McHenry resigned from the cabinet, and Secretary of State Pickering was dismissed by the President. But the aggressive conduct of the extremists within the administration had already dissipated the popular support for Adams based on his prudent handling of American-French relations.[94]

"Nothing can equal the discomfiture of the _friends of order_," Senator Mason gleefully reported, "at the rapid change in public opinion which has already I trust operated their downfal [_sic_], and is still progressing. N.Jersey & Delaware are like to follow the example of New York," he believed, "and even in Connecticut the delusion is vanishing fast." In Philadelphia on the Fourth of July 1800 only the Republicans held a parade and celebration; "the other party gave no demonstrations of joy, the church bells were silent, & the [Federalists] were generally attending to their daily occupations." Moreover "Since the late changes in the cabinet, & in politics at large, life has become not only tolerable, but somewhat comfortable."[95]

Once it was taken for granted that Jefferson would be

---

[94]Pickering to William L. Smith, 7 May 1800, William Loughton Smith Papers, LC; Page Smith, _John Adams_, 2 vols. (Garden City, N.Y., 1962), II, 1028, 1033. See also Liston to Grenville, 6 May 1800, Br. State Papers, Liston Corresp., LC.

[95]Mason to Monroe, 23 May 1800, Monroe Papers, LC; Elijah Griffiths to Jefferson, 8 July 1800, TJ-LC.

elected President, the Federalists fell to battling for the custody of their party. Hamilton and his allies decided to run their own presidential candidate, General Charles C. Pinckney of South Carolina. "Zeal and fortitude," according to Hamilton, "are more than ever necessary. A new and more dangerous Era has commenced. Revolution and a new order of things are avowed in this quarter. Property Liberty and even life are at stake." Yet Adams was seeking "to curry favor with the Jacobins" and to entice Republican leaders into a coalition of moderates against the extremists in both parties. The Hamiltonians were enraged when he pardoned John Fries and the two others condemned to death for treason, and disgusted that the suit against Duane for publishing Ambassador Liston's purloined letters "would not _be pushed_!" during the President's desperate campaign for re-election.[96]

The hot-tempered Adams condemned the Pinckney faction with "the grossest invectives," Robert Liston reported, and "has even gone so far as to throw out the cant invectives employed by the Jacobins,--that they are a Faction, led by British influence and British intrigue. Indeed his language to the Democrats" in his campaign speeches and writings "would almost tempt one to believe that he had in fact conceived the wild idea of throwing himself into the arms of that party, in order to secure the office of Vice-

[96]Alexander Hamilton to James McHenry, 15 May 1800, James McHenry Papers (photostat, second series), LC; Liston to Grenville, 30 May 1800, Br. State Papers, Liston Corresp., LC; New York _American Citizen_, 2 May 1801. See also Pickering to William L. Smith, 7 June 1800, William Loughton Smith Papers, LC; Oliver Wolcott to James McHenry, 26 Aug. 1800, James McHenry Papers (photostat, second series), LC.

President, and to disappoint his federal rival."[97]

While a struggle for the soul of Federalism went on among the party leaders, the apathetic Federalist voters were quietly becoming reconciled to the prospect of a Republican victory. In Philadelphia "the Feds have exhibited a degree of order & civilization, not before witnessed for many years," a Republican recorded, and the Federalist Benjamin Rush agreed that "A spirit of moderation, & mutual forbearance begins to revive among our citizens." Dr. Rush, the friend from Revolutionary days of both Adams and Jefferson, confided to Jefferson in August that he was well thought of among the Federalists. "Judge Peters," he related, "spoke of you yesterday at his table in my hearing, in the most respectful and even affectionate manner."[98]

In December 1800 when the electoral vote was completed, Jefferson had defeated Adams by seventy-three to sixty-five. Because the vice-presidential candidate Aaron Burr had an equal number of votes, the election was submitted to the House of Representatives, but the Federalist members failed in their attempt to elect Burr and thwart the public's clear intention. William Duane went to the new capital at Washington after the opening of Congress to report the election in the House and to be present for the inauguration of Thomas Jefferson.

---

[97] Liston to Grenville, 5 July 1800, Br. State Papers, Liston Corresp., LC. See also Liston to Grenville, 29 May 1800, ibid.

[98] Elijah Griffiths to Jefferson, 8 July 1800, TJ-LC; Rush to Jefferson, 22 Aug. 1800, TJ-LC. See Liston to Grenville, 8 Oct. 1800, Br. State Papers, Liston Corresp., LC, on the Aurora's effective pre-election campaign exposing alleged financial peculation by Pickering and other government officers.

John Adams, reflecting bitterly on the election a few weeks following his retirement, blamed his defeat on foreign meddlers who "have a strange, a mysterious influence in this country. Is there no pride in American bosoms?" he demanded. "Can their hearts endure that Callender, Duane, Cooper, and Lyon, should be the most influential men in the country, all foreigners and all degraded characters?" Yet the Federalists had brought on their own defeat, Adam believed, by their pro-British sympathies and their vanity. "If we had been blessed with common sense," he insisted, "we should not have been overthrown. . . . A group of foreign liars, encouraged by a few ambitious native gentlemen, have discomfited the education, the talents, the virtues, and the property of the country."[99]

---

[99]Adams to Christopher Gadsden, 16 Apr. 1801, C. F. Adams, ed., Works of John Adams, IX, 584; Adams to Benjamin Stoddert, 31 Mar. 1801, ibid., 582.

CHAPTER III

QUIDS AND DEMOCRATS

The inauguration of Thomas Jefferson on March 4, 1801, was celebrated by the Republicans in Philadelphia with a grand parade through the city, followed by festive dinners and self-congratulatory toasts. For weeks beforehand while the outcome of the presidential election in the House of Representatives was still unknown, the Federalist newspapers had warned peaceloving citizens to be on guard, for the Aurora writers were "labouring with all their might to excite sedition and rouse the desperate to insurrection" if the Federalists dared to elect Aaron Burr. But on the jubilant Fourth of March, the Gazette of the United States had grudgingly to admit the absence of "those excesses which many of the peaceable citizens had long apprehended from *such* a collection on *such* an occasion."[1]

The parade was led by the Militia Legion, the group which had formed following the brutal beating of Duane, and which in the presidential election had "had its use in the general scale."[2] Duane himself was in Washington for the inauguration. As the military host marched past they looked so clean, mocked a Federalist

---

[1] Gaz. of the U.S., 18 Feb., 5 Mar. 1801.

[2] Thomas Leiper to Jefferson, 8 Mar. 1801, TJ-LC.

satirist, that one might suppose them gentlemen. But

. . . now a wild, untutor'd train,
A foreign, outcast, downcast band,
(Who robbed the gallows, in their native land,)
Deplor'd the absence of their chief Duane--
Fit crew for such a captain, by my soul!--
If in procession I had been,
I should have marched behind these men,
If I would keep my purse, or body whole--

Following the militia came the party leaders and the multitude of happy citizens. Alexander James Dallas, the foremost Republican lawyer, was flanked by two lesser attorneys, Charles Swift and John L. Leib.

And now a trio, D_ll_s, Sw_ft and L__b,
Drew ev'ry eye on ev'ry side;
Was it because, their dress denied
That they belonged to such a ragged tribe?
Or was it not, because some thought,
They could not in the open day,
(And that too in the public way)
Mid such a crew be caught?
. . . .
Indeed, Good A. J. D. you were asham'd
With such a mob to go,
But then, in truth, you cannot well be blam'd,
The mob would have it so;
Or give you no more of those shining fees,
That often reach C. Sw_ft in shape of Glo'ster cheese.

When the parade ended the Republicans dispersed to their separate celebrations.

The mob now parted, each one to his hole,
To hail Democracy and drain the bowl,
The better part, as so themselves they call
At Francis's Madeira sipp'd,--
A foreign squad, in brandy dipp'd
Their snouts at Cordner's factious hall--
While yet another and more numerous train,
In Whiskey toasted, in the fields, M'K[ea]n--
We thought till now, as 'tis in Hell's deep shades,
That faction's children, own'd no diff'rent grades.[3]

---

[3]Gaz. of the U.S., 11 Mar. 1801.

The Federalists at the moment of Jefferson's inauguration, beguiled by "his benevolent, conciliatory, yet manly address," were uniquely candid concerning Republicanism's "different grades." The advocates of Jefferson "very obviously consisted of two classes of men," according to one analyst, distributable "under the general heads of Democrats and Jacobins." The former group included "all the well informed, well disposed citizens" in the Republican party, and "under the latter head was crowded the rubbish of our community, consisting chiefly of united Irish—fugitives, and anglo-democratic outlaws," and including "the refuse of our native vulgar, whose occupations and amusements unavoidably expose them to the contagion of those profligate intruders."

The inaugural celebration in Philadelphia, "Ephraim" maintained, bore out the contention of an inherent rift between Republicans; "conscious of their different qualities and views they very naturally divided" and went with their own sort, the democrats to Francis' Union hotel and the jacobins to a tavern on Chestnut street "with fare adapted to their taste and circumstances." "The Democrats passed the evening in innocent hilarity, and drank to toasts dictated by benevolence and a spirit of conciliation," toasts "such as might be drank by Americans." But the jacobins, "the vile excrements of popular governments in all ages," at their dinner headed by Thomas Cooper and Dr. James Reynolds, "breathed nought but the foul breath of sedition and insurrection," and offered toasts "such as might be relished by any United Irishmen, French Jacobins, and fugitive members of the English Corresponding Society."[4]

II

The alleged breach in Pennsylvania's Republican party was real enough, as experience in office was soon to show. Only the extremism and dissension among the Federalists themselves had theretofore obscured it, causing the Republicans to act as a united political family. In Philadelphia the breakup of the famous Democratic Society of Pennsylvania in 1794 was an old wound only superficially healed. The Whiskey Rebellion in western Pennsylvania in the summer of that year, when Democratic farmers had refused to pay the federal excise tax, had gravely jeopardized the right of peaceful political opposition. "The mad conduct of the insurgents at Pittsburgh is the natural fruit of their democratic clubs," in the opinion of most Federalists and of President Washington himself. The mother club in Philadelphia had been particularly blamed. "The country people have no clubs to carry points, and they universally detest them," according to the Gazette of the United States, as designed "by intrigue and management in the cities to lead the country people by the nose."[5]

In September 1794 the President had mobilized troops to march to the scene of disorder. In debating its response to the emergency, the Democratic Society foundered. A moderate wing led by Alexander J. Dallas thought that the use of federal military force was unneces-

---

[4]Ibid., 9, 11, 12 Mar. 1801.

[5]Ibid., 2 Sept., 30 Dec. 1794.

sary, that the civil authorities could restore order in western Pennsylvania and prosecute the offenders in the state's courts.[6] The members in favor of a more radical statement of position had been led by Benjamin F. Bache and a German physician turned politician, Michael Leib, who in 1799 was elected Congressman from Philadelphia county.

In the Society's meeting on September 11, Dr. Leib introduced three resolutions as a proposed statement of policy. The motion to consider them passed by one vote, thirty to twenty-nine. The first two resolutions, which supported and commended the Governor of Pennsylvania for his efforts to restore order, were carried without serious controversy. But "On going to the 3[d], an unusual warmth took place among some of the members, and the President suddenly and unexpectedly quitted his seat," disrupting the proceedings until "the Society called Cit[n]. Bache to fill the Chair pro tempore." The third resolution denounced "the intemperance of the Western citizens, in not accepting the equitable and pacific proposals made to them by the Government," and charged that "such an outrage upon order and democracy, so far from entitling them to the patronage of Democrats, will merit the proscription of every friend to equal liberty." While it was under debate, the President and twenty-nine members walked out of the room. The thirty who remained then "coolly and dispassionately discussed" the resolution, and it was withdrawn. But the damage to the Society was already done. In the following

---

[6]George Mifflin Dallas, Life and Writings of Alexander James Dallas (Philadelphia, 1871), 150-151.

weeks the President and the angry members did not return; many of the officers resigned, and the club continued as a remnant until it disbanded soon after.[7]

The members who had favored a strong statement against the insurrection were those, like Bache, who had most cause to fear their own denunciation as dangerous radicals. Many of them, including Michael and his brother John L. Leib, enlisted as volunteers on the western expedition, "to teach those lawless scoundrels west of the Allegheny that our Country is not to be a prey to anarchy." It was said that "'The Democratic Society of Pennsylvania could have made a quorum in the field.'" But to Federalists the "uncommon pains . . . to make us believe in the sincerity" of their patriotism, merely revealed "a consciousness of cause for suspicion; while those who have been uniform" in their support of government "deal with ease and confidence on an established credit." Some members "took arms against the insurgents" as "Incendiaries are sometimes the first to cry fire; by this means they expect to escape detection."[8]

The unintentional destruction of the Democratic Society created an unseen resentment of Michael Leib among other Republican leaders. A. J. Dallas was cool; Senator George Logan began to

---

[7]Minutes of the Democratic Society of Pennsylvania, 141-146, HSP.

[8]Michael Leib to Lydia Leib, 20 Oct. 1794, Society Collection, Leib-Harrison Family Papers, HSP; Gaz. of the U.S., 11, 19, 30 Dec. 1794. See also ibid., 17 Sept. 1794; Porcupine's Gaz., 25 Mar. 1799; Michael Leib to Lydia Leib, 5, 11 Oct. 1794, Soc. Collection, Leib-Harrison Family Papers, HSP.

despise him, and most important, Albert Gallatin felt bitterly aggrieved by his actions. Gallatin, the foremost Republican leader in western Pennsylvania, had taken the lead in urging the government to act with moderation, and although he later regretted his position then, he never forgave Leib for taking the opposite ground against him.[9] The ramifications of that resentment were to be felt throughout Pennsylvania Republicanism during Jefferson's administration, when Leib became a Philadelphia Congressman and Gallatin the Secretary of the Treasury and arbiter of the state's patronage.

In 1799 the selection of Thomas McKean as the Republican candidate for Governor made future schism within the party inevitable. McKean, a signer of the Declaration of Independence and for twenty years the Chief Justice of the Pennsylvania Supreme Court, had been a strong Federalist until his conversion only three or four years before. The Chief Justice was an aging but ambitious man. "Who would believe," a sarcastic Federalist demanded, "that this pure patriot, this honest democrat, this unassuming, humble republican, had, so long ago as ten years, projected the visionary scheme of mounting to the supreme executive magistracy of Pennsylvania?" At that time "his vanity led him to believe, that the honest and industrious citizens [the Federalists] would have supported him." But they had always rebuffed him because of his "oppressive and capricious" disposition. As Judge he had long "outraged jurors, insulted witnesses, and scandalously abused lawyers."

---

[9] _Aurora_, 30 Oct. 1815.

An aggrieved Republican demanded, "Did you ever know a man who had less command of his temper?" In both opinions and habits he was "known to be . . . the most arrogant, selfish, and intolerant aristocrat that Pennsylvania ever gave birth to." If the Federalists had nominated him "they would have been laughed at for their political stupidity, in fixing upon the most furious despot (in real character) perhaps in the state; and he would not have got one anti-federal vote." Rejected by his own party, McKean had turned to the Republicans and "stoops to their filthy embraces, that he may make them the instrument of his elevation." But his "supplicating and servile deportment, to the seditious horde of democrats" would not alter the habits of a lifetime, and "they will, when too late, have equally to lament . . . the common ruin that will overspread us."[10]

The nomination of McKean violated one of the strongest bonds of Republicanism in Pennsylvania--the defense of the democratic state Constitution of 1776, Benjamin Franklin's Constitution, against the conservative alterations made in the state constitutional convention of 1790. "All the old constitutionalists . . . are the present republicans," the Federalists said, and they considered themselves "as a band of brothers." Yet the party's circular letter calling for the election of McKean was signed by six Republicans--A. J. Dallas, Tench Coxe, Peter Muhlenberg, Michael Leib, Samuel Miles and William Penrose--who were all "turn-coats, except

---

[10]John Adams to Christopher Gadsden, 16 Apr. 1801, C. F. Adams, ed., Works of John Adams, IX, 584; Gaz. of the U.S., 6, 12, 14, 16 Aug., 9 Sept. 1799; Porcupine's Gaz., 15 Aug. 1799.

one," Leib, who had been a constitutionalist in 1790. At that time McKean himself "not only opposed the Constitution by bellowing against it in Philadelphia," recalled a disgruntled western Republican, but "he and some others rode through some of the interior Counties for the purpose of making converts to his opinion," and "ever and anon he was shewing his dislike to it . . . until finally he was most instrumental in its overthrow."[11]

In the constitutional convention McKean had been chairman of the committee of the whole and "could scarcely suffer any one to speak, if he did not favor his opinions." Among the innovations he had desired, in a system to replace Pennsylvania's unicameral legislature, were property qualifications for the office of Governor and Senator, senatorial districts representing property interests equally with numbers of population, and the indirect election of Senators by special electors. The "most attentive research," according to the Federalists, would not disclose "a single vote made by him, against those parts of the constitution which most tend to royalty and aristocracy."[12]

During the gubernatorial campaign of 1799 the Federalist newspapers gleefully exposed McKean's record in the constitutional convention. At one point in debate he had dismissed a popular objection to one of the proposed changes as "the feeble noise occasioned by the working of SMALL BEER." "What!" Peter Porcupine exclaimed, "compare the remonstrance of the people, whose voice has

---

[11]Gaz. of the U.S., 6, 28 Aug. 1799.

[12]Ibid., 16, 28 Aug. 1799.

been called the voice of God; compare the voice of his SOVERIGN LORD AND MASTER; compare this awful voice to '_the feeble noise occasioned by the working of small beer._'" Cobbett and other writers repeatedly assured the Republicans that if McKean were elected "it is but reasonable to presume, that he will pay little attention to the _feeble noise of poor_ SMALL BEER." But the Republicans saw their first great victory on the horizon, and they were not to be distracted by reasonable doubts about their candidate.[13]

Before the nomination Leib and William Duane had taken the lead in advocating the candidacy of General Peter Muhlenberg, a Revolutionary hero and the most popular German in Pennsylvania. "So perfectly was a great number of the 'Jacobin' party convinced of the personal objections which might be urged against the Chief Justice," the Federalists reminded, that "a considerable schism is well known to have taken place between the adherents of Muhlenberg and McKean." But because of "the obstinate refusal of the vain old man to withdraw his pretentions . . . he was finally fixed on as the '_Republican_' candidate" and loyally supported.[14]

McKean was chosen because of his great prominence in the state and because he had the support of A. J. Dallas, "the Life and soul of the Republican cause of Pennsylvania." Dallas had come to the United States from Jamaica at the end of the Revolution as "an indigent fortune-hunting stranger," in the opinion of the Federalists, who never doubted the ability of this "arrogant, assuming

---

[13]_Porcupine's Gaz._, 10 June 1799.

[14]_Gaz. of the U.S._, 14 Aug. 1799.

foreigner," but deeply resented his having "risen, so easily, from rags and infamy, to wealth and a conspicuous office." Like the Geneva-born Gallatin, Dallas had never had a choice of political parties because of the extreme nativism of the Federalists. The Republicans had eagerly welcomed his talents as a lawyer and a political organizer.[15]

As a young attorney Dallas became a protege of Governor Thomas Mifflin, who appointed him to the second highest office in the state, that of Secretary of the Commonwealth. Mifflin as Governor was disavowed by both political parties and by 1799, near the end of his term of office, he was said to be "intoxicated every day, and most commonly every forenoon." Consequently Dallas and Judge McKean possessed "the efficient powers of the government," and they "mean to have it understood," a Federalist warned, "that they are determined to support all the turbulent and flagitious of the community." The Republicans could hardly have refused their proffered aid. But from Western Pennsylvania came a slight rumble of discontent with the decision in Philadelphia to nominate McKean upon the urging of Dallas. "Mr. Dallas has always behaved civil to me in his office, and I thank him," a westerner wrote to a trusted Philadelphian. "But I always considered him as a man disposed to carry his talents to the best market, and I think, considering all things, he has had a good slice of our goose pye."[16]

---

[15]Thomas Leiper to Jefferson, 11 Feb. 1801, TJ-LC; Gaz. of the U.S., 11 Sept. 1799.

[16]Oliver Wolcott to Alexander Hamilton, 1 Apr. 1799, John C.

During McKean's first year and a half in office, with Dallas as his Secretary of the Commonwealth, the course pursued by the Governor was unsatisfactory to both Federalists and Republicans. In 1799 when Hamiltonian extremism was destroying the party in power, there had been rumors of a coalition between the Adams Federalists and the McKean Republicans. In Philadelphia McKean, Dallas and Mathew Carey, the Irish publisher and bookseller, had been special guests at a dinner meeting of the Sons of St. George, an aristocratic Anglo-Federal organization, where they drank to "The King of Great Britain, the Scourge of anarchy and despotic tyrants." "This is pretty company for the _Sons of St. George_," William Cobbett protested; "for my part, I would sooner dine with _the Sons of the Dragon_." John Adams allegedly had pardoned the convinced traitor John Fries of Pennsylvania after "the _coalition_ took place" and "the President was visited by Governor M^c^Kean." But McKean followed his "proffer of conciliation" to the Federalists with a policy of removals from office which enraged them. The lesson was remembered in 1801 when the opportunity arose to substitute Aaron Burr for Jefferson as President of the United States. Burr would not disown the Republicans, James Bayard had warned, but "would be disposed and obliged to play the game of McKean upon an improved plan, and enlarged scale."[17]

Hamilton, ed., _The Works of Alexander Hamilton . . ._, 7 vols. (New York, 1850-1851), VI, 406; _Gaz. of the U.S._, 6 Aug. 1799.

[17] _Porcupine's Gaz._, 22, 24 Apr. 1799; Timothy Pickering to William L. Smith, 7 June 1800, William Loughton Smith Papers, LC; _Gaz. of the U.S._, 1 May 1801; James A. Bayard to Alexander Hamilton, 8 Mar. 1801, J. D. Hamilton, ed., _Works of Alexander Hamilton_, VI, 523.

The removals of existing officeholders greatly pleased the Pennsylvania Republicans, but gradually they became dissatisfied with the tendency of the new appointments. It became apparent that McKean's motive in selecting replacements was not to reward the party faithful but to achieve personal power. He removed his own "graceless nephew" Joseph Hopkinson for his political sins, but his sons, other relations and friends, including many Federalists, received generous executive patronage. At one of the "jacobinical dinners" honoring Jefferson on March 4, 1801, a toast was offered to "'The Governor of Pennsylvania, firm, virtuous, and enlightened, *may he apply a balm to the wounds of party spirit.*'" "We see no occasion for their beginning so soon to insult" McKean, the *Gazette of the United States* commented. But "This is the uniform course pursued by Jacobins--as soon as they have made use of a tool till their purpose is answered, they begin to censure the operation of it, and presently cast it away." Because of his removals policy, McKean had seen "the desertion of his former friends, for whose loss, the clumsy and perfidious adulation of the Jacobins, and the disgraceful panegyrics of Duane are his sorry consolation." And now "he is at full leisure to contemplate his situation, and lament, as it is said, he pathetically does."[18]

III

In the first days following Thomas Jefferson's inauguration,

---

[18] McKean to Jefferson, 7 Mar. 1800, TJ-LC; *Gaz. of the U.S.*, 9 Mar., 1 May 1801. See also John Beckley to Jefferson, 27 Feb. 1801, TJ-LC; Duane to Jefferson, 10 June 1801, TJ-LC.

anxious but hopeful Federalists watched intently for signs revealing the tendency of the new administration. "Every supporter of Mr. Jefferson . . . is not a Jacobin," an optimistic Philadelphian reminded. "The seeds of dissention . . . are not so deeply sown in our country as . . . gloomy foreboders would represent." But the jacobins "are all in astonishment at finding the federalist no less solicitous, than heretofore, to support the government with dignity and honour." They thought "that a mysterious kind of metamorphosis would take place in the two parties" by which they would suddenly "become honourable men and supporters of government," and "the Federalists would, by an irresistable fatality, sink down" to their former level.[19]

William Duane was said "to rave and roar" at the Federalists' refusal "to exchange characters with Jacobin blackguards," and "The Aurora abounds with Letters from Washington" advising the President upon his line of conduct; "it is evident," John Ward Fenno concluded, "that the writers are afraid of a system which will ensure to Mr. Jefferson the support of all friends to the United States." One New England observer was wildly pessimistic in his predictions: "The _Aurora_ of Irish Duane tells the men of property to take warning if they please, take shelter they cannot. The people . . . are going now to reign." But cooler heads were comforted by the thought that "men in and out of office are very different things." As one worldly Federalist observed to a Republican friend, "I believe you are a little more _peopleick_ than myself, but that will wear off

---

[19]_Gaz. of the U.S._, 9 Mar., 13 Apr. 1801.

after carrying your share of the government for awhile."[20]

Duane's standing with the President was jealously watched as an index to Jefferson's intentions, but opinions on the matter fluctuated wildly. The "Editor of the Aurora boasts, and perhaps truly," one commentator feared, "of more extensive and liberal support than is afforded to the Editor of any other Gazette in the United States!!" Yet Duane was "but the cats paw of the faction," according to another view, "and is used for whatever purposes his masters have occasion. Persons of more consequence than he, have recently been at Washington, and he has had abundant opportunity to learn his lesson." It was rumored that after the inauguration Duane would "relinquish the management of the Aurora to his son, for the purpose of some more elevated station in the affairs of the Republic. It is hinted," said Fenno maliciously, "that he has been named as Consul to CALCUTTA, but that, from *personal* considerations and *important private* concerns, he begs leave to decline the honor of the appointment." When the *Aurora* failed after the fourth of March to appear printed in an improved typeface, as promised, one Federalist paper took it as evidence that "Jasper" instead of being patronized by the new administration was dropped and despised by "all but the very dregs of the faction."[21]

---

[20] *Ibid.*, 4, 19 Mar. 1801; Jonathan Roberts to Jonathan Roberts, Sr., 10 Dec. 1800, Jonathan Roberts Papers, HSP; James A. Bayard to Caesar A. Rodney, 24 Feb. 1804, James A. Bayard Letterbook, NYPL.

[21] *Gaz. of the U.S.*, 30 Jan., 16 Feb. 1801; *Relf's Philadelphia Gazette*, 13 Mar. 1801.

Many Federalists believed that the incorrigible editor would soon turn against Jefferson. After the Aurora criticized a minor administrative decision, the Gazette of the United States announced triumphantly: "It was predicted that this Irishman would turn his hoof at the new government, he hates all government, because none has yet been found degraded enough to employ his services, or wicked enough to sanction his crimes." But to the Federalists' regret, Duane continued to be an arch defender of Jefferson, and when James T. Callender began to abuse him, the Aurora revealed that as early as 1798 Callender's bad character had been known to the Republicans. The Federalist papers refused to believe it and happily repeated Callender's "unmerciful castigations upon poor Duane, whom he calls a Presidential Bagpipe."[22]

For Jefferson the relationship with Thomas Paine was even more embarrassing. Since the publication of The Age of Reason in which Paine had sought to lay "the axe to the root of revealed religion," his works were "held in the utmost contempt and abhorrence" among Christian Americans. He wanted to leave France and return to the United States, but when it was discovered that the new President had offered him passage on a government vessel, the public outcry was so intense that he delayed his return until late in 1802. William Duane became one of his warmest friends in the new capital at Washington; he was one of the few who still honored the eloquent revolutionary who had outlived his usefulness. Duane tried to dissuade Paine from continuing to publish the series of letters he

---

[22] Gaz. of the U.S., 12 May 3, 7, 28 Sept. 1802.

wrote upon his return, addressed to the United States citizens, which attacked the Adams administration and dared to criticize the late George Washington. "I have fairly told him that he will be deserted by the only party that respects him or does not hate him--," the editor informed Jefferson, "that all his political writings will be rendered useless--and even his fame destroyed." But Paine silenced him at once by saying that when he began _Common Sense_, Benjamin Rush "told him that there were two words which he should avoid by every means as necessary to his own safety and that of the public--_Independence_ and _Republicanism_."[23]

President Jefferson's continued friendship with these men was thought in some quarters to be "humiliating to the pride of the United States." When a New England Congressman called at the executive mansion to pay his respects, he found Paine in the same room behaving with familiarity, and "Duane is another of the Great man's associates. . . . In times like these, _posts of honor are private life_." "When the first Magistrate of the Nation lives in habits of intimacy with such men as Duane & Thomas Payne, we may with propriety say, _We have fallen on evil times_."[24]

Interestingly, James Madison was not subjected to the same hostile scrutiny. When Duane was introduced to the Secretary of

---

[23] _Ibid._, 15 July 1800; Duane to Jefferson, 27 Nov. 1802, TJ-LC; Alfred Owen Aldridge, _Man of Reason: The Life of Thomas Paine_ (London, 1960), 275-276; William M. Van der Weyde, ed., _The Life and Works of Thomas Paine_, 10 vols. (New York, 1925), X, 95-175.

[24] William Plumer to Oliver Peabody, 22 Dec. 1802, William Plumer Papers, LC; Plumer to Edward L. Livermore, 21 Dec. 1802, _ibid._; Plumer to John Norris, 20 Dec. 1802, _ibid._

State by a mutual acquaintance, a Federalist paper commented: "It must be mortifying to a man of Mr. Madison's gentlemanly manners, that his situation exposes him to the impertinence of such creatures." Later events were to reveal that for moderate republicans of both political parties, the Father of the Constitution was a more congenial leader than was the author of the Declaration of Independence.[25]

Duane's true status with the members of the government and its leading friends was less elevated than most Federalists imagined. The patronage he received was less than he had hoped for, and in dealing with the many lawsuits against the Aurora for stories published in the party cause, he was largely left to defend himself. "I confess I do not feel as easy under these prosecutions as I was accustomed to do," he wrote one year after the Republicans took office. "I formerly considered myself embarked in a cause in common with the most upright and virtuous portion of the community." But "A few persons only have proved that they were such as I conceived them," and he felt abandoned. "When I see all my countrymen at peace," he confided to Jefferson, "and republicans diffusing concord and harmony, under the reign of liberty and moderation—I cannot but think it hard, that I alone should still remain the victim."[26]

In 1801 three federal suits for libel were pending against Duane. He had been indicted for publishing the stolen letters of

---

[25] Gaz. of the U.S. for the Country, 11 Dec. 1801.

[26] Duane to Albert Gallatin, 15 Mar. 1802, Albert Gallatin Papers, New York Historical Society; Duane to Jefferson, 10 June 1801, TJ-LC.

the British Ambassador Robert Liston, and for a story declaring that Secretary of State Timothy Pickering had directly encouraged the separation from France of the rebellious colony of St. Domingo. On these two charges he had never been tried, presumably because of President Adams' changed attitude toward both the British Ambassador and Pickering. The third case was the celebrated Senate prosecution for the Aurora's discussion of the partisan motives behind the bill to alter the method for counting electoral votes. Duane's intended defense against this charge was to prove the truth of the alleged libel. In October 1800 a commission was empowered to receive testimony in Washington from members of Congress called as witnesses by the defense to affirm the events described by Duane. The case was scheduled to be tried by the circuit court sitting at Philadelphia in May 1801.[27]

In the meantime the sedition law expired, but under the terms of its enactment cases already initiated were to be continued. The victorious Republicans had long denounced the law as unconstitutional, but it was soon apparent that there was to be no mighty repudiation for the sake of principle. The new Republican Congress did not meet until December 1801, and then it chose not to reopen a controversy safely closed or to rehabilitate the character of its victims. Thomas Cooper always thought it a misfortune for civil liberties that "this very objectionable law was not repealed, but was permitted to expire by its own limitation." Matthew Lyon was

---

[27] New York American Citizen, 2 May 1801. See also Duane to Monroe, 23 Oct. 1800, Monroe Papers, NYPL.

disgusted at the failure of Congress "to do justice to the sufferers" after discussing a plan for compensation, in spite of Jefferson's support of the measure. "I have also divined," Lyon told Cooper, that the President's draft of his message to Congress in December 1803 contained such a recommendation which "was struck out, and I could guess by whose advice." Evidently he meant Gallatin.[28]

President Jefferson in 1801 prepared a message to the Senate explaining his views and actions in the case against Duane, but it was not sent, probably upon the advice of Gallatin or Madison. The President also intended to discuss the sedition law in his first annual message to Congress and drafted a strong statement of his view that the authority to find an act unconstitutional rested equally with all three branches of government, acting in their separate functions. But after he submitted the message to Madison and Gallatin for revisions, the subject was deleted. Gallatin thought that Congress might consider the discussion improper and questioned whether a majority in the current Senate had originally opposed the law.[29]

Although members of Congress and the administration were reluctant to reaffirm the party's opposition to the sedition law, President Jefferson had determined to nullify the unconstitutional

---

[28]Cooper, Two Essays, 38; Lyon to Cooper, 20 Dec. 1803, Joseph Clay Papers, NYPL.

[29]Jefferson to the Senate, draft, [Nov. 1801], Paul Leicester Ford, ed., The Writings of Thomas Jefferson, 10 vols. (New York, 1892-1899), IX, 257-258 n.; Jefferson to Gallatin, 12 Nov. 1801, TJ-LC; Adrienne Koch, Jefferson and Madison; The Great Collaboration (New York, 1950), 227-228.

act on his own responsibility. When Duane was in Washington at the time of the House election and inauguration, Jefferson had told him that "whenever in the line of my functions I should be met by the Sedition law, I should treat it as a nullity," and that the President could stop proceedings in a case by requesting the federal district attorney to enter a noli prosequi in the suit. In the case of the Senate prosecution, special care would need to be taken "out of respect to that body" to determine "whether there was any ground of prosecution in any court & under any law acknoleged of force." If the sedition law was its only foundation, the case could be dismissed.[30]

Yet during the spring circuit, without preliminary inquiry, Duane's case came up for trial as scheduled. Publicly Duane remained calm and explained that "No step has been taken . . . because a case of such a delicate nature required the deliberation of the whole body which the executive deems it proper to consult." But privately he thought that Jefferson's wishes were being violated and that bringing the case to trial would be a "recognition of its validity." His suspicions fell upon the new Attorney General, Levi Lincoln of Massachusetts. He believed that Lincoln was not eager to reveal his disapproval of the sedition law to his "Eastern friends," and "therefore his instruction to Mr. Dallas were not so strong, as were necessary, or so precise as the spirit of your intentions demanded."[31]

---

[30] Jefferson to Duane, 23 May 1801, Society Miscellaneous Collection (Morris Duane), HSP.

[31] N.Y. Am. Citizen, 2 May 1801; Duane to Jefferson, 10 June 1801, TJ-LC.

A. J. Dallas in March had resigned as Governor McKean's Secretary of the Commonwealth and accepted the position of federal District Attorney for the Eastern District of Pennsylvania. As such he was responsible for the disposition of the suit. He was also Duane's private attorney but could not represent him in the trial. His counsel therefore was a young lawyer, Mahlon Dickerson, who "From the rising young men" was the "only one who is decidedly republican that displays talents," but who was unable to win over the experienced Jared Ingersoll, "a man who entertains the most incurable hatred for me," Duane told Jefferson. Strangely, Dallas neglected to submit the sedition proceedings to a grand jury to consider whether any valid law applied to the alleged offense, thus failing to serve the interests and views of either his client or the President.[32]

Duane was right that Attorney General Lincoln's instructions had been inadequate. "The President has judged it inexpedient" to continue sedition proceedings, he informed Dallas, "except that one" commenced against Duane by the Senate, and therefore Lincoln instructed him to stay or discharge "all such as may be depending" against him "except that above mentioned" or others with special circumstances. Dallas replied that Duane was to meet a "prosecution at <u>common law</u>, for violating Liston's letters," but Lincoln was "at a loss what direction to give" him, "The President being absent," and therefore recommended "a continuance of the cause," which was granted.[33]

---

[32]<u>Ibid</u>.; Duane to Jefferson, 18 Oct. 1802, TJ-LC.

[33]Levi Lincoln to Dallas, 25 Mar. 1801, TJ-LC; Madison to Jefferson, 17 July 1801, TJ-LC.

In explaining to Duane why he had to face trial for seditious libel, President Jefferson gently placed the responsibility for the oversight upon the editor, who had not "furnished as specific a list of the prosecutions as would enable me to interpose with due accuracy." But the President told Gallatin that he had not instructed the Attorney because he had assumed that Dallas would arrive at the same position independently, and he did not want to become involved unnecessarily. Jefferson was forced to take the risk of censure wholly upon himself however and was fully exposed to the enmity of the Federalist press in Philadelphia.[34]

At the court hearing on May 12 the defense was fortunately granted a postponement. The commission to receive evidence had not been able to act because one member appointed by the prosecution had refused to serve and the other, Harrison Gray Otis, had failed to attend. Thomas B. Adams, the son of the ex-President, thought that "the bare-faced impudence of Duane in making this a pretext for postponing . . . ought not to have availed him." Only Justice Samuel Chase, he thought, had been properly firm in these matters, and if his precedents had applied "the trial must have proceeded. But who can bear to be libelled in the Aurora?" The Gazette of the United States also thought it should be emphasized that "it was for no very great merit on the part of Paddy that he got off."[35]

---

[34]Jefferson to Duane, 23 May 1801, Soc. Misc. Collection (Morris Duane), HSP; Jefferson to Gallatin, 12 Nov. 1801, TJ-LC. See Gaz. of the U.S., 27 Apr., 15 May 1801; Gaz. of the U.S. for the Country, 10 Aug., 4 Sept., 22 Oct., 12 Nov. 1801.

[35]N.Y. Am. Citizen, 2 May 1801; T. B. Adams to William S. Shaw, 14 May 1801, Miscellaneous Papers (Bound), Mass. Hist. Soc.; Gaz. of the U.S., 18 May 1801.

These vindictive views were in part shared by the three Judges. Richard Bassett declared that the defendant should show proof that the missing evidence was material to the defense and gave his opinion against the postponement. The others, William Tilghman and William Griffith, expressed doubt that Duane had used "all diligence and good conduct" to obtain the evidence, yet the commission's failure "was not imputable to his neglect," and they therefore concurred that the case should be postponed until October. But the condition was set, Duane informed the President, that it was "then to be tried peremptorily!!!"[36]

Jefferson soothed the worried editor and assured him that "you have time to explain your wishes to me." In consultation with Dallas, Duane formally solicited a _noli prosequi_, and in July the President asked Madison to instruct the District Attorney to enter a new prosecution of the offense under an applicable state law or to drop the suit. "This was done and the grand jury finding no other law against it declined doing anything under the bill."[37]

In a less celebrated case also tried in May 1801, Duane experienced much greater harrassment and chagrin. Levi Hollingsworth, a prominent flour merchant and sometime chairman of the Federalist party's corresponding committee, sued Duane for publishing on January 8, 1800, the charge that at a public auction a friend of Hol-

---

[36] _Ibid._, 13 May 1801; Duane to Jefferson, 10 May 1801, TJ-LC.

[37] Jefferson to Duane, 23 May 1801, Soc. Misc. Collection (Morris Duane), HSP; Duane to Jefferson, 10 June 1801, TJ-LC; Madison to Dallas, 20 July 1801, TJ-LC; Jefferson to Edward Livingston, 1 Nov. 1801, Jefferson Papers, Mass. Hist. Soc.

lingsworth had threatened to throw into the river anyone who bid against the merchant. Duane later admitted that "'To give the Devil his due it was not Levi,'" but another member of the Hollingsworth family. "The suit went on, notwithstanding this polite apology." Afterward Duane always felt that he had received unusually harsh punishment for mistaking a man's Christian name.[38]

The purpose of the Hollingsworth prosecution was not to recover damages for libel, but to have Duane declared an alien by suing him in a federal court. If the court accepted the jurisdiction as a case between a citizen and a foreigner, Duane would lose the privileges of American citizenship which he had exercised since his return to his native country in 1796. The inspiration for the suit was not Hollingsworth's alone, but a party measure, and Duane particularly blamed Jared Ingersoll as "the instigator of the attack." The idea undoubtedly originated with the knowledge that former Secretary of State Pickering had suggested to President Adams that Duane be deported under the terms of the alien act.[39]

On the first hearing in circuit court Duane protested the jurisdiction and a postponement was granted until the May term. With Dallas acting as his counsel, Duane then filed a sworn affidavit that he was a native born citizen and submitted a precedent in which an American who had resided in Europe was allowed to be a citizen by the vote of Congress. The prosecution brought witnesses to testify

---

[38]Duane from [Levi Hollingsworth], n.d., Soc. Collection, HSP; <u>Aurora</u>, 14 July 1806. See also <u>ibid</u>., 19 May 1801; <u>Gaz. of the U.S.</u>, 7 Aug. 1799.

[39]Duane to Jefferson, 10 June 1801, TJ-LC.

that they had known Duane as a boy in Clonmel, including one "poor devil of an Irishman" whom Hollingsworth brought thirty or forty miles and kept locked up all night with a "centinel over him," lest he escape and talk to Duane. But when he was brought into court the next morning, "the poor fellow was completely drunk" and the trial had to be adjourned briefly.[40]

After hearing the evidence, the Judges gave the opinion that although it appeared that Duane had been born in the present state of New York, he had left America prior to the Declaration of Independence and therefore was a British subject. The jury was sent out and "immediately returned with the verdict," the Gazette of the United States announced triumphantly, "that William Duane was NOT a citizen of the United States." But "the fault is not in him," James Cheetham's American Citizen sympathized, "but in imperious circumstances beyond human control. In this case he is more an object of commiseration than abuse."[41]

The evening the verdict was announced, Caleb Wayne published an abusive commentary in celebration of the decision. The government had been mistaken, he wrote, in not deporting Duane long ago. Americans should "collect and burn" those sheets of the Aurora "containing the black catalogue of toasts in which the memory of Washington is insulted and our liberty and government degraded," in his

---

[40]Duane to Judge Richard Peters, Jr., 11 Jan. 1801 (misdated 11 Jan. 1800), Richard Peters Papers, HSP; Aurora, 19 May, 29 Sept. 1801.

[41]Ibid., 19 May 1801; Gaz. of the U.S., 19 May 1801; N.Y. Am. Citizen, 23 May 1801.

opinion, "by being named in conjunction with this worthless and despicable out-cast of a foreign land, who is now proved to have neither part nor lot in these matters."[42]

The next morning Duane replied with a series of short paragraphs on the irony of the Anglo-Federalists choosing to humiliate him in that particular way.

> Infinite pains, expence, and zeal were employed to confer the last stroke of infamy on an American, by stigmatizing him with the title of a British subject!
>
> The open and uniform adherents of the British government, concurring in the sentiment that to be a British subject is infamous!

Without naming any names Duane insisted that "Old Tories" had been most active in pressing the case against him. He concluded with an allusion to the midnight Judges and the Federalist dominated jury which had found the verdict: "Struck Juries and Mr. Adams' Judiciary Law, giving very happy exemplification of the moderation and the kind of justice which republicans are to expect from their adversaries!"[43]

A motion for contempt of court was filed against Duane that day on behalf of Hollingsworth, and he was ordered to reappear in the circuit court on Friday, May 22. Two of Hollingsworth's three attorneys, incidentally, Jared Ingersoll and Edward Tilghman, had declined President Adams' offer of the new judgeship which was held by William Tilghman, Edward's brother, then presiding in the third circuit at Philadelphia. A. J. Dallas declined to defend Duane

---

[42]Gaz. of the U.S., 19 May 1801.

[43]Aurora, 20 May 1801.

against the charge, but proposed to file a countersuit for contempt of court against Caleb Wayne for his article of May 19. Duane then decided to appear on his own behalf, "considering the business as wholly a party litigation, but upon consultation was advised to appear with counsel, lest it should be construed into a slight or want of respect for the forms of legal proceeding." Therefore Mahlon Dickerson appeared for Duane against the battery of Federalist lawyers. On Saturday morning the Court heard an additional observation by Dallas, "(not as a justification, for he disavowed that, but) as an extenuation of Duane's offence!!" He was then declared guilty of contempt of court and sentenced to thirty days imprisonment beginning immediately.[44]

President Jefferson was informed of the editor's plight and began to consider whether he should issue a pardon. The Attorney General was absent from Washington and he wanted the advice of a professional lawyer, so he sought the opinion of Robert R. Livingston. "I am obliged to decide for myself in a case of law," he explained, "which, in whatever way I decide, will make a great deal of noise." Duane had been imprisoned for "printing matters, not pretended to be untrue," and Jefferson inquired whether truth could be considered either a contempt or a libel. If so under British common law, could it be so in the United States, "the constitution of which inhibits any law abridging the freedom of the press?" Finally he asked, "If it may be a contempt even in the U. S., may it not be

---

[44]Smith, John Adams, II, 1064; Gaz. of the U.S. for the Country, 28 Aug. 1801; Aurora, 25 May 1801.

pardoned by the President" under his constitutional authority? "If either of these questions be answered in the affirmative, Duane may be relieved by pardon."[45]

Livingston in his reply earnestly tried to dissuade the President from doing anything to aid Duane. He did not share Jefferson's doubts whether British common law jurisdiction was admissable in American courts, and the objection based upon the guaranteed freedom of the press "appears to me rather restrictive" on the powers of legislation. He agreed that the President possessed the authority to pardon a contempt. "But viewing the subject as very important, so far as it relates to you personally," Livingston thought it his duty to "take the liberty to advise on the expediency of granting the pardon contemplated." If Jefferson went ahead, the measure would "awaken all the acrimony of the Tory party, give them the aid of the Judges & the lawyers without cordialy [sic] interesting republicans" in its support. "The administration is yet new, & the ground delicate," he admonished, and Jefferson should do nothing to "afford advantages to your enemies."

In Philadelphia Livingston had already discussed the case with Dallas, Peter S. Duponceau and several other gentlemen. "Upon the whole I found the general sentiment of the republicans that I had conversed with to be unfavourable to Duanes conduct on this occasion." Dallas and the others had concurred in the opinion that the

---

[45]Jefferson to Livingston, 31 May 1801, Ford, ed., Writings of . . . Jefferson, IX, 257 n. This letter is mistakenly identified as referring to the Senate prosecution of Duane for seditious libel, ibid.

court's judgment "in the original cause was perfectly right; & that the verdict could not have been other than it was." They also told him that the "libel on the court was . . . gross, & violent." That was a somewhat harsh description of Duane's allusive ironies, but only later was he to realize that the legal fraternity shared a stronger bond than the brotherhood of party. Nor did Duane learn that his own attorney had helped to prejudice the case against him, and he continued to be grateful for Dallas' legal counsel.[46]

In the end the contempt conviction was not pardoned, and Duane received "a month's lodging at the public expense." But "Even since I have been confined," he told Jefferson proudly, the Republicans came to him for political information. "I am neither shaken in my principles nor broken in spirit," he assured the President. "But after the turbulent contest which I have gone thro' with this most remorseless of factions, and injured as I have been in the stigma put on me, . . . I am shocked--I begin to feel the injury I have sustained," he admitted, "and to consider that it has been done, because I was not base--but because I have been formidable to oppressors."[47]

The incident exposed a division of sentiment among members of the Republican party, between those who would no nothing to rescue Duane and those who would seek him out even in jail. The differing attitudes within the party toward its most useful editor were also re-

---

[46]Livingston to Jefferson, 31 May 1801, TJ-LC. See Duane to Jefferson, 10 June 1801, TJ-LC.

[47]Ibid.; Aurora, 29 Sept. 1801.

vealed by the limited patronage that he received. After the Republican triumph Duane had hoped to move the Aurora to the new capital at Washington, so that it might serve as the party's national organ in victory as it had in the years of strife. But the party leaders tactfully declined his services and asked him to "sustain the Aurora at Philadelphia." Duane willingly accepted the flatteringly worded rejection.[48]

The editor approved by the party leaders to establish its Washington press was a competent but non-controversial journalist, Samuel Harrison Smith. A Philadelphian, Smith was socially prominent but safely obscure politically. His very lack of notoriety, in contrast with Duane, was probably his greatest asset for the role. It is uncertain who was Smith's principal sponsor in establishing the National Intelligencer; probably Jefferson, Madison and Gallatin agreed in endorsing the choice. Smith was secretary of the American Philosophical Society when Jefferson was its President, and Smith's wife, in her memoirs, recalled that his decision to move to Washington had been influenced by Jefferson. Gallatin acknowledged that he "and others" had encouraged Smith.[49]

From this first favor Smith enjoyed an unending flow of rewards, liberal printing patronage and a special relationship to the

---

[48]Duane to Gallatin, 13 Dec. 1801, Albert Gallatin Papers, NYHS.

[49]Mott, Jefferson and the Press, 47-48; Noble E. Cunningham, Jr., The Jeffersonian Republicans in Power; Party Operations, 1801-1809 (Chapel Hill, 1963), 260; Margaret Bayard Smith, The First Forty Years of Washington Society . . ., Gaillard Hunt, ed. (New York, 1906), 9; Gallatin to Jefferson, received 15 Dec. 1801, TJ-LC.

sources of news, while the relatively little received by Duane rapidly became less and less. When he agreed to continue in Philadelphia, "it was intimated to me . . . that some means would be found to recompense me," and from a conversation with Nathaniel Macon, who became Speaker of the House of Representatives, he had inferred "that if I bought a press [in Washington], I should have the printing of the House [Journals]." Early in 1801 the optimistic editor borrowed twenty-two thousand dollars and established two businesses on Pennsylvania avenue, a printing office and a shop for selling books and stationery. He envisioned himself in the future commuting frequently between Philadelphia and the capital, enjoying the confidence of the Republicans there and serving their interests in the Aurora. Financially the paper maintained his family but "affords no surplus, even to discharge old debts." But with official patronage of his Washington establishments, "I may still thrive," he told Jefferson. To a new business correspondent he disclosed his expectations: "there can be no doubt," he promised, "of my arriving at such a rank in the bookselling and stationary [sic] business as must render my correspondence a very eligible one to any man in trade in London."[50]

Duane's prospects received a sharp setback in December 1801 when the first Republican Congress opened and he did not receive the

---

[50]Duane to Gallatin, 13 Dec. 1801, Gallatin Papers, NYHS; Duane to Jefferson, 10 June 1801, TJ-LC; Duane to Joseph Nancrede, 30 Sept. 1801, Pers. Papers Misc. (Duane), LC. See also Duane to Joel Barlow and Fulwar Skipwith, 2 Jan. 1801, ibid. On the National Intelligencer's relations to the administration see Cunningham, Jeff. Repubs. in Power, 258-267.

expected contract for publishing the House Journals. He came to Washington to solicit the job and was informed that it had been awarded to Samuel Harrison Smith, and he was to have "only" '<u>such part of the printing as M^r. Smith cannot execute</u>.'" Duane immediately protested the injustice to Secretary of the Treasury Gallatin, who as the foremost Pennsylvanian in the government was unofficially responsible for the problems of patronage in his state.[51]

Gallatin informed the President of Duane's grievance and placed the blame for it upon John Beckley, the House Clerk. "Why Mr Beckley did not divide the printing between Mr Duane and Mr Smith I do not know," he commented, "but I am sure that most of our friends are so chagrined at it, that they speak of altering the rules of the House, so as to have the printer appointed by the House and not by the clerk." The Washington publisher deserved support but not "an exclusive monopoly," the Pennsylvanian objected. "He has already the printing of the laws and of every department; and the Congress business might have been divided." Duane had earlier applied to Madison for the printing of the laws and the State department printing, but his request had been rejected.[52]

Perhaps Beckley was responsible for giving the House contract to Smith, and evidently neither Jefferson nor Gallatin was consulted, but it appears doubtful that it was his personal decision. He had known Smith's family for at least a decade, but he had been

---

[51]Duane to Gallatin, 13 Dec. 1801, Gallatin Papers, NYHS.

[52]Gallatin to Jefferson, recvd 15 Dec. 1801, TJ-LC; Duane to Madison, 10 May 1801, Madison Papers, LC.

an intimate of Benjamin F. Bache and was a close friend of Duane. The Virginian introduced the editor to Madison soon after the administration opened. From the cordial relations between the two later, it was evident that Duane never suspected Beckley of willfully defrauding him.[53]

The unfair distribution of patronage was partially rectified soon after when the Senate awarded Duane a portion of its printing. Two years later, when Republican unity and good will was beginning to erode, Duane openly challenged Smith for the contract to publish the Senate Journals. They had hitherto been "printed by a person of adverse politics," he said of the moderate Smith, "with whom, however, I did not think it delicate to be a competitor before this period." With this appeal the Senate awarded him the printing of its Journals for that session. Long before Jefferson retired from the Presidency however, the controversial editor was divested of any contracts for official printing. Yet the enduring Federalist hostility to him allowed John Quincy Adams to assert that in 1801 Duane "came in for his share, and more than his share, of emolument and patronage" and "obtained by extortion almost the whole of the public printing."[54]

---

[53]Jefferson to Jonathan B[ayard] Smith, 26 Apr. 1791, Henley-Smith Family Papers, LC; Porcupine's Gaz., 16 May 1797, 10 Aug. 1798; Beckley to Jefferson, 27 Oct. 1801, Jefferson Papers, Mass. Hist. Soc.; Gaz. of the U.S. for the Country, 11 Dec. 1801; Duane to Joseph Clay, 12 Dec. 1805, Clay Papers, NYPL; Beckley to Duane, 4 Mar. 1806, Del. Hist. Soc.

[54]Duane, Circular Letter to U.S. Senators, 14 Oct. 1803, "Letters of William Duane," Massachusetts Historical Society Proceedings, 2d Series, XX (1907), 280; N.Y. Am. Citizen, 13 Jan. 1802;

Duane did receive the promise of trade for his stationery business. "I believe you may be assured of the favor of every department here," the President told him, although "My custom is inconsiderable & will only shew my desire to be useful to you." The President ordered many books through him, and Duane also became one of the agents for securing books in Europe for the new Library of Congress. His best hope for executive patronage was from the member of the cabinet from Pennsylvania, and early on Gallatin told him that he wished "to be useful to you whenever consistent with propriety," and that Duane could "reasonably count on" almost all the stationery business from his department. The first large contract Duane received was from the Treasury department, for 400,000 sheets of paper to be delivered by November 15, 1801.[55]

The editor immediately encountered difficulties in meeting the obligation, for he was new to the business and had dangerously over-extended his credit in purchasing his Washington property. After a few words exchanged among Federalist businessmen in Philadelphia, one sub-contractor withdrew his services after he had agreed to terms. Duane had to ask Gallatin in September for three thousand dollars in advance payment, which "would put me above the reach of

---

William Plumer to Edward L. Livermore, 21 Dec. 1802, Plumer Papers, LC; Cunningham, Jeff. Repubs. in Power, 270; Aurora, 1 Aug. 1805; J. Q. Adams, Memoirs, IV (12 May 1820), 112.

[55]Jefferson to Duane, 23 May 1801, Soc. Misc. Collection (Morris Duane), HSP; Duane to Jefferson, 10 May, 10 June 1801, 18 Oct. 1802, TJ-LC; Jefferson to Duane, 23 Apr. 1802, 27 Nov. 1804, TJ-LC; Gallatin to [Duane], 5 July 1801, Gallatin Papers, NYHS; Cunningham, Jeff. Repubs. in Power, 269.

those people who now oppose me with more success than I could have possibly expected. The steps they have taken," he told the Secretary, "are too shocking to trouble you with the relation of them." Although Gallatin was disposed to be cooperative, Duane was not able to fulfill the contract on schedule.[56]

In December when he lost the bid to print the House Journals, he feared that the news would jeopardize his financial standing in Philadelphia and asked for a large advance for stationery that "I might at least console myself in preserving my credit." Gallatin asked the President to transmit Duane's application "to the several heads of Department. . . . We may in the Treasury purchase a part," he said, "but cannot until Congress shall have made an appropriation; our's being exhausted." The Pennsylvanian began to show signs of wishing to disengage himself from any continuing responsibility for the patronage of the trouble-ridden editor. During this period of Duane's frenzied attempts at enterprise, some Philadelphians thought that the Aurora lapsed from its high standard of political reporting. Perhaps it was best for his lasting reputation as a journalist that he failed in business.[57]

In March 1802 when his entire property came under attachment for payment of six hundred dollars damages to Levi Hollingsworth, Duane renewed his plea to Gallatin. "Such attentions as can be

---

[56]Duane to Gallatin, 12 Sept. 1801, Gallatin Papers, NYHS.

[57]Duane to Gallatin, 13 Dec. 1801, ibid.; Gallatin to Jefferson, recvd 15 Dec. 1801, TJ-LC; Mathew Carey to Jefferson, 24 Apr. 1802, TJ-LC.

shewn me in the pursuits to support my family will . . . be of particular value," he told him, "as I have neither the ordinary shames of other men, nor the ordinary security for my industry--and this thro' no dishonorable conduct of mine." But the Treasury department placed no new orders with Duane, and a few months later he was told by a friendly informant that Gallatin suspected him of over-charging and acted as if he might cut off his contract. The Federalist papers had thrown out hints that "it would be well to know the price that is paid" for this stationery.[58]

Although the Secretary said that the rumor was "altogether unfounded," Duane's patronage steadily dwindled and within a year or two was terminated. According to the account of John Quincy Adams, Duane had "soon encroached upon the powers of indulgence to his cravings which the heads of Departments possessed, and quarrelled both with Mr. Madison and Mr. Gallatin for staying his hand from public plunder." Duane was "prodigal and reckless," as Adams asserted, but he was not greedy. "Duane appears not to have any idea of the value of property," a Philadelphian said of him long after, contrasting him with a rival editor who was "very well convinced that it is 'the one thing needful.'"[59]

Another aspect of party favor in which Duane's interests were sacrificed to those of the over-privileged S. H. Smith, was the fur-

---

[58]Duane to Gallatin, 15 Mar., 12 Aug. 1802, Gallatin Papers, NYHS; Gaz. of the U.S. for the Country, 10 Aug. 1801.

[59]Gallatin endorsement on Duane to Gallatin, 12 Aug. 1802, Gallatin Papers, NYHS; J. Q. Adams, Memoirs, IV (12 May 1820), 112; Edward Fox to Jonathan Roberts, 2 June 1812, Roberts Papers, HSP.

nishing of exclusive government news to the National Intelligencer. Duane had his own private sources of news, especially among his friends in Congress, and the Aurora maintained its position as a national Republican organ which was read by party leaders along with the quasi-official Washington paper. But he resented being kept in ignorance about controversial policies which as a loyal editor he was laboring to defend. Gallatin he thought was "too much reserved" about disputed Treasury matters, forcing editors to rely on their own "instincts and experience" to frame a case.[60]

In 1803 when important diplomatic information was given to the National Intelligencer, Duane asked Secretary of State Madison to furnish a statement for the Aurora. He further proposed that a system should be adopted for supplying appropriate facts to key newspapers for publication. In this way he suggested the "mortification and uncertainty" of pro-administration editors would be "rendered less painful." Duane frankly admitted that "I feel my situation much more irksome and discouraging as an Editor than when my life was in hourly danger and my only source of information was from the blunders or the audacity of those who were in power."[61]

Madison submitted the complaint to the President, who replied that Duane's intense partisan spirit was admirable but untrustworthy, making him "improper to be considered as speaking the sense

---

[60]Duane to [C. A. Rodney], 29 Sept. 1802, General Manuscript Collections (Duane), Columbia University.

[61]Duane to Madison, 3 Aug. 1803, "Letters of Wm. Duane," Mass. Hist. Soc. Procs., 2d Series, XX (1907), 279.

of the government." Therefore Madison drafted an answer to Duane rejecting the scheme. Jefferson approved the reply and sent it on but commented to Madison, "Duane is honest, & well intentioned, but over zealous. These qualities harmonize with him a great portion of the republican body. he deserves therefore all the just & favorable attentions which can properly be shewn him."[62]

IV

The distinctions among Republicans between the "moderates" and the "high-fliers," as Jefferson came to term them, troubled the administration from the outset. There were differences in temperament, between bold and cautious men, and differing conceptions of what the victory signified. Men like Duane, who had criticized President Washington for his seeming indifference to the social fulfillment of the Revolution, saw it as a mandate for change of much that had been instituted during the Federalist years in power. Others thought that the public had rejected extremism and entrusted the Republicans to restore political tolerance and moderation. The competing views of the party's mandate came into conflict immediately on the question of the removal from office of Federalist office-holders.

During the previous administrations Republicans had been systematically excluded from the government bureaucracy. The problem arose whether the injustice should be rectified by a general sweep

---

[62] Jefferson to Madison, 16 Aug. 1803, TJ-LC; Madison to Jefferson, 21 Aug. 1803, TJ-LC; Jefferson to Madison, 29 Aug. 1803, Madison Papers, LC; Irving Brant, James Madison, 6 vols. (Indianapolis, 1941-1961), IV, 151; Cunningham, Jeff. Repubs. in Power, 271.

of the Federalists from office, by a more restrained removals policy, or by the appointment of Republicans only upon the appearance of casual vacancies. Those who counseled the President to be liberal in dismissing undesirables, neither hoped nor wished for reconciliation with the Federalists. The party would attack Jefferson as much for one removal as for three hundred, someone pointed out accurately. As Jefferson himself complained a year after taking office, "They still hold nine tenths of the offices of the US. and cry out as if they had nothing because they have not the other tenth also."[63]

But there were other, highly influential Republicans who feared removals from office and the permanent disaffection of Federalist voters as a threat to the national safety. A. J. Dallas thought that the party should hold wide the "door of reconciliation" to the opposition, lest "the Parties . . . continue almost equally to divide the nation." In that event, he believed, "every Federalist will become a Conspirator; every Republican will be a tyrant;—and each general election will involve the hazard of civil war." Wilson Cary Nicholas of Virginia offered the same urgent advice to government: "the mischievous division of the people of America into nearly equally balanced parties" should be "entirely extinguished," and "it depends very much upon the temper of the administration for the next four years." If the parties were perpetuated, he believed, echoing the warning of George Washington's farewell address, it

---

[63]John Beckley to Jefferson, 27 Feb. 1801, TJ-LC; Stevens T. Mason to Monroe, 5 July 1801, Monroe Papers, LC; Thomas Leiper to Jefferson, 26 Aug. 1802, TJ-LC; Jefferson to Leiper, 6 July 1802, Arents Collection, NYPL. See also Gaz. of the U.S., 7 Apr. 1801.

would lead to "despotism" or to sectional "dissolution."[64]

President Jefferson's own opinion about removals, and about the desirability of attracting old opponents to the Republican party, fluctuated during his term of office. In his view there were not two but four political categories: monarchical federalists, republican federalists, sweeping republicans, and moderate and genuine republicans. The philosophy which in general guided his decisions in relation to removals was that "while we push the patience of our friends to the utmost it will bear, in order that we may gather into the fold all the republican federalists possible, we must not, even for this object," he commented to Gallatin, "absolutely revolt our tried friends. It would be a poor maneuvre [*sic*] to exchange them for new converts."[65]

The opposing opinions among leading Pennsylvanians on the question of removals became apparent very early, although it did not lead immediately to a breach of good relations. The *Aurora* was in favor of sweeping removals, and the editor sent Gallatin a folder labelled "Citizen W. Duane" in bold Gothic letters, containing a careful listing of all the clerks in the executive departments with a personal and political analysis, as for example, "Three Execrable Aristocrats," "Two Paltry fools," "A notorious Villain," "If possible worse;" or "Nothingarian," "Nincumpoop," Oliver Wol-

---

[64]Dallas to Gallatin, 14 June 1801, Gallatin Papers, NYHS; Nicholas to Madison, 1 May 1801, Rives Collection, Madison Papers, LC.

[65]Jefferson to Gallatin, 14 Aug. 1801, Gallatin Papers, NYHS. See Cunningham, *Jeff. Repubs. in Power*, 12-70.

cott's dear nephew, and "Two misguided Youths." Secretary Gallatin as it happened was the strongest influence within the administration for moderation and a non-partisan spirit. At a moment when Jefferson had decided to yield to the strong Republican sentiment for putting more of their members in office, Gallatin prepared a Treasury circular to Customs Collectors, who were almost all Federalists, directing them to choose subordinates in the future on the basis of "integrity and capacity" alone. Jefferson suggested postponement and it was never sent.[66]

The President and Gallatin also engaged in a "family controversy" over the reinstatement of three clerks dismissed by the previous administration for furnishing secret information to the Aurora. Their stolen Treasury documents had raised suspicion of misappropriation of funds by Timothy Pickering and others. The charge was a misinterpretation of the government's accounting system, but a highly effective issue in the 1800 campaign. "These publications do harm with the ignorant, who are the greatest number," Alexander Hamilton had complained and "in a very belligerent humor" had considered suing Duane.[67]

---

[66]Duane to Gallatin, [1801], Gallatin Papers, NYHS; Leonard D. White, The Jeffersonians: A Study in Administrative History, 1801-1829 (New York, 1951), 152; Cunningham, Jeff. Repubs. in Power, 25.

[67]Gallatin to Jefferson, 14 Sept. 1801, Henry Adams, ed., The Writings of Albert Gallatin, 3 vols. (Philadelphia, 1879), I, 49-50; Duane to Jefferson, 10 May 1801, TJ-LC; Gaz. of the U.S. for the Country, 22, 24 Sept., 7 Nov. 1801; Robert Liston to Lord Grenville, 8 Oct. 1800, Br. State Papers, Liston Corresp., LC; Alexander Hamilton to Oliver Wolcott, 3 Aug. 1800, J. C. Hamilton, ed., Works of Alexander Hamilton, VI, 450.

Jefferson wanted to re-employ the partisan clerks, but Gallatin opposed it. Their rejection would have no "other effect abroad," he promised, "except giving some temporary offence to Duane, Beckley, [Israel] Israel, and some other very hot-headed but, I believe, honest Republicans." In compromise they were hired for different posts than they had held previously. The former Treasury clerks received an army commission and a distant consulship, and the dismissed State department clerk, William Lee, was employed by the Treasury where in time he rose to the position of Second Auditor.[68]

The collaboration of Secretary Gallatin and his like-minded friend A. J. Dallas had for some years an overriding influence on federal patronage in Pennsylvania. Write "by every Post," Dallas had told him when Gallatin went to Washington. "I wish to know all your opinions, that I may give them any little aid in my power." From other sources the President received the report that in Philadelphia "the Custom house Officers are an Eye sore" to the Republicans, and "Nothing will appease the people here but a complete sweep of the Customhouse." But Dallas advised against any removals in the Port of Philadelphia and even petitioned for reinstatement in office of a Federalist friend who had been replaced by a popular Republican.[69]

---

[68]Gallatin to Jefferson, 14 Sept. 1801, Adams, ed., Writings of Albert Gallatin, I, 49-50; Carl Russell Fish, The Civil Service and the Patronage (New York, 1905), 47; Duane to Jefferson, 1 Mar. 1801, 5 June 1824, TJ-LC.

[69]Dallas to Gallatin, 21 Feb. 1801, Gallatin Papers, NYHS; Matthew Lyon to Jefferson, 4 Apr. 1801, TJ-LC; Duane to Pierce Butler, 12 Nov. 1801, TJ-LC; Dallas to Gallatin, 14 June, 18 Aug. 1801, Gallatin Papers, NYHS. See also Duane to Jefferson, 10 June 1801, TJ-LC.

Dallas himself was both federal District Attorney and the city Recorder, and for him officeholding was an embarrassment of riches. Because of his lucrative law practice, "Neither of my offices are worth holding," and the Pennsylvania legislature soon forced him to relinquish the state appointment. The clamor for removals, in his opinion, was disgraceful because it was linked to the prayer for appointment. "Acquiesce in the cry, but reject the prayer, will be clamor be diminished?" No:-," he answered, "the Republicans have been as much dissatisfied with the selection from their own corps, as they could be with the continuance of the Federalists in office."[70]

Although Gallatin admitted that "the Republicans expect a change in Philadelphia," his influence dissuaded the President from making any immediate removals in the Customs House there. Gallatin at first sought to explain his views to the Aurora editor and to obtain the crucial support of his newspaper. "I am not without hopes," he told Duane in July, "that the final results & temperate decisions here will eventually prove beneficial & popular." And when Duane visited Washington in August, the Secretary took "an opportunity of showing the impropriety of numerous removals. He may think the reasons good," Gallatin commented, "but his feelings will be at war with any argument on the subject."[71]

---

[70]Dallas to Gallatin, 30 Sept., 14 June 1801, Gallatin Papers, NYHS; Sanford W. Higginbotham, The Keystone in the Democratic Arch: Pennsylvania Politics, 1800-1816 (Harrisburg, 1952), 40.

[71]Gallatin to Jefferson, 17 Aug. 1801, Adams, ed., Writings of Albert Gallatin, I, 39; Gallatin to [Duane], 5 July 1801, Gallatin Papers, NYHS.

The editor tried to understand the administration's viewpoint and when Republicans in Philadelphia questioned him about the delay in removals, he answered that nothing would be done hastily. "As they are so kind as to repose considerable confidence in my opinions, I apprehend these assurances tend to quiet them in some measure." But within a year after the party took office, the differing views on the subject were a major cause for mutual suspicion among the state's Republicans. When an unpopular appointment was announced, Thomas Leiper wrote to Jefferson that he was sure Gallatin and Dallas had "settled the whole business and that you are not to blame in any part of it." But he warned the President that confidence in both was declining in Pennsylvania, and Gallatin, "Your confidential friend we blame here for keeping so many of John Adams' friends in office."[72]

The first public controversy among Pennsylvania Republicans came over the repeal of the Judiciary Act of 1801. The Federalists' belated new system of judgeships was universally viewed by Republicans as a shameful stratagem to put more tories into offices for life and to further increase the power of the judicial branch of government, which was totally dominated by Federalists. "There is great solicitude here, as to the probability of a change in the Judiciary system," Dallas wrote from Philadelphia. "Every day brings fresh proof, that every legal and fair mode should be adopted, to give the Republicans some share in the administration of justice."[73]

---

[72] Duane to Jefferson, 10 June 1801, TJ-LC; Leiper to Jefferson, 26 Aug. 1802, TJ-LC.

[73] Dallas to Gallatin, 30 Sept. 1801, Gallatin Papers, NYHS.

When Congress opened in December a bill to revoke the act of the previous session was the first important party measure. Public support for the action was abundantly evident; the Pennsylvania legislature passed a joint resolution instructing its Senators and requesting the Representatives to vote for the repeal. Yet there were Republicans in Congress who doubted "the propriety" of the immoderate measure, until the Federalists took the initiative in political hostility by securing a writ of mandamus against Secretary Madison to compel him to deliver a commission to one of the "midnight appointees" whom the President intended to exclude from office. The "conduct of the Judges on this occasion," wrote Senator Stevens T. Mason, "has excited a very general indignation and will secure the repeal of the judiciary law of the last session. about . . . which some of our republican friends were hesitating."[74]

During the Senate debate on repeal, Pennsylvania's Federalist Senator James Ross introduced a memorial from the Philadelphia bar asking that the new judiciary system be retained because of its efficiency. Amazingly, the memorial had been signed by several prominent Republicans, including District Attorney Dallas and the state Attorney General, Joseph B. McKean, the son of the Governor. They apparently had cooperated for professional reasons without considering the political implications of their action. Tench Coxe explained to Philadelphia's Congressman William Jones that the mishap occurred from lack of prior agreement. But the Republican

---

[74]Higginbotham, Keystone, 42; Mason to Monroe, 21 Dec. 1801, Monroe Papers, LC.

signers regretfully had been "placed in a kind of collusion" in the minds of "the greater part of the republican interest here, who are, as I am told, full of feeling." According to Duane, "The Judiciary business . . . nearly destroyed M^{r}. Dallas," but he managed to remove "a great portion of the odium" by writing a partisan address which was widely circulated.[75]

Duane was in Washington to hear the debate on repeal, and his response to the "curious memorial" was scathing. In justifying their interference, the lawyers "state themselves called upon by their professional duty," he said; "(how their professional duty comes to have a concern with the passing of laws, God only knows! For no one can discover.)" But it reminded Duane of Andrew Jackson's observation that the unanimity of the Philadelphia bar demonstrated that there was one thing on which all lawyers were agreed, "that of getting at the fees." More courts meant more lawsuits, and "they considered it a professional duty to support a source of profit." Yet "Great stress was laid upon the memorial of the Philadelphia bar" in the Senate debate, "as if lawyers, and lawyers only, were competent to decide upon a point, in which the whole people were more deeply interested, if not in a pecuniary, at least in a political view." The judiciary law was repealed in spite of the unexpected party division. After witnessing the debate Duane reflected that "The present age is as much in danger from lawyers, as the three last have been the victims of priests," and that the

---

[75]Coxe to Jones, 4 Feb. 1802, Soc. Collection, HSP; Duane to Jefferson, 18 Oct. 1802, TJ-LC; Higginbotham, Keystone, 42, 45-46.

excessive independence of the judicial branch of government was a flaw in the American system.[76]

V

The "differences of opinion & interest which seem to be springing up" in Pennsylvania were from his election onward "subjects of uneasiness" to Jefferson. For "if that state splits," he told Duane, "it will let us down into the abyss. I hope so much from the patriotism of all, that they will make all smaller motives give way to the greater importance of the general welfare." In Pennsylvania by 1801 Republicanism was unquestionably the general persuasion, and Gallatin thought for that reason that the state was "fixed" for the party. There was not "in the whole state a single individual," in his opinion, "whose influence could command even now one county, or whose defection could lose us one hundred votes at an election." Yet he acknowledged that his sanguine analysis depended upon the continuance of Jefferson at the head of the party, and "the danger would be great should any unfortunate event deprive the people of your services."[77]

To help the President keep up with the status of political rivalry in Pennsylvania, Duane furnished him with a guide to five leading Republicans--Dallas, George Logan, Michael Leib, Tench Coxe and Peter Muhlenberg--who "may be said to hold the principal weight."

---

[76]Aurora, 6, 8, 9, 10, 12, 15 Feb. 1802.

[77]Jefferson to Duane, 23 May 1801, Soc. Misc. Collection (Morris Duane), HSP; Gallatin to Jefferson, 14 Sept. 1801, Adams, ed., Writings of Albert Gallatin, I, 50-51.

1	Mr Dallas	-----	offended with 2, unreservedly opposed to 4,--cold to 3 & 5
2	Dr Logan	-----	Violently hostile to 1; D^o 3 & 5; good understanding with 4
3	Dr Leib	-----	Hostile to 2;--familiar with 1 & 4; common cause with 5
4	Mr Cox	-----	Estranged but willing to be friends with 1; friends with 2; familiar and friendly with 3 and 5
5	Mr Muhlenburg	-	Friendly with all--but displeased with 2; and rather distant than familiar with 4.

In brief Logan and Coxe were in friendly alliance, as were Leib and Muhlenberg, and Dallas was aloof from them all. Less modestly Duane would have added himself as the sixth force, and toward all he continued to express warm regard.[78]

George Logan was the first to imperil the precarious unity when in the autumn of 1802 he attempted to purge Congressman Leib from the ticket. The two had been enemies since 1794, the year that Leib's radical resolutions concerning the Whiskey Rebellion led to the dissolution of the Democratic Society of Pennsylvania. Moreover they were direct rivals for the leadership of Philadelphia county. The congressional district included the urban neighborhoods just outside the city limits to the north and south, as well as a number of rural townships dotted with small farms. Logan was a gentleman farmer devoted to the improvement of agriculture and enjoyed political influence among his rural neighbors. But Leib came from the densely populated Northern Liberties of the city, inhabited mostly by craftsmen, which for years had been the most broadly organized democratic constituency in eastern Pennsylvania and perhaps

---

[78] Duane to Jefferson, 18 Oct. 1802, TJ-LC.

in the state. According to the Federalists, the "despots of the Northern Liberties" marched in ranks to the polls.[79]

Logan's influence locally was declining relative to Leib's, and he had the additional worry of Leib's intimacy with General Muhlenberg. Logan hoped to succeed his friend Thomas McKean as Governor, but Muhlenberg, McKean's rival in 1799, possessed greater statewide support and influence because of his Revolutionary record and because of the state's large German population. In Duane's opinion Logan himself destroyed his gubernatorial prospects; the attempt to destroy Leib "will shut him out from every hope of that kind."[80]

In September 1802 after the county nominations had been entered, thirty Republicans met at the Rising Sun tavern and resolved to replace the Congressional candidate. Their hostility to Leib encompassed his personality, his morals and his style of politics. Leib was an intelligent and witty man with a keen taste for political manuevering, and also something of a dandy, whose most gallant gestures were bestowed upon the voters. The Federalists called him a "democratic blockhead" who was known for "his affected flouncing and bouncing and shuffling and tergiversating." Until he was

---

[79]Thomas Leiper to Jefferson, 16 Aug. 1804, TJ-LC; Gaz. of the U.S., 1 Jan. 1799. See Frederick B. Tolles, George Logan of Philadelphia (New York, 1953), 141, 145, 233-234, 245-246.

[80]Duane to Jefferson, 18 Oct. 1802, TJ-LC. See also Logan to Jefferson, 10 May 1801, TJ-LC; Thomas Leiper to Jefferson, 19 Sept. 1802, TJ-LC; Duane to C. A. Rodney, 29 Sept. 1802, Genl. MSS Collection (Duane), Columbia. On Logan-Muhlenberg rivalry for election to U.S. Senate, 1801, see Higginbotham, Keystone, 32-34.

elected to Congress in 1799, they had dismissed him as one of the "stupid creatures" who served as "puppets" to Dallas and Coxe. Noting that Dallas in Jamaica had once acted the role of Archer in The Beaux' Stratagem, someone recommended that the next time he "get his friend Leib to act the part of SCRUB." Leib "is his man; he is pretty well in his own clothes, but in the habilment of Brother Scrub, would exhibit a vulgarity that would set the whole house in a roar." Nonetheless "By constantly cringing to the follies and inflaming the passions of the mob," Leib was elected to high office. Thereafter his enemies, in place of hilarity and ridicule, substituted charges of criminality.[81]

For ten years Leib had been involved in a property suit which threw a shadow over his political ambitions and was to continue to jeopardize him politically during the whole of his career. When Leib was a young physician in 1784, he had attended Colonel Joseph Penrose before his death. He was related to the Penrose family, and the Colonel had placed six thousand dollars worth of government loan office certificates in his hands. Years later after the public debt had been funded, he sold the certificates through a broker in New York. The family learned of the transaction and sued him for recovery of the sum. Leib said the certificates had been payment for his medical services, but the heirs contended that they had merely been placed in his trust. Perhaps the intended arrangement had been for Leib to hold the then worthless notes in lieu

---

[81] Ibid., 44-45; Gaz. of the U.S., 17 Apr., 1, 24 Aug., 4 Sept. 1799, 2 Jan. 1800; Porcupine's Gaz., 19 Apr. 1799.

of cash payment and to receive a portion of the proceeds if and when they became valuable.[82]

From 1790 onwards the suit was continued until finally in 1801 Leib arranged a settlement out of court. He paid the Penrose family part of the sum demanded, and it furnished him with a statement attesting to his good character and exonerating him from any imputation of misconduct. Leib and his followers published the testimonial abroad and celebrated his political reprieve. But the affidavit was only as good as the public's willingness to believe it. The Federalists certainly would not accept it, and the thirty Republicans at the Rising Sun meeting were ready to announce their disbelief. It was revealed sometime after the settlement that the two male heirs had agreed, one willingly and one because he was drunk, but that the three women when they learned of it had been angry with their men. And so the old charge was reopened of "an infamous breach of trust, _to say no more_, committed upon _helpless female orphans_" (all middle-aged).[83]

The party leaders, especially Dallas and the city's Congressman William Jones, stopped the revolt against the county nominee. Leib's supporters came out in force to a second meeting at the Rising Sun, but Dallas persuaded them to withhold divisive state-

---

[82] Philadelphia _Freeman's Journal_, 13, 14 June 1804; _The Following Testimonials of the Conduct and Characters of Dr. Michael Leib and Colonel William Duane are Taken from the Records of the Supreme Court of Pennsylvania_ ([Philadelphia], 1816), pamphlet, HSP.

[83] Leib to Gallatin, 8 May 1801, Gallatin Papers, NYHS; _Gaz. of the U.S._, 4 Sept. 1799, 17, 23, 25 Apr. 1801; _Freeman's Journal_, 20 Aug. 1804.

ments, and he wrote a set of mild resolutions endorsing the official candidate. Leib was out of trouble and his re-election to Congress assured. But to obtain the support of Dallas and Jones, he may have promised or at least intimated that he would not be a candidate at the next term. The movement to purge him from the Republican party was just getting underway.[84]

In view of these circumstances Leib decided to take the initiative and appeal for popular support. Rather than wait for the moderates to attempt privately to ease him out, he would expose their lukewarm Republicanism to the public view. To do this he initiated a citizens' campaign to petition the President requesting more removals from office in Philadelphia. "It is truly astonishing that there should be found men among us," he said, "and professors of democratic principles too, who exert themselves to counteract the wish of the people of our State--The President is much importuned by such men to continue the present incumbents in office." Jefferson wanted to remove "the obnoxious men among us, and . . . only wants a pretext for so doing," Leib continued, but he was dissuaded by such appeals. "He ought to know the public sentiment on this point, not only that he may act conformably to the public will and interest," Leib declared, revealing his real meaning, "but that he may in future know how to appreciate the opinions of such characters as advise him to act in opposition to the statements of the people."[85]

---

[84] Thomas Leiper to Jefferson, 19, 22 Sept. 1802, TJ-LC; Freeman's Journal, 25 Aug., 12 Sept. 1804.

[85] Leib to Mathew Carey, 12 Dec. 1802, Lea and Febiger Papers, HSP.

Leib's colleague William Jones tried to counteract the campaign by "the office-hunting caitiffs." He drafted a letter to the President denying that the Republican Congressional delegation from Pennsylvania was in any way dissatisfied with his conduct. Jones and six other Congressmen signed it, and it was shown to Leib, who apparently agreed to sign a modified version. But instead he "sent a mutilated extract to the City which was first noticed <u>in the Aurora</u> and then in the resolutions of a Ward meeting denouncing the authors and dictating to the President."[86]

During March 1803 meetings were held in each of the wards of Philadelphia to choose members of a committee which would prepare the memorial on the removals question. Congressman Jones was disgusted and contemptuous, and although he believed the affair would end "in the disgrace and confusion" of the agitators, he deplored the trend of politics both in Philadelphia and the state legislature. "I am sick of City (and I may say of Lancaster) Republicanism," he confided to John Randolph.

Jones attended one of the ward meetings held "in the corner of a corner Tavern," which was chaired by Joseph Scott, the clerk of the Common Council. In 1799 Scott had been tried and found not guilty of assault, for standing guard while a fellow Irishman beat up one of the Federalist editors. The ward meeting increased Jones' distaste for the noisy democrat who said "'as I hope for salvation and may I never stir of this spot alive' [he] never was an alien one

---

[86] Jones and others to Jefferson, draft, 12 Feb. 1803, Uselma Clarke Smith Collection, HSP; Jones to John Randolph, 19 Mar. 1803, <u>ibid</u>.

hour of his life, <u>except forty out of forty three years</u>," Jones added. "The Lees of our City have been disturbed by Michael Lieb's [<u>sic</u>] shaking the cask," Jones concluded, "but they will succumb in due time, and I hope without injuring the liquor by their accidity."[87]

A. J. Dallas took the whole affair more calmly. "The Ward Meetings are a nuisance," he thought, "and will bring the Republican interest into some discredit," but they were "composed of very few indeed" and would not be taken seriously by men of character. The "only real mischief to be apprehended," he warned, "is the disgust excited in the minds of men like Capt. Jones." Gallatin agreed and advised the President, "I foresee a schism in Pennsylvania: the most thinking part of the community will not submit to the decrees of partial ward or township meetings; and yet the violent party will have a strong hold on public opinion," by representing their opponents as the friends of the Federalist officeholders.[88]

"I have for some time been satisfied," Jefferson replied mildly, that "a schism was taking place in Pennsylvania between the moderates and high-fliers." The same thing would occur in Congress, he predicted, when a leader for the high-fliers appeared, and in other states when the Republicans became strong enough not to fear another enemy. "I hope those of Philadelphia will not address on the subject of removals," he admitted; "it would be a delicate operation indeed."[89]

---

[87]<u>Ibid.</u>; <u>Gaz. of the U.S.</u>, 10 Apr. 1799.

[88]Dallas to Gallatin, 30 Mar. 1803, Gallatin Papers, NYHS; Gallatin to Jefferson, 21 Mar. 1803, Adams, ed., <u>Writings of Albert Gallatin</u>, I, 118.

[89]Jefferson to Gallatin, 28 Mar. 1803, <u>ibid</u>., 120.

When Jefferson received the memorial from Philadelphia, he decided to reply to it in a private letter to William Duane. Apologizing for "the trouble which this communication proposes to give you," he asked him to convey his remarks on the subject of removals to the committee members individually, without allowing the letter out of his hands lest "it should get into those of the common adversary, & become matter for . . . malignant perversions." Jefferson's response to the request for more removals was substantially different from that of Gallatin, his chief adviser on Pennsylvania, and the Secretary's friends Dallas and Jones. Whereas they condemned the desire as shabby self-seeking, he endorsed the concept of "giving republicans their <u>due proportion</u> of office." He had preferred the "milder measure of waiting till accidental vacancies" occurred, he explained, except in the cases of the least deserving officers and those most actively opposed to the government, who had been removed. But under this policy, he said, there were only 130 Federalists left in the 316 offices for which the President had appointive power. He cited figures for Philadelphia to show the greater amount of money and patronage in the control of Republican officers relative to the remaining Federalists. In short the administration's record on removals had not been excessively moderate.[90]

He sent the draft of the letter to Gallatin and asked for his advice. They had agreed that there should be no formal reply but he justified his idea of an informal response through Duane.

---

[90] Jefferson to Duane, draft, 24 July 1803, TJ-LC.

"Some apprehensions may perhaps be entertained that if the schism goes on, he may be in a different section from us." But "if there be no danger in this, he is the one I should prefer," and "I am strongly of opinion it will do good."[91]

Gallatin did not agree and recommended that the answer be withheld. "If a letter shall be written, I think that, if possible, it should be much shorter than your draft, and have perhaps less the appearance of apology." He reiterated his own distaste for the whole subject of party patronage, which made it appear that the "hard struggle" for Republican supremacy was not for principles but for "the sake of a few paltry offices,--offices not of a political and discretionary nature, but mere inferior administrative offices of profit." A friendly letter to Duane would be indiscreet, he suggested. "Unforseen circumstances may produce alterations in your present view of the subject, and if you should hereafter think proper to act on a plan somewhat different from that you now consider as best, a commitment would prove unpleasant."

Gallatin justified his advice with a fatalistic political analysis. "Either a schism will take place, in which case the leaders of these men would divide from us," in his opinion, "or time and the good sense of the people will of themselves cure the evil. I have reason to believe the last will happen," he assured the President," and that the number of malcontents is not very con-

---

[91]Jefferson to Gallatin, 25 July 1803, Gallatin Papers, NYHS.

siderable, and will diminish."[92] The real tendency of events in Pennsylvania was the opposite of his description, which merely reflected his intimacy with Dallas and his personal prejudice. In counseling the President to silence, the Secretary served the interests of his own particular friends in Pennsylvania, but he did Jefferson a disservice. The advice was taken and the letter to Duane suppressed, but the President forfeited an opportunity to confirm the affection and loyalty of the majority of Republicans in Pennsylvania.

Several months later Gallatin and Duane engaged in a quarrel which terminated friendly relations between them. About February 1804 when Duane was visiting Washington, the Secretary suggested in conversation that the _Aurora_ might stand aside and allow the doomed Congressman Leib to fall before the Rising Sun movement. In reply Duane "made use of highly indecent and insolent language to a secretary," it was rumored, for he regarded the proposition as an insult to his integrity. The Congressman had formerly been closely associated with Bache politically; he had nurtured good relations with Bache's successor, and the warmhearted Duane had an ardent sense of loyalty. Moreover Leib was devoted to increasing the people's role in politics, and from Duane's viewpoint an attack on him was an attack upon the best aspects of Republicanism. He interpreted Gallatin's suggestion as proof that a third party was forming in Pennsylvania, which intended to exclude the democrats

---

[92]Gallatin to Jefferson, 11 Aug. 1803, Adams, ed., _Writings of Albert Gallatin_, I, 134-135.

and make peace with the Federalist party.[93]

This fateful interview, with its often regrettable consequences for both Duane and Gallatin, took place because of an exchange between Leib and the President of which Duane may have been unaware. Anticipating possible defeat at the next election because of the Penrose scandal, Leib decided to retire from Congress and applied to Jefferson for an appointment in the Philadelphia Customs House. The President rejected his request and apparently advised him to appeal in candor to the people for a vindication of his character.[94]

"He is determined to consider me as his patient," Leib complained, "notwithstanding the explanations I gave him." "I am not disposed to lessen your confidence or your hope," he told Caesar A. Rodney, "by any description of the physician; but you must promise me to refrain from laughter, if you see my name exhibited in the newspapers as one of the applicants to the chinese for the removal of _mysteries_." He pondered bitterly the probable consequences of a disclosure of his rejection. "I much regret the cause which produced the application to T Coward J.," he told Rodney, who had acted on his behalf with Jefferson, and if it "shall be produced against me as a charge of disqualification for a seat in Congress," he threatened, "you must consider your self liable for all the consequences."[95]

---

[93] _Freeman's Journal_, 7 July, 11 Sept. 1804.

[94] Joseph Clay and others to Jefferson, 23 Jan. 1804, Gallatin Papers, NYHS; _Freeman's Journal_, 4 Sept. 1804.

[95] Leib to Rodney, 16 June 1804, Rodney Papers, Del. Hist. Soc.

Undoubtedly Jefferson and Gallatin conferred about Leib and his role in the developing party division. If the President during the first years of his administration had dealt directly with party matters in Pennsylvania, rather than acting through the Secretary of the Treasury, the events there might have been somewhat less violent. The revolt against the unpopular Governor McKean was inevitable. But if Jefferson himself had talked to Duane about the controversial Congressman, it might have averted the intensely bitter feud between Duane and Gallatin, which hurt them both politically. Duane certainly would have defended Leib and told the President that he was merely the intended first victim among the democrats, but he would not have suspected Jefferson's motives in the affair as he rightfully did Gallatin's. And in that case he might not have linked himself so inextricably with the fate of Leib, in unequal alliance.

Duane has been much blamed in his own time and historically for his enmity toward Gallatin, which injured the brilliant Secretary's political reputation in Pennsylvania. But Gallatin himself was responsible for his political failures. He was not an innocent victim of intra-party fighting, but a powerful ally of the aggressive "moderates." When he represented trans-Allegheny Pennsylvania in Congress, he had appeared to be an heroic frontier statesman, but after he entered the government he allowed his ties with the region to lapse. From the summer of 1802 onward he did not return to Pennsylvania even briefly, but spent his vacation in New York City, stopping on his way just long enough to visit the Dallas family in Philadelphia.[96]

Gallatin's greatest weakness as a politician was his own aversion for that role. A European intellectual essentially, the Genevan was ascetic in his habits, cool and reserved by temperament, and often mistrustful and distant even with political allies. An important Pennsylvania supporter after visiting Gallatin reported, "I had full & fair opportunity as there was nobody present but his lady who seems by no means inattentive to politics." But "I do not know how it was but in the sequel he seem'd not so communicative as in the beginning." Baffled but respectful, the supporter concluded that "a continuation of the intercourse would be profitable to me but perhaps ultimately inconvenient." Duane enjoyed repeating an anecdote which parodied the Secretary's private life. "A Droll fellow . . . drove the stage coach from Washington towards Baltimore" one night when the editor was leaving the city, and a traveller sitting beside him asked "'who lives in that house?' —'Lives!' said the driver 'Lives!' Why nobody lives there,' 'Theres light in the house' said the traveller.—O yes, the Secretary of the Treasury and his family breathe there' said the Driver," to the great amusement of Duane.[97]

Gallatin was often inept when he attempted to maneuver po-

---

[96]Henry Adams, The Life of Albert Gallatin (Philadelphia, 1879), 303.

[97]Jonathan Roberts to Matthew Roberts, 25 Nov. 1811, Roberts Papers, HSP; Duane to [Henry Dearborn], 3 July 1810, Pers. Papers Misc. (Duane), LC.

litically because the distasteful duty offended his pride. For example he wanted to enlist the services of the talented Joseph Clay, a well educated Philadelphian of good family who had been Bache's close friend. When Clay was suggested as a possible candidate for Collector, Gallatin called him "certainly the most capable" of those named and proposed to Jefferson that some station for him be found because the middle states, he said, had such a limited number of "young men of true merit and some scientific knowledge." Yet when Jefferson offered the consulship at Lisbon and Clay declined, Gallatin evidently was insulted by the rebuff. "If practicable, it is desirable that we could collect around us men of [superior] abilities," he commented the next time Clay was proposed for a post.[98]

In 1802 Clay was elected to Congress from Philadelphia to replace William Jones who had decided to retire. The Secretary now said that he was "the only man of superior weight and talents who appears to be closely united with Leib and Duane," and expressed the belief that he would have a good influence on his "intimate friend" Duane. Clay would soon be "perfectly reconciled to us," according to Gallatin, and "It is highly probable that Duane, who may be misled by vanity and by his associates, but whose sincere Republicanism I cannot permit myself to doubt, will adhere to us

---

[98]William Jones to Dallas, 3 Aug. 1801, Gallatin Papers, NYHS; Gallatin to Jefferson, 17 Aug. 1801, Adams, ed., Writings of Albert Gallatin, I, 38-39; Jefferson to Gallatin, 21, 28 Aug. 1801, ibid., 40-41; Gallatin to Jefferson, 1 Oct. 1801, Gallatin Papers, NYHS.

when his best friend shall have taken a decided part."[99]

Gallatin desired to enjoy the advantages of good political relationships without the willingness to nurture them. He failed to understand the personality of Clay, a timid man with a domineering, unkind father, who thrived on guidance and reassurance from others. Duane and Leib gently steered him politically for several years, until in Congress he was drawn into the orbit of the brilliant John Randolph, the foremost enemy of the administration.

In his relations with Duane, Gallatin at first sought in a highly self-conscious manner to maintain a useful alliance. Their acquaintance was "modern & requires, perhaps, that I should explicitly say, that although I may not have agreed with you in every thing," he acknowledged, "I feel a sincere esteem for your talents & firmness, a conviction that few men have been either more useful or more persecuted than yourself," and a willingness to reward him. "Perhaps I say more than is necessary," the Secretary worried, answering a letter he had neglected for two months during the period when Duane was tried for sedition and imprisoned for contempt of court. But "ever since your letter has remained unanswered, I felt that we had fought with different arms but in the same cause, that whilst I was a member of the Administration, the unrelenting spirit of persecution," he realized, "had pursued you out of your birth right & into a jail--and that you might construe my silence into neglect."[100]

---

[99]Gallatin to Jefferson, 11 Aug. 1803, Adams, ed., Writings of Albert Gallatin, I, 134-135.

[100]Gallatin to [Duane], 5 July 1801, Gallatin Papers, NYHS. The name of the recipient of this letter has been carefully removed from the manuscript.

Gallatin struggled to break through his natural reticence and caution in order to keep the loyalty of the excitable Duane. But the flamboyant editor's personality and politics were too repugnant. In 1802 Duane wrote that he had been told Gallatin was angry with him, and "I have thought indeed that on some late occasions I perceived a distance, a coldness, and reserve toward me different from the affability of two or three years ago." Gallatin denied it and noted, "On the whole I suspect that Mr. Leib must be at bottom of this." But he did nothing to restore Duane's confidence or to retrieve him from a dangerous association with Leib.[101]

When the two finally quarreled and broke, the results were injurious to them both. "From the day that Gallatin proposed to me to proscribe Leib," said Duane, "for what or why I could not learn, I found myself in a state of proscription, and the ground I stood on at Washington as it were frittering away from under me." Gallatin also lost, by the defeat of his political friends in Pennsylvania. His view of these events, looking back at them, was that "the thirst for offices" had "created a schism in Philad[a]. as early as 1802. Leib, ambitious, avaricious, envious & disappointed blew up the flame, and watched the first opportunity to make *his* cause a general one." Governor McKean provided that by his vanity, his nepotism and indiscretion, and "Want of mutual forbearance amongst the best intentioned and most respectable republicans has completed the schism. Duane, intoxicated by the persuasion that he alone had overthrown federalism," in Gallatin's opinion, "thought

---

[101] Duane to Gallatin, 12 Aug., 1802, *ibid.*

himself neither sufficiently rewarded nor respected; and possessed of an engine which gives him an irres[i]stible control over public opinion, he easily gained the victory for his friends."[102]

In Philadelphia the Republican schism became open and bitter in the election of 1804. The enemies of Congressmen Leib were increased in numbers and better organized, and they undertook an intensive campaign using their own newspaper, the Freeman's Journal. They first attempted to eliminate Leib from the Republican ticket by secretly dominating the ward and district meeting which would choose members of the nominating committee. When that failed because Leiper, Duane and others discovered and exposed the plan, they nominated a rival candidate in the general election, William Penrose. The burden of their campaign was that Leib had been morally disqualified for office by the Penrose scandal. Leib's supporters necessarily defended at length his personal character, but among themselves the democrats emphasized a different theme--it was his superior political qualifications which mattered. At a dinner party Duane said, according to a shocked member of the opposition, that "morality is not a necessary qualification in a legislator."[103]

In this campaign the divided Republicans received new names to identify them, Democrats and Quids. The latter advocated

---

[102] Duane to C. A. Rodney, 1 July 1808, Rodney Papers, Del. Hist. Soc.; Gallatin to John Badollet, 25 Oct. 1805, Gallatin Papers, NYHS.

[103] Freeman's Journal, 26 June, 20 July 1804; Higginbotham, Keystone, 70-71.

moderation, or "a halfway-house between virtue and vice, between truth and falsehood. . . . What an hermaphrodite thing, partaking of two characters, and yet having neither! A tertium quid from the combination of good and evil." It was Tench Coxe who christened the third party and the ever changeable Coxe who led it in the campaign against Leib in 1804. Behind Coxe's leadership was the influence of his good friend George Logan.[104]

The Quid faction in Philadelphia was a small minority of the Republican party, but powerful beyond its numbers because of the individual prestige of its supporters. Mathew Carey, Stephen Girard, Manuel Eyre, Sr., Thomas M. Souder, Samuel Wetherill, Jr., and Clement Biddle Penrose were among those who lent their names to the movement. Another was Blair McClenachan, who had resigned as President of the Democratic Society of Pennsylvania after Leib and Bache introduced their radical proposals. On the whole the men who planned the revolt against Leib represented the small commercial wing of the Republican Party. Shipbuilders, auctioneers and merchants engaged in the city's rich international trade were prominent in the campaign for Penrose. Most of Philadelphia's merchants were Federalists, but those few who considered themselves Republicans evidently favored a policy of greater moderation toward the defeated opponents. According to Duane, the Quids "had determined to make their peace for their former offences against federalism--and to expiate their devotion to the lower orders."[105]

---

[104] Ibid., 63, 69; Aurora, 22 June 1803; Thomas Leiper to Jefferson, 16 Aug. 1804, TJ-LC.

[105] The generalization is based upon a comparison to the

The Quids could defeat Leib only with the support of the Federalists, which they welcomed. Indeed the tone of the Freeman's Journal was often indistinguishable from familiar Federalist diatribes. Duane was denounced for his "chequered life" in Calcutta, for "a certain history of two acts" in Britain, and for allegedly lying to a federal court in claiming United States citizenship. "I have often asked myself . . . how it came to pass," said one Quid essayist, "that William Duane, a stranger, without fortune, illiterate, nay, without a single adventitious circumstance to usher him into public notice, possesses such influences in the state, and control over the democratic portion of the community?" Federalist readers were delighted with "the climate" of the Freeman's Journal. "Even Duane pants, & thinks the air sultry." Thomas Leiper, the chairman of the city's General Ward Committee, was objective and accurate when he wrote Jefferson, "Believe me Sir the question is not Leib[,] it has now become a party question[;] if we cannot vote in Leib as a member of Congress I shall say the republicans have lost their election."[106]

The three Congressional candidates from the city and county of Philadelphia and adjacent Delaware county were voted upon in all three districts. Leib was the only one opposed, by Penrose, because

---

names of the Quid leaders, in Freeman's Journal, 30 June, 10 July 1804, with their occupations listed in the 1804 Philadelphia city directory, HSP; Aurora, 10 Oct. 1804.

[106] Freeman's Journal, 23 July, 18, 20, 23, 24 Aug., 14 Sept. 1804; Elias E. Ellmaker to Nicholas Biddle, 13 July 1804, Biddle Family Papers, LC; Leiper to Jefferson, 16 Aug. 1804, TJ-LC.

the Federalist party had not nominated any candidates. As predicted, "the whole federal influence of this district, with the exception of the majority of the people called Quakers, residing in the city, and of about six respectable persons" turned out and voted for the third party ticket. The Quids did not deny it, but avowed that the Federalists had merely voted against the candidates they disliked most.

In the city Leib was defeated in all the better neighborhoods, and in High street ward, the most exclusive, he lost by 44 votes to 174 for Penrose. But the Republican total went up as the counting continued, for the Federalists came out in the "fair weather which prevailed until noon; and as the republican force is not so generally of the fair weather class," they turned out "in the evening, and after the hours of industry." Leib won in the working class wards on the northern and southern edges of the city and carried Philadelphia by eighteen votes. He lost heavily to Penrose in rural Delaware county, but regained in the strongly Democratic urban districts of Philadelphia county. His own constituency, the Northern Liberties, gave him a margin of 600 votes, and he was re-elected to Congress by a scant 300.[107]

In the violence of this campaign Duane and A. J. Dallas bitterly severed their relations. "He has attacked me," Dallas objected, "as the Author of an Address, which I never saw, till it was in the press." Upon reading this accusation Dallas cancelled

---

[107] Aurora, 10, 11 Oct. 1804; Freeman's Journal, 10 Oct. 1804.

his subscription to the Aurora as "a duty to himself, and his family." He stiffly requested the bill if money were owing, and if there was credit standing "M^r. Duane may consider this note as a receipt in full."[108]

Dallas' actual role in the organization of the third party is unclear. Thomas Leiper exonerated him at the time, but later declared that he had been the movement's secret manipulator. Dallas for as long as possible professed his devotion to Republican unity, although he shared the hostile opinion of the embattled Congressman. When his brother John L. Leib was nominated as a commissioner of bankruptcy, Dallas urgently objected. "A man more destitute of talents, and -----, does not exist among us. He is mean, noisy, and mischievous." Gallatin dutifully passed on the report that "Great apprehension is entertained at Philadelphia" about the nomination, as Leib was considered "destitute of talents and integrity," and "certainly he is not respectable."[109]

The Aurora penetrated Dallas' public neutrality by its pressure, and he prepared to take the offensive. To Gallatin he confided, "Thank Heaven our Election is over! The violence of Duane has produced a fatal division. He seems determined to destroy the republican standing and usefulness of every man who does not bend

---

[108]Dallas to Gallatin, 16 Oct. 1804, Gallatin Papers, NYHS; Dallas to Duane, draft, 20 Aug. 1804, Dallas Papers, HSP.

[109]Leiper to Jefferson, 16 Aug. 1804, 23 Mar. 1806, TJ-LC; Dallas to Gallatin, 18 Aug. 1803, Gallatin Papers, NYHS; Gallatin to Jefferson, 20 Aug. 1803, Adams, ed., Writings of Albert Gallatin, I, 139.

to his will." He had attacked Dallas; "He menaces the Governor. You have already felt his lash; and, I think, there is reason for M^r. Jefferson himself to apprehend, that the spirit of Callender survived."[110]

VI

Thomas McKean in 1805 was to stand for election to a third term as Governor of Pennsylvania. He had been re-elected in 1802 with only nominal opposition from the Federalists and with scant enthusiasm in his own party, but since then he had become embroiled in an increasingly virulent clash with the Republicans in the legislature on the issue of judicial reform. Moreover the Governor admittedly had supported the plan to oust Leib, and he and other "officers of Government who it is supposed head the party" were implicated in the creation of a Quid faction in Lancaster county and in the spread of "a third Party, who call themselves the moderation, which it is thought is forming in Pennsylvania." After his re-election, "In his address to the Legislature he breathes the spirit [of] union & reconciliation . . . An event which I most devoutly deprecate—," an assembly leader complained; "The moment it takes place true sound Republicanism is at an end in Pennsylvania." Observing the schism develop, General William Irvine, who had moved lithely from friendship with Alexander Hamilton to patronage from Thomas McKean, advised his less experienced son, "Join not warmly

[110]Dallas to Gallatin, 16 Oct. 1804, Gallatin Papers, NYHS.

in any party, til it is absolutely necessary, mind your own business."[111]

By 1804 it was evident that the Republican representatives from central and western Pennsylvania would not support McKean again no matter what his party label. But the opposition of the *Aurora* made the threat of defeat far more serious, and the Governor and many of his friends, including Dallas, laid the blame for his troubles wholly upon Duane as the secret author of a conspiracy. "We have had stormy weather here," McKean wrote from Lancaster, "but are now more calm, and would be soon enjoying prosperous gales, were it not for incendiary diabolical News-publishers." They "I fear, will soon require legislative correction," said McKean, who was contemplating a little sedition law to protect state officials from political libel.[112]

"The extensive Circulation of the Aurora & the implicit Confidence put in it may do infinite Mischief" in the gubernatorial election, feared one McKean supporter. "I sincerely lament the depravity of that man[;] he has been usefull to this country & thereby acquired the Confidence of the pecple," he admitted, "which now when he has forsaken the interests of the State renders him the more dangerous." The Governor's friends could attempt to counteract

---

[111]Caesar R. Wilson to Col. Thomas Rodney, 10 May 1803, Rodney Family Papers, NYPL; Nathaniel B. Boileau to Jonathan Roberts, 10 Dec. 1802, Roberts Papers, HSP; William Irvine to Callender Irvine, 15 Apr. 1803, William Irvine Papers, HSP.

[112]Thomas McKean to George Logan, 15 Feb. 1805, Logan Papers, V, 61, HSP; Higginbotham, *Keystone*, 114, 123.

"the evil effects of his poisonous columns" only by the use of handbills, "no paper having an extent of Circulation or a standing with the Community Capable of rebutting his pernicious doctrines."[113]

A. J. Dallas, with "the thunders of the Aurora . . . daily rolling over my head," began to develop an opinion violently hostile to the political power of newspaper editors, which in the end disillusioned him with the Republican party and drove him out of active politics. He commiserated with Gallatin, who confessed his discouragement with the political trend. "Perhaps the crisis is arrived," Dallas commented, "when some attempt should be made to rally the genuine Republicans, round the standard of reason, order, and law. At present we are the slaves of men, whose passions are the origin, and whose interests are the object of all their actions." He specified, "I mean your Duanes, Cheethams, Leibs, &c," who rule through the tyranny of the press.[114]

Dallas hoped to find a means to destroy that influence, but Andrew Gregg, more politically astute, discouraged him from a "project" to expose the names of untrustworthy journalists. He pointed out that there was no reason to think that the gullible public would stop believing in those men. "For my own part," Gregg said, "I really can discover no practicable means in the present state of things, other than better information gradually communicated thro' other channels, and so rescuing the people from their

---

[113] John Kean to Dallas, 20 Mar. 1805, Dallas Papers, HSP.

[114] Dallas to Gallatin, 21 Dec., 26 Jan. 1805, Gallatin Papers, NYHS.

delusion. Does not something like this," he added, "already discover itself in the City and in most of the eastern counties. In the Center of the State" the Aurora in 1805 was the only paper in circulation and there its influence "principally discovers itself."[115]

Duane's power to affect the Governor's destiny put McKean, never mild, into a fury of loathing. Duane, he informed the President, was a Porcupine, a Callender, a Cataline, a Judas. He blamed the Republican schism upon the editor's campaign for Leib in the Congressional election; "in his zeal for the Doctor he endeavored to injure all his other friends who opposed his election. Few men can bear prosperity," the Governor commented; "M^r. Duane seems to me to be one of the number. He affects to consider his importance, as an Editor of a News-paper, to be superior to the Governor of a State, or even of the President of the United States." Yet his influence, McKean admitted, "has been more powerful than could rationally have been supposed." To this outburst from the Governor of Pennsylvania, ostensibly to defend himself against an accusation by Duane, President Jefferson replied calmly assuring him that he ignored "vague insinuations without foundation, or built on suspicion."[116]

The emotion expended in the estrangement among Republicans was more extreme than in the strife with the Federalists because of the mutual sense of betrayal. In Washington Michael Leib and Joseph Nicholson had an argument that "proceeded to blows!" Duane asked

---

[115]Gregg to Dallas, 16 Nov. 1807, Dallas Papers, HSP.

[116]McKean to Jefferson, draft, 18 Feb. 1805, Thomas McKean Papers, HSP; Jefferson to McKean, 3 Mar. 1805, ibid.

Joe Clay to send him the true story since "I did not think it delicate to ask Leib." Duane himself was the cause of a fight in the Philadelphia Coffee House when a prominent Federalist, Major William Jackson, taunted a Quid, Daniel W. Coxe, with the accusation that Duane was a friend of the President. Coxe said no, "that he despised me," but Jackson offered contradictory evidence; "at length J. gave C. the lie, and Coxe slapt him on the cheek--they had two or three boxing bouts." Someone "caused a ring to be formed, and the poor Major was most severely mauled kicked and cuffed!" The incident led to a duel a few days later in the state of Delaware in which the Federalist Jackson was again the victim. A bullet went through his right cheek and out the left, knocking out two or three teeth.[117]

The developments within Pennsylvania's Republican party created fresh possibilities for the Federalists. Former Congressman John Rutledge planned a visit to Philadelphia, but "I suspect that I shall find that City sadly changed since the prosperous days of the republic which we passed there so happily," he wrote Robert Goodloe Harper. "Federalism seems truly humbled there & the utmost ambition of our former friends will be content, I learn with excluding Duane & his Gang from the supreme Power." In the gubernatorial election "They of course will cooperate indirectly with Dallas," who thus "triumphs over the Men who he finds compelled to be subservient to his aggrandizement. This, I think, is all wrong," said Rutledge. "No consequence . . . can be more pernicious than the

---

[117]Duane to Joseph Clay, 12 Dec. 1805, Clay Papers, NYPL; William J. Duane to Clay, 16 Dec. 1805, ibid.

alliance of Federalists with these third party men under any circumstances." In his opinion, the Quids should be taught a lesson that "those who cajole the People" can not "calculate upon our interference to prevent their becoming the first Victims to their own folly & intrigue." If not "they will think it a sure game to mount the Ladder by any Means, even the most infamous, & oblige the federalists to support it with their Shoulders." Rutledge's advice for the gubernatorial election was that "The federalists should be neutral, in which event Duane would succeed, & though a reign of profligate anarchy might be expected to ensue, good would finally result."[118]

The issue which divided Governor McKean and the Democrats and revealed their differing philosophies was that of judicial reform. While the legislature sought a means to reduce the power of the judiciary, the Governor wanted to increase the numbers of Supreme Court judges and circuits. The domination of the courts by Federalists intensified the concern with the question, but the reformist members would not be satisfied with merely placing Republicans in judicial office. To the consternation of Republican lawyers, most of whom became Quids, the Democratic farmers in the legislature wanted to make important changes in the nature of the judicial system.

They believed that the courts were needlessly complex, leading to long and expensive litigation even in minor property suits.

---

[118] Rutledge to Harper, 3 Aug. 1805, Robert Goodloe Harper Papers, LC.

In most civil cases, they thought, the truth would easily emerge upon an examination of all the facts. But lawyers and judges tended to obscure the truth with irrelevancies which impeded and often denied justice. The farmers sought to institute a simpler alternative for settling disputes, voting to extend the jurisdiction of justices of the peace over property suits and to provide for settlement by arbitration. The Governor vetoed all these measures, but by the 1804 session of the legislature, the Democratic reformers had the strength to override his vetoes by an overwhelming margin.[119]

Duane was not personally convinced that the farmers had found a panacea in demanding a system of local justice, because of the danger of establishing a set of petty tyrants. But he certainly agreed that the existing judicial system distorted the ideal of equality before the law by its reliance on legal intricacies unknown to the layman and on the eloquence or craft of lawyers. The party who could pay higher fees for better counsel was the more likely to obtain judgment. The awareness of this inequity, and the resentment of the aristocratic pretensions of lawyers, were fundamental to all the measures for judicial reform. One act vetoed by McKean made it illegal to employ counsel in cases for arbitration. Some persons suggested that legal fees should be set by official

---

[119] Higginbotham, Keystone, 49-58, 67-67; Elizabeth K. Henderson, "The Attack on the Judiciary in Pennsylvania, 1800-1810," Pennsylvania Magazine of History and Biography, LXI (Apr. 1937), 113-136; [Jesse Higgins], Sampson Against the Philistines . . . (Philadelphia, 1805), is the most complete contemporary statement of the case for local justice; it has sometimes been wrongfully ascribed to Duane, who published it. The Aurora during 1804 and 1805 was a repository of letters on the judiciary.

standard and that higher payment be regarded as a bribe, or that employment of more than one lawyer be prohibited. Many individuals favored creating equal opportunity for justice by socializing the legal profession. Lawyers would receive salaries paid by the state, and the courts would assign free counsel to both plaintiff and defendant.[120]

In 1803 the legislature was asked to interfere in an unusual case of judicial arrogance. Thomas Passmore, a Philadelphia merchant, had received in arbitration a favorable judgment for a claim against an insurance firm. When Andrew Pettit and Andrew Bayard announced their intention to appeal the decision, Passmore became angry and posted on the notice board of the City Tavern some unkind remarks about Bayard. Thereupon A. J. Dallas, the attorney for Pettit and Bayard, asked the Supreme Court to hold Passmore in contempt. He was questioned and found innocent of willfully attacking the court or a case in progress, but he refused to apologize to Bayard as requested, so he was found guilty of contempt of court and sentenced to fifty dollars fine and thirty days in prison.

Passmore protested the action in a memorial to the state assembly. From it came two recommendations, for an inquiry into the judges' conduct, and for a law defining the powers of a court to punish for contempt. The bill defining contempts was unfortunately defeated by a tie vote on its final reading, but the inquiry was continued to the next session, when the three judges who had con-

---

[120] Aurora, 4 Jan. 1803, 22 Mar. 1804.

victed Passmore were impeached for exceeding their powers. The Senate set the trial for January 1805.

The Supreme Court judges retained Dallas and Jared Ingersoll to defend them, but the assembly had some difficulty in securing a prosecutor. Several prominent Republican lawyers refused to take the case, but finally the legislators retained Caesar A. Rodney of Delaware, who had succeeded Dallas as Duane's attorney. In the trial the defense argued that the judges' conduct was justifiable within the terms of the common law, and that their action if mistaken was not culpable. The vote on removal from office was a bare majority against the judges; since a two-thirds majority was necessary to convict, the judges were acquitted.[121]

Duane was enraged by the decision which proved the futility of impeachment as a means to protect the public from judicial abuses. The lesson was again illustrated a few weeks later with the acquittal by the United States Senate of Samuel Chase, the notorious Supreme Court Justice, who during the period of the sedition law "had waged a merciless war against the printers." Dallas, although a witness for the prosecution, succeeded in thwarting the will of Jefferson and gaining Chase's acquittal by his moderate testimony that the Justice's conduct in the Fries trial had been arbitrary but perhaps not criminal. His influential testimony was in harmony with a Quiddish mood among some Republicans in Congress, who were alarmed by the demand for democratic innovations in Pennsylvania and elsewhere, and were increasingly reluctant to antagonize the Federalists.

---

[121]Higginbotham, <u>Keystone</u>, 55-57, 66-67.

"All parties appear to wish it had never been commenced—," wrote one Federalist during the Chase trial; "I believe we shall not hear of another very soon."[122]

The defeat ended the attack on the judiciary in national Republican policy, but in Pennsylvania the Democrats became even more determined to effect judicial reform, by revising the constitution if necessary. The miscarriage in the Passmore case demonstrated the potential for tyranny. The court had reached out into the private life of a citizen wholly ignorant of any wrongdoing, summoned him to appear and answer for opinions not expressed within the hearing of the court and not intended to reflect upon it or to be disrespectful, but which the court construed to be a contempt of its prerogatives. Yet the judges guilty of this arbitrary conduct were protected from censure because they had acted within the bounds of the definition of contempts under British common law. They could not be convicted of criminal behavior; therefore their life tenure as judges continued.[123]

---

[122] _Aurora_, 30 Jan. 1805, 22 Mar. 1804; Raymond Walters, Jr., _Alexander James Dallas, Lawyer--Politician--Financier, 1759-1817_ (Philadelphia, 1943), 131-132; William Plumer to Daniel Plumer, 25 Feb. 1805, Plumer Papers, LC.

[123] The vague, extensive common law definition of contempt was superseded by an Act of 1831 which limited contempt to disobedience to a judicial process and to misbehavior in the presence of the court, "or so near thereto as to obstruct the administration of justice." In 1918 the Supreme Court expanded the "so near thereto" doctrine, but reversed itself in 1941 by a five to four decision in the case of Harry Bridges v. California, in which the Court declared that unless the danger to the administration of justice was "extremely serious," the broader definitions was an invasion of the constitutional right of freedom of the press. Edward S. Corwin, _The Constitution, and What It Means Today_ (Princeton, 1946), 113-114.

British common law readings were admitted into American courts generally, not through constitutional or legislative deliberation, but as a result of judicial practice. The use of anachronistic precedents, not suited to America's republican government, sometimes permitted judgments which violated the civil rights guaranteed in the Constitution. During the Adams administration, common law prosecutions for seditious libel were a graver threat to the freedom of speech and press than was the written sedition law, which stipulated that the truth would not be considered a libel. The common law followed Lord Mansfield's doctrine, the greater the truth, the greater the libel. Thomas Jefferson, conscious of the many discrepancies with constitutional liberties, thought that the British common law should not be argued in American courts except where it had been adopted by statue. His Republican legal advisers however strongly discouraged that viewpoint.[124]

In Pennsylvania during Governor McKean's administration there was a persistent effort by Democratic legislators to uproot the custom, by enacting legislation to prohibit the reading of foreign precedents in the state's courts. In 1800 and 1801 bills for that purpose were defeated. In 1807 the measure finally passed but was vetoed by the Governor and failed to pass over his veto.[125]

---

[124] Aurora, "Montezumazin," 15, 17, 18 Mar. 1800; Jefferson to Robert R. Livingston, 31 May 1801, Ford, ed., Writings of Thomas Jefferson, IX, 257 n.; Jefferson to Gallatin, 12 Nov. 1801, TJ-LC; Robert R. Livingston to Jefferson, 31 May 1801, TJ-LC. See Leonard Levy, "Liberty and the First Amendment, 1790-1800," American Historical Review, LXVIII (Oct. 1962), 22-37.

[125] Henderson, "Attack on the Judiciary," Pa. Mag. of Hist. and Biog., LXI (Apr. 1937), 117, 132.

Duane thought that common law jurisdiction, combined with the life tenure of judges, was at the heart of judicial tyranny. In his opinion the common law was "the entailed curse of ages. It was an "incoherent and inscrutable code" formed from a "collection of precedents derived from times of darkness and superstition," whereas the law should be appropriate to a given society and its institutions; "no part ought to be adopted to times which no longer carry respect for the intelligence of the times, . . . but which like the errors of the abstract sciences are long and deservedly obsolete." The power of judges to impose the unwritten code, selecting at will from among contradictory decisions, made "our boasted liberty," he thought, "a mere sound dependent on the *mercy*--the *discretion*--the *caprice*--the *malice*--or the *family interests* of any men vested with juridical authority."[126]

The best protection against such tyranny, in his opinion, would be a modification of the independence of the judiciary which would make judges ultimately responsible to the people. To achieve this the rule of tenure should be altered, either to limit the term of office by fixed appointment or election, or to make judges removable by the legislature for offenses not necessarily criminal. In a democracy, he argued, no branch of government should be independent of the people's supervision. The idea of checks and balances between branches was an insufficient protection, because of a possible tendency for officers to cooperate in self-seeking. Only

---

[126] *Aurora*, 30 Jan. 1800, 1 Feb., 30 Jan. 1805.

the people could protect themselves, "because they alone are interested." He thought that every officer in the political system should be "at certain reasonable periods, according to the nature of the trust reposed in him . . . again submitted to the ordeal of public opinion, and elected or appointed, or rejected, upon the true principles of democracy—utility to the people." In the case of the judiciary the principle of "good behavior" should be abandoned. "There are wrong ways of doing right things," he argued; an officer might become insufferable although acting within the law. "To be a good judge, it is not only necessary that a man should be wise and impartial, but the people must think him so."[127]

The failure to convict the judges impeached in the Passmore case convinced the Democratic majority in the legislature that it was necessary to alter the constitutional provision for judicial tenure during good behavior. A state convention for this purpose, it was thought, might also decrease the Governor's excessive power of appointment and reduce the four-year term for the state senate. The proposal for a constitutional convention became the key issue in the gubernatorial campaign between Thomas McKean and an obscure German legislator from rural Northumberland county, Simon Snyder. The Democrats in caucus had agreed upon Snyder a day after Duane arrived in Lancaster to confer with them.[128]

---

[127] William Duane, Experience the Test of Government: In Eighteen Essays (Philadelphia, 1807), 7-9, 14-16. This pamphlet is the best summation of Duane's views on judicial and constitutional reform.

[128] Higginbotham, Keystone, 80-84, 87-89; The Tickler, 17 Oct. 1810.

A. J. Dallas took the lead in organizing the Quids into a Society of Constitutional Republicans pledged to defend the existing law and to re-elect McKean. Active with him in the Society were George Logan and William Jones, and most of the other men who had opposed Leib for Congress the year before, including Eyre, Wetherill and Carey. There were also some new names, such as Peter S. Duponceau and Jonathan Bayard Smith, the father of S. H. Smith, Duane's successful rival for government patronage. Acting upon Gallatin's advice, the Quids avoided "an absolute rejection" of a convention in principle, but opposed an immediate call as "the usurpation of a minority."[129]

Underlying the dispute about judicial and constitutional reform were fundamental differences in Republican philosophy. The Quids on the whole were men who received offices or were familiar with authority and who regarded their elevation as natural; they thought it appropriate for the better classes to administer the government, with benevolent disposition, on behalf of the less fortunate. The Democrats had cherished a different ideal--"_may the sovereignty of the people endure for ever_."[130]

To a man of Governor McKean's temper it was intolerable that the "chimerical experiments" and "giddy innovations attempted in our legislature" could not be checked, with "my knowledge, acquired with great labor, study & reflection, and the advantage of a long & public

---

[129] G. M. Dallas, _Life of A. J. Dallas_, 92; Dallas to Robert Smith, 11 Apr. 1805, _ibid._, 117; Gallatin to Dallas, 30 Mar. 1805, Simon Gratz Collection, HSP.

[130] _Aurora_, "Regulus," 25 Mar. 1805.

life." Dallas was a cooler personality, but truly horrified by the implications of the 1805 campaign. "It is avowed here, and it will be in practice by the reformers everywhere," he warned a non-Pennsylvanian, "that lawyers, men of talents and education, men of fortune and manners, ought not to participate in the formation, or in the administration of a democratic government." According to one Democrat, the Quids feared reform "because those who riot in luxury and extravagance upon the miseries of the community, must be compelled to pursue some honest profession--to labour or to starve."[131]

The demand for a convention led to an open debate on the merits of the Constitution of 1790 in comparison with the more democratic document of 1776. "The present constitution," according to McKean, who had been one of its chief authors, was "the production of as patriotic learned and enlightened men, as, perhaps, ever assembled for a similar purpose," and "approached as near to perfection as any that ever did, or now does, exist in the world." Thomas Paine wrote a series of articles expressing a different view, which were published in the Aurora and circulated as a pamphlet which was to be his last. "At the time this Constitution was formed," he declared, "there was a great departure from the principles of the Revolution" by the men in power. The reactionary revisions of that period were again assailed by Pennsylvanians as well as by Paine.[132]

---

[131] McKean to George Logan, 19 Feb. 1803, Logan Papers, HSP; Dallas to Robert Smith, 11 Apr. 1805, in G. M. Dallas, Life of A. J. Dallas, 117; Aurora, "Regulus," 27 Mar. 1805.

[132] McKean to Dallas, 25 May 1805, Aurora, 3 June 1805, quoted in Higginbotham, Keystone, 85; Thomas Paine, "To the Citizens

According to one critic, Duane's "present hobby horse seems to be to make the people believe that democracy consists in the sole government of the house of representatives." Benjamin Franklin's Constitution of 1776 with its unicameral legislature had tended to that view. The changes effected in 1790 had dispersed the assembly's power by expanding executive authority, creating a senate with superior privileges and introducing life tenure for judges. The reformers wanted to restore the spirit of the abandoned document. Duane and Thomas Paine both advocated a bicameral legislature, but with equal houses chosen by annual election. "Like the continual motion of the sea, which preserves its sweet and its saline particles from evaporating," the editor suggested, "so does a continued rulling of the democratic waters prevent their stinking, stagnating, or being converted into a pestilential pool of monarchy, aristocracy, or priestcraft." In Dallas' view, "The object is to reduce government to its elements, rendering the immediate agency of the people perpetually necessary to every executive, legislative, elective, and judicial purpose."[133]

The attack on Pennsylvania's Constitution, its defenders were quick to point out, had threatening implications for other states and for the United States Constitution as well. "After

---

of Pennsylvania on the Proposal for Calling a Convention," Aug. 1805, Philip S. Foner, ed., The Complete Writings of Thomas Paine, 2 vols. (New York, 1945), II, 992-1007; printed in Aurora, 31 Aug., 4, 7 Sept. 1805.

[133]Matthew Lyon in Freeman's Journal, 10 Sept. 1804; Aurora, 1 Apr. 1805; Dallas to Robert Smith, 11 Apr. 1805, in G. M. Dallas, Life of A. J. Dallas, 117.

effecting the object here," Dallas predicted, "it will be enforced by the additional weight of a precedent" elsewhere; "and we have already seen that the federal constitution is upon the same ground, the butt of active hostility." The state and national documents had been written during the same period and in the same political mood. The admirers of the state Constitution of 1776 praised the Articles of Confederation also for the spirit of equality therein, while admitting that they had been faulty in detail. The federal convention had been necessary, Duane thought, but there was "an artificial, as well as a real pressure, upon the public" at the time. In Pennsylvania, wrote Paine, judges alone were given tenure during good behavior, "I suppose, because lawyers have had the formation of the judiciary part of the Constitution." The malice toward lawyers and other men of wealth and attainments, Dallas thought, was the foundation of all the criticism of the existing documents. "The framers of the federal constitution, as well as the State constitution, are denounced because they were of that description."[134]

In the Pennsylvania legislature a few years later a proposal to amend the federal judiciary article brought out a bold hostility to the United States Constitution which shocked the Federalists and Quids to the core. In a very popular speech "Leib called _it_ an _affair_ of compromise," one reported, "the work of a secret divan, produced amidst distractions and distresses artificially created for the purpose of introducing monarchy &c." But the revival of old

---

[134] _Ibid._; _Aurora_, 22 Mar. 1805, 10 Dec. 1810; Paine, "To the Citizens of Pa.," P. S. Foner, ed., _Writings of Thomas Paine_, II, 1003-1006.

anti-federalist feelings was usually brief and not intended as a program for action. "The federal constitution was formed, imperfect indeed; but containing in it the means of perfection," Duane wrote, and "the good genius which has presided over the destinies of America, has uniformly produced out of premeditated evil greater good."[135]

In the gubernatorial campaign the two wings of the Republican party both coveted the support of the President, who carefully maintained his neutrality. He had to be extremely cautious in all his dealings with Pennsylvania since "Our friends . . . seem to have got into such a jumble of subdivision," and he admitted, "I can not put pen to paper to a member of either party without scolding." But Jefferson was philosophical about political tendencies which disagreed with his own wishes. "That all our constitutions are perfect no man will say," he commented on the movement for a convention in Pennsylvania. "When time shall have been given by reason & discussion to convince the majority of this, that majority will carry an amendment into effect quietly. but they will not be forced," he objected. "he who would do to his country the most good he can, must go quietly with the prejudices of the majority till he can lead them into reason."[136]

In Philadelphia George Logan and Michael Leib exchanged

---

[135]John Sergeant to Thomas Biddle, 10 Jan. 1808, Gratz Collection, HSP; Aurora, 10 Dec. 1810. See also Jonathan Roberts to Jonathan Roberts, Sr., 8 Jan. 1808, Roberts Papers, HSP; Roberts to Matthew Roberts, 28 Jan. 1808, ibid.

[136]Jefferson to Thomas Leiper, 11 June 1804, Jefferson Papers, Mass. Hist. Soc.; Jefferson to C. A. Rodney, 23 Oct. 1805, Gratz Collection, HSP.

charges of unfair tactics in the campaign. According to Leib, Logan used Jefferson's name and claimed to have a letter from the President endorsing McKean. Jefferson replied to these complaints with a carefully phrased denial and a statement of his neutrality, but soon he received an anonymous charge that Leib was going from tavern to tavern in the city and the Northern Liberties showing his letter from the President. "He enjoins secrecy on those to whom he shews it," meeting the requirement that it not be published, "but cares not how many see the letter; perhaps near a thousand persons of the lowest class of society have already seen it. Those who are your <u>real</u> friends here," the complainant said, "cannot but regret that you should correspond in any shape whatever with so noted a liar and abandoned villain."[137]

The Quids felt that the President's endorsement rightfully belonged to the incumbent and that by his neutrality he awarded an advantage to the other side. "Duane's assertions, that he possesses the confidence, and acts at the instance, of the President, will buoy him upon the surface, for sometime longer," Dallas complained. "While he has influence, the state, the United States, will never enjoy quiet. I hope, therefore, and there is every reason to expect, that his present machinations will be exposed and defeated, as a prelude to his fall."[138]

---

[137]Leib to Jefferson, 22 July 1805, TJ-LC; Leib to C. A. Rodney, 18 Dec. 1805, Rodney Papers, Del. Hist. Soc.; Jefferson to Leib, 12 Aug. 1805, TJ-LC; Unsigned letter to Jefferson, 24 Aug. 1805, quoted in Cunningham, <u>Jeff. Repubs. in Power</u>, 219.

[138]Dallas to Gallatin, 4 Apr. 1805, Gallatin Papers, NYHS.

But Dallas' tacit request that Gallatin use his influence with the President for this purpose did not succeed. The situation had changed since 1803 when Jefferson withheld a friendly letter to Duane upon Gallatin's advice. The President had begun to make his own political decisions about the state. Previously the Secretary had tried to prepare the way for a commitment to the Quids, but in 1805 the two of them never discussed the gubernatorial campaign. "We have it here," Thomas Leiper wrote soon after, "that Gallatin is excluded from your Councils . . . . this is agreeable to 7/8 of my Political friends for we believe he was and is the Head of the third party."[139]

McKean was returned to office in the election on October 8, but in long term significance, it was a Democratic triumph. With the Aurora, Duane "easily gained the victory for his friends. I call it victory," Gallatin explained, "for the number of republicans who have opposed him rather than supported M'Kean do not exceed one fourth or at most one third of the whole; and M'Kean owes his re-election to the federalists." The Quids had been rejected by the party they claimed to represent, and the future belonged to the hated radicals.[140]

"If Mr. Jefferson, and his powerful friends at Washington,

---

[139] Jefferson to William Wirt, 3 May 1811, Wirt Papers, Md. Hist. Soc.; Leiper to Jefferson, 23 Mar. 1806, TJ-LC.

[140] Gallatin to John Badollet, 25 Oct. 1805, Gallatin Papers, NYHS; Jonathan Roberts, Memoirs, 1799-1830, 2 vols., HSP, I, 110; Leib to C. A. Rodney, 18 Dec. 1805, Rodney Papers, Del. Hist. Soc.; Leib to Rodney, 9 Jan. 1806, Gratz Collection, HSP.

in the year 1805, had not given their countenance to the presumptions of the Aurora, the evils of the present time would not have happened," wrote the disenchanted Dallas a few years later. "I do not say this by way of reproach," he maintained, "but to point out the true cause, why no man of real character and capacity, in the Republican party of Pennsylvania, has the power to render any political service to the Administration." In that state an era had come into being which honored the principle of the sovereignty of the people.[141]

---

[141]Dallas to Gallatin, 21 Apr. 1811, Gallatin Papers, NYHS.

CHAPTER IV

THE DUANE-LEIB PARTY

The Democratic party in Philadelphia, led principally by Duane and Leib, was founded upon the idea of active participation by the voters in election campaigns and in all aspects of political life. The techniques of "demagoguery" were scorned by the Federalists and distasteful to the Quids, but their evident success won grudging admiration from those men, which was to transform in time the gentlemanly style of politics which they preferred. The Federalists "should no longer be the champions of a fallen administration," John Rutledge advised in 1803, "but of the people--of the masters of Jefferson Duane Leib & the other rascals who tyranise over the people--If Jefferson cannot be ousted but by this sort of cant why we must have recourse to it."[1]

The organization of a political party which sought direct involvement of the citizens in large numbers had been initiated for Philadelphia in Leib's Northern Liberties, called "the cradle of democracy" by its friends. There "all the elections, with few exceptions," someone complained in 1800, were conducted with rigid discipline and unseemly ardor. The volunteer militia were used for "forming men in military array, and marching them to the election

---

[1]Rutledge to Harrison Gray Otis, 3 Apr. 1803, Harrison Gray Otis Papers, Mass. Hist. Soc.

ground with drums beating and fifes playing, men armed, mounted on horseback, sounding trumpets and parading thro' the streets." Leib in part had inherited his leadership there as a relation of the Constitutionalist leader of the 1780s, Samuel Coats, but he had gained the loyalty of the district for himself for "he was the first to bellow at town meetings, and to harrangue at taverns," and the first to call upon the voters at their businesses and shops, with flattery and hints of favor. Once a mob of rowdy Democrats celebrating an election triumph went to Leib's house at two in the morning and wanted to pull him in a carriage through the streets, but he escaped it was said through "abject entreaties."[2]

The people of the Northern Liberties were particularly susceptible to democratic appeals, for the district was crowded and poor. The inhabitants were mostly mechanics, who tended to live there because they could not afford the more expensive housing in the city proper. The liberties were not subject to the city ordinance which required the construction of brick buildings; one of Leib's finest speeches, someone jibed, was "<u>in defence of wooden houses</u>." Perhaps a majority of the residents were of the middling sort; there was virtually no upper class, but "hundreds, and thousands, of the poor." Southwark was a similar district, below the city on the Delaware river, but less politically important at this time because its population was much smaller. After 1812 Southwark grew more than other parts of Philadelphia because of the wartime

---

[2] <u>Gaz. of the U.S.</u>, 4 Sept. 1799, 17 Feb. 1800; <u>The Tickler</u>, 30 Sept. 1807, 19 Oct. 1808; <u>Spirit of the Press</u>, Dec. 1806.

expansion of the shipbuilding industry there. Pennsylvania's second and more famous demagogue, Joel Sutherland, came from that district.[3]

Federalists discounted automatically the politicians' concern for the people as hypocrisy and sham. For example in 1802 there was an outbreak of yellow fever which was the most serious since the terrible epidemic of 1798, and by early August the Philadelphians were "flying in all directions" to escape. The Aurora moved out to Frankford for six weeks, and Duane "excited, and spread the alarm to answer his party views at the coming election," his enemies were convinced. The merchants and civic leaders resented his warnings as "calculated to injure the city" and feared that they would "make a most unfavorable impression on the minds of persons at a distance." Although they were confident that "the City is as healthy as it is possible for it to be," the danger in the epidemic was not there, but in the congested Northern Liberties. Since the contagious district could not be quarantined and many of its inhabitants could not afford to leave town, the county hospital was "prepared for the poor who fled from the scene."[4]

---

[3]The Tickler, 16 Sept. 1807; Richard Rush to Benjamin Rush, 6 June 1812, Rush Papers, Library Company of Philadelphia. John Palmer, Journal of Travels in the United States of North America, and in Lower Canada Performed in the Year 1817 . . . (London, 1818), 254, contains comparative figures for 1810 on the population and the numbers of houses and stores in the city and the northern and southern liberties.

[4]William Irvine to Callender Irvine, 4 Aug. 1802, Irvine Papers, HSP; Julia Rush to James Rush, 7 Sept. 1802, Manuscripts Collection, Lib. Co. of Phila.; John Thomas Scharf and Thompson Westcott, History of Philadelphia, 1609-1884, 3 vols. (Philadelphia, 1884), I, 513; Higginbotham, Keystone, 59-60. See also Richard Rush to James Rush, 7 Aug. 1802, Rush Papers, Lib. Co. of Phila.

For many years after the advent of Republican government it remained fashionable to denounce Democrats as a class in outrageously slanderous terms. The Federalists made only feeble efforts to contest elections with the party in power and were content to contrast their own respectability with the Democratic rabble. On election days when the party members loitered in groups, there were frequent jokes expressing alarm at the derelicts, pickpockets and escaped convicts to be seen in the streets. At a standing division of the voters in one ward, a person who stood with the minority was consoled to contrast his group with "Milton's fallen angels" on the other side, including a watch-thief married to a prostitute, he said, and a "Lounging youngster, married to a rampant widow, old enough to be his mother."[5]

The favorite joke about the Democrats was their love of drink. A recipe for party leadership was offered as follows: To bad character, greed and ambition, add "a loud voice, to rouse attention in the sleeping drunkard, and a hard head to keep sober 'till midnight." Pour them "into the first grog-shop you meet (say John Miller's;) let them ferment 'till the watch goes twelve; the *scum* will then sink, and you will fall under the table, to rise in the morning an acknowledged *Friend of the People*." One sad tale was told of a "Victim of Democracy" who voted for Jefferson, read the *Aurora* and became a shambling alcoholic as a result, because his companions did not think it drunkenness "to get a little fuddled every evening." Although the Federalists had loved to ridicule "the gin-

---

[5] *The Tickler*, 12 Oct., 25 Nov. 1807, 5 Oct. 1808.

drinking pauper who is said to conduct Bache's paper," Duane's enemies could only accuse him of astonishing sobriety; "what are we to expect from a man who can drink three bottles of stimulus after dinner without being merry."[6]

In spite of the snobbish contempt for its membership, the Democratic party was organized in a highly responsible and effective manner. After Duane, Leib, Leiper, Joseph Clay and a few others at the top, the second order of leadership generally was formed by master craftsmen who had thrived in their trade. On the whole the party tended to represent Philadelphia's mechanic classes, ranging from lowly carters and sweepers through prosperous masters with many employees, as opposed to the commercial and professional interests of the Federalists and Quids. The official nominating machinery, the General Ward Committee in the city and the county conferees, was reinforced by a number of political clubs which met year around to keep up the party spirit and which performed zealous service on election days. The True Republican Society founded in the 1790s was still active, and the Society of the Friends of the People, established for the gubernatorial campaign of 1805, continued after that event. One of the most resented of the party groups was the Democratic Young Men, because it served so conspicuously in distributing election tickets outside the polls and getting out the party vote. Some thought it highly improper to allow boys under twenty-one to participate in politics.[7]

---

[6] Ibid., 30 Sept. 1807, 2 Oct. 1811; Gaz. of the U.S., 2 Dec. 1799; Freeman's Journal, 25 Aug. 1804. See also Gaz. of the U.S., 5 Aug., 30 Nov. 1799, 11, 16, 22 July 1800.

[7] See for example Spirit of the Press, 5 Oct. 1805; The

The Tammany Society or Columbian Order was the most important of the political clubs. It had been established in 1795 with a franchise from the Society in New York, to take the place of the recently disbanded Democratic Society of Pennsylvania. Philadelphia's Republican leaders were all members of Tammany until after the election of 1799, but when Governor McKean entered office some of the moderates began to drop out, believing that its work was done and that a secret society was no longer needed. More moderates resigned as the democratic members became assertive and troublesome, and Edward Pole was supplanted as Grand Sachem by Michael Leib. The new regime admitted only "welding-hot democrats" and excluded the educated men of property "who view the poor, their children." The Society followed the traditional "Indian" rituals, as in New York, when it met at one of the several taverns which were designated as Tammany wigwams. The members were organized into seventeen tribes named for each of the states, and Duane was sachem of the New York tribe.

Tammany's acceptance of aliens who were not yet qualified for naturalization was the most bitterly resented feature of the hated club. "Men who could not, under our laws, be citizens for years, readily found seats in this honourable body, where the influence over the elective franchise has been greater than in any other known association in this country." By what right, someone demanded, did Duane and "other adopted brethren claim affinity with St. Tammany? We

---

Tickler, 10 Oct. 1808. On the party machinery see Higginbotham, Keystone, 21, 36-37, 62, 70, 139 and passim.

never heard that he ever visited Ireland." But "It was now not necessary to be an American to become a son of Tammany," another pointed out, "for the magic yell of wiskinky, so savage was it, could convert the sons of Erin into Aborigines of the American wilds, though the sun of America had not yet warmed them to their hearts."[8]

Other fraternal groups, ostensibly non-political, played their own role in the party structure. William Binder, one of Leib's closest associates in the county, was president of the United German Benefit Society, a benevolence club which paid benefits to the sick or deceased. The St. Patrick's Benevolent Society was formed in 1802 as a substitute for the older, somewhat staid Hibernian Society. Its stated purpose was to pay the sickness and funeral expenses of members. But when a slander on its politics occurred, it required two letters to the President of the United States to straighten out the matter. One member wrote to ask if Duane had ever said that "the members of the St. Patrick society . . . were all Federalists and consequently inimical to our present happy Government." William John Duane had applied for membership, he explained, and "I am apprehensive that the above (false I hope) insinuation made to Us by the Members of the rising sun faction may operate so forcibly upon our true Democratical Members as to cause his rejection." Jefferson denied the charge, sending his reply through Leiper for safety, and not long after the elder Duane became

---

[8] Spirit of the Press, 28 Sept. 1805, May 1807; Freeman's Journal, 10 Apr. 1805, quoted in Francis V. Cabeen, "The Society of the Sons of St. Tammany of Philadelphia," Pa. Mag. of Hist. and Biog., XXVII (1903), 45.

president of the society. He and his son dominated the club politically for many years.[9]

Indirectly the militia was as valuable as Tammany and its brother clubs, for the Philadelphia Militia Legion was plainly a Democratic political army. The volunteer regiment formed in 1799 after the beating of Duane by militia officers had superseded the Federalist "McPherson's Blues," commanded by William McPherson, a Philadelphia Customs official. Its members had been excessively eager volunteers on the Northampton expedition to put down Fries Rebellion, but when the political atmosphere changed and war with France was averted, the Blues abandoned the field to the Republican Legion.

The services of the volunteers were welcomed by the state for they helped to meet the state's obligation at their own expense. The Legion's elected officers received commissions from the Governor, and the state agreed to furnish muskets for use in drill; but the companies purchased their own uniforms and ran their own affairs. According to law, all men who had resided in Pennsylvania for more than six months were required to be enrolled in the militia and to appear for discipline on designated training days or pay "a pecuniary equivalent for personal service." But in practice only those who chose to actually served because the fine was not enforceable.[10]

---

[9] James Mease, <u>The Picture of Philadelphia</u> . . . (Philadelphia, 1811), 283-284, 287; John Hill to Jefferson, 4 May 1804, Jefferson Papers, Mass. Hist. Soc.; Jefferson to Leiper, 11 June 1804, <u>ibid</u>.

[10] <u>Pennsylvania Archives</u>, 4th series, "Papers of the Governors," 12 vols. (Harrisburg, 1900-1902), IV, 529.

The Legion was a fine social club for Democratic young men who enjoyed learning the military art in the company of their friends. They took their drill seriously and were considered an elite corps, in comparison with the drafted or enrolled militia which seldom met and had no uniforms for parade. The regiment always marched on the Fourth of July, and for other important occasions, such as the celebration of the Louisiana Purchase and Tammany's annual anniversary holiday in the spring. Its activities tended to be particularly noticeable in the fall, shortly before the elections in October. In 1803 the men conducted their first mock battle as a public spectacle at the raceground south of Pine street.

When the Republican party took office, the public's willingness to organize and serve in the militia began to be restored. At the end of 1800 "a numerous and effective enrollment" had increased the militia to 80,000 throughout the state, and two years later 90,000 were enrolled. Philadelphia furnished Pennsylvania's First Division, composed of two brigades, one from the city and the second from the county. The militiamen elected their own officers, but the jobs generally were filled by those who expressed willingness to serve, since they paid no salary but required much time and some expense. Within a short time militia office and political ambition were equated in the public mind, and the list of regimental officers read like a roster of the Democratic party. In 1807 Michael Leib, who had not previously been active, was elected Brigadier General of the county brigade. In Philadelphia "the military and civil authorities appear to stand pretty much upon the same footing," someone jibed, "with a little inclination to bend in favour of the latter."[11]

The ignorance and incompetence of the officers was savagely lampooned in the less respectable Federalist journals. In a typical parade drill, it was suggested, the captain kept his eyes on his drill book to see what he should do next, while the men freely offered their advice, then stopped for a drink until the captain politely cajoled them to return. An alleged meeting at the "Sign of the Cock and Breeches" proposed to the legislature a radical reform in the militia law--no more food, cigars or alcohol to be permitted in the ranks. Someone recommended that one of the Legion companies be engaged to teach the militia officers their duty.[12]

Governor McKean in his first years in office was pleased with the revived interest in the militia and urged the legislature to be liberal in its support of the "patriotic ardour," for "the efforts of individuals, in such a cause, can never be completely successful without legislative aid." But when the Republican schism became apparent, the Governor's enthusiasm began to flag. "Of the conduct of the Militia," he told the legislature in 1804, "it would be ungrateful to speak in any terms, but those of respect and praise." The next year and each year thereafter he urged a complete reform of the law, to bring the militia under "the immediate care of

---

[11] Ibid., 461-462, 503-504; [Robert Waln], The Hermit in America, on a Visit to Philadelphia . . . (Philadelphia, 1819), 22. See also The Tickler, 28 Oct., 4 Nov. 1807, 26 Oct. 1808.

[12] Ibid., 21 Oct. 1807; Spirit of the Press, Dec. 1807.

the government," and to prescribe universal "rules and principles" by which it would act. Privately he admitted that he was most annoyed by the section of the law which stated that officers were to be elected. With such a provision neither "subordination nor discipline" could be maintained; "besides, Youths between 18 & 21 years of age, day-laborers, journey-mechanics & artisans and aliens, who have resided six months only in the State &c.," he complained, "appear incompetent to make a proper choice of a General or Inspector of a Brigade, or indeed of any commissioned officer in the militia."[13]

McKean's distrust was understandably aggravated by the Legion's refusal to salute the Governor in the parade on July 4, 1805. The honorary commandant, a former Revolutionary officer, strongly urged them to observe the simple military courtesy, but the board of officers voted on it and refused. "To avoid so disagreeable a dilemma, the general declined the command, and the governor retired from the city on that day."[14]

Duane complained that the Governor sought to "dispirit" and "retard" the militia's organization and expressed his faith in America's use of the system, which discouraged the development of standing armies and the likelihood of war. The "declarations of men in the regular military service, too plainly indicate the danger from large military establishments; men educated in a profession

---

[13]Pa. Archives, 4th series, IV, 430, 461-462, 479, 503-504, 546, 571, 584, 622-633, 651; McKean to Maj. Genl. Joseph Hiester, 31 July 1807, Gregg Collection, LC.

[14]Spirit of the Press, 14 Sept. 1805; Duane to Jefferson, recvd 5 Dec. 1805, TJ-LC.

wish to exercise it," he shrewdly pointed out. Duane himself was actively engaged in the militia service, first as Captain of the Legion company of Republican Greens, which was reputed to wear the most resplendent uniforms in the corps. Later he became Colonel of the 25th regiment of Pennsylvania's First Division. His company of volunteers was attached to the unit, commanded by Duane's friend Bartholomew (Bat) Graves, but his affection for the Greens brought him out to march with them when they were on Legion parade. "Colonel Captain" Duane admitted that he would have preferred to continue with his company rather than to accept the "drudgery" of the regimental command, if it were not for the "political use" of the job. "The duty however gives me better ideas of matters which I find useful as an Editor."[15]

The militia became highly unrespectable in the eyes of the Federalists when the Democrats began to serve. McPherson's Blues had been disbanded and no new Federalist companies were formed. The only fashionable corps which continued was the First City Troop of cavalry; consequently it became in time one of the most famous of socially exclusive institutions in Philadelphia. For the "young tradesmen" and other inferior Federalists in the city, the volunteer fire companies replaced the militia as fraternal associations offering an agreeable social life. The directorship of a fire company was said to be "the summit of the hopes and wishes of one half the clerks,

---

[15] Duane to Jefferson, 8 Dec. 1806, TJ-LC; Spirit of the Press, 2 Apr., Aug. 1806; The Tickler, 12, 28 Oct., 18 Nov. 1807.

counter-hoppers, and quill-drivers in the city."[16]

The disapproval of the militiamen ranged from contemptuous descriptions of them as shabby soldiers and buffoons, to allegations that they formed a Praetorian band which might impose tyranny at will. Governor McKean, annoyed beyond all restraint by the increasing political pressure against him, in 1807 sought a warrant for the arrest of Michael Leib on a charge of conspiracy. Joseph Hopkinson, appearing for Leib, censured the indelicacy of the application, and before the court had made a decision, the request was withdrawn. "If the warrant had been granted, in less time than twice twenty-four hours," Duane allegedly threatened, "we would have had seven hundred men at Lancaster. . . . We would have pressed all the wagons and carriages in Philadelphia, and made the cartridges and cast the balls in the wagons coming up." On that occasion "The thunder and blitzen of the Northern Liberties, the wild Irish of Irishtown, and all the butchers of Philadelphia would have turned out."[17]

President Jefferson honored the militia in 1807 when he appointed General John Shee as Philadelphia's Collector of the Port. The aging Shee, who had been a family friend of the Leibs for many years, was the first Commandant of the Legion and from 1802 Major General of the First Division. Jefferson had appointed him to head the Indian department, but Shee preferred not to move to Washington,

---

[16]Palmer, Journal . . . 1817, 282; [Waln], Hermit in America, 204-208.

[17]U.S. Gaz., 30 Mar. 1807, quoted in Scharf and Westcott, Hist. of Phila., I, 529; Spirit of the Press, Apr. 1807; Higginbotham, Keystone, 127.

and he was given time to decide whether he should move or resign. Meanwhile Governor McKean punished him for political disloyalty by removing him from his state office as head inspector of flour. When the vacancy in the Collectorship occurred, Tom Leiper wrote to recommend John Steele, but Jefferson explained that Shee's situation was not satisfactory to him, and "as I suppose Genl. Shee the person whom it is most material to take care of," he had decided to appoint him. Leiper quickly concurred; the arrangement "is more agreeable to me than what I was soliciting for." The appointment was clear evidence, "A Disciple of Washington" pointed out, that Jefferson was devoted to the jacobins in Pennsylvania; he urged the Quids to abandon hope in the President and come in with the Federalist party.[18]

The most deeply resented aspect of the Democratic party organization was its tendency to promote an Irish-German coalition. In 1799 the Republicans were accused of exploiting "the particular nature of the population of Pennsylvania," and "They say, it was the Germans and the Irish who put M'Kean into office." "A considerable portion of the inhabitants of the interior parts of the State are natives of Ireland, or of Irish extraction," Ambassador Robert Liston explained, "and these, besides that they favoured Mr. McKean as a countryman, are, with few exceptions, at perpetual variance

---

[18]Michael Leib to Lydia Leib, 5 Oct. 1794, 19 June 1800, Soc. Collection, Leib-Harrison Family Papers, HSP; Leib to C. A. Rodney, 9 Jan. 1806, Gratz Collection, HSP; Duane to Jefferson, recvd 5 Dec. 1805, TJ-LC; Leiper to Jefferson, recvd 20, 28 Aug. 1807, TJ-LC; Jefferson to Leiper, 21 Aug. 1807, TJ-LC; U.S. Gaz., 16 Oct. 1807.

with the present system of administration."[19]

"A still larger proportion of the Settlers are Germans, or immediate descendants of Germans." They composed nearly one-third of the state's total population, and among the pre-Revolutionary settlers they were the most nationally conscious group. On the whole the natives of English origin tended to be Federalists and Quids and the Scotch-Irish to be Democratic, but for them the relationship between nationality and politics was less conspicuous. The evidence of elections in these years shows that the Germans were the most likely to act as a unit.[20] They were "a race of men bred up in a state of extreme ignorance," according to Liston, "which renders them the easy dupes of democratick artifice.--The greater part of them cannot read," he asserted, and "they have scarcely any notions on the general subject of Government, except a confused idea, that a Republick differs so much from a monarchy, that it ought to be free from wars and free from taxes." In his opinion, "The Demagogues" callously exploited "their acquaintance with the sentiments of these simple people."[21]

The combination of the "Irish interest" and the "German interest" became steadily more pronounced under the leadership of Duane and Leib. Through his association with Peter Muhlenberg, Leib

---

[19] Gaz. of the U.S., 22 Nov. 1799; Liston to Grenville, 5 Nov. 1799, Br. State Papers, Liston Corresp., LC.

[20] See for example the experience in the gubernatorial election of 1805, Higginbotham, Keystone, 97-98, 100.

[21] Liston to Grenville, 5 Nov. 1799, Br. State Papers, Liston Corresp., LC.

possessed a strong claim to the loyalties of the German voters. They "are a very powerful Body and their incress are more rapid than any other people," Tom Leiper informed Jefferson, "and they will stick together. Muhlenberg & Leib are some where about the Head of them and they have no political ideas abstracted from each other." It appeared to him that Leib was "first in command"; in the Federalists' opinion, Muhlenberg "has a head; and so has a pin."[22]

In Philadelphia Duane was the hero and undisputed leader of the immigrant Irish. In 1798 he had been arrested at St. Mary's Catholic church for protesting the alien laws; later a federal court declared that he was an alien despite his native birth, and in 1802 he became a naturalized citizen. The Quids feared his influence with the new citizens and tried to injure his popularity by spreading the story that he was not a good Irishman, but "a faithful and loyal British subject," because he had signed the London Corresponding Society's remonstrance to the King and parliament against the infamous treason and sedition laws of 1795. One person who had called Duane an enemy to Irishmen sued him for an assault in the "dead of night," but the case was dismissed because no witnesses would corroborate the story. Nonetheless the Quid paper claimed possession of a letter in which Duane said the rascal was "too contemptible for any other treatment than a kicking, I met him in the street and gave him a couple of remembrancers."[23]

---

[22]The Tickler, 2 Aug. 1809; Leiper to Jefferson, 19 Sept. 1802, TJ-LC; Gaz. of the U.S., 17 Apr. 1799.

[23]Freeman's Journal, 20, 23, 24 Aug., 4, 5 Sept. 1804.

The naturalized citizens formed potentially a minority interest of considerable political significance. The number of new immigrants arriving in Philadelphia each year was probably about 1500 and perhaps half or more remained in the city.[24] A high proportion of the newcomers were adult males, which increased their political importance relative to the total population, about 110,000 in the city and county. The Irish were a large majority of the immigrants, and might have formed the whole judging from the resentment by the native Philadelphians; the epithet "foreigner" almost invariably meant "Irish." The English immigrants generally were exempted from group prejudice; they were less troublesome politically than the gregarious Irish, and they apparently benefited from Philadelphia's "most strange, infatuated, and unmerited preference in favour of the English."[25]

A special naturalization law enacted in 1804 made possible an abrupt increase in the numbers of new citizens. The act exempted aliens who had arrived between 1798 and 1802 from the requirement of declaring in an American court five years in advance their intention to become naturalized. The justification for the special arrangement was that the persons arriving in those years had been reluctant to call attention to themselves as foreigners during the lifetime of

---

[24]United States Bureau of the Census, Historical Statistics of the United States, 1789-1945 (Washington, D.C., 1949), 19; Marcus Lee Hansen, The Atlantic Migration, 1607-1860; A History of the Continuing Settlement of the United States (Cambridge, Mass., 1940), 90; Palmer, Journal . . . 1817, 291-292; John Bristed, America and Her Resources . . . (London, 1818), 20.

[25][Waln], Hermit in America, 127.

the threatening alien law. For them it was declared sufficient to bring a witness into court to testify to their residence in the United States for the required five years.

Politically the chief beneficiaries of the law were expected to be the Democratic parties of Philadelphia and New York, for about half the emigrants to the United States arrived at those two ports. Senator DeWitt Clinton sponsored the bill which reduced the naturalization period from fourteen to five years, and soon after he resigned to become Mayor of New York. The following year Congressman Leib introduced the proposal for the special exemption from first papers, as a further corrective of Federalist injustices concerning naturalization. Both Clinton and Leib became heroes with the Irish as a result, and the later political cooperation of those two men in part reflected the similar nature of their parties in the country's two largest cities.[26]

Leib's bill was defeated in 1803 because of insufficient groundwork. Leib originally introduced a petition from aliens in Carlisle county, Pennsylvania, which the House refused to receive because it contained objectionable language, presumably reflecting harshly on past members of Congress who had enacted the alien law. It was withdrawn and identical petitions from other Pennsylvania communities were revised and presented with the "exceptionable passages taken out." Roger Griswold of Connecticut demanded an in-

---

[26]Hansen, The Atlantic Migration, 90; Gustavus Myers, The History of Tammany Hall (New York, 1917), 30; Alvin Kass, Politics in New York State, 1800-1830 (Syracuse, 1965), 86.

vestigation of this, for the alterations had evidently been made in Washington. But Leib defended himself and explained that the changes had been made by William Duane and Congressman-elect Joseph Clay, who were there as an authorized committee.

On February 21 the bill was defeated with only 37 voting for it and 42 opposed. Many Republican members had failed to vote. The northern sponsors, especially Leib, had been careless in not making sure of the support of their southern colleagues who had no direct interest in the bill. The next year the measure was again introduced, after better preparation among the Republicans, and it passed easily, 65 to 38. The Senate concurred without debate.[27]

In Philadelphia and elsewhere committees on naturalization were formed to help eligible residents take advantage of the special law. The Aurora assured the aliens that their Democratic friends would instruct them in how to apply and see to it that they had but a "very trifling expence." The service became a regular feature of the Duane-Leib organization, and the committee was always active shortly before elections. According to angry nativists, the special naturalization law was scandalously abused, and hundreds of unqualified persons became citizens through false testimony by paid witnesses that they had lived in the United States for five years. It was claimed that for the gubernatorial election of 1808 the Democrats in Philadelphia had more than five hundred aliens naturalized in the final two weeks, and one-third of them were not qualified.[28]

---

[27]Annals of Congress, 7th Cong., 2nd sess., 569-581; ibid., 8th Cong., 1st sess., 297, 1195.

[28]Aurora, 16 July 1806, 5 Oct. 1810; The Tickler, 5, 8, 10, 19 Oct. 1808.

The issue of national origins as a divisive factor among Republicans was revealed in 1804 with the emergence of the Quid faction. The Freeman's Journal made clumsy efforts to discourage the development of an Irish-German coalition. It censured Duane for setting himself up as a dictator to the Irish, and denied that Leib was persecuted because he was German, but its hostile words were interpreted as being insulting to those groups. Belatedly the Quid paper tried to repair the damage with articles on the nation's friendship for Ireland and on the great contributions of the Germans to American life.[29]

The immigrants were often blamed for dividing the Republican party. An English visitor complained, "there is nothing to prevent an Irishman or a German, a fiery red-hot zealot, from taking the lead in all discussions, browbeating, and giving the tone to the rest." To this tendency the state of Pennsylvania was "peculiarly exposed," he commented, "having long been the rendezvous . . . of all European emigrants, more especially Germans." The Virginia Republican Thomas Ritchie also blamed the issue of nationality for Pennsylvania's troubles. There would be no third party movement in Virginia, he maintained, because there the Germans and Irish could not be organized into "clans and tribes for political purposes."[30]

---

[29] Freeman's Journal, 20, 23 July, 3, 10, 12, 15 Sept. 1804.

[30] Augustus John Foster, Jeffersonian America, Notes on the United States of America Collected in the Years 1805-6-7 and 11-12 by Sir Augustus John Foster, Bart., Richard Beale Davis, ed. (San Marino, Calif., 1954), 274; Charles H. Ambler, Thomas Ritchie: A Study in Virginia Politics (Richmond, 1913), 31-32.

In both Philadelphia and New York there was a strong nativist reaction against the rising influence of foreign-born voters. In 1806 Mayor Clinton of New York stopped a riot against the Irish near St. Peter's Catholic church, and in the city elections the following spring a nativist ticket appeared but was unsuccessful. Stories of the aggressiveness of foreigners seeking to dominate American politics were matched by earnest proposals that they be relegated to an inferior status. The fear of continued emigration from Europe and its political consequences was often explicit in these remarks. How many of the "old stock" of "real 76ers" would be alive in thirty years, one Revolutionary veteran was said to have asked another. "Oh, more than there are now," he replied, "unless the non-intercourse or non-importation acts should be made perpetual." A snob from Baltimore complained that mobs of dishonest Irishmen were trying to set themselves up as gentlemen; "Billy O'Dunn is the prototype of our hero."

> But why should Bill be sounded more than Kanneday,
> Sound them, and Kanneday doth become the mouth as well;
> Kanneday will lye and cheat, as soon as Billy![31]

The nativists insisted that Europeans "must be combed of their prejudices" before they could comprehend America's interests. Their tendency to form themselves into national groups, "sometimes for purposes of benevolence, sometimes for military tuition and parade, sometimes for conviviality, and sometimes for political conference," was cited against them as proof that they were not yet

---

[31]Louis Dow Scisco, Political Nativism in New York State (New York, 1901), 18, 19; The Tickler, 19 Apr. 1809, 31 Oct. 1810.

fully loyal. "When shall we see the day . . . that the Germans and the Irish will feel themselves more honoured by the title of AMERICANS than by any other?" A. J. Dallas' son thought that the nativism was understandable because the immigrants themselves seemed determined "to avoid sinking into a homogeneous mass." Why should Americans ignore the question of birth, "while they, in whose favor we should do so, insist thus upon retaining it as a link of concern, a shibboleth, and a pride?"[32]

The strongest underlying motivation for the nativist attack was the fear of increasing radicalism. The "dregs of Europe" beclouded American minds with the "mists of _foreign democracy_." The relationship of Duane and Leib for example was an "instance of the baleful effect of foreign depravity introduced into the garden of Columbia."[33]

The tightly organized Democratic party in Philadelphia, with its excellent machinery for turning out a large vote, also initiated the dubious practice of manipulating the official election procedures so as to obtain the best possible results. According to Pennsylvania law, a man was eligible to vote when he had resided in the state for two years and in his district for six months, and he had paid the poll tax. Elections were conducted by secret ballot, in theory, but a visitor who had observed elections in Pennsylvania commented that if "it ever became really worth while to use bribery

---

[32] _Ibid._, 2 Aug. 1809; _Spirit of the Press_, Oct. 1808; G. M. Dallas, _Life of A. J. Dallas_, 74.

[33] _Spirit of the Press_, Nov. 1806; _The Tickler_, 12 Oct. 1807.

. . . I have no doubt . . . that the system of the ballot will be no defense against it." A Philadelphian who blamed foreign-born politicians for all election fraud remarked bitterly, "we may only wait a few years, and then hear of votes being bought and sold, with as much facility as Bank Stock." The essential flaw in the system was that elections were conducted and the results judged, not by a non-partisan board, but by the majority party as one of the spoils of victory.[34]

In Philadelphia inspectors of the general election were chosen ten days before by special election in each of the wards and townships. The ward elections were fiercely contested and often considered more important than the general election itself, because the winning slate of inspectors could vitally affect the final outcome. On the designated Friday afternoon in late September, the local constable in each ward opened the polls for the annual preliminary contest. A standing division of the voters present at that time determined which party's judges would conduct the day's balloting. For this reason the constable's politics were important; he could hurry or delay the opening of the polls to serve the interests of his party. In South Mulberry one year the Friends of the Constitution had carefully assembled at two o'clock in threatening numbers, so Constable John S. Malone waited to allow time for the "whippers-in" to shout through the ward and gather the Democrats. By the time

---

[34]Foster, Jeffersonian America, 238; The Tickler, 5 Oct. 1808. The description of Philadelphia's election system which follows is based upon widely scattered information and hints in contemporary sources, especially newspapers.

he "began to count the parties" it was nearly three o'clock and the Democrats had an enormous majority. In order to carry their inspectors in wards where the outcome was doubtful, it was charged, the Democrats would move in voters from the safe districts of the Northern Liberties and Southwark. The men would reside in the neighborhood for a few days in sleeping quarters provided for them, so that they might claim to live in the ward when they went to the polls.[35]

After the Duane-Leib party began it, all factions in Philadelphia adopted the practice of making their greatest effort for victory in the preliminary ward contests. An innocent Englishman who visited the city in 1817 just before the gubernatorial election was "astonished to witness the anxiety felt by leading men, that *their* party should be elected *inspectors*." The eventual victory "seemed, in fact, in their estimation, actually to rest upon" it. He expressed surprise at this concern, when the method of election was by secret ballot, but a friendly acquaintance took him aside afterwards and explained "that the fact of the inspectors being on one side or the other had been calculated to make a difference of upwards of 200 votes in a particular section!"[36]

In the general election the inspectors could manipulate the outcome by the use of their discretionary power to receive or reject votes. "The means by which an inspector can effect this, though the

---

[35] *The Tickler*, 5 Oct. 1808.

[36] Henry Bradshaw Fearon, *Sketches of America* (London, 1818), 139-140.

mode is by ballot, is said to be remarkably exact." Although a prospective voter's intentions were ostensibly secret, "it is evident that in reality the conferees must be able to make a pretty good guess upon the subject." When a citizen arrived to vote, the "election ground" outside the polling place was a noisy, chaotic scene where rival "committees of vigilance" instructed their partisans and confused the opposition if possible. These men offered him a sheaf of ballots for each office and each party, and he had to select those he wanted. A favorite trick was the introduction of false ballots with misspelled names to deceive ignorant or hurried voters. By the time he entered the polling place with his bundle of ballots in his hand, the inspectors could readily foresee his intentions.[37]

The citizen's name was then checked in the tax assessor's book, and he was permitted to vote if all was in order. Depending upon his party, the inspectors might challenge him or neglect to question him closely concerning his age, his place of residence, his naturalization if foreign-born, or the date he had paid his taxes. Many Federalists believed that aliens were permitted to vote in Democratic strongholds, and that two, three or four persons might use one set of naturalization papers for identification, while the Aurora warned the foreign-born to bring their citizenship papers to the polls with them, or they would be deprived of their voting rights.[38]

Under Pennsylvania law, boys between the age of twenty-one

---

[37] Ibid.; Foster, Jeffersonian America, 238.

[38] Ibid.; The Tickler, 8, 10 Oct. 1808.

and twenty-two who were the sons of electors in the district were permitted to vote without having been assessed for taxes. The provision could be corrupted to allow voting by minors, and in 1806 it was alleged that the Democrats sent many minors from the city and southern districts to vote in the Northern Liberties, where they could expect a friendly reception from the inspectors. In that election, it was charged, "Paupers, boys of eighteen years of age, and even NEGROES . . . were suffered to vote." (Free Negroes were not legally barred from voting, but they were excluded by custom.) The most flexible device the inspectors possessed was that of the tax assessment. The law required that the voter be assessed six months prior to the election, as proof of his residence in the district for that period, but the entries in the tax book tended to fluctuate according to political expedience.[39]

II.

The flourishing party organization created by Duane and Leib received its first setback in 1807 because its leaders appeared to some to be ambitious and greedy. The leading Democrats in the legislature feared Leib's personal pretensions, and some Philadelphians resented Duane's hot temper and dogmatic pronouncements. By an accidental sequence of events in the winter of 1806, Leib's rivals for statewide power received a secret invitation from Philadelphia to establish a newspaper in the city, and the Democratic party there began to be destroyed from within.

---

[39] Ibid., 12 Oct. 1807; Spirit of the Press, Oct. 1806.

Final victory over the Quids at the next gubernatorial election was almost certain, and a geographical contest for domination was developing between men of similar principles and goals. The rural Republicans had always accepted in the past a large measure of leadership from the metropolis. The influence of A. J. Dallas in securing McKean's candidacy had burdened them for nine years with a hated Governor; after 1804 the leading influence passed from Dallas to Duane, whose newspaper was the rallying point for the Democratic opposition. But with victory in sight the farmer-legislators challenged the tendency to domination by a minority of presumptuous Philadelphians.

The key to the situation was the candidacy of Simon Snyder. When the Democrats had agreed upon him in 1805, the Northumberland county representative was completely unknown outside the legislature, and one of his chief assets as a candidate was that he symbolized the "clodhoppers" or "clodpoles," as McKean had characterized the Democrats in a damaging outburst of bad temper. Snyder was chosen because he was German, and because the far better known German Republicans, Peter Muhlenberg and Joseph Hiester, were not available at that time.

Hiester had indicated that he would not run against McKean, and when the Democratic caucus in Lancaster was in the process of selecting a candidate, the newspapers announced that Muhlenberg had been elected president of Dallas' Society of Constitutional Republicans. Leib exploded, "If I had been there by G_d Muhlenberg should not have had anything to do with it," and shortly after he returned to Philadelphia, the General declined the honor. The *Aurora* said that Muhlenberg had been named without his knowledge or consent, and that it was a trick by Dallas to destroy him as a potential candidate. Nonetheless Muhlenberg later endorsed McKean, to the *Aurora*'s consternation, and his influence was crucial in the Governor's reelection. Jokes at the time said that the General's unexpected independence had occurred because he was away from the city and able to think for himself when he acted. But later Leib was held responsible by the suspicious Snyderites, and even Tom Leiper complained that Leib had "been making apologies for Muhlenberg."[40]

General Muhlenberg's defection and the sudden prominence of Snyder threatened to destroy Leib's hopes for dominating the German political interest. The Philadelphians would have preferred to substitute another candidate for 1808, but it was argued that "as Snyders name has been up, and attachments of course formed, . . . it would be extremely dangerous to change the object;" he "is become so identified with the principles that if you change the one you jeopardize the other." When Leib tried to discourage Snyder's rising prestige and popularity, the country Democrats in the legislature turned upon him with venomous charges of party disloyalty, and accused him of secretly hoping for McKean's election in 1805 in order to gain time in which to replace Snyder with himself or a candidate of his own choosing. At first Duane's popularity was not affected;

---

[40]Higginbotham, *Keystone*, 85, 87-89; *Democratic Press*, "Honestus," 24 Sept. 1807; *Spirit of the Press*, 5 Oct. 1805; Leiper to Jefferson, 23 Mar. 1806, TJ-LC.

his efforts to defeat the Governor had been unquestionably genuine. But when he persisted in defending his beleaguered friend, Duane was warned that he showed "absurd taste" in choosing a pet as dangerous as a copperhead.[41]

If Snyder were elected, his close friend Nathaniel B. Boileau was generally expected to dominate his administration. From Montgomery county, Boileau was an outstanding leader in the legislature and had been especially outspoken on the issue of judicial reform. In 1806 Leib challenged Boileau's leadership directly when he declined to run again for Congress and instead entered the legislature at the head of the assembly delegation from Philadelphia county. "Boileau was the most popular man, but Leib had strength enough to defeat his wishes," recalled an independent Republican, who reflected, "In those two men, we see an instance of where to very moderate capacities, & acquirements, was joined an immoderate desire to fill the first places."[42]

In his first session Leib took the lead in the "dirty intrigue, to destroy each other." He opposed the choice of Snyder to run for House Speaker on the pretext that he could not be elected,

---

[41] Jesse Higgins to Jonathan Roberts and Matthew Roberts, 8 May 1807, Roberts Papers, HSP; Samuel Maclay to Jonathan Roberts, 2 Feb. 1808, *ibid.*; *Democratic Press*, 25, 30 Sept. 1807. The charges against Leib were disclosed in *ibid.*, "Veritas," 26, 28 Aug., 2, 10, 19, 28 Sept. 1807; *ibid.*, "Honestus," 22, 24, 29 Sept. 1807; *ibid.*, 11, 15, 18, 19, 21, 23, 24, 26, 29 Sept., 1, 5 Oct. 1807. For a full discussion of Leib's actions and the resulting attack upon him see Higginbotham, *Keystone*, chapter VI.

[42] *Ibid.*, 81-82; Jonathan Roberts, Memoirs, I, 113, 119-120, HSP.

and later he prevented the possible selection of Boileau as United States Senator. When his colleague John Thompson left the assembly chamber and went home, he said, with a toothache or gumboil, the Federalist-Quid candidate Andrew Gregg was elected by one vote. But Leib had miscalculated and his schemes were quickly and harshly turned against him. In January 1807 the Democratic caucus authorized an investigation and prepared a secret report which censured his conduct.

By the opening of the next session the somewhat chastened Leib was ready to cooperate with Snyder. But Boileau jealously prevented it and destroyed the opportunity for party unity. "From the best information I can obtain & the best observation I have been able to make," wrote Jonathan Roberts of Montgomery county, "this evidence of Leibs condens[cens]ion was the [signal] for the Boileau-ites to detach Snyder from a good understanding with Leib." Early in the session the House debated Leib's resolution recommending a federal convention to amend the judiciary article of the Constitution, which in the end was defeated by a tie vote. Boileau's speech in favor was intended to close the debate on the motion, but a young Philadelphia lawyer, John Sergeant, then "proceeded in the most jesuitical style to do away the effect of Boileaus speech."

The next morning Sergeant continued and "indulged himself with great Libertys toward Leib," the favorite target for the Federalist and Quid speakers. When he sat down "Leib rose & in a speech of two hours length displayed powers of mind I did not believe he posses'd," Roberts admitted. "The faces of his opponents tho' some of them are pale enough naturally did not want for colour while he was speaking[;] I do not think they will often provoke him--This speech," Roberts believed, "will make Leib the premier of his party--At replication he is certainly the great Leviathan but he is cruel & vindictive as well as ambitious."

Leib's "celebrated speech" heightened the fears of his rival, "& it really appear'd to awaken a disposition in the Boileauites to effect a coldness between him & Snyder." The sincerity of his support was open to question. "It was easy therefore to awaken Snyders jealousy & to sting his pride by artful representations." The Speaker was prevailed upon to call the intemperate Philadelphian to order; a little later he rebuffed him in the matter of a committee assignment. "Leib could not be blind to what was going on around him," and a new division in the Republican party between the country Democrats and the Philadelphians was inexorably emerging.[43]

The prestige of the Aurora as the party newspaper for the whole state inevitably suffered from the Leib-Boileau quarrel. Since Leib went to Lancaster, a Snyderite estimated, Duane's popularity had sunk by fifty per cent. The editor was accused of abandoning "his most intimate friends" if they would not "obsequiously submit, to be the instruments" of Leib's ambition. "He who will not bow to The Brothers, is denounced." But Leib should be supported, one Philadelphian claimed, because "he has always been a bone of contention;

---

[43]Jonathan Roberts to Jonathan Roberts Sr., 8 Jan. 1808, Roberts Papers, HSP; Roberts to Matthew Roberts, 28 Jan. 1808, ibid.

therefore, if he were laid aside, we would have no school for oratory."[44]

In spite of the conflict with the country Democrats, Duane and Leib with prudent behavior should have continued for many years to share an important influence in state affairs because of their leadership of the well-organized Democratic machine in Philadelphia. But Duane's quick temper when his political ideas or acts were challenged led him into two quarrels with important Republicans in the city, with disastrous consequences for the harmony of the local party. The trouble began in October 1806 when the narrow victory of Frederick Wolbert as sheriff was contested by the Quid candidate, William T. Donaldson, who charged that fraud had occurred in the election procedures. The Governor appointed an investigating commission, whose membership was notably conservative; the Democrats charged that it had been selected by Attorney General Joe McKean, who also served as counsel for Donaldson. In January the commission reported that it had found ninety-one illegal votes; therefore the Governor voided the election and declared that the incumbent sheriff would remain in office until the following October.[45]

Duane and Leib demanded that the Governor issue the sheriff's commission to Wolbert, and when he refused they threatened to impeach him. Within the next few months the issue developed into a personal conflict between McKean and the two Philadelphians which exceeded the

---

[44] Democratic Press, 23, 25 Sept., 1 Oct. 1807.

[45] Spirit of the Press, Oct. 1806; Higginbotham, Keystone, 121-122, 125-126.

violence of the 1805 campaign. The Governor began three libel suits against the Aurora and attempted unsuccessfully to censor it by forcing the editor to post bond for his future good behavior. When that failed McKean proposed general legislation on newspaper libels, to provide prior censorship when a paper was judged to be turbulent. Thomas McKean, Jr., challenged Leib to a duel but was refused; then his second, Richard Dennis, tried to challenge Duane, Leib's second, but failed. The Governor sought to prosecute the two on a charge of conspiracy for attempting to force him to issue Wolbert's commission, but he was unsuccessful.[46]

Leib carried out the threat of impeachment proceedings against the aged Governor, who had only eighteen months remaining in his constitutional term of office. Because he was ill, the inquiry was temporarily suspended "lest he should die and his death be attributed thereto," but when his health had improved sufficiently, Leib's committee completed the investigation and reported six counts for impeachment. The report was approved by the committee of the whole, but the matter was postponed until the next session. The following January the Federalist-Quid coalition succeeded in ending the impeachment proceedings by a general postponement.[47]

The noisy controversy between Duane and Leib and the Governor

---

[46] Ibid., 114, 123-125, 127, 143; Duane to C. A. Rodney, 20 Mar. 1807, Genl. MSS Collection (Duane), Columbia; Duane to Rodney, 28 Jan. 1807, Gratz Collection, HSP; McKean Papers, IV, 5-7, HSP; Aurora, 12, 15 Jan. 1807.

[47] Duane to Rodney, 28 Jan. 1807, Gratz Collection, HSP; Duane to Rodney, 20 Mar. 1807, Genl. MSS Collection (Duane), Columbia; Higginbotham, Keystone, 126-127, 149-150.

dwindled away without any significant conclusion, except for the libel suits against the Aurora which continued in the courts for some time longer. The Philadelphians' purpose in the futile conflict was to maintain their position of leadership among the state's Democrats and to serve notice that the McKeanites would not be welcomed back into the Democratic Republican party. They injured themselves by their extremism, opening the way for a future understanding between the Quids and the Snyderites.

Trapped in the middle of the violent quarrel over the sheriff's election was the incumbent officer, John Barker, one of the gentlest men engaged in politics. When Wolbert's victory was first contested, Leib and Duane had asked Barker to go to Lancaster and urge the Governor to issue the sheriff's commission. He went but McKean dismissed him with an outburst of invective against the Philadelphia leaders. After he returned to the city, rumors were published concerning an attempt "to terrify, or seduce [the Governor], or something of that kind, by the medium of general Barker." The sheriff, who also commanded the city militia, was a highly popular Democrat known for his generous and easy-going personality, and he heartily disliked being implicated in an alleged plot against the chief executive. He wanted to reveal the full story of his interview with the Governor, but Duane apologetically declined to publish his account in the Aurora. He therefore took his letter to Poulson's American Daily Advertiser, and Duane angrily replied in the Federalist paper that Barker was politically confused.[48]

[48]Ibid., 122-123; Aurora, 12 Feb. 1807; Spirit of the Press, Feb. 1807.

The differing personalities of Duane and Barker had caused them to clash publicly once before, when at a town meeting in 1804 the sheriff unexpectedly expressed the view that the Aurora should not reply to the Quids' slanders, but ignore them as beneath notice. At this Duane broke in with an impassioned defense of his newspaper and had to be restrained by the chairman, while at the side John Leib was heard to mutter, "Damn Barker, he's a damned old rascal." The damage was repaired a few days later with explanations in the Aurora from both Duane and the sheriff.[49] Their quarrel over Wolbert's commission was not smoothed over but grew steadily more damaging, as friends of Barker, especially Jacob Vogdes, told the editor that he was mistreating him. Duane's instinct, when he was questioned and placed in the wrong, was to become intensely self-defensive and to lash out at his enemies.

Meanwhile Duane became involved in another quarrel, with the federal marshal John Smith, a McKean supporter who wanted to return to the majority party. The Marshal "is now with us," Leiper wrote after the gubernatorial election, "and would have been always had it not been for Dallas." In November 1806 the city's General Ward Committee met with representatives from the county to prepare a memorial to Thomas Jefferson asking him to consent to run for a third term as President. On the subject of the address there was more unity than on any previous political action, according to Leiper, but the memorial was finally signed by only the chairman and the secretary.

---

[49] Freeman's Journal, 7, 8 Sept. 1804; Aurora, 8 Sept. 1804.

Two delegates, Tench Coxe and John Smith, disliked the harsh language denouncing Federalist officeholders, and several objected to signing in company with one or both of those men. The distrust of Coxe was general for he had a long history as a political changeling, but Duane led the protest against fellowship with the Marshal.[50]

Smith had been one of the founders of the Militia Legion, and a few weeks later at a meeting of the board of officers, he and Barker's friend Vogdes, who was captain of the Columbian Blues, turned on Duane violently for his vindictive and dictatorial behavior. Following this encounter the editor feared a duelling challenge. "I have . . . judged it more prudent to remain at home than go abroad much," he confided to Caesar Rodney, "because every idea of Justice is out of the question for me as you know." Duelling was illegal, "and tho' I might be killed and my family ruined without justice . . . if I were to wound or kill one of them even in defending myself, a prison and a gibbet would be soon provided for me by corrupt Sheriffs & Marshals &c."[51]

Duane's simultaneous quarrel with Barker gave Smith a splendid opportunity to regain public favor by becoming the champion of the abused sheriff. Rather than emphasize his own mistreatment by the Aurora editor, he promoted the belief that Duane had done great injury to the popular Democrat. Smith's son-in-law was Richard Dennis, who had been second for Thomas McKean, Jr., and who was trying to

---

[50]Leiper to Jefferson, 23 Mar., 21 Nov. 1806, TJ-LC. On Smith's appointment as marshal see Leiper to Jefferson, 8 Mar. 1801, TJ-LC; Cunningham, Jeff. Repubs. in Power, 30-31.

[51]Duane to Rodney, 28 Jan. 1807, Gratz Collection, HSP.

provoke his own duel with the editor. Dennis showed "very great solicitude" in the case, said Duane disdainfully, and was one of the authors of "The publications which have been circulated with so much zeal . . . with the name of poor, miserable, infatuated Barker." When a grand jury indicted McKean, Jr., and Dennis, upon Leib's complaint, for breaking the law against duelling, Barker and Vogdes were among the citizens who signed their memorial of protest to the Governor.[52]

Duane dismissed the affair as a trick by the Quids to regain the confidence of the Republican party. Is "Mr. Smith," he asked, "acting under the advice or with the knowledge and connivance of the great puppet worker Dallas?" Although Dallas was not involved, Duane's suspicions were essentially correct for there emerged from the incident a new faction in Philadelphia composed of repentant Quids and disgruntled Democrats, which was christened the Quadroons by the Aurora. Rather than destroy the opportunity by apologizing to Barker, Duane foolishly and unkindly increased his criticism. "Gen[eral] Barker was yesterday boasting," Duane wrote to Rodney at the end of January, "that if I went to Washington there were two or three persons in Congress determined to shoot me. These are strange things," he concluded.[53]

---

[52] Ibid.; Aurora, 15 Jan. 1807; Richard Dennis and Thomas McKean Jr. to Thomas McKean, [1807], McKean Papers, IV, 7, HSP.

[53] Aurora, 15 Jan. 1807; Duane to Rodney, 28 Jan. 1807, Gratz Collection, HSP; Democratic Press, 3 Sept., 5 Oct. 1807. This judgment disagrees with that of Higginbotham, Keystone, 137, that the "assertion appears to have little foundation."

During these uneasy days in January, when Duane stayed indoors as much as possible and avoided receiving suspicious messages, "some influential Democrats" in Philadelphia wrote to the editor of the Northumberland Republican Argus, John Binns, and invited him to establish a newspaper in the metropolis. Binns, who was a close friend of Simon Snyder, a representative from Northumberland county, went to Lancaster to ask the opinion of Snyder, Boileau and others, and they encouraged him to accept the invitation. For the country Democrats it was a lucky opportunity to promote Snyder's candidacy within Leib's home territory. Snyder later denied that he had assisted in establishing Binns' Democratic Press "for the purpose of putting down Duane and myself," Leib wrote to Jonathan Roberts, but "Would you believe it, when I tell you" that while the new paper was attacking Leib daily, Snyder wrote to Binns saying "that the press must not fall, and that he would contribute towards its support to the extent of his means!"[54]

When Binns came to Philadelphia in February he solicited support both from Duane and from Duane's enemies. His own primary interest was supporting Snyder not destroying the Aurora, which was the "ablest and most influential Republican paper in Pennsylvania," he wrote long after, "and probably had as much, or more, influence with that party in the Union, than any other paper then published." But Duane was the "fast and faithful" friend of Leib, who was "gen-

---

[54]Binns, Recollections, 191-192; Leib to Roberts, 16 Dec. 1809, Roberts Papers, HSP; Higginbotham, Keystone, 137. See also Roberts to Jonathan Roberts Sr., 13 Dec. 1807, Roberts Papers, HSP.

erally believed" to oppose Snyder, and hence the beginning of a long and bitter rivalry.[55]

At first Duane generously helped Binns become established in the city, sponsoring his membership in Tammany and the Society of the Friends of the People and inviting him to join his company of Republican Greens. In March about one hundred Democrats gathered at John Miller's tavern to hear Binns swear "upon the altar of my conscience" that his purpose in establishing a new paper was not to oppose Duane and Leib but to serve as an auxiliary to the Aurora. Two months later the Democratic Press opened the "paper War" with Leib, attacking his conduct in the legislature and opposing his re-election.[56]

Ironically the first victim of Binns' Press was not Leib but Duane. The fierce campaign against the assemblyman by a combined Quid and Quadroon effort could not overcome the overwhelming strength of the Democratic party in Philadelphia county, and although Leib ran last on the assembly ticket, 175 votes behind the leader, he was safely re-elected. However the addition from the previous year of five hundred new voters, mostly in the rural areas, cut the Democratic majority in the county by half, from about one thousand to five hundred.

In the city also there was a huge increase in the numbers voting; nearly eight hundred more persons than had voted for Governor

---

[55] Binns, Recollections, 191-192.

[56] Democratic Press, 25 Sept., 5 Oct. 1807; Philadelphia Evening Star, 1 Aug. 1810; Leiper to Jefferson, 28 Aug. 1807, TJ-LC.

came out for the purpose of defeating Duane as a candidate for the state senate. Although the Federalists and Quids together had carried the city in 1805 and 1806, they increased their margin in this election, and the *Aurora* described the results as "the first federal triumph in this district, since the election of Thomas Jefferson." It blamed John Binns for inspiring the moribund party; "when he began to squirt his filth at some of the members of the democratic party, their drooping spirits began to revive, and like a scattered covey of partridges, they began at once to whistle for each other."[57]

The real inspiration to the Federalists was not Binns but the chance to humiliate the *Aurora* editor. Duane's candidacy for the state senate was the first and the last time that he sought elective office. Although he complained of persecution, Duane himself had underestimated how much he was hated. He had wanted to run for Congress to take the place of his friend Joe Clay, who was retiring to become cashier of the new Farmers and Mechanics bank. But in September when he returned from Richmond, where he had gone to observe the treason trial of Aaron Burr, his friends told him that he was not eligible because he had not been a citizen for the required seven years. The senate nomination was belatedly given him as a consolation, but became instead a source of chagrin.[58]

---

[57] *Freeman's Journal*, 17 Oct. 1807; *Democratic Press*, 14, 16, 17 Oct. 1807; *Aurora*, 15, 20 Oct. 1807; Higginbotham, *Keystone*, 99, 117, 144.

[58] Duane to Rodney, 20 Mar., 23 Nov. 1807, Genl. MSS Collection (Duane), Columbia; *Democratic Press*, 11 Sept. 21 Oct. 1807; *The Tickler*, 16, 23 Sept. 1807.

The campaign against the editor was intensively nativist in spirit. It was the most serious, open expression of such feelings since the United Irish rebellion of 1798 had inspired the legislation of the alien laws. In Philadelphia in 1807, as in New York, the elections disclosed a public reaction against the special naturalization law of 1804, which had suddenly increased the influence of foreign-born voters. In New York the nativist ticket was defeated at the polls, but in Philadelphia the sentiment triumphed, because of the opportunity to reject the presumptuous Irishman who had set himself up as the leader of the naturalized citizens. Duane's quarrel with John Barker increased the resentment, for Barker was a Revolutionary veteran who had fought at Trenton, Princeton and Brandywine, but when he was appointed Major General of Philadelphia's militia division in the summer of 1807, the Aurora denigrated his past military service.[59]

A few days after Duane's candidacy was confirmed, a new paper was established in the city upon principles "purely American--excluding all foreign partialities or prejudices." The Tickler, edited by George Helmbold, alias Toby Scratch-em, joined the Spirit of the Press, edited by the hunchbacked Richard (Dicky) Folwell, in a viscious campaign against the Aurora editor. These savagely humorous journals, founded upon a bigoted hatred of all Democrats but Duane especially, were not acknowledged organs of any party, but they were read in Philadelphia. In a special Congressional election

---

[59] Spirit of the Press, July, Oct. 1807; Pennsylvania Archives, 6th series, 15 vols. (Harrisburg, 1906-1907), IV, 758, 770; Scharf and Westcott, Hist. of Phila., I, 528.

a year earlier, five hundred Federalists to show their contempt for the Democratic party had voted for Folwell, "a poor _unfortunate maniac_ who is the unhappy object of sport for the idle boys of the town."[60]

Duane's nomination threatened to "tarnish the American name," according to Helmbold and Folwell, and had been pushed through by his cohorts, "The scum of Europe, rascals, runaways/ whom their o'er cloyed country vomits forth." Lack of a decent national pride in American youth, they charged, was responsible for the shameful partiality to strangers; "they consider foreigners more wise and infallible, in the science of government concerns, than their fathers, who established the present system of government." But if the naive young Democrats understood the "subtle machinations of Europeans," they "would let them know, that we are not beholden to Europeans: that we can manage our affairs without their advice and assistance." To begin the Philadelphians should rebuff William Duane.[61]

In the city on October 13 "the contest was the most ardent ever witnessed." "Hundreds were induced to come out and vote against Wm. Duane, who for many years have never put in a single ticket. When out," the _Democratic Press_ complained, "they voted the whole ticket," contributing to the Democratic defeat. Duane ran far behind his party and lost by a humiliating 1,240 votes to Edward Heston, an ill-educated farmer from Blockley township. Duane retained the

---

[60]_The Tickler_, 16 Sept. 1807; _Aurora_, 28, 29 Nov., 1 Dec. 1806.

[61]_The Tickler_, 7 Oct. 1807; _Spirit of the Press_, Oct. 1807.

loyalty of most of the Democrats, but he was crushed by the influx of Federalist and Quid voters bent upon putting the editor in his place.

He carried the Northern Liberties and Southwark, but lost in the rural districts of the county, and he won only four of the fourteen wards of Philadelphia, North and South Mulberry, on the northwestern edge of the city, and the southwestern Cedar and Locust, which were becoming the center of Irish population. In the better class wards in the central part of the city, he was defeated by margins of three to one. And in his own neighborhood, High street ward, still considered the most fashionable, Duane received 46 votes to 260 for Heston.[62]

The defeat was celebrated with malicious glee in some quarters. Grief-stricken wakes were cheerfully imagined by Helmbold and Folwell, who fancied that Duane had died from the shock and that "Poor Peggy is inconsolable." He was attended by Dr. Leib "with the utmost affection," and "his nurse was granny Leiper." But a few days later Colonel Duane marched on parade with his "former dear green boys," then side-stepped from the ranks, it was reported, to receive the batallion's salute as it passed the _Aurora_ office. The editor's attorney, Walter Franklin, was among the supposed friends "engaged in the dirty work carried on here in October." Duane intended to say nothing to him about it, "but he saves me the mortifi-

---

[62] _Democratic Press_, 14 Oct. 1807.

cation of suppressing by never having been inside my doors since the Election!"[63]

At the beginning of November it was announced that Duane's twenty-seven year old son would become editor-in-chief of the Aurora. The paper would "go on in the same track," and it was generally supposed that "the veteran still loads and aims his boy's musket, who merely pulls the trigger." William John's name remained on the masthead for fourteen months while his father sought a temporary retirement from political journalism. "The young man is to be pitied," thought Enos Bronson, "for we are told he is a lad of some genius."[64] Duane's purpose in the arrangement was to gain time in which to work on a wide range of publishing projects, by which he hoped to rescue himself from the long-standing debt for his now useless property in Washington. The Aurora was not profitable, partly because of unpaid subscriptions, and he still owed 18,000 dollars, although he complained that much more was due him "for the public [service] of which the public seem to care as little about as if I had been the greatest rascal in the Universe." The planned "occupations require seclusion," he explained, "and I have effected it by the change of names in the paper."[65]

---

[63]Ibid., 22 Oct. 1807; The Tickler, 21 Oct. 1807; Spirit of the Press, Nov. 1807; Duane to Rodney, 23 Nov. 1807, Genl. MSS Collection (Duane), Columbia. See also Freeman's Journal, 14, 15 Oct. 1807.

[64]Duane to Jefferson, 16 Oct. 1807, TJ-LC; Spirit of the Press, Nov. 1807; The Tickler, 4 Nov. 1807; U.S. Gaz., 10 Oct. 1807.

[65]Duane to Jefferson, 16 Oct. 1807, TJ-LC; Duane to Rodney, 23 Nov. 1807, Genl. MSS Collection (Duane), Columbia.

CHAPTER V

PRESIDENTIAL POLITICS

The Republican party nationally faced a critical test of its strength and unity in the forthcoming presidential election. The beloved Jefferson was all but certain to retire at the end of his two terms in office, and there was no one else "in whom we can repose so much confidence," Thomas Leiper told him frankly. "The Pivot we have been running upon is yourself." The question arose whether the successful alliance of Virginia with New York and Pennsylvania could survive without him or would founder on the inability to agree wholeheartedly upon a candidate.

For Pennsylvania the *Aurora*'s position was crucial. That paper "with all its indecency," a Philadelphian warned James Madison, "is worth for our purpose all others," for it was read "in every hovel of Pennsylvania." Fortunately for the party leaders as well as for the editor, Duane's relations with the national administration were now better than at any time since the early days of Jefferson's term of office.[1]

The break with the party in 1806 by John Randolph, the eccen-

---

[1]Leiper to Jefferson, 23 Mar., 21 Nov. 1806, TJ-LC; Admiral Thomas Truxton to Madison, 17 Mar. 1808, Madison Papers, LC.

tric, intellectually powerful Congressman from Virginia, had tested the fidelity of Duane and of all Republicans. Previously the Aurora had warmly supported Randolph's often controversial opinions, especially his sharp criticism of the government commission which had agreed to a compromise settlement with the claimants in the case of the Yazoo land frauds. Consequently Duane was widely expected to follow the Virginian into self-imposed exile, but his enemies within the party were to be disappointed.

When Randolph quarreled with Jefferson concerning foreign policy, the circumstances were so shadowed by mystery and confusion that Duane almost strayed from the President unwittingly. Randolph objected to what he considered an aggressive, even belligerent attitude toward the European powers by the American government. He denounced specifically the government's effort to acquire Florida by the use of pressure on Spain. In January 1806 Congress went into secret session to consider the administration's request for a special appropriation of two million dollars for the possible purchase of Florida. When Randolph failed to defeat the measure, he retaliated by spreading his own version of the secret proceedings to the public.[2]

Duane, although totally ignorant of the subject in dispute, spontaneously sympathized with Randolph and repeated his views, to the consternation of Congressman Leib. "Duane is laying about him," he told Caesar A. Rodney, "and is dealing out blame to those who have never been questioned as to their principles, or as to their interest

---

[2]See Henry Adam, John Randolph (Boston, 1882), 154-190.

in the honor of the present executive." Leib apprehended dismal political consequences from Duane's indiscretion since his paper "is considered as the mirror of the sentiments of our party," and he urged Rodney to enlighten the editor. "It will not be necessary that he should be informed that I have interfered," Leib cautioned, "as he may, perhaps, take it ill that I did not write to him."[3]

Duane received Rodney's hint, with many others, and he reacted to the thickening intrigue with his instinct for candor. He wrote directly to the President for information concerning the many damaging rumors about him and the cabinet which were current in Philadelphia. The most recent and alarming report was the charge that Jefferson and James Madison had approved the expedition against South America by General Francisco Miranda. Duane told the President that he had refused to believe reports that Rufus King of New York had served as agent between Madison and Miranda. But, he confessed, the "story was told in a manner to excite attention and to shake incredulity." Duane warned Jefferson that the anxiety created "among those who love you & had not strength of mind to resist it is not to be described."[4]

Jefferson responded immediately and warmly to the candid inquiry. "It is a proof of sincerity which I value above all things," he told the editor; "if my friends will address themselves to me directly, as you have done, they shall be informed with frankness & thankfulness." Reassuring Duane on every point, the President

---

[3]Leib to Rodney, 8 Feb. 1806, Gratz Collection, HSP.

[4]Duane to Jefferson, 12 Mar. 1806, TJ-LC.

declared the report that Miranda's expedition was "countenanced by me" to be "an absolute falsehood." He confirmed Duane's information that John Randolph had attacked the administration, and told the Anglophobic editor that Randolph wanted the government to ally with Britain and to go to war with Spain "& consequently France." "This perhaps is not the only ground of his alienation," the President admitted, "but which side retains its orthodoxy the vote of 87 to 11 republicans may satisfy you."[5]

The considerate, friendly attention which Jefferson always gave to his supporters was perhaps his strongest asset as a politician, and in the case of the warm-hearted Duane it was precisely what was needed to reaffirm his loyalty. John Randolph was disgruntled by the lost opportunity, but affected mere disgust. Joseph "Nicholson, who has been in Philadelphia lately, writes me that the Aurora refused to give circulation to anything against the powers that be," Randolph informed James M. Garnett. "This perfectly corresponds with my own observations on that paper & its Editor," he assured his friend. "It seems that N. applied to know whether some communication of his would be inserted, and the reply was, 'not if against the administration.'"[6]

Just at this point, Aaron Burr's mysterious and ominous movements in the Southwest gave Duane a splendid opportunity to demonstrate his devotion to President Jefferson. The Pennsylvania edi-

---

[5]Jefferson to Duane, 22 Mar. 1806, TJ-LC.

[6]Randolph to Garnett, 4 June 1806, John Randolph-James M. Garnett Letterbook, Library of Congress.

tor's zeal to defend the government against the conspiracy became almost ludicrous. He forwarded to Washington secret particulars regarding Burr's movements and plans which he had received from correspondents, and he offered his own military services for the capture of the conspirators. After Burr was arrested, Duane sent his second son Patrick on a trip from Pittsburgh to New Orleans so that he could provide the government with an estimation of the state of public opinion in the Southwest.[7] Duane had sound personal reasons for his extraordinary interest in the case of Aaron Burr. In 1802 Burr had solicited support from the Aurora though his associate Matthew L. Davis, and Duane had been waiting to reply to the insult. Moreover Burr's personal associations in Pennsylvania had been generally with members of Governor McKean's party. His friends in Lancaster were "pretty near the government," and Duane took pleasure in identifying the fugitive as "the emperor of the quids."[8]

Duane also sought to serve the President by harrying the Marquis de Casa Yrujo. The Spanish Ambassador was persona non grata in Washington, but he refused to go home. He remained instead in Philadelphia with his American wife, Sally McKean, the daughter of the Governor, and wrote anonymous letters to Federalist newspapers criticizing United States' foreign policy. In his last significant

---

[7]Duane to Jefferson, 4 Nov., 8 Dec. 1806, 1, 8 July 1807, TJ-LC; Duane to Rodney, 5 Aug. 1807, [1 Jan. 1808], Genl. MSS Collection (Duane), Columbia; Duane to Secretary of State Robert Smith, 24 Mar. 1811, ibid.

[8]Duane to Abraham Bishop, 28 Aug. 1802, Pers. Papers Misc. (Duane), LC; Jonathan Roberts to Jonathan Roberts, Sr., 8 Jan. 1808, Roberts Papers, HSP; Aurora, 12 Dec. 1806.

act as ambassador, Yrujo successfully subverted Miranda's expedition to South America by warning officials in the Spanish colonies.[9]

The news of the capture of Miranda's ship the Leander reached the United States in early July 1806. Duane feared that Yrujo, from personal pique, would use the occasion to urge his government to hostile relations with America. Great Britain would be the lone beneficiary of a war between her mutual enemies Spain and the United States. Indeed Duane believed that the British cabinet itself had planned Miranda's expedition as a means of embarrassing United States-Spanish relations. Hence the Aurora charged that unfriendly representations by Yrujo concerning the affair would further the schemes of "his coadjutors the British agents."

The Aurora's criticism of Yrujo continued during the next few weeks until the Spanish minister filed two suits for libel, compelling the editor to pass an afternoon in jail. Yrujo objected to the paper's description of him as a "privileged spy." He brought his second action for the remark that he was a prospect for a "strait waistcoat," Duane's comment on the report that the Spanish community in America deprecated the strange behavior of its ambassador.[10]

Yrujo was taking a risk in suing the editor, for the Aurora's observations however defamatory came uncomfortably close to the truth about him. The disgraced ambassador did engage in espionage from his home in Philadelphia. Yrujo's intimacy with Johathan L. Dayton,

---

[9] See Brant, Madison, IV, 188-212, 323-325, 332-333.

[10] Aurora, 3, 19, 21 July, 12, 13 Aug. 1806.

Burr's partner in conspiracy, had just been exposed and his reputation could not afford an investigation into the nature of the friendship. The Spanish government was more circumspect than its minister; it rejected the recommendation of a pension for Dayton and cautioned Yrujo against implication in the plot against the Southwest. Duane's reflection on the state of Yrujo's mind was more clearly libelous, but not entirely indefensible.[11]

Two things encouraged Yrujo to take Duane into court. His father-in-law was the Governor, and Governor McKean thought Yrujo's suits would aid his campaign to suppress the Aurora. McKean during the same period sued Duane on three separate charges of libel, and proposed a revision of the libel laws which would provide a system of prior restraint of licentious newspapers.[12]

The ambiguity of the libel law itself was another encouragement to Yrujo and to all potential plaintiffs. There was at that time no law in Pennsylvania which specifically provided that the truth of a statement could be introduced as a defense against the charge of libel. The common law definition of libel as a publication which tended to defame was all that the courts had to go on. Criminal libel, or the defamation of public officials, was no more clearly defined, so that mere political criticism could be construed as constituting a libel. Each court acted on its own discretion.

---

[11] Ibid., 29 July 1806; Brant, Madison, IV, 341-342; Hubert Bruce Fuller, The Purchase of Florida (Cleveland, 1906), 166-168, 170.

[12] Aurora, 13 Aug. 1806; Higginbotham, Keystone, 114, 123.

Yrujo, who was represented in the case by his brother-in-law the Attorney General of Pennsylvania, had cause to hope for a friendly court.[13]

Duane suffered from this system and the proliferation of lawsuits it encouraged. Since 1798 he had been sued several dozen times, but was convicted only occasionally. Some suits were necessarily dropped or dismissed, because of the tendency to scatter charges like buckshot, many of them repetitious or insubstantial. Most of the disputes dragged on from one court session to the next, sometimes over many years, so that Duane felt he inevitably lost whatever the judgment. He regarded lawsuits as his peculiar "entailed estate," and complained to Jefferson that he was constrained to stay within "the range of the courts of law, in which I am doomed I fear to linger out my life."[14]

By a twentieth century definition of libel, which allows a wide range to political comment, William Duane would seldom have been convicted or even sued. The *Aurora*'s criticisms were exaggerated and frequently cruel, but they were always political. Duane prided himself on his refusal to publish personal abuse. A few days before he called the Spanish Ambassador a "privileged spy," Duane had censured a correspondent for sending him anecdotes about Yrujo

---

[13] *Ibid.*, 123-124, 181-182; Frank L. Mott, *American Journalism* (New York, 1941), 172; Frederick Hudson, *History of American Journalism, 1690-1872* (New York, 1873), 741-742, 744; *Aurora*, 13 Aug. 1806.

[14] *Ibid.*, 12, 13 Aug. 1806; Duane to Jefferson, 4 Feb. 1809, TJ-LC.

which were "too indelicate for this paper."[15]

Duane's enemies were often less decorous. The editor had to sue Caleb Wayne of the United States Gazette, who wrote that Duane had left Ireland in flight because he raped a girl who subsequently died. This story never stopped circulating in Philadelphia. Duane also sued Richard Folwell for calling him the bastard son of a camp follower in the French and Indian war. Both suits were inconclusive, and Folwell continued to publish his lewd fantasies about Duane's past, sometimes illustrated with woodcuts.[16]

With Yrujo's suits Duane had the problem that his hints were only clever guesses. He did not have the information which would have proved their truth. Yrujo thought Duane's damaging innuendos were based on facts divulged to him by a member of the Spanish legation in Philadelphia. He consequently requested the official's recall to Madrid and meanwhile put the man under a virtual house arrest. Actually Duane knew much less than the Marquis feared. It appears, Duane wrote Jefferson, "that I must have penetrated the Spanish mysteries of State. Your eminent situation may perhaps enable you to judge what the secret really is; for tho' it seems I discovered it, it remains a secret to me to this moment."[17]

Jefferson was indignant at the possibility that America's

---

[15] Aurora, 14 July 1806.

[16] Scharf and Westcott, Hist. of Phila., I, 509; Duane from [Levi Hollingsworth], n.d., Society Collection, HSP; The Tickler, 30 Sept., 12 Oct. 1807, 6 Dec. 1809; Spirit of the Press, Aug., Oct. 1806, Aug. 1807, Aug. 1808.

[17] Duane to Rodney, 28 Jan. 1807, Gratz Collection, HSP; Duane to Jefferson, 2 Nov. 1806, TJ-LC.

hapless hospitality to the Spanish Ambassador could extend to rewarding him damages in an American court. In February 1807 he requested Caesar A. Rodney, his new Attorney General and Duane's former lawyer, to have the case removed to the United States Supreme Court, which held jurisdiction over cases involving ambassadors, and subsequently dismissed. Unluckily for Duane, though fortunately for United States-Spanish relations, Madrid acted on Washington's request for Yrujo's replacement before Jefferson's instructions had been carried out. As an ordinary resident alien, Yrujo could bring suit in the state courts. His case against Duane lingered in the Pennsylvania courts for the next several years.[18]

Some good came out of the quarrel with Yrujo, for it reaffirmed the cordial relations between Jefferson and Duane. The President appreciated Duane's motive in attacking a man who had assaulted himself, and the editor was naturally grateful for Jefferson's effort to help.

At this time the administration faced an emergency in foreign relations, caused by the renewal of the European war and the refusal of either Britain or France to respect the rights of neutrals. In the summer of 1807 the sinking of the American *Chesapeake* by the British *Leopard* brought the two countries to the point of war. The crisis strengthened the party loyalty of the Anglophobic Republicans such as Duane who favored a strong stand against the

---

[18] Jefferson to Rodney, 5 Feb. 1807, Rodney Papers, Del. Hist. Soc.; Fuller, *Purchase of Florida*, 168; Lewis Mayers, *The American Legal System* (New York, 1955), 7-9; *Aurora*, 2, 5 Mar. 1808; Duane to Jefferson, 4 Feb. 1809, TJ-LC.

former colonial rulers, and the editor urged the President to send him "hints that may be useful for the public service." In December Congress enacted Jefferson's proposal for a general embargo on shipping as a means of retaliation without war. Duane was highly pleased with the decisive action and maintained complete faith in the measure after many Republicans had begun to regret it, because of the hardship imposed on American commerce. The *Aurora*'s zealous defense of Jefferson's Embargo renewed the hatred of Duane in Philadelphia's commercial community. It would "perhaps be too hard upon him," one letter writer acknowledged, "to assert he is in the pay of the great European Napoleon, but as we cannot be hung for thinking, I shall indulge my thoughts as I please."[19]

II

Meanwhile the presidential election was approaching and the Republicans had the difficult task of selecting a successor to Jefferson, someone of national stature and popularity who could hold the party together and maintain its electoral dominance. Secretary of State Madison was generally regarded as the likely candidate, but he was suspected of quiddish tendencies. Consequently some of the party's ardent democrats hoped to forestall the President's retirement. By 1806 public opinion was "taking a strong and decisive direction towards demanding M^r. Jeffersons continuance another term

[19]Duane to Rodney, 23 Nov. 1807, Genl. MSS Collection (Duane), Columbia; "Veritas" to the Editor of the *True American and Commercial Advertiser*, 30 June 1808, Bradford Collection, Unbound Correspondence, HSP. See also Duane to Jefferson, 8 Dec. 1806, 1, 8 July 1807, 12 Jan. 1808, TJ-LC; Jefferson to Duane, 20 July 1807, 17 Mar. 1808, TJ-LC; Duane to Rodney, 20 Mar. 1807, Genl. MSS Collection (Duane), Columbia; *U. S. Gazette*, 10, 17 Oct. 1807.

of 4 years," according to John Beckley, "as the only means of preventing a schism in the republican party," for "Madison, is deemed by many, too timid and indecisive as a statesman, and too liable to a conduct of forbearance to the federal party which may endanger our harmony and political safety." In Philadelphia Duane and Thomas Leiper led the General Ward Committee in adopting a unanimous resolution calling upon the President to accept a third term, and later a similar resolution passed the Pennsylvania legislature. But it was a futile effort for the aging President keenly wished to retire from public service, and the party leaders were forced to try to agree upon a successor.[20]

The disaffected John Randolph was determined to exploit the potential mistrust within the party, and at any cost politically to defeat the chances of James Madison. He believed that the administration had betrayed the party's agrarian principles, and he fixed the blame upon Madison for all that he disapproved in its actions. For example, although Secretary Gallatin had also been a member of the Yazoo commission, Randolph blamed Madison alone for the settlement which rewarded the speculators in Yazoo lands. His preferred presidential candidate for 1808 was the Virginian James Monroe, but he would have been satisfied with the election of Vice President George Clinton of New York, who was more popular in the northern states.[21]

---

[20]Beckley to James Monroe, 13 July 1806, Monroe Papers, NYPL; Leiper to Jefferson, 23 Mar. 1806, 28 Aug. 1807, TJ-LC; Philadelphia, Pa., Democratic-Republicans to Jefferson, 12 Nov. 1806, TJ-LC; Jefferson to Leiper, 22 Dec. 1806, TJ-LC.

[21]Randolph to Rodney, 12, 28 Feb. 1806, Rodney Family Papers, LC.

Randolph's hopes inevitably depended upon cooperation from the Democrats of Pennsylvania, whose electoral behavior after Jefferson's retirement could not be predicted with certainty. The Virginian estimated that the state would be safe for any Jefferson-backed candidate except Madison. Indeed there was a noticeable coolness toward the Secretary in Pennsylvania, a coolness which Madison appeared to reciprocate. The Democrats there tended to associate him with Dallas and the Quids, and Madison did nothing to alter that image. Duane made several attempts over a period of years to establish contact with the Secretary of State, but Madison responded always with indifference.[22]

Randolph believed that Pennsylvania's indifference to Madison could be turned into active opposition by an effective propaganda campaign. For this he needed the Aurora. "There is," he wrote Rodney, "(a great deal) rotten in the state of Denmark. We have no press:—& besides are tongue-tied & hand-cuffed." Randolph was willing to forget his personal dislike for Duane in the interest of a higher service. As Henry Adams put it:

> of all northern democracy, the democrats of New York and Pennsylvania, the Cheethams and Duanes, had been most repulsive to Randolph, but in his hatred for Mr. Madison he was now ready to unite with these dregs of corruption.

But the dregs were not ready to unite with Randolph. The proposition was rejected by Duane in an interview with Randolph at the end of May 1807, when the editor arrived in Richmond to witness

---

[22] Adams, Randolph, 215; Leib to Rodney, 19 May 1808, Gratz Collection, HSP. See Duane to Madison, 10 May 1801, 3 Aug. 1803, 10 Aug. 1805, Madison Papers, LC; Madison to Duane, draft, 20 Aug. 1803, ibid.

the treason trial of Aaron Burr. "Duane is here," Randolph wrote Joseph Nicholson, who had warned him of Duane's fidelity to the President. "Knowing what you do you will suppose that in any communication with him I would be guardedly circumspect." His caution was doubled by the knowledge that Wilson Cary Nicholas, Madison's principal campaign manager, was in Richmond at the same time and also testing out Duane's opinions. "Some important result is no doubt to flow from this conjunction," Randolph wrote James Monroe, reflecting bitterly on the advanced state of intrigue and hypocrisy prevailing in politics.[23]

Randolph however was not so circumspect in his conversation that Duane failed to understand his meaning. Some years later, in attacking Randolph's personal organ <u>The Spirit of '76</u>, he revealed that "he could have filled the station which it now occupies," a friend reported to the Virginian, but he had been "too public-spirited to yield to an attempt which you once made to buy him up."[24]

Before Duane left Richmond it was obvious to Randolph that the two could make no agreement. Their mutual distrust had been intensified by their opposite response to the treason trial in progress. As a member of the grand jury, Randolph formed a lasting aversion to General James Wilkinson, the chief witness for the prosecution, and pressed for an indictment of the General. Duane also

---

[23]Randolph to Rodney, 12 Feb. 1806, Rodney Family Papers, LC; Randolph to Nicholson, 31 May 1807, Joseph H. Nicholson Papers, LC; Randolph to Monroe, 30 May 1807, quoted in Adams, <u>Randolph</u>, 215-216; <u>ibid</u>., 214.

[24]James M. Garnett to Randolph, 15 Apr. 1811, Randolph-Garnett Letterbook, LC.

became acquainted with Wilkinson during the Burr trial, and he conceived a loyalty to the mysterious soldier as intense as was Randolph's hatred.[25] The only alliance contracted as a result of Duane's trip to Richmond was the marriage of his eldest daughter Catharine, who accompanied him on the trip, to Thomas Jefferson Morgan, the son of Colonel George Morgan, who appeared as a witness in the trial.[26]

Despairing of the Aurora, Randolph agreed to support another newspaper in Philadelphia, the new Democratic Press of John Binns. On the understanding that the Press would oppose Madison in 1808, Binns received a spate of new subscriptions. The paper initiated an early and strenuous campaign for George Clinton for President.[27]

The man who recommended Binns to Randolph was Joseph Clay, one of Duane's closest friends. But Clay's devotion to John Randolph superseded other loyalties. Duane, Leib and Caesar Rodney had all pushed and guided him politically until he went to Congress in 1803. The father-dominated Clay found in Randolph a man with whom he could identify, for he was entranced by the Virginian's intellectual brilliance and strength. Philadelphia was somewhat embarrassed by her Congressman's unorthodoxy, but continued him in office with the blessing of Duane and Leib. Clay's new loyalty however inevitably

---

[25]Randolph to Garnett, 31 Aug. 1808, 7 Apr. 1811, ibid.; Garnett to Randolph, 29 Mar. 1811, ibid.; Annals of Cong., 10th Cong., 1st sess., 1261; Adams, Randolph, 220-221; Aurora, 26 Jan. 1808, 1, 5, 12 Jan. 1811.

[26]North American, 8 Dec. 1907; Freeman's Journal, 25 Aug. 1807.

[27]Higginbotham, Keystone, 156-157; Randolph to Garnett, 31 Aug., 12 Sept. 1808, Randolph-Garnett Letterbook, LC.

compromised his membership in the "wretched triumvirate!"[28]

The Aurora meanwhile gave no hint which of the three potential candidates the editor preferred. To him the essential consideration was the continuance of Jefferson's foreign policy, but he did not say whom he considered the President's rightful successor. If he had expressed his wholly personal preferences, the aloof Madison probably would have come last in the Aurora's reckoning. Although he did not know James Monroe, he was inclined to trust him because of the latter's onetime intimacy with Senator Stevens T. Mason of Virginia. The libertarian Mason, Duane's first mentor in Republican politics, had died soon after the party came into office.

Vice President Clinton in age, experience and service possessed claims to the Republican nomination which equalled those of Madison, and he was a favorite of the Northern Democrats. The Pennsylvanians especially felt a fraternal bond with the New York party, for the Clintonians had upheld Jefferson against Burr and dealt a blow to the Quids' pretensions. Michael Leib as well as Joe Clay hoped to persuade Duane to endorse George Clinton. He plyed him with information more optimistic than it was accurate, including the report that the Republicans would unite on a ticket of Clinton for President and Madison for Vice President. Duane was somewhat tempted to believe the Clintonian-inspired rumor that Philadelphia would be restored as the national capital; it "would cer-

---

[28]Ibid.; A. J. Dallas to Gallatin, 11 Mar. 1806, Gallatin Papers, NYHS. See Joseph Clay to Duane, 2 Mar. 1801, ibid.; Gallatin to Jefferson, 17 Aug. 1801, Adams, ed., Writings of Albert Gallatin, I, 39; Leib to Rodney, 16 June 1804, Rodney Papers, Del. Hist. Soc.; Jefferson to Duane, 28 Mar. 1811, TJ-LC.

tainly be an advantage to me," he admitted. "But whatever is is right." Barraged by contradictory rumors about the presidential nomination, the editor entreated Attorney General Rodney to "give me such information as may keep me from mistakes at least, on a matter of so much moment at this time."[29]

On February 1, 1808, Duane's confusion was dispelled by the news that a Congressional caucus had nominated James Madison for President and George Clinton for Vice President. A week later Duane went to Washington by prior intent, where he had an appointment with the President for February 9. There can be little doubt that the conversation with Jefferson overcame the editor's misgivings and fixed the *Aurora* for Madison. Duane was elated by his interview with the President, reporting home that Washington was "full of intrigue," with "third partyism on the rise," but that there was "one man here who sees & knows all these things and deplores what he sees, but labors only by good deeds to counteract them."[30]

It is very likely that during this interview Jefferson revealed to Duane his intention to recommend the editor for a military commission in the special Army to be created for the duration of the national emergency. Congress appropriated funds for the extraordinary units in April, and in July Duane received a commission as

---

[29]Duane to Rodney, [1 Jan. 1808], Genl. MSS Collection (Duane), Columbia. See also Duane to Rodney, 20 May 1808, *ibid.*; Leib to Rodney, 19 May 1808, Gratz Collection, HSP; Randolph to Joseph Clay, 15 Feb. 1808, Alderman Library, University of Virginia.

[30]*Aurora*, 1 Feb. 1808; [Duane to Jefferson, Jan. 1808], fragment, Misc. Papers (Duane), NYPL; Duane to Messrs. Binny and Ronaldson, 9 Feb. 1808, Lib. Co. of Phila.

Lieutenant Colonel, commanding a regiment of riflemen. His officers below the rank of major were politically congenial, and although the commission was insignificant to him as a job--the salary was less than he paid his chief clerk--it was highly gratifying as an honor. Of my "confidence in yourself," Jefferson assured Duane later, "the military appointment . . . was sufficient proof, as it was made, not on the recommendations of others, but on our own knolege [sic] of your principles & qualifications."[31]

The pro-Randolph group in Philadelphia conceded the Aurora to Madison even before the editor's journey to Washington. Randolph responded cynically to the news. "And so D___ has gone over to the Philistines! all his pledges to the contrary notwithstanding," he answered Joe Clay. "As Sir Peter Teazle sez, 'damn all sentiment.'" Clay asserted that Pennsylvania would go for Clinton in spite of the Aurora, and Randolph grasped at the optimistic prediction, for, as he reminded Clay, "everything is in the hands of Pennsylvania."[32]

III

The Aurora did not immediately disclose the editor's decision to support Madison. The sentiments of most of the Duane-Leib party in Philadelphia were in favor of Clinton, and a premature declaration would have split Duane's political family and possibly would have

---

[31]Jefferson to Duane, 12 Aug. 1810, TJ-LC. See also Jefferson to Duane, 11 Mar. 1809, TJ-LC; Duane to Jefferson, 4, 28 Feb. 1809, TJ-LC; Duane to Rodney, 29 Mar. 1810, Genl. MSS Collection (Duane), Columbia; Spirit of the Press, Dec. 1807, Aug. 1808.

[32]Randolph to Joseph Clay, 15 Feb. 1808, Alderman Library, Univ. of Va.; Adams, Randolph, 233.

isolated Duane and nullified his effort. The paper did offer a straw which could have shown how the wind blew: it admitted correspondence condemning the proposal to transfer the national capital from Washington back to Philadelphia, a Clintonian stratagem to attract votes in Pennsylvania.[33]

The Aurora mystified the partisans of Madison and Clinton equally, and both camps were pessimistic. In March Admiral Thomas Truxton of Philadelphia, a bit panicked, reminded Madison that it was crucial to secure the paper's allegiance and suggested that this was a task for "Democrats of the first water." At the same time Philip Nicholas in Richmond gloomily observed the optimism of Randolph's party, based on its confidence that Pennsylvania and New York would go for Clinton. Nicholas himself conceded the Leib party to Clinton and unwisely fastened his hopes for Pennsylvania on the moribund Quids. Meanwhile in Washington the Clintonian Congressman James Sloan of New Jersey was worried because, as he told young John Quincy Adams (erroneously), Duane was "coming out in the Aurora very strong for Madison." Sloan however still thought that Clinton would carry Pennsylvania.[34]

Throughout March and April Duane acted privately on behalf of Madison, in association with Tom Leiper. Once he had accepted the fact of Jefferson's retirement, Leiper endorsed Madison without

---

[33] Aurora, 17, 18, 19 Feb. 1808.

[34] Truxton to Madison, 17 Mar. 1808, Madison Papers, LC; Philip N. Nicholas to Wilson Cary Nicholas, 17 Mar., 1808, Wilson Cary Nicholas Papers, LC; J. Q. Adams, Memoirs, I (19 Mar. 1808), 522.

question and with some enthusiasm for the man's own merits. The General Ward Committee of Philadelphia, chaired by Leiper, elected a Madisonian delegation to the convention in Lancaster which would nominate the presidential electors. Leiper and Duane headed the delegation and at least two of its three other members could be relied on to follow them. As it turned out, the Philadelphia group had no opportunity to express its preference. The convention was anxious to display its unanimity for Simon Snyder for Governor, and therefore avoided disagreement on the presidential question by nominating an uncommitted slate of electors. Leiper and Michael Leib both became candidates for the electoral college. Still the opportunity remained open for the Philadelphians to influence the state's vote for President, through the committee of correspondence appointed by the convention. The seven members were all Philadelphians of the same faction, Duane, Leiper, Leib and four lesser leaders of their party.[35]

Immediately after the state convention adjourned, Duane executed an unexpected manuever which not only resolved the disagreement among the city Democrats but also advanced Madison's candidacy nationally. On March 18 the Aurora predicted that all of Pennsylvania's twenty electoral votes would be cast for Madison, and that he would carry the nation with relative ease. Nevertheless, to "promote a completely unanimous vote," Duane suggested a concession to the great popularity of the Clintons. Since Vice President George Clinton "appears disinclined to serve again in that station," Duane

---

[35] Aurora, 22 Feb., 10 Mar. 1808.

asked, why not nominate DeWitt Clinton in his place? "We suspect no measure could be more effectual in allaying angry passions."

Some of Madison's partisans suspected a Clintonian trick. "I see Duane has been got to propose the compromise which was always the object," wrote a disgusted anti-Clintonian from New York. Madison's advisers should not be frightened by George Clinton's threatened presidential candidacy, he warned, into accepting a shabby accommodation with the Clintons which would be unworthy of Madison. These suspicions may have been accurate, and Duane's suggestion a sincere attempt to find a solution which would satisfy Leib and the other Clintonians in his party.[36]

But the actual effect of the proposal was such that the Clintonians had far better cause to suspect a plot against them. The Madisonians "have not only insulted the Vice President by attempting to put the Secretary over him," a New York Congressman complained, "but they have actually attempted to play upon him little & mean dirty tricks." Immediately following the appearance of the *Aurora*'s comment that George Clinton seemed "disinclined" to serve again as Vice President, a deputation of four Madisonians called upon him and inquired directly whether he intended to accept the caucus nomination for that office. Clinton was inevitably trapped by the question, either into denying the authority of the caucus and staking all his hopes upon the Presidency, or into maintaining his claim to the second position and fatally compromising his presiden-

---

[36] J. N. [James Nicholson?] to [W. C. Nicholas], 30 Mar. 1808, W. C. Nicholas Papers, LC.

tial pretensions. He replied as evasively as possible, but finally he told his visitors that he was not in the "habit of disobeying the voice of the people when constitutionally expressed." Madison's representatives gave Clinton's answer to the press, with ample flattery to the New York patriarch and with the conclusion that Clinton would run for Vice President and not for President.

Soon after this interview, Michael Leib acknowledged defeat of his efforts for Clinton and fell into line with his colleagues Duane and Leiper. The alacrity with which the Madison men acted to turn the Aurora's proposal to their own advantage strongly suggests that they were expecting it, but it is unlikely that Duane was in their confidence during the campaign. Probably the maneuver for a compromise which resulted in political embarrassment to Clinton actually originated with Senator Samuel Smith of Maryland, who hoped that "the old man" would decline and make way for a younger Northern candidate. His political intimate General Wilkinson, who was also friendly with both George Clinton and William Duane, cautioned Smith that "to make you vice president things must take their course silently," and promised that "I shall for this End do what is necessary in philadel[a]."[37]

John Binns' Democratic Press meanwhile was leading the van for Clinton as agreed. It unequivocally condemned the Congressional caucus and even denounced James Madison. Binns' position made Leib's

---

[37]Josiah Masters to Edmond C. Genet, 29 Mar. 1808, Edmond C. Genet. Papers, LC; Aurora, 8 Apr. 1808; James Wilkinson to Samuel Smith, 2 Nov. 1808, James Wilkinson Papers, Darlington Memorial Library, University of Pittsburgh.

decision easier, since the editorial policy of the Press in sum, on national, state and local issues, was hurrah for Clinton and Snyder and down with Michael Leib. Binns and John Geyer, the printer of the German paper, were "riding the country to stir up division," Duane informed Caesar Rodney, "which has effectually aroused D^r. Leib, who will now come forward in his strength with us as usual."[38]

Leib still believed that Madison was the candidate of the Quids and would have liked some proof of his affection for Democrats. The proof he most desired, but did not get, was the removal from office of Philadelphia's federal marshal, John Smith, who had organized the Quadroon revolt in the last election. Nonetheless Leib sent the President a "tribute of respect and affection," and Jefferson responded immediately, with gratitude and with surprising candor on the subject of the Embargo and foreign affairs, the subject on which the national administration and the Duane-Leib party were most congenial.[39]

By the end of April it was safe for Duane and Leiper to make their campaign public. The committee of correspondence met and called a Philadelphia town meeting for May 16, so that citizens could express their opinions on the choice of candidates for President and Vice President. The Aurora in the days preceding the scheduled meeting was extraordinarily careful to guide the public toward the

---

[38]Higginbotham, Keystone, 136-140, 156-157; Duane to Rodney, 20 May 1808, Genl. MSS Collection (Duane), Columbia.

[39]Leib to Rodney, 19 May 1808, Gratz Collection, HSP; Leib to Jefferson, 20 June 1808, TJ-LC; Jefferson to Leib, 22 June 1808, TJ-LC.

choice of Madison while seeming to make no interference with the public will.[40]

On May 5 Duane published his first editorial in support of Madison. He shared with his readers, as with old friends, his opinion that "the happy policy which has preserved the peace and prosperity, of the United States, and the respect of the universe, will be best ensured and promoted by the candidate recommended to be put in nomination" by the members of Congress. Madison was a man of proved ability, the editorial went on; moreover Madison possessed a "prepared knowledge of the general state of the world, which is not to be immediately caught, and embraced, and acted upon like [a] mathematical problem." Having made his point, Duane apologized for his intrusion. "Menaces and intrigues have forced us to this early declaration, which we should not have otherwise found it necessary to make."

The masterpiece of public persuasion was the anniversary celebration of the Tammany society four days before the town meeting. Most of the men in Tammany still favored Clinton in their hearts. The True Republican society, a brother to Tammany, at its annual dinner on May 3 toasted Duane and the *Aurora* with nine cheers, but gave six cheers to Clinton and no toast at all to James Madison.

The Tammany dinner was as sober in its political calculation as it was convivial socially. The committee excluded all names but Thomas Jefferson from the written toasts, and volunteers were not admitted. The first toast was: "The people--Their will the law,

---

[40] *Aurora*, 3, 5, 7, 10, 12 May 1808.

and none to represent them who will not obey it."[41]

Midway through the dawn to dark festivity, Michael Leib delivered the traditional "long talk." Gently and subtly, the Grand Sachem asked support for Madison for President in view of the crisis in foreign affairs. "While all hearts would have united" in support of Jefferson, "our confidence and our affections are variously drawn towards a successor," Leib acknowledged. "Serious injury to the public interest may arise from jarring and discordant opinions among men of the same family." Consequently "brothers," Leib concluded, "let our efforts be directed to promote harmony," let us encourage "charity and not intolerance." The society ordered the publication of the address for the general public, and it appeared in the Aurora on Saturday May 14.

On Monday afternoon the Democrats met at the State House as requested to express their opinions on the national candidates. The committee of correspondence had authorized John Leib to write resolutions supporting Madison and Clinton, the caucus nominees, and these were read to the audience as the first order of business. Joseph Clay rose at once and opposed the resolutions in a twenty minute speech, concluding with a request for the postponement of the town meeting until October 3. "As no one else appeared disposed to rise," Duane reported to Rodney, "I replied to him in a speech of about three times the length." Duane's rebuttal reached an impromptu peroration when he challenged the audience with the crucial question:

[41] Ibid., 5, 14 May 1808.

"Will you support as at all times you have done the choice of the majority--or bow to the will of John Randolph & Co." The applause at this point was so hearty that Duane abruptly rested his case. "Our friend Joe attempted a reply but gave it up in five minutes," he told Rodney, and the occasion ended as a "triumph for us." Only twenty-five men voted with Clay against the resolutions.[42]

The Philadelphia town meeting in effect carried Pennsylvania for Madison. The committee of correspondence circulated the news of the victory, and within the next few weeks county meetings all over the state endorsed Madison and Clinton, acting upon the advice of the committee. The only serious holdout was Northumberland county, the home of John Binns before he moved to Philadelphia in 1807. Binns himself admitted defeat in late July and with his defection the opposition movement collapsed. Joe Clay offered Randolph all the hope he could summon, "but since the desertion of Binns we have no press &c!"[43]

IV

Madison either did not notice or did not care what had occurred in the Pennsylvania campaign. He had no close acquaintance with any of the Democrats in Pennsylvania, and the advice he received from his friends about that state was notably uninformed. Even before Madison was inaugurated as President, the new party forming

---

[42]Duane to Rodney, 20 May 1808, Genl. MSS Collection (Duane), Columbia.

[43]Randolph to Garnett, 31 Aug., 12 Sept. 1808, Randolph-Garnett Letterbook, LC; Higginbotham, Keystone, 160-161.

around John Binns was striving to identify itself as his sole support in Philadelphia, and it was succeeding because it had the sanction of the Quids, Madison's only trusted friends in Pennsylvania. Madison's accustomed indifference to William Duane did not falter at any time, before or after the election.[44]

It was of course Thomas Jefferson who won Pennsylvania for Madison. The idea of Madison as Jefferson's legitimate heir was a major reason for the victory, but it was not the President's only contribution to the campaign. Jefferson took at least three executive actions during 1808 which were intended to influence the vote in Pennsylvania. In July Duane's military commission was announced. "I cannot write-," spluttered Randolph at the news, "Lieut-Col Duane!!!"[45]

The Collector of the Port of Philadelphia, the Democrats' beloved General John Shee, died during the summer, and Jefferson was presented with the problem of deciding on a major appointment just before the national election. Albert Gallatin warned him that it was "morally impossible to make an appointment that will not displease some section of the Republicans." Under the circumstances, he advised, "I think it will be best not to be too hasty in filling the place." Gallatin hoped for the eventual selection of William Jones, who was a Quid, and he believed that the deputy Collector,

---

[44]Duane to Madison, 3 Aug. 1808, 1 Feb. 1809, Madison Papers, LC; Duane to Rodney, 13 Feb. 1809, Genl. MSS Collection (Duane), Columbia; Duane to [Henry Dearborn], 27 July 1809, Pers. Papers Misc. (Duane), LC; Brant, Madison, V, 272-273.

[45]Randolph to Garnett, 24 July 1808, Randolph-Garnett Letter-took, LC.

Edward Fox, a man who was highly offensive to the Democrats, would serve ably in the interim. Jefferson ignored the advice to delay and announced his nomination almost immediately. His choice was John Steele, the candidate urged by Tom Leiper, and a man whose prominence was based on a direct conflict with Governor Thomas McKean.[46]

As insurance for Madison in trans-Allegheny Pennsylvania, which was holding out its support in the expectation of a bribe, the executive branch permitted a slight alteration in the route of the new National Road so that it would go through the town of Washington. The change was recommended by Leiper, by Duane, whose new son-in-law was a young lawyer in Washington, and also by Albert Gallatin, but Jefferson acquiesced with reluctance and distaste.[47]

Alexander Dallas was appalled by the President's behavior and disgusted with his administration generally, but especially with the Embargo. "I verily believe," he confided to Gallatin, "one more year of writing, speaking, and appointing, would render M^r. Jefferson a more odious President, even to the Democrats, than John Adams. My only hope is," he went on, "that M^r. Madison's election may not be affected, nor his Administration perplexed, in consequence of the

---

[46] Gallatin to Jefferson, 6 Aug. 1808, Adams, ed., Writings of Albert Gallatin, I, 402; Duane to Jefferson, 9 Aug. 1808, TJ-LC; Leiper to Jefferson, recvd 20 Aug. 1807, 21 July, recvd 18 Aug. 1808, TJ-LC; Leiper to Madison, 9 Aug. 1808, Madison Papers, LC; Higginbotham, Keystone, 162.

[47] Duane to Rodney, 20 May 1808, Genl. MSS Collection (Duane), Columbia; Leiper to Jefferson, 21 July 1808, TJ-LC; Leiper to Madison, 9 Aug. 1808, Madison Papers, LC; Gallatin to Jefferson, 14 Sept. 1808, Adams, ed., Writings of Albert Gallatin, I, 417; Philip D. Jordan, The National Road (Indianapolis, 1948), 79-80.

growing dissatisfaction, among the reputable members of the Republican party."

After the government announced its nomination for the post of Collector, leaving Dallas' son-in-law Richard Bache among the disappointed candidates, Dallas no longer trusted Madison either. Secretly he informed Gallatin that he intended to resign his position as federal district attorney. He cited Leiper's influence on Jefferson and "others" as evidence that he and the Jefferson administration were irreconcilable. After November balance and perspective returned; Dallas did not resign; but Madison could be grateful to Jefferson's flurry of favoritism to the Democrats for his twenty electoral votes from Pennsylvania.[48]

---

[48] Dallas to Gallatin, 30 July, 5 Dec. 1808, Gallatin Papers, NYHS.

CHAPTER VI

THE DEMOCRATS DIVIDE

Simultaneously with Madison's election, Simon Snyder became the new Governor of Pennsylvania, elected in an overwhelming triumph by the Democrats which confirmed their hold on the Republican party in Pennsylvania and destroyed the pretensions of the Quids. In other states, direct popular participation in government was not received as a public ideal until much later, but in Pennsylvania the notion of caretaker republicanism was vanquished in 1808. After that election, any person with political ambitions automatically avowed his respect for democratic values, and new issues and difficulties began to dominate the state's politics.

The triumphant Democratic Republican party, so effectively unified throughout the years of struggle against McKeanism, immediately fell victim to the rising jealousies between its city and country members. The rivalry between Leib and Nathaniel Boileau for personal influence in the legislature had foreshadowed a party division, and it appeared doubtful whether the new Governor could hold his supporters together. Snyder's first executive appointments made it evident that he did not intend to try. Although "reward sweetens labor," he acknowledged, "this cannot be extended to all who may be deserving, and some may not be willing to console themselves with the reflection of having deserved well of their country." The state's second highest position, that of Secretary of the Commonwealth, went to his friend Boileau, and in Philadelphia he rewarded so many "Quadroons" that Leib maintained "Had he rushed blindfold into the street, and seized the first passing in his way, the chance would have been more favorable to a good choice." The next year Leib himself was made the new United States Senator, an act intended as a consolation and as a banishment from Pennsylvania.[1]

If the obscure "Clodhopper" Simon Snyder had been elected in 1805, he would have owed his victory to the Aurora. At that time Duane had been the single most powerful political influence in Pennsylvania in the opinion of Gallatin, Dallas and others. But in the interim, although his newspaper continued its predominance, the country Democrats in the legislature had found a new rallying point in the person of their narrowly defeated candidate. Duane's great popularity in the interior was inevitably overshadowed by the deeply felt affection for Snyder, whose victory gave the farmers their first freedom from Philadelphia's long political domination. At this moment in their political development, the city and country Democrats were not separated by any important idealistic differences, but became hopelessly divided by regional and personal jealousies.

Snyder revealed his unfriendly intentions toward Duane soon after his inauguration when he refused to dismiss the two suits against Duane by the Marquis de Casa Yrujo, as Jefferson had in-

---

[1]Snyder to N. B. Boileau, 31 Oct. 1808, Correspondence of Simon Snyder, HSP; Leib to Jonathan Roberts, 6 Aug. 1809, Roberts Papers, HSP. See Higginbotham, Keystone, 179-181.

tended to do had they appeared in a federal court. This was the one favor Duane wished from the new Governor, but "he affects scruples about his authority by the constitution." Consequently, "I must continue to run the gauntlet of the courts, under Snyder's administration as well as under McKean's."[2]

The Governor's favoritism to the Quadroons and neglect of the established leadership in Philadelphia quickly made it evident that he would stake his political future in the city upon the emergence of a new party owing allegiance to him personally. With his victory the prestige of his friend John Binns rose immeasurably, and he relied upon the hope that the Democratic Press could supplant the Aurora as the state's foremost Democratic newspaper. For the present the Snyderites sought to undermine Duane's position without attacking him personally and perhaps alienating individual Democrats who could be won away from his leadership.

Marshal John Smith, who had so effectively championed General John Barker, was unscrupulous enough to recognize that Duane was financially vulnerable and might be driven out of business. "My unfortunate compliance," the editor complained, "with the invitations of the heads of departments" in 1801 to establish a printing and stationery office in Washington, "involved me in a debt that has hung upon my industry and resources ever since and placed me largely at the mercy of the banks." His major loans were from the Farmers and Mechanics bank in the city, where Smith was a large stockholder and

---

[2]Duane to C. A. Rodney, 13 Feb. 1809, Misc. MSS Collection (Duane), Columbia; Duane to Jefferson, 4 Feb. 1809, TJ-LC.

a member of the board of directors. When a Federalist bank in New England turned up and purchased a bad debt of Duane's from Calcutta, Smith used the opportunity to attempt to ruin his credit and his public standing. In a board of directors meeting, Duane told Caesar Rodney, "this minion had . . . the infamy to declare that I was in desperate circumstances, and that before Debt here I owed a large debt in England!" Duane denied that he had ever owed "a dollar in England," but fortunately he had a formidable defender at the meeting in Joseph Clay, who had retired from Congress to become the chief officer of the new bank. Because of their disagreement on the presidential election, Duane and Clay had "not had any intercourse since his return from Congress," but he had "the generosity to contradict this villainous invective," and his word was sufficient to forestall the threat. It was perhaps not coincidental that at the next Farmers and Mechanics bank election, Smith and John Barker were not returned as directors.[3]

The personal pressure on Duane kept him on edge and "for a long time," he wrote a friend, "you may have perceived in the stupidity of the Aurora the state of my mind." In fact, he confided, "an attempt has been made in several ways at once to ruin me." Behind Smith's mean tricks he saw the schemes of A. J. Dallas, for "you know who was John Smiths patron and adviser heretofore," he reminded Caesar Rodney, "and whose toad eater and agent he is now." This enemy, "not content with plundering my industry goes into my

---

[3]Duane to Rodney, 1 July 1808, Rodney Papers, Del. Hist. Soc. See also Duane to Jefferson, 4 Feb. 1809, TJ-LC.

family and attempts to tear asunder the dearest of all my affections."

His son William John had married Deborah Bache in 1805, and her brother, Richard Bache, Jr., was married to Sophia Dallas, the daughter of the federal district attorney. "Dallas governs old [Richard] Bache," and, according to Duane, it was he who was responsible for an attempt to estrange William John from his father, "under the color of advancing his interests by inducing him to _study the law_." The son, more conservative in temperament, did not share his father's loathing of the legal profession, but he regretfully declined the opportunity out of respect for his father's feelings. But "I yet apprehend," Duane confided to Rodney, "that it will go into that channel and that we shall be separated."[4]

II

A contest of political strength between Duane and Simon Snyder was ultimately weighted in favor of the Governor because of his extensive patronage and broad executive powers. But the _Aurora_ still possessed great prestige throughout Pennsylvania, and Duane could hope at least to harry the Governor into abandoning the Quadroons in Philadelphia and compromising favorably with the yet powerful Duane-Leib party. By mere chance however an incident in the spring of 1809 all but destroyed Duane's popularity in the interior, seriously injured the strength of his party in the city, and elevated the Governor to an unassailable position.

---

[4]Duane to Rodney, 1 July 1808, Rodney Papers, Del. Hist. Soc. See also [Duane], _Biog. Memoir of W. J. Duane_, 11-12; Gillespie, _Book of Remembrance_, 36-37.

The Olmstead case, a test of state's rights against the power of the federal government, was the first crisis in the new administrations of both President Madison and Governor Snyder. Logically one or the other should have suffered a loss of prestige, but they both emerged unharmed, and the chief victim of the affair was Duane, a bystander.

During the Revolution young Gideon Olmstead and three other Americans held prisoner aboard the British *Active* had heroically escaped, surprised their captors and taken control of the vessel, but before they could sail their prize into port, two privateers appeared and insisted upon escorting the sloop into Philadelphia. The admiralty court of Pennsylvania divided the prize four ways, giving only one quarter to the heroes, one quarter to each of the privateers, and one quarter to the state treasury. The court of appeals of the Continental Congress overruled the judgment, awarding the whole to Olmstead and his fellows, but it took thirty years for them to recover their money from Pennsylvania.

In 1803 Olmstead won judgment in federal district court against the estate of David Rittenhouse, the late Treasurer of Pennsylvania, who had been stakeholder of the disputed prize money. But the state legislature intervened with a special law which forbade payment on the judgment, and gave the state's protection to Rittenhouse's executrixes, his daughters, Mrs. Elizabeth Sergeant and Mrs. Esther Waters. The case was carried to the Supreme Court and in February 1809 Chief Justice John Marshall issued a peremptory mandamus, ordering the district court in Philadelphia to carry out the 1803 decision.

The new Governor reacted to the challenge with hasty defiance, ordering the Philadelphia militia to stand ready for resistance, before he had related the matter to the legislature. As soon as he acted it became clear that Snyder had made a mistake, and everything the state did thereafter was for the purpose of helping the Governor to save face. The mood of the legislature had changed drastically from that of 1803, because the Republicans did not want to injure the national administration's ability to deal firmly with the foreign emergency. After deliberating a full month the legislature adopted a set of mild resolutions which did not sanction the Governor's threatened use of force. Shortly before its adjournment, it appropriated a sum of money large enough to repay Olmstead and proffered it to the Governor to use at his discretion in meeting contingencies arising in the case.[5]

By the beginning of April Snyder was ready to submit if he could do so without admitting his error. Mrs. Sergeant and Mrs. Waters, ostensibly under the Governor's protection, desperately wanted him to agree to pay, pleading that the state "possesses other means to assert and maintain its own rights, than by making them the victims of the contest." Admitting that the legislature had cleared the way, Secretary Boileau replied that the Governor "thinks, under existing circumstances, it would be premature in him at this time, to exercise that discretion in the manner you have hinted." Boileau's meaning was made clear in the instructions he sent the

---

[5] See Higginbotham, Keystone, 183-198, for a full account of the case, and a differing interpretation.

following day to Attorney General Walter Franklin. If Rittenhouse's daughters were arrested for defiance of the federal court order, he was to apply immediately on their behalf for a writ of habeas corpus. But "In the meantime, should your application fail, arrangements will be made to pay the money. If you should succeed," Boileau ended halfheartedly, "then it is hoped, that the just rights of the state will still be preserved." Governor Snyder expected to lose, but he would not make an outright surrender if he could justify his defeat as a gesture of gallantry to rescue the ladies.[6]

The Olmstead case would have been quickly terminated and forgotten, had it not been for the strange turn of events in Philadelphia. The federal officer responsible for executing the court order was the United States Marshal, John Smith, whose political interest was at variance with his duty. John Binns suggested that he relinquish the task to someone "approved by the Governor's friends," but when Smith took the idea to Dallas, the District Attorney rejected it with indignation. On Saturday, March 25, the Marshal made his first attempt to serve process at the house of Mrs. Sergeant and Mrs. Waters and was turned away, "at the point of the bayonet," by a guard of militiamen. A more resolute officer perhaps could have penetrated the display of resistance, if not then certainly at any time thereafter, for the city's militia was divided and increasingly demoralised by the "disagreeable . . . service."[7]

---

[6]John Sergeant to Snyder, 5 Apr. 1809, Pa. Archives, 4th series, IV, 695-697; Boileau to Sergeant, 7 Apr. 1809, ibid., 699-700; Boileau to Franklin, 8 Apr. 1809, ibid., 700.

[7]Walters, A. J. Dallas, 153; Michael Bright to Boileau, 25 Mar. 1809, Pa. Archives, 4th series, IV, 693-694.

Duane was doing his best "to draw the citizens from the cause" and to persuade his friends in the Militia Legion not to cooperate in Governor Snyder's folly. General Michael Bright, the militia commander for the city, reported frankly that the efforts of "a certain class," Duane and his colleagues, "to prejudice the minds of the people against the measure" had "too much prevailed" and gravely hindered his execution of the Governor's orders. Several Legion companies had "absolutely refused to serve their tour of duty," and others had furnished only a few of the required number. The men who did turn out felt themselves exploited because of the difficulty in obtaining replacements, and growing "tired of service," they insisted "that the general militia ought to take their part of duty." But in fact only the voluntary corps of the Legion were sufficiently organized and trained to be useful, and General Bright was forced to depend upon their compliance, while increasingly doubtful of his ability to maintain a full complement of guards at "Fort Rittenhouse."[8]

After March 25 the house at Seventh and Arch streets became the scene of nightly revels by citizens who gathered to ridicule the guardsmen. Mrs. Sergeant and Mrs. Waters were so disgusted with the "disorder and tumult in their neighbourhood" and so thoroughly "tired of their confinement" that they finally threatened to flee

---

[8]Bright to Boileau, 25, 31 Mar. 1809, <u>ibid</u>., 693-696; Bright to Snyder, 13 Apr. 1809, <u>ibid</u>., 704. See also Richard Bache, Jr., to Walter Franklin, 27 Mar. 1809, Soc. Misc. Collection, HSP; Duane to Rodney, 13 Apr. 1809, Genl. MSS Collection (Duane), Columbia.

to Lancaster and wait there until the Governor released the money to pay Olmstead.[9]

Meanwhile the federal officials had adopted a course of action which was certain to settle the affair in the government's favor. President Madison sent Attorney General Rodney to confer with Dallas, after Smith's failure to serve the summons, and Rodney strongly recommended prosecuting Bright and the guardsmen for their resistance. The legal reply to their military threat was completely dispiriting to the Pennsylvanians; "it would have been much more dignified for us," lamented Abner Lacock, the western leader, "to have been vanquished in the field, . . . than to have been foiled by unprincipled Judges armed with sophistry[,] subtilty & tergiversation."[10]

General Bright and eight militiamen were arrested, indicted by a grand jury, and ordered to appear for trial on Monday, April 17. It "has damped the spirits of the militia of this district," Bright reported, "owing to their being liable to prosecution." He did not mind for himself, maintained the disconsolate General, but "I feel for" the others, all poor men with families. "I wish the business could be settled," he confessed, "provided it could be done with honor to the state." Governor Snyder and Secretary Boileau knew that they were defeated, and they authorized Attorney General

---

[9]John Sergeant to Snyder, 5 Apr. 1809, Pa. Archives, 4th series, IV, 696-697. See also Bright to Boileau, 31 Mar. 1809, ibid., 696; Bright to Snyder, 13 Apr. 1809, ibid., 703-704.

[10]Brant, Madison, V, 29; Lacock to Jonathan Roberts, 10 July 1809, Roberts Papers, HSP.

Franklin to arrange the surrender, salvaging the state's rights "to the utmost of your power."[11]

It appeared that Marshal John Smith would be forced to admit victory. His personal conduct during the affair, either through "stupidity or wickedness," had tended to alienate the favorable public opinion. But he could no longer forestall the humilitation of Governor Snyder and the consequent damage to the Snyderite faction in Philadelphia. After the court appearance on April 17, the militia guard would collapse completely, and there would be no remaining obstacle to the delivery of the original summons.[12]

At the last moment however the Marshal saved the state from an open surrender, through connivance with the Attorney General. Walter Franklin informed the Sergeant family that the Governor would pay the money if the ladies would first allow themselves to be arrested, and they were eager to fulfill the bargain. It was agreed that the guard would be withdrawn "on some pretext or other," and the Marshal received this information, "(whether official, or not, we cannot say)," the Aurora reported. Smith "took the hint" and finally executed his mission, by stealth, two days before the inevitable legal victory.[13]

On the evening of April 14, after quelling the usual riot,

---

[11] Bright to Snyder, 13 Apr. 1809, Pa. Archives, 4th series, IV, 703-704; Boileau to Franklin, 11 Apr. 1809, ibid., 701-702.

[12] Aurora, 13 Apr. 1809. See also Duane to Rodney, 13 Apr. 1809, Genl. MSS Collection (Duane), Columbia; Brant, Madison, V, 29.

[13] Aurora, 17 Apr. 1809.

the guard officer "ordered a file of men" into the Sergeant's yard to search for intruders. There he was confronted by Mrs. Sergeant, while her sister encouraged her from a doorway; she said "that 'she wished that the marshal would take me and the whole of the guards, and put us in jail.' Disregarding her language," the officer recorded, "I immediately placed two sentinels in the yard." Mrs. Sergeant had failed, but "a short time after" one of her sons came out "and requested that I would withdraw the sentinels, pledging at the same time his honor that he would keep close doors, and let no one in," so the officer agreed to the courtesy. At dawn John Smith quietly entered Cherry alley, came over the back fence, entered the house and arrested Mrs. Sergeant. Attorney General Franklin then played out the farce by suing for a writ of habeas corpus, and when this was denied Governor Snyder sent the payment of 14,378 dollars due to Gideon Olmstead, in order to release her from personal suffering.[14]

The Olmstead affair was settled, but not so neatly as had been planned by the federal authorities, and District Attorney Dallas concluded that it was still necessary to assert the rights of the federal government by punishing General Bright and the guardsmen. Marshal Smith's shabby ruse had prevented the natural completion of this lesson, but Dallas evidently was not conscious of the betrayal.

---

[14]Charles W. Westphal, adjutant, 25th regiment, Pa. militia, Evening Report, 14 Apr. 1809, Morning Report, 15 Apr. 1809, Pa. Archives, 4th series, IV, 704-705; John Sergeant to Snyder, 15 Apr. 1809, ibid., 705-706; Snyder to Franklin, 23, 24 Apr. 1809, ibid., 707-709; Duane to Rodney, 17 Apr. 1809, Genl. MSS Collection (Duane), Columbia.

Nonetheless he and others were surprised and chagrined to find that public opinion in Philadelphia, which had never defended the state's position against Olmstead, suddenly began to champion the threatened militiamen. Thanks to Smith, they had not been forced into submission, but merely tricked through an undignified stratagem. Overnight they became heroes, and the myth of a gallant stand against the state's enemies began to form in the public memory. By the time their trial was completed, Dallas told the court that he could not recommend leniency because "alas! the defendants seem rather to exult than to grieve at their situation."[15]

On May 2 General Bright and eight men were convicted of resisting a federal officer and were sentenced to a fine and one month's imprisonment. Duane and Leib immediately wrote to President Madison urging him to pardon the offenders. Public feeling was changing, they explained, from disapproval of the outrage upon the law to pity for those now suffering under it. Since the United States had won its point, the politically healthy thing for Pennsylvania would be to release the prisoners. President Madison did remit the sentences, but when the men came out of jail after six day's imprisonment, it was as triumphant martyrs in the cause of state's rights.[16]

This strange end to the case was understandably perplexing

---

[15]Dallas to Rodney, 17 Apr. 1809, Rodney Family Papers, LC; Walters, A. J. Dallas, 154; G. M. Dallas, Life of A. J. Dallas, 110.

[16]Duane to Madison, 3 May 1809, Madison Papers, LC; Leib to Madison, 3 May 1809, ibid.

to outside observers. "I had seen with much pleasure that the dispute with Pennsylvania was likely to go off smoothly," the retired Jefferson wrote to the President, "but am much mortified to see the spirit manifested by the prisoners themselves as well as by those who participated in the parade of their liberation." Duane and Leib of course tried to expose the traitorous role of the federal Marshal in accomplishing the pyrrhic victory, but they were not taken seriously, and in 1811 over their protest President Madison reappointed John Smith on the recommendation of Dallas and Gallatin.[17]

For Duane the outcome of the Olmstead case was a precipitous loss of popularity in the interior of Pennsylvania. He had devoted himself to upholding the government's position, then against all reasonable expectation Governor Snyder had emerged the real winner in the confrontation with Madison. When the Philadelphians attempted to get a legislative investigation of the Governor's dangerous, unauthorized action, the country Democrats voted their approval of his conduct by an overwhelming majority. "They really divide the responsibility so with him," observed an assemblyman, "as to leave him little or nothing to bear & wanting nothing to justify him." Although at the time they had not endorsed the action, they now felt "It has become necessary for the country democrats to assert their independence or give themselves up to be governed by a few men in the city."[18]

---

[17] Jefferson to Madison, 22 May 1809, quoted in Brant, Madison, V, 30. See Duane to Rodney, 29 Mar. 1810, Genl. MSS Collection (Duane), Columbia; Thomas Leiper to Madison, 14 Jan. 1811, Madison Papers, LC; Leib to Madison, 7 Feb. 1811, ibid.; Duane to D. B. Warden, 6 Apr. 1811, David Baille Warden Papers, LC.

[18] Jonathan Roberts to Matthew Roberts, 13 Jan., 4 Feb. 1810, Roberts Papers, HSP.

"As to Duanes influence in the western country it is at an end," in Abner Lacock's opinion. "I do not believe he has five democratic friends in this business west of the mountains[;] in short he is considered a traitor in the light of [James] Calender." Lacock admitted "I consider this as a great misfortune," for "democracy is wounded in the house of its friends," and he did not underestimate the significance of the loss to the Snyder party of "Duane (the ablest printer in the Union)."[19]

In Philadelphia the Olmstead case was seriously damaging to the Duane-Leib party organization, because it destroyed the political usefulness of the militia. When General Bright and his guardsmen were transformed in the public mind from dupes into heroes, Duane's supporters within the militia, who had advocated civil over military obedience, naturally had to pay the consequences. Duane's friend Colonel Jonas Simonds of the 50th regiment was selected to be a scapegoat. The bulky Simonds was a Customs House employee and had once been threatened with dismissal, according to Duane, "only for being seen in my store!" Now for having requisitioned an outsize bathtub from the county hospital, the "whale-belly colonel" was placed under military arrest and "put into Coventry" by his officers.[20]

The ten-year-old Philadelphia Legion was destroyed by the Olmstead contention. "The Snyder men . . . have succeeded," the editor informed Caesar Rodney, "in breaking up our militia Legion

---

[19]Lacock to Jonathan Roberts, 10 July 1809, ibid.

[20]Duane to Rodney, 20 Mar. 1807, Genl. MSS Collection (Duane), Columbia; The Tickler, 6, 13 Sept. 1809.

. . ., a corps the political and useful local influence of which you are not ignorant of." At the annual parade on the Fourth of July 1809 the member companies sympathetic to Governor Snyder publicly seceded from the volunteer army. Duane disregarded the offenders as a few "undisciplined companies," but another observer described the "remains of the legion" as a sorry "remnant." Neither the commandant nor the first major, a Quadroon leader, "chose to exhibit themselves in their proper places," and Duane's protege Major Bartholomew (Bat) Graves had to take command of the proceedings. After the parade the estranged companies retired to separate celebrations, toasting General Bright or Duane and Simonds, according to their loyalties. "The Philadelphia militia legion; may it never be undermined by those who marshalled it;" punned the Philadelphia Volunteers, "nor the officers of the government be engaged in disorganizing the supporters of social order in the days of terror." But within a year the organization was dissolved by "the work of John Smith," who had been one of the founders. As a reward, according to Duane, Smith was taken in as a major in a new voluntary association of cavalry formed by "Robert Wharton and that nest of tories for the sole purpose of distracting and destroying the republicans."[21]

III

The failure of the Legion marked the end of the Irish-German

---

[21] Duane to Rodney, 29 Mar. 1810, Genl. MSS Collection (Duane), Columbia; The Tickler, 12 July 1809; Evening Star, 10 July 1810; Scharf and Westcott, Hist. of Phila., I, 544.

coalition which Duane and Leib had created in Philadelphia, and the beginning of a new ethnic division in the city's politics. The Olmstead case had greatly intensified the tendency to mutual suspicion between the two groups of Democrats, because the Irish-dominated militia companies, influenced by Duane, had generally refused to turn out as guards to support the cause of the German Governor. The naturalized citizens, Bright had reported to Secretary Boileau, "are led to believe, that the oath by them taken, was to support the constitution of the United States, and not that of the state of Pennsylvania." Consequently after General Bright's triumph a party of over-excited celebrants proposed, "May the Americans and _Dutch_ unite, and ______ the _United Irish_."[22]

Simon Snyder's rise to prominence inevitably destroyed Duane's and Leib's hopes for their coalition. When the Governor became the arbiter of German orthodoxy, Senator Leib was quickly branded as an apostate and forced to plead that he was a "good German." Even in Philadelphia, Snyder soon supplanted Leib in popularity with the German voters, who were the first group to join the Quadroons in the new Snyderite party. John Binns soon after his arrival in the city had won over John Geyer, the editor of Philadelphia's only German-language newspaper, and the hasty creation of a German _Aurora_ could not undo the damage. Geyer was suitably rewarded by the Governor for his part in disintegrating the city's Democratic organization.[23]

---

[22]Bright to Boileau, 31 Mar. 1809, _Pa. Archives_, 4th series, IV, 695-696; _The Tickler_, 7 June 1809.

[23]See for example [Leib], "Letter to the Germans of the

The trouble between the Germans and the Irish began in 1808 during the Democratic campaign for Governor. While Duane complained that "the Dutch" were "a weak reed . . . to depend on," the Germans suspected wrongly that the Irish would betray the candidate. The Irish in turn were worried by rumors of German hostility. In Lancaster two or three young men whose job in the campaign was to persuade the foreign-born to vote for Snyder, were said to be swearing privately that when he was elected, every Irish clerk would be turned out of office.[24]

The Militia Legion was the first party organization to suffer from the rising distrust because the Quadroons within it had deliberately "set on foot a scheme for sowing distraction between the Irish & Dutch." The trouble was "actually affected," according to Duane, "by John Smith, Jacob Vogdes, and a man called Major Dennis who married Smiths daughter." Major Lewis Rush, who had withdrawn as a bank endorser for Duane, became their valuable ally. "You'd be astonished," Duane told Rodney, "to know the lengths to which these people have gone;" they "nearly produced bloodshed" between the Irish and the Germans in the Legion manuevers on June 22 at Frankford Creek, in which Colonel Duane commanded one division against the attack led by Rush. Unfortunately "the sacredness of the day has not prevented them from menacing a renewal" of the warfare on the Fourth

---

County of Philadelphia," Philadelphia Pennsylvania Democrat, 4 Oct. 1810; The Tickler, 17 Oct. 1810.

[24] Ibid., 5 Oct. 1808; Duane to Rodney, 20 May 1808, Genl. MSS Collection (Duane), Columbia.

of July. "I dread the repeat," admitted Duane, who had sponsored the idea of the mock battles now made all too real. Richard Folwell, who was among those who resented the large Irish participation in the militia, congratulated Rush's American-born Germans for the "dreadful engagements on the Rhine."[25]

Philadelphia's Irish phobia, so evident among the Federalists in 1798 and the Quids in 1805, was to some degree shared by many Democrats as well. As the city's Snyderite party became established with the "German interest" as its base, it attracted others who resented the Irish for their political precocity and success. Duane enjoyed his role as paterfamilias, and he tended to favor his countrymen because of the warmth of their attachment to him. The "first division" of his "bodyguard," a nativist taunted, had "arrived from Londonderry in August last." The enthusiasm and unity of the naturalized Irish made them a conspicuous political force. When they decided to boycott a Democratic candidate on one occasion, they had reduced his total by one thousand votes. But the Snyderites gradually succeeded in isolating Duane and his followers by playing upon the fear that the Irish meant to control the Democratic party. "The Sons of St. Tammany of St. Patrick--May they ever be an united family," vowed the worried Duaneites, "and bear in mind that division would give a triumph to the foes of both--the enemies of freedom."[26]

---

[25]Duane to Rodney, 1 July 1808, Rodney Papers, Del. Hist. Soc.; Spirit of the Press, Oct. 1808. See also Scharf & Westcott, Hist. of Phila., I, 534-535; Aurora, 4 May 1808; The Tickler, 18 Nov. 1807.

[26]Ibid., 10 Oct. 1808; Duane to Rodney, [1 Jan. 1808], Genl. MSS Collection (Duane), Columbia; Aurora, 21 Mar. 1811.

The naturalized English were particularly active in helping to organize the Snyder party, and Duane and Leib (who would never publicly accuse the Germans) often denounced them by nationality for their contribution to political turmoil in the city. The Governor appointed "an impertinent english youth, a notorious and insolent quid," as clerk of the Mayor's court in Philadelphia, and "Another english boor" became inspector of weights and measures. The most influential and most hated of the English-born politicians was Matthew (Mat) Randall, a broker, who with his son Josiah was associated politically for twenty years with John Binns. Duane of course felt the new development as an additional persecution, and complained bitterly when Marshal Smith prepared a jury list for a trial against them in which "out of 48 names there are only 3 republicans, and there are eleven Englishmen, besides Tories."[27]

The political role of the newly-arrived English was not generally noticed, because they were largely protected from group slander by the Anglophilia of the Federalists. When nativists decried the participation by foreign rabble in American politics, they usually made it clear that they meant the Irish. And if a naturalized citizen from England should be disapproved of for his politics, he would not ordinarily be abused for his nationality. A Connecticut newspaper editor observed that the three most troublesomely independent Republican papers in the nation, the Aurora, the Richmond

---

[27]Leib to Jonathan Roberts, 6 Aug. 1809, Roberts Papers, HSP; Duane to D. B. Warden, 6 Apr. 1811, D. B. Warden Papers, LC. See also Pennsylvania Democrat, 29 Dec. 1809, 27 Apr. 1810; Aurora, 25 May 1811.

Enquirer and the Baltimore Whig, were all edited by Irishmen, while the placid National Intelligencer was "happily" edited by an Englishman, Joseph Gales.[28]

Another factor which tended to obscure the English-Irish conflict in Philadelphia was that John Binns, the best known leader of the Snyderites, was himself an Irishman. Moreover Binns was no ordinary Irishman but one whom the English had tried for treason because of his activities with the United Irish during the war with France. The Duane men nonetheless ruthlessly sought to denationalize him; after he was expelled from the St. Patrick's Benevolent society, he sued in a state court to gain readmission. And "The story of his career in his own country" was revised and retold as a "dark and disgraceful" episode of betrayal, because he had been acquitted of treason and another man hanged. On one occasion in Chestnut ward, "DUANE told him that murder and perjury were written in his countenance." In reply "this miserable piece of tainted flesh belched out its congenial abuse," but Duane rebutted "by levelling at the animal's head the nearest candlestick. There was then some confusion," a reporter acknowledged, "but it soon subsided."[29]

Binns was unwilling to concede the Irish voters to Duane without a struggle, and he retaliated by reviving the accusation that

---

[28] The Tickler, 18 Sept. 1811.

[29] Pennsylvania Democrat, 6 Apr. 1810; Philadelphia Whig Chronicle, 16 Oct. 1812; Evening Star, 28, 30 July 1810. The Francis Place Papers, British Museum, contain material on Binns' political activities in England.

Duane's accountant, James Robinson, was an Orangeman. This "is the most detestable imputation that could be affixed to his character," admitted an old party man, who feared the reflection upon "the integrity of the Editor of the Aurora." Binns' purpose, according to Robinson himself, was "to pull down the colonel," because he "perhaps . . . expects to make converts of the Irish, and . . . Mr. Duane happens to be a little popular with that class of citizens."[30]

During the early years of the rivalry, Duane easily retained the loyalty of the Irish and largely excluded Binns from a share in the affections of his countrymen. John Quincy Adams later recorded in his diary an interesting error in fact about the competing editors. "Pennsylvania," he wrote, "has been for about twenty years governed by two newspapers in succession: one, the Aurora, edited by Duane, an Irishman, and the other, the Democratic Press, edited by John Binns, an Englishman."[31]

The rival Democratic parties contended for the loyalties of the Scots. Binns had a fiercely effective proselytizer in young Geordy Palmer, while the "Juvenile Sons of Erin" called upon ancient Celtic ties: "Scotia Minor—descended from the same stock; may her hardy sons unite with those of Scotia Major." The ethnic conflict among the naturalized British unfortunately introduced the need for a verbal distinction between the Scotch-Irish and the mere Irish population in Pennsylvania. All were Democratic Republicans, and

---

[30]Evening Star, 28, 29 Sept. 1810. See also The Tickler, 26 Sept. 1810.

[31]J. Q. Adams, Memoirs, IV, 112-113.

the naturalized Irish had presumed the existence of a fraternal bond with the older residents and talked of the political interests of "the Irish peopled counties." But soon after the Democratic schism in Philadelphia, an outsider apologized for calling one of the Quadroon converts an Irishman when he was "only a Chester county Irishman," that is, Scotch-Irish.[32]

The danger of religious prejudice entering politics was implicit in the situation. The immigrants, mostly Catholic, were becoming isolated from their Protestant countrymen who had lived longer in America. The earliest manifestation of the problem came several years later in the gubernatorial election of 1823. But during Duane's years of active leadership, religious differences were never allowed to become a political issue. Duane himself was a lapsed Catholic, in lifelong rebellion against his religious instruction, and almost fanatically secular, ever on guard against expressions of Christian hypocrisy. Moreover the United Irish movement which was the political heritage of many immigrants had been founded by Protestants, upon the principle of religious tolerance and mutual cooperation for the sake of national independence. The Irish nationalism among the Protestant emigres was evident in the Duane-Leib party. Dr. James Reynolds, although no longer active, was still a member, and a newcomer like James Wilson (the grandfather of Woodrow Wilson) was as proudly Irish as he was stanchly

---

[32] Aurora, 4 Apr. 1811; Duane to Rodney, 20 May 1808, Genl. MSS Collection (Duane), Columbia; The Tickler, 2 Aug. 1809, 23 Oct. 1811.

Presbyterian. Wilson, who arrived in 1807, became foreman on the *Aurora* and later its acting editor before establishing his own newspaper in Ohio. Honoring the man who gave him a start in journalism and in politics, he named his first child William Duane Wilson.[33]

---

[33] Josephus Daniels, *The Life of Woodrow Wilson, 1865-1924* (Chicago, 1924), 28-31.

CHAPTER VII

OLD SCHOOL VERSUS NEW SCHOOL

The factional division among the Democrats of Philadelphia, created by the feud between Governor Snyder and "the Brothers" Duane and Leib, and exacerbated by ethnic jealousies, was gravely aggravated by a new development in the city's experience, the manufacturing boom which occurred as a result of the national Embargo. The moratorium on international trade, intended to force the warring Europeans to respect America's rights as a neutral, produced hardship and depression in other regions of the country. But in Philadelphia the suffering in the merchant community was offset by a new prosperity among the precocious master mechanics. Foreign commerce had so dominated the city's economy that it was felt to be "an injurious influence upon our internal concerns and improvements." "It is now, therefore," advised William John Duane, "when foreign trade, the cause of domestic apathy, is nearly annihilated" that the citizens should act to develop their domestic interests. Indeed he believed there was "a revolution . . . really, however imperceptibly, going on" in Pennsylvania.[1]

---

[1]William John Duane, Letters Addressed to the People of Pennsylvania Respecting the Internal Improvement of the Commonwealth; by means of Roads and Canals (Philadelphia, 1811), 12, 53-54. See Louis M. Sears, "Philadelphia and the Embargo of 1808," American Historical Association, Annual Report, 1920 (Washington, 1925), 251-263.

In Philadelphia the political effect of this "revolution" was a deeper division of the Democrats, according to their roles in the emerging economy. Duane's Irish "bodyguard," as the newest and poorest element of the city's population, was the least able to take advantage of the new opportunities. The Quadroon faction on the other hand tended to include the most successful master mechanics, who were ready to advance into manufacturing. And as incipient entrepreneurs they found a firm basis for cooperation with the prosperous Quids, who also sought the support and favor of the Snyderite state legislature. These ambitious men quickly became known as the "New School" among Democrats, while Duane and his party proudly took the name of "Democrats of the Old School."

"We behold in a temporary suspension of our commerce an ephemeral & doubtful evil producing a great, a growing & a lasting good," Jefferson's partisans in Philadelphia wrote to commend the President upon the Embargo policy. They predicted an exploration of "the prolific sources of our internal wealth" and the application of "industry & ability" in ways "which while they benefit the enterprising, enrich our country with solid wealth & make her more independent & happy." Governor Snyder too took notice that the threat of war had created a new "zeal and exertion to supply our wants by home manufactures" and asked the legislature to "devise means to encourage it." An upsurge in schemes for transportation development tripled the number of corporation grants during this period.[2]

---

[2]Philadelphia, Pa., Democratic-Republicans to Jefferson, 1 Mar. 1808, TJ-LC; Pa. Archives, 4th series, IV, 677-678; William

"The manufacturing system progresses in this State beyond all conception," Duane wrote to a friend in Virginia. By 1810 the value of Pennsylvania's manufactures was estimated at more than forty-four million dollars, nearly 25 per cent of the national total. And more than one third of the state's manufactured goods was produced in the city and county of Philadelphia. Bustling activity and optimism were apparent everywhere but near the waterfront. Paul Beck, a Democrat turned New Schooler, quickly achieved wealth and local fame by developing a shot manufactory, to end the reliance upon Europeans for the weapons of war. Factories opened for the production of red and white lead and oil of vitriol, and in another application of elementary chemistry the distilling industry flourished, ending the dependence upon imported beverages. Duane praised this pioneering enterprise, which gave farmers a market for their grains as well as providing "profitable employment" for many people. An unprecedented building boom reflected Philadelphia's growing prosperity. According to Democratic sources, two thousand brick houses were built within the city limits in two years after 1808, more than had been constructed during the four years preceding.[3]

The Embargo created a boom psychology in Philadelphia because it suddenly and artificially released capital which had been

---

Miller, "Business Corporations in Pennsylvania, 1800-1860," Quarterly Journal of Economics, LV (1940-1941), 156-158.

[3]Duane to Isaac Briggs, 6 July 1811, Isaac Briggs Papers, LC; Thomas Law to Jefferson, 13 Apr. [1811], TJ-LC; J. Leander Bishop, A History of American Manufactures from 1608 to 1860, 3 vols. (Philadelphia, 1864), II, 173; Scharf and Westcott, Hist. of Phila., I, 528, 531-532; Foster, Jeffersonian America, 270-271; Evening Star, 6 Oct. 1810.

absorbed in foreign commerce and made it available for investment in domestic enterprise. Duane's son pointed out in an article for the Aurora that "at the present moment when capital is chiefly withdrawn from the ocean," private savings represented "an extraordinary resource of very great magnitude." And "It is an interesting fact," a Bucks county man observed, "that a great number of persons have directed their whole capital whether large or small from their accustomed occupations, into various branches of the arts never before attempted in this country." Moreover "The embargo created such a want of employment for money, as rendered it difficult for the Banks to loan out the funds they had at command." Rather than allow their capital to remain idle indefinitely, the banks for the first time offered loans to individuals for investment in manufacturing. Mathew Carey later observed that there had "existed a scarcity of money, more or less great according to circumstances," two or three times each year "during the very long period, in which I have carried on business in this city, . . . except during the embargo."[4]

The repeal of the Embargo in 1809 restored the demand for commercial capital and threatened the new class of investors in Philadelphia, which needed long-term credit for the expansion of manufacturing. According to a Federalist scoffer, "Bank offals" and "money hawks" desperately seeking the renewal of their discounts

---

[4]W. J. Duane, Letters . . . Internal Improvement, 25; Samuel D. Ingham to Jonathan Roberts, 22 Nov. 1811, Roberts Papers, HSP; Mathew Carey, Letters to Dr. Adam Seybert, Representative in Congress for the City of Philadelphia, on the Subject of the Renewal of the Charter of the Bank of the United States (Philadelphia, 1811), 17. See also Aurora, 7 Feb. 1811; Louis M. Sears, Jefferson and the Embargo (Durham, 1927), 108.

presented a spectacle at the Coffee Exchange daily as they pursued any potential endorser, whether friend or stranger. The tightening of credit became more serious as the local banks responded to curtailment by the expiring Bank of the United States, and in 1810 and 1811 the "pressure" in the money market was generally acknowledged to be "considerable."[5]

The mechanics and manufacturers of Philadelphia reacted to this situation with a demand for new banks in the city which would serve their interests. The old institutions--the North American, Pennsylvania, and Philadelphia banks--were effectively the exclusive property of the privileged merchant community, and the new Farmers and Mechanics bank, established in 1807 and chartered in 1809, was not adequate to the needs of the enterprising Democrats. The enthusiasm for banking reached a peak in February 1810 with the organization of a Mechanics bank for the western wards of Philadelphia. When the stock went on sale by public subscription at the Statehouse, the mob of expectant buyers was so immense that an estimated six hundred to seven hundred persons failed to gain entry to the building. One well-known citizen was reported to have lost his hat and wig while trying to enter through a window on the south side of the Statehouse. A more dignified group of disappointed gentlemen retired to the Coffee House, where they founded a second institution, to be called the Commercial Bank, and before noon on the same day subscribed one million dollars capital.

---

[5]<u>The Tickler</u>, 9 Aug. 1809; Carey, <u>Letters to Dr. Adam Seybert</u>, 17; James Mease to Jonathan Roberts, 11 Jan. 1811, Roberts Papers, HSP.

While the banking mania raged, five other banks were talked of for Philadelphia, and reports from other towns indicated that the phenomenon was sweeping Pennsylvania. In March the legislature attempted to check the rampage by prohibiting unincorporated banks and banking associations from issuing paper money. But the enthusiasm was irrepressible and more schemes were continually generated, while the already organized institutions prepared to apply for charters, which they hoped to obtain with the aid of money "judiciously bestowed" upon the legislature.[6]

II.

The sudden infatuation with banking as a means to sustain industry presented Philadelphia's quarreling Democrats with a new and permanent source of disagreement. Men who had been genuinely united only a few years earlier by their common faith in political egalitarianism found themselves increasingly separated by conflicting concepts of what the egalitarian ideal implied for the economic sphere. The New School among them was eager to create new banks and expand credit facilities in order to encourage greater equality of opportunity and to assure suitable rewards for individual initiative. Duane and his Democrats of the Old School shared those values, but they were more deeply concerned with the need to establish institutions with broad and lasting social benefits. The banking schemes, in their opinion, were an incitement to the worst sort of selfish

---

[6]Aurora, 7 Feb. 1810; Pennsylvania Democrat, 9 Feb. 1810; The Tickler, 14, 28 Feb., 28 Mar., 18 Apr. 1810; Scharf and Westcott, Hist. of Phila., I, 546.

individualism, at the expense of the general welfare.

The difference in emphasis in part reflected the particular interests of each party's membership. Both schools represented the mechanic classes and strongly supported the development of manufactures, and both were coolly indifferent to the distress suffered by merchants because of the interruption of foreign commerce. But the New School party as it developed tended to attract the most prosperous masters, while the Old School became increasingly a party for the journeyman class of workers.

The quasi-official society for the encouragement of domestic manufactures was dominated by Quid and Quadroon politicians like Mathew Carey and Hugh Ferguson, whereas when William Duane organized a memorial to ask for the protection of infant industries, it was on behalf of the city's weavers, mostly recent emigrants from Ireland. In 1810 the journeyman printers of Philadelphia attempted to organize for higher wages but were defeated by an association of the city's booksellers, which refused to hire any man involved in the protest. Mathew Carey was the dominant figure in the employer's combination, although the "honorable" and "liberal" portion of the master printers, according to Duane's protege George White, had readily agreed to the "trifling" and deserved increase in wages.[7]

The tendency to class division between the two schools of Democrats was apparent to outside observers. Duane's party continued to receive the familiar taunts by snobbish nativists about the rabble

---

[7] Aurora, 12 Jan. 1811; Evening Star, 30 Oct., 5 Nov., 1810; The Tickler, 26 Oct. 1808.

of "Dammany Howl." When the editor in 1811 organized a series of ward meetings to oppose the rechartering of the Bank of the United States, the *Tickler* pronounced his attempt a miserable failure because not more than five of the sixty-five delegates selected to draft the planned memorial could be in any way affected whether the Bank continued or not. One ward sent three tailors in its delegation, and another could not act because only five drunken men turned out to the meeting. The "influential" and "decent" Democrats had spurned Duane's effort.[8]

The jokes about the New Schoolers tended to ridicule their rising expectations and ludicrous gentility. General Michael Bright, the Snyderite hero of the Olmstead affair, who received a state appointment as inspector of flour, was a "*gentleman* biscuit baker, got above his profession," as was Peter Christian, a New School politician who had formerly "danced attendance" at the "Aurora book-store morning levees." Conrad Weckerly, a Northern Liberties' Democrat who was said to be worth 100,000 dollars but who could be upset by the loss of a few cents at shuffleboard, moved into the new wing of the party. The *Tickler* reported that he planned to enlarge his goat farm and intended to ask the Snyderite legislature for an exclusive privilege to make camels-hair shawls from goat's wool.[9]

Duane and his friends were conscious of the effect of prosperity upon the men who were deserting them to join the Governor's

---

[8] *Ibid.*, 26 Sept. 1810, 20 Feb. 1811, 13 Oct. 1813.

[9] *Ibid.*, 5 Oct. 1808, 17 Oct. 1810; *Spirit of the Press*, July 1811.

party. Captain Lewis Rush, an early Quadroon who had helped to undermine the Militia Legion, had also withdrawn as an endorser of Duane's bank loans, shortly before the trouble at the Farmers' and Mechanics' bank, instigated by Marshal Smith. Rush was "no doubt, as honest a skin dresser as there is in the state," according to one Old Schooler, but "He measures his understanding by the length of his purse." "Once he was only silly, but now money has made him an ideot." The type-founders firm of Binny and Ronaldson, which supplied the Aurora, thrived during this period of business expansion, but the partners were an unfortunate illustration of "fortunes caprices," in Duane's opinion. "They have acquired fortune by industry, and it has ruined them as men. I never knew men more estimable for simplicity and probity--they are now the reverse."[10]

The public image of the New School Democrats as more respectable than the Duaneites was enhanced by the participation of most of the former Quid faction. Although A. J. Dallas had remained aloof from local and state politics since his distasteful experience in the gubernatorial election of 1805, Duane was convinced that he was "the secret spring" behind the machinations of John Smith, his "open instrument." In his opinion the emerging party was simply the "Dallas & Co. machinery . . . in full motion again." John Binns was "now as great an Eulogizer of Dallas" as the Quid editor William McCorkle during the McKean administration.[11]

---

[10]Duane to C. A. Rodney, 1 July 1808, Rodney Papers, Del. Hist. Soc.; Evening Star, 29 Sept., 6 Oct. 1810; Duane to Jefferson, 25 Jan. 1811, TJ-LC.

[11]Duane to Rodney, 1 July 1808, Rodney Papers, Del. Hist. Soc.; Duane to Rodney, 13 Feb. 1809, Genl. MSS Collection (Duane), Columbia.

Duane's allegation of conspiracy was unfair to Dallas, who had genuinely retired from party politics, but it was correct in spirit as a comment upon the nature of New School Democracy. The Constitutional Republican party had been clearly rejected by the people of Pennsylvania and the Quids had no political future outside the statewide Snyderite party, as reconciliation with Duane and Leib was impossible from either viewpoint. Since their strength was largely in Philadelphia, the Governor and his friends could readily accept the Quids' cooperation without disturbing their control of the legislature or affecting the loyalty of the western farmers.

To improve his ties with the metropolis, Snyder in 1811 appointed the prominent young New School politician Richard Rush, son of Dr. Benjamin Rush, as his Attorney General. Rush soon after resigned to accept a federal appointment, and a spokesman for the Governor solicited the advice of Edward Fox, who recommended the choice of "some respectable old gentleman," like the Federalist Jared Ingersoll. A few days later Snyder "sent him the Commission. Will wonders never cease," Fox marvelled. In these circumstances even an austere Gallatin-Dallas Republican like Fox could reconcile himself to the Clodhopper Governor. "I believe that his having been advocated by Duane and Leib in 1804 & 5 gave [an] impression not very favorable to his future administration," but Fox admitted that time had altered his opinion. Charles Jared Ingersoll, the son of the Attorney General, was another important convert to Democracy of the New School. He and Richard Rush, who had been childhood friends and Princeton classmates, both abandoned the politics of their prominent Federalist families and enthusiastically associated themselves with the ungentlemanly John Binns in a self-proclaimed political triumvirate.[12]

The reunification of the Quids and Snyderites in Philadelphia was hastened by their mutual interest in manufacturing. The Philadelphia Manufacturing Society, an investment company formed in direct response to the Embargo, was wholly dominated by former Quids who became New Schoolers. The brewer Thomas F. Gordon, son of Elisha Gordon, and Binns' devoted colleague Josiah Randall, son of the broker Matthew Randall, illustrated the ease of movement into the new party. The Samuel Wetherills, Senior and Junior, who were then beginning to establish the family's immense fortune through the manufacture of chemicals, were among the New School's proudest acquisitions from the Constitutional Republican party.[13]

Perhaps the most useful, certainly the most controversial of all the converts were Tench Coxe and Mathew Carey. The two were close friends and had generally acted together in local politics, with Coxe taking the lead in the early years, as in the conspiracy to oust Michael Leib from his seat in Congress. Both men were interested in influencing public policy toward banking and manufacturing, and Carey for that reason began about 1810 to take a more public role in politics, which exposed him for the first time to the malice of Old School Democrats, with which Coxe was long familiar. "If . . .

---

[12]Fox to Jonathan Roberts, 13 Dec. 1811, Roberts Papers, HSP; Fox to Roberts, 25 Dec. 1812, _ibid._ See the letters of Rush to Ingersoll in the Charles Jared Ingersoll Collection, HSP.

[13]_Aurora_, 9 May 1808; _The Tickler_, 5 Oct. 1808, 7 June 1809. See _ibid._, 1808 to 1811 _passim_, for identity of and commentary on the New School men.

Carey had been contented to mind his own business," one asserted, "he might have passed out of the world with at least the reputation of not being silly--thousands of people mistook him to be a man of sense; but he has put an end to this delusion." The two men contributed occasional articles for the Democratic Press, and supported Binns' political regime with their substantial influence. Indeed it was rumored that they had been deeply involved in the mysterious origins of that newspaper. Carey was reported to have predicted with confidence in May 1807 that Binns would take a "'decided part against both Leib and Duane, as soon as he got his paper fairly a-going,'" because, "said Mr. Carey, 'he has made such pledges to Mr. Coxe and myself as no man can violate.'"[14]

When the banking mania hit Pennsylvania in 1810, the city's two Democratic parties had nearly opposite reactions to the phenomenon. The New School party became the sponsor and the political beneficiary of the interest in obtaining bank charters from the legislature, while the Old School condemned the enthusiasm as ill-conceived and dangerous. The "whole property of this flourishing state, and all its useful industry and frugal habits," the Aurora predicted, was "about to be sunk into the den of sordid speculation; to the ruin of innocent private families, to the enrichment of the cunning and profligate; and to the total discredit" of Pennsylvania. If the legislature succumbed to the demands upon it, "paper, which has worked so many wonders, will be so plenty presently, that no man,

---

[14] Aurora, "Sangrado," 18 Jan. 1811; Evening Star, 1, 29 Aug. 1810.

but one who feels qualms of conscience, or 'that damn'd starving quality called honesty,' need be without an estate." Duane in his newspaper continually warned the farmers of Pennsylvania that country banks would be directly hostile to their interests; their dependence on short-term credit would inevitably lead to wholesale foreclosures, and "landed property will in a very short time change proprietors and owners." Indeed the state was "menaced with a total revolution of property, by the infatuation which has seized the people."[15]

John Binns, in sharp contrast with Duane, fully approved the multiplication of banks which occurred during this period, even looking back after the fact of the panic and depression which they created. Countless farmers were ruined by the enticement to seek credit, he acknowledged, but the farms sold at sheriffs' auctions were later improved by their purchasers, he reasoned; strangers moved into Pennsylvania, and "The titles to land became more clear, settled, and certain." In Binns' opinion, the misfortunes of individuals were more than offset by the benefit to the state as a whole through the enterprise which the banks stimulated.[16]

New School and Old School thought on the banking question were not radically separated, endorsing wildcat speculation on the one hand or hard money conservatism on the other. The responsible men in both parties anticipated an increased use of paper money in the future, solidly backed by specie deposits. There was however a clear difference in emphasis, between the New Schoolers' essential

---

[15] Aurora, 7 Feb. 1810, 13, 19, 24 Jan. 1811.

[16] Binns, Recollections, 232-234.

optimism about the opportunities which the new banks would open and the Old School men's fear of the social ills which they might perpetrate.

Tench Coxe for example warned of the need to demand adequate specie reserves, to limit the profit margin allowed to the stockholders, and to tax the excess profits, but with those safeguards he was confident that "we shall have more benefit" than harm from the proposed new charters; "the floods of paper will be restrained, & property & morals will be securer--This will be progress in Good, which is the best course of man and of Government." Mathew Carey, whose primary concern at this time was promoting the recharter of the United States Bank, also at least publicly advocated the simultaneous expansion of the state's banking facilities. "He would talk by the hour about banks and banking--discounts and deposits," scoffed an Old Schooler, "as rapidly as if he knew anything about it." Publishing his views in the Democratic Press and elsewhere, Carey sought to reassure his fellow New Schoolers and the Snyderites generally that a renewed national bank would not interfere with their wish for increased credit through local institutions.[17]

Duane and his partisans generally could not share in the mood of carefree optimism. "If we could only be brought to hesitate," Duane pleaded, "when we come to act on public transactions, so as to consider before we act; many of the evils of society would be guarded against." His description of the ruinous effects of the rage for

---

[17]Coxe to Jonathan Roberts, 3 Dec. 1810, Roberts Papers, HSP; Aurora, "Sangrado," 18 Jan. 1811; Carey, Letters to Dr. Adam Seybert, 33-38, 60-61.

banking did not seem exaggerated to most Old Schoolers, many of whom were more pessimistic than he about the economic consequences of an increased dependence on paper money. The editor Lewis P. Frank recommended that the city's mechanics especially read a pamphlet by Benjamin Davies, published at New York, called The Bank Torpedo or "Bank Notes proved to be a Robbery on the Public & the real cause of the distresses of the poor." Davies proved to his satisfaction that paper money led inevitably to inflated prices and the need for higher wages to offset them. Duane however was unconvinced by such hard money dogma. "Davies & Carey are fanatics of different sects," he concluded. The former "appears to be a very well disposed benevolent kind of a jumper in politics, but his torpedo . . . is perfectly harmless." In time the editor came to agree with the New Yorker's old-fashioned doctrine.[18]

Duane's own views on banking were moving backward relative to the general trend of opinion. Early in the decade when most Democrats distrusted banks as aristocratic, monopolistic institutions, Duane thought that the expansion of credit facilities would convert banking into a public blessing. When the Philadelphia bank applied to the state legislature for a charter and the Bank of Pennsylvania opposed it, requesting instead its own enlargement and exclusive privileges, Duane admitted extensive correspondence to the Aurora denouncing the monopolists. The editor himself accused them of a "disposition to treat your brethren as bastards, and cut them

---

[18] Aurora, 25 Dec. 1810, 24 Jan. 1811; Pennsylvania Democrat, 2 June, 23 Oct. 1810.

off from the equal inheritance of a common right."

Somewhat tentatively he postulated a laissez-faire philosophy as a solution to the problem of future incorporations. "Would it not be proper, at once, to say . . . [that] trade is the affair of individuals, the conduct of which is best trusted to private interest which is ever sufficiently regardful of itself. Besides," he suggested casually, "as it would be best that every branch of commerce should be kept full, how can this be so but at the hazard sometimes of overflowing the measure?" The fears of paper money and the faith placed in the exchange of coin were merely "the prejudices of superficial men," he thought then, since "the coin is in fact a measure of proportion and holds its value dependent upon credit and convention, as much as a hogshead measure or Bank-note." "Yet paper assured upon the credit of reputable members of society," he argued, "is surely of equal convenience and as secure as any other medium of traffic."[19]

Incidentally Michael Leib at this time had similar ideas about the democratic value of encouraging banking expansion. In Congress he unsuccessfully suggested the development of a scheme to deprive the Bank of the United States of its position as exclusive depository for the government, by allowing customs officials to deposit the tax revenues either in the national bank and its branches or in any chartered bank, at their discretion. "His object was to equalise the benefits," Leib explained, "and not to permit that institution to monopolize an enormous profit from the treasure of the nation." Thomas Paine, who when he was in Washington had stayed at the same

---

[19] Aurora, 17, 20 Dec. 1803, 21 Feb. 1804.

boardinghouse as the Philadelphian, was alarmed by Leib's ideas, and warned President Jefferson of the inflation and speculation which would follow from the Congressman's admitted aim to "unfetter the bank institutions generally." Paine perhaps justifiably suspected "the Doctor's motion . . . [to be] an unwise attempt at popularity among those interested in . . . banks." By 1810 when these ideas came to be widely shared among Democrats, the time had passed when Michael Leib could have benefitted from them politically. Whether or not his own thinking on the subject changed radically, as Duane's did, he was a leader in a party whose members increasingly deplored any form of favoritism toward banks and bankers.[20]

Duane's personal experience with credit during the years since Jefferson's election had a great deal to do with altering his views on finance. Acting upon the promise of extensive government patronage, he had borrowed 22,000 dollars to establish an office in Washington, and by 1808, with his patronage cut off completely, he still owed 18,000. He survived John Smith's scheme to drive him into bankruptcy, but he felt that it was essential to do something "to sell myself out of the hands of the Banks here, who worry me every day." He was particularly vulnerable because of his dependence upon endorsers, who supported his loans as a political favor to the editor. But as the New School emerged and attracted many of the more prosperous Democrats, "men who have heretofore placed their names on my paper," Duane complained, "have been . . . induced to withdraw"

---

[20] Annals of Cong., 8th Cong., 2nd sess., 860; Paine to Jefferson, 25 Jan. 1805, Foner, ed., Writings of Thomas Paine, II, 1463.

as endorsers, until he was left finally with only two remaining backers. In this situation he felt "constantly harrassed with this bank influence," and feared that any setback in his affairs would lead to immediate foreclosure on his loan and a sheriff's auction of the Aurora. Consequently there was sharp conviction behind his editorial warnings to farmers to beware of the involvement in a system which was intended to serve the needs of commerce and was fundamentally unsuited to their interests.[21]

Although Duane by 1810 had abandoned his cheerful confidence in egalitarian banking, he had not arrived at a fixed opinion about a policy for the future. "It is a subject upon which it is very difficult to say what is best," he commented to Caesar Rodney. "The advantages of Banking regulated with discretion, are incalculably great to society, in the existing state of the world and the predominancey of commerce. The danger is in the abuse," he now believed, "and what is there that is not subject to abuse?" The Aurora denounced the plethora of banks suddenly formed in Philadelphia and elsewhere, and scoffed at the wild expectations of fabulous profit to the stockholders. But the editor primarily objected to the impulsive haste of their organization and the confusion which they created for the legislature and the people of Pennsylvania. It was necessary for the state to ascertain the proper limits of banking, to determine a safe amount of capital by a study of its population and resources, and for this purpose he earnestly recommended caution and delay

---

[21] Duane to Roger [C. Weightman], 20 Dec. 1808, Madison Papers, LC; Duane to C. A. Rodney, 1 July 1808, Rodney Papers, Del. Hist. Soc.; Duane to Jefferson, 4 Feb. 1809, TJ-LC.

regarding any new incorporations.[22]

The Old School's pessimistic approach to the banking question by no means implied a lack of confidence in rapid economic expansion for Pennsylvania. The party was as keen as the New School to promote industrial development, which would create new markets for agriculture. But Duane and his son William John, who had entered the legislature in 1809 and was said to be writing for the Aurora on state politics, were formulating a party policy on these issues which they intended as an alternative to the banking schemes. Instead of reliance upon private credit as an economic stimulus, they proposed the public investment in a general plan of transportation, which would enlarge the capital resources of the state as a whole and benefit all its citizens uniformly.[23]

William Duane Senior had been an advocate of public expenditures on transportation improvements long before that idea became politically respectable. In 1801 the Aurora had objected to the incorporation of a turnpike company as inappropriate under a Republican state administration. "It says, 'The roads are free as air,'" reported the scandalized Gazette of the United States. "The Aurora concludes by stating, that a Turnpike is a great political evil, and hopes, that, 'now the government of the United States is lodged in the hands of men devoted to the good of the whole,"' the Federalist

---

[22] Duane to Rodney, 29 Mar. 1810, Genl. MSS Collection (Duane), Columbia; Aurora, 24 Jan. 1811. See also ibid., 10 Jan. 1811.

[23] On W. J. Duane see Jonathan Roberts to Matthew Roberts, 7 Dec. 1809, 13 Jan., 13 Dec. 1810, Roberts Papers, HSP.

journal quoted sardonically, "the roads, instead of being made and paid for by those who derive advantage from them, 'will be improved and supported out of the Federal Treasury.'"[24]

The editor's son in 1810 published a series of articles on internal improvements, later circulated as a pamphlet, intended to convince the public and the legislature of the need for state investment in road and canal companies. He had retreated from his father's idea of exclusively public construction because it was unrealistic in view of the lack of any action in this direction. He acknowledged the existing distrust of corporations, among old Republicans, but argued that they could be made to serve the public interest, and pointed out that he would sympathize with the conservative legislators' bias if they were to show a preference for public action, instead of merely doing nothing. William John advocated a system of cooperation between the state and private construction firms, by which each would own stock in a given project, but eventually the full ownership would revert to the public.

Reviewing the potential sources of income to finance such investment, the editor's son defended the right to tax against the traditional prejudices against taxation. Like his father he believed that the object of government was to "diffuse the greatest possible happiness amongst the whole people." And to be happy men required civilization; they needed to raise a surplus to exchange for conveniences, and education for their children, in order to increase

---

[24]Gaz. of the U.S., 12 Mar. 1801.

the blessings of civilization. "It is the business of government," he declared, "so to manage the affairs of the state as to facilitate the means of the citizen for making this surplus." That autumn the thirty-year-old legislator was elected to his second term in the assembly, and was appointed chairman of the Committee on Roads and Internal Navigation. His promotional zeal probably influenced the decision in the following session to appropriate 825,000 dollars for investment in the development of transportation.[25]

III

William John's essays were published in the Aurora during August and September, just prior to the annual election in 1810, which "On the whole" was "a contention for measures as well as men." But much the noisiest issue of the campaign was the exchange of accusations between the allegedly powerful "officeholders" and the "disappointed office-seekers" on the other side. The politicians of the two schools were engaged in a crucial struggle to establish one set or the other as the legitimate leadership of a single Democratic party. The Governor's faction had been active in the city for three years, but had not yet won an election victory over the well-organized Duane-Leib party, which retained the loyalty of the majority of Democratic voters. The Snyderites were in command everywhere else in the state and anticipated that "all will be well at the next

---

[25] W. J. Duane, Letters . . . Internal Improvement, 20-21, 23-25, and passim; James Weston Livingood, The Philadelphia-Baltimore Trade Rivalry, 1780-1860 (Harrisburg, 1947), 51.

election, except in the City & County of Philadelphia." But the New School there succeeded after an extraordinarily strenuous campaign in breaking through the last resistance to the Snyderite ascendancy.[26]

The banking enthusiasm which had stirred Philadelphians to frenzied activity early in the year played a role in procuring the New School's victory in the autumn election. Duane complained privately that the "Banks of which so many were set up here had their origin in political objects," but he made no public accusation beyond that implied in an election day editorial denouncing "Paper Credit" as a "hundred headed monster," bringing "terror, dismay and desolation in its train." Elsewhere in the state in this election there was evidence that the promise of friendly support to incorporations was helping to return some candidates to the legislature. By 1812 this trend throughout Pennsylvania was so pronounced that "We are now told there shall be no distinction at the next election but the advocates for new Banks and the opposition." Indeed "this has been the secret spring of action these two years," wrote a Philadelphian, "but not publicly avowed before." In time however the Democratic involvement in state banking became so evident a feature of the political life of Pennsylvania that a Federalist wit commented that flourishing tradesmen and mechanics sought above all to give their children education, without which "it is impossible to attain any eminence, beyond that of an assessor, a colonel, a magistrate, or a bank director."[27]

---

[26]Aurora, 21 Sept. 1810; Nathaniel B. Boileau to Jonathan Roberts, 19 Aug. 1810, Roberts Papers, HSP. See Evening Star, 19 July-23 Oct. 1810; Higginbotham, Keystone, 213-218.

[27]Duane to C. A. Rodney, 29 Mar. 1810, Genl. MSS Collection

The essential New School-Old School confrontation in their struggle for dominance was the campaign in the Northern Liberties, where the infant Bank of the Northern Liberties had a concealed role in producing the New School's triumph. The bank had sprung to life in the aftermath of the Mechanics bank riots, when the public had fought for the privilege of investing, and in early March it organized itself extra-legally and began issuing notes and making discounts. At that time 10 per cent of its subscriptions had been paid in, a total of 10,625 dollars, which the bank loaned out during its first week of operation. Later that month its activities were checked by the emergency legislative action to bar the issue of bank notes by unincorporated institutions. The directors began at once to plan their campaign to obtain a charter, organizing petitions from the district and proposing financial incentives which might be offered to the legislature. Most important they urgently promoted the election of the New School's assembly candidates from the county.[28]

The mutual understanding between the bank and the local Snyderites was not revealed during the campaign by the worried Old Schoolers, who were struggling to retain the loyalty of the Northern Liberties' Democrats generally. But when the election result was known, they bitterly predicted that "The Bank of the Northern

---

(Duane), Columbia; Aurora, "H," 28 Sept., 3, 4 Oct. 1810; N. B. Boileau to Jonathan Roberts, 19 Aug. 1810, Roberts Papers, HSP; John Connelly to Roberts, 3 Apr. 1812, *ibid.*; [Waln], *Hermit in America*, 93.

[28]John T. Holdsworth, *Financing an Empire: History of Banking in Pennsylvania*, 2 vols. (Chicago, 1928), I, 303-305. See also Minutes of the Stockolders of the Bank of the Northern Liberties, 1811, in Roberts Vaux Papers, HSP.

Liberties is sure of a charter." Although "how many were purchased" by it could be only "conjectured," the promise of incorporation apparently had succeeded in luring enough influential local Democrats into the new party to help sway other voters. Perhaps its most important effect was in helping the New School to create a formidable ward organization, whose intensive campaigning succeeded for the first time in carrying the district which had been Michael Leib's personal constituency since the 1790's. The defeated Old School loyalists deplored the selfish motives of the new set of rival ward leaders. After the Snyderite victory in the county, George White's *Evening Star* listed the names of the men who expected to receive patronage jobs in reward for their efforts. In addition "A President, and a batch of directors, cashier, tellers and clerks [for the Northern Liberties bank] form no inconsiderable item in the account of corruption."[29]

The fierce struggle for the district began on the Fourth of July and grew steadily more intense until it reached its climax on September 28 in the contest for inspectors of the general election. While the traditional leaders scoffed at their rivals "private or public begging," they desperately attempted to counteract the pressure by their own campaign efforts. Duane and the *Aurora* remained surprisingly aloof from this election, because of the editor's preoccupation with national issues and with his own projects to rescue himself financially. But Michael Leib took direct charge of the

---

[29] *Evening Star*, 16 Oct. 1810.

campaign for Philadelphia, and the evening Old School newspaper, the <u>Pennsylvania Democrat</u>, was supplemented by the new <u>Evening Star</u>, "a paper of politics corresponding as far as different persons of the same principles can agree with the general politics of the AURORA." Meanwhile "Never was there such pains taken, as these <u>patent democrats</u>" of the New School took to influence the voters; "they had committees to traverse the western wards, and the eastern lanes and alleys" of the city and "every street, lane, alley and bye-corner of the Northern Liberties."[30]

By the Friday of the inspectors election the Snyderites were trained and commanded like Hessians or Swiss mercenaries, according to the Old School leaders, who themselves had a "committee of vigilance" three hundred strong in the northern district. "Violence, previously threatened and predicted, was the order of the day," when the Snyderites refused to accept the constable's verdict that the Old School voters had won the standing division to elect the judges of the ward contest. They rushed into the polling place, pulled down the judges' stand, and continued to riot until past three o'clock when they were offered a compromise which restored peace to the neighborhood. By that time, according to the <u>Aurora</u>, many good Democrats had left the election ground, and others had stayed away altogether, with the result that the aggressive New Schoolers carried their slate of inspectors, and the subsequent triumph in the general election was all but a foregone conclusion.[31]

---

[30] <u>Ibid</u>., 6, 17 July, 5 Sept. 1810; <u>The Tickler</u>, 17 Oct. 1810.

[31] <u>Aurora</u>, 27 Sept., 1 Oct. 1810; <u>Evening Star</u>, 29 Sept. 1810.

That Sunday Michael Bright entertained a crowd of people waiting at the ferry with the maliciously gleeful story that "when Leib and [Frederick] Wolbert heard that the Arabs had carried the election in the Northern Liberties, they cried like children; or what was tantamount to it." The Evening Star rejoined that the gossip was ridiculous, since Leib was "not a candidate for any elective office, and, therefore, . . . cannot be personally triumphed, even in an Arab triumph." But the Federalists saw the result differently: "thus ends one of the most complete dictatorships ever exercised in this country by any man," intoned the Tickler. "This tyranny . . . was long tolerated by the people—nay, they even appeared to delight in being dictated to by Leib," the editor admitted, "and often would they rattle their political chains with frantic joy, and shout hosannas to their tyrant." But the defeat by the Snyderites in his own constituency revealed that he had not "obtained a lease-hold for life" on the "blind confidence" of "the weak, credulous, ignorant, and designing part of the community."[32]

Duane's disciple George White, who had edited the campaign newspaper and had worked harder than anyone to defeat the Snyderites' challenge, made a scathing prediction for the future. With the success of the New School of Democratic politicians, "Banks are now to swarm upon us like locusts did over the face of Egypt, and our substance is to be eaten out by them, and beggary is to become a fashionable thing. Idlers and speculators, who are too lazy to work," in his opinion, "are to become depradators upon the public in the

---

[32] Ibid., 1 Oct. 1810; The Tickler, 17 Oct. 1810.

shape of stockholders and bank directors, and the hope of living upon the labors of others promises to palsy the industry of the community." White believed that "Our republican principles are in the market." In future they "are to be bought and sold by a bank charter, a directorship or a discounter; instead of labourers we are to have a new swarm of brokers, and this new south sea bubble is to prostrate the principles and the industry of the commonwealth."[33]

---

[33] Evening Star, 16 Oct. 1810.

CHAPTER VIII

GALLATIN AND THE BANK

Shortly after the defeat of his party by the infant Bank of the Northern Liberties, Duane personally challenged a far more powerful adversary in Philadelphia, the Bank of the United States. The charter of the national bank was to expire in March 1811, but it had appealed to Congress for a renewal of its privileges, with the support of Secretary of the Treasury Gallatin and the administration. Duane was determined to oppose that possibility at any cost, and from November onward the _Aurora_ was editorially dedicated to the single goal of helping to destroy the Bank. Ultimately the aggressive campaign had unexpected and lasting repercussions upon the Republican party and its once favorite editor. President Madison was forced to rearrange his cabinet in response to the seeming threat from the still powerful newspaper, while Duane himself risked and lost much of his remaining influence and prestige.

Although he was unshakeably opposed to recharter, Duane had not arrived at a fixed philosophy about the relationship of the government to banking. He did propose an alternative to the United States Bank, which he urged President Madison to consider, but events later forced him to abandon his faith in this solution. By 1810 Duane was in full retreat from the laissez-faire notions he had espoused briefly early in the decade, and convinced that the free development of banks should be checked by the controlling influence of the federal government. This he thought could be accomplished through the creation of a standard national currency, which would automatically limit the expansion of locally-circulated bank paper, by the demand for convertibility.

But the editor's conservative wish to protect the public from exploitation was to some degree compromised by his equally fervent economic nationalism. The Embargo had stirred his dreams of a mighty internal empire, and he wanted to believe that it was possible to promote rapid expansion and development, through governmental encouragement and through the magic qualities of credit, without yielding to the accompanying evils of speculation and profiteering. During this period he reconciled his conflicting wishes by the belief that the increased use of paper money could be socially beneficial if there were a central monetary policy established in the public interest. To achieve this, in his opinion, it was essential to destroy the privately owned and operated Bank of the United States, which was guided solely by the profit motive, and to replace it with a genuinely national institution.

In his editorial debates of the issue, Duane sought especially to refute the arguments of two locally important advocates of renewal, Mathew Carey and Dr. Erich Bollman. Carey's numerous essays and speeches in favor of the Bank attracted wide notice because of his high political standing in the community, as a prominent businessman as well as a leading New School Democrat. The European-born

Bollman was a commercial adventurer who had acquired notoriety by his involvement in Aaron Burr's conspiracy and had no political influence in Philadelphia, unless among the Federalists who in any case generally favored recharter. But Bollman's Paragraphs on Banking had an intellectual impact on the discussion because it was the only pamphlet, in Duane's opinion, "in which the subject and principles of banking and credit are discussed with any thing like a competent knowledge of the subject." His own thinking on the issue was deeply influenced by Bollman's ideas, in spite of his disagreement with the writer's conclusions.[1]

Duane and Mathew Carey were both amateurs in economics, and at this time probably were about equal in their theoretical understanding of financial matters. Nonetheless as political rivals they delighted in ridiculing each other's intellectual efforts. Carey began the feud with a gratuitous slur on the influence of newspaper editors upon questions of public policy, but Duane and his partisans retaliated with a fury which no doubt made him regret his involvement. When Carey mocked Duane's "profound, convincing, and unanswerable arguments" against recharter, the editor dismissed him as a man

---

[1]Mathew Carey, "Desultory Reflections upon the Ruinous Consequences of a Non-renewal of the Charter of the Bank of the United States," 2nd ed. (Philadelphia, 1810), pamphlet, University of Chicago; Carey, Letters to Dr. Adam Seybert; [Erich Bollman], Paragraphs on Banks, 2nd ed., improved (Philadelphia, 1811); Aurora, 25 Dec. 1810. On Bollman see Fritz Redlich, Essays in American Economic History: Eric Bollman and Studies in Banking (New York, 1944), 1-106; Joseph Dorfman, The Economic Mind in American Civilization, 1606-1865, 5 vols. (New York, 1946-1959), I, 484-499. There is no adequate discussion of Carey's views on banking, but see ibid., I, 342; Kenneth W. Rowe, Mathew Carey: A Study in American Economic Development, The Johns Hopkins University Studies in Historical and Political Science, series LI, number 4 (Baltimore, 1933), 59-64, 68-69, 72.

of "shallow understanding, incompetent to reason on the simplest subject."[2]

A band of loyal Old School men invaded the crowd of "quidnuncs, brokers, and shavers" at the Coffee House, in order to heckle a speech by Carey in favor of renewal. The baiting succeeded in drawing an outburst against "some tool of Duane" in the audience, and an expression of surprise that any reader of the Aurora was allowed entry to the Coffee House. This gave the Old Schoolers an opportunity to remind Carey of his own radical activities in the 1790s, in opposition to William Cobbett. "I suppose . . . [Duane] will some day endeavor to collect a mob as you did, to pull down Porcupine's house," someone called out. "You were a democrat then," someone else shouted. "Mat. whisked about, and furiously roared out, what scoundrel is that. What party do you belong to now, said another--poor Mat. was like a whirligig," his speech was ruined, and the meeting on behalf of the Bank ended in a shambles.[3]

Carey's arguments in support of recharter emphasized the Bank's practical value and the danger that its dissolution would lead to general curtailment and recession. If he was concerned at this time, as he came to be later, with the problem of creating a stable currency, he avoided revealing that purpose in his public statements on the issue. On the contrary he specifically denied that the United States Bank had a central banking function for the

---

[2]Carey, Letters to Dr. Adam Seybert, vi-vii, 48; Aurora, 4 Jan. 1811. See also ibid., 25, 27 Dec. 1810, 22, 25, 31 Jan. 1811.

[3]Ibid., "Sangrado," 28 Jan. 1811.

nation, and contrasted its innocent business motives with the political influence to be feared from a government-sponsored institution. He preferred to renew the charter of the private company because "the true motto of Banks, I take to be the reply made by a wise old merchant to . . . Colbert . . . when he enquired what government could do for trade and commerce--_Laissez nous faire--leave us to ourselves_."

It is difficult to judge the depth or sincerity of Carey's reasoning on the matter, because clearly he was seeking to influence the opinions of men who distrusted the United States Bank because they thought it too powerful. In advocating recharter, "I unfortunately differ from a large portion of the political party to which I belong," Carey acknowledged, but "I leave to time to decide whose ideas are most correct on the subject." In addition to the traditional hatred of the Hamiltonian creation, shared by Democrats generally, there was a rising sentiment among New Schoolers in favor of liberating the state banks by striking down the monopolistic national institution.[4]

"I take it for granted," John Binns wrote to a new Pennsylvania Congressman, "that you have a deep and irremoveable impression that Congress have no right to grant Charters of Incorporation; if it has the State Legislatures have not," he reasoned. "Two independent sovereignties cannot justly legislate on the same subject within the same jurisdiction." After recharter was defeated, Binns supported the Bank's unsuccessful application for incorporation in Pennsylvania, because

---

[4]Carey, _Letters to Dr. Adam Seybert_, 31-32, 65.

it did not interfere with his philosophy that the banking business should be left for the states to manage.[5]

Probably Carey supported the United States Bank primarily because of his awakened interest in the development of manufacturing. He was concerned with the problem of establishing adequate credit facilities as a stimulus to rapid economic expansion. Unlike Duane and the great majority of Democrats, Carey had no prejudice against foreign investors as men who sought to drain profits away from the country for their personal enrichment. Two thirds of the Bank's stock was held by foreigners, but the capital which they furnished to Americans contributed far more to the economy, Carey pointed out, than was removed in payments abroad on interest and dividends.[6]

A few of Philadelphia's entrepreneurial Democrats were persuaded by this viewpoint, and some leading New Schoolers, including John Barker and Jacob Vogdes, organized a meeting of master mechanics and manufacturers to express their support for recharter. They "are to represent the great succour, aid, and comfort which they have received from the bank," scoffed the _Aurora_, "the vast sums lent to manufacturers, and the great patronage which every thing American has received by the patronage of this bank," But each signer "flatters himself" that he will be remembered gratefully with loans in the future, because instead of the "usual phrases of _dam'd_ _rascally_ _democrats_, &c," the Bank directors "are now meanly and _disgustingly_

---

[5]Binns to Jonathan Roberts, 30 Nov. 1810, Roberts Papers, HSP; Thomas J. Rogers to Jonathan Roberts, 26 Jan. 1812, _ibid._; Higginbotham, _Keystone_, 225.

[6]Carey, _Letters to Dr. Adam Seybert_, 58-60, 63.

obsequious, to the republicans." The false hopes would be quickly crushed upon renewal, Duane predicted.[7]

The accusation that the United States Bank was in reality a "British Bank" with interests hostile to the nation was the argument "most relied upon" by its enemies, "constantly reiterated, and more than any other calculated to excite against it popular prejudices," in the opinions of Carey and Bollman. Certainly no one worked harder than the Aurora editor to exacerbate those feelings. Fully two thirds of his "twenty reasons" for opposing recharter were based upon a xenophobic resentment of its English connections. Duane no doubt understood the propaganda value of his arguments, but he unquestionably shared the prejudices of his readers against any form of dependence upon the British. It "would be worth the sacrifice of a sum of ten times the bank capital," in his opinion, to extinguish "the baleful influence which has existed hitherto under the all polluting auspices of that bank."

Carey insisted that it would be capricious and unethical to exclude the foreign investors arbitrarily, but Duane scoffed that "this compassionate man, for he is all bowels, has transferred all the stock bought by [Alexander] Baring, into the hands of numbers of widows and orphans, and persons in an advanced stage of life--who will . . . die of the fall of stocks." The argument that foreign investment contributed more to the economy than it extracted in profits was unconvincing to the Anglophobic editor. "We do not say

---

[7]Scharf and Westcott, Hist. of Phila., I, 548; Aurora, 25 Jan., 9 Feb. 1811.

that no part of the use of this capital remains; we know very well that part of it does," he acknowledged; "but we also know that its pestilential influence is felt through every gradation of society;" by the tradesman, the storekeeper, the shipbuilder and the merchant, by "the press in its corruption--the election in its votes--and even in the halls of congress and on the desks of the treasury--it is felt."[8]

The Aurora explained that Alexander Hamilton's Bank had been from its foundation an institution entrusted with the task of helping to sustain a foreign policy based upon subservience to the reactionary government of Great Britain. "For What Was The Revolution Accomplished?" the editor asked. Devotion to America or to England had divided the political parties from the beginning, by his analysis. But the commercial vassalage to Britain entailed upon the nation by the Jay Treaty had not been successfully challenged until the Embargo policy of President Jefferson. Erich Bollman attempted a disinterested reply to this conspiracy theory of an international monied faction devoted to "the overthrow of republican government." If the United States Bank had exerted an influence for friendly American-British relations, he reasoned, it was not because it had English stockholders, "but because it is a bank." Whatever her politics England "fights, after all, in the cause of laws," while the regimes of France "spread insecurity and terror." He would be less surprised, Bollman said, "to see butchers turn zealous advocates for

---

[8] Carey, Letters to Dr. Adam Seybert, 63; [Bollman], Paragraphs on Banks, 2nd ed., 116; Aurora, 8 Nov., 15, 28 Dec. 1810.

vegetable diet, than to see banks espouse the cause of revolutionary troubles or military sway."[9]

But Duane's objections to the British connections went deeper than mere prejudice and suspicion. He understood the Bank's commercial usefulness for facilitating international exchanges, and for that reason wanted no renewal of its charter. To him the end of the United States Bank was one essential feature in a general redirection of American foreign and economic policy. Since the repeal of the Embargo "we have been inundating the country with British manufactures," making New York City for example into a "reservoir of British excrement," and the ease of commerce was "running the balance of trade against the nation, from 30 to 40 millions per annum." This continuing indebtedness to Britain, rather than the ten million dollars capital in the Bank, threatened to inflict a permanent colonial status upon the United States, in Duane's opinion.

The solution he believed was a radical turning away from the ocean toward internal development under the influence of government policy. The Embargo had been unpopular, he thought, only because it was misunderstood and misrepresented. "A person could hardly fall sick or dislocate a limb, that it was not placed to the account of the embargo." But that policy was an admirable alternative to war with Great Britain and would have succeeded, he declared, "if it had been enforced and adhered to for a little while longer." In any case to Duane the measure illustrated the tremendous influence for

---

[9] Ibid., 13 Dec. 1810, 26 Jan. 1811; [Bollman], Paragraphs on Banks, 2nd ed., 119.

good which the government could have upon the economy. He envisioned the defeat in Congress of the United States Bank's appeal for recharter as the dawn of an enlightened nationalistic policy.[10]

If there had been no English stockholders and no threat of war with Britain, Duane undoubtedly would still have opposed the Bank's renewal. His Anglophobic sentiments were genuine, but he was more fundamentally concerned with the anti-democratic political implications of employing a private corporation to conduct public business. This did not mean that he thought any form of national bank was unconstitutional. It "cannot be supposed," he reasoned, "that a supreme government exercising the exclusive power of coinage of gold and silver, and copper, is divested or not invested with the power of coining paper also." His unorthodox reply to the question of constitutionality was an adaptation of Dr. Bollman's theory that the United States Bank functioned as a national mint, because paper money had become the country's real currency, and that a "change of the circulating medium" was the "real point in question" in the debate on recharter.[11]

Duane agreed with this formulation of the problem, but rejected Bollman's conclusion that the United States Bank was indispensable for providing a standard circulating medium, and formulated his own alternative system of currency and finance for the nation. The editor had read the Paragraphs on Banks in manuscript, for the

---

[10] Aurora, 18 Jan., 7 Feb. 1811.

[11] Ibid., 4 Jan. 1811; [Bollman], Paragraphs on Banks, 21, 46-47, 49, 73.

author had submitted it to several printers, and later complained that "some of the expressions and ideas, contained in it, have made their appearance in the newspaper publications of one of them." Bollman argued persuasively that "petty local institutions" were responsible for the "abuse of banking," although Duane at this time thought him too extreme in suggesting that they be treated as "nuisances." The states needed "the power of creating a banking credit," in Duane's opinion, in order to protect them from the exclusive powers of the general government, "if abused," or the monopolistic domination of the Bank of the United States."[12]

Although he admired Bollman's precocious understanding of monetary theory, the editor quarreled with what he considered his poor grasp of political priorities. "The author appears . . . not to have considered the principles of popular government," he chided, "with the same attention as he has studied the principles of credit." Bollman admitted that the existing United States Bank was not his ideal institution, declaring that "I should like best to have a national bank, created, like the judiciary by the constitution itself and independent of government." In Duane's opinion an institution established on those principles would "secure an eternal jubilee to treason and disaffection to the government."

Bollman himself discounted the political criticisms of the petitioning Bank as meaningless partisanship, and urged that these superficial considerations be relinquished in favor of a more sophisticated appreciation of its value. "For the business which

---

[12] Ibid., iii, 55-56, 60-61; Aurora, 4, 7 Jan. 1811.

the United States bank now does <u>must</u> be done by some institution or other," he reasoned, "And which ever institution suceeds to its business will succeed to its principles and spirit." Suppose the present owners were wholly displaced by Republicans, he argued, the new men would soon "feel the tendency of things to be stronger than the drift of their political creed and would find themselves pushed, without knowing how, into the track of their predecessors." Bollman advised the political zealots to take the world as they found it; "since you cannot do without the thing how can you get rid of its spirit?" Suppose "shoemaking unavoidably led to federalism [then] must the people go barefoot?" It might be possible to dismantle the Bank safely, he conceded, and to introduce a new circulating medium, but "what is to be gained? what good end is to be achieved by all this trouble?"[13]

To Duane the answer was self-evident, the establishment of a financial system in the public interest. He instinctively rejected Bollman's cynicism as contrary to the idea of democratic self-government. In his opinion it was possible to create an institution which would have "all the advantages of a bank, without any of its disadvantages," and from which "<u>the whole profit would go to the public</u>." The essential requirement was to supplant the narrow private interests and profit motive which dominated the United States Bank with a system of public ownership and control, by using the western lands as the basis of credit. "To any banking institution not founded on the

---

[13]<u>Ibid</u>., 7 Jan. 1811; [Bollman], <u>Paragraphs on Banks</u>, 48, 56, 72-73.

landed security of the United States we are hostile," he told his readers.

Duane's idea that the public lands somehow could be converted into a capital fund for banking was based upon the success of Pennsylvania's loan office in the eighteenth century. The colony had granted long-term mortgage loans to farmers on low interest, without suffering depreciation of its legal tender or loss of faith in the public credit. The editor insisted that the lands were not only equal to specie reserves but "the best possible basis of credit," because they had intrinsic worth rather than merely conventional value. His plan did not specify for certain whether the government should simply issue money on its own credit, backed by land, as had been attempted in the eighteenth century, or whether it should mortgage the lands by the sale of stocks or bonds to obtain a cash fund for its operations. The first solution was "probably sufficient," he suggested, but the second had the advantage of being "certain of immediate accomplishment." In outlining tentative arrangements based on this alternative, Duane anticipated that the mortgage-holders could be reimbursed in cash or lands for their investment and the federal government would retain the ownership of the institution.

From this beginning he sketched a grand design of public banking and control of the currency. An institution with headquarters in Washington, functioning as an executive agency and responsible to Congress, would be the depository of the public funds, and would issue federal notes in denominations of not less than twenty dollars, which would circulate nationally in all government transactions. It would also fill the role of the United States Bank in making loans to the government, but whether such an institution would engage in private banking functions as well, extending credit to individual citizens, Duane did not specify. His failure to be explicit on this question reflected the mental conflict he was experiencing between his faith in economic progress and his distress over currency inflation. He imagined that his land bank scheme could lead to rapid development of the interior without the evils of land speculation, and refused to admit the possibility that a lapse in the public credit would leave the government at the mercy of its bondholders. His suggested safeguards against this hazard were unconvincing.[14]

Dr. Bollman, in a postscript to his Paragraphs on Banking, objected that the Aurora's proposal had "inconveniences so obvious that the idea must be abandoned on the slightest investigation." The public lands could not serve as the basis for a financial system, he explained, because "Equality of intrinsic or representative value is one of the essential characters of a good circulating medium." If the government pledged its lands "specifically," making "each note a title to a designated tract," the plan would fail through its own inequity. But if it used the lands "collectively," by forming a mortgage pool for banking, "the security would not be greater than that of government generally." A public agency could not replace the

---

[14]Duane to James Madison, 5, 8 Dec. 1809, Madison Papers, LC; Aurora, 28 Dec. 1810, 10, 11, 28, 29, 30, 31 Jan. 1811. See also Bray Hammond, Banks and Politics in America: From the Revolution to the Civil War (Princeton, 1957), 11-12, 30; Fritz Redlich, The Molding of American Banking: Men and Ideas, 2 parts (New York, 1947), I, 205-208.

Bank of the United States in his opinion because the public credit was "not equal to that of a private banking institution." Duane had not succeeded in his efforts to solve the dilemma by harmonizing political ideals with economic realities.[15]

II

In late February 1811 the Senate decided, by the single vote of Vice President George Clinton, to deny the Bank of the United States a renewal of its charter. Duane joined in the general rejoicing with a sense of personal triumph. During the winter of the Bank debate he had "passed thro' the most laborious and intense application that I have experienced in any period of my life," he told Thomas Jefferson. The journeyman printers had been on strike and his foreman out for months with pneumonia, so that the editor "unassisted by a single individual" had to write every story for a newspaper containing "more manuscript matter than any . . . in the country." But he felt that "My labor was rewarded by the cessation of the Bank and by a consciousness that my humble efforts had contributed something to that effect."[16]

Secretary of the Treasury Gallatin had urgently sought the continuation of the Bank as necessary to the work of his department, and he strongly suspected that its defeat was the result of political opposition to him personally. The campaign against the Bank in the Senate was led by the same men who consistently labored to embarrass

---

[15] [Bollman], Paragraphs on Banks, 2nd ed., 110-114.

[16] Duane to Jefferson, 15 Mar. 1811, TJ-LC.

the Secretary and his proposals, Samuel Smith of Maryland, William Branch Giles of Virginia, and Michael Leib of Pennsylvania. The Clintons of New York had joined the cabal against Gallatin on the Bank issue, and it appeared that even President Madison could become the victim of a Clinton-Smith alliance in the next presidential election. During these months the *Aurora* had attacked Gallatin with unprecedented fury and personal abusiveness, and the Secretary understandably regarded its campaign as an integral part of the Senatorial conspiracy against him. "No man can doubt by whom this machinery is put in motion," John Randolph warned him through Joseph Nicholson. In view of the *Aurora*'s evident wish to oust him from the cabinet, Gallatin could "no longer hesitate how to act" toward his enemy the Secretary of State, Robert Smith, the brother of the powerful Senator. Gallatin agreed and decided that he must force the President to choose the services either of himself or of his cabinet rival. "He assigned as the chief reason of his offence against him, that he was the author of many anonimous publications written against Him" in the *Aurora*.[17]

Gallatin's anger was justified but he was mistaken in his conclusion that the intrigues of Robert and Samuel Smith were behind Duane's publications. The editor was loosely associated with the Baltimore men through his friendship with Leib and Giles, and by his opinion that "the Republican party must go to destruction if M^r^

---

[17] Randolph to Nicholson, 14 Feb. 1811, in Adams, *Randolph*, 239-240; Elizabeth Donnan, ed., "Papers of James A. Bayard, 1796-1815," American Historical Association, *Annual Report, 1913*, 2 vols. (Washington, 1915), II, 484-485; Brant, *Madison*, V, 265-270, 276.

Gallatin continues, and that Mr Madison will be thrown out at the next election" if he did not renounce the Secretary's influence. But Duane had "never corresponded with either" of the Smiths, nor "received any favors," and "whatever there has been between them and me, has partaken more of injury to me (as far as it could go) than favor."

The editor distrusted the brothers because in the early years of the decade, when Quids and Democrats had struggled for dominance in the Republican party, they had been friendly to the Mc-Kean administration in Pennsylvania. He believed that Madison, Gallatin, and the Smiths had once been linked in "a *little cabal*, which aimed to influence all public affairs in their own favor." The secret party "had a sort of beginning" in the Congress of 1796, according to the editor. "It was composed of an interest in four states—N. York[,] Penna.[,] Maryland and Virginia. Ed. Livingston & A. Burr were the Yorkers—Gallatin and Dallas were the Pennsylvanians. The Smiths of Maryland and the Nicholases of Virginia." Since achieving office and power, "the aim of every man of them," this "little cabal has been curiously unsorted" and "they are now in conflict." But Duane claimed that "*it would not surprize me much to see the fragments reunited*."

In the Senate Michael Leib was actively cooperating with Samuel Smith on political measures, but Duane denied that he was influenced by his friend's activities. "Dr. Leib . . . and I have agreed and disagreed in politics now fourteen years," he assured Henry Dearborn, "without the one having ever changed the opinions of the other."

They had shared "fundamental principles" and seldom differed on "measures of policy," he commented, "but we have seriously differed about men, many times, & act as distinctly upon each his own judgment, as any two men of opposite politics." Duane refused to believe however that his friend had been taken in by the untrustworthy brothers. "I know what their deportment was towards Dr Leib when he was in Congress, and it can scarcely be supposed that he can forget it. . . . If they were sincere before, they must be inconsistent now," in Duane's opinion; "if they were hypocrites before they cannot be sincere now. Leib is not a man of dull capacity, he sees and decides as soon as any man I know."

Duane's own solution to the rivalry between Gallatin and Robert Smith was to "dismiss both" the cabinet officers. He was opposed to "playing off one minister against another," he declared, because both were so swollen with vanity and love of power that collision between them was inevitable. "I say it will be impossible that the measures of policy devised by the President, if they were the most wise that wisdom could suggest, can escape collision between such conflicting passions."[18]

During the period of the recharter debate the *Aurora* was unquestionably slanderous toward the Secretary of the Treasury. It accused Gallatin of supporting the Bank because he was personally "deeply involved" in profitable land speculation and because he was in sympathy with pro-British intrigues against full American inde-

---

[18] Duane to [Henry Dearborn], 3 July 1810, Pers. Papers Misc. (Duane), LC.

pendence. Duane portrayed the Secretary as an evil genius whose manipulations of national policy had caused "the corruption which is now undermining the rights of this nation, sapping the foundations of representative government--prostituting great national interests to the enrichment of the few, and the total disregard of the great mass of people." He acknowledged that "The man who dares to utter truths like these holds himself up for the butt of malignity," but "What we can do we shall do" in order "to awaken the nation to the conduct of those entrusted with their power."[19]

Duane did not oppose the Bank because he hated Gallatin, as the Secretary imagined, but attacked the Pennsylvanian with growing violence only because his position on recharter was intolerable. The editor had almost mellowed toward Secretary Gallatin as his political power had declined in the last years of Jefferson's administration, when he no longer influenced the President's decisions on patronage, and when the Dallas party had been vanquished within Pennsylvania. At least the Aurora did not assail him. And in 1809 when Duane proffered to Madison his scheme for a national land bank, he suggested that his anonymous ideas be entrusted to the Secretary for fuller development, since to a mind like Gallatin's "such a plan would at once present itself in a manner that would give it form and efficacy." But Duane was bitterly disillusioned anew by Gallatin's views on foreign policy and by his plea for renewal of the United States Bank charter. He began to cast doubts even on the Secretary's reputed brilliance, and declared that it was "cowardly in Mr. Gallatin," the

---

[19] Aurora, 7 Jan. 1811.

Spirit of '76 lampooned him, "to entrench himself behind his talents and virtues, when it is known by all the world, that his adversaries have few or none of these impenetrable kind of troops" at their disposal.[20]

Duane blamed Gallatin exclusively for the administration's retreat from a strong policy of resistance to British violations of the neutral rights of America. His "situation in the cabinet . . . furnished him with ample means of frustrating the wise policy of Mr. Jefferson" and destroying the Embargo through "hypocritical secret intrigues." That is "Mr. Gallatin was guilty of an egregrious treachery in telling the truth," the Spirit of '76 commented, "by saying that taxes or loans were the only sources of revenue, when it was evidently his duty to tell a lie in order to save the embargo." Later Gallatin wrote the legislation which repealed the non-intercourse act and reopened trade with France and Britain.[21]

But to Duane and others the final proof that the Secretary was secretly pro-English was the revelation by a Parliamentary inquiry into the conduct of Robert Erskine, its recalled minister, that Gallatin had told Erskine "that he Mr. G. had been years employed in efforts to wean Mr Jefferson from his French attachments." The former President was not offended by the indiscretion but the Aurora and other papers assailed Gallatin's "scandalous conduct." In their private correspondence in this period, Jefferson expressed at some

---

[20]Duane to Madison, 5 Dec. 1809, Madison Papers, LC; Aurora, 4 Apr. 1811.

[21]Ibid., 7 Feb., 4 Apr. 1811.

length his essential agreement with Duane's Anglophobia, and the editor could contrast his hero's sentiments with the Secretary's apparent friendliness toward the former colonial rulers. Finally when Gallatin became the administration's spokesman for the British Bank, Duane declared that nothing "shall induce us to sacrifice principles to support men who betray all principles," not measures or money or "the apprehension of another proscription like that of 1798."[22]

In March Gallatin decided to take action against the ill treatment of him in the Aurora by retaliating against Robert Smith, his cabinet rival. He submitted his resignation to Madison, and as he expected the President declined it and immediately asked for the Secretary of State's resignation. He offered Smith the post of Ambassador to Russia to assuage him, and Smith at first accepted but then rejected the courtesy, presumably after consultation with his brother. The Smiths had decided to fight the President over the dismissal by an appeal to public opinion. In addition to their organ, the Baltimore Whig, three independent newspapers which hitherto had attacked Gallatin without criticizing President Madison now had to decide between him and the dismissed officer. The Boston Patriot and the Richmond Enquirer quickly retreated from a confrontation with the Republican President, and ultimately only the Aurora chose to censure Madison for his submission to the powerful influence of the Secretary of the Treasury.[23]

---

[22]Duane to [Henry Dearborn], 3 July 1810, Pers. Papers Misc. (Duane), LC; Jefferson to Duane, 13 Nov. 1810, TJ-LC; Aurora, 7 Jan. 1811. See Walters, Gallatin, 231-234; Brant, Madison, V, 161-163.

[23]Ibid., 282-283, 291-294; Walters, Gallatin, 241-243; Aurora, 24, 25 Apr., 2, 3, 4, 6, 7 May 1811.

When the cabinet crisis broke, Duane was deeply involved in a personal crisis over money. He had applied to the Comptroller of the Treasury for 1,000 dollars owed to him on a former contract, but Secretary Gallatin interfered and stopped the payment for a prior investigation of Duane's accounts with all the executive departments. To Duane who believed that Gallatin for seven years had "persecuted me with the spirit of an assassin," these "artful intrigues" had been "set on foot to destroy my paper and beggar my family." On March 12 he received notice that the needed payment had been cancelled, and the following day Thomas Leiper and Joseph Clay both informed him of their intention to withdraw as his bank endorsers, for sums of 3,000 and 5,000 dollars respectively. These two had been his close personal and political friends for more than a decade. "I am the same in every respect, but they are no longer my friends-," he told Thomas Jefferson; "in short they menace me at this moment with ruin."[24]

"Leiper who has stood firm since the revolution became the advocate of the Bank" and withdrew his support from Duane for that reason, the editor explained to Henry Dearborn. Jefferson agreed that in "looking about for a motive, I . . . supposed it was to be found in the late arraignments of mr Gallatin in your papers." He was surprised at this form of disapproval from the tobacco merchant. Duane's services should not be "effaced" by one disagreement; "thus I think, and thus I believed my much esteemed friend Lieper [sic] would have thought," Jefferson admitted. The stubborn Scotsman may

---

[24]Duane to D. B. Warden, 6 Apr. 1811, D. B. Warden Papers, LC; Duane to Isaac Briggs, 6 July 1811, Isaac Briggs Papers, LC; Duane to Jefferson, 15 Mar. 1811, TJ-LC.

have been particularly annoyed with the editor because he believed that the Aurora was helping to destroy the only defense against the state banking mania. "Leiper says that in writing against the Bank I was writing against my own interest," Duane related to Dearborn, "& must therefore be a dangerous man, since none but a mad man would do so."[25]

Joseph Clay on the other hand informed Duane by messenger that "The causes of my refusal are the groundless and unwarrantable attacks in the Aurora on my friends; particularly on Mr. Randolph." The editor had been striking at the Virginian for his part in the current court martial of General James Wilkinson, whom Duane idolized as the man who saved the country from the plot of Aaron Burr. Moreover Gallatin and Randolph had once been close friends and the Aurora linked them together in a fantastic conspiracy theory of pro-British interests undermining the national welfare. After Robert Smith was fired he ascribed "the whole of the . . . commotion & changes in the cabinet to Gallatin & yourself-," a friend told Randolph incredulously; "but I cannot understand whether he accuses you of influencing Gallatin, or Gallatin of operating on you." Duane was hurt that Joe Clay could choose to sacrifice him because of a greater loyalty to the Virginian; "we were friends when he did not know John Randolph, and even when he despised John Randolph and declared him to be no republican."[26]

---

[25]Duane to Dearborn, 19 Mar. 1811, Henry Dearborn Papers, Mass. Hist. Soc.; Jefferson to Duane, 28 Mar. 1811, TJ-LC.

[26]Duane to Jefferson, 15 Mar. 1811, TJ-LC; Aurora, 1 Jan., 28 Feb. 1811; James M. Garnett to John Randolph, 15 Apr. 1811, Randolph-Garnett Letterbook, LC; Duane to Dearborn, 19 Mar. 1811, Dearborn Papers, Mass. Hist. Soc.

Faced with imminent bankruptcy, Duane appealed to Jefferson to help him, and the former President warmly agreed to do so. "The zeal, the disinterestedness, and the abilities with which you have supported the great principles of our revolution," he assured him, "the persecutions you have suffered, and the firmness and independence with which you have suffered them," were all valid claims upon the Republicans. Jefferson was careful to stipulate however that his aid was not an endorsement of the editor's opinions on Albert Gallatin. He thought that he knew "his character more thoroughly than perhaps any other man living," but "everyone, certainly, must form his judgment on the evidence accessible to himself, and I have no more doubt of the integrity of your convictions, than I have of my own."

In view of the danger from Europe, Jefferson urged the editor to yield some of his stubborn independence and to cooperate more fully with President Madison and the Republican administration. Jefferson believed that "the last hope of human liberty in this world rests on us." "If we schismatize on either men or measures, if we do not act in phalanx, . . . I will not say our <u>party</u>, the term is false and degrading, but our <u>nation</u> will be undone, for the republicans are the <u>nation</u>." Rather than "each one pursuing the path he thinks most direct," he should uphold the leaders and "things may here & there go a little wrong. it is not in their power to prevent it. but all will be right in the end, tho' not perhaps by the shortest means." Yet Jefferson still did "homage to every one's right of opinion. if I have indulged my pen therefore a little further than the occasion called for," he apologized, "you will ascribe it to a sermonizing habit, to the anxieties of age, perhaps to its garrulity, or to any other motive" rather than to lack of "esteem & confidence" in the editor.

Duane had asked if it might be possible to raise a loan for him in Virginia by subscribing a number of endorsers, and Jefferson agreed to undertake this project to help him. Peter Carr, his nephew and secretary, circulated the request within Albemarle county, and ten or twelve persons quickly consented. But "The truth is that farmers, as we all are, have no command of money," and "our support can be but partial." The Richmond banks and Richmond endorsers were necessary in order to raise any substantial sum for the editor. For this purpose Jefferson wrote to enlist the aid of William Wirt in the project. The Aurora "has, unquestionably rendered incalculable services to republicanism, through all its struggles with the federalists, and has been the rallying point for the Orthodox of the whole Union. It was our comfort in the gloomiest days," he reminded the young attorney, "and is still performing the office of a watchful Sentinel. We should be ungrateful to desert him, and unfaithful to our own interests to lose him."[27]

Wirt was delighted to be of service to Jefferson, but rather dubious about helping Duane. "You may rely upon it that D's name has no magic in it here-," he replied; "he is considered as the foe of M^r. Madison." But Jefferson's distinction between "the past fidelity

---

[27]Jefferson to Duane, 28 Mar. 1811, TJ-LC; Jefferson to Wirt, 30 Mar. 1811, Wirt Papers, Md. Hist. Soc.

and present aberration of the Aurora is just, liberal and magnanimous--and the sentiment might, perhaps, be spread by the contagion of your letter." Wirt made an experiment without it, and "the answer was that D. could not want friends, since his alliance with the S____s." But when he showed the letter to one person, William H. Cabell, "The effect was to dispose him to lend D. $500." Wirt concluded that with Jefferson's direct backing "something important might be done for D." in Richmond.

While these arrangements were underway, the Aurora for the first week of April arrived in Virginia, and all efforts for Duane were cancelled. The editor had unequivocally declared his position on the cabinet crisis, in support of Robert Smith and against Madison. "The paper is now regarded as an opposition one," Wirt informed Jefferson. The latter had said he "should have no hesitation in abandoning" Duane, should he "push his state-partyism against mr Gallatin to an opposition to the President," and Wirt advised that "he merits abandonment" on that principle. "Every Gentleman who mentions this Subject in my hearing speaks with the warmest resentment against D. Believe me, Sir, it is impossible to do any thing for him here, now."[28]

Jefferson agreed and sought to extricate himself as gracefully as possible. He sent Madison a full account of his involvement, with the apology that "I should not at a later moment" have acted "exactly

---

[28]Wirt to Jefferson, 10, 17 Apr. 1811, ibid.; Jefferson to Wirt, 15 Apr. 1811, TJ-LC. See also Jefferson to Wirt, 3 May 1811, Wirt Papers, Md. Hist. Soc.; Wirt to Jefferson, 19 May 1811, ibid.

as I did." His explanations to Gallatin, intended to soothe injured feelings, were rather less candid about his aid to the editor. To Duane himself Jefferson wrote a final plea for party regularity, arguing the surprising doctrine that newspaper editors had an obligation similar to that of members of Congress. Duane did not reply immediately because he was hurt by Jefferson's disapproval, but when they resumed correspondence Jefferson expressed his "regret that I had inadvertently said or done any thing which had given you uneasiness. I pray you to be assured that no unkind motive directed me, and that my sentiments of friendship and respect continue the same."[29]

Duane delayed for a week before taking a stand on the cabinet crisis, until the threat of bankruptcy had been averted. The mystery of how his financial troubles were settled has led contemporaries and historians both to the suspicion that the _Aurora_ editor sold his services to the Smith faction. When the _National Intelligencer_ first reported that Robert Smith had been offered an appointment to Russia, Duane expressed disbelief that President Madison would treat the Secretary of State "with such indelicacy." Two days later he admitted that it "appears to be true" about Smith's "banishment to Siberia," and promised that "We shall have a great many things to say on these subjects, at a more fit season." On April 3 the editorial column bannered "Clear the Decks!" and announced that "The secretary

---

[29]Jefferson to Madison, 24 Apr. 1811, TJ-LC; Jefferson to Duane, 30 Apr., 25 July 1811, TJ-LC; Duane to Jefferson, 5 July 1811, TJ-LC. Compare Jefferson to Gallatin, 24 Apr. 1811, with Jefferson to Robert Smith, 30 Apr. 1811, and Jefferson to Duane, 28 Mar. 1811, TJ-LC.

of the treasury has succeeded completely" in his plots to gain mastery over the cabinet and the mind of the President. "I believe M[r] Gallatin not only to be a villain of the darkest hue," he wrote privately to D. B. Warden, "but I think the safety of the national liberties depends upon his expulsion from power," and "if he be not removed that he will drag down M[r] Madison with him." Not until April 5 did the Aurora publish anything in defense of the dismissed Secretary Smith, and then it declared that "We are authorized to state" his list of reasons for disagreement with President Madison. The President replied to the inaccurate information in this article by a memo to Smith directly. In the same day's issue, a cryptic phrase told Tom Leiper and Joe Clay that Duane's bank loan had been accommodated.[30]

It was Michael Leib who became the editor's new endorser. Leib apparently came home from Washington during the first few days of April, bringing the information from Robert Smith and other political gossip which began to appear in this week's issue. With his signature Duane's loan was transferred from the Farmers and Mechanics bank to the Bank of Pennsylvania. The editor was "compelled to borrow at a disadvantage" and had no reason to hope that his "difficulties and embarrassments" were over, but at least he had avoided the disaster of a foreclosure on the Aurora.[31]

---

[30] Aurora, 27, 29 Mar., 3, 5, Apr. 1811; Duane to Warden, 6 Apr. 1811, Warden Papers, LC; Brant, Madison, V, 291-296.

[31] Duane to Jonathan Smith, Cashier, Penn[a] Bank, 7 Dec. 1811, Gratz Collection, HSP; Duane to D. B. Warden, 6 Apr., 21 July 1811, Warden Papers, LC. See Aurora, 8 Apr. 1811, with note from [A. J. Dallas], in Gallatin Papers, NYHS; Brant, Madison, V, 293-294.

Yet clearly he was a little ashamed of his capitulation to his friend's judgment in favor of upholding the Smith faction. "The essays concerning R. Smith in the Aurora are not written by me," he confessed to Warden, but the author was as "respectable a gentleman" as could be found in the camp of "the Smiths." Possibly it was Baptis Irvine, whom Duane respected and who had written to the editor from Baltimore during the week in which he made his decision. It bothered Duane enormously to be in any way subject to another's opinions, and he said that in the fall he would sell off his personal property "even at half price rather than not be independent." "I know no public man. I have no confidence in any," he wrote bitterly the day following his public declaration in Robert Smith's favor; "nor could I ever again repose confidence in the professions of any political character--I have found them base and perfidious all round--there is not a particle of difference between them." But "it is impossible they can deceive me again."[32]

The proud editor proclaimed that the Aurora would stand "indifferent to all parties" in the future, and "maintain those principles which they all betray. This . . . is an explicit declaration of my feelings and my determinations." Thomas Jefferson warned him that "The example of John Randolph, now the outcast of the world, is a caution to all honest and prudent men, to sacrifice a little of self-confidence, & to go with their friends," in spite of differences

---

[32]Duane to Warden, 6 Apr., 29 May, 21 July 1811, Warden Papers, LC. See Baptis Irvine to Jonathan Roberts, 30 Nov. 1810, Roberts Papers, HSP.

of opinion. Duane had "for some time required a lesson on the subject of modesty," in William Wirt's opinion, "which the people will now give. He thinks that we will follow him--So thought J. R.--and D., like him, will find his mistake." Wirt believed that Duane's comments on Madison treated him "with an impudence of contempt so open and daring, that I suspect the federalists spoke the truth in calling D. an Irishman." John Randolph himself was delighted by the "great mortality of the poor dear Irish (patriots, <u>note</u> as imported) from hot weather & cold water (not <u>whiskey</u>)" in the "torrid zone of Philad[a]." When the <u>Aurora</u> stood alone in defense of the dismissed Secretary of State against a popular Republican President, it exposed the frailty of the editor's remaining influence. "Duane . . . is as harmless a creature as lives," Randolph concluded from the episode; "entirely insignificant."[33]

---

[33]Duane to Warden, 6 Apr. 1811, Warden Papers, LC; Jefferson to Duane, 30 Apr. 1811, TJ-LC; Wirt to Jefferson, 17 Apr. 1811, Wirt Papers, Md. Hist. Soc.; Randolph to James M. Garnett, 29 July 1811, Randolph-Garnett Letterbook, LC.

CHAPTER IX

PRELUDE TO WAR

Duane's obstinate gesture of protest against the power of Albert Gallatin was physically, financially and politically exhausting, and "has left me," he confided to Jefferson, "like a man after a severe disease, with an unusual degree of debility." In peacetime his action might have served as the beginning for a coalition of Northern Democrats which could present a formidable challenge to President Madison. But with the nation at the point of war, Republican unity was essential, and Duane merely isolated himself by his insistent stand upon principle. "I have during these ten years," he lamented, "been in the situation of a man who in a small company saw himself exposed to the vollies of a numerous enemy, and the little band either sinking one by one into the slumber of death or flying into the arms of the enemy"; until at last, he admitted, "I find myself . . . standing almost alone."[1]

He was determined to prepare for a solitary future by getting "out of the power of villains" who controlled his bank loans and then to go on with the *Aurora* as the "occupation for the remainder of my days." For ten years he had found it "impossible to get out of debt with the paper of greatest circulation in the country,"

---

[1]Duane to Jefferson, 17 July 1812, 15 Mar. 1811, TJ-LC.

and because he was never "much of a pecuniary calculator," he had attempted to procure the needed income through schemes which only increased his difficulties. Since his first financial scare, in 1808, he had carried through a prodigious assortment of publishing projects, which demonstrated his amazing energy and wide interests, but which unfortunately merely added to the burden of his large unsaleable book stock.[2]

During this period he edited from European works an introduction to army tactics, entitled The American Military Libary, and issued A Military Dictionary, which was intended as a compendium of elementary useful knowledge. He also completed and issued four volumes of his projected edition of the writings and memoirs of Benjamin Franklin, and published a textbook for adults based upon the course of study in Joseph Neef's school, where his five year old son Edward was a student. The school had introduced the new methods of Johann Pestalozzi to Philadelphia. The most successful of Duane's projects was an American edition of Count Destutt de Tracy's review of Montesquieu's Spirit of the Laws. Thomas Jefferson had asked him to publish it, but found himself collaborating more than he intended, in order to improve the rough translation by the inexperienced young man whom Duane employed. The "review" came out in July 1811, when Duane's financial troubles were at their worst, and luckily he was able to sell all the copies to another dealer. Although they went "for the price of print and

---

[2]Duane to Jefferson, 15 Mar. 1811, 23 Jan. 1809, 17 July 1812, TJ-LC. See also Duane to D. B. Warden, 21 Mar., 6 Apr., 21 July 1811, D. B. Warden Papers, LC.

paper," he was content, since "every *cent* then was in effect as good as a dollar when I did not want the dollar."[3]

After the 1811 affair Duane reversed the direction of his efforts from audacity to austerity. He sensibly decided to abandon his unprofitable ventures into publishing and the book business, and although he had little success in selling his stock even below wholesale prices, he did rid himself of five printing presses, and kept just one, for the *Aurora*. He had to give up the plan suggested by Jefferson to publish "Baxter's Hume," an edition of David Hume's history of England with corrective political commentary by the editor. In April 1812 he finally managed to sell his house and lot on Pennsylvania avenue in Washington to Joseph Gales of the *National Intelligencer*. These sacrifices did not clear off the debts, but they did reduce them sufficiently to relieve the pressure on him.[4]

In Duane's political failure, John Binns saw a unique opportunity for his own advancement and for the *Democratic Press* to rise and replace the *Aurora* in national prestige. "It seems to be neces-

---

[3] *The American Military Library; or, Compendium of the Modern Tactics* . . . , 2 vols. (Philadelphia, 1807-1809); *A Military Dictionary* . . . (Philadelphia, 1810); *An Epitome of the Arts and Sciences* (Philadelphia, 1811); Benjamin Franklin, *The Works of Dr. Benjamin Franklin, in Philosophy, Politics and Morals* . . . , 6 vols. (Philadelphia, 1808-1818); [Antoine L. C. Destutt de Tracy], *Commentary and Review of Montesquieu's Spirit of the Laws* . . . (Philadelphia, 1811); Duane to Jefferson, 17 Aug., 29 Oct. 1810, 25 Jan., 15 Mar., 5 July 1811, 14 Feb. 1813, TJ-LC; Jefferson to Duane, 12 Aug., 13 Nov. 1810, 18 Jan., 28 Mar., 25 July 1811, 22 Jan. 1813, TJ-LC.

[4] Duane to Jefferson, 17 Aug. 1810, 17 July 1812, 14 Feb. 1813, 11 Aug. 1814, TJ-LC; Jefferson to Duane, 12 Aug. 1810, TJ-LC; Duane to Monroe, 6 Feb. 1825, Monroe Papers, NYPL.

sary that he should be thought as great a man as the other," Edward Fox commented with disgust when Binns in 1812 secured a meaningless state commission as an aide to his friend Governor Snyder. He "never would have thought of Military honours," Fox was certain, if "Duane had not been appointed a Lt. Colonel" by Jefferson. "But I suspect," he commented wisely, "that Binns and Duane have very different dispositions. Duane appears not to have any idea of the value of property; I believe Binns is very well convinced that it is 'the one thing needful.'"[5]

The Democratic Press had not established a reputation in Washington as a newspaper of national stature, although "As the paper of our state it is caught up as all in all here." Binns' personal advocates in the capital, it was admitted, "have been among men rather silent or at least retired in their habits, moving in limited circles only," and "have been no match" for Duane's friends and other detractors. But after Richard Rush went to Washington as Comptroller of the Treasury, Binns stood an excellent chance to obtain the sponsorship of Albert Gallatin.[6]

Binns had never met the Secretary, but during the cabinet crisis of 1811 he risked an obsequious letter of self-introduction. Writing carefully in his ill-educated hand, he struggled for the polite tone appropriate for a cabinet minister, but blundered as he warmed to accusations against Frederick Wolbert, "one of the humble

---

[5]Fox to Jonathan Roberts, 2 June 1812, Roberts Papers, HSP.

[6]Richard Rush to Charles Jared Ingersoll, 11, 26 Feb. 1812, Ingersoll Collection, HSP.

toad-eaters, excuse the expression Sir, of D[r]. Leib." In his hatred of Duane, the fastidious Gallatin was ready to unite even with Binns, and to offer federal patronage if it would help the *Press* to supplant the *Aurora*. Gallatin was "not a man to lose sight of such an object when once he entertains it," and Binns soon received his first small printing contract from the Treasury department.[7]

A political union of Gallatin and Binns was the ultimate in Quadroonship, by the Old School's definition, but the vulgar journalist had the indispensable aid of two gentleman Democrats, Charles Jared Ingersoll, who wrote all the national news for him, and Richard Rush, who was his inspired advocate in Washington. When Rush became Comptroller, Gallatin was "as friendly as can be and shakes assent to all I say," he reported to his cohorts. "Sure, perfectly sure I am," he told Ingersoll, "that he is the explicit advocate, understandingly as well as at all times and zealously, of the democracy *of our state* in all its *strength and soundness*"; that is, of Governor Snyder and his administration. "Go to our chestnut street friend [Binns]," Rush commanded, "and, together, make your own prudent use of this."[8]

Rush's appointment in 1811 to the second highest federal office held by a Pennsylvanian enhanced the growing prestige of the New School Democrats. Moreover in his advice on appointments and military commissions, he promoted his party's advantage with ingenu-

---

[7]Binns to Gallatin, 27 Apr. 1811, Gallatin Papers, NYHS; Rush to Ingersoll, 9 June 1812, Ingersoll Collection, HSP.

[8]Rush to Ingersoll, 26, 28 Feb. 1812, *ibid*.

ous enthusiasm. His Federalist father, Dr. Benjamin Rush, implored him to come home and abandon the insecure life of a politician, but he replied, "Is my own decided, constant, daily, hourly, happiness to go for nothing in the scale against Philadelphia, Philadelphia, Philadelphia?" Rush maintained a strict standard of political qualification in recommending appointment to office, in spite of the embarrassment of aristocratic friends seeking preferment, his father's censure, and sentimental lapses by Charles Ingersoll. He hoped particularly to improve the New School's standing in the crucial Northern Liberties, and for that reason urged a major appointment for William White, an impecunious preacher who had forsaken the pulpit for politics. His father was scandalized, but he insisted that "Parson White of Walnut Street," the Bishop of the Episcopal church and a family friend, "is not a better man than parson White of the northern liberties."[9]

Rush assiduously promoted the interests of the Democratic Press, which he was certain could attain a prominent national reputation during the coming war with Britain. "Its centrality--being lord of the ascendant at such a centre, and at such a time, will be ever broadening its claims to . . . [federal patronage] and every other kind of distinction." Binns jealously believed that "the Aurora is in favor of Washington. Indeed it is not so," Rush insisted. "There are an hundred reasons why it will continue to be

---

[9]Rush to Benjamin Rush, 4, 6 June 1812, Rush Papers, Lib. Co. of Phila. See also Rush to Benjamin Rush, 11, 16 May 1812, ibid.; Rush to [John Binns], 9 July 1812, Gratz Collection, HSP; Rush to Ingersoll, 20, 26 Apr., 15 June 1812, 17 Jan., 2 Sept., 19 Oct., 9, 10, 11, 14, 18 Nov. 1813, Ingersoll Collection, HSP.

read; but by the great bulk of our party, it is thought of here just as it is in Pennsylvania."[10]

II

Duane of course keenly regretted the attrition of his political influence, for he was as gregarious as he was intractable, and had a fondness for involvement in vital affairs which it now appeared would be permanently frustrated by his break with the Madison administration. To him public service was the standard for judging a man's life. In the approaching war with England, he hoped to redeem himself and to perform a service to his country which would be welcomed at last. He threw himself into the war effort with frenzied dedication, although "I presume since I have been considered in the opposition," he complained, "it would not be consistent with affairs of state to give the writings of a suspected heretic in politics any countenance in war." Duane was sometimes an amusing figure in a ludicrous war, but on the whole his notions can be exonerated more readily than can the war itself.[11]

After the Chesapeake crisis of July 1807, Duane began to study the art of war intensively, with the goal of broadening the public's knowledge. He had been collecting European books on military theory, and had permission from Secretary of War Henry Dearborn to use the War Office library. He intended to cull the essence of foreign military lore, chiefly French, for the instruc-

---

[10] Rush to Ingersoll, 6 June, 26 Apr. 1812, ibid. See also Rush to Ingersoll, 1, 11, 26 Feb., 9 June, 5 Dec. 1812, ibid.

[11] Duane to Jefferson, 17 July 1812, TJ-LC.

tion of a civilian republic, and among his first efforts was the translation and abridgment of the works on tactics by the great French theorist Count Guibert. "I have conversed much with General Wilkinson on the subject," Duane told Jefferson at the outset of the project, "and meet his ideas as far as I was competent to discourse with a man of practical experience."[12]

Duane's chief interest in military studies was the problem of training and discipline, because he understood and enjoyed the leadership of men. The frequent drills and parades of the Philadelphia Legion had made it a unit vastly superior to the ordinary militia. Duane had introduced the plan of expanding the training to include actual battle maneuvers, upon the principle that experience would conquer fear. Unfortunately the Legion had been destroyed by its internal political dissension, and among non-Democrats the "volunteer system" had "fallen into disrepute." When the war started, it was "almost in vain" in Philadelphia "to attempt to withstand the popular opinion, which was decidedly averse to military parade," according to the Federalist Condy Raguet.[13]

Duane had received some practical military experience as Lieutenant Colonel in charge of a rifle regiment, one of the special units created by Congress in 1808 with temporary appropriations for the period of national emergency. "Not one of the field officers we have appointed know any thing of Duty," General Wilkin-

---

[12]Duane to Jefferson, recvd 5 Dec. 1807, TJ-LC.

[13][Condy Raguet], A Brief Sketch of the Military Operations on the Delaware During the Late War . . . (Philadelphia, 1820), 7.

son confessed to Samuel Smith, "except a Lt Col Whiting of Massachusetts & my friend Duane." In accepting the commission Duane had made it clear that he could not afford to be stationed at any distance from Philadelphia. Consequently Fort Mifflin, the dilapidated, largely abandoned base outside Philadelphia, became the site of his military pursuits.[14]

He increased his own knowledge of the techniques of training and discipline, and personally regarded the results as a model achievement. "The federalists of this city did not like to see such . . . well disciplined elegant and well behaved men as I marched through Phil[a]. the 4th of July last," he boasted to Caesar Rodney in early 1810. These men became "in less than three months taught by me competent to join any army."

But the ambitious scope of Duane's undertaking soon had him in trouble with the War department. As highest ranking officer attached to Fort Mifflin, Duane took upon himself full responsibility for the command and included in his program of strenuous drill the existing garrison of regulars, an artillery company, as well as his own enlisted regiment. Anticipating a need for Fort Mifflin in case of war, he planned capital improvements of its wretched facilities, and began on his projects before funds had been authorized. The War department, overwhelmed by Duane's unmilitary and costly display of independence, took action to limit the energetic Colonel's authority.

---

[14]Wilkinson to Samuel Smith, 2 Nov. 1808, James Wilkinson Papers, Darlington Memorial Library, University of Pittsburgh; Duane to Jefferson, 4 Feb. 1809, TJ-LC.

An order of November 7, 1809, restored command of Fort Mifflin to a professional army officer. Colonel Duane, now outranked by a Captain Reed, was enraged by the interference with his program of discipline, and complained that the responsibility returned to an officer who had commanded the garrison for nine years and admitted himself that he had not trained two men who could "sponge a gun." The clumsy manner of communicating the order made it more obnoxious. Instead of notifying Duane formally, the Secretary of War informed him privately through one of his own junior officers. The Secretary presumably thought it would appear less harsh in this manner, but Duane took it as an insulting personal rebuke.

The incident was an example of the notorious timidity of Secretary William Eustis. Dr. Eustis, almost a stranger to Duane, had succeeded Henry Dearborn in the War department when Dearborn chose to retire. Duane refused to forgive Eustis, despite the Secretary's attempts to explain and apologize, and declined to be consoled by assurances that the ruling had not been aimed at him personally. I feel "the more injured," he stubbornly maintained, "because I learn that the order of 7th of November 1809, has been circulated through the army as far as Orleans and Portsmouth." The only acceptable apology would have been a reversal of the order,

> placing me as I ought to be in the full possession of an authority which I never abused, but which under my direction rendered Fort Mifflin what it never was before, and which if I had not been so unkindly checked would have made it still more creditable to the government.

Since such an order was not forthcoming, Duane had resigned his commission before the Fourth of July 1810.[15]

But he continued his study of military discipline. In the spring of 1812 he was approaching completion of the work which was to become the most successful of his military writings. In April that year he went to Washington to arrange for the sale of the last of his property there, and for two weeks enjoyed the sensation of involvement in the fascinating turmoil of preparation for war. In the company of James Wilkinson, he fancied himself at the very center of events. General Wilkinson had recently undergone a long investigation of his past career and associations, but in February 1812 a military court had acquitted him on all charges. He returned to Washington exonerated, and with his position as the nation's highest ranking officer enhanced by the approach of war.[16]

While in Washington in April with access to important persons, Duane printed and circulated a brief pamphlet outlining his views on the proper organization and discipline of the Army, based on his book knowledge of European practice. His friendship with William Giles, the chairman of the House committee on military

---

[15]Duane to Rodney, 29 Mar. 1810, Genl. MSS Collection (Duane), Columbia. See also Duane to Jefferson, 16 July 1810, TJ-LC; Evening Star, 28 July 1810; 18th Congress, 1st session, Letter from the Secretary of War, Transmitting Information Respecting the Original Amount of a Judgment Lately Obtained by the United States, in the District Court of the Eastern District of Pennsylvania, against Colonel William Duane . . . (Washington, 1823), pamphlet, HSP.

[16]Duane to Jefferson, 17 July, 20 Sept. 1812, TJ-LC; Rush to Ingersoll, 20 Apr. 1812, Ingersoll Collection, HSP; Aurora, 1, 3, 5, 12 Jan., 13, 17, 19 June 1811; B[aptis] Irvine to Wilkinson, 28 Feb., 7 Mar., 31 Aug. 1811, James Wilkinson Papers, Chicago Historical Society; C. J. Ingersoll to Wilkinson, 14 Mar. 1812, ibid.; Annals of Cong., 12th Cong., 1st sess., 2125-2137.

affairs, no doubt helped him receive a hearing for his views, and according to him the memorandum produced an "extraordinary effect . . . on men's minds." He claimed a personal victory when Congress enacted on June 26 "a law correcting almost every thing pointed out as to the organization." Undoubtedly the provision of the act most satisfying to Duane was its final section, which stipulated full integration of the "additional military force" raised by the Act of April 12, 1808, into the regular military establishment. The inferior status imposed by Secretary Eustis in his order of November 1809 was legally eliminated.[17]

In June 1812 Duane's Handbook for Infantry was published, and he sent copies to the House of Representatives and to the various state governors. The House referred the manual to its military committee which simply reported back a recommendation that the President be authorized "to prescribe from time to time, the discipline for the regular troops and militia of the United States." But the resolution was tabled upon its first reading. Governor William Plumer of New Hampshire, who had despised Duane in former days, acknowledged receipt of his "valuable treatises on military discipline" with the gratifying compliment that "Your attention to this important science, merits the consideration & grateful acknowledgment of the public." The state legislature had postponed consideration, but "The only objection stated, was not against the principles or details of the work, but that it was not the same system of

---

[17] Ibid., 2332-2334; Duane to Jefferson, 17 July 1812, TJ-LC.

discipline as established by the United States."[18]

Duane's Handbook for Infantry, which later became official, was intended as a manual for the elementary training of soldiers. Its one hundred pages of drill formations were prefaced by general commentary in which Duane explained that the book was a revised version of the French discipline system of 1791, incorporating the improvements developed, especially by the French in the course of the war in Europe. "All the mystery of military discipline," Duane quoted the great French soldier Count Saxe, "is to be found in the legs, and he who thinks otherwise is a fool." The Handbook followed this precept and excluded or de-emphasized all aspects of training which did not prepare the soldier for battlefield action. Marching, facing and wheeling, the author explained, are the three elements on which "the whole art of military action depends." He recommended that head and shoulder drill and the ceremonial "manual exercise" be postponed until the trainees had mastered the use of their legs. The manual eliminated exercises wholly useless in action such as the "slow step" and the old-fashioned "oblique step," which in practice had been supplanted by use of quarter and half face.

The militia veteran and the late Lieutenant Colonel inserted his own prefatory advice "On the Manner of Conducting Drills." The officer, he commented, should drill his troops personally, in order to learn the "habit of command," and he should be both firm

---

[18] Annals of Cong., 12th Cong., 1st sess., 1566, 1571; Plumer to Duane, 5 Jan. 1813, William Plumer Papers, LC.

and cheerful in demeanour. The secret of good leadership, Duane thought, was in the perfect balance of these antithetical qualities, stumbling neither into autocracy nor into lack of authority. In his reflections Duane exposed his own love of teaching, of the idea of soldiering, and of the values in the relationship between older and younger men.

III.

On June 18, 1812, the United States declared war upon Great Britain in retaliation for the years of violation of American neutral rights. The Aurora, which had always advocated a strong stand against British insults, had argued for many months before that war or submission were the only remaining choices. For Duane, as for other Republicans, it was belated disillusionment with French intentions toward the United States which convinced him that it was imperative to go to war. For more than two years after the repeal of the Embargo, he had expounded his faith that a return to that policy could still rescue the nation's honor. But in 1811 new insults by Napoleon exposed the fraudulence of the promises in the Cadore letter, which had declared an end to commercial depredations. With this Duane concluded that the United States Congress through its timidity and selfishness had dissipated the chance to make effective economic retaliation, and the nation was bereft of an honorable alternative to war.

Duane was profoundly optimistic about the future significance of a victory over Britain. "Such a change as I anticipate," he speculated in a letter to Thomas Jefferson, "will cast upon our shores the riches and the wreck of British intellect, arts, sciences and manufactures." He foresaw a vast immigration to America from England, especially by workers, who would bring their skills and talents with them. The "day is not distant," he predicted, "when all that England had to boast of will cease to exist there and be transferred hither. . . . We are destined to be the residuary legatees of British literature, science, commerce, navigation and perhaps power and policy!"[19]

But America was not prepared for war in 1812, in spite of the long anticipation, and for that reason many who approved the undertaking in principle honestly doubted the capacity of Madison's administration to carry it through. "What is thought amongst you of the Secretary of War and the Aurora?" asked a Philadelphian, worried by the paper's reports of his incompetence. Congressman Jonathan Roberts expressed his frank opinion that Eustis "is a dead weight on our hands. . . . His unfitness is apparrent [sic] to every body but himself & to himself I apprehend it will ever be a secret." But "how he is to be gotten off I know not."[20]

A large minority in the Senate, including both Senators from Pennsylvania, opposed the House of Representatives' declaration of total war and nearly succeeded in blocking the resolution. Michael Leib was a principal floor leader for the delaying maneuvers, which appeared startlingly inconsistent in view of his long

---

[19]Duane to Jefferson, 17 July 1812, TJ-LC.

[20]Edward Fox to Roberts, 13 Jan. 1812, Roberts Papers, HSP; Roberts to Matthew Roberts, 27 Mar. 1812, ibid.

advocacy of a militant policy. "Doctor Leib . . . is opposed to war!! and against England!!!!" Richard Rush sputtered; "a measure he has been labouring for fifteen years!" But it was a presidential election year and "He is as angry with Mr Madison as with governor Snyder, and will be alike hostile to any measure they are known to wish."[21]

In Jonathan Roberts' judgment, Leib was "a devoted Clintonian." But he observed that the Philadelphian was "rather coming" around as he found that "his frowns cannot put down all that displeases him." In the presidential caucus in May, although "his heart is with [DeWitt] Clinton . . . he was forced to attend . . . & vote for Madison or be set down a malcontent without the means of mischief."[22]

As Congress moved toward its decision for war, in Philadelphia "Wagers not a few are laid on Leib's vote," John Binns reported. The Senator voted finally in favor of the declaration, and another Philadelphia commented that he had known that Leib would not oppose the war ultimately. "The great fear was their being able to carry some measure of less force; so that the Clinton faction might have room to come out with the remainder: because," he asserted shrewdly, "it is evident that war was their wish--but not a war by the powers that be. If you had stopped short of what you

---

[21]Rush to Benjamin Rush, 13 June 1812, Rush Papers, Lib. Co. of Phila. See Roger H. Brown, The Republic in Peril: 1812 (New York, 1964), 111-115.

[22]Roberts to Matthew Roberts, 20 June, 20 May 1812, Roberts Papers, HSP.

have done, in even so small a degree," he told Congressman Roberts, "the Clinton's would have come out red hot." As it was "they will now be at some loss," he thought, "for they cannot oppose the measures agreed upon, and I look upon them now as in the back ground completely."[23]

But DeWitt Clinton was not willing to abandon his hopes to defeat Madison, and he allowed his presidential candidacy to become a forum for protest against "Mr. Madison's War." He sought to appeal simultaneously to the Federalists, who opposed any war against England, and those Democrats from the middle states who distrusted Madison and thought that a stronger leader could prosecute the war with more vigor. The state of Pennsylvania was the key to the presidential contest. Madison retained the loyalty of the southern states, while Clinton could depend upon the twenty-nine votes from New York, which had placed him in nomination, and had an excellent chance to sweep Federalist New England. But the northern opposition "cannot (I think) be successful," in Samuel Smith's opinion, "unless Penn[a] should join in it--& I do not believe she will."[24]

Duane and Leib for the second time took opposite views on the presidential candidates. In 1808 Duane had supported Madison and had won over the reluctant Leib, in spite of their mutual affection for the New York patriarch George Clinton. The Vice President

---

[23]Binns to Roberts, 19 June 1812, *ibid.*; Edward Fox to Roberts, 24 June 1812, *ibid.* See also Fox to Roberts, 16 June 1812, *ibid.*; John Randolph to Edward Cunningham, 24 June 1812, John Randolph Papers, LC.

[24]Samuel Smith to John Spear Smith, 13, 18 June 1811, Papers of Samuel Smith, LC.

died in April 1812, and his nephew DeWitt fell heir to the family's political interest. When the Aurora announced a non-partisan meeting to honor the dead Vice President, John Binns "suspecting the motives and the objects . . . took no notice of it in the Press and privately opposed it," with the result, he boasted, that "not 50 people met [,] nothing was done, and every man slunk away as if he had done something he was ashamed of."[25]

Binns was wrong in his accusation that Duane sought to launch a campaign for DeWitt Clinton in Pennsylvania. In spite of his differences with the President upon domestic issues, the editor quickly concluded that the war effort required the incumbent's continuation in office. But he implied his support rather than endorse Madison's administration directly, and concentrated his editorial attention on the problems of the war itself. Consequently much of the public believed that he was working with Michael Leib as a secret manipulator of Clinton's campaign in Pennsylvania.

The Aurora's news reports about military preparation and the early battles were so alarming that they were taken as evidence that Duane wished the defeat of Madison. "Duane's plan," according to Edward Fox, "is to know more, or to seem to know more of army affairs than any other person, printers or any other:--he thinks by this to raise a kind of popularity, and to gain his ground again." Fox acknowledged that "He has many friends among the officers who write him," but personally believed that "he makes free with their

---

[25]Binns to Roberts, 26 Apr. 1812, Roberts Papers, HSP.

letters and fits the publication to his purpose!"[26]

The paper kept up its demand that the President dismiss the inept Secretary of War. "I certainly dreaded the effect of a war under such incompetent hands as D^r. Eustis, and I dread it still," Duane admitted to Jefferson at the outset. A former military surgeon, Eustis had been in peacetime "a pleasant gentlemanly man in society; & the indecision of his character," Jefferson recalled, "rather added to the amenity of his conversation." Duane's friend General Zebulon Pike, who liked Eustis, admitted that "I do not think he was calculated to be at the head of the W[ar] Department at the present day. as a man he was personally firm: as a public officer trembling at every act."[27]

As the Secretary's incapacity became increasingly evident, friends of the administration privately expressed their concern and anxiety and hinted that the presidential election could be adversely affected. "Our friends . ... must do something great and brilliant," warned A. J. Dallas, lest the public conclude that the ability to wage war "does not correspond with the spirit that declared it." Duane himself saw "no probability of any correction but in some fatal disaster when public indignation will force the imbecile man to abandon a station which he ought never to have accepted."[28]

---

[26]Fox to Roberts, 23 Nov. 1812, _ibid_.

[27]Duane to Jefferson, 17 July 1812, TJ-LC; Jefferson to Duane, 1 Oct. 1812, TJ-LC; Pike to C. A. Rodney, 24 Jan. 1813, Charles B. Pike Collection, Chicago Hist. Soc.

[28]G. M. Dallas, _Life of A. J. Dallas_, 128; Duane to Jefferson, 17 July 1812, TJ-LC. See also Rush to Ingersoll, 2 Aug., 9, 18 Sept., 6, 10 Oct. 1812, Ingersoll Collection, HSP.

Madison undoubtedly knew that the War department's blunders jeopardized his chances for re-election, and for the President's sake, if not for the country's, Secretary Eustis should have offered to resign. But this he was not willing to do, at least not before the election, Rush informed Ingersoll, from "obstinancy, or pride, or what you will," and President Madison chose not to force the issue. "To dismiss," Rush explained, "would look like bowing to the Aurora--and therefore probably will, for the present at least, be staved off by the same feelings." Madison's sensitivity to appearance was costly to the nation. The first year of the war was disastrous, and the defeats of 1812 did lasting harm to the war effort.[29]

The hope that the nation could slide safely through the period of the election, with the voters in ignorance of the extent of military bungling, was shattered in August by Brigadier General William Hull's incredible surrender at Detroit without a battle. The blame lay primarily in the ill-conceived and inadequate plan of campaign. Although Duane had been "among those who from the beginning considered this expedition ought never to have been undertaken," his newspaper rallied behind the government. Now "The executive will determine to expel the enemy from the continent," it promised, "and take the measures competent to the event," so that finally "the disaster at Detroit will prove a most fortunate event for the American people."[30]

---

[29] Rush to Ingersoll, 2 Aug. 1812, ibid.

[30] Aurora, 31 Aug., 3 Sept. 1812; Julius W. Pratt, "William Hull," DAB, IX, 364.

Privately Duane offered his sympathy and support to President Madison, and he appended a cheerful postscript on the election campaign in Pennsylvania. The Federalist and Clintonian delegations meeting at Lancaster "have quarreled and separated in ill-blood--without agreeing on any object relative to the . . . Presidential election--a good omen." But on the same day he wrote to Jefferson that "a change in the War Department appears to me indispensable to the public safety and the security of the approaching Election."[31]

Jefferson offered what optimism he could, but the news of Detroit had destroyed his confidence that the United States would easily conquer Canada. The former President was forced to deny the hopeful rumor that he would return to the government as Secretary of State. "I am past service," he told Duane;

> the hand of age is upon me. the decay of bodily faculties apprises me that those of the mind cannot be unimpaired, had I not still better proofs. every year counts by increased debility, and departing faculties keep the score--the last year it was the sight, this it is the hearing, the next something else will be going, until all is gone.

Although Jefferson sympathized with Duane's anxiety about the War department, he counselled him to be patient. "I have so much confidence in the wisdom & conscientious integrity of mr. Madison," he wrote, "as to be satisfied that, however torturing to his feelings, he will fulfill his duty to the public & to his own reputation by making the necessary change." Indeed "he may be preparing it while we are talking about it."[32]

---

[31]Duane to Madison, 20 Sept. 1812, Madison Papers, LC; Duane to Jefferson, 20 Sept. 1812, TJ-LC.

[32]Jefferson to Duane, 4 Aug., 1 Oct. 1812, TJ-LC.

The public morale suffered another shock two weeks before the election. News arrived that the New York militia had refused to cross the state border into Canada to reinforce the troops at the Battle of Queenstown, and the American force was in consequence defeated. Duane, writing to James Monroe, implored the government to use "the occasion . . . to bring the subject to a solemn and decisive issue." A policy of conspicuous and rigorous punishment of the offenders, he thought, "would aid to restore confidence in the army, which I can assure you is very much depressed." Most important it "would give a marked tone of *decision* to the *executive government*."[33]

Although Duane had adopted a forbearing attitude toward Madison, a great many persons blamed the "languour of the war" upon the President's inept leadership. "It is admitted by Mr. Madison's friends that he has no talents for war," one Old School leader asserted, and Secretary Eustis remained in office because of his poor judgment. Therefore let us "permit Mr. Madison to depart in peace, to cultivate his farm," he advised the voters.[34]

In Philadelphia all branches of the Republican party had formally united for the purpose of supporting the war. They nominated a single slate of state and local candidates, in order to prevent a victory by the reviving Federalist party. In spite of continued bickering between the "*two printers*," which would teach "the folly of *spoiling* printers, and making them the leaders (or the

---

[33]Duane to Monroe, 23 Oct. 1812, Monroe Papers, NYPL.

[34]Philadelphia *Whig Chronicle*, "Phocion," 30 Oct. 1812.

drivers, rather) of the party," the party unionists believed that "it never will be in the power of Duane Binns or Leib to divide us again."[35]

The Old School Democrats distrusted the arrangement which allowed the Snyderites to take advantage of their cooperation and make raids upon their membership. Leib's friend George Bartram, the son of John Bartram, the famous botanist, had "thrown a huge somerset into the arms of John Binns, and slap dash he stalked off a commissioner." They feared that other "democrats were about throwing a somerset after the fashion of colonel Bartram, into the embraces of that sweet scented shrub--John Binns." In the Northern Liberties the Old School rebelled and nominated its own slate for state assembly, which rejected four of the six "union" candidates. The official Republican ticket won over the Federalists, but the Old School bolters polled a majority in the northern district.[36]

A local movement in favor of DeWitt Clinton for President was launched immediately following the state election with the appearance of the _Whig Chronicle_. The editor was George Goodman, an official of the Liberties and an officer of Michael Leib's Tammany society. According to rumor, money for the publication came from William Binder, an old Liberties politician and an intimate of Leib and Duane. The paper was dubbed "Michael's Chronicle" by the _Democratic Press_, but Leib remained out of view.[37]

---

[35]Edward Fox to Roberts, 27 May 1812, Roberts Papers, HSP; Thomas Leiper to Madison, 16 Aug. 1812, Madison Papers, LC.

[36]_Whig Chronicle_, 28 Oct. 1812; _Aurora_, 19 Oct. 1812; Higginbotham, _Keystone_, 264-266.

[37]_Ibid._, 268, 372n.

The *Chronicle*, an evening newspaper, apologized for supplementing the morning "AURORA, a paper in talent, principle, and merit, not surpassed, if equalled, in the United States." Its deference went beyond simple flattery, for the paper used Duane's statements as authority for its endorsement of Clinton. The *Aurora* had established beyond doubt, it contended, that two members of the President's cabinet were unacceptable to the American public. The editor promised he would vote for Madison if Albert Gallatin and William Eustis were removed before the election.

The Congressional caucus system of nomination for President, according to Clinton's personal representatives in Pennsylvania, should have been the foremost issue of the national election. Clinton hoped by attacking the caucus to draw together the Democratic factions of the middle states in an expression of resentment against an eliteist Republican Establishment. The *Whig Chronicle* asserted that the choice was between sycophants and "real democrats who have their country's welfare at heart." It ignored the Federalist party's overwhelming support of Clinton's candidacy, and earnestly stated its conviction "that Mr. Clinton is a pure decided and energetic democrat of the good old school."

Unlike Madison, Clinton would prosecute the war with great vigor, the *Chronicle* promised. The objection that "This is Not the Time" for change was a refrain which traditionally had prevented all reforms, the editor argued, and why was the current administration, or the state of Virginia, better qualified to lead in the present time? "Why is Mr. Clinton less fit than Mr. Madison," he demanded. "Is it because he is descended from the Irish and supported by the PATRIOTIC EMMET?"[38]

Probably it was the *Whig Chronicle*'s misuse of his name which forced Duane to make an explicit declaration in favor of Madison one week before the election. He had previously stood aside from the campaign because "it presented to my mind only a choice of difficulties." If in November 1812 war had not yet been declared, Duane disclosed, he would have supported Clinton, but it became the public's duty to support the government once the war was in progress. Moreover Clinton's supporters were "at the most extravagant variance among themselves," he pointed out, and "there must be insincerity or treachery in one of the two classes of his advocates."[39]

Other Old School Democrats who remained loyal to President Madison urged the Northern Liberties men not to revolt from the Republican union. The evening *Star of Liberty*, edited by Britton Evans, former co-editor of the *Evening Star*, began publication in order to challenge the contention that Clinton would be a more forceful war leader. The Federalists claimed that he would bring peace, and "It is a foul cause that must be supported by falsehood and deception." The Old Schoolers of Southwark in a public meeting denounced Clinton as a "*political backslider*" who had defected to the Federalist party.[40]

---

[38]*Whig Chronicle*, 14, 16, 30 Oct. 1812; Higginbotham, *Keystone*, 259-260, 263.

[39]*Aurora*, 24 Oct. 1812. See also *ibid*., 25 Aug., 9, 13, 21, 29, 30 Oct. 1812.

[40]*Ibid*., 29 Oct. 1812; Philadelphia *Star of Liberty*, 3 Nov. 1812.

The state of Pennsylvania, as apprehended, decided the outcome of the presidential contest. DeWitt Clinton carried New England and New York; if in addition he had won Pennsylvania's twenty-five votes, he would have become President by a majority of eleven in the electoral college. The revived Federalist party in the state campaigned strenuously for Clinton and nearly tripled its vote over the election of 1808. Nonetheless his vote in Pennsylvania fell short of Madison's total by 20,000; more than sixty per cent of the voters chose to retain the incumbent President.

In his campaign plans, Clinton had relied upon a Democratic revolt from the administration on domestic issues, but no revolt materialized. The Federalists were strong in Philadelphia, but a unified Republican effort produced a local triumph for the President. Even in the Northern Liberties, there was no Democratic division to mar the victory. James Madison received more than 1600 votes in the district, which represented the combined strength of the Old School and the New School Democrats, while Clinton received only 726 votes there, less than the total potential vote of the Federalist residents.[41]

The Old School party needed to relieve the tensions among its members created during the presidential campaign. The Philadelphia returns demonstrated that "the democrats are invincible," according to the _Evening Star_, but the outcome did not prove DeWitt Clinton no Democrat, the _Whig Chronicle_ insisted. However the latter urged the public to rally behind the majority choice, and Evans'

---

[41]Higginbotham, _Keystone_, 176, 268; _Aurora_, 19 Oct., 4 Nov., 1812.

Star placed the entire blame for the Clintonian movement upon the guile of the Federalist party. Some of Clinton's "warmest and most affectionate disciples denounce his nomination," it revealed, "as being impolitic and replete with distrust and ill success. What confidence can be placed in a faction whose principal intentions are to divide and destroy the interests, union and welfare of the country?" Both of the Old School evening papers stopped publication soon after the election.[42]

The rivalry of the Chronicle and the Star had spoken of course for the conflicting views of the Old School's principal leaders. It was the first serious difference between Duane and Leib in a decade of close cooperation in politics. The result in part was a triumph for Duane's leadership; certainly if the Aurora had supported the Clinton movement, the party's role in the election would have been quite different. But primarily the party members themselves wanted to express their support for the war against England, and could not be distracted by the introduction of extraneous issues. Duane and Leib did not quarrel over their differences, but they were no longer in complete harmony, and after the opening of Congress, they did not write to or see one another for more than a year.[43]

IV.

Secretary Eustis resigned from the War department in Decem-

---

[42] Whig Chronicle, 2, 4, 9 Nov., 23 Dec. 1812; Star of Liberty, 5, 14 Nov. 1812; The Tickler, 10 Nov. 1813.

[43] Duane to Madison, 22 Jan. 1814, Madison Papers, LC.

ber after the President was safely re-elected. Although his departure had been inevitable, his successor was not yet selected, and there was a further two months delay because of the difficulty of finding a candidate willing to accept the position. Secretary of State Monroe had helped direct the department for several months before the resignation, but Monroe refused to accept a permanent appointment. Henry Dearborn and William H. Crawford also refused, in succession. The President and Secretary Gallatin were reduced to discussing the relative merits of two New Yorkers, Governor Daniel Tompkins and General John Armstrong. Madison disliked Armstrong, but Gallatin greatly preferred him to Tompkins, who had no military experience, and the President therefore reluctantly appointed him to be the new Secretary of War.[44]

The public on the whole welcomed the appointment of Armstrong, because it had faith in his military competence. General Pike, writing from the Canadian front where he was killed soon after, highly approved the selection. "Gen[l] Armstrong . . . is in my estimation," he told Caesar Rodney, "one of two men who comes within my knowledge of all America the most proper for that appointment. The other is Wilkinson." Pike knew that the dislike and distrust of Armstrong was because of his authorship in 1783 of the infamous "Newburgh Letters." "Grant that he wrote them," Pike observed philosophically: "This act is like the original Sin, expiated by long faithful and important Services." General Pike thought he saw a political advantage in the appointment of Armstrong because his

---

[44]Brant, Madison, VI, 126-129.

"age and future prospects preclude any visionary schemes of Greatness." But James Monroe, from the moment that Armstrong accepted the cabinet post which he had refused, regarded him as a rival for the presidential nomination in 1816.[45]

John Armstrong had barely taken office in Washington when he appointed William Duane as Adjutant General of the fourth military district. "Of all extraordinary things that is the most extraordinary," averred Richard Rush. The decision apparently had been as secret as it was sudden, and Rush first heard news of it from Binns in Philadelphia. "Although on the spot I assure you, and it seems strange," he replied, "I have not yet heard a breath of it at Washington. I saw all the great folks at the drawing-room on Wednesday, but heard no syllable of it."[46]

Duane and Armstrong were only slightly acquainted, but they had a bond in their mutual friendship with General Wilkinson. Michael Leib was "warmly attached to Gen. Armstrong in politics," and the Aurora had been friendly to the controversial New Yorker when he returned from France in 1810 and was criticized for his conduct as the American Ambassador. Armstrong then had been suspected of harboring presidential ambitions, for he had claims to "favorite son" support from the two largest states in the union. He had moved from his native Pennsylvania to New York when he

---

[45]Zebulon Pike to C. A. Rodney, 24 Jan. 1813, C. B. Pike Collection, Chicago Hist. Soc.; Henry Adams, History of the United States, 9 vols. (New York, 1889-1891), VI, 426-428.

[46]Rush to Ingersoll, 20 Mar. 1813, Ingersoll Collection, HSP.

married the sister of Robert R. Livingston. But if Armstrong hoped by appointing Duane to renew his ties with Pennsylvania, he showed poor political judgment. In 1804 when he left for France, the editor had been the state's most influential Democrat, and after his return he apparently failed to comprehend the radical change in Duane's status.[47]

The commission of Duane created such intense resentment among important Pennsylvanians that General Armstrong was abashed and attempted to rectify his mistake by the use of polite deception. Charles Ingersoll, who had arrived in Washington as a new member of Congress, interviewed him on the subject, and the Secretary disavowed personal responsibility for the choice. Ingersoll was willing to accept his explanation, but Binns was not so easily reconciled. "I am led to believe that he has not dealt candidly with you," Binns retorted. "I am quite certain, I speak from personal knowledge, that Gallatin never did in any way, manner or form, acquiesce in Duane's appointment. He never knew of it until it was announced." Binns grudgingly promised to "try to agree with you, for the present at least, in thinking that Armstrong has been partially misled."

Armstrong next attempted to improve on his vague story that

---

[47]Duane to D. B. Warden, 24 Aug. 1809, 6 Apr., 21 July 1811, n.d.[1811?], D. B. Warden Papers, LC; Duane to Jefferson, 25 Jan. 1811, TJ-LC; Henry Dearborn to Jefferson, 14 Apr. 1811, TJ-LC; Jefferson to Madison, 24 Apr. 1811, TJ-LC; Duane to C. A. Rodney, 29 Mar. 1810, Genl. MSS Collection (Duane), Columbia; [Senator] John Smith to Gallatin, 15 Apr. 1811, Gallatin Papers, NYHS; Evening Star, 8 Dec. 1810; Aurora, 21, 29 Mar., 15 May 1811, 22 Aug. 1812; Brant, Madison, VI, 203.

he had acted on the advice of other officials, and declared that Duane had been appointed at the request of the Commander of the fourth military district, General Joseph Bloomfield. This explanation Binns happened to know was untrue, because he had been the first person to inform Bloomfield of the appointment. He would be more willing to trust the new Secretary of War, Binns maintained, if Armstrong would simply acknowledge that he had appointed Duane "from personal attachment or a conviction of his ability or any other honest motive."[48]

General Armstrong was burdened by the acquisition of Duane's enemies, but Duane himself ultimately suffered by association with Armstrong. Ironically, he had intently hoped that Monroe would head the War department, while Richard Rush, who became a trusted companion of the future President, had supported Armstrong's appointment.[49]

Undoubtedly the person who suffered most because of Duane's military appointment was Secretary of the Treasury Gallatin. His recommendation had made Armstrong the Secretary, yet Armstrong "smote" him "in the onset of . . . patronage." Gallatin's distress with the appointment, together with his discouragement about financing the war, caused him to leave Washington in voluntary exile. He

---

[48]Binns to Ingersoll, 31 May, 19 June 1813, Ingersoll Collection, HSP. See also Binns to Ingersoll, 9, 14 June, 11, 13 July 1813, _ibid_.

[49]Duane to Madison, 20 Sept. 1812, Madison Papers, LC; Duane to Jefferson, 20 Sept. 1812, TJ-LC; Jefferson to Duane, 1 Oct. 1812, TJ-LC; Rush to Ingersoll, 1 Dec. 1812, Ingersoll Collection, HSP.

elected to serve in the delegation to Russia, which would attempt to arrange for the Czar's mediation of the war. Gallatin realized that his diplomatic mission would mean the appointment of a new Secretary of the Treasury, and his own retirement to private life, but he did not mind, he confided to his brother-in-law James Nicholson. "I will acknowledge to you that Duane's late appointment has disgusted me so far as to make me desirous of not being any longer associated with those who have appointed him." A. J. Dallas was outraged by the treatment of his friend, "Degraded and disgraced, in the face of the world, by the machinations of his Enemies, and the *delicacy* of his Friends."[50]

Albert Gallatin chose to end a long and distinguished public career, in which he had served as chief adviser to two Presidents, because of a personal feud with a newspaper editor. His resentment of the Philadelphia *Aurora* had increased immeasurably as a result of its harsh criticism of his policy on the United States Bank, and he had successfully retaliated against Duane then by causing the removal of Secretary of State Robert Smith. During that public controversy Dallas had cautioned him that, since "a newspaper government is the most execrable of all things," he should "think less of the denunciations of Duane and of the blandishments of Binns." But the normally cool and rational Gallatin had lost control of his feelings where the *Aurora* editor was concerned. In 1813 when Armstrong was being considered to head the War department,

---

[50]Dallas to William Jones, 22 July, 2 Aug. 1813, Uselma Clarke Smith Collection, HSP; Gallatin to Nicholson, 5 May 1813, Gallatin Papers, NYHS.

the President had objected that he had a difficult personality. Gallatin had replied that any trouble which the Secretary of War could create would be most felt by the Treasury department, and he was prepared to cope with it. When it developed that the trouble was not administrative or financial but personal, Gallatin preferred to abandon his career rather than serve in the same cabinet with an associate of William Duane.[51]

---

[51]Dallas to Gallatin, 24 July 1811, quoted in Adams, Life of Albert Gallatin, 442; Brant, Madison, VI, 127.

CHAPTER X

ADJUTANT GENERAL DUANE

On March 24, 1813, Duane received his commission as a United States Army Colonel and the assignment as Adjutant General of the fourth district. He confided the news to his friend Allan McLane, the Collector at Wilmington. "I suppose I shall have to put on a blue coat," he wrote, elated at the opportunity for military service; "it would suit my domestic affairs better to stay where I am, but none of us can live above a thousand years and a half." The fourth district's responsibility was the protection of the Delaware river region, including especially the cities of Philadelphia and Wilmington. Since its headquarters was Philadelphia, Duane did not have to leave the city, but he turned over the _Aurora_ to his Irish protege James Wilson, who continued as editor for the duration of the war.[1]

The War department also announced in March that Duane's _Handbook for Infantry_ "will be received and observed as the system of Infantry discipline for the Army of the U.S." Just "as Gibbon, the Captain of Hampshire Militia, says he was useful to Gibbon, the historian of the Roman empire," John Quincy Adams commented sarcastically, "so Duane, the Colonel, was a useful auxiliary to

[1]Duane to McLane, 3 Mar. 1813, Allan McLane Papers, NYHS.

Duane, the printer, for fleecing the public by palming upon the army, at extravagant prices, a worthless compilation upon military discipline that he had published."[2]

Former President Adams was equally indignant at the editor's return to favor. "Duane is a general, and more than a General," he objected, because he had the ear of Secretary of War Armstrong. "'Forgotten Pensilvania!!,'" Adams exploded, when Richard Rush complained of his state's lack of patronage; "will you say, Gallatin Armstrong, Duane, are not Pensilvanians? Armstrong was born in Pensilvania . . . Gallatin and Duane have been created and preserved and most bountifully rewarded and most sedulously promoted by Pensilvania."[3]

Duane's role in the war, as a person in a position of confidence, depended upon the military fortunes of his patron General Wilkinson. "For God's sake tell me," Wilkinson had written earlier, "am I not to be permitted to have a dash at John Bull?" He and Armstrong had been friends since the Revolution, when they served together under General Horatio Gates, and Duane expected that the Secretary would give him the opportunity to show his military genius. The war was going badly on both the Western and the northern fronts, "but things by land will now be under better auspices--," Duane was confident, "and I look forward with a recruited spirit."[4]

---

[2]The (Philadelphia) Wanderer, 24 Mar. 1813; J. Q. Adams, Memoirs, IV (12 May 1820), 112.

[3]Adams to Rush, 6 Sept. 1813, J. H. Powell, ed., "Some Unpublished Correspondence of John Adams and Richard Rush, 1811-1816," Pa. Mag. of Hist. and Biog., LX (Oct. 1936), 448.

[4]Duane to McLane, 5 Feb. 1813, McLane Papers, NYHS.

He thrust himself into his own military duties with an enthusiasm which easily exceeded his responsibilities. As Adjutant General, he was the chief administrative aide to the commanding general of the district, General Joseph Bloomfield. Bloomfield was a Revolutionary veteran and the former Governor of New Jersey, but aging and "content to stay near home," according to Charles Ingersoll. Duane thought that he was not competent to serve in action, "independent of the effects of age which is already dotage." Duane and Bloomfield had a cordial relationship, but Duane was eager for organizational reforms which would create a more efficient army, and he felt frustrated by the General's conservatism and lack of vigor. He "has not the remotest idea of modern principles," complained the Adjutant, "nor of that distribution of the duties which renders ten thousand men as manageable as one."[5]

Duane himself acted with his customary amazing energy, and took all the initiative that his situation permitted. The circumstance of war unfortunately encouraged his natural tendency to extravagance. At his own expense, he ordered the construction of a magnificent mahogany bureau for the Adjutant General's office, which cost two hundred dollars for "the workmanship alone for journeyman's wages." Its two dozendrawers secured with multiple locks could contain many more secrets of war than Colonel Duane was likely to find in his possession.[6]

---

[5]Charles J. Ingersoll, _Historical Sketch of the Second War Between the United States of America, and Great Britain_ . . . , 2 vols. (Philadelphia, 1849), I, 100; Duane to Jefferson, 26 Sept. 1813, TJ-LC.

[6]Duane to Daniel Parker, 8 Oct. 1819, Daniel Parker Papers, HSP.

Both privately and officially Duane sought to help Robert Fulton promote the acceptance of his new weapon, the torpedo. The editor had met Fulton after he returned to the United States and in 1810 demonstrated his invention to American officials. The naval authorities had opposed the development of the weapon, but Fulton kept working with a coterie of civilian enthusiasts, including Duane, who had conducted a torpedo experiment at Fort Mifflin while still a Lieutenant Colonel. Some members of Fulton's band had participated in Aaron Burr's conspiracy, which was distasteful to Duane, who resented their hatred of Wilkinson for exposing them.[7]

Fulton's torpedo was not a propelled weapon, but a floating mine loaded with gunpowder which exploded upon impact. The inventor had developed a submarine, the *Nautilus*, anticipating its use to plant his "clockwork torpedoes," or time bombs, under the hull of a ship. But he used surface boats in the practical development of the weapon. In his plan, a boatman would fire a harpoon into the bow of a ship at anchor, and a torpedo attached by lines would float under the hull and explode when the set time had elapsed.[8]

Duane may have helped to organize a company of volunteers to conduct torpedo raids on British ships in the Delaware river. Soon after receiving his commission, he instructed Colonel McLane,

---

[7]Francis F. Beirne, *The War of 1812* (New York, 1949), 196-198; *The Tickler*, 14 March 1810; Duane to McLane, 6 Feb. 1814, McLane Papers, NYHS. See also Duane to D. B. Warden, 29 May, 21 July 1811, D. B. Warden Papers, LC.

[8]Benson J. Lossing, *The Pictorial Field Book of the War of 1812* (New York, 1868), 236-242; William B. Parson, *Robert Fulton and the Submarine* (New York, 1922), 151-153.

who had been placed in command of the defense of Wilmington, to "secure means of exact information to be had daily or at shorter periods if possible of the _number_--and _sales_--and positions of the enemy . . . ships of war in the waters of the Delaware, so that I may be constantly apprized thereof." Duane met McLane a few days later aboard the Delaware revenue cutter off Fort Mifflin to discuss the confidential project. As the plan moved along swiftly, he became concerned "to secure some situation as retired as possible and as close to the scene of action for 18 or twenty men--hardy rough seamen--who with clean wholesome food can live anywhere." But Duane's exhilaration at the prospect of torpedo warfare on the Delaware was premature. The river was not a major channel for enemy ships, and if a marine unit did actually operate there, it never achieved a position of significance in the war.[9]

The chief hope of Fulton's supporters was to see the torpedo introduced in the defense of Chesapeake Bay, where its effectiveness could adequately be demonstrated. In February 1813 Duane appealed to Governor James Barbour of Virginia to authorize the creation of marine units on the Chesapeake as a state military project. There must be a large number of experienced men "_along shore_ on your waters who would embark for a small monthly pay in these _guarda costas_," Duane argued. Fulton would supply "the machines," which he had ready for use, and would send a trained man to handle the equipment. Duane was certain that the national government would

---

[9]Duane to McLane, 3, 10 Apr. 1813, McLane Papers, NYHS; Alfred T. Mahan, _Sea Power in Its Relations to the War of 1812_, 2 vols. (Boston, 1905), II, 158-159.

assume the entire expense of the project once the weapon had been demonstrated in action by some "gallant Virginians." Meanwhile it should be kept a secret, he cautioned, because of the danger of spies and because the "honor to the state would also be more decisive." But the Governor of Virginia did not respond to the appeal by Duane, who had also sent a message of encouragement from Fulton.[10]

The importance of submarine warfare was in fact never demonstrated during the War of 1812. The occasional attacks with Fulton's torpedoes, led by volunteers or amateurs, were of slight military significance and did not effect a change in United States Navy policy. The incidents of damage to British ships by underwater explosion led to protests against the torpedo as an instrument of barbarous warfare. The American peace party joined the British in condemning the weapon, but the _Aurora_ replied, what was the difference between the use of artillery "under air" and "under water?" Privately Duane blamed the national administration for its failure to recognize the significance of the weapon in a war for freedom of the seas against the world's supreme naval power.[11]

Philadelphia was in a state of public alarm in March 1813 when Duane assumed his commission as Adjutant General. There were numerous reports of British ships sailing on the recently thawed Delaware river, and the city was wholly without protection since

---

[10]Duane to Barbour, 24 Feb., 10 Mar. 1813, James Barbour Papers, NYPL. See also Robert Fulton, autograph memorandum entitled "Details for using the Torpedoes," 5 Aug. 1813, Pierpont Morgan Library, New York.

[11]Beirne, _War of 1812_, 196-198.

the few United States troops stationed at Fort Mifflin had been ordered to the northern front. Duane wrote to Secretary Armstrong with several proposals for defending the city, but the harried Secretary was not sympathetic. The fears in Philadelphia, he advised coolly, "do not I think, grow out of as comprehensive a view of what the enemy wish to do and can do, as might have been expected." He agreed to request the Governor of Pennsylvania to call up one thousand militiamen to active service, but the measure was "a mere soporific to quiet the present spasms of the city," he admitted. "With the exception of those renowned places, Sag Harbor, New Beford, &c., no place has made so much noise as Philadelphia," complained the Secretary. "Pour a little oil on the waves of folly and of faction, for the latter are at the bottom."[12]

By late April it was clear that the crisis was false, and there was time to plan for the permanent defense of Philadelphia. The best defense would have been the fortification of a particular island in the Delaware located several miles below Wilmington. It was commonly known as the Pea Patch, in honor of its swampy fecundity, but it was strategically situated for the resistance of entry up river, at a point where the river simultaneously narrowed and made a sharp bend. In April Duane and Allan McLane toured the area with General Bloomfield, and plotted a rough survey of the fortifications needed on the island and along the adjoining shores. The city council of Philadelphia agreed without hesitation to appropri-

---

[12]Armstrong to Duane, 21 Mar. 1813, in Scharf and Westcott, Hist. of Phila., I, 563n.

ate 20,000 dollars for the works on the Pea Patch. But when a full study was made by a Captain of the Army Engineers, the complete cost was estimated at 65,000 dollars. The project suffered an indefinite delay while the Philadelphians waited for the citizens of Delaware to contribute to the financing.[13]

As months passed and nothing was accomplished, Duane began to goad Allan McLane to force some action from the people of Wilmington. "What are the people below about," he asked. "Now is the time to move upon the Peapatch." If the fort were constructed, Duane claimed, "Delaware State would become of double consequence--and the commerce and navigation of the Delaware become five fold--and it would become an important naval port." But the fortifications had not yet begun when the next spring thaw was approaching. With "no time to be lost." Duane "proposed sending all deserters there to work on erection of the work," and boasted that with two hundred men "I could run up a noble work in four weeks," and "keep them well fed and well worked and they would be out of the range of whiskey and become healthy men also." But here "every thing goes by intrigue," he lamented, "and I fear nothing will be done."[14]

Philadelphia was given "Some sense of protection" in the autumn of 1813 when the 32nd regiment of Pennsylvania militia was stationed near Derby, six and a half miles south of the city. A

---

[13]David B. Tyler, The Bay & River Delaware, A Pictorial History (Cambridge, Md., 1955), 95, 111, map, frontispiece; Duane to McLane, 24 Mar., 10 Apr., 29 June 1813, McLane Papers, NYHS.

[14]Duane to McLane, 11 Jan., 15 Feb. 1814, ibid. See also Duane to McLane, 6 Feb. 1814, ibid.

troop of "dismounted cavalry" and an artillery company with two field pieces were attached to the infantry regiment by the Adjutant General. The commander of the regiment was Colonel Samuel E. Fotterall, a veteran of the defunct Militia Legion, who had been much respected among officers of that political corps for his military proficiency. Most of the officers were Old School Democrats, and the regiment named its bivouac "Camp Duane."

Duane was delighted by the opportunity to direct their training. In evolution of the line, he boasted,"they are preferable to any Regiment in the Service without exception," and in camp they would "learn the firings, and the method of preparing ammunition and the preservation of it and their arms." If any enemy movement should occur in the area, he would "give the troops an idea of rapid movement in actual service." Some Federalist disbelievers taunted the "great tactician" for his fantasies of heroism. They expected him to ask Madison "to confer the rank of Commander in Chief on his wise head. Lord what a splutter he would make in Canada."[15]

That winter General Wilkinson was to command a northern invasion directed at Montreal. Duane followed his progress with devotion and related his information to Allan McLane, who was an old friend of the General. Wilkinson was a soldier "that you and I would love to see and be near," he commented regretfully, but "the fates ordain otherwise and we must do as well as we can where it

---

[15]Scharf and Westcott, Hist. of Phila., I, 566; Duane to McLane, 4 Oct. 1813, McLane Papers, NYHS; Philadelphia Voice of the Nation, 16 Dec. 1813.

has been ordered that we should be." Although Duane saw his hero as "something like a man of business," who "does not linger on the road while duty calls him to action," Wilkinson took five months to proceed from New Orleans to the Canadian border. He was widely reported to be marching northward from dinner party to dinner party, but Duane suspected that the delay was caused by intrigue. "Wilkinson's orders were dispatched on the 4th March from Washington," he told McLane. "Somehow, it was the 9th May before they reached Orleans!"[16]

Wilkinson became ill when he arrived at Sackett's Harbor, and the campaign was delayed further. He had made a secret night mission to Fort George, and the resulting "fatigue of 67 hours laid him up for three days," but "he was recovering and at work in his tent," Duane reported. In November the campaign was again set back by a violent, damaging storm, and Wilkinson himself "was confined to his pallet the whole time." But when the troops were resupplied and the General "had recovered health and no less of Spirit," the movement on Montreal was at last underway. "We shall have a very popular war the moment Wilkinson's despatch arrives," Duane was certain.[17]

Instead the news arrived that the long delayed campaign had collapsed without a battle. According to Wilkinson, the cause of

---

[16]Duane to McLane, 4 Oct., 29 June 1813, McLane Papers, NYHS; James Ripley Jacobs, Tarnished Warrior: Major-General James Wilkinson (New York, 1938), 284-286; McLane to Wilkinson, 25 Mar. 1812, Wilkinson Papers, Chicago Hist. Soc.

[17]Duane to McLane, 4 Oct., 19 Nov. 1813, McLane Papers, NYHS.

the debacle was the insubordinate conduct of General Wade Hampton. "Wilkinson ordered Hampton to join him at a point designated for a union of force and joint attack on Montreal," Duane explained in a "Private and Sacred" letter to Allan McLane. "Hampton replied that he did not approve of that point and went off another way-- The force of W alone must have been sacrificed had he gone, he halted, and found Hampton actually in winter Quarters! I need not say more."[18]

Duane's distraction over "the unhappy state of things northwardly" was relieved some weeks later when he heard from Wilkinson. Writing "with his own pen and a good stiff neat hand," he answered Duane that he was "getting better and in excellent spirits--full of confidence." But Wilkinson's superiors in Washington were not. Secretary Armstrong, the chief supporter of the long controversial general, reacted bitterly to his failure as a betrayal of trust. "The effort which has been secretly in motion," Duane told McLane, "has been to set Armstrong & Wilkinson at variance, and make them destroy each other." In the past "the lure has been seen and it has failed," he added, but now Armstrong would be lucky if he "escapes the toils laid for him."[19]

In January Duane saw Morgan Lewis when he passed through Philadelphia, and Major General Lewis, who was Armstrong's brother-in-law and an old friend of Wilkinson, told him "openly and unreservedly, that it was determined at Washington to destroy Wilkinson

---

[18]Duane to McLane, 27 Nov. 1813, <u>ibid</u>.

[19]Duane to McLane, 27 Nov. 1813, 11 Jan. 1814, <u>ibid</u>.

--Who had determined it--or how it was to be done--or for what crime," Duane observed sourly, "he did not say nor give me any light to see through. It is an enigma in an enigmatical period." But within weeks the thing was accomplished. "Wilkinson's army (by order) has been divided," Duane bleakly informed Colonel McLane in February; "one half sent to Sackets Harbor[,] the other to Plattsburg--and what is contemplated God alone knows for I do not nor can hear of any who does." His worst fear was that "they are all <u>full of peace</u>."[20]

The break between Armstrong and Wilkinson terminated Duane's friendly association with the War department. He wanted to stay out of the quarrel, but he would not sacrifice his friendship with Wilkinson to satisfy the angry Secretary. "I do not know that you are aware of a change of disposition toward me," he wrote to warn a friend on the staff of the War department, assuring him that he would expect no further accommodation "should there be the least probability of its proving unpleasant to you."[21]

II.

Simultaneously with Wilkinson's fall from favor, Duane's role as Adjutant General was further compromised by a domestic political conflict. An untimely vacancy in a major patronage position broke the tenuous harmony of the Republicans in Philadelphia. Postmaster Samuel Patton died at the beginning of January 1814, and A. J.

---

[20]Duane to Daniel Parker, 24 Jan. 1814, Parker Papers, HSP; Duane to McLane, 15 Feb. 1814, McLane Papers, HSP.

[21]Duane to Parker, 29 Mar. 1814, Parker Papers, HSP.

Dallas immediately informed his good friend William Jones, Gallatin's successor as Secretary of the Treasury, that his son-in-law Richard Bache, Jr., "will be a candidate, I find, to succeed him." The next day he wrote again in alarm to report the rumor that Gideon Granger, the Postmaster General, had promised the office to Senator Leib when there was a vacancy. Protesting this possibility "with all my soul," Dallas asked the Secretary to tell Madison, Monroe and Granger that the appointment would destroy all public confidence in the mails, and that he personally would never again send a letter addressed in his own hand.[22]

On January 4 the death of Patton was announced officially, and the Post Office department received several applications for his position. The next afternoon Charles Ingersoll, who had been elected to Congress with the cooperation of the Old School Democrats, presented the Pennsylvania delegation's recommendation of Richard Bache. Although no success as a lawyer, Bache had been shrewd enough to become the first member of the Dallas family to join actively in the New School party. On the Fourth of July past he had been the featured speaker at the party's Independence Day celebration.

That evening Granger received a recommendation for Leib from "some of the old standard republicans of the Senate and House." But a host of Pennsylvanians descended upon him to express their unalterable objections. First came Congressman Jonathan Roberts

---

[22]Dallas to Jones, 2, 3 Jan. 1814, Uselma Clarke Smith Collection, HSP.

and then Senator Abner Lacock leading a delegation, which threatened that Granger would lose his cabinet post if he failed to appoint Bache. On January 7 Ingersoll introduced a resolution in the House to investigate the powers of the Postmaster General and to study the expediency of removing his appointive power and giving it to the President.

In these circumstances Granger waited and did nothing. The President interviewed him on the subject in late January and "from the tenor of his conversation I inferred whom he would appoint," said Granger. Dolley Madison thought that the Postmaster would do the right thing eventually, since "It would indeed be an insult to *us* all, to give it to *the other*." Her confidential assurances that Bache would get the post were addressed to Hannah Gallatin at the home of the Dallases in Philadelphia, "*but only* for your eyes," she cautioned.

Meanwhile Ingersoll was growing impatient. He called on Granger again to demand Bache's appointment, but refused to disclose his plans for his unfriendly bill, saying "*he should take his own time to bring it forward*." Consequently Granger still did nothing, and on February 5 the angry freshman Congressman introduced additional legislation for a full investigation of the Post Office department. He received immediate action--the appointment of Michael Leib as Postmaster of Philadelphia.

The next day President Madison dismissed Granger from the cabinet. He named Return J. Meigs, one of his wife's relations, to succeed him. Granger lost the position of power which he had held since 1801 because of his favoritism to Leib, just as Secretary of State Robert Smith had fallen three years earlier because he was suspected of association with Duane.[23]

Leib had resigned from the Senate to accept the appointment, since he knew he could not be re-elected by the legislature. He was allowed temporarily to continue in the office, despite a fierce campaign for his removal. But the affair did not quiet down, as the administration had hoped, but fully reawakened the factional rivalries in Philadelphia. The trouble came at the worst point in the war, when the maximum in cooperation was needed.[24]

The defense of Philadelphia was continually hampered by old jealousies and mutual suspicions. John Binns, an aide to Governor Snyder with the rank of a militia Colonel, used his political influence to harrass Duane whenever possible. "What think you of my being summoned before a pettey justice of the peace," the Adjutant exclaimed to Daniel Parker, "for the paltry sum of 5 $" for an expenditure for which "the brother officer would not pay the Bill, tho I had duly signed it!" And another officer addressed "a formal letter to me to know under what authority I acted."[25]

---

[23]Gideon Granger to John Todd, 7 Feb. 1814, Gratz Collection, HSP; Mrs. Madison to Mrs. Gallatin, 21 Jan. [1814], Gallatin Papers, NYHS. See also Henry Clay to William H. Crawford, 10 May 1814, James F. Hopkins, ed., _The Papers of Henry Clay_ [_Clay Papers_], series in progress, 3 vols. published (Lexington, Ky., 1958-1963), I, 897; Brant, _Madison_, VI, 243-245.

[24]_Aurora_, 12, 19 Feb. 1814; Duane to Madison, 22 Feb. 1814, Madison Papers, LC; Thomas Leiper to Madison, 22 Feb. 1814, _ibid_.; John Binns to Madison, 11 July 1814, _ibid_.

[25]Duane to Parker, 24 Jan. 1814, Parker Papers, HSP.

Even the outlook on military events was affected by political loyalties. Binns was hostile toward General Wilkinson and honored William Henry Harrison, whom Duane detested. "God is my judge," he avowed, "I would not trust a corporal's guard nor the defense of a henroost to him against any equal number of men." He blamed Harrison for the "sacrifices in the west" in the winter of 1813, and declared "I shall be very well content if Harrison after spending a million of dollars in his erratic course returns with the western youth safe to their homes." The General was later successful at the Battle of the Thames, but if he "continues to eat his way all over the country," a friend wrote to the Adjutant, "he will hardly have time to return to the frontier at the opening of the next campaign." When Harrison passed through Philadelphia in December 1813, he was adulated by Binns and the New Schoolers and, Thomas Leiper warned Madison, "I am told one of his party told General Harrison he should be our next President." Armstrong and Harrison were personal rivals, and Duane claimed that the *Democratic Press* began to attack the Secretary because "Harrison set it going." Armstrong refused to promote the successful General, and the insulted Harrison resigned his Army commission.[26]

The Democratic rivals Duane and Binns were both resentful

---

[26]B[aptis] Irvine to Wilkinson, 7 Mar. 1811, Wilkinson Papers, Chicago Hist. Soc.; Duane to Parker, 24 Jan. 1814, Parker Papers, HSP; Duane to Jefferson, 14 Feb. 1813, TJ-LC; Parker to Duane 11 Dec. 1813, Parker Papers, HSP; Leiper to Madison, 22 Feb. 1814, Madison Papers, LC; Freeman Cleaves, *Old Tippecanoe: William Henry Harrison and His Times* (New York, 1939), 157, 213-216. See also *ibid*., 108-109, 121; Duane to McLane, 3 Mar. 1813, McLane Papers, NYHS; Duane to Parker, 5 Dec. 1813, Parker Papers, HSP.

of the participation of Federalists in the war effort. In 1813 when it was believed that Philadelphia was threatened, some of the city's young gentlemen began to organize for the first time, but the New School's association of Democratic Young Men rushed its own volunteers to Fort Mifflin as soon as they learned that the Federalists were active. Duane was annoyed that General Bloomfield accepted the services of the "Volunteer association composed of the sons of Tories and Aristocrats . . . at the very moment they were defaming the government." According to Duane, the group not only behaved disgracefully in camp and were "a curse to the neighborhood," but they willfully ruined their weapons "and dam[n]ed them as Democratic arms."[27]

Duane was highly vindictive toward British residents, Anglo-Federalists, and the whole of New England. He suspected the presence of traitors and continually sought evidence that aliens were engaged in spying. But neither District Attorney Dallas nor Marshal John Smith were cooperative. "It is useless to give any information to our _prefect_ in this city," he complained, because Dallas might object "that it was _putting him to a great deal_ of trouble." And "the marshal is a contemptible spaniel of his and unfit to be trusted with the care of even an oyster cellar." When Philadelphia sent Thomas Cadwalader on a mission to the War department, Duane denounced him as "an austere aristocratical man sour and sick at being on the common floor, when he thinks he should be on an ele-

---

[27]Scharf and Westcott, _Hist. of Phila._, I, 562-563, 563n; Duane to Jefferson, 26 Sept. 1813, TJ-LC.

vated platform like his sisters husband the British Minister Erskine. I cannot permit myself to believe," Duane concluded, "that he wishes England better than America, but I have no doubt he loves England better than any man in the administration--and would spare no pains to give the British a political ascendancy in the U. States."[28]

The Federalists themselves indulged in a resurgence of nativist feelings, especially against the Irish, whom they blamed for the war with England. When a public work day was declared to construct redoubts to protect the city, the naturalized "Sons of Erin" furnished 2,200 workers, more than any other group of association. But there was a strong feeling in the city that "Poor Americans" did all the fighting for "a crew of imported incendiaries like Col. Pokeberry [Binns] and the Calcutta Polerider [Duane], whose stripes in European and Indian jails they are to avenge under the name of free trade and sailor's rights." On the Fourth of July 1813 the "Cossack Society," as the Sons of St. George were then known to the Democrats, drank a toast to "the brave American soldiers and seamen who have bled in battle; such blood was too precious an oblation for the doubtful claims of strangers." James Wilson commented, "We are credibly informed that there were foreigners (and Irishmen too!) present at the Cossack dinner when the toast was given . . . showing the contempt in which they were held." Presumably he meant New Schoolers, who instead of "taking the hint," drank to the insult, but Wilson warned that they would gain nothing "for their prostitution."[29]

---

[28]Duane to McLane, 3 Mar. 1813, McLane Papers, NYHS; Duane to Parker, 31 Aug. 1814, Parker Papers, HSP.

[29]Scharf and Westcott, Hist. of Phila., I, 574; The (Philadelphia) Corrector, 16 Sept. 1814; Aurora, 21 July 1813.

The resentment of the war led to a growing demand that the foreign-born be excluded from American politics. Charles Biddle, a prominent Federalist, attended a meeting of volunteers where he found the city's "warmest Democrats"; he was welcomed and "unanimously called to the chair," but he quickly became disgusted by the performance of Joseph de Puglia, a New School politician. The "little, dark-looking foreigner came forward" to present resolutions denouncing the "traitors" abroad in "our beloved country." "It provoked me to hear a fellow lately come among us talk of our 'beloved country,'" Biddle admitted. Another Philadelphian who complained of finding "foreigners elbowing everybody down" wherever he went, proposed that in future the test of a political candidate should not be his party, but "is he an American, in birth as well as principle?" According to Wilson, the Cossacks had declared "that no foreigner (which means no Irishman) shall have an office whilst an Englishman or a tory can be had to fill it."[30]

III.

Duane became disheartened by the animosities at work in the city and in Washington. One year after receiving his commission, he declared that "I should resume a private station immediately if Gen. Bloomfield were here to take charge of the papers &c." The "difficulties in the way of duty are disgusting," he complained; "I find nothing but obstacles in my way." Moreover he thought that

---

[30]Ibid.; Charles Biddle, Autobiography of Charles Biddle, Vice-President of the Supreme Executive Council of Pennsylvania; 1745-1821 (Philadelphia, 1883), 336-338; Voice of the Nation, 17 Aug. 1813. See also ibid., 31 Aug., 8 Dec. 1813.

"it is not men who possess the kind of zeal which actuates me that are wanted--I do not mean literally wanted--but in the idiom of looked for or selected."[31]

But Duane did not resign and he could not forget his constant worry about American strategy. "I dream sleeping and waking of these things," he admitted. If only Congress had gone "right to work" at the outset, he lamented, "raised a sufficient army, disciplined them properly, and put them under adequate general officers --we should have been in complete possession of all Canada at this time." From his experience in the fourth district, he continued to send suggestions for reforming the system of recruitment. In the spring of 1814 for example Philadelphia sent "a very fine detachment" to the north, but "if we had only Cash in the hands of Recruiting officers, we would have sent in my opinion 2000 instead of 700."[32]

Frustrated in his duties as Adjutant, Duane returned to his "hobby horse--writing military books!" He planned "to put the whole French Infantry System in a fit state for use and service," in a book which would supersede his Handbook for Infantry, the official manual, commonly ignored. He used his one week furlough in June to begin work on the project and expected to have "an Infantry system system from the company to the Brigade ready in a few weeks--the labor of my lamp when every one else is asleep."[33]

---

[31]Duane to Parker, 29 Mar., 24 Jan. 1814, Parker Papers, HSP.

[32]Duane to Parker, 13, 27 May 1814, 5 Dec. 1813, ibid. Duane's correspondence with Parker in ibid. contains several undated "proposals" intended for consideration by the War department.

[33]Duane to Parker, 4, 21 June, 3 July 1814, ibid.

Meanwhile the British were winning the long war in Europe and would soon be free to turn their attention to the American enemy. "What will our administration now say to affairs in Europe?" Duane worried. "Will they repose upon British magnanimity or American courage?--If they trust the former farewell to national virtue and security--If they call forth the spirit of the nation," he believed, "we shall stand the most distinguished and prosperous nation that has existed." But Gallatin was a member of the American diplomatic mission, and "I fear there is more than one Talleyrand in the world." "My opinion is we shall have a sharp war--a contest for our liberties." In "such an event," he told Daniel Parker, "I shall look for a more efficient station, I do not mean of rank, but where I can render more efficient service--I shall plant my progeny on the Muskingum and take the fortune of war myself."[34]

The threat of British attack on the Atlantic seaboard was steadily mounting, and all the eastern cities remained undefended. In late July Duane visited Washington to see his friends in Congress and the War department and to observe for himself the preparations for defense of the capital. On his return he toured Fort McHenry near Baltimore, where encampment was in progress, and was dismayed by the general incompetence; the platoon officers were "miserable bipeds" and the militiamen uninstructed. Moreover he had counted every tent in camp and watched every battalion on parade without once being questioned, and "Admiral Cockburn might

---

[34]Duane to Parker, 8 June, 3 July 1814, ibid.

have done the same with the greatest ease."[35]

On August 19 British sailors landed at Chesapeake bay and began to march toward the capital. Five days later, at Bladensburg, the entire American defense force was disgracefully routed, and the city of Washington suffered a totally humiliating conquest. Throughout the eastern United States the apathy and confusion of two years of war were suddenly transformed to panic-stricken activity.

In Philadelphia the city, state, and federal officers simultaneously undertook discordant preparations for the defense of the region. "I could wish to be any where," Duane admitted, "rather than in this scene of conflicting authorities." During the war thus far the Pennsylvania militia had done nothing, either in service of effective training, and in Philadelphia itself, according to Condy Raguet, the only activity had been the recruitment of regular soldiers and the formation of a few volunteer companies. But now all authorities contended for control of the small supply of arms and material. Duane thought that the district staff should have complete supervision of the defense planning, and when the Governor was granted free use of the federal arsenal, the Adjutant objected that "I shudder at the consequences." It would mean "an empty arsenal in the spring," when "the utmost efforts of the nation will be required." With all the rival activity in progress, the city's preparations for defense were behind those of New York and Baltimore, Duane acknowledged, and Philadelphia would be lucky if "the

---

[35]Duane to Parker, 10 Aug. 1814, _ibid_.

enemy suffers us to remain unmolested this fall."[36]

The most serious contention was between the district office, which had the responsibility of defending the entire Delaware river region, and the Committee of Defense in Philadelphia, which wanted to abandon "the lower country" in order to provide for the city's safety. The Federalist-dominated Committee of Public Safety, as Duane called it, had been formed during the crisis and granted authority to act independently of the city council, which Duane admitted was "a weak, nerveless and consequently a pernicious body." The committee planned a line of defense along the Schuylkill river, immediately to the west of the city, and wanted the militia and volunteers to remain in Philadelphia. General Bloomfield resisted its demands with superior "firmness and judgment," in Duane's opinion, and the committee therefore sought his removal as district commander. Meanwhile Bloomfield created a camp thirty-six miles southwest of the city and dispatched several of the volunteer companies under the command of a federal officer.[37]

The main defense was to be at Marcus Hook, twenty miles south of the city on the Delaware. Governor Snyder had mobilized 10,000 state militiamen, and in early September the unit began arriving in the neighborhood of Philadelphia. General Bloomfield

---

[36] *Ibid.*; Duane to Monroe, 10 Aug. 1814, Monroe Papers, NYPL; [Raguet], *Brief Sketch of the . . . Late War*, 21-22. Governor Snyder refused to send the militia out of the state to aid in the defense of Washington; Beirne, *War of 1812*, 270.

[37] Duane to Parker, 31 Aug. 1814, Parker Papers, HSP. See also Duane to Parker, 10 Aug. 1814, *ibid.*; Scharf and Westcott, *Hist. of Phila.*, I, 572; [Raguet], *Brief Sketch of the . . . Late War*, 23, 96.

intended to bypass Duane, whose duties as Adjutant General included "Instruction of troops" and "Arrangement of troops in order of battle," either to avoid displeasing Governor Snyder or because Duane lacked enough military experience. But the officer whom he requested to "lay out the camp" at Marcus Hook declined the duty, and Bloomfield therefore ordered Duane to take charge of the encampment. Another officer was recalled temporarily to Philadelphia to take over the Adjutant's office.[38]

Duane was enchanted to be at last on active service. After three weeks' "Hard tour of duty," he reported that there were 5,000 men in camp, "all from the plough," and "not one man from the General to the private who knew a single part of military duty of any kind--I had to mark off the ground," he told Daniel Parker, "switch the tents with my own hands--dig their sinks, and fireplaces--parade and detail their guards--post their sentinels--go the rounds night and day--wet and dry--drill the officers--drill the non com[d] officers and drill the soldiers." In short he had to be "the first man on parade and the last man to repose. But I never enjoyed better health nor higher pleasure--nor was there ever finer materials[,] officers only excepted."[39]

From the outset he encountered difficulties with the state

---

[38]Duane to Monroe, 17 Sept. 1814, Monroe Papers, NYPL; Louis Bache, defendant, Proceedings of a General Court Martial . . . Marcus Hook . . . October 1814; Whole Evidence and Documents (Philadelphia, 1815), appendix 2, p. 9, appendix H, p. 7, pamphlet, University of Chicago; [Raguet], Brief Sketch of the . . . Late War, 30n.

[39]Duane to Parker, 26 Oct. 1814, Parker Papers, HSP.

officers who owed political as well as military allegiance to Governor Snyder. Throughout the war Duane had railed against the Army's inefficiency and poor organization, and he intended to make his camp a model of discipline. The troops had to learn "that when they come into service for war, they must not expect to act like militia in peace." But when he insisted upon full compliance with military regulations, in mustering them into the national service, the officers of one regiment refused to obey him and nearly produced a mutiny.

The trouble came when he attempted to re-organize Louis Bache's volunteer regiment from Bucks county. The unit was top-heavy with officers and had only enough privates to form three companies, but the members considered themselves exempted from interference because they were volunteers. Duane felt no malice toward them; in fact Louis Bache "unfortunately was a valued friend of mine own and a connexion by marriage." But he was rigid in his demand that they comply with regulations. Finally at the parade ground on October 14 he counted off Bache's detachment into three companies and called for officers to take the command. Six officers in turn refused him and he placed them each under arrest and ordered them home. The following day Duane himself was relieved of duty; five hundred militiamen jeered him out of camp, and the story of his "retreat from Marcus Hook" followed him ever after.[40]

---

[40]Duane to Parker, 26 Oct., 2 Nov. 1814, ibid.; L. Bache, defendant, Proceedings of a Genl. Ct. Martial, 18, 24, 29, 32, 34, 45, and passim; Aurora, 15 Nov. 1814; Democratic Press, 13 Oct. 1814. See ibid., 9 Oct. 1816; Franklin Gazette, 5, 6, 17 Oct. 1818.

Both Bache and Duane were repudiated for their conduct in the affair. In a court-martial, Bache was convicted of mutiny, disobedience and insubordination, and dismissed from the United States service. Duane had been technically in the right, but needlessly officious under the circumstances. His superior officer countermanded the order for the re-organization, and a month later the War department withdrew the regulation upon which he had acted.[41]

The incident could perhaps have been averted if General Bloomfield had not just then been succeeded by General Edmund P. Gaines, recently wounded in the northern fighting. Gaines was not familiar with the political hazards of his new assignment. Governor Snyder and Nathaniel Boileau, the Secretary of the Commonwealth, were the forces behind Bache's insubordinate conduct, and they supported his contention that he was not bound to obey the United States officer, because the Governor and General Bloomfield had a private understanding that there would be no re-organization. They claimed that Gaines had "tacitly assented" to the arrangement. But Bloomfield did not corroborate Snyder, and if an agreement existed, Duane was not informed of it.[42]

The Adjutant General was not restored to duty in Philadelphia, but posted to Camp Billingsport, New Jersey, "'to chop blocks

---

[41] Aurora, 15 Nov. 1814; Duane to Parker, 2 Nov. 1814, Parker Papers, HSP.

[42] James W. Silver, Edmund Pendleton Gaines, Frontier General (Baton Rouge, La., 1949), 50; Snyder to Boileau, 21 Oct., 1 Nov. 1814, Correspondence of Simon Snyder, HSP; L. Bache, defendant, Proceedings of a Genl. Ct. Martial, 12, 18, 24, 26, 27, 30, 36, 40, appendix H, 7.

with a razor'--." His office was temporarily taken over by an acting Adjutant, James N. Barker, the son of John Barker, the former sheriff, while Duane was assigned to discipline men who "neither believe it necessary nor tolerable." He confessed, "I am sent on a sort of penance, or to expiate I suppose the political sins of my past life." When he returned to Philadelphia in mid-November, he became ill because of the change from camp air to a "close room and blankets."

His only remaining hope for service was that his new book on infantry discipline would be officially adopted. But influential persons who "hate me with the malevolence of sin and death" would probably bear a preponderant weight in the decision, he predicted. And "after all perhaps it is so much the best for me. If my book does not obtain, I shall consider it as a hint to have done" and to resign the commission. "I will not receive pay for nothing."[43]

IV.

Miraculously the war ended a few months later without loss of territory and with a glorious victory by General Andrew Jackson at the Battle of New Orleans. Duane and his patrons Armstrong and Wilkinson all suffered varying degrees of disgrace for their efforts. The Secretary of War was dismissed for the ignominious defeat at Washington; Wilkinson was acquitted of negligence but forced to retire from the service, and Duane's military works were rejected for use by the Army.

[43]Duane to Parker, 2, 13 Nov. 1814, Parker Papers, HSP.

In November Congress had authorized the creation of a board of tactics to decide upon a uniform system of discipline. Duane was not appointed to the board as he thought he should be, and until January he could not raise the money for the journey to Washington to represent his interests. General Winfield Scott was the chairman of the board of officers which included General Gaines, Colonel Thomas Cushing and several others. There was a mutual enmity between General Scott and the *Aurora* editor, and in his own camp Scott had discarded Duane's *Handbook* and declared, Duane was told, "*that he would sooner resign his commission than suffer his men to be disciplined by any system of Duane's*." The board rejected the earlier manual as "archaic," and it did not choose to adopt his recently published *System of Infantry Discipline*. Scott apparently objected that it did not incorporate Napoleon's revisions of the French system, but Duane thought that the "proscription" was because of "the inveterate hatred of persons who have no justifiable ground even of resentment against me."[44]

Although he had promised himself that "I shall not break my heart" over it, he was embittered by the decision which placed him once again in financial jeopardy. The happiness of his "precious family, already too much tossed about by the storms and the treachery of politics--and the labors of fifteen years of my own life,

---

[44]Winfield Scott, *Memoirs of Lieut.-General Scott, LL.D. Written by Himself*, 2 vols. (New York, 1864), I, 154; Charles Winslow Elliott, *Winfield Scott, The Soldier and the Man* (New York, 1937), 190; Silver, *Gaines*, 51; Duane to Parker, 15 Nov., 9, 22 Dec. 1814, 3 July 1815, Parker Papers, HSP; Duane to Monroe, 2 Feb. 1815, Monroe Papers, NYPL.

are all too deeply involved to suffer me not to feel great disquietude." He was left with thousands of useless copies of the Handbook, plus the loss involved in the publication of the second manual, to be added to the burden of his past indebtedness. "It is to me another crisis in a life of unblemished efforts to pursue the paths of virtue and honor with independence of mind and without ostentation or meanness."[45]

After the war General Wilkinson came to Philadelphia to write his memoirs, and was regularly an honored guest at the Tammany Society and the Sons of St. Erin. A. J. Dallas wanted him sent abroad, to avoid "active mischief" through the Aurora, but the General refused the positions that he was offered. Before Wilkinson left Washington he was "busily employed in intrigues to keep himself in office." In the reduction of the Army there were to be only two Major Generals, and "the current of opinion . . . sets pretty strongly in favor" of Jacob Brown and Andrew Jackson. Therefore "one, at least, of these, must be broke down and he has fastened upon the former." "Duane who may be regarded as squire to the Don" was said to be "on the point of clipping the wings of all our Niagara Eagles, and shewing that there was no merit there but among the rank and file. The object of all this," according to John Armstrong, "is to bring others down to the level of the knight and then to plead thirty years service against the mere vulgar and unfounded prejudice of the day."[46]

---

[45] Ibid.; Duane to Parker, 25 Nov. 1814, Parker Papers, HSP. See also Duane to Parker, 14 Jan. 1820, ibid.; Franklin Gazette, 6 Oct. 1818.

[46] Thomas Robson Hay, "General James Wilkinson--The Last

Wilkinson was forced to retire, but the *Aurora* kept up its insistence that General Jackson alone deserved preeminence as an American hero. According to John Binns, "One of the most contemptible poltroons that ever disgraced the army . . . has the superlative vanity to deem his meed of praise necessary to fill the measure of Gen. Jackson's happiness and secure his standing." But in the presidential campaign of 1828 it was remembered that Jackson had first been proposed as a candidate of Colonel Allan McLane at a dinner in Philadelphia.[47]

Phase," *Louisiana Historical Quarterly*, XIX, No. 2 (Apr. 1936), 409-414; Dallas to Monroe, 28 May 1815, quoted in Jacobs, *Tarnished Warrior*, 316; Armstrong to Lt. Col. [James] Hamilton, 18 Apr. 1815, Society Collections, Chicago Hist. Soc.

[47]*Democratic Press*, 9 May 1815; *Philadelphia Mercury*, 17 Nov. 1827.

CHAPTER XI

PRINCIPLES AND NOT MEN

During the first years following the war with England, Duane played a valuable role politically as an honest maverick, independent of the self-satisfied Republican establishment. His predictions of economic disaster and his deepening pessemism about the moral future of America were at odds with the prevailing mood of confidence and enterprise. But there was a growing minority which had begun to share the concerns that had troubled him for many years and which welcomed the *Aurora*'s candor amidst so much hypocrisy and cant.

The country was said to have entered upon an Era of Good Feelings, because the party system had been finally broken down and the Republican Ascendancy was complete. To Duane it meant "the frustration of all the good that has arisen out of the triumph of 1800." The party of Jefferson had succumbed and the party of Gallatin had taken its place. The perversions of Republicanism he blamed upon "the policy of *courting enemies* and *sacrificing friends*" which had been "carried to such a height" during Madison's administration. By 1816 for example the young Federalist Nicholas Biddle could easily transfer his loyalties, since "the ruling party has outgrown many of the childish notions with which they began their career 20 years since." Duane had chided Jefferson about the "fatal policy, which your goodness will excuse me for saying was too much countenanced by yourself," for "it is too plain that we are not all republicans nor all federalists." Some men were "indifferent to social and moral obligations" and governed only "by their fears or interests; to place men of such character on a level with men of principle or virtue is to reduce virtue and vice, patriotism and perfidy to a common standard of merit.[1]

The event which revealed unmistakably the change in Republican philosophy was the party's establishment of a Second Bank of the United States. The war had thrust the nation into an almost desperate financial condition; the government was impoverished and the currency dangerously inflated and fluctuating. Alexander Hamilton had met a similar crisis following the Revolution by summoning the financial strength of private business and international bankers to the support of the public credit. In 1814 President Madison's Secretary of the Treasury, A. J. Dallas, recommended the same solution, to be accomplished through the creation of a second national bank. In his opinion the currency depreciation was so severe that it was beyond the government's power to remedy, and only the use of stable outside sources could restore financial confidence.

Dallas offered a scheme for a new bank which provided for greater government participation, as a safeguard to the public interest, but his plan was opposed and defeated. A new school of Republicans in Congress, led by John C. Calhoun of South Carolina, preferred

---

[1]Duane to Jefferson, 26 Sept. 1813, TJ-LC; Biddle to B. Henry, draft, 27 Nov. 1816, Nicholas Biddle Papers, LC.

to incorporate a private institution on the Hamiltonian model, unhampered by partnership with the government. Reluctantly President Madison acceded to their demands, and in April 1816 Congress chartered the Second Bank of the United States, a Republican resurrection of its Federalist predecessor.[2]

Duane had condemned any plan for another bank as an intolerable sacrifice of the public's control over the public interest. The Secretary of the Treasury "instead of pursuing the glorious purpose of establishing a system consistent with the principles of the government," had devised a scheme for a so-called "national institution" which in reality would be "the property of a combination of speculators!" As financial agents for the government, these profiteers would be "invested with all the power, patronage, credit, confidence, and even the gratuitous receipt, possession, and use of public treasure," and the public in turn denied "the power, . . . possession and use of its own treasure!" In Duane's opinion, a Congress which would delegate its own authority to private individuals who were not subject to public approval or censure was shamefully "indifferent to its power and its place in the orbit of the constitution." "If there be so little capacity in congress as not to discern this shameful imposition-- . . . melancholy indeed must be the prospects of the lovers of a representative democracy."

As an alternative to the Bank, Duane revived his suggestion of 1811 that the federal government issue Treasury notes which would

---

[2]Ralph C. H. Catterall, The Second Bank of the United States (Chicago, 1903), 1-21.

serve as a national currency. The extreme inflation since that period in fact made the idea highly impracticable, but Duane refused to accept the evidence that private financial resources were necessary to establish monetary stability. How could notes "with a security commensurate and durable as the government itself, be pernicious, or of less value as a currency, than the notes of any private bank," he asked, "since no bank existing or to be created could survive the overthrow of the government?"[3]

The editor was stubborn in the defense of his proposal because of his absolute conviction that the money power must not be yielded to private interests. For the same reason, the Old Republican chairman of the House Ways and Means committee, Duane's friend John Eppes of Virginia, also favored the issue of Treasury notes as a solution to the financial crisis. As Duane, he suggested the stability of the notes should be supported through the creation of internal taxes.[4] This was an extraordinary departure from strict constructionist tenets, but Eppes preferred to impose direct taxes rather than deprive the people of their right to democratic control over their interests through their elected representatives. The nationalistic Duane and the Old Republicans of Virginia often agreed on public measures, because they shared a common sense of priorities in American politics.

To Duane the question of the Second Bank of the United

---

[3]Aurora, 18, 19, 21 Dec. 1815, 3 Jan. 1816, "National Finance," 18 Dec. 1815-4 Jan. 1816.

[4]Catterall, Second Bank, 7, 9-10.

States was crucial to the country's future economic development. During the war the creation of vast numbers of small state banks which could not maintain a specie standard had encouraged pernicious monetary speculation, and, in Duane's opinion, "public virtue appeared on its last legs." Fortunately "the sudden and unexpected news of peace, interposed and save the country for the moment, from the renewal of such scenes of speculation as disgraced and corrupted the nation in 1790-91." But the establishment of another national bank would "not only . . . overdo the system of banking, already enormously overdone; but . . . open a vast scheme of iniquitous gambling, by which public morals, already deplorably decayed, will receive a new and afflicting aggravation."

The new Bank would thrust the nation into a depression, he predicted, through excessive issues of paper money. In his opinion bank capital was already greater than the economy could absorb, and "Society, like the human body, can bear only a certain quantity of aliment with health; even some privation is more salutary than excess." His conservative view was in sharp contrast with that of his old rival Mathew Carey, who insisted that the national bank was necessary because the existing banks could not satisfy the increasing demand for credit. Unlike Carey, Duane did not anticipate dependence upon bank capital to promote rapid industrial expansion, but envisioned a more gradual increase in the real wealth of the nation as the basis for economic progress.

In his opinion the most useful aid to economic development would be the construction of transportation facilities. In the

Aurora he outlined a scheme for a national internal improvements fund with which to connect the country "from the extremities to the centre." The government would "determine the place, direction, form, and quantity to be executed annually of each road and canal," and would be reimbursed for its subsidy by the increased sales of public lands and by taxes upon the enhanced value of tillage and "the cultivation of lands, now wild and unproductive." The expanding agricultural market would "give a new activity to society, and create new means, with new wants which would encourage industry to supply them."

Duane believed that "Great as is the evil of those numerous institutions," the state banks, Congress should "apply a gentle . . . corrective, or curative course of policy, rather than throw the nation into further affliction," by expanding the banking system. The existing banks were "like certain diseases engrafted on society, which must be endured," until society itself could effect a cure through time and work. If as he suggested the government would sponsor "powerful and extensive activity" for internal improvements, it would "gradually augment the capital of the landholder and cultivator," he believed, "so much as to convert the *paper stock* of those numerous banks, into a more substantial solid value, in place of the spurious credit which now composes so much of the circulating medium of the country."[5]

---

[5] *Aurora*, 19, 22 Dec. 1815, 3, 4 Jan., 10 Apr. 1816; Mathew Carey in *U. S. Gazette*, 6 Apr. 1816.

II.

Politically the incorporation of the Second Bank was a symbolic event which sharply divided the members of the postwar Republican Establishment from Duane's Old School Democrats and the growing numbers of would-be reformers. Congress, in adopting this solution to the financial crisis, had placed a mistaken notion of convenience above the demands of social decency. Instead of encouraging a return to a high standard of public morality, the legislators had deliberately incited the public to nurture ambitions for speculative profit in the future. These "modern" Republicans had abandoned the party's original principles, in Duane's opinion, because of the inclusion of ex-Federalists among them, because of their delusion that Federalist ideas and institutions were harmless when under Republican control, and because of their personal expectations of profit from the banking system. The new slogan of the *Aurora* became "Principles and Not Men," and the editor steadfastly predicted that by such behavior "the people will become disgusted with their rulers, and begin to doubt the duration of a government capable of countenacing such abuses."[6]

In Pennsylvania soon after the war there emerged an anti-caucus movement, composed of a coalition of groups which opposed for differing reasons the monolithic party in power. The caucus system of nominations, under the one party rule then prevailing, virtually eliminated the meaning of the process of popular election and replaced it with government by an oligarchy of party

---

[6] *Aurora*, 10 Apr. 1816.

leaders. The *Aurora* had expressed sentiments against the caucus as early as 1805; and in 1812 the Democrats for DeWitt Clinton had attempted without success to introduce it as an active issue in politics. But not until 1816 did the Pennsylvania men, for the first time in the history of American politics, succeed in making the caucus system a major issue.

The movement could loosely be termed Clintonian. The New Yorker more than any other national figure could hope to benefit from the success of its efforts. And it tended to encourage cooperation between the groups which he had sought prematurely to ally in his campaign of 1812, the Federalists and the Independent Democrts.

This was particularly important for Philadelphia, where a "union of faction and federalism" was said to be in progress. In that city the Federalist party had survived the war and was uniquely strong; it had regained control of the city government in 1814 because of renewed Democratic division and had much to gain from tacit cooperation with the Old School. For the Federalists' survival the anti-caucus movement was essential in order to break down the concept of Republican Ascendancy, which postulated a consensus so general that it could absorb all men of good will.

There were two sorts of Federalists who refused to submit to political reconstruction: the traditional "high-toned" or Hamiltonian type, such as Enos Bronson of the *United States Gazette*, which still dominated the city party, and another variety, neither rich nor aristocratic, whose economic views were more conservative than the doctrines prevailing in the majority party. Condy Raguet was the prime exemplar of the second type. Raguet, who had been a local military hero in the late war, was probably the most popular Independent Republican in the county of Philadelphia, as well liked among the Old School Democrats as by the members of his own party. In 1818 he was elected to the state senate along with Michael Leib on an Amalgamation ticket, and ran well ahead of Leib and the two Patent Democrat candidates in the Old School stronghold, the Northern Liberties.

Raguet's popularity was closely related to his outspoken expression of his conservative views on banking. Like the Old Schoolers, he was opposed both to the Second Bank of the United States and to the proliferation of state banks, and he acted upon these convictions after becoming a member of the senate. Raguet had been the principal founder of the Philadelphia Saving Fund society, the first American imitation of a Scottish institution intended to provide a secure depository for the savings of working men, safe from the threat of loss through speculative manipulations. Raguet's hostility to the paper banking system admittedly had originated in a concern with the need of merchants to have more stable conditions for commerce. But the Federalist shopkeepers and the Old School mechanics during the economic boom of the postwar period had similar fears and interests.[7]

---

[7]_Franklin Gazette_, 17 Oct. 1818; [Condy Raguet], _An Inquiry into the Causes of the Present State of the Circulating Medium of the United States_ (Philadelphia, 1815), 37-42, 47-55, and _passim_; Horace W. Lippincott, _Early Philadelphia: Its People, Life and Progress_ (Philadelphia, 1917), 263-266; Elizabeth Donnan, "Condy Raguet," _DAB_, XV, 325-326.

The Old Schoolers had long acknowledged that the Federalist party had an "honest and well meaning part . . ., that is the middling and poorer class of people . . . unwilling to go all lengths with the 'better blood.'" Duane distinguished between the city's "ultras," and the "liberal" Federalists who lived in the county. There the party's amalgamation with the Old School became highly advanced; according to a New School or Patent Democratic source, the county Federalists had abandoned their party name at Duane's insistence and agreed to the term Independent Republicans. They "bear their ignominious dependence with patience and fortitude." As the weakest party in the county, the "liberal" Federalists had a practical reason for their moderate attitudes; but there was a genuine difference between them as a group and their fellow Federalists in the city. Social prestige in Philadelphia required residence within the limited bounds of Pine and Vine streets, whereas the communities beyond the city limits to the north and south had always been modest. Probably the Federalists there were mostly small merchants, and they did not emulate the old "high-toned" views of the party's lawyers, businessmen and members of prominent families, who lived within Philadelphia proper.[8]

The principal agent of cooperation between the Old School and the Federalists was Michael Leib, who had an understanding with DeWitt Clinton. In 1815 Clinton asked him to have Thomas T. Stiles "send me his True American," a paper consistently ultra-Federalist

---

[8]Aurora, "Brutus," 21 Sept. 1810; Franklin Gazette, 12 Oct. 1818; Burt, Perennial Philadelphians, 529.

but potentially useful to the anti-caucus movement.[9] In local politics, the Federalists and the Old School tended to cooperate by standing aside from serious competition in the other party's stronghold. In the city the Old School was the weakest of the three parties, but its continuing dissension with its Patent Democratic rivals allowed the Federalist party to maintain control of the city government. The Federalists in the country on the other hand did not nominate a state assembly ticket, which greatly enhanced the chances of the Old Schoolers.

Leib had returned to Philadelphia from Washington in 1814 when he received the highly controversial appointment as Postmaster. He was removed from office in January 1815, less than one year later, by Madison's new Postmaster General, but he became briefly once more the storm center of local politics. Duane was primarily interested in large political ideas, and during the war years especially he had ignored the practical needs of the party. Leib, with his keen interest in the details of politics, set about the task of reconstructing the party's crumbling organization. He revived the moribund Tammany society, placing his brother-in-law John Harrison in the position of Grand Sachem, and he restored the Old School's electoral strength in the Northern Liberties. In 1815 the party took full full control of the district's Board of Commissioners, and Leib was unanimously elected its President.[10]

---

[9]Clinton to Leib, draft, 11 Sept. 1815, DeWitt Clinton Papers, Columbia University.

[10]U. S. Gazette, 10 May 1815; Democratic Press, 4, 5, 8, 11 May 1815.

Leib's alleged collusion with the Federalists was the source of criticism within his own party as well as censure by the Patent Democrats. According to Binns' Democratic Press, "some of Duane's personal friends circulate that he will abandon Leib. One thung is clear, either Duane must abandon Leib," in Binns' opinion, "or he will himself be abandoned by the few democrats who yet think he is not entirely lost to the party." But Duane dismissed the accusation that "Dr. Leib has turned federalist!" as another slander in the long history of "personal hostility" to him.[11]

In fact the charge of Old School-Federalist collusion was grossly exaggerated, for the two parties had great difficulty in finding a common basis for action. It was in their mutual interest to cooperate for the purpose of crushing the Republican Ascendancy, but they were separated not only by old suspicions and hatred, but by still existing fundamental differences in motivation. The problem was illustrated by the experience concerning the establishment of the Second Bank of the United States.

Federalists and Old Schoolers alike were opposed both to the creation of the Second Bank and to the vast increase in country banks which had occurred during the war. Philadelphia's merchants resented the erratic policies of the feeble institutions, which greatly impeded the orderly process of business. But they feared the political implications of a new national bank, potentially an instrument for continued domination by the Republican party. The friends of freedom would prefer that the government controlled a

---

[11]Ibid., 18 Oct. 1815; Aurora, 25 Oct. 1815.

huge mercenary army, Enos Bronson declared dramatically, rather than "such an enormous machine as that contrived by Mr. Dallas." In their opposition to the Bank, some Federalists considered seriously the alternative of Treasury notes proposed by Duane. "I have believed, that the project proposed by W. D. could not possibly succeed," wrote Charles Chauncey, "but some of my friends, I find, believe otherwise." Chauncey himself was convinced "that W. D.'s plan will greatly increase, instead of diminishing, the difficulties, which at present exist."[12]

In 1815 the Old School supported the Federalists' nominee for Congress from the city in the belief that he would oppose the Second Bank. The lawyer John Sergeant was seeking office for the first time, and his qualifications, the Aurora declared, were that he had "never been for sale," nor involved in land or stock speculations.[13] After Sergeant was elected, Duane regarded him for a time as a link with the affairs of government. The hope was much encouraged by Sergeant's brother-in-law, Joseph Reed.

Reed, the city recorder, was a director of the Commercial bank, a member of a good family and well connected with influential friends. But he was a devoted Clintonian, and after the war had actively associated himself with the Democrats of the Old School and become a friend of Duane. Reed showed the editor the letters

---

[12]Chauncey to John Sergeant, 14 Jan. 1816, John Sergeant Papers, HSP; U. S. Gazette, 11 Jan. 1816. See also ibid., 4, 8 Apr. 1816; Condy Raguet to Nicholas Biddle, 19 Jan. 1816, Biddle Papers, LC.

[13]Aurora, 4 Oct. 1815. See also Democratic Press, 14, 18, 20 Oct. 1815.

he received from Sergeant, and Duane wrote directly to the young Congressman, enthusiastically relating his political views. Reed himself nurtured the idea that John Sergeant could become the anti-caucus candidate for Governor of Pennsylvania and be elected by a "united federal vote with that portion of the democrats who have . . . given you their support."

But the Democrats of the Old School were quickly disenchanted with the Congressman when he failed to oppose the creation of the Second Bank. "If I understood Duane," Reed wrote to Sergeant in 1816, "his ideas were very much the same as your own before you left us.--that a national bank would only increase the evil already very great." Reed attempted to dissuade Sergeant from adopting a politically damaging position, reminding him that Duane was "very anxious that you should have nothing to do in the Bank." He urged Sergeant to write and ask Duane for a copy of the currency proposal which he had sent to the President. "He will be as he always is, flattered by these attentions, by which he is more easily governed than by other methods of treatment," Reed cynically but shrewdly observed.

During the session as it became clear that Sergeant was likely to approve the Bank charter, his brother-in-law increased the hints concerning his political advantage. "Is not Duane uncommonly powerful" on the subject? "I am sorry to see so much and so well said against a Bank," Reed professed, "for after all I cannot help wishing to see a proper one established _especially in Phil^a._" He pointedly informed Sergeant that Binns had published a "feeble, contemptible attack" upon him.[14]

Despite the flow of advice from Reed, the Congressman voted finally in favor of the incorporation. Soon after he accepted a commission from the Bank to travel to Europe and seek capital from foreign investors. Moreover he was named to the first board of directors, but was forced to decline the appointment because of the prior commission. No more was spoken of Congressman Sergeant among the Philadelphia Old School Democrats. Nonetheless he easily retained his seat in Congress with the vote of the locally powerful Federalist party. The Federalists rapidly lost their original distrust of a new national bank as their own partisans purchased a large proportion of the stock and gained a dominant influence in its operation.

This early disillusioning experience was the Old School's only attempt to support a Federalist candidate for office. In the same election Michael Leib failed to be elected to the legislature in spite of Federalist votes in his favor. But "The Union looks to higher objects than this district," the Democratic Press warned its partisans, and "until the Presidential and the Gubernatorial election are over, the Union in this district will be kept together." Binns predicted that "After those periods it will crumble."[15]

III.

The Presidential election of 1816 did not appear to offer a

---

[14]Duane to Sergeant, 27 Jan. 1816, Sergeant Papers, HSP; Reed to Sergeant, 28 Feb., 2, 5 Mar. 1816, 5 Feb. 1817, ibid.

[15]Democratic Press, 14, 18 Oct. 1815.

practical opportunity for the Pennsylvanians to express their sentiments against the encroaching oligarchy of the Republican party. There was no national candidate available to represent the anti-caucus position. Moreover the anti-caucus Democrats did not object personally to the Congressional nominee, James Monroe. Duane for one admired Monroe's performance in the war cabinet, and he greatly preferred Monroe as a candidate to the opponent who very nearly defeated him in the caucus, the despised William H. Crawford.[16]

The grievances felt by the Old School Democrats were primarily against the Fourteenth Congress and its betrayal of Republican principles. The postwar Congress had chartered the Second Bank of the United States; it had dismissed an investigation into the misconduct of the Post Office department, thereby condoning the practice of using public funds for profiteering and favoritism. And it had ended its session by voting to double the salary of Congressmen under the guise of altering the mode of compensation. In brief the members had displayed "an unprecedented example of mental and moral incapacity," in Duane's opinion, in adopting "a course of measures . . . so much at variance with the principles and policy heretofore professed," and "repugnant to the national prosperity and character."[17]

Resentment was widespread against the Fourteenth Congress, especially for the Compensation Act. "The Salary bill--has been toasted till it is black," Duane declared after observing the

---

[16] Aurora, 18, 23 Apr., 31 May, 11, 19 July, 5 Aug. 1816.

[17] Ibid., 24 Apr. 1816.

sentiments expressed in various parts of the country on the Fourth of July. "The late festival shews the public opinion on that point. We are glad to perceive that our solid interests begin to claim more attention than mere party names," he commented, "that simplicity of manners, frugality, home manufactures, &c. are favorite subjects."[18]

The Old School Democrats reserved a special category of reproach for the outgoing President. In their opinion Madison had betrayed his own principles and the nation's faith when he signed the act establishing a national bank, a measure which he had always declared to be unconstitutional. Michael Leib made this duplicity the major theme of his "long talk" at the Tammany society anniversary in May. "Brothers, let us ask ourselves this question," he began, "are we in a better condition now as a people and a political party, than we were under the administration of president Adams?" Conditions had actually worsened, Leib replied, because hypocrisy had been added to the people's burden. "President Adams did not pretend to be the friend of a representative democracy."[19]

The Presidential candidate who could best have represented the will of the anti-caucus men was the late George Clinton. In 1816 the name of "the great, and the good, and the ever-to-be-lamented Clinton" was summoned as frequently as that of any living politician. In contrast with Madison, Clinton had possessed the courage in 1811 to veto the Bank of the United States by his cast-

---

[18]Ibid., 11 July 1816.

[19]Ibid., 13 Apr., 26 June 1816.

ing vote as Vice President. Moreover the Pennsylvanians could not forget that Clinton would have been their choice for President in 1808, but from a spirit of good will which now appeared to have been mistaken, they had agreed to support the choice of the party caucus.[20]

A friendly correspondent in 1816 wrote to Duane to testify that "a short time previous to the election of Mr. Madison, I heard you declare, . . . your preference of Mr. Clinton." The correspondent also recalled, quite wrongly, that Duane had published it. "I was struck with the blunder you had committed," he remembered, "in declaring for one, who, . . . would be distanced in an electioneering, or any other race, with our present worthy chief magistrate." In retrospect he congratulated Duane for his valor. "You might have kept the secret of your preference to yourself--and your not doing so seems to acquit you of the sinister, and courtly means imputed to you." The totally false but flattering reminiscence was not corrected by the editor.[21]

DeWitt Clinton would have been a direct beneficiary of the nostalgia for his late uncle, but he was not in a position to run for president in 1816. He had seriously damaged his reputation by the ill-advised campaign of 1812. And he suffered the loss of unified support from the Democratic party of his own state through the rise of a talented rival, Martin Van Buren. Van Buren's influence made New York Governor Daniel Tompkins the state's favorite son in

---

[20] Ibid., 21 Apr., 26 June, 19 Aug., 24 Oct. 1816.

[21] Ibid., "Washingtoniensis," 19 Aug. 1816.

1816, and eventually Tompkins became the vice presidential nominee on the caucus ticket with James Monroe.[22]

For a time Clinton apparently entertained hopes of making the race, and he looked to Pennsylvania to aid him. Michael Leib visited New York at the end of October 1815 and conferred for several days with him and his friends. Especially important in these interviews was Sylvanus Miller, one of Clinton's most intimate political advisers and the confidential link between Clinton and the Pennsylvanian. Soon after his return, Leib traveled from Philadelphia to Pittsburgh visiting political leaders there and along the way. The apparent end of these activities, the construction of a Clintonian party in Pennsylvania, was frustrated however by the New Yorker's enforced decision not to attempt the presidential contest.[23]

A later attempt to draft Clinton, according to the Aurora, was not successful. In April 1816, after Monroe's nomination but before Congress had adjourned its session, it was "rumored that there will be a very formidable opposition to the caucus recommendation, at Washington." In such a protest movement, Duane reported, Nathaniel Macon of North Carolina or another of the strict constructionists would be the vice presidential nominee. "Mr. Clinton of New York, was spoken of as a candidate for president." But, "it is said he refused to be put in nomination."[24]

---

[22]See Robert V. Remini, "New York and the Presidential Election of 1816," New York History, XXXI (July, 1950), 308-324.

[23]DeWitt Clinton Diary, 29 Oct.-3 Nov. 1815, NYHS; Aurora, 27 Dec. 1815.

[24]Ibid., 27 Apr. 1816.

When Clinton declined to sacrifice himself in the cause, the possibility of an anti-caucus ticket appeared to be dead in Pennsylvania. But it was dramatically revived in August when the movement gained a symbolic leader, the revered Charles Thomson, who had been Secretary of the Continental Congress throughout the Revolution. "Two literary gentlemen," curious for Thomson's opinion, called on the eighty-seven year old patriarch at his farm several miles west of Philadelphia. They asked, should the next president be from Virginia or perhaps from another state? Thomson

> immediately replied, "I would give my vote for
> DE WITT CLINTON.
> I have been acquainted with the politics of that family for half a century. I always respected his uncle; and I consider *him* as a man of talents and principles worthy of the school in which he was brought up."

The publication of his statement in the *Aurora* on August 2 created an immediate sensation. "The communication . . . has put the vermin who feed upon the sores of society, in terrible disorder," Duane reported. "They appeared in the streets yesterday, like rats running from a house on fire."[25]

The visit to Charles Thomson was followed by a meeting at Lancaster which called for an anti-caucus convention to meet at Carlisle in mid-September. The Carlisle meeting was small and disappointing, but it did adopt an unpledged electoral ticket headed by Thomson, which was intended to serve as a protest against the system of caucus nominations. The ticket was published only two weeks before the presidential election, and its sponsors admitted

---

[25] *Ibid.*, 2, 3 Aug. 1816.

that it could not be expected to do well. But they maintained that the attempt would be salutary. "What if we do not now succeed in enlightening the public judgment?" wrote a Pittsburgh man to the *Aurora* editor. "We must begin at some time to oppose the pernicious tendency of caucusing, and the earlier the better."[26]

The Monroe-Tompkins men labored to expose the anti-caucus appeal as a fraud intended to conceal ignoble motives. They charged that it was Federalist inspired, which was untrue, and that it was a Clintonian subterfuge. In fact several avowed Clintonians were active in the movement, including Leib and especially Joseph Reed, who was the principal organizer of the Carlisle meeting and probably the person who had obtained the support of Charles Thomson. After the convention it was rumored that the "Clinton project . . . was completely mortified at Carlisle," but the delegates swore that they had never intended to nominate a particular candidate. The sentiments of the majority of anti-caucus men were probably similar to those of Duane, who was partial to the New Yorker but who was not an active Clintonian. "Upon the merits or claims of Mr. Monroe, or Mr. Clinton, the editor has not yet offered an opinion," he wrote three months before the election; if his opinion were required, he would not hesitate." But since Clinton was not a candidate there was "a want of motive to offer an opinion on the question."[27]

---

[26] *Ibid.*, 14, 26, 31 Oct. 1816; Philip S. Klein, *Pennsylvania Politics, 1817-1832: A Game Without Rules* (Philadelphia, 1940), 79-83.

[27] C. J. Ingersoll to Richard Rush, 23 Sept. 1816, Ingersoll Collection, HSP; *Aurora*, 5 Aug. 1816. See also *ibid.*, 19, 21, 22, 26 Oct. 1816; *Democratic Press*, 26 Oct. 1816.

The choice offered by the independent electoral ticket, the Aurora and the Carlisle leaders repeatedly stated, was not between James Monroe and any other candidate, but between "caucus usurpation or free election." Since Monroe's victory was certain, there was no reason whatever to fear giving one's vote in protest against the method of his nomination. The Aurora warned that "corruption has already made the business of caucussing so perfect, that in a little time it would be utterly useless to make opposition."

> Why should our country fare better than all the rest? Is there any thing in our air, or soil, or woods, that is an antidote to corruption? Are we alone to escape the machinations of the enemies of civil liberty?[28]

The election on November 1 was a stunning victory for the anti-caucus cause. In a tiny election turnout, James Monroe carried the state of Pennsylvania by a mere 8,000 votes. The Monroe ticket received 25,473 votes, to 17,492 votes for the ticket of unpledged electors. In Philadelphia, which James Madison had carried by more than 2500 votes in 1812, the independent electors received a majority over the caucus ticket of 1265 votes.[29]

Nicholas Biddle sought to console his friend Monroe with the information that only about one-third of the potential electorate had voted in the election, because confidence in Monroe's success "prevented the majority from making any exertion." Biddle assured Monroe of his "confirmed popularity" in Pennsylvania and explained that "the opposition . . . was owing in a great degree to

---

[28] Aurora, 28, 31 Oct., 1 Nov. 1816.

[29] Ibid., "Jackson," 5 Nov. 1816.

the prevailing dislike to [sic] the interference of members of Congress in the choice of a President."[30]

IV.

The unexpected triumph for the anti-caucus cause gave a tremendous lift to the movement and enhanced the possibility of upsetting the Snyder party in the next gubernatorial election. In Philadelphia there was a resurgence of strength in the Old School party, reflected in the "propitious" results of the 1816 elections. The Old Schoolers had increased their strength relative to the Snyderites throughout the city and county, and with the aid of Federalist voters had elected their county assembly ticket for the first time since the war.[31]

Duane's renewed participation in state politics, which the Aurora had ignored for years, contributed enormously to the Old School's restoration. "The Aurora is active, malignant, and within the banks of the Schuylkill & Delaware, efficacious too," warned Charles Ingersoll. "That paper is too powerful for the [Democratic] Press." William John Duane, who had completed his law studies and had been admitted to the bar in 1815, was an able and enthusiastic member of the Carlisle movement and the author of a number of excellent essays in defense of the cause. "The son writes as much and better than the father," in Ingersoll's opinion, "and they have nothing else to do but to compose their paragraphs & columns."

---

[30]Biddle to Monroe, 25 Nov. 1816, Monroe Papers, NYPL.

[31]Aurora, 10 Oct. 1816; Democratic Press, 9, 10, 11 Oct. 1816.

Binns on the other hand "is not only alone, without the same readiness with his style," Ingersoll admitted, "but engrossed besides with a power of advertising patronage and other means of making mony [*sic*] to which he bends his force."[32]

Governor Simon Snyder was serving his third term in office and constitutionally would be forced to retire at the end of 1817. His popularity, especially in the rural areas of central and western Pennsylvania, had unified the statewide Democratic Republican party for more than a decade. But it was questionable whether the Snyder party could remain dominant without the personality of Snyder, especially in view of the development of divisive economic issues. Duane of course thought it necessary to break up the longstanding establishment in Harrisburg, or "*Sycophantsburg*" as he called it, and continually pressed the question, "*Shall Simon Snyder nominate his successor*?" By July 1816 the fierce electoral agitation had understandably confused many people into "the mistaken impression that the election for governor of Pennsylvania takes place in the present year. It does not take place till the fall of 1817," the *Aurora* clarified.[33]

The anti-caucus theme had a deeper significance than the mere demand for rotation in office so as to share in the spoils of victory, as it was characterized by its detractors. Rather it reflected a rising concern with the moral consequences of a system

---

[32]Ingersoll to Richard Rush, 23 Sept. 1816, Ingersoll Collection, HSP.

[33]*Aurora*, 20 July, 23, 24 Oct. 1816.

which encouraged flagrant opportunism by men in politics. Vast economic rewards were available to unscrupulous sycophants of the "Republican" party through their manipulation of the power of bank incorporations. In 1814 the legislature had chartered forty-two banks in a single action, to supplement the total of four banks then legally functioning in Pennsylvania. The wildly speculative institutions were at extreme variance with the agrarian principles formerly espoused by the Snyder party. But members of the legislature were deeply involved in the interests of the banks they chartered.

"The revolution in the meaning of names is curious," observed the Aurora. "In former times many who were in heart monarchists assumed the name of federalists; in the present times the name of democrat is used to cover shaving and peculating and cheating the public." In Duane's opinion, the nation was experiencing the repetition of an endless struggle. "In all ages: there was a basic political division between "the few" and "the mass"; so it was in 1776 and again in 1800 when "the mass resolved to put things to rights once more." But "As soon as these few were displaced there arose another few from amongst the old mass," who again had to be made subservient to the interests of the whole society.[34]

The resentment of the Forty-two Bank act contributed greatly to the chances for an anti-caucus victory in the gubernatorial election. "Any democrat of good qualifications out of the city will easily put a period to the Snyder dynasty," in the opinion of

---

[34]Ibid., 4, 10 Oct. 1817.

Hugh Hamilton, editor of the Harrisburg Chronicle. Hamilton was a former Federalist who became a Democrat of the Old School and whose editorial views on economic questions closely coincided with those of Duane. Writing to a Philadelphian, Hamilton warned that the anti-caucus men could win only "if there is a proper understanding between the city & the country," for "you can form no idea how your brokers have incensed the country against anything in the city."[35]

Joseph Reed believed, after "inquiries on the subject," that "nothing but a good candidate is wanting to command success." Yet that "it must be admitted, is difficult to find." The two leading prospects for the anti-caucus nomination were Andrew Gregg and Joseph Hiester. In Reed's opinion "neither . . . have those high commanding qualifications necessary for the high station of Governor of this Great State." Gregg was the favorite in central Pennsylvania; but he seemed reluctant to run and was unlikely to win, because he had opposed the war with England while in the Senate. Consequently, at a convention in Carlisle in March 1817, after desultory consideration of other candidates the anti-caucus party nominated Joseph Hiester by acclamation.[36]

Congressman Hiester was a rich, elderly German farmer from Berks county, who had served in the Revolution with the rank of captain. He had been a respected figure in Pennsylvania political

---

[35]Hamilton to John Sergeant, 4 Jan., 11 Mar. 1816, Sergeant Papers, HSP.

[36]Reed to Sergeant, 5 Feb. 1817, ibid.; Klein, Pa. Politics, 84-88. See also Hugh Hamilton to John Sergeant, 12 Mar. 1816, Sergeant Papers, HSP.

life since the 1780s, serving in the convention which ratified the United States Constitution, and in the state constitutional convention of 1790. In the early 1800s Hiester had been a close friend of the late General Peter Muhlenberg, and he had been suspected along with Muhlenberg of cooperation with Michael Leib to construct a German political party in the state. Old School influence was strong in the convention which selected him as a candidate in 1817. Hiester's chief merit was his personal reputation for being honest, frugal and decent, together with his military service in the Revolution. Throughout the state he was sentimentally endorsed as the "*last old revolutionary character . . . likely to be a candidate for governor*."[37]

Although Hiester had been nominated by Democrats, his candidacy was highly acceptable to the Federalist party because of his Revolutionary service and his "unimpeachable moral character." The party openly endorsed him and campaigned enthusiastically on his behalf. Consequently in Philadelphia, at least, the Patent Democratic opponents ignored the merits of the two candidates and campaigned almost exclusively against Federalism itself and against the threat of revived Federalist power if Joseph Hiester were elected.[38]

---

[37]Meadville *Crawford Messenger*, 5 Sept. 1817, quoted in James A. Kehl, *Ill Feeling in the Era of Good Feeling: Western Pennsylvania Political Battles, 1815-1825* (Pittsburgh, 1956), 198; *U. S. Gazette*, 1 Oct. 1817. See also *Aurora*, 30 Sept., 4 Oct. 1817.

[38]*U. S. Gazette*, 12 Oct. 1816, 27, 29 Sept., 1, 4, 11, 13 Oct. 1817; *True American*, 4 Sept. 1817; *Poulson's American Daily Advertiser*, 2, 3 Oct. 1817; *Democratic Press*, 3-15 Oct. 1817.

The candidate of the Snyder party was William Findlay, who had been state treasurer since 1809. To Duane and the Old School Democrats, Findlay was an outstanding example of the emerging system of collusion between politics and business. It was he who had written the bill creating "that great hot-bed of aristocracy--that poison of Pennsylvania legislation, the mammoth banking law." Governor Snyder himself had always opposed the new banks, and the act of incorporation had passed over his veto. Formerly Duane had unjustly accused him of "secret connivance," but during the gubernatorial campaign he blamed only Findlay and alleged that in 1814 the Treasurer had told Snyder that he ought to resign because of his obstinacy on the banking question and allow Findlay to become the candidate for Governor. Findlay's advocates, according to the *Aurora*, were the entrenched office-holders, plus "a few lawyers of *questionable* character," and "a host of bank *stock-holders* and *bank directors*, erected under his influence and engaged in his support."[39]

In the summer of 1817 the Hiesterites uncovered a scandal which graphically illustrated their objections to the Findlayite branch of the Democratic party. Thomas Morgan, Duane's son-in-law from Washington, Pennsylvania, revealed his knowledge of an incident of Findlay's dishonesty. In February 1815, a period of gross fluctuation in bank values, the Treasurer had accepted 8,000 dollars worth of depreciated western bank notes in exchange for a treasury draft on the Bank of Pennsylvania in Philadelphia. The recipient, General Thomas Acheson, a merchant from the town of

---

[39] *Aurora*, 10 Apr. 1816, 21, 31 July 1817.

Washington, had no official business with the treasury, but was given the gratuitous profit of about 650 dollars simply as a favor from his friend the Treasurer. When the story was disclosed, the Findlayites denied it, but Morgan and the Hiesterites had a number of corroborative witnesses because General Acheson had widely boasted of his good fortune.[40]

The Acheson incident suggested the need for a thorough investigation of the Treasurer's past conduct. "I have not the smallest doubt but that exchanges of the public money, upon a stupendous scale, will be established," wrote "Aristides." He recommended that every draft upon a Philadelphia bank which was not explicitly accounted for should be examined for evidence of "a similar purpose of favoritism and corruption." The Hiesterites also assembled some evidence that Findlay himself had used the state funds to conduct his affairs. Periodically he had borrowed large sums from banks in Harrisburg, and the "time and manner of borrowing and repaying" led political sleuths to the conclusion "that the *public money was made use of*, during the intervals between the annual settlements of accounts" by the Auditor-General.[41]

The charges against the Treasurer were similar to those a year earlier of misconduct in the federal Post Office department. Congress in 1816 had ordered an investigation of the evidence that during the war officers of the department had sold drafts on the

---

[40] *Ibid.*, 24 June, 15, 31 July, 14, 15 Aug. 1817; *Democratic Press*, 7 Oct. 1817.

[41] *Aurora*, 31 July, 2 Oct. 1817.

post office valued at par in exchange for the depreciated notes of District of Columbia banks. The Assistant Postmaster General, Abraham Bradley, Jr., was also President of Washington's Union bank, which had profited enormously through the receipt of the departmental drafts. But the Congressional investigating committee had quickly dismissed the charges. It acknowledged that the unfortunate arrangement had enriched some individuals and banks, but concluded that there was no proof of a dishonest intent.

Duane's *Aurora* had been intensely interested in the Post Office investigation and was utterly contemptuous of the result. The editor analyzed and revised the committee's report to satisfy his own unshaken conviction that "the treasury of the post office is employed as a *shaving shop*--the public money, and the privileges of the office, are employed in usury, and in *loans to members of congress*, and in profiting the public agents." The chairman of the committee which exonerated the department was a Congressman from Pennsylvania, Samuel D. Ingham of Bucks county. Ingham was also a key supporter of Findlay and the leader of the Findlayites in the state's Congressional delegation. Duane reiterated his opinion of Ingham formed by the Post Office affair during the gubernatorial campaign.[42]

The Patent Democrats, taken by surprise, attempted to ignore the charges against their candidate, and intensified their

---

[42]*Ibid.*, 5, 6, 9, 10, 11, 12, 13, 29 Apr., 1 May, 5 Aug. 1816; *Weekly Aurora*, 7 Oct. 1816. See also Duane to John Sergeant, 27 Jan. 1816, Sergeant Papers, HSP; Samuel D. Ingham to C. J. Ingersoll, 16 Apr. 1816, Ingersoll Collection, HSP.

campaign against the Hiesterite link with the Federalist party. The one exception was Mathew Carey, who tried to explain away the Acheson exchange. Carey was chairman of the committee of correspondence for Findlay and had placed him in nomination at Harrisburg. He dismissed the problem of unequal exchange as a relatively harmless adjunct of the banking system and "repeatedly said that there was more stress laid on the transaction than it deserved." The derision which met Carey's rationale indicated that his silent colleagues had adopted the more prudent course.[43]

In the final months of the gubernatorial race, the issue of Findlay's misconduct as Treasurer dominated the anti-caucus campaign. The *Aurora* had raised the issue but other newspapers throughout the state took it up with increasing fervor, and the Federalists, for their part, were delighted to publicize the allegations of Republican malfeasance in office. The Clintonian organ the New York *Columbian* predicted on the basis of the information from the state that Findlay would be defeated because of "his artful and complicated money transactions, &c."[44]

The potential significance of a victory for Joseph Hiester had been increased immeasurably by DeWitt Clinton's recent election as Governor of New York. Appealing successfully against the use of the legislative caucus, Clinton had gained the nomination in a

---

[43]*Aurora*, 10 July, 14 Oct. 1817; *Democratic Press*, 7 Oct. 1817; *True American*, 25, 30 Sept. 1817.

[44]*Aurora*, 1, 4 Oct. 1814; *U. S. Gazette*, 27 Sept., 1 Oct. 1817; *True American*, 2-30 Sept. 1817; Kehl, *Ill Feeling*, 196-198; New York *Columbian* quoted in *U. S. Gazette*, 13 Sept. 1817.

statewide convention and gone on to a sweeping victory. "A new state of things has arisen in New York," wrote William H. Crawford. "DeWitt Clinton again wields the influence." Already calculating the effect upon the presidential succession, Crawford predicted that the new Vice President Daniel Tompkins "will become a cipher in the politics of New York before the end of four years. His chance of the Presidency I consider as gone, never to return. Clinton will again appear the Northern favorite." Moreover in Pennsylvania the "rapidly amalgamating" Old School men and Federalists, Crawford believed, "may eventually become very formidable, if not triumphant. In that event . . . Clinton would receive the suffrage of that State." Charles Ingersoll also thought that "Should Mr. Hiester succeed . . . the plan would be a coalition with Governor Clinton to secure all the Eastern and middle States . . . for his presidency in 1821."[45]

"The most hard-fought electioneering campaign we have ever seen is going on in Pennsylvania," observed the Columbian. Writing from Boston, Duane's old friend Henry Dearborn cancelled his subscription to the Aurora because he thought that the editor was indulging in "unqualified abuse" of Findlay and imputing evil motives to all opponents indiscriminately. But Richard Rush was dissatisfied with the indifferent attitude of most non-Pennsylvanians toward the state's gubernatorial election and particularly

---

[45]Alvin Kass, Politics in New York State, 1800-1830 (Syracuse, 1965), 82; Crawford to Albert Gallatin, 23 Apr. 1817, Adams, ed., Writings of Albert Gallatin, II, 36-37; Ingersoll to Richard Rush, 23 Apr. 1817, in William M. Meigs, The Life of Charles Jared Ingersoll (Philadelphia, 1900), 106.

annoyed with the National Intelligencer for calling it a mere "family dispute." In Rush's opinion, which he expressed frankly to the President, it was the most important event then pending in the United States. Should Findlay lose, he warned Monroe, "I am quite unable to say what will be the fate or direction of national politics, for years to come."[46]

Rush believed that the Era of Good Feelings in the country, ushered in by Monroe's unopposed victory in 1816, was gravely threatened by Pennsylvania's anti-caucus movement. Thomas Jefferson admitted that he had been "charmed to see that a Presidential election now produces scarcely any agitation"; but Rush was worried. "There is something in the seeming unanimity and calm of the present moment, that fills me with anticipations. It cannot last. Tornadoes that will sweep in opposite courses, may be generating."[47]

In spite of Findlay's shortcomings as a candidate, the Snyderites still had the tremendous advantage of their Democratic Republican orthodoxy, which meant a great deal especially west of the mountains. Thomas Sergeant, Findlay's unofficial campaign manager, predicted that the "tramontane vote" would "devour" Hiester's majorities east of the Susquehanna. "To surrender all this side of

---

[46]New York Columbian quoted in U. S. Gazette, 13 Sept. 1817; Dearborn to Duane, 7 Oct. [1817], Pers. Papers Misc. (Dearborn), LC; Rush to Monroe, 28 Sept. 1817, Monroe Papers, LC. See also Rush to C. J. Ingersoll, 16 May 1817, Ingersoll Collection, HSP; Rush to James Madison, 6 Sept. 1817, Richard Rush Papers, 1812-1847, HSP; Rush to [Joseph] Gales, 27 Sept. 1817, Lewis Biddle Collection, HSP.

[47]Rush to Jonathan Roberts, 3 July, 11 Aug. 1817, Roberts Papers, HSP; Jefferson to Gallatin, 16 June 1817, Ford, ed., Writings of Thomas Jefferson, X, 92.

the Allegheny into Mr. Hiester's hands is giving up a very strong first position," remarked Charles Ingersoll.[48] But the western Democrats were equal to Tom Sergeant's expectations. Joseph Hiester carried Philadelphia, Pittsburgh, and much of eastern Pennsylvania, but by compiling immense majorities beyond the mountains, Findlay carried the state by a scant 7,000 votes.

The most consistent patterns of the Hiester-Findlay election was a division between densely populated communities, which voted for Hiester, and sparsely populated rural areas, which went to Findlay. Farmers who lived in relatively isolated districts, apparently unaffected by the issues of the anti-caucus men of Philadelphia and Pittsburgh, retained their loyalty to the principle of Republican unity and voted for the candidate of the Snyder party.[49]

Richard Rush warned the President that Findlay's victory had been obtained only by the most arduous effort, "and the majority will not be large." William Crawford too told the absent Albert Gallatin that "the result . . . is not considered brilliant. Should that State fall into the hands of the Quids and Feds," Crawford feared, "DeWitt Clinton enters the list this time three years with Mr. Monroe. The change is certainly possible."

A more disinterested observer, Thomas Jefferson, confessed that he was puzzled by the political future. "That federal for-

---

[48] Ingersoll to Rush, 23 Apr. 1817, Meigs, Life of C. J. Ingersoll, 106.

[49] Klein, Pa. Politics, 95; Kehl, Ill Feeling, 198-199, cf. 203.

tress which we had to storm, . . . is now compleatly mastered," he wrote to an old colleague, "and all, within & without, is quiet. What is next? What are to be our future parties?" Jefferson found "a strange jumble at present. Duane is making common cause with the federalists. [John] Randolph is federal by nature and by his passions. [Henry] Clay is on the start somewhere. I do not know where the Clintons are," he admitted, "of such medley complexion are the parties of that state." Jefferson was certain of one thing only, that new parties would emerge, "for parties must be wherever men are free, and wherever their minds and faces are unlike."[50]

---

[50]Rush to Monroe, 17 Oct. 1817, Monroe Papers, LC; Crawford to Gallatin, 27 Oct. 1817, Adams, ed., Writings of Albert Gallatin, II, 55; Jefferson to Henry Dearborn, 17 May 1818, TJ-LC.

CHAPTER XII

THE PANIC OF 1819

The election of William Findlay led to a shift in political influence in Pennsylvania away from the rural "Clodhoppers" who had revered Simon Snyder into the hands of the sophisticated Philadelphians who were Findlay's key supporters. The most important office under the Governor, that of Secretary of the Commonwealth, went to the city lawyer Thomas Sergeant, who was a younger half-brother of the Federalist Congressman John Sergeant. In Philadelphia itself the Findlayite victory affected the nature of the political factions, for a small group of young politicians took control of the New School Democratic party and purged John Binns from its leadership. The Patent Democrats, as the Old Schoolers called them, were also known as the Family party, because of the convolutions of kinship among its leaders. Tom Sergeant and his brother-in-law Richard Bache, who had become the city Postmaster upon Leib's removal, and Bache's brother-in-law George Mifflin Dallas formed the nucleus in the city. In Pittsburgh the party was represented by Dallas's brother-in-law William Wilkins.[1]

The paternal figurehead of the Family party was Alexander James Dallas. The elder Dallas, who had led the Quid party in 1805

---

[1]See Klein, Pa. Politics, 96-112, for a general discussion of politics during William Findlay's administration.

in support of Governor Thomas McKean, had retired from politics after the election of Snyder in 1808, during "the reign of newspaper editors," Binns and Duane. Although he disdained Binns, Dallas was on excellent terms with Binns' intimate colleagues Richard Rush and Charles J. Ingersoll, and after Dallas entered President Madison's cabinet in 1814 he cooperated with Rush concerning patronage in Pennsylvania. When Dallas chose to retire after two years as Secretary of the Treasury, upon completing his goal of creating a Second Bank of the United States, Rush proposed that the Philadelphia New Schoolers nominate him for Congress. When the General Ward committee carried through the suggestion, Duane blamed the lack of "any delicacy at all" by George M. Dallas and Richard Bache, for Dallas had been "proposed and nominated by the votes of his own son and son-in-law!" But Dallas declined the proffered nomination and politically he was wise to do so, as the Old School Democrats would certainly have caused his defeat in the general election. He was eulogized by the Democratic Press upon his retirement from the Treasury and return to the practice of law in Philadelphia. A few months later, in February 1817, he died unexpectedly. At the time of his death, A. J. Dallas' reputation was at its highest, and he was almost restored to the political esteem which he had enjoyed in the early 1800s.[2]

---

[2]G. M. Dallas, Life of A. J. Dallas, 129-130, 141; Rush to Ingersoll, 21 June 1816, Ingersoll Collection, HSP; Ingersoll to Rush, 23 Sept. 1816, ibid.; Aurora, 7, 8 Oct. 1816; Democratic Press, 8, 16 Oct. 1816; John Jacob Astor to Albert Gallatin, 1 Feb. 1817, Gallatin Papers, NYHS; Joseph Reed to John Sergeant, 5 Feb. 1817, Sergeant Papers, HSP; Jonathan Roberts to Nicholas Biddle, 30 Jan. 1817, Biddle Papers, LC. On patronage see Rush to A. J.

The restoration of Dallas and the rise of his family and its friends to political dominance during the Era of Good Feelings illustrated the truth of Duane's analysis of politics in Philadelphia. Throughout the era of Binns' prominence, Duane had contended that the Quids were truly the preponderant influence in the New School Democrats and that A. J. Dallas, even in apparent retirement, had always been the "great manager." A "new _puppet_ plays nothing but the _old farce_," Duane commented in 1816, on a "stripling" enlisted in the service of Dallas; "put down _Leib_ and _Duane_ has been the cry of [Alexander J.] Macsycophant and Co. for fourteen years, and it is now _newly fitted up and played_ like the pieces formerly at the _old Theatre_ to amuse the democrats."[3]

The Findlayite leaders in Philadelphia were the younger generation of Constitutional Republicans. "In 1805, Tom Sergeant, Dick Bache, and the whole family compact, in all its ramifications of affinities, even unto the 45th degree of cousinship, were active and furious quids." These young politicians had the full support of the older Quids, and during the campaign of 1817 they could be seen with Tom Sergeant and others in planning sessions at the White Horse tavern or working over "musty papers" at the city library. Together they were "the very essence of patent democracy."

There was for example Edward Fox, Tom Sergeant's uncle, formerly a close associate of Dallas and Thomas McKean. Tench Coxe

---

Dallas, letters 1812 to 1815 _passim_, Lewis Biddle Collection, HSP; Ingersoll to A. J. Dallas, 18 Dec. 1813, 8 Apr. 1816, Ingersoll Collection, HSP.

[3] _Aurora_, 13 Aug. 1816.

and Mathew Carey, who had consistently supported every movement in opposition to Leib and Duane since the Rising Sun conspiracy of 1802, moved with ease from the New School Democrats into the Findlay party. "Can it be wise or discreet," Sergeant asked, "to keep alive & perpetuate our hostility to quids? . . . their errors, if errors they can be called, were those of opinion on a few local points, long since consigned to oblivion; and," in his opinion, "they themselves have, within a few years been the pride and ornament of democracy."[4]

The Family's assumption of political leadership was generally accepted by the New School Democrats, even by those who had first invited John Binns to move to Philadelphia and establish a newspaper. General John Barker and United States Marshal John Smith, the key figures in the 1807 movement to oppose Duane from within the Democratic Republicans, were both attached to the Findlay party. The Marshal's brother Robert Smith was a brother-in-law of William Findlay and a party leader in the legislature. Old General Barker was the Family party's favorite Revolutionary hero; on election eve in 1817 he had opened the ball held in honor of Findlay. The General's son James N. Barker prospered in politics as a loyal Family man. First appointed a city alderman by Governor Findlay, Barker eventually became Mayor and then Collector of the Port of Philadelphia. Somewhat resembling in nature his gentle father, James Barker was a cautious and indecisive man, but his

---

[4]Philadelphia Independent Balance, 11 Aug. 1819. See also Aurora, 10, 14, 15 July, 9 Sept., 7, 14 Oct. 1817; Harrisburg Chronicle, 22 Mar., 9 Aug. 1819; Democratic Press, 4 Oct. 1817.

opinions were supplied him by George M. Dallas.[5]

The elimination of John Binns was quickly accomplished by creating a new newspaper to replace the Democratic Press as the party organ. Binns had possessed one crucial political asset, his personal friendship with Simon Snyder. When Governor Snyder's constitutional term was approaching its close, he did not sufficiently appreciate that he was dispensable. His domineering and vulgar personality was offensive to a great many persons within his own party, and he had no compensating talents as an effective newspaper editor. The first indication of a movement to overthrow Binns was an attempt in the Pennsylvania legislature in 1816 to defeat his re-election as a state director of the Bank of Pennsylvania. Some Snyderite legislators from the country were shocked by the vindictive sentiments of the Philadelphia representatives. The attempt was abandoned, reportedly at the request of William Findlay, and the assault on the editor postponed until after the gubernatorial election.[6]

On February 22, 1818, the Franklin Gazette began publication in Philadelphia under the editorship of Postmaster Richard Bache. The prospectus declared that the paper would be "free from that licentious attack on reputation, which converts political controversy, into personal slander." From this an editor in Washington,

---

[5] Aurora, 15 Aug., 6 Oct. 1817, 23 Oct. 1820; Independent Balance, 19 Feb. 1823; Fearon, Sketches of America, 139-140. On James N. Barker see George M. Dallas to Samuel D. Ingham, letters 1825 to 1831, passim, Dallas Papers, HSP.

[6] Matthew Roberts to George Weaver, 23 Dec. 1816, Roberts Papers, HSP; Aurora, 22 July 1817.

Pennsylvania, inferred that the Democratic Press from its "indelicacy of style, rudeness of clamour, and want of talent and fair reputation, has been condemned as worn out." To former President Madison, Bache wrote that he hoped by abolishing abusive writing to "relieve my native State from what may at present be termed, the horror of an election."[7]

Within a few months the break between Binns and the Family leaders became final. In April Binns asked Tom Sergeant, the Secretary of the Commonwealth, to appoint him as a city alderman and Sergeant refused. Binns attacked the Secretary, repented his support for Findlay, and found himself politically abandoned. One friend who remained loyal to Binns was Richard Rush, but Rush had gone to London as the American Ambassador and was not in a position to help in political matters. In a letter to Richard Bache soon after the Franklin began publication, Rush hopefully directed: "Remember me particularly to our friend Col. Binns." The enclosed "political information . . . is for his confidential ear in like manner as for yours. Your two papers work together I feel sure. We must never forget the services of his," Rush admonished. "It is impossible that I ever can." The editor stopped sending the Franklin to Rush soon after. By the time he had been in London for a year, the homesick Rush was completely out of touch with Pennsylvania politics. The State department sent him a file of the Nation-

---

[7]"Prospectus," Franklin Gazette, enclosed in Richard Bache to Jefferson, 3 Jan. 1818, TJ-LC; Washington Gazette quoted in U. S. Gazette, 30 Jan. 1818; Bache to Madison, 8 Jan. 1818, Madison Papers, LC. See also Nicholas Biddle to John Forsyth, 6 Feb. 1818, Biddle Papers, LC.

al Intelligencer, but he never saw a Pennsylvania paper and even Philadelphia papers "reach this country but sparingly." He admitted, "I grieve at the misunderstanding which has grown up between the Editors" Bache and Binns, "and trust, . . . that as I left them, so on my return I shall find them friends again."[8]

John Binns never submitted to the judgment of political exile. Five years later the Patent Democrats were still struggling to eject him from the political scene. "Binns will not give up--he will die in the last ditch," complained one frustrated Family leader. Binns continued to command the loyalty of a factional party which represented several hundred votes and was apparently particularly strong in the fiercely democratic southwestern wards of the city. Recent immigrants from Ireland were probably the largest element in Binns' following. William Duane was the hero of an earlier generation of Irish immigrants who had arrived in the Federalist era or during the presidency of Thomas Jefferson. But during the years of Simon Snyder's administration, Binns had begun to attract the newer arrivals from his native country.

For a number of years after 1818 the Family party had to compete for Democratic votes with two factional parties, Old Schoolers and Binns men. "It is a curious fact that altho at the polls we have given in double the number of votes that the two united factions . . . did at the two last elections," a Family leader complained in 1823, "yet at the ward meetings, and at town meetings,

---

[8]Franklin Gazette, 31 Oct. 1820; Rush to Bache, 4 Aug. 1818; extract copy in John Binns folder, Society Collection, HSP; Rush to Jonathan Roberts, 8 Dec. 1819, Roberts Papers, HSP.

they can manage to bring forward such a number of the canail more than we can, that they have often beaten us at those places." He took comfort however in the proof "that our men are the genteelist and most respectable of the party; men who will not come out where their [sic] is a collection of the offscourings of the party," but who would faithfully go to the polls on election day.[9]

Samuel Cooper, a loyal Binns man, described the same situation from a different point of view. The Family men were "pretended democrats," explained the untutored but eloquent Cooper, "who would sacrafice their own farther [sic] to make room for themselves." When Binns exposes their hypocrisy, "then [sic] open the cry of Irish Irish. Americans to your Posts. We are no longer to be dictated to, we have Americans enough to Edit papers[,] he won't do the renigado &c."[10]

In 1818 an important member of the Family party who was not related by blood or marriage to the other leaders was the thirty-two year old Nicholas Biddle. However Biddle was socially intimate with the entire Dallas clan and had been privy to the plans for founding the *Franklin Gazette*. Indeed it would perhaps be fair to say that John Binns had been expelled in order to make the party safe for Nicholas Biddle. "I have thought for some time," George Dallas boasted in 1819, "that the Democratic party was quietly, but certainly, under going a purification and a regeneration." The

---

[9]John Lisle to George Bryan, 25 Jan. 1823, George Bryan Papers, HSP.

[10]Cooper to George Bryan, 14 Aug. 1823, *ibid*.

party was regaining, Dallas believed, "a character and dignity of which the meddling cunning of printers has deprived it for many years."[11]

The single most important cause of Biddle's conversion to Republicanism was his friendship with James Monroe, formed in London when the young Princeton graduate was on his grand tour and Monroe was the American Ambassador. When Monroe was elected President, Biddle predicted that he would "have the fairest field of administration . . . since the time of Washington." Another reason for Biddle's changed opinion of the Republican party was his great admiration for the service of A. J. Dallas as Secretary of the Treasury, in creating the much needed Second Bank of the United States. In addition to the Dallas and Bache families, Biddle had a number of friends among the Democratic politicians, notably Charles Ingersoll and the fatherly Jonathan Roberts, then a United States Senator from Pennsylvania. Biddle also had a warm friendship with Mathew Carey, who regarded the younger man as something of a political protege. Biddle should use his talents in government, Carey urged, because good men had been too passive and it was "working our perdition."[12]

---

[11]G. M. Dallas to [Samuel D. Ingham], 20 July 1819, Dallas Papers, HSP; Biddle to John Forsyth, 6 Feb. 1818, Biddle Papers, LC.

[12]Biddle to B. Henry, draft, 27 Nov. 1816, _ibid_.; Carey to Biddle, 4 Feb. 1815, _ibid_. See also Biddle to Jonathan Roberts, draft, 14 Dec. 1815, _ibid_.; Roberts to Biddle, 27 Dec. 1815, 14 Jan. 1817, _ibid_.; Biddle to John Forsyth, 13 Oct. 1819, _ibid_.; Richard Bache to Biddle, 17 Mar. 1817, _ibid_.; M. Thomas to Biddle, 10 Mar. 1817, _ibid_.; Biddle to Monroe, 10 Apr. 1817, Monroe Papers, NYPL; Captain J[ames] Biddle to C. J. Ingersoll, 4 Aug. 1817,

A practical reason for Biddle's change of party was that he was highly ambitious politically. By 1818 he had nourished for nearly a decade the hope of election to Congress. In 1810 a group of Federalist friends had offered to nominate him and he accepted, but the plan had to be abandoned because Biddle at twenty-four was constitutionally too young for the office. Instead he agreed to stand for the Pennsylvania legislature, where his maiden speech, delivered on his twenty-fifth birthday, was a brilliant and impassioned defense of a recharter of the First Bank of the United States. Biddle served a term in the state senate in 1814-15, his last political activity as a Federalist. In 1816 Biddle was proposed as a Republican candidate for Congress, but the nomination was blocked in the General Ward committee by delegates from the Old School. Disappointed, Biddle agreed again to go to the state capital, but he resigned his senate seat halfway through his elected term rather than endure a second dreary winter in Harrisburg.[13]

In 1818 Biddle was given another chance to begin his political career in Washington, when the Philadelphia Patent Democrats nominated him for Congress. The _Franklin Gazette_ adopted the lofty editorial position that a good man could not decline to vote for the statesmanlike Nicholas Biddle. Nonetheless Biddle's candidacy was the most hotly contested of the Family's nominations. No doubt

---

Ingersoll Collection, HSP; Biddle to Carey, 31 Jan. 1815, Nicholas Biddle Personal Letters (film), HSP.

[13]Biddle to Mr. Watts, 5 Oct. 1810, _ibid_.; Biddle to Isaac Weaver, 18 July 1817, _ibid_.; Richard to Leech to Biddle, 30 Dec. 1817, Biddle Papers, LC; Thomas P. Govan, _Nicholas Biddle, Nationalist and Public Banker, 1786-1844_ (Chicago, 1959), 30-34, 52.

with the help of some Federalist votes, Biddle ran first on the Findlay Congressional ticket, but the ticket lost to a combined Federalist and Old School slate. "We did our best to send you Nicholas Biddle in Congress," Charles Ingersoll wrote to the President, "but we were totally vanquished, as I feared we should be." From Washington Congressman John Forsyth sent his condolences to the city and county of Philadelphia.

With the Findlay party increasing in strength in the state overall, Ingersoll anticipated "salutary influences on the disorordered politics of this district." He thought that Biddle "may certainly be chosen on another trial if he is disposed for it." Biddle was so disposed, and he again headed the Family slate of Congressional candidates in the election of 1820. But the result was identical; he polled the most votes on a losing ticket. Without the support of the Old Schoolers, the Democrats could not elect their candidates in the Federalist dominated city. The Family had been mistakenly confident that their star acquisition would be popular with all Republicans because of his brilliance. When he was defeated, the _Franklin Gazette_ and Biddle himself maintained that it was not for personal reasons, but because he "was well disposed to the administration of the general government." This explanation was not true of the Old School Democrats who clearly disliked Biddle for other reasons. According to "Brutus" in the _Aurora_, the true vocation of this politically ambitious gentleman was to be an idle aristocrat. The much praised Biddle, he asserted, was a man of mediocre talents, guilty of vacillation in his political loyalties, and morally disqualified for office because President Monroe had appointed him a year earlier to the board of directors of the "unlawful mammoth bank."[14]

Biddle made one more unsuccessful attempt to gain office as a Patent Democrat when in 1821 he sought election by the Pennsylvania legislature to the United States Senate. Two years later Biddle became president of the Bank of the United States. He drifted away from his association with the Family party, having finally acquired by appointment the national political influence which he could not attain by popular election.[15]

During the period when the Family party was assuming leadership of the New School, the Democratic party of the Old School was also experiencing changes in leadership and nature. Michael Leib, for more than fifteen years co-equal in leadership with William Duane, had almost disappeared from the party councils by 1819. As early as 1815 Leib had become seriously ill, and four years later his enemies announced that he was "now tottering on the verge of the grave." Meanwhile he had been elected to two terms in the state assembly, but one supporter confessed that his performance in the legislature had "by no means equalled our expectation," perhaps primarily because of the state of his health.

Although Leib had made few friends in the legislature,

---

[14]Franklin Gazette, 10, 13, 17 Oct. 1818, 4, 11 Oct. 1820; Ingersoll to Monroe, 22 Nov. 1818, Monroe Papers, LC; Forsyth to Biddle, 16 Oct. 1818, Biddle Papers, LC; Biddle to Monroe, 8 Oct. 1820, quoted in Govan, Biddle, 69; Philadelphia National Gazette, 7 Oct. 1820; Aurora, 2, 3 Oct. 1820.

[15]C. B[iddle], Jr., to Nicholas Biddle, 12 Nov. 1820, Biddle Papers, LC; "C." to Biddle, 18 Dec. [1820], ibid.

Joseph Reed hoped that this "perhaps may not be the case with the people on whom his efforts may probably have more weight and influence than on the members."[16] The ex-Federalist turned Democrat pointed out that "this indeed is his calculation and many attempts have been made with that view." The political technique newly observed by Reed was an old one for Michael Leib. Throughout his career as a legislator, Leib had introduced measures for their popular effect which he knew had no chance to become law, while giving his best energies to highly practical political ends. During five years in the United States Senate, Leib's most successful effort had been to eliminate the federal office of Purveyor held by his old enemy Tench Coxe and to prevent Coxe from obtaining another job. In the 1817 session of the Pennsylvania legislature one of Leib's proposals was to lower the salaries of all the major officeholders under the state executive. "But the resolution was literally laughed out of the House." Later Leib sponsored a successful measure which reduced the income of the Attorney General, Amos Ellmaker, as punishment for Ellmaker's part in effecting Leib's removal as Postmaster of Philadelphia in 1815.[17]

Michael Leib was not highly popular with the younger generation of Old School Democrats. Originally, loyalty to Leib had been a _sine qua non_ of party membership. He had been the first politician in Philadelphia to speak of "the sovereignty of the

---

[16] _Aurora_, "Letter from Harrisburg," 27 Dec. 1815; Philadelphia _American Centinel_, 12 Oct. 1819; Joseph Reed to John Sergeant, 5 Feb. 1817, Sergeant Papers, HSP.

[17] _Ibid._; Harrisburg _Chronicle_, 24 May, 30 Aug. 1819.

people," and men who remembered him as "the vital spirit of democracy" had always forgiven such shortcomings as his penchant for personal vendettas. But there was a new generation of Old School Democrats, men who had joined the party because they agreed with its ideas as expressed in Duane's Aurora. They did not choose to overlook the distinction between Leib's professions and his political actions.

The final precipitous decline of Leib's influence became apparent in the election of 1818 when he ran for the state senate. In that election the Old School Democrats and the Federalist party integrated their tickets for the first and last time. Leib was nominated by both parties in the county of Philadelphia, and after bitter objection the city Federalists conceded and accepted Leib as their candidate. The subsequent election was a disaster for Leib and consequently for his party. He was elected, but only because of the votes of Federalists in the city. In the county Leib ran last of the four Senate candidates, and worst of all he was last in his own constituency, the Northern Liberties. Undermined by Leib's unpopularity, the Old School assembly ticket in the county, which had won in the two preceding years, was defeated by the Patent Democrats. Clearly the strategy of amalgamation with the Federalists had been a failure. Several hundred accustomed Old School voters rebelled and either stayed home from the polls or voted for the Family candidates. The campaign of 1818 was the last to be designed by Michael Leib. He was too sick to attempt another comeback. In 1819 the Patent Democrats gained full control of the Board of Commissioners in the Northern Liberties.[18]

With Leib's retirement from political leadership, the co-operation of the Old School and the Federalists broke down. The process of amalgamating had exactly coincided with the years of Leib's return to local politics, 1814 to 1818. The following year Duane deferred to the strong sentiment within the party against working with the Federalists and helped to organize a "unity" ticket in the city, which carried Philadelphia for the Democrats for the first time since 1813.

With the loss of Leib's Northern Liberties as a political base, the Old School Democrats led by Duane became identified more explicitly as a movement for protest and reform. The Aurora again became a forum for dissenting opinion, as it had been during the administration of John Adams, but for a smaller minority. Among the new leaders of the party who joined Duane after the war was his old friend James Thackara, the Republican engraver who had paid Duane's rent in 1798 when the immigrant printer was destitute. Thackara, who had become curator of the Pennsylvania Academy of Fine Arts, returned to politics after a long retirement as an Old School man, but in outlook he was more conservative than the party. He more closely resembled an Old Republican of the agrarian or Virginia variety. The artist was as outspoken as he was independent, and after he was elected to the legislature in 1818, "Mr. Thackara opposed" became a refrain of the House proceedings.[19]

---

[18]The (Philadelphia) Union, 1, 10, 15 Oct. 1818; American Centinel, 16 Oct. 1818; Franklin Gazette, 29 Sept., 3, 5, 6, 12, 13, 15, 17 Oct. 1818.

[19]Harrisburg Chronicle, 1, 11, 25 Feb., 1, 4, 8 Mar. 1819;

The Family party found Thackara intolerable; they thought him vulgar, impudent, and a poor representative of his city constituency. When the Democratic coalition was agreed upon for 1819, the Family attempted to oust the engraver from the ticket and proposed in his place the wealthy chemicals manufacturer Samuel Wetherill, who had been one of the founders of the New School. This motion by George Dallas in the town meeting to endorse the candidates inspired an impromptu oration from William Duane. He defended the "blunt honesty and integrity" of Thackara, and explained that "For Mr. Wetherill he had a very great respect; but he was a bank director . . . and that was a sufficient objection to him." To the Old Schoolers present the statement was simple dogma, but it puzzled the Family members. "As to bank directors," avowed the next speaker for Wetherill, "he could not see why that subject had been mentioned."[20]

II.

By 1818 economic conditions in the United States had begun to confirm the Aurora's familiar gloomy forecasts that national disaster would result from the postwar economic trends. The country was indulging in a false prosperity which steadily grew more

---

Robert D. Crompton, "James Thackara, Engraver, of Philadelphia and Lancaster, Pennsylvania," Journal of the Lancaster County Historical Society, Vol. 62 (April, 1958), 65-95; Joseph Jackson, Early Philadelphia Architects and Engineers (Philadelphia, 1923), 151; James Thackara, Thackara's Drawing Book for the Amusement and Instruction of Young Ladies & Gentlemen in the Pleasing and Elegant Art of Drawing (Philadelphia, [1813]).

[20] Franklin Gazette, 6 Oct. 1819; American Centinel, 4, 5, 8 Oct. 1819.

precarious. With the return of peace in Europe, America immediately had begun to import immense quantities of manufactured goods from abroad. At the same time it had lost all the commercial advantages which it enjoyed while the European powers were at war. The result was a huge trade imbalance. The extravagance was supported through a vast expansion of credit by the nation's banks. Although in February 1817 the banks returned theoretically to a specie basis, payments of hard money remained almost completely nominal. Consequently, with no effective check on the volume of their notes in circulation, the banks extended discounts freely to an unprecedented scale. In "the cupidity of [extravagant] habits, it was calculated that paper discounts would supply the failures of commerce," Duane remonstrated; "the Banks discounted, and we imported 80,000,000 of dollars worth of your luxurious muslins, shawls, leghorns and all the frippery of your Paris and London fashions--while our annual exports averaged 40,000,000."[21]

While the nation headed toward depression, the government was too engrossed with privilege and intrigue to be concerned, according to William Duane. Following the inauguration of President James Monroe, the *Aurora* observed a courteous interval of several months before commenting on the new administration. But by the time of the President's first annual message in December 1817, Duane discerned that Monroe had no plans to take action which might restore health to the faltering economy. The baseless optimism of Monroe's message to Congress distressed him. "The public is very

---

[21]Duane to D. B. Warden, 16 May 1819, D. B. Warden Papers, LC.

solemnly informed by the chief magistrate," the Aurora commented sourly, "that 'at no period of our political existence had we so much cause to felicitate ourselves at the happy condition of our country.' That the chief magistrate believed this to be the true state of our country," Duane acknowledged, "there cannot be the least doubt; but that he was deceived, . . . is as demonstrable as that water descends, or that air ascends." In Philadelphia at that moment there were 16,000 persons unemployed because of shutdowns at the iron foundries in the suburbs. The total of unemployed industrial workers, according to Duane, numbered in the millions.[22]

Although harsh, the Aurora's appraisals of the government and the economy were honest and realistic. Other newspapers, more loyal to the Republican party, were slow to recognize the growing economic imbalance. For example Niles' Weekly Register, published in Baltimore by Hezekiah Niles, affirmed the President's sanguine judgments for as long as possible. However during 1818 Niles became convinced that the inflation of bank credit was leading the country toward a crisis. Without criticizing the government, Niles began an editorial discussion of the banking situation which made his newspaper famous as a critic of the economy of the period.[23]

The long range solution to the balance of trade problem was a fully protected domestic economy. On this the editors Niles and Duane agreed. In the middle and northern states the desire for a

---

[22]Aurora, 5 Mar. 1817, 19, 21, 22 Jan. 1818.

[23]Niles' Weekly Register, XIII (20, 27 Dec. 1817), 257-259, 282, XIV (7 Mar. 1818), 20.

self-sufficient American system of industry and commerce, excluding foreign participation, was widely expressed and not limited by party. It was a simple truth of society, the Aurora insisted, "that the country must be most prosperous which provides every thing within itself." The legislation of a high tariff to protect weakened home manufactures would be a practicable beginning toward the visionary goal.[24]

In Pennsylvania, the state most advanced in manufacturing, there was general dissatisfaction with the inadequate tariff law of 1816. Although it was the first avowedly protective tariff act ever passed by Congress, it provided substantially less protection than the wartime emergency measure which had doubled all existing duties for the duration of the war. Many Pennsylvanians, Duane among them, had pleaded for the retention of the "double duties" until an effective substitute measure was framed. Within the state the popularity of this appeal had given strength to the emergent anti-caucus movement. The issue formed the basis for an Independent Republican party in Pittsburgh, where Henry Baldwin, who became the leading anti-caucus man in the West, was first elected to Congress in 1816 as a direct reaction against the inadequate new law. As a Congressman Baldwin became the principal spokesman for establishing a barrier to foreign competition. The Findlay Democrats were equally eager for a higher tariff; Mathew Carey's essays on the subject soon made him the most famous tariff advocate in the

---

[24]Aurora, 26 June 1818. The tariff and other forms of economic protection and encouragement were discussed in the Aurora continually during the years of Monroe's administration.

nation. For the most part the rival branches of the Democratic party in Pennsylvania cooperated on the tariff question with relatively little friction. Baldwin and Carey worked together in preparing the highly protective tariff bill of 1820, which failed to pass Congress, and Carey's Philadelphia Society for the encouragement of domestic manufactures sent John Harrison, a prominent Old Schooler, to Washington as its representative to testify on behalf of the unsuccessful legislation.[25]

Meanwhile the institution which the government had created to restore national monetary stability, the Second Bank of the United States, was engaged in contributing on a vast scale to the increasing currency inflation. Under the inept management of its first President, William Jones, the Bank was operating in a manner directly contradictory to its intended purpose. In March 1818, after little more than one year of business, the Bank's total accommodations stood at fifty million dollars, which was approximately twenty-five times the amount of its specie. The Central Bank in Philadelphia provided no policy and exercised no control over its fourteen branches, and in the South and West their reckless conduct encouraged wildcatting by the other banks and created a highly dangerous business atmosphere.

---

[25]Kehl, Ill Feeling, 111, 115; Malcolm Rogers Eiselen, The Rise of Pennsylvania Protectionism (Philadelphia, 1932), 36-41, 64; Duane to John Sergeant, 27 Jan. 1816, Sergeant Papers, HSP; Duane to D. B. Warden, 16 May 1819, D. B. Warden Papers, LC; Baldwin to Carey, 26 Feb., 1 Mar., 1 May 1820, Edward Carey Gardiner Collection, HSP; Harrison to Carey, 13 Sept. 1819, 24, 27 Jan. 1820, ibid.; Harrison to Lydia Leib Harrison, 12 Jan. 1820, Soc. Collection, Leib-Harrison Family Papers, HSP.

A combination of ignorance and greed were responsible for the Bank's disastrous policies. The guiding principles under President William Jones were the desire to maintain a high price for the stock and to furnish a large dividend to the shareholders. Certainly in its first years of operation the Second Bank of the United States tragically confirmed the Aurora's charge that it would not serve as a national institution but as the privileged property of a band of speculators.[26]

In January 1818, when the Bank appeared to be flourishing and had just declared a semi-annual dividend of four per cent, the Aurora began publishing a series of essays on its conduct which astounded the public. The articles described the Bank's unwise and excessive discounting with such detailed knowledge of transactions and board decisions that the charges of mismanagement by the directors were taken seriously almost at once. One skeptical writer lampooned the frightening evidence, advising "Run! Run! Beware of the Bank of the United States!" But the True American called upon the Bank's officials to refute the disclosures, reminding them that the public had never intended "to create an institution to support Stock Jobbers," and that the Bank would "soon be unpopular" if the accusations were true. In succeeding weeks the Philadelphia newspapers generally were inundated with letters and essays in response to the continuing series in the Aurora, many of them in defense of the Bank.[27]

---

[26]Catterall, Second Bank, 27-39.

[27]Aurora, "Brutus," 23 Jan. 1818 and ff.; True American, 28

The author of the controversial series signed himself "Brutus." His identity became a subject of intense interest in Philadelphia, and Duane was harassed with demands that he reveal his name. Refusing on principle to expose a contributor, the *Aurora* editor reminded the public that in 1799 he had been beaten by a gang of thirty men for such a refusal, but had not yielded the information. Duane moreover affected not to know himself who was the author, and the ruse was carefully maintained. After months of speculation, the identity of "Brutus" was still unknown. In May Duane announced that about fifty different persons had been named as the author, including several directors of the United States Bank, one Congressman, a distinguished member of the state legislature, three merchants, two eminent brokers, and about a dozen persons with no knowledge of the subject whatever. The Petersburg *Intelligencer* had narrowed the contest down to five: "two disgraced generals [James Wilkinson and John Armstrong], a lame bookseller [Mathew Carey], a quack doctor [Michael Leib] and a speculating attorney [Joseph Reed]." Eventually the enemies of "Brutus" abandoned the fruitless guessing game and concluded that the mysterious writer was William Duane himself.[28]

In fact the author of "Brutus" was not Duane, but an unknown twenty-eight year old named Stephen Simpson. Simpson was later to

---

Jan., 14, 16 Feb. 1818; *Franklin Gazette*, 12, 14, 21, 23 Sept. 1818; *Niles' Weekly Register*, XIV (7 Mar. 1818), 21.

[28]*Aurora*, 10, 25, 27, 28 Apr., 9, 13 May, 25 June 1818; *Independent Balance*, 6 May 1818, 4, 11 Aug. 1819; *Franklin Gazette*, 9 Oct. 1818; C. J. Ingersoll to Monroe, 29 Oct. 1820, Monroe Papers, NYPL.

become famous as the author of the radical manifesto, the *Working Man's Manual*. The pseudonym he selected, that of the hero-traitor Brutus, was an unrecognized clue to his identity. Shortly before he began his detailed disclosures of mismanagement, Simpson had resigned as a note clerk in the Second Bank of the United States. Young Simpson had been placed in the Second Bank to begin a career as a banker through the influence of his father, George Simpson, who had been Cashier of the First United States Bank and of its successor, Girard's Bank. Stephen admired his father's careful banking practices, but not those of his employers in the Second Bank.

Moreover Simpson was a romantic who did not want to be a banker but a writer of fiction in the fashion of his hero Lord Byron. He had already attempted without success to found his own literary journal before he volunteered to write on banking for the *Aurora*. Simpson's political idealism was as thoroughgoing as his romantic philosophy; his range of interests was typical of a younger generation of intellectuals in politics, which was to come to maturity during the Presidency of Andrew Jackson. For three years, from 1818 to 1820, "Brutus" contributed almost daily to Duane's newspaper, establishing himself in a new career as a political journalist. He became the *Aurora*'s principal writer on national politics, while Duane devoted his attention to other subjects, especially Latin America. From his earliest essays, "Brutus" denounced the Monroe administration for its oligarchical "clanship" and for sustaining the hated Second Bank for use as a "political machine." Simpson was an extremely excitable and fiery young man, and his writing was more virulent than that of Duane. James Monroe bitterly resented the invective of "Brutus," which he believed was written by Duane, and he formed an intense dislike of the Old Republican editor.

Although Duane was thirty years older than Stephen Simpson, the two were similar in temperament and worked closely and well together. Simpson became very active in the Old School party in addition to writing for the *Aurora*, and was the most valuable addition to the leadership since 1810 when William John Duane had made the decision to stand by his father. Simpson and the younger Duane were the party's heirs apparent in the event of the editor's retirement.[29]

In July 1818 the board of directors of the Bank of the United States recognized for the first time that the Bank was in danger. Belatedly admitting the wisdom of conservative policies by the national institution, the directors ordered a curtailment of the discounts. In succeeding months they adopted increasingly severe measures in an effort to force retrenchment by the branches. The Central Bank struggled to save itself from the consequences of

---

[29]Broadus Mitchell, "Stephen Simpson," *DAB*, XVII, 183-184; Henry Simpson, *The Lives of Eminent Philadelphians, Now Deceased; Collected from Original and Authentic Sources* (Philadelphia, 1859), 893-894; Edward Pessen, "The Ideology of Stephen Simpson, Upper Class Champion of the Early Philadelphia Workingmen's Movement," *Pennsylvania History*, XXII (October, 1955), 328-340; Dorfman, *Economic Mind in Am. Civ.*, II, 645-648; Stephen Simpson, *Biography of Stephen Girard* (Philadelphia, 1832), 114-116; Simpson, *The Author's Jewel, Consisting of Essays, Miscellaneous, Literary and Moral* (Philadelphia, 1823).

the branches' hitherto unchecked liberality and at the same time sought to use the resources of the branches to rescue its own financial position. The policy was successful from the point of view of the directors, but in the end it was disastrous for the nation. The unexpected stringency of the United States Bank, and its demand for payments in specie, forced all banks to curtail discounts and reduce their paper circulation, and the contraction of credit gradually brought business to a standstill.

Congress authorized an investigation of the Bank in November 1818 on the motion of Representative John C. Spencer of New York, and it appeared possible that the hated institution would lose its charter. The criminal frauds in the branch at Baltimore were as yet unknown, but the committee headed by Spencer found massive evidence of mismanagement and also discovered four violations of the terms of incorporation. Although the specific violations were trivial, they provided legal justification for Congress to revoke the institution's charter in retribution for its unethical and harmful conduct. In the floor debate the Bank's defenders, relying on their superior technical understanding of banking and finance, undermined the force of the investigation's findings. Moreover the Bank's President William Jones, when he resigned in January, provided a scapegoat to bear the guilt of former wrongdoing. In the end Congress took no action to punish the Bank. Even the Clintonian Congressman Spencer, Duane confided to a friend in February, "after obtaining and meriting public gratitude has been prevailed upon to join in sustaining the Bank--upòn the plea that many people would be ruined--while he loses sight of the ruin of the whole country by that [institution]."[30]

In March 1819 the United States Bank was rescued both politically and financially. In cooperation with the national administration, the Directors selected Langdon Cheves of South Carolina as the new President, to be entrusted with the responsibility for lifting the Bank from jeopardy. Cheves arrived in Philadelphia on March 6 and immediately undertook ruthlessly efficient measures to restore the Central Bank's financial security, albeit at the expense of the branch banks and the surrounding countryside.

A few days after the arrival of Cheves, Philadelphia received the news of the Supreme Court's unanimous opinion in the case of McCulloch versus Maryland. Chief Justice John Marshall had ruled that it was unlawful for a state to tax the national bank or its branches, declaring it an unconstitutional interference with the sovereign power of the central government. The decision upheld the long disputed constitutionality of the Bank itself. The creation of a national bank was authorized, Marshall declared, by the clause of the Constitution which granted Congress the power to take whatever action was "necessary and proper" in the pursuit of its enumerated powers. The Court's opinion elevated the Bank to an unassailable legal position, depriving the states or the people of any means to protect themselves against it.

In the Aurora both Duane and Simpson attacked the decision

---

[30]Catterall, Second Bank, 51-67; Govan, Biddle, 57-59; Duane to Alden Spooner, 15 Feb. 1819, B. V. Spooner Collection, NYHS.

with an almost unprecedented fury. "Brutus" analyzed Marshall's opinion in detail, reasserting the unconstitutionality of the Bank or of any chartered corporation. "As equality of rights is the grand basis of our revolutionary constitution," Simpson reasoned, "every infraction of that equality, by inferring peculiar privileges . . . must necessarily be a contravention of the supreme principles of our government!" Although "Brutus" challenged the accuracy of the legal opinion, he also reminded the public that the Supreme Court's authority was merely judicial. "The great political question of the constitutionality of this bank is still open," he asserted; the people or Congress "possess full and competent powers to pronounce it an unconstitutional abortion of avarice and ambition."[31]

Duane had intended to allow "Brutus" to speak for him on McCulloch versus Maryland, but his own strong feelings on the subject broke through in a bitter commentary. He avowed that the protection of a people was not in a written constitution, but in the intelligence of society for guarding against corruptions and tyrannies. Although John Marshall's opinion could easily be destroyed by logical argument, he believed, the blame for the decision fell ultimately upon the people, who were "so infatuated or degenerate, as to be thus opinionated and sophisticated into subservient depradation." But, he told himself,

> what avails preaching to a people eaten up with egotism--poisoned by their own vanity, and persuaded, in the very act of their degradation and misery, that they surpass all other

---

[31] Aurora, 16, 18, 20, 24, 26, 29, 31 Mar., 2 Apr. 1819.

> people in wisdom, and all other people in--possessing a representative government--.

Duane had been scolding the American people for nearly a decade, but he had never before sounded so near to despair. "The survey of human society and of nations for ages past," he reflected, "does not uniformly present the charms of Arcadian innocence, . . . and the verdan [sic] fields and the cheerful skies realizing an Elysium; appear as rarely and as evanescent in the chart of history." So too the promise of a golden age to appear in America was fading. "At the present moment," he believed, the hopes of the Revolution "are surrounded by mists and darkness." In the United States "the government is retrograding"; principles succumb to power, "selfishness undermines and supercedes society in its most interesting points--deceit and corruption have taken the place of the frankness and disinterestedness, which . . . accomplished the revolution." Over all this Duane mused,

> it would seem as if there were ebbs and flows in human institutions, which have their periods governed by some remote moon; and that having reached a given height to recede again was an inherent quality of its nature.

"We did not intend to advert to these facts," Duane apologized for his commentary, "but the predominant feeling will force its way where the soul is free."[32]

The impassioned response to the Court decision by both Duane and Simpson reflected their mutual belief that the Bank of the United States was the very antithesis of the spirit of the Revolution. There were two reasons for this conviction, which

---

[32] _Ibid._, 17, 19, 20, 23 Mar. 1819.

Duane had developed and explained at length over a period of years. Politically he believed that the creation of a private monopoly to conduct public business was an intolerable violation of the principle of self-government. Simpson echoed him when he called the Republican Fathers of the Second Bank, Albert Gallatin and A. J. Dallas, "the *political* assassins of American liberty."[33] Morally Duane felt that in establishing a national bank the government had erected an official monument to speculation; its existence was a declaration that personal selfishness had replaced disinterested patriotism as the national spirit. Consequently the Supreme Court's decision in *McCulloch* versus *Maryland*, which exalted the Bank, signified to Duane that the era of the Revolution had closed.

III.

By the spring of 1819 the United States presented a "uniform picture of growing distress." The severely contractionist policy of the United States Bank forced a sharp curtailment of bank credit generally. At the same time, because of a sudden drop in European demand for American agricultural produce, there was a very rapid decline in the prices of export commodities. The market depression, combined with the pressure by banks for immediate cash payment on loans, threatened the nation's farmers with forfeiture of their property on a colossal scale. Manufacturing and trade were already in a disturbed condition, and when agriculture was struck, the country plunged into its first major depression.

---

[33] *Ibid.*, 3 Mar. 1819.

"The whole country from Orleans to Portland is in an agony," the *Aurora* reported in April. "Bankruptcy pervades every quarter of the union." President Monroe however still spoke hopefully of the "propitious state" of the nation. "It is a melancholy and a cruel state," Duane commented, "in which no man can foresee where calamity is to stop, nor discover in the government the capacity or the disposition to alleviate public sufferings."[34]

Yet in the face of real adversity, the Democrats of the Old School, who for years had been prophesying ruin, brightened in outlook and became remarkably cheerful. "During the first years of the peace and tariff," the *Aurora* reflected, "there seemed to be no end to *importation*, to *shopkeeping*, to *speculations* on vanity and slops of all kinds, and the '*blest paper credit*'--and by their united operation, national reputation and public prosperity are absolutely *banked out*." Yet the state of moral and economic exhaustion offered the first real hope for social regeneration. The Old School Democrats believed that the calamities of 1819 occurred because the people had been beguiled by the appeal of luxury and extravagance, and they had forewarned like Old Testament prophets that "it is in your heavy afflictions only that a cure can be found."[35]

The Old School men thought that the people would comprehend through the experience of hardship that the national goals had be-

---

[34] Duane to D. B. Warden, 16 May 1819, D. B. Warden Papers, LC; *Aurora*, 7 Apr., 20 May 1819.

[35] *Ibid.*, 1 Dec. 1818, 7 Apr. 1819. See for example *ibid.*, 3 Dec. 1818, 6 Jan. 1819.

become perverted. They would repent their apathy and greed and reaffirm their faith in the republican values of honesty and frugality. The Old Schoolers yearned for a restoration of the social environment of the Revolution, for they idealized that period as a time when the sense of fraternity had governed human relationships. "Anaxagoras" even suggested the creation of an orthodox system of national dress. Although it would not be welcomed, he acknowledged, by "some of those mushrooms of pride and folly, who wish to distinguish themselves by their extravagance and dissipation," he believed that it would be "a bold step towards republican simplicity and republican dignity and morality."[36]

The means to social restoration envisioned by the Old Schoolers was the complete eradication of the paper system and a return to a hard money economy. Similar proposals in response to the Panic were current in almost every state, and the phenomenon frequently has been explained as a consequence of mere superstition, ignorance and fear of the modern world. This was not the case for the Democrats of the Old School. Their radical, single-minded program for reform reflected the sophistication in the ways of bankers which they had acquired in their urban experience. Stephen Simpson, still known only as "Brutus," was the party's leading theorist on questions of banking and credit. Few persons had less cause to fear banks than Simpson, who had been reared in a mansion owned by the First Bank of the United States and who could have enjoyed a comfortable career as a banker simply by sup-

---

[36] *Ibid.*, 25 Sept. 1819.

pressing his conscience and eschewing dangerous political opinions. The Old School's rejection of the paper system was not by prejudice but by deliberate choice. William Duane himself arrived at a hard money position only after 1817.

Since 1801 Duane had passed through a personal cycle of experience and thought on the question of currency and credit which was a precursor of a similar national cycle, not completed until the 1830s. In the halcyon days of Jefferson's first administration, Duane had hailed the possibilities for expanding the nation's enterprise by democratizing the banking facilities. Within a few years his own excessively optimistic use of credit had brought him to the brink of ruin, and the experience permanently affected his attitude toward borrowing and the lure of banks. As early as 1810 he began to warn against excessive paper issues by the growing numbers of state banks and against a dependence upon credit. At that time he advocated a national paper currency issued by the federal government, which he believed could restrain inflationary issues by private institutions and furnish the country with a non-fluctuating medium.

Following the War of 1812, Duane for a period held an oddly inconsistent position. He denounced the plan for a national bank of issue, yet clung to his proposal of Treasury notes, refusing to concede that it would be an equally inflationary measure. Duane did not turn to a hard money position in 1815 because he believed, correctly, that the extreme scarcity of specie in the country meant that the adoption of hard currency would plunge the nation into depression. He still hoped that a conservative government policy on currency could effect a gradual return of stability.

Between 1817 and 1819 however Duane became a thoroughgoing hard money man. The safe return by the banks to a specie paying basis in February 1817 encouraged him to believe that the trend could be strengthened. Moreover the successful revolutions in South America awakened the hope that the silver mines would be reopened and that in the future the supply of specie would be abundant. The onset of the Panic and depression removed another barrier to reform; there was no need to fear a disordering of the economy by change. Finally, Duane had at last abandoned his confidence in the will or the capacity of government to furnish a completely stable currency. At almost sixty he began to expound his new orthodoxy, that gold and silver alone possessed the absolute inviolability which characterized a proper medium of exchange.[37]

The Old School Democrats rejected the paper credit system not because they were blind to its potential to accelerate expansion but because they possessed a clear vision of its capacity to produce class division. "The _paper system_ first split the nation into two separate classes, with incompatible and repugnant views," wrote Stephen Simpson for the _Aurora_. "Of all _political curses_ and _corruptors_, banks and stocks are the causes, as they become

---

[37] _Ibid._, 29 Apr., 31 July, 14 Aug. 1816, 21 Feb. 1817, 22 May 1819; _ibid._, "National Insanity, Proved," 10, 13, 14, 15, 16, 19, 21, 23, 26, 28, 30 Apr., 5 May 1819; _ibid._, "Review of Malthus," 18, 23, 25 Oct., 4, 7, 8, 9, 10, 11 Nov. 1820; [Duane], _Notes Relating to the Gold and Silver Coinage_ ([Philadelphia, 1831]), pamphlet, LC.

the *focus* of them."[38]

The summons to a restoration of republican virtue was not an appeal to sentiment or religious piety, but an expression of a deep political conviction that freedom was founded upon equality. In the Old School philosophy, the existence of a classless society was a fundamental precondition of popular democracy. The genius of democracy, in their conception, was not the equivalence of legal status or of formal rights, but the genuine equality among citizens in their capacity and their power to influence the decisions of the society. An economic system which fostered cupidity, permitting unscrupulous individuals to amass wealth by exploiting the labor and diminishing the property of their fellow citizens, threatened the basis of democracy. "You are aware that our republican government was established for the happiness and freedom of the people," Stephen Simpson lectured the Bank President, Langdon Cheves. "How those objects are accomplished by a system of *paper frauds*, which immediately generates an aristocracy of wealth, a distinction of *ranks*, and a class of *idlers* is sufficiently obvious. *Luxury* and *vice*," in his opinion, "are not less foes to liberty, than they are to happiness. . . . A servile respect to the exterior appearance of *property* and *wealth*, has become the bane of the republic." A return to the moral ideals of industry, thrift, decency and magnanimity, was politically essential in order to maintain the relative equality of condition which made democracy meaningful.[39]

The charge that division existed between the interests of

---

[38]*Aurora*, 26 Nov., 6 Dec. 1819. [39]*Ibid.*, 24 June 1819.

the idle few and the industrious majority was not of course a description of class warfare in a modern sense. But neither was it merely a complaint against aristocracy. The Old School Democrats indeed objected to the monopoly and special privilege awarded by the grant of banking charters. But they believed that those characteristics were natural features of the institution of banking itself and could not be subjected to democratic reform.

In 1817 a Harrisburg subscriber wrote to the *Aurora* to protest the growing tendency for banks to fall under the control of particular families, as sons joined or replaced their fathers on the boards of directors. Duane responded that the writer was mistaken in directing his complaint at "hereditary preferments." The banking institutions in themselves formed "a *privileged order* possessing exemptions and powers unknown to any other order of man; it is the privilege of trading upon credit to any extent, without any individual being responsible in his property for his dealings." No man possessing such a privilege, Duane reasoned, not even the correspondent from Harrisburg, could be expected to forego the opportunity of passing it on to his children.

The *Aurora* frankly asserted that the grant of limited liability to corporations made possession of a bank charter a "*license to cheat*." Hence "can it be at all surprising that the *privilege is used*--it is not proper to say, it is *abused*." During 1817 and 1818, before the Panic had convinced him that note issue banking should be eliminated altogether, Duane had advocated a return to the system of full liability as the best means of restraining the banks. "Make the estates of _bank traders_ like all other traders _responsible_ for their debts, and their own interests will prevent excesses." If the stockholders were made "_accountable to the last cent_," he had argued, "then banking would be as salutary as it is now _afflicting_."[40]

A misinterpretation of the party's motives in assailing the banks could have arisen from their use of language. The Old School Democrats continued to employ an eighteenth century epithet, aristocratic, to describe a distinctively nineteenth century problem, the corporate power and privilege enjoyed by business. Thus for example the banking act of 1814, which placed credit facilities within the reach of virtually every Pennsylvanian, was denounced by one Old Schooler as a "great hot-bed of aristocracy." By this he meant that the banks were a device which would convert lucky or unscrupulous democrats into rich men. The encroachment of plutocracy was what the Old School most feared.[41]

The power of the banking system to effect rapid changes of fortune was a socially divisive force of unlimited potential. A degree of disparity among men the Old Schoolers accepted as inevitable because of the natural differences in intelligence, talents and ambition. "The very efforts of industry would soon produce inequality of possessions," Simpson acknowledged in the _Working Man's Manual_, but "this inequality would never attain to a pitch to inflict misery or to produce extortion." Simpson's _Manual_, written a decade later, was a fully developed exposition of the ideas he

---

[40] _Ibid._, 27 Feb. 1817, 3 Dec. 1818. [41] _Ibid._, 31 July 1817.

had expressed in the Aurora during his years as "Brutus." "The difference between the powers of man," Simpson insisted, "is not so great, as to produce a vast disparity in their productions and acquisitions, without the intervention of some agent of a character extraneous to industry and skill."

In the United States a tradition was emerging which permitted "the distribution of property by law instead of industry." The privilege of incorporation favored the new business class with opportunities for self-aggrandizement which were totally unrelated to merit. "If law had never interfered with labour, or fortified capital by charters and privileges," Simpson wrote in 1829, "usury and extortion, with their concomitants and consequences, would be unknown in this prosperous country."[42]

The Democrats of the Old School were perhaps shortsighted to regard the paper banking system as the sole threat to an egalitarian society and to ignore the potential for class division which was inherent to industrialism. In their experience however the evil custom of turning privilege into profit was overwhelmingly illustrated by the banking corporations; whereas in the field of manufacturing the use of incorporation was almost unknown. Internal improvements companies received legislative charters, but these enterprises generally paid very low if any dividends. The stockholders appeared more public benefactors than profiteers.

Opposed to schemes which encouraged the accumulation of

---

[42]Stephen Simpson, The Working Man's Manual: A New Theory of Political Economy on the Principle of Production the Source of Wealth (Philadelphia, 1831), 52, 125, 127.

capital, the Old School Democrats conceived of the future industrial society as a counterpart of the agrarian past. The development of manufacturing as they imagined it, carried on by skilled craftsmen, would not alter the social structure in which the majority of men were small property owners. Although the Democrats of the New School and the Old School alike supported a protective tariff, the Panic of 1819 revealed a conscious distinction in their conceptions of industrial development. Mathew Cary blamed the depression entirely upon the lack of protection for manufactures and at that time began his single-minded campaign to promote tariff legislation. On this issue Duane and Carey quarreled anew, for Duane censured Carey's failure to deal with the more important cause of the Panic, the paper banking system.[43]

Stephen Simpson too "gave a free expression of ridicule and contempt" to the petition by Carey's society for the protection of manufactures urging Congress to provide relief. The petition stated, Simpson exclaimed, "that the evils chiefly arose from the fetters and restraints imposed upon the *discounts of the banks*, by the drain of *specie*! This society too," Simpson complained, "*professed* to promote manufactures; and are for advancing them by a still further extension of *paper credits*." According to Simpson, the well-meaning but ignorant petitioners did not understand that banks and manufactures "are as now constituted, as adverse to each other, as the poles, their interests are fundamentally incompatible." The inevit-

---

[43]Duane to Carey, 14 Feb. [1822?], Edward Carey Gardiner Collection, HSP.

able rise in prices which accompanied a system of bank credits, Simpson declared, was a positive deterrent to the development of manufacturing. "It is true," he acknowledged, "that by the natural growth of _trade_, agriculture and manufactures, and the consequent augmentation of _gold and silver money_, provisions and labor would be enhanced in price." But this would not be pernicious, he explained, for "the increase of dearness would in that case be _gradual_--it would be _permanent_; it would pervade _every thing_; and would not be liable to _fluctuation_." Moreover "being bottomed on _solid wealth and labor_, it never could lead to poverty."[44]

Hard money enthusiasts, resentful of government favoritism, often were advocates of a philosophy of laissez-faire. However the Old School party was a decided exception. This "_let us alone_ is a sophism-," Duane declared emphatically; "whatever is the interest and happiness of society must not be _let alone_." Duane and his party believed that there were ways in which the government could act in the economy without discrimination; for example by uniform support for a general transportation system. More important, Duane believed that the principle of equality upon which the United States was established imposed a philosophy of positive action by society to protect all its members.[45]

The editor rejected the notion that individuals could best protect themselves through enlightened self-interest as a theory

---

[44] _Aurora_, 24 June 1819.

[45] _Ibid._, 20 Apr. 1818. See Arthur M. Schlesinger, Jr., _The Age of Jackson_ (Boston, 1945), 314-317; Murray N. Rothbard, _The Panic of 1819, Reactions and Policies_ (New York, 1962), 186.

which peopled the world with men of the imagination. A more realistic view demonstrated that "the great mass of every country may be considered as composed of indigent, simple, ignorant, or rash, and inconsiderate persons" who could be confused and exploited. He believed that laws to prevent exploitation should be rigorously applied, "for if society be a compact, in which the protection of all the members be the end and obligation; surely laws and institutions should operate in that manner which protects the weakest." Duane denied that such regulations were an unjust infringement of personal liberty. The "blessings of society," he argued simply, "are not to be procured but by sacrificing private or partial interests, to those of the whole community."

Duane opposed the theory of laissez-faire capitalism with a conscious assertion of neo-mercantilism adapted to a democratic state. The modern English economists, or "Economistics" as Duane called them--Adam Smith, Jeremy Bentham, Thomas Malthus and others--were guilty of "inversions of the natural order of thinking," in his opinion. The consideration of profit to the individual rather than concern for the general good was the foundation of their arguments. Whereas "The constitution of society contemplates a family with interests and duties in common, of which the law is the sole rule of action." Adam Smith had accomplished the sophistic revolution. Before him for two thousand years "political economy was considered as being the science of government itself"; but since the publication of the falsely named <u>Wealth of Nations</u>, the ancient principle of commonwealth had been abandoned by economic theorists.[46]

---

[46] <u>Aurora</u>, "National Insanity Proved," an analysis of Jeremy

The outstanding exception among British intellectuals to the new consensus was the social planner Robert Owen. In Duane's opinion the communal experiments by Owen, designed to discover a mode for preserving human happiness in an industrial society, shed "A Flood of Light on the Wealth of Nations." Duane avowed that Owen had conceived "a design much more rational and noble than that which has given immortality to Lycurgus, or Confucius, or Solon." His experiments proved that human beings need not be limited by the circumstances of their birth, for their capacities could be profoundly influenced by environment and education. "In fact," Duane commented, "the 'mind must be born again' by a new training from infancy, on the principle that the character of man ever has been and ever must be formed _for_ him." He believed however that such action should not be the work of individuals but of the whole society.[47]

IV.

In Pennsylvania at the beginning of the Panic there was a genuine possibility of action for reform. The legislature, which was beginning to show its independence of Governor Findlay, enacted a measure calling upon the other states to join with Pennsylvania in assembling a national constitutional convention for the purpose of ridding the country of the Second Bank. More important, it

---

Bentham's _In Defense of Usury_, 10, 13, 14, 15, 16, 19, 21, 23, 26, 28, 30 Apr., 5 May 1819; _ibid_., "Review of Malthus," 18, 23, 25 Oct., 4, 7, 8, 9, 10, 11 Nov. 1820; [Duane], _Notes Relating to the Gold and Silver Coinage_, pamphlet, LC; Duane, _Visit to Colombia_, 547.

[47] _Aurora_, 19 Mar.-18 Apr. 1817, 24 Apr. 1819. Duane claimed that his was the only newspaper in the United States which published the essays of Robert Owen; _ibid_., 9 Apr. 1817.

adopted a highly controversial proposal to reform the operation of the state banks; by this act each of the Forty-two banks of 1814 was required to return to a specie basis by August 1, 1819, or forfeit its charter. Some Findlayite representatives attempted to undermine the measure by substituting a much longer grace period, while Duane's old friend James Thackara argued that specie payments should begin immediately.[48]

The Old School men candidly exhorted the populace to take full advantage of the opportunity to force a series of bank failures which would clear the way for a return to hard money. "_The first day of August next_ will be ever memorable in the annals of the state," wrote "Bellisarius" for the _Aurora_, "as one which will behold the axe laid to the root of an evil not less destructive of liberty and of the peace of society than the unjustifiable requisitions of the most unlimited aristocracy." On that day "_all the state banks will be in the power of the people_," and "Fair Play" called for a just retribution. "We do not aim at stirring up a spirit which shall lead to a premeditated run upon the banks," claimed "Bellisarius"; yet forbearance toward them would be a crime against the commonweal. The difficulties experienced because of bank failures, he argued, would be far less serious than the suffering created by their frantic struggle for survival. "Let but the object of the struggle cease to exist, and the long agony will be over."[49]

---

[48]Harrisburg _Chronicle_, 1, 8, 15 Feb., 7 June 1819.

[49]_Aurora_, 3, 6, 13 July 1819.

The ultimate desire of the Old Schoolers was for nothing less than "the total prostration of the banking and funding system." "Brutus" avowed it to be the solemn duty of the people's representatives in the states and in Congress "to abrogate all bank charters within their jurisdictions." Congress had the power to repeal the charter of the United States Bank "simply on the great principle of public good." But if necessary in order to defy the Supreme Court, "THE STATES MUST ASSEMBLE IN CONVENTION--and the people vote the monster to the tomb." The sacrifices would be momentary, Simpson pleaded, and the benefits ever enduring. "Let us, in the name of heaven, for once be true to our fame as American republicans[,] to our country and to our revolution."[50]

The opportunity for reform presented by the specie law of 1819 was almost completely frustrated by Governor Findlay's lack of cooperation. Findlay, who had been the "prime agent in saddling this state with a litter of 42 banks," was unwilling to enforce the stringent legislation against them. Although several closed voluntarily or suspended operations because of the Panic, none was sued for forfeiture of its charter. The banks complied nominally with the regulation, and the state did not force the issue. In December 1819 Governor Findlay announced that the purpose of the act had been accomplished and that no future action for enforcement would be necessary. He admitted that the lack of a uniform currency was a continuing "inconvenience," but submitted his opinion that it might "be most prudent to permit the fluctuating paper of our dif-

[50] Ibid., 26, 29 Nov. 1819.

ferent banks to find its level through natural rather than artificial channels."

Although he disapproved of using the state's powers to effect a reform of the currency, Findlay thought that it would be "practicable and expedient for the commonwealth to co-operate in the general effort to revive credit and arrest the progress of distress." By his emphasis he succeeded in turning the legislature's attention away from the fundamental problem and toward the consideration of temporary relief measures to help the state's debtors. The Governor proposed the creation of a loan office, which would borrow inactive capital on the credit of the state and re-loan it upon mortgage security. "This would not only prevent many sacrifices of property by legal process," he pointed out, "but essentially aid in giving new life and activity to numerous pursuits of productive industry, and facilitate the progress of restoration." He also supported the bill for a minimum appraisal law, which was introduced by two representatives from strong Findlayite constituencies. The law would have stayed execution for debt if the creditor refused to accept an official value placed upon landed property.[51]

The most outspoken and controversial critic of debtor's relief was William John Duane. The younger Duane had been elected to the legislature in Philadelphia's Democratic unity victory of 1819 and was appointed chairman of the special committee on the

---

[51] *Ibid.*, 3 Dec. 1818; *Pa. Archives*, 4th series, V, 152-155; Rothbard, *Panic of 1819*, 38, 73. See also Jonathan Roberts to Matthew Roberts, 8 Jan. 1820, Roberts Papers, HSP.

general state of the domestic economy. At the end of January the Assemblyman submitted a report which opposed the loan office or any other schemes for relief, except for a program of road and canal construction to provide jobs for the unemployed. Within the assembly there was a surprised and angry reaction, and a minority member of Duane's committee moved that the House refuse to publish the report. The motion passed, 49 to 40, in a clearly partisan vote between the supporters of William Findlay and of Joseph Hiester.

In W. J. Duane's opinion, a relief program would be unjust as well as unsound economically. It would tend to benefit that portion of the community which had contributed to the general distress by indulging in ambitious schemes for expansion. Although a loan office could help many honest farmers, Duane acknowledged, it would not aid those distressed persons who did not possess land to mortgage, and its long term credit arrangements would be subject to abuse by unscrupulous debtors. Moreover honest creditors were also suffering because of the Panic. The concerns which Duane expressed reflected his experience as a Philadelphian and as a politician of the Old School. Residing in a major center of speculative enterprise, most Old School men were aware that debtors often were the exploiters rather than the exploited. In the midst of the Panic one astute _Aurora_ essayist called for the reform of the bankruptcy law, to stop its misuse by persons who deliberately sought to cheat their creditors while secretly providing well for themselves.

The Assemblyman's strongest objection to Governor Findlay's plan for a loan office was that it would help to restore paper money circulation and to renew the dependence on the credit system. In his characteristically milder manner, William John Duane expressed the hard money views of his father and other Old School leaders. In the Aurora at the same period, "Brutus" denounced with inspired fury the introduction into Congress of a scheme for national monetary expansion. Simpson believed that an irrevocable choice was at hand between hard money and the paper system: "the American people are now to come to a final determination; and pronounce upon their liberty, property, and happiness, for all future time."

In Pennsylvania the chief division of sentiment on relief legislation was between eastern conservatives and western debtors. Many rural representatives who were neither Findlayites nor friendly to the private banks, sought to justify the loan office by denying that it was "a banking system." The Philadelphia Federalists however, like the Old School Democrats, regarded it as a dangerous instrument of monetary expansion. The two Federalists in the legislature who were most popular with the Old School, Representative William Lehman and Senator Condy Raguet, shared with W. J. Duane the task of undermining the relief proposals.[52]

In March 1820 Findlay's loan office bill was defeated by a tie vote, and the session ended in an impasse, without major legislation. The Governor was to stand for re-election in the autumn,

---

[52]Rothbard, Panic of 1819, 39-40, 72-76, 165, 191; the author of the Duane Report is incorrectly identified as Duane Senior in ibid.; Aurora, 24 Sept., 17, 27 Dec. 1819. See also Niles' Weekly Register, XVII (11 Dec. 1819), 242-243; Harrisburg Chronicle, 15 Mar. 1821.

and the "spirit of <u>independence</u>" displayed in the House of Representatives was a bad sign for the Findlayites. "The confidence of a large portion of the freemen of the interior," an anti-caucus man reported, "is unquestionably <u>withdrawn from the present administration</u>."[53]

V.

Governor Findlay's prestige suffered a steady and well-deserved decline throughout his term of office. The *Aurora*'s charge that he had been guilty of gross conflict of interest while state Treasurer had failed to defeat him in 1817, but appeared certain to help prevent his re-election. Esteem for Findlay personally had never been high, even among his own supporters. "I am glad that the party has been successful," Director of the Mint Robert Patterson remarked candidly in October 1817, "although mr. Finley [*sic*] does not seem to me to be entitled to the place, either by his talents, his character, or his service." During the next three years more evidence accumulated to justify the doubts about Findlay's ethics. A legislative investigation revealed that the Governor and his top adviser, Secretary of the Commonwealth Thomas Sergeant, were extorting graft from the applicants for auctioneers' commissions. Findlay had forced one applicant "to loan money to his brothers insolvent" business, and Sergeant had refused a commission to another who would not promise to employ Samuel Fox, the Secretary's cousin. The successful applicant gave Fox a post with a salary of two thousand dollars annually.

---

[53]Rothbard, *Panic of 1819*, 75; *Aurora*, 16 Dec. 1819.

The "singularly obsequious" committee which investigated the bribery concluded that Sergeant had shown praiseworthy generosity to his cousin and was not guilty of criminal behavior. But Senator Jonathan Roberts, the veteran Snyderite politician, believed that "the attempt at suppression will work more mischief than they are aware of." Indeed in his opinion "the game is up with Findlay." Although officially exonerated, the Secretary was forced to resign his position because of the public reaction to the scandal. "What man . . . has passed through more mental and bodily suffering," George Dallas sympathized with Sergeant, "than accompanied him through his short political career! He seems to have got rid of it all by getting rid of his office. Nevertheless, he is watchful, ardent, and active."[54]

The united Democratic Republican party created under Governor Snyder could not withstand the assaults on conscience by the Findlay administration. "In this distracted state I do not know what we should do without you as a point of alliement [sic]," Charles Ingersoll wrote to President Monroe, explaining the Pennsylvania situation. "The present Governor, who was chosen by too precarious a majority, has given his enemies such occasions of disparaging him," that he would be likely to lose if Ex-Governor Snyder

---

[54]Patterson to Jonathan Russell, 26 Oct. 1817, Jonathan Russell Papers (photostats), Mass. Hist. Soc.; Jonathan Roberts to Matthew Roberts, 22 Dec. 1818, 2 Jan. 1819, 21 Feb. 1820, Roberts Papers, HSP; G. M. Dallas to [Samuel D. Ingham], 20 July 1819, Dallas Papers, HSP; Klein, Pa. Politics, 98-105. See also Thomas Sergeant to Thomas J. Rogers, 21 Jan. 1819, Dreer Collection, HSP; Harrisburg Chronicle, 18 Mar. 1819; Aurora, 18 May, 13 Oct. 1819; Independent Balance, 24 June, 14 July, 4, 11 Aug. 1819.

were to be run against him, which at that time appeared probable; "and between their respective partisans the powerful republican ascendancy of Pennsylvania may be brought into jeopardy."[55]

The "curious spectacle" predicted by Ingersoll of at least three candidates for Governor in 1820 did not materialize, for Simon Snyder died in November 1819. Findlay was assured the nomination as the only Democratic Republican candidate, to run against the Independent Republican, Joseph Hiester. But he had forfeited the support of a number of old Snyderites of high standing, including Jonathan Roberts and the former state Auditor George Bryan. Senator Roberts not only rebuffed the many entreaties to campaign for him, but admitted that "as I stand advised I cannot vote for Findlay." "There seems no redeeming spirit about the governor-," he commented. "He stands in the naked imbecility of folly surrounded by men as or more foolish than himself & all equally selfish." Although Roberts declined to predict the election's outcome, he suspected that the Governor "cannot stand a canvass--Every day will weaken his standing." Nonetheless the Senator did not intend to vote for the anti-caucus candidate, and he was certain that "Findlay will have by some means . . . a majority of the party in number and respectability--Not that they approve his conduct but from the circumstances of things."[56]

---

[55]Ingersoll to Monroe, 10 Aug. 1819, Monroe Papers, NYPL. See also Thomas Cadwalader to Richard Rush, 25 Sept. 1819, Cadwalader Collection, HSP.

[56]Jonathan Roberts to Matthew Roberts, 16, 27 Feb., 29 Apr. 1820, Roberts Papers, HSP.

The gubernatorial election of 1820 was a repetition of 1817; the candidates, the issues, and the regional divisions of strength remained the same, but the final result was reversed. The conservative Joseph Hiester, as in 1817, was supported jointly by Federalists and the anti-caucus factions, and carried the southeastern counties of Pennsylvania. William Findlay, whose strength had been in the western and southern regions of the state, polled a total number of votes almost identical to that which had narrowly elected him three years earlier. But in 1820 about eight thousand persons who had not turned out in the previous election went to the polls and voted for Hiester.

The Independent Republican's strength increased in the south central and southwestern counties especially. Historians of Pennsylvania politics have noted that the shift in support occurred, characteristically, in communities with relatively dense population. The sparsely populated rural counties retained their loyalty to Findly, the orthodox Republican candidate.[57] The significance of the gubernatorial election appears to be that there was a strong public reaction to the Panic of 1819 in the regions most seriously affected by the Panic, which surmounted the traditional concept of Republican unity. The victory of Hiester was a triumph for the anti-caucus Democrats' view that Federalism was moribund and that important new issues, created by economic change, unavoidably divided the members of the nominal Republican party.

---

[57]Klein, Pa. Politics, 95, 108-109; Kehl, Ill Feeling, 203.

CHAPTER XIII

A VISIT TO COLOMBIA

The revolution in the colonies of South America for independence from Spain was a subject of deep interest to the United States. The rebellion had begun during the long European war when Spain itself was an occupied country, the battleground for Europe. With peace and the restoration to the throne of King Ferdinand VII, Spain attempted by military force to restore its authority in the American colonies. But it was too late; Spain was too weak, and she had no allies willing to fight for her lost territories. By 1819 the final victory of the republican armies appeared inevitable.

The people of the United States were naturally sympathetic to the republican aspirations of South Americans, and they urged immediate recognition of the revolutionary governments. The United States government however was understandably reluctant to offend Spain, for the acquisition of East Florida was yet to be accomplished. The Monroe administration, although privately sharing the sympathy for the rebels, endeavored to enforce upon the American people a strict neutrality in the colonial war and to placate the Spanish suspicions of the American interest. Protest against this unpopular policy was loosely directed by Speaker of the House Henry Clay, who hoped to use the issue to serve his presidential ambition.

William Duane was keenly interested in the South American Revolution, and he took an active role in advocating United States' support of the infant republics. The *Aurora* in 1810 was one of the first newspapers in the country to notice the opening of the rebellion, and in 1817 Duane began a systematic study and thorough editorial coverage of the embattled colonies. Between 1817 and 1822, when Duane retired as an editor, the *Aurora* was unsurpassed as a source of information on South America.[1]

The President and the Secretary of State dismissed Duane's concern with American policy for South America as mere political hostility. The *Aurora* "was incessantly pouring upon me the most violent and groundless abuse," complained John Quincy Adams, who believed it to be "the most slanderous newspaper in the United States." President Monroe agreed that "for years, [not] a day passed but his newspaper has been filled with abuse and slander upon the Administration." But the President maintained that Duane's "abuse was a recommendation," that "to be reviled by him was a certificate of good character."[2]

In truth Duane would have felt and acted as he did on South America regardless of who was in office. The editor was not within the political orbit of Henry Clay. The two were acquainted only slightly, and Duane suspected Clay's politics because of his vote in favor of creating the Second Bank of the United States. Al-

---

[1]See Hyman German, "The Philadelphia 'Aurora' on Latin American Affairs," *Pennsylvania History*, VIII (April, 1941), 110-130.

[2]J. Q. Adams, *Memoirs*, IV, 507-508, 514.

though Duane respected Clay for taking a strong stand on South America, he did not use the Aurora to publicize the Speaker's role.[3]

Duane was however a warm friend of another Congressman from Kentucky, who was also a zealous supporter of the Latin republics, Colonel Richard Mentor Johnson. In Congress Johnson's position on crucial national issues had coincided with the views of Duane; he had strenuously protested the demise of Jefferson's Embargo and had opposed a recharter of the First United States Bank. After the war, in which he became a national military hero, Colonel Johnson voted against the Second Bank, but advocated a protective tariff and favored government expenditures for national improvements.[4]

On the South American issue, Colonel Johnson was a spokesman for an unofficial group of citizens and Congressmen who sought to influence American policy without directly clashing with the administration. The circle included David Trimble of Kentucky, who preferred Richard Johnson to Henry Clay as the political leader of his state, and the Clintonians John C. Spencer of New York and Henry Baldwin of Pennsylvania. Dr. William Thornton, the chief of the Patent Office, and Baptis Irvine, the itinerant editor, were associated, and William Duane was a sub-rosa member of the group. "I am in a state of political outlawry with the members of the administration," Duane apologized to the wife of General Jacob Ripley,

---

[3]Aurora, 30 Mar., 1 Apr. 1819.

[4]Duane to Jefferson, 5 June 1824, TC-LC; Thomas P. Abernethy, "Richard Mentor Johnson," DAB, X, 114-116; Leland Winfield Meyer, The Life and Times of Colonel Richard M. Johnson of Kentucky (New York, 1932), 66, 75, 142.

who sought his help for a political prisoner, "and could render no service whatever thro' them. The general can tell you how I stand with what is called the Cabinet."

"Anything that I can do is by stealth or without being seen," explained the editor, by interceding with friends who had influence in the capital. In this way he had aided in the rescue of Richard W. Meade, an American merchant from Pennsylvania who for two years was held a political prisoner in Spain. The American government demanded and secured his release, "but it was not until the Cabinet was alarmed lest Congress should take the merit of the case out of its hands." By the end of 1818 the administration adopted sterner measures to protect the rights of American citizens held prisoner by the Spanish. The first act under the new policy was to send a ship of war to Havana to demand the release of William D. Robinson, an American merchant in South America who was a personal friend of Duane. The Spanish Ambassador Don Luis Onis agreed to cooperate, but objected that "Robinson was a very bad man, and had been guilty of extreme misconduct in Caraccas." Secretary Adams himself distrusted Robinson and thought him (as he did Duane) to be "essentially an adventurer."[5]

Duane's earnest support of the South American rebels reflected his commitment to the idea of democratic revolution. Duane believed that it was the destiny of the United States, which had achieved independence through the aid of France, to help other sub-

---

[5]Duane to Mrs. Love Allen Ripley, 22 Dec. 1818, Gratz Collection, HSP; J. Q. Adams, <u>Memoirs</u>, IV, 144, 221, 229, 251, 503, V, 36.

ject peoples in turn. By supporting the South Americans, the United States could make moral reparation for its failure in the 1790s to honor its alliance with France. Yet concern with the acquisition of Florida had been permitted to overwhelm America's obligation to the cause of freedom. "It is lamentable to see a nation which has existed free and independent only 35 years from the close of the war for its independence," Duane commented, "which has given the example and furnished as it were, the _universal_ and _common law_ of revolution, all at once falling into the iniquitous duplicity and treachery of the old systems of machiavelism and oppression," attempting to flatter and appease the despotic Spain, while abandoning the people who fought for liberation from Spanish tyranny. But "we are a pious money loving people," Duane observed bitterly, who have enjoyed generosity from others and now have nothing to spare but "sympathy," and "that of the kind which we find in the memorable old song of _moderation_."

> There was an ancient gentleman, who had a good estate,
> Who kept a sumptous house, and lived at a plentiful rate;
> And kept a porter to relieve the poor daily at his gate,
> Which the porter always did, by a--_sympathetic_ thump of a
> stone on the pate.
> Moderation! Moderation! O! wonderful republican moderation![6]

To the moderate Republicans who directed American affairs, such as John Quincy Adams, the notion of a national responsibility to radicalism was foreign and repugnant. Secretary Adams describing Baptis Irvine might equally have written of William Duane: "He is one of the men with whom this age abounds--a fanatic of liberty

---

[6] _Aurora_, 2 Feb., 30 Mar. 1818.

for the whole human race-- . . . . He is by birth an Irishman, and has no native American feelings." Therefore "like all the European republicans whom I have known," Adams observed, "he habitually thinks of liberty as a blessing to be acquired, and never as a blessing to be enjoyed."[7]

The sense of continuity between the Revolutions in North and South America was real to Duane. He had known in the 1790s the first generation of political exiles in the United States, Latin Americans who like himself were in flight from a wave of repression in their own countries. Soon after Duane arrived in Philadelphia, he recorded later, "I became acquainted with some men of virtue and intellect, who were preparing the way for that revolution in South America, which is now realized. Those intimacies," he explained, "had, by exciting my sympathy, led me to bestow more earnest attention on the history, geography, and the eventual destiny of those countries." Pedro Gual, who became the first minister of foreign affairs of Simon Bolivar's Republic of Colombia, was among the exiled patriots whom Duane had known when Gual and his family were living "in adversity" in Philadelphia.[8]

Duane's closest association with the Southern Revolution was through his friendship with Manuel Torres. Torres, who lived in exile in Philadelphia from 1796 until his death in 1822, became the first diplomatic representative from a South American republic to be received by the government of the United States. In New

---

[7]J. Q. Adams, Memoirs, IV, 444-445.

[8]Duane, A Visit to Colombia, iii, 458.

Granada (later a province of the Republic of Colombia), Torres had been rich and well-educated; trained as a military engineer, he had served as confidential secretary to the Spanish viceroy. In 1794 however he was imprisoned with other "conspirators" for plotting the "emancipation of South America." Influential friends arranged his escape and he fled to the United States. His fortune dwindled, and for his efforts "to furnish the patriots with supplies," the Spanish confiscated his estate, but he had the satisfaction of contributing to the Revolution by "unceasing correspondence and counsels, from Mexico to La Plata and Chili," Duane proudly recalled. "To him all the agents from all sections of South America resorted as the FRANKLIN of the southern world." Torres' closest friend in the United States had been William Duane, and Duane felt himself honored by the association. "His talents as a mathematician and his general learning were transcendant," he reminisced of Torres. Although he had met the "ablest men" of three-quarters of the world, Duane declared, he had never met Torres' intellectual equal.

In his opinion, "No man understood . . . more profoundly" the common interests of the two Americas; "no man that ever existed devoted himself with more zeal[,] disinterestedness and wisdom," Duane believed, "to promote the consummation of that great American cause of which he has spoken with intuitive wisdom from the first to the last hour of an intimacy of about twenty years." From his friend, Duane acquired his own deep conviction of the future commercial and political importance of South America to the United States, and this became the central theme of his exhortation for a change in foreign policy.[9]

From 1817 onward the editor argued, shrewdly and persuasively, a viewpoint which became the unconscious basis of the Monroe Doctrine: that no European power would attempt to interfere in the former Spanish colonies. The members of the Holy Alliance, although perhaps sympathetic to the re-establishment of monarchy, lacked the money or the ships to undertake a project of redemption in South America. And Great Britain, the only nation which possessed the power to act, lacked the incentive to do so. Britain's sole interest in South America, Duane continually asserted, was in exploiting its commercial possibilities; in the interest of maintaining open markets there, Britain would oppose renewed political domination by any foreign power. Duane believed that the United States could defy Spain with complete impunity. The only threat to the United States' position in South America would arise from the commercial rivalry of Great Britain; because of proximity the United States possessed a natural advantage, which it should not jeopardize through short-sighted diplomacy.[10]

Duane thought that the Florida question dominated American policy quite unnecessarily, and he had been opposed to any negotiations for the territory. Spain could not hold Florida, yet did not intend to give it up, in his opinion, but only to use the issue as

---

[9] _Ibid._, 609; _Franklin Gazette_, 16 July 1822; Duane to Monroe, 15 July 1822, Monroe Papers, NYPL.

[10] _Aurora_, 10, 19 June 1817, 7, 9, 10, 11, 25, 26, 27, 28, 30, 31 Mar., 2, 4, 7, 9, 13 Apr. 1818; Duane, _The Two Americas, Great Britain, and the Holy Alliance_ (Washington, 1824).

a tactic to deflect American support for the rebelling colonies. The United States government should simply wait until the South Americans themselves took Florida from the Spanish and offered it to the United States. Opposed however to this aggressive philosophy, which advocated open defiance of the European powers, was the viewpoint of responsible moderates that the country had to deal candidly with the "legitimate" owner of Florida in order to retain the respect of Europe. The opinion of Nicholas Biddle, who mistrusted expansionism altogether, was an extreme example of this view. "We have already enemies enough abroad," Biddle advised the President concerning Florida; "the impression to be created in Europe by any movement, may well be weighed in deciding on it."[11]

The alleged American neutrality in the South American conflict Duane regarded as hypocritical, for the government treated the impotent Spain as if it were a great power and ignored as nonexistent the established republican governments. He blamed the double standard on Secretary of State Adams, whom he correctly estimated to be the principal creator of foreign policy. In December 1817 an incident occurred which to Duane outrageously illustrated the duplicity of the government's position. United States' forces seized the former Spanish territory of Amelia island, located in the St. Mary's river off the west coast of Florida, which just six months before had been invaded and occupied by a group of international volunteers in the name of the South American Revolu-

---

[11]Aurora, 25, 28 Feb., 23 Apr. 1817; J. Q. Adams, Memoirs, IV, 53; Biddle to Monroe, 19 Feb. 1816, 30 July 1818, Monroe Papers, NYPL.

tion. The government defended the seizure by two contradictory arguments. President Monroe declared that Amelia had fallen into the hands of private adventurers who were using the island as a base for slave trading, smuggling and piracy. But the administration also cited the secret law of 1811, which declared that the United States would not tolerate the transfer of Florida territory to any foreign power.[12]

In a long editorial campaign the Aurora bitterly attacked the American action at Amelia island. The justification by the principle of "no transfer" to a foreign power belied the charge of mere adventurism and served as evidence of a conscious act of hostility against the South American rebels. The Aurora explicitly disputed the President's allegations of misconduct on Amelia, using information which probably had been supplied to Duane either directly by some of the South American diplomatic agents or indirectly through Manuel Torres.[13]

The original occupation of Amelia island had in fact been authorized by several South American officials in the United States. The island was to be used for privateering against the Spanish and it was hoped as a base for a future invasion of mainland Florida. The Monroe administration denied that the patriot agents possessed

---

[12]Joseph Byrne Lockey, Pan Americanism: Its Beginnings (New York, 1920), 183-195; Charles Carroll Griffin, The United States and the Disruption of the Spanish Empire, 1810-1822 (New York, 1937), 103, 110-112, 140-142, 148-149, 255; Samuel Flagg Bemis, John Quincy Adams and the Foundations of American Foreign Policy (New York, 1949), 307-308, 345, 349. These authorities agree in accepting the correctness of the government's action.

[13]See Aurora, 13 Jan.-3 Mar. 1818.

the authority for their action, and Duane denied that Monroe's government had the power to decide on their status. In truth the agents had apparently acted without instructions, and under pressure from the United States, their governments eventually disavowed any interest in the island.

The administration recovered quickly from the Amelia affair. A group of South American residents protested to the State department; a few newspapers raised questions about the seizure, and Henry Clay in "private company" was "indefatigable . . . in expressing disapprobation of that transaction." But most newspapers readily accepted the explanations offered by the President, and the general public was not troubled by the event, which ended with the United States in possession of a new bit of Florida territory.[14]

A few months later the Florida issue erupted into an international crisis. In April 1818 General Andrew Jackson, in pursuit of the Seminole Indians, crossed the territorial boundary, marched deep into Florida, and finally besieged and conquered the Spanish fort at Pensacola. Jackson began his return home in late May, and in June the public received the first news of the invasion.

Duane's instinctive reaction was to support Jackson absolutely. In addition to admiring and trusting Jackson personally, he strongly approved the General's aggressive demonstration of Spanish weakness and his subversion of the official policy of friendly negotiation. Duane anticipated governmental censure of

---

[14]J. Q. Adams, _Memoirs_, IV, 30-31, 46, 53, 60, 71, 89-90; _Niles' Weekly Register_, XIII (20 Dec. 1817), 258.

the action at Pensacola. In mid-June the Aurora reported that "The ministerial papers have begun the cry against general Jackson. His offense is his splendid public services." The attack was politically inevitable, maintained the editor, because the name of Jackson had been spoken of for the Presidency and consequently inspired fear among "those creatures that derive their nurture about the public dunghill."[15]

The pressure for the punishment of Jackson, from within the cabinet and from advisers like Nicholas Biddle, was however resisted by the President and the Secretary of State. In July the administration decided upon a compromise position; the government would relinquish the Spanish forts, but defend General Jackson. Duane ridiculed the government's retreat into wily diplomacy from the straightforward course which Andrew Jackson had provided. Secretary Adams, Duane mocked, would answer the complaints of Ambassador Onis with a manifesto interpreting the capture of Pensacola as part of a "pacific operation of diplomacy" and a friendly act toward Spain. Its theme was "explained in a scarce book--called, The Prince." Duane imagined that when Adams and Onis met "they must have laughed in each other's faces."[16]

The Pensacola dispute continued into the following session of Congress, where a demand was raised for the investigation and censure of Jackson's conduct. The jealous hostility toward Jackson by Secretary of the Treasury William Crawford was the source of the trouble, it was revealed in the Aurora in a letter from Nashville.

---

[15]Aurora, 13 June 1818. [16]Ibid., 3, 14 July 1818.

"That Crawford has been all along inveterate against Jackson, . . . I have not seen adequate proof," John Quincy Adams commented on the charge by Duane's Nashville correspondent. "But since the publication of that letter, it is impossible to avoid perceiving that he is so." The two Senators from Pennsylvania, Abner Lacock and Jonathan Roberts, both Crawford supporters, were important participants in the attempt to condemn Jackson, but the majority opinion in Pennsylvania clearly favored the General. Henry Baldwin was among the Congressmen who spoke warmly on Jackson's behalf.[17]

Because President Monroe had at least partially upheld Jackson, the Pensacola debate in Congress became a contest for or against the executive. Some of the anti-caucus men in Pennsylvania, who were strong defenders of Jackson, were not happy to find themselves _ipso facto_ on the side of the government. Hugh Hamilton's Harrisburg _Chronicle_ denounced the _National Intelligencer_ editors and others for using Jackson's heroism as a subject for party feeling. "The character of General Jackson is a guarantee for the contempt in which he holds these attempts of the administration papers."[18]

Speaker of the House Henry Clay, who welcomed any opportunity to criticize the Monroe administration, joined avidly in the movement to censure Andrew Jackson. Clay's position was highly inconsistent with his former professions. Allegedly the chief advo-

---

[17] J. Q. Adams, _Memoirs_, IV, 214. See also Jonathan Roberts to Nicholas Biddle, 20 Jan. 1819, Biddle Papers, LC; Jonathan Roberts' Memoirs, II, 125-139, HSP; Harrisburg _Chronicle_, 22 Mar. 1819.

[18] _Ibid._, 28 Jan. 1819.

cate of the South American republics, he now condemned the event which had done more to aid in the cause of their liberation from Spain than any previous action by the United States. Duane had been uncertain in his opinion of Clay, but at this time he turned against him with the pronouncement that "Clay of Kentucky has lost himself on the Seminole question." In Congress Colonel Richard Johnson broke with his friend Clay on the Pensacola issue and was among the most effective of the defenders of Jackson.

The censure attempt failed and the affair ended as a personal triumph for Jackson. The General's tour of the eastern cities of Baltimore, Philadelphia and New York, shortly before the conclusion of the Congressional debate on Pensacola, proved beyond doubt Jackson's enormous popularity with the nation. "The crowds who call to pay him the honest homage of respect is [sic] I may say excessive," Duane complained mildly to Alden Spooner, the day following Jackson's arrival in Philadelphia, "as the morning has been a round of introductions and the access to his quarters a crowded thoro'fare, like the emptying of a church or a theatre. The general's health," Duane went on, reminding Spooner that he had known Jackson when he was in the Senate in 1797, "is such that no man who was acquainted with him twenty years ago, can discern any difference but a sprinkling of gray hairs. His honors sit easy upon him--," observed the editor; "there is not that superciliousness & arrogance & vanity in him that is to be seen in persons who have stuffed themselves into a reputation which history will consign to [execration]."[19]

[19]Duane to Spooner, 15 Feb. 1819, B. V. Spooner Collection, NYHS.

In February 1819, simultaneously with Jackson's victory in Congress, the United States concluded a treaty with Spain for the total acquisition of Florida. Secretary of State Adams had succeeded in eliciting highly favorable terms from Ambassador Onis, including a declaration of the western boundary of the Louisiana Purchase which relinquished all Spanish claims in the Northwest to the United States. Although the American government had disavowed Jackson's invasion, Secretary Adams skillfully used it as the basis for a virtual ultimatum to Spain either to govern Florida or to give it up. Within a few months the Spanish government came to terms and ceded Florida to the United States in exchange for five million dollars in American claims to be assumed by the American government.

Following the Adams-Onis treaty, Duane had no further quarrel with government policy on South America, for future good relations with the southern republics seemed assured. He even yielded a grudging respect to John Quincy Adams for the Florida settlement and for his defense of Andrew Jackson. Still the Secretary was the son of John Adams and a man of "royalist predilections"; "we shall speak of the *son* as we spoke of the *father*," Duane promised, "such as the one was and the other is." The feeling of mistrust was fully reciprocated by Adams.[20]

II.

In late 1819 Duane's friend Manuel Torres became the diplo-

---

[20]*Aurora*, 13 May 1819. See also *ibid*., 6 Mar., 9 June, 1818, 25 Feb., 19, 30 Mar., 1 Apr., 14 May 1819.

matic representative to the United States from the Republic of Colombia. The Republic, formed by the ex-colonies of Venezuela and New Granada, was the creation of Simon Bolivar, the Liberator. Torres, who was given the rank of charge d'affaires, had been instructed by his government "to open and extend friendly relations between the two countries to the utmost of his power." In presenting his credentials to President Monroe and Secretary of State Adams, Torres attempted to make it clear that he would not be politically troublesome to the administration. Colombia did not intend to "press unseasonably" for recognition or to do anything "which might give dissatisfaction to the Government of the United States." But Torres informed the American Secretary that "the object of his Government," in mutual understanding with Buenos Ayres and Chili, "was the total emancipation of all South America."[21]

Simon Bolivar was at that time preparing to carry the revolution into Peru, and in January 1820 Torres proposed that the American government sell surplus arms on credit to Colombia for use by Bolivar. Before the proposal came before the cabinet for consideration, Colonel Richard M. Johnson, who had recently become a Senator from Kentucky, called upon Monroe and Adams to present two requests on behalf of Duane. The editor desired either the commission to sell arms to the South Americans or a diplomatic appointment to Colombia. The President and the Secretary were shocked at the apparent collusion. The "project of furnishing ten thousand stands of arms to Venezuela for the sake of making a profitable

---

[21] J. Q. Adams, Memoirs, IV, 440, V, 113.

job to Duane" disgusted Monroe, and John Quincy Adams was smugly disdainful. "To this complexion ninety-nine hundreths of the South American patriotism, and which has for these three years been flaunting in such gorgeous colors in this country, must come at last!"[22]

Torres and Johnson, who cooperated on South American affairs, did want to help their old friend who was "now poor and embarrassed, and involved in a lawsuit with the Government." Duane and the War department had failed to negotiate a satisfactory settlement of his military accounts for his service as Adjutant General; the differences concerned especially his expenditures as quartermaster. The confusion in part arose from the tumultuous urgency of the crisis of 1814, when Duane had sought to secure ammunition and order tents and supplies for the ten thousand man militia camp created for the defense of Philadelphia. Throughout his service however Duane had been engaged in a private struggle against the "odious tyranny practised in the accountants office over every officer in the army who is not . . . [a] sycophant." He had predicted in 1814 that in settling his military accounts he would feel that authority "with a vengeance."

The War department originally charged Duane with the sum of nine thousand dollars outstanding; this was corrected down to seven thousand dollars, and the government prepared to sue for recovery of that amount. However Duane "had found a receipt from his successor for three thousand dollars of the money," and the total was

---

[22]<u>Ibid</u>., IV, 507-508, V, 45.

again reduced. In October 1819 the United States entered suit against Duane for 4,317 dollars. Colonel Johnson believed that if Duane "knew anything about the way of keeping accounts he would be able to show that he had also paid all the remainder of the balance." Although Johnson thought that Duane "had been in some respects ill used by the Government," John Quincy Adams was convinced that "if there had been anything wrong in the War Department with [Duane], it had been in the forbearance to sue him for the balance due, too long."[23]

For Senator Johnson it was a delicate mission to approach Monroe and Adams to ask a favor for William Duane. Adams prided himself on keeping his feelings in check, but his true thoughts must have been transparent. He told Johnson that he "retained no resentment . . . whatever" against Duane for his "violent and groundless abuse" and "should be ready and willing to render him any service in my power." President Monroe was rather more candid in remarking that "Colonel Johnson might have been more worthily occupied than in becoming the medium of such proposals." But Johnson managed his difficult assignment with tact, honorably fulfilling his responsibility to Duane without himself offending the President or the Secretary. "Johnson is a man who can refuse no favor to any person," Adams charitably concluded. "He would recommend

---

[23]*Ibid.*, IV, 507-508, V, 112; *Pa. Archives*, 6th series, VII, 3, 7; Duane to Monroe, 17 Sept. 1814, Monroe Papers, NYPL; Duane to Daniel Parker, 24 Jan. 1814, Parker Papers, HSP; Duane to Jefferson, 5 June 1824, TJ-LC; 18th Cong. 1st sess., *Letter from the Secretary of War, Transmitting Information Respecting . . . William Duane*, pamphlet, HSP.

ten persons for one and the same place, rather than say no to any one of them."[24]

Monroe and Adams discussed the requests at length, and Adams was clearly gratified by the President's frank expression of enmity toward the editor. Monroe reasoned that an appointment to a man who had continually criticized the administration would give a general disgust to the people of this country, who would universally consider it as buying off his opposition." The Secretary transposed this imagined public inference into settled fact about Duane's intention; "his present proposal is substantially to sell his silence," Adams recorded in his diary. "The President offers nothing for it but his contempt." John Quincy Adams believed that Duane was "always for sale to the highest bidder," but that opinion was the opposite of the truth about Duane's fiercely independent career.

In talking with Adams about the President's refusal, Colonel Johnson commented that "Duane was a man of great information and considerable talents, but without judgment." A proof of that, he acknowledged, "was in his complaints against the President in the very letter by which he was soliciting favors from him." Duane had based his pretensions to an appointment upon his past work and sacrifices for the Republican party and had chided Monroe for his neglect. "The services of which he boasted," in Monroe's opinion, "were nothing but twenty years of perpetual abuse upon the best men

---

[24]The conversations of Adams with Monroe, Col. Johnson and others concerning Duane are recorded in J. Q. Adams, Memoirs, IV, 507-509, 514-515, 519-520, 526-527, V, 43, 45-47, 111-113, 117-118.

in the country." Monroe moreover quite properly felt that personally he owed nothing to the editor.

Apart from the obvious political objection, Duane would have been an excellent choice for a diplomatic post in South America, especially Colombia. He had many friends among the revolutionaries, including Colombia's Foreign Minister, Pedro Gual. He had studied South American affairs with his typical industry and thoroughness and was as well informed about them as anyone in the United States. And he had taught himself to read and speak Spanish.

President Monroe offered to place Duane's requests before the cabinet, but Colonel Johnson declined the gesture and retrieved from Secretary Adams the two letters from Duane which contained his proposals. In spite of Johnson's discretion, rumors began to circulate in the capital. "Duane is said to have actually offered himself . . . upon terms," a Washington newspaper reported; he asked "ready money."[25] Senator Jonathan Roberts and Congressman John Sergeant separately approached Adams to ask that Duane's letters be made public. "The President also . . . told me," Adams recorded, "that he wished copies of them had been taken." The effort to discredit the editor seemed useless to Adams. "Duane has no character to lose," he reasoned. "He is known to be unprincipled, poor, and for sale. . . . To prove him venal and profligate would only show him fit for the trade which he pursues, of disseminating slander."

Duane, with his application rejected and a lawsuit pending against him, was in serious financial trouble. He had never been

---

[25]Washington Gazette, quoted in Aurora 27 June, 1 July, 1820.

able to live within the income of the Aurora. His wife Margaret had been "accustomed to a life of plenty and educated in habits more elegant than prudent," and the family gradually had exhausted her portion of the Markoe fortune. Duane had four daughters to support, the eldest nineteen and the youngest only seven, and his adolescent son Edward was just ready to enter college.[26]

The government suit threatened to ruin Duane by causing the final collapse of his always precarious credit. In October 1820 a preliminary judgment was obtained against him "which was all founded on technicalities," Duane complained, "and without regard to the facts upon the face of written and contemporary statement." From then on the federal District Attorney, Charles Jared Ingersoll, "appeared to delight in vexatious notifications of a judgment hanging over me," Duane objected, "and alarming those to whom in the way of business I had transactions of credit, such as the paper maker, the typefounder, and the ink maker." In November Manuel Torres kindly promised him a large personal loan, and a few weeks later Duane was forced to ask him for five hundred dollars in cash, for he had received a bill which "is in fact a notice of execution if not paid--instanter."[27]

Duane's political enemies were highly pleased by his personal misfortune. "Brutus is a profligate," Charles Ingersoll wrote to the President. "About the time that he made overtures to

---

[26]Duane to Jefferson, 5 June, 8 Nov. 1824, TJ-LC; Duane to Alden Partridge, 15 July 1820, Pers. Papers Misc. (Duane), LC.

[27]Duane to Jefferson, 5 June 1824, TJ-LC; Duane to [Manuel Torres?], 14 Dec. 1820, Pers. Papers Misc. (Duane), LC.

you last winter for an appointment out of the country he was sued on a balance . . . reported against him at the Treasury." Judgment had been found against him; "and all he can do, according to his own code of morals, as he can not escape from the country, is to utter loud denunciations against those who govern it. I understand," Ingersoll told Monroe, "that he is extremely straitened, and, probably, desperate."[28]

The high quality of the Aurora which Duane had maintained since 1798 began to decline rapidly in the next two years. In 1821 Duane reduced the subscription rate and changed the print to a smaller typeface; the following year he was forced to adopt a much cheaper grade of paper. The editorial quality of the Aurora also sharply declined. "Brutus" contributed seldom and in 1822 retired from the paper altogether, as Stephen Simpson prepared to begin his own journal. Duane himself wrote principally about South American affairs, which dominated the newspaper. But apart from these articles, Duane wrote less and less original material and for the first time in his journalistic career began to rely heavily on material culled from other sources.

The War department made a settlement with Duane in May 1822. It reduced the claim by nearly two thousand dollars, leaving a total balance against him of 2,621 dollars. Even the reduced sum was beyond Duane's means, and he felt that he had been disgraced, placed in the class of a public defaulter. The judgment "was the immediate cause of my selling off all of [the] property that I had

---

[28]Ingersoll to Monroe, 29 Oct. 1820, Monroe Papers, NYPL.

in 1822," he explained later to Thomas Jefferson, "and paying to the last dollar of the produce." Duane had no credit whatever and was in constant financial peril. "To avoid all this," he told Jefferson, "I resolved to sell all and begin the world anew in my 64th year."[29]

In July Manuel Torres died, less than a month after he had been officially received by President Monroe as charge d'affaires from the Republic of Colombia, in the first formal recognition of a South American republic by the United States. Torres had suffered from chronic asthma, especially during the American winters, and when he went to Washington for the recognition ceremony Duane knew that he was dying, but Torres said he had waited thirty-five years for that day, and he would go. After his return to Philadelphia, Torres "lingered out the interval," his body gradually succumbing but his mind clear until the last. Duane was with him when he died and immediately afterward he wrote, as Torres had requested, to inform President Bolivar and to express Torres' gratitude to President Monroe, Secretary Adams and Henry Clay. Torres' will made Duane the sole executor of his private papers and executor with Richard W. Meade of his public papers.[30]

During the summer Duane was given the opportunity he had wanted to visit South America. He was invited by "some gentlemen

---

[29] Letter from the Secretary of War . . .; Duane to Jefferson, 5 June 1824, TJ-LC.

[30] Franklin Gazette, 16 July 1822; Duane to Monroe, 15 July 1822, Monroe Papers, NYPL; Duane to Henry Clay, 15 July 1822, Hopkins, ed., Clay Papers, III, 261-262; Duane, Visit to Colombia, 608-609.

who had furnished supplies to the Colombians . . . to visit that country to settle and obtain the amount of their accounts," Duane informed Thomas Jefferson. "I accepted their proposal to defray all my expenses, pay a weekly allowance to my wife during my absense, and allow me a commission on all I should settle in behalf of the claimants."[31]

It was necessary before Duane could depart to complete the sale of the Aurora. Fortunately he had several possible buyers because the presidential election two years away created interest in the acquisition of a newspaper once so influential as the Aurora. A "Baltimore negotiator" desired to buy it as an organ for John Quincy Adams, and partisans of Henry Clay were also interested in the disposition of the paper. Duane rejected an offer by a man from Harrisburg, "whose faculties are not adapted to a city, or to sustain such a paper with any credit or effect." Duane's personal choice as his successor was his former protege James Wilson, who was "able & virtuous and as if he breathed my own spirit." Wilson, who had edited the Aurora during the war while Duane was on active service, had moved in 1815 to Steubensville, Ohio, where he established the Western Herald. He was eager to return and take charge of the Aurora, but encountered difficulty in selling his own paper in Steubensville. Duane helped him to find a loan of two thousand dollars in order to go through with the purchase, but just a few weeks after Duane left for South America, Wilson was forced to resell the Aurora because it become impossible for him to leave Ohio.

---

[31]Duane to Jefferson, 5 June 1824, TJ-LC.

The new publisher was a Philadelphia classics teacher, John Sanderson.[32]

III.

Duane published his final issue of the Aurora on September 30, 1822, and on October 2 sailed from New York for Caracas with his daughter Elizabeth and his step-son Richard Bache. Twenty-one year old Elizabeth, the eldest child of Duane's second marriage, "was threatened with consumption," Duane explained, "and, like my daughter Katherine much attached to me, solicited to accompany." Lieutenant Bache, a recent graduate of West Point, went along with the idea of volunteering his military service in the revolution, a cause "not less holy than that which fifty years ago called forth the exertions of his forefathers." However he "soon perceived that the war was drawing too near its close to justify a stranger in entering upon a new career."

Throughout the nine month long journey, Duane was received by the South Americans with greater respect and courtesy than he was accustomed to in the United States. The Colombians were well informed of his devotion to the cause of their independence. In a remote city in the Andes, for example, Duane met an admirer who knew his life story and was eager to talk with him about history and political philosophy. The first Congress of the Republic of Colombia in 1821 had honored Duane for his service to South America "by a vote of thanks, and the epithet benemerito." The "demonstra-

---

[32]Duane to A. McIntyre, 14 Sept. 1822, Gratz Collection, HSP; John C. Wright to Henry Clay, 2 Nov. 1822, ed., Clay Papers, III, 309; ibid., 310n.

tions of respect by the public authorities have no personal reference to the writer, an unknown individual," Richard Bache was careful to observe in his account of the journey, "but were the outpourings of grateful feelings towards the chief of the party, whose exertions in favour of their country prompted the people to this expression of their regard."

Duane and his family sailed as guests of the Colombian government aboard the *Hercules*, a new corvette constructed in New York for the Colombian navy. Their only fellow passenger was Senora Antonia Bolivar, sister of the President, who with her two children was returning to her native country after nine years exile. On October 18 the vessel landed at the port of LaGuayra, where the Duanes were gratified "to find, very unexpectedly, several acquaintances and friends waiting to greet us, some of them from Caracas, fifteen miles distant." In his first impression of South America, Duane was struck by the oriental look of the streets and buildings and continually reminded of his life in Bengal thirty years earlier. Aging and worldly, he was generally more tolerant of different habits and strange experiences in South America than young Richard Bache, who had lived all his life in Philadelphia. Duane had even mellowed somewhat toward the Roman Catholic church, of which Bache was still deeply suspicious.

The Duane family remained more than three weeks in Caracas, preparing for their overland journey to Bogota and enjoying a lavish social life with the foreign and creole community in the city, which was made especially festive by the celebration of Senora

Bolivar's homecoming. Colonel Duane, a handsome man who had grown more distinguished in looks as he grew older, was a welcome figure in the ballroom. Indeed he was equally popular with the ladies of Caracas and Bogota and the Indian women in remote villages of the Andes. The secret of his success was that he appreciated "the sight of agreeable women" and always "addressed them as they should be addressed, beautiful or ugly, with courtesy."

The stay in Caracas was the most enjoyable period of the entire trip to South America; "intimacies had been formed; and attentions, kindness, and hospitality, had been so constant and so generous," Duane remembered, "that the approach of the period of departure on our journey became irksome." On November 12 the Duane party set out on the southward journey to Bogota, a distance of more than one thousand miles to be travelled on the backs of mules, "passing five great ranges and seven lesser ranges of the Andes." A large party of friends, in keeping with local custom, escorted the Duanes out of Caracas and lunched with them at the first resting point, nine miles from town. They took their final opportunity to warn the family of the extreme difficulties to be encountered.

"We could scarcely credit the assertion . . . that the disgusting fare now presented [at lunch], and the miserable hovel which sheltered us, would prove highly acceptable before we got to our journey's end," Richard Bache remembered ruefully. "We felt inclined to attribute the friendly remonstrances, now urgently repeated, against our undertaking the journey, to a polite expression of concern for our welfare," he recalled, "an over estimate of the difficulties, and an under valuation of our capability of enduring fatigue." Duane's memories of the trip were more cheerfully philosophic. The "admonitions and persuasions were so unceasing . . . that, although there was really no exaggeration in the description," he admitted, "we found ourselves less disconcerted when the toils, privations, and fatigues, were realized, than we might have been."

Miss Elizabeth in particular had been entreated to remain in Caracas with her friend Josephine, the daughter of Senora Bolivar, or with the family of General Lino Clemente, whom the Duanes had known in Philadelphia. Everyone told her "that no lady had ever attempted such a journey before," and that for a girl of "delicate frame" and failing health it would be truly hazardous. But "her usual reply was that she had her father and brother with her, that she could go any where they could go, and live upon whatever would subsist them." And Elizabeth was right; she learned to sit her mule all day like a soldier and could still find energy in the evening to display her Philadelphia finery to the giggling and awestruck girls of the village. Duane himself happily acknowledged that his favorite daughter "made the journey with much less fatigue than I did" and was "not only restored to health but to robust florid health by a journey on mules of more than 1400 miles."

Although the most difficult part of the trip was in the mountains of western Venezuela, in some ways the first four days were the hardest. They pushed themselves too fast and were forced to stop after only one hundred miles for eleven days at Valencia. The mules had developed sores from improper loading and needed to rest. Then ironically, while descending from a rooftop where the family had been enjoying the view, Duane made a misstep on a landing whose boards had been stripped for fuel, plunged through the staircase, and "found myself seated on the ground floor." The injury was not serious, but he was badly bruised, an "inconvenience" which for several weeks "rendered any other than a sitting position desirable."

Fortunately their host at Valencia, the commandant, questioned the two servants they had hired in Caracas and discovered "that although they both professed to be so well acquainted with the country, as to undertake to be our guides, neither of them had ever been farther south or west than Truxillo," less than one-third the distance to Bogota. The commandant offered them the service of his orderly sergeant, "who had five times passed the whole route," and the Duane family accepted with gratitude, "though far short of the thanks we afterward found to be justly due." Sergeant Maurice Proctor was an uncommonly gregarious and resourceful Englishman from Suffolk "whose passion was rambling," they discovered, "and who had become so much naturalized to the climate, food, and people of the Sierra, was so well known every where on the road, that this little jaunt, of 1300 miles, was as welcome to him as a party of pleasure." By the commandant's direction the sergeant was to receive no salary, "and in truth, it was not necessary . . ., for he considered the permission to go with us as a favour to him."

Duane knew that a sergeant "is as proud of his rank, and tenacious of his command, as a general," and therefore placed

Proctor "in command of the rest of the suite." He had to manage "the knavish dispositions of our two hired *assistientes*," and also to direct the various muleteers and their assistants who changed with each exchange of mules. With these responsibilities "the sergeant was in his element, and conducted things as if he was on military service." Proctor spoke Spanish "with more fluency than correctness, . . . and never failed to make himself understood, and nine times out of ten agreeable," except when it became necessary to deal with a "supercilious" local official or a "pilfering muleteer." Then "he not only took care to make known his own importance, and his ribbon and medal or Darabobo, but the importance of the *Coronel de los Estados Unidos del Norte* to whom he was attached by the commandant of Valencia." Fortunately for the Duane family, the sergeant "knew every body, every where; he knew where to procure what we wanted, and always on cheap terms; and without him," Duane acknowledged, "it is morally certain, we should not have been able to find our way in three months."

On one occasion the servant Vincente and Valentine, a muleteer, evaded the watchful Sergeant Proctor and contrived to fall behind the party, unfortunately keeping the baggage with them, in order to spend the night at a Spanish camp where they could indulge their passion for dancing fandangoes. The two escaped to dances in the evening whenever possible, and on the march Vincente was frequently found "in a deep sleep on his mule, to which he had committed himself and his fortunes implicitly." Valentine, the "troublesomely clever muleteer," was "a sturdy patriot," Duane noted, who could tell the heroic deeds "of all the eminent Colombians within a hundred miles" of their route. "He was not bashful in relating his own exploits in two campaigns, nor that among the muleteers he was considered no small character." Although Valentine boasted that "he was considered the best dancer among the numerous circle of his acquaintance," he acknowledged "that Vincente, your _assistiente_, . . . beats me hollow." When Valentine with his mules was about to part from the Duane party, "he made an apologetic confession" of his tricks and misdeeds and declared "that he never travelled with any people more to his satisfaction, and if it were possible he would like to go the whole world over with us. Poor Vincente," Duane sympathized,"was disconsolate at being separated from a man who had the candour to acknowledge him his superior at a fandango."

Eighty-four days after they set out from Caracas, the Duane party on February 3, 1823, entered the capital at Bogota. Duane proceeded directly "to the government house, where I was received . . . with the most unaffected kindness" by Pedro Gual, the foreign minister. The family remained nearly three months in the city, and the "novelty of a young lady from North America, having accomplished a journey over the Eastern Cordilleras," Duane recorded, "together with the good wishes of those members of the government to whom I had been known personally, or by reputation, during the revolution . . . made our residence an interesting resort of the principal ladies and gentlemen of Bogota."[33]

---

[33]The account of the journey is based on Duane, _A Visit to Colombia_ (622 p.); [Richard Bache], _Notes on Colombia, Taken in the Years 1822-3, With an Itinerary of the Route from Caracas to Bogota_;

The United States' diplomatic representative to Colombia, Colonel Charles Todd of Kentucky, was especially cordial to the family during their visit. Although Todd had received the position for which Duane had applied in 1820, the two enjoyed good relations. "I might refer you to Col Duane for detailed information with respect to the State of Affairs here," Todd wrote to Henry Clay soon after Duane left Bogota, "and his opinions would be entitled to great consideration, having devoted many years to the acquisition of an extensive knowledge of the Country and in Support of the Cause."[34]

While Richard and Elizabeth enjoyed themselves with the young people of the capital, Duane was occupied with the business he had come to deal with, recovering debts to American merchants from the Colombian government. Eventually he succeeded in settling a large portion of the accounts, "to the amount of $104,000," but he was troubled by the "deliberate mode of business" of the board of liquidations. Fortunately the board met in the public library and Duane, always a bibliophile, had ample time to inspect the large collection of valuable Spanish works on history and geography mixed in with much Roman Catholic "dogmatic rubbish." Most of the Colomian officials, Duane complained, "are not men of business as business is done with us. They are, however, compared with the

---

and an Appendix. By an Officer of the United States' Army (279 p. + map, Philadelphia, 1827); Duane to Jefferson, 5 June 1824, TJ-LC.

[34]Todd to Clay, 8 May 1823, Hopkins, ed., Clay Papers, III, 414.

Spaniards prodigious men."[35]

With a new life to make following his retirement from the Aurora, Duane had the distinction of being the first person to propose formally to the Colombian government the construction of a canal across the Isthmus of Panama. "The [London banking] house of Goldsmidt . . . was to be my back, along with a House at Rotterdam and another house at London," Duane later explained to Thomas Jefferson. His application requested "authority and protection on a trigonometrical survey, between the two seas, at the expense of the undertakers; and after making the survey, to commence opening a canal from sea to sea." The contractors requested in return "a power to levy a small toll on ships passing through that canal." The project failed, Duane explained, because the government at Bogota, although enlightened, made unreasonable stipulations because they underestimated the difficulties of the undertaking. Colombia would have granted a contract to Duane upon the terms that the survey be completed within two years and that he furnish "adequate securities" before the survey had been conducted for the final execution of the canal.[36]

Although Duane was completely happy with his trip to Colombia, the net effect of his visit was the loss of his grand illusion about the South American Revolution. "Col Duane, if he were to meet with you," Charles Todd wrote to Henry Clay, "would undeceive

---

[35]Duane to Jefferson, 5 June 1824, 20 June 1826, TJ-LC; Duane, A Visit to Colombia, 477-478.

[36]Ibid., iv; Duane to Jefferson, 20 June 1826, TJ-LC; Aurora, 16 June, 1834.

you with respect to many matters about which, he says, he has been heretofore under misapprehensions.--He would tell you," continued the disenchanged Todd, "that though the Country is separated from Spanish dominion and Misrule, yet that Spanish duplicity in the Governors and Spanish superstition in the people are but too painfully prevalent." After his return Duane wrote to Jefferson about the Colombians:

> They have a passionate desire to imitate the U.S.--_only where some habit has_ rendered it convenient not to follow it too closely. The trial by jury and the freedom of the press they _adore_--if you believe them, but are utterly uninformed of the spirit and nature of the former as well as of the latter. I witnessed some very curious transactions in relation to both.[37]

Duane became a member of a tacit fraternity of former enthusiasts of the Revolution who had become disillusioned through their own experiences in South America. In 1828 the German Wilhelm von Humboldt wrote to him from Caracas to utter his complaints against "these Spanish creole republicans." Duane himself never abandoned hopes for the South American republics. But he predicted in 1834 that the conflicts created there by personal ambitions "are not likely to end, until all those born under the monarchy have passed away,--exactly like the _Tories of our Revolution_--the sources of all the troubles which followed the peace of 1783."[38]

On April 27 the Duane family left Bogota and began the difficult northward journey down the Magdalena river. It took three

---

[37] Todd to Clay, 8 May 1823, Hopkins, ed., _Clay Papers_, III, 414; Duane to Jefferson, 20 June 1826, TJ-LC.

[38] Humboldt to Duane, 21 Aug. 1828, Alexander von Humboldt Papers, American Philosophical Society; _Aurora_, 10 Sept. 1834.

weeks to travel the distance of 765 miles by small boats and mules to the city of Carthagena, on the Gulf of Darien in the Carribean sea. While they waited for a ship to carry them back to the United States, the family was entertained by Duane's good friend William D. Robinson. They sailed on June 10 "and reached N. York on the auspicious 4th July."

CHAPTER XIV

THE OLD SCHOOL FINDS A CANDIDATE

When William Duane sold the Aurora and left for South America in 1822 the Democrats of the Old School disappeared from Philadelphia politics. Three months after Duane's departure, his colleague of twenty years in politics, Michael Leib, died after a long illness. "Our Republican Brothers have no other alternative," Stephen Girard wrote to Caesar Rodney, "but to console themselves by going arm in arm to his burial." The Old School party for many years had been all but synonymous with Duane's newspaper, which had given to a small reform-minded minority the opportunity to be widely heard. But the Aurora's "old practice of dividing the democratic family," the Franklin Gazette was pleased to report, had caused the editor's financial failure and driven him into "voluntary exile from his home and friends, to seek something more profitable among the republican emperors of the south."[1]

In the local elections that year the Old School's assembly ticket made a feeble showing in the country, and the attempt by William John Duane to organize a protest vote in the city was a miserable failure. The belated formation of a ticket by the "mechanicks, manufacturers, and Hucksters," to demand greater represen-

---

[1]Girard to Rodney, 29 Dec. 1822, Rodney Family Papers, LC; Franklin Gazette, 8 Oct. 1822.

tation for "the manufacturing interest" and "the proscription of lawyers from public employments," was really the work of a "trio of lawyers," the *Franklin* scoffed, who united "in calumniating their own profession." The Democrats of Philadelphia, conceding the election in advance to the dominant Federalists, took little interest in either side of the intraparty contest. George M. Dallas polled an unimpressive total of 1300 votes for Congress, but W. J. Duane, from a party which could bring out about eight hundred votes in the city, received a vote of less than one hundred. "WILLIAM J. DUANE, the *favorite and flatterer of faction*," the *Franklin Gazette* exulted, "has collected together the miserable cohort of NINETY-THREE deluded followers."[2]

The decline of the Old School party began with the victory of Joseph Hiester in the gubernatorial election of 1820. The anti-caucus coalition of reform Democrats, Federalists, and high tariff men in the west, could not survive the unpopularity of the Governor almost as soon as he was in office. In 1821 the Patent Democrats regained the majority in the state assembly and insulted Hiester directly by electing his defeated opponent, ex-Governor William Findlay, to the United States Senate. General Hiester, the Revolutionary veteran and simple German farmer, was abused as Governor for the very qualities which had been praised in him as a candidate. In the campaign his supporters had boasted of his scrupulous honesty and lack of personal ambition, in contrast with the corruption and

---

[2]*Ibid.*, 27 Sept., 4, 9 Oct. 1822; *Independent Balance*, 9 Oct. 1822.

intrigue of the Findlay administration, but when he became Governor they found him timid, vacillating and excessively good-natured. While his enemies joked cruelly about "the wonderful vigor, . . . and the profound ability of the 'old gentleman' and his cabinet!" his disappointed friends admitted that he was "disqualified by nature, habits and education, for the stormy and arduous duties of his station."[3]

The Hiester administration was in fact a period of useful reform, but it was a negative reformism which did not inspire public enthusiasm. Hiester was the first public official to speak out against the manipulation and abuse of election procedures, and he sought especially to reform the graft-ridden system of executive patronage. In order to combat the growing misuse of public funds, he proposed extending the bonding requirements to more officeholders. And he substituted a general retailers' tax for the special auctioneers' commissions, which had been surreptitiously bought and sold during the previous administration. But the "shop tax" was unpopular and hurt the Governor politically.[4]

Hiester wanted the state to divest the Governor of his extensive patronage under the Constitution of 1790. Meanwhile he struggled to be fair and impartial in the distasteful duty of filling the appointive positions. "The hinges of his policy are safety and

---

[3] _Franklin Gazette_, 6 May 1822; Philadelphia _Columbian Observer_, 20 Apr. 1822.

[4] Klein, _Pa. Politics_, 113-117; _Pa. Archives_, 4th series, V, 244-247, 280-296, 379-396, 450-461; _Franklin Gazette_, 8 Oct. 1822.

ease to himself," complained a former supporter. "He studies _to balance two parties_; and to offend none." Hence he rarely announces a single appointment "but makes them _by pairs_, taking one from each party." The anti-caucus Democrats were dismayed by the Governor's numerous appointments of Federalists, which appeared to confirm the Patent Democrats' contention that anti-caucus sentiments were a sham.[5]

The Duane family was well treated by the Hiester administration. William John became the prosecuting attorney for Philadelphia; Thomas Morgan, the editor's son-in-law, was made prothonotary of the court in Washington country, and Duane himself was appointed a city alderman. "Why don't their friend Binns cry out against _family compacts_?" asked the _Franklin Gazette_. "Why don't the Aurora declaim, as it used to, against _office holders_?" When the anti-caucus Democrats began to repudiate the Hiester administration, the Duanes' patronage became an embarrassment and a political liability. "_The Aurora_ has been for a year past almost as silent as the grave touching the politics of Pennsylvania," wrote John Norvell, who had succeeded Richard Bache as editor of the _Franklin_. "That miserably imbecile administration, which he labored so incessantly for so many successive years to put into power, has looked to him in vain for support in its difficulties with the public."[6]

Stephen Simpson, who had no office or status to protect,

---

[5]_Columbian Observer_, 20 Apr. 1822.

[6]_Franklin Gazette_, 26 Apr., 6 May, 8 Oct. 1822; W. J. Duane to Joseph Hiester, 24 June 1828, Gregg Collection, LC; Kehl, _Ill Feeling_, 165.

openly expressed his disillusionment with Governor Hiester, who "acts by starts and fits, according to the impulses that move him," bound to the Republicans by affection but inclined to the Federalists by "connections and circumstances. . . . He has long ceased, therefore, to act on principle." When for example he received two acts reapportioning Congressional districts, equally bad, he vetoed one and signed the other, because he "had not the heart to return two Bills. . . . Alack-a-day," lamented Simpson, "what a vigilant guardian of the Constitution!"[7]

II.

The limitations of Joseph Hiester were not unexpected, but it had been the fate of the anti-caucus movement since 1816 to have a program without a candidate. The Democrats of Pennsylvania of either New or Old School had produced no statesmen of impressive stature. To compensate for internal weakness, the Findlay party clung to its attachment to the national administration of James Monroe, and the Hiesterites looked with hope to DeWitt Clinton of New York. The admiration for Clinton had been a strong link, perhaps the strongest, which held together the anti-caucus coalition, but by 1822 Clinton's political prospects appeared to have reached an unhappy ending.

In the philosophy of Duane's Old School Democrats, Clinton possessed in a large degree the qualities of an ideal statesman. He was as Governor of New York a vigorous, intellectually powerful

---

[7] Columbian Observer, 20, 27 Apr. 1822.

executive, who advocated and undertook direct action to promote the general welfare. His grand design of the Erie canal was a unique illustration of the Old School's ideal of broad public planning. Moreover the New York canal commissioners, in their first report, had rejected the idea of using private companies to build the canal, which "would defeat the contemplated cheapness of transportation," and emphasized the importance of state construction in order to safeguard the public interest.[8]

Clinton had shared the Old School's early concern with the inflation created by excessive bank issues, and in his first gubernatorial address in January 1818 he had called for "the immediate and correcting interposition of the legislature." Lecturing the representatives on the tendency of the paper system to create a "fictitious and deceptive" prosperity, inevitably followed by panic and hard times, he had suggested that future incorporations of banks should be carefully restricted, to defeat speculative motives and serve only "the exigencies of commerce, trade or manufactures." Looking forward he had wondered "whether a much greater augmentation of such institutions may not in course of time produce an explosion that will demolish the whole system."[9]

Clinton was widely respected for his talents and ideas but he was disliked in his home state because of his arrogant personal-

---

[8]Guy S. Callender, "Early Transportation and Banking Enterprise in Relation to the Growth of Corporations," _Quarterly Journal of Economics_, XVII (1902), 155.

[9]For the text of Clinton's address see _Niles' Weekly Register_, XIII (14 Feb. 1818), 406-412. See also _ibid_., XIV (14 Mar. 1818), 39-42; _U. S. Gazette_, 4 Mar. 1818.

ity. Jabez Hammond expressed the belief that "Clinton was a sincere friend to the equal rights, prosperity and happiness of the mass of men," but acknowledged that he "possessed habits of thinking of himself and a deportment which rendered him unacceptable to them." Perhaps he was unfortunate, Hammond shrewdly observed, to have acquired political influence and power when quite young because of his association with his uncle, "but which he might have imagined he possessed in consequence of personal merits which those around him discovered." In political dealings he generally overestimated his influence, and frequently he offended his own supporters by his coldness and reserve; "his manners were such that men who resorted to him in friendship & with a wish to support him, came from him not only disgusted but changed from friends to enemies." The estrangement in 1822 of Martin Van Buren, who developed a strong rival party in New York state, was to destroy Clinton's presidential pretensions.[10]

In Pennsylvania the personal objections to Clinton were unknown. His first public visit there was not until 1825. On that occasion the citizens of Philadelphia "were very highly gratified with your presence among them," Clinton was assured in a flattering report, and "manifested this feeling with a degree of warmth quite unusual, and indeed without example." Yet the effect of the personal

---

[10]Jabez D. Hammond, _The History of Political Parties in the State of New York from the Ratification of the Federal Constitution to December 1840_, 2 vols. (Albany, 1842), II, 273-275; Rufus King, notes on conversation with Chief Justice Ambrose Spencer, 26 Aug. 1821, Charles R. King, ed., _The Life and Correspondence of Rufus King_ . . . (_Rufus King Correspondence_), 6 vols. (New York, 1900), VI, 398.

appearance was that "Clinton has lost character here--His public speeches were poor--and he read them off."[11]

In 1817 Clinton had been elected Governor of New York and for a time it had appeared that he would be an active candidate to succeed Monroe. "An attempt will . . . be made to cut short the reign of eight years," one New Yorker suspected; "we have so many great men who are growing old, and cannot wait." Clinton, "the man mountain," according to his supporters "is a towering genius and will . . . soon put everything to rights." The campaign would soon open, he predicted; "in fact a little brush fighting has already commenced, sentinels are placed, & the spies are out." Money would be spent for newspaper support; "little typers Gentlemen will be spread all over the land, as small puffers," and "Duane Leib & Co will puff in great style, & make such noise, with threats & coaxing, to gain the Clodhoppers of Pennsy^a."[12]

The support of Pennsylvania was crucial to the hopes of the New York Governor, and since the retirement of Simon Snyder the "Clodhoppers" there were potentially vulnerable. Even William H. Crawford, whose political plans required faith in a united Republican party, had to admit that because of the scandalous conduct of the Findlay administration, "Old Pennsylvania Democracy seems to be going the way of all the earth." Clinton's worried rivals saw the

---

[11]John Sergeant to Clinton, 13 June 1825, Clinton Papers, Columbia; G. M. Dallas to S. D. Ingham, 14 June 1825, Dallas Papers, HSP.

[12]E. Sage to John W. Taylor, 15 Mar. 1818, John W. Taylor Papers, NYHS.

shadow of his ambition behind every issue which excited the public. The Clintonians in Congress were the first to rise to the defense of Andrew Jackson when he came under attack for his unauthorized invasion of Florida during the Seminole war. The subsequent "ogling and love-making" between Clinton and Jackson disgusted William Crawford, who thought it "a connection which had originated in unprincipled ambition on the one side and the most vindictive resentment on the other." However when the Monroe administration itself was attacked and decided to uphold the General, the political gains from the affair were neutralized.[13]

The Congressional investigation of the Second Bank of the United States in the winter of 1818 was proposed and conducted by a political intimate of Clinton, John C. Spencer of New York. Friends of the Bank were quick to inform the President of the sinister political motives behind the investigation, and the administration cooperated fully in the successful efforts to save the institution. Later Congressman Spencer sponsored the resolution calling for a report from the Secretary of the Treasury on the state of the national currency. The resulting document convinced one Senator that Crawford was incompetent to deal with the nation's fiscal problems. But John Quincy Adams discerned that Crawford had avoided commitment on any important question because he suspected that the object was to ensnare him in a "disclosure of some doctrine which would affect his popularity."[14]

---

[13]Crawford to Gallatin, 24 July 1819, Adams, ed., <u>Writings of Albert Gallatin</u>, II, 117.

[14]Jonathan Roberts to Nicholas Biddle, 20 Jan. 1819, Biddle

In 1819 a totally unexpected question suddenly broke before the public--whether slavery would be admitted or prohibited in the territories of the United States. When Missouri territory applied to Congress for admission to statehood, Representative James Tallmadge of New York proposed a law to prohibit further introduction of slaves into Missouri and to provide for the manumission at twenty-five of the children of slaves already living in the territory. The Tallmadge amendment carried in the House but was defeated in the Senate, and the Missouri question was postponed until the following session.

We see "the congress of this republic," the _Aurora_ commented, "under a constitution that _guarantees a republican constitution to every state_," not merely doing nothing but actually "rejecting a proposition that was to preclude the extension of slavery." Duane's reaction expressed the feelings of countless Pennsylvanians. "The _slavery of man_," he wrote, "is abhorrent to every noble and honorable feeling"; justice and Christian law demanded that "its progress should be arrested, and means should be adopted for its speedy and gradual abolition--for its utter extinction." For it was absurd to say, wrote "Hancock" in the _Aurora_, that "FREEDOM and SLAVERY can exist long in the same country."[15]

Old Republicans, like Duane and Thomas Leiper, who had helped to create the Pennsylvania-Virginia axis, were shocked by

---

Papers, LC; Biddle to Monroe, 24 Jan. 1819, Monroe Papers, LC; J. Q. Adams, _Memoirs_, V (25 Mar. 1820), 37.

[15] _Aurora_, 5 Mar., 23 Nov., 7 Dec. 1819.

the revelation that the South intended to cherish its offensive institution. "I have been informed formerly by a great number of Virginia Gentlemen that they were Cursed with that thing called Slavery," Leiper wrote to Thomas Jefferson; "notwithstanding the members of Congress to the south of the Potomac all voted in favor of Extending it to Missouri." It was justly said, he concluded, that "a Tree is known by its Fruit not by its Blossoms!!"[16]

Many Northerners hoped that the public expression of their moral convictions could influence the next Congress to accept the terms of the Tallmadge amendment. In Philadelphia a mass meeting for this purpose was led by the Federalists Jared Ingersoll and Horace Binney. At Harrisburg when the legislature opened, Assemblyman William John Duane proposed that it instruct the state's delegation to Congress to vote against the admission to statehood of any territory which did not provide for the restriction of slavery. The resolution stated unequivocally the constitutional right of Congress to legislate for the territories and declared that the spread of slavery should be stopped at the banks of the Mississippi river. It was quickly passed by a unanimous vote of both houses.[17]

In New York the Missouri question became the subject of unseen political manuevering between Clinton and Van Buren's Bucktails. The Governor embraced the proposal of James Tallmadge, who had long been a member of the Clinton party, and sought to identify

---

[16]Leiper to Jefferson, received 27 May 1823, TJ-LC.

[17]Aurora, 23, 24 Nov. 1819; Freeman's Journal, 16 Dec. 1819; Glover Moore, The Missouri Controversy, 1819-1821 (Lexington, Kentucky, 1953), 176.

himself with the cause of slavery restriction. By this time he badly needed a means to improve his standing, for he would be a candidate for re-election in May 1820. The Bucktails had won the elections for the legislature the previous spring, and William Crawford believed, "with great apparent satisfaction," that "this would put Clinton down, never to rise again."

The Governor in his annual address in January called for action to support the restriction principle, and the legislature complied, instructing its delegation in Congress to oppose the creation of slave states. "I was not favorable to his recommendation," Martin Van Buren admitted, "but unwilling to give him the advantage of wielding so powerful an influence against us as it would have proved to be, if we had opposed it." Because there was no roll call in the Senate, Van Buren was not forced to vote for the resolutions; nonetheless he felt apologetic to the South thirty years later for allowing himself "to be prevented by political and partisan considerations . . . from meeting them by open opposition." In self-justification "I can only say . . . that I acted on the defensive, and that I had no hand in bringing the matter forward."[18]

In Washington where the admission of Missouri was under debate, the effect of the Pennsylvania and New York resolutions was to convince some Northern Caucus Democrats that the subject should be closed through agreement to a compromise. A Boston Congressman

---

[18]J. Q. Adams, Memoirs, VII (6 May 1819), 359; John C. Fitzpatrick, ed., The Autobiography of Martin Van Buren, American Historical Association, Annual Report, 1918 (Van Buren, Autobiography), 2 vols. (Washington, 1920), II, 99-100, 138.

was convinced that the restriction ferment "is altogether an intrigue of DeWitt Clinton's to get over the State of Pennsylvania." Many believed, as Van Buren did, that the purpose of the agitation was "to bring the politics of the slave states and the standing of their supporters in the free states into disrepute."[19]

The Federalists' opposition to slavery extension was interpreted as a disingenuous effort to get back into power. A rumor spread in Washington that an understanding existed between Clinton and the New York Federalist Rufus King, an ardent defender of restriction. "The latter is to be Pres^t^ & the former Secretary of state with right of succession after four years." The story was absurd for King despised Clinton and was on excellent terms with the anti-restrictionist Bucktails. "Mr. King's views towards us are honorable and correct," Van Buren assured a political colleague. "The Missouri Question conceals so far as he is concerned no plot."[20]

"Clinton had enough to do to maintain himself as Governor of New York, and would certainly have no party to make him President at the next election," John Quincy Adams pointed out to a concerned Monroeite. Yet Clinton's prospects might be better if the slavery question should cause a sectional division. A worried Southerner predicted that "Duane & his party (& the feebleness of the present administration has given Duane & his friends strength)

---

[19] Ibid., 137; W. Tudor to Rufus King, 12 Feb. 1820, C. R. King, ed., Rufus King Correspondence, VI, 273.

[20] Rufus King to John A. King, 18 Mar. 1820, ibid., 317-318; Jonathan Roberts to Matthew Roberts, 27 Feb. 1820, Roberts Papers, HSP; Van Buren to M. M. Noah, 17 Dec. 1819, in Van Buren, Autobiography, 139.

will support Clinton"; he presumed New York would support him, and the Northwestern states, "Ohio, Indiana, Illinois are not sufficiently enlightened to free themselves from this pretended Crusade for African emancipation--They hate us, not because we have slaves, but because they have none."[21]

These political fears operated in the debate on Missouri. To Senator Jonathan Roberts, a Crawfordite devoted to the notion of the Republican Ascendancy, the crisis which the nation faced was not a decision on the future of slavery, but the threat of an interference with the presidential succession. In his opinion, "the catastrophe is to be averted only by a speedy settlement of the question--This the republicans all feel." On March 2 the House of Representatives, in a dramatic reversal of its previous position, abandoned restriction for Missouri and voted to admit it as a slave state with the provision that in future slavery would be prohibited in the Louisiana Purchase north of the line 36° 30'.[22]

In the New York elections in May the Bucktails pledged themselves to defeat the Governor and "effectually settle the question of Mr. Clinton's future prospects." Their candidate was Monroe's Vice President, Daniel Tompkins, and they calculated upon the prestige of the national administration. The President should "interest himself" in the Bucktails' progress, Van Buren reasoned, for

---

[21] J. Q. Adams, Memoirs, VII (6 Dec. 1819), 470; Henry Clay from unknown, New Orleans, 26 Apr. 1822, Hopkins, ed., Clay Papers, III, 200.

[22] Jonathan Roberts to Matthew Roberts, 27 Feb. 1820, Roberts Papers, HSP.

"It appears to me that to check Mr. Clinton's career is a matter of as much interest to our sister States as to us." During the campaign the Clintonians protested against interference from Washington, but Van Burean was dissatisfied that he did not receive more open help.[23]

The Governor defied the predictions and survived the Bucktail onslaught, although by a mere 1,500 votes. Probably he owed his narrow victory to his position on the Missouri question. Vice President Tompkins was believed to be opposed to the restriction of slavery, and the Bucktails had failed to neutralize the issue by securing an endorsement of Tompkins from the leading restrictionist Rufus King. The Vice President was certain to win, Van Buren had coaxed, "& all that is necessary to make his majority overwhelming is a strong & unqualified expression of your sentiments." When King refused to comply, apparently because of his greater commitment on the issue of slavery, Van Buren's estimate was shown to have been overly optimistic.[24]

The re-election triumph, Clinton's friends tactfully told him, would provide only a brief respite from the opposition's malice. "They feel their defeat to the pith of their bones and to the core of their hearts, but are recovering from their dismay and hope to revolutionize every thing" by a state constitutional convention,

---

[23]Van Buren to Rufus King, 19 Jan., 12 Mar. 1820, C. R. King, ed., Rufus King Correspondence, VI, 252-253, 304; Aurora, 29 Jan., 4 Feb. 1821.

[24]Van Buren to King, 12 Mar. 1820, C. R. King, ed., Rufus King Correspondence, VI, 304. See also ibid., 231-232, 232n., 263-264, 288-289, 295,299n., 318-319, 322, 327; J. Q. Adams, Memoirs, V, 37-38.

warned Charles Haines, former secretary to the Governor. To prepare for renewed struggle, the party needed an editor, "a man of boldness, vigor, and courage," for its newspaper the Columbian. Haines reported, "I have written to Duane, on this point," for a recommendation.[25]

The settlement of the Missouri question by compromise ended the Republican fears of a presidential contest in 1820. Although it was understood that "his next four years will not be years of peace," Monroe would have no opposition for a second term; "none is expected even from New York," reported Senator King, "whose Legislature in all probability will be anti-clintonian." Although isolated groups of Clintonians in New York, Pennsylvania and Ohio showed a disposition to censure the slave-holding President, none attempted to oppose his inevitable re-election. The lone exception was the Old School party in Philadelphia.[26]

The Aurora maintained the attack on slavery extension as if that question were still open and charged that the slave interest alone would be served by continuing the Virginian as President. The author of the Aurora campaign was not Duane but his anonymous colleague Stephen Simpson, or "Brutus," who wrote so effectively on the issue of banking. The young radical hated Monroe for his indolence and apparent indifference to social and economic problems,

---

[25]Haines to Clinton, 24 May 1820, Clinton Papers, Columbia.

[26]Jonathan Roberts to Matthew Roberts, 27 Feb. 1820, Roberts Papers, HSP; King to Jeremiah Mason, 4 May 1820, C. R. King, ed., Rufus King Correspondence, VI, 337; Moore, Mo. Controversy, 324-325, 339-340.

and as his essays against the President became increasingly harsh and personal, even friends of "Brutus" cautioned that he needed to temper his judgments.[27]

Action on the presidential election was postponed until after the gubernatorial contest, for many Hiester supporters favored Monroe, notably John Binns' faction. The first meeting was announced for the afternoon of Saturday, October 21, at the State House. The invitation was to persons opposed to the extension of slavery, and the intention was to adopt an electoral ticket in opposition to the caucus nominee. But many Monroe supporters attended, both Family party and Binns men, claiming the invitation was inclusive, and turned the occasion into a fiasco for the Old School. The intruders, a procured mob of office hunters, officeholders, brokers and bank dependents, according to the Aurora, so dominated the proceedings that the friends of reform "quietly adjourned" to Overholt's tavern to complete their meeting.

During the tumult at the Mayor's Court Room, Duane became involved in a stormy argument with a "beardless young man," James Biddle, over the merits of Monroe. In denouncing his foreign policy he called the President a "tool of George IV," and for this emotional outburst was censured by newspapers from Boston to Washington, D. C. The Franklin Gazette in defending Biddle displayed some of the latent nativism which had bee an element in the creation of the Family party. Shall "the son of a revolutionary officer" not be permitted to speak, it asked, "when that privilege

---

[27] Aurora, "Senex," 4 Nov. 1820.

is conceded to one, born in another country, and who was not the self-created immaculate guardian of our political institutions . . . until sometime after that struggle?"[28]

The effect of the State House meeting was to leave the Old School stranded with their cause. The "incendiary attempt . . . here to connect your name with the question of slavery," Charles Ingersoll wrote to assure the President, "as far as the public indications go, . . . has proved a disgraceful abortion." The New School Democratic newspapers, which had remained silent on the restriction question, now openly defended the people of the South. The misfortune of slavery has been "entailed" upon them and "they cannot perhaps get rid of it without the most awful hazards," the Franklin sympathized; moreover the Missouri question had been settled and could not be reopened "without in fact hazarding the agitation of the union to its centre." The Federalists also disavowed any connection with the October 21 meeting, so foreign to the "noble convocation" a year before, in "spirit & aim," in "complexion & result."

The blame for the turbulent assembly all fell upon Duane, and Ingersoll thought that even that "shameless desperado must feel ashamed and mortified at the result." Duane did not attempt to shift the responsibility, although probably it was not he but Stephen Simpson who planned and organized the disastrous affair. It was Simpson's first attempt at practical politics and the mismanage-

---

[28] Ibid., 27 Oct. 1820; Democratic Press, 23 Oct., 1 Nov. 1820; Franklin Gazette, 31 Oct., 1 Nov. 1820.

ment showed his impetuosity and lack of experience. He was to do a great deal better three years later on behalf of Andrew Jackson. The greatest blunder was to schedule the meeting for the same day as an excursion and barbecue to celebrate the victory of Hiester. The Old Schoolers cheerfully toasted Clinton, Duane and "Brutus," while their leaders were being routed from the State House.[29]

The indignant defense of the President against his accusers did not excite public enthusiasm for voting on November 3. The Democratic turnout was very light and there was little Federalist participation. "The Clintonian ticket, manufactured at the self-styled anti-slavery meeting," received about one-third of the total vote in the Northern Liberties and Southwark, and about forty per cent in the city. Duane was not displeased by the result of the Old School's protest; "the ticket was meant to declare, that there was in Pennsylvania a spirit which was devoted to principle, and uninfluenced by the corruptions of men. But in the opinion of one old Philadelphia Democrat, "Duane & Co[mpan]ys" opposition to Monroe "was rediculusley managed." Simpson's hard campaign exclusively on the slave issue was discernibly hypocritical, for it was clear then and later that his true concern was with the sufferings of free labor. James Ronaldson thought that as a result of this campaign, "Duane has lost all his influence."[30]

---

[29]Ingersoll to Monroe, 29 Oct. 1820, Monroe Papers, NYPL; Moore, Mo. Controversy, 188-189; Franklin Gazette, 1 Nov. 1820; National Gazette, 25 Oct. 1820; Aurora, 26 Oct., 6 Nov. 1820.

[30]Ibid., 6 Nov. 1820; Franklin Gazette, 4 Nov. 1820; James Ronaldson to Richard Ronaldson, 7 Nov. [1820], MSS Collection, Lib. Co. of Phila.

After 1820 the success of Clinton's enemies in New York completely undermined his chances for a presidential nomination. The Bucktails even cut short his gubernatorial term by a year under the new state constitution. In April 1822 he announced that he would not again be a candidate, "having discovered," scoffed the *Franklin*, "after a conviction that he could not be re-elected, that *there was great virtue in the principle of rotation in office*!" In New York "an impression almost universally prevailed, that the Clintonian party could not regain its ascendancy," and "it was dissolved" by general, tacit consent.[31]

III.

The political outlook for Pennsylvania in 1822 appeared highly propitious for the Family party of George Dallas and his relations and friends. The anti-caucus movement, the chief obstacle to Family power, lost its momentum after the election of Hiester and appeared to founder under the misfortunes of its favorite DeWitt Clinton. In Philadelphia the Family's control of the Democrats seemed all but complete; the "fag end of factions" were an annoyance but no threat. Moreover "some of the Binnites have [joine]d us," John Lisle reported, but he admitted, "very few if any" Old School men; "perhaps they may come [in] before the 4th July, if not they will either [have] to amalgamate themselves with the Federalists or keep quiet, as we shall not notice them as a party." The Family's position of dominance at Harrisburg seemed

---

[31]*Franklin Gazette*, 20 Apr. 1822; Hammond, *Hist. of Pol. Parties*, 91, 97-98.

almost equally assured, after the Findlayites regained the majority in the legislature in 1821. Nothing on the horizon appeared likely to obstruct their drive toward the consolidation of statewide power, and with complete confidence they prepared to dictate Pennsylvania's choice for the presidency in 1824.[32]

These expectations were dramatically overthrown by the emergence as if from nowhere of a massive public movement for the candidacy of General Andrew Jackson. The origins of the Jackson movement have always remained obscure, but I believe it rose like a phoenix from the ashes of Old School Democracy. The candidacy almost certainly began in Philadelphia among former Old Schoolers; it was probably transmitted by them to their anti-caucus colleagues in the west, who made it public, and it immediately captured the imagination of the state's farmers, who turned "Jackson Fever" into a national epidemic.

Before the Jackson campaign began in early 1823, it appeared that the presidential contest in Pennsylvania would be between William H. Crawford and John C. Calhoun. Secretary of the Treasury Crawford was a Southern candidate, born in Virginia and determined to follow in the line of Virginia Republican Presidents, unbroken since Jefferson, by means of a Congressional caucus nomination. Secretary of War Calhoun, from South Carolina, was considered one of the "Northern" candidates, with John Quincy Adams and Henry Clay, because he favored the tariff and other progressive economic measures. Moreover "M^r. Calhoun's family was originally from Pennsyl-

---

[32]Lisle to George Bryan, 13 June 1822, George Bryan Papers, HSP.

vania & he was educated in Connecticut & it is supposed his feelings are Northerly which may give him some advantage in that part of the Union."[33]

Of the three Northern candidates Calhoun was the youngest, the least experienced and the least known, but he was the choice of the Family party, in large part because of the personal devotion of Samuel D. Ingham. The friendship of Calhoun and Congressman Ingham of Bucks county began in 1814 when they served together on the House committee which aided Secretary of the Treasury A. J. Dallas in creating the Second Bank of the United States. William Duane's enmity to both men dated from the same period. He thought that Calhoun had been a sycophant to Dallas in the disappointed hope of succeeding him in the Treasury department. Although "the son of a most worthy and open-hearted Irishman," Calhoun had been ruined by his education at Federalist Yale; "his politics hang very loose about him--and indeed he cannot be properly accused of _any principles_--but an inflexible devotion to No. 1 indifferent alike to everything else."[34]

Over the years the _Aurora_ had freely expressed its contempt for Ingham, who seemed to be an expert in concealing or diminishing the misdeeds of his political fellows. As chairman of the House committee on post offices, he had thwarted the investigation into the misuse of Post Office department funds. When the _Aurora_ exposed

---

[33]R. H. Walworth to A. C. Flagg, 28 Dec. 1821, Azariah C. Flagg Papers, NYPL.

[34]_Aurora_, 6 June 1818. See also _ibid_., 27, 31 July 1816, 16 May 1818, 2 Oct. 1819.

the fraudulence of the committee's proceedings, Congressman John Randolph and others agreed that its information was correct. In 1819 Ingham was appointed United States Marshal at Philadelphia when Duane's old enemy John Smith was removed because his accounts were more than fifty thousand dollars in arrears. Only a month later Ingham was needed by the Findlay administration to take over as Secretary of the Commonwealth when financial scandal forced Thomas Sergeant to step down one position, to Attorney General.[35]

When the new Secretary became "the great butt of political attack," he felt disposed to sue his tormentor Duane, but George Dallas advised against it. "I am candidly, and perhaps very unlawyerlike, of [the] opinion that you should for the present, at least, give up all idea of prosecution or civil suit. . . . Our Secretary of State must sue no one," Dallas believed. He had clearly learned a great deal about Democratic politics from his father's mistakes. "You will give cause to the cry of persecution," he told Ingham in 1819, "and the Old School, at this hour ready to fall to pieces, will rally at the sound of their old watch-word, and be more devoted to their arch leader than ever."[36]

When Calhoun became the candidate of the Family party, Adams and Clay were virtually eliminated from the Presidential con-

---

[35] _Ibid._, 6, 9, 10, 11, 12, 13, 29 Apr., 1 May, 7 Oct. 1816, 2 Oct. 1819; James M. Garnett to John Randolph, 31 Mar. 1820, Randolph-Garnett Letterbook, LC; Thomas Sergeant to Thomas J. Rogers, 21 Jan. 1819, Dreer Collection, HSP; C. J. Ingersoll to Monroe, 16 Jan. 1819, Misc. MSS (Ingersoll), NYHS; Monroe to C. J. Ingersoll, 23 Jan. 1819, Ingersoll Collection, HSP.

[36] Dallas to [Ingham], 20 July 1819, Dallas Papers, HSP.

test in Pennsylvania. Adams would not in any case have been supported by the Democrats, for the recollection of his father's administration was too keen, and he was himself disliked because of his rather forbidding personality. He was "cold--unsocial--unpopular--irritable," according to one Washington observer, and consequently "has no party--no support--few friends." Although Adams clearly thought that he should be the next President, he took a perverse pride in his lack of political appeal. "This utter inability to support my own cause passes . . . for simplicity approaching to idiotism," he acknowledged, but he derived moral satisfaction from standing above the standards of others. During the Congressional session of 1822 "there was so animated a recruiting service and so general an enlistment," he complained, "that Duane and [Thomas] Ritchie had good reason for concluding that I . . . was *hors de combat*." "In the hour of need I found no one to defend me but myself, and so I well know it will be again."[37]

Henry Clay on the other hand could have expected broad Democratic support from Pennsylvania, but it never developed. "It is a little remarkable," he commented late in the campaign, "that my support of the Tariff has excited against me in the South, a degree of opposition, which is by no means counterbalanced by any espousal of my cause in Penns[ylvani]a." Clay was widely respected, but did

---

[37]James Tallmadge to DeWitt Clinton, 11 Feb. 1818, Clinton Papers, Columbia; J. Q. Adams, *Memoirs*, VI, 43, 244-246, and *passim*; J. Q. Adams to Robert Walsh, 21 June 1822, Worthington Chauncey Ford, ed., *Writings of John Quincy Adams*, 7 vols. (New York, 1913-1917), VII, 270-272; J. Q. Adams to Louisa Catherine Adams, 12 Sept. 1822, *ibid.*, 304-305.

not inspire the intense commitment from any group which would have been necessary to launch a campaign. When Josiah S. Johnston of Louisiana came in the summer of 1824 to try to salvage the situation, he reported to Clay from Philadelphia that "your affairs have been trusted to providence." Johnston thought, probably correctly, that Pennsylvania "might have been secured at a proper time & this state would have secured you" the presidency.[38]

Clay had calculated upon the ultimate support of the Family men, believing that their movement for the youthful Calhoun was "artificial and will be short lived." He waited and nurtured his good relations with the Family and other Findlay supporters, such as Nicholas Biddle and Mathew Carey, now largely retired from practical politics. John Norvell, the editor of the Franklin Gazette, encouraged him to believe that his patience would be rewarded; "though, from local causes, I cannot afford you direct aid at present," he told Clay, "you may rely upon it that we have never lost sight of you." The party was pledged to Calhoun, whose "talents and patriotism amply qualify him for the station. With equal talents, if not superior, longer service, and stronger party attachments, you have the personal preference of many of us." Although Langdon Cheves warned him that "the Franklin hangs on with all the tenaciousness of a first love . . . to our friend Calhoun," Clay followed Novell's advice that if he pursued a conciliatory policy toward the other northern favorites, it was "more than probable

---

[38]Clay to Josiah S. Johnston, 3 Sept. 1824, Hopkins, ed., Clay Papers, III, 827; Johnston to Clay, 4 Sept. 1824, ibid., 829.

that you will become the candidate in opposition to Mr. Crawford, and be elected." The judgment agreed with Clay's own conviction: "In my conscience I believe the people of Penns: generally prefer me to any other, and greatly to Mr. Crawford."[39]

Crawford's lack of popularity was so pronounced that Norvell thought that he could not "without the aid of a congressional nomination, command two thousand votes in this great republican commonwealth." He was resented not only because he based his pretensions upon the Virginia succession, but because he appeared to be devoid of other qualifications. At best he was considered "a safe and judiciary statesman without possessing the first order of talents," and at worst shamefully ambitious and incompetent. Duane had blamed the "disgraceful" state of national finances upon his lack of "capacity or judgment" as Secretary of the Treasury. Moreover the editor distrusted him because of his friendship with Albert Gallatin, who eventually became the vice presidential nominee on the Crawford ticket. Duane thought Gallatin originally had placed Crawford in the Treasury department as "a pawn, to cover his castle, until an occasion for a good move should offer to castle the king."[40]

A major campaign began for Crawford in spite of his evident unpopularity, a few months after the Family started to promote Cal-

---

[39] William Creighton, Jr., to Clay, 2 May 1822, *ibid*., 205; Norvell to Clay, 14 Nov. 1822, *ibid*., 322; Cheves to Clay, 9 Nov. 1822, *ibid*., 316; Clay to Cheves, 5 Oct. 1822, *ibid*., 292. See also Clay to Biddle, 28 Jan. 1823, *ibid*., 355; Josiah S. Johnston to Clay, 19 Aug., 4, 11 Sept, 1824, *ibid*., 815-816, 829, 836-837.

[40] Norvell to Clay, 14 Nov. 1822, *ibid*., 321; Jonathan Roberts from unknown, 12 Mar. 1824, Roberts Papers, HSP; Duane to D. B. Warden, 7 May 1821, D. B. Warden Papers, LC.

houn. An important reason for this was his broad support from other states and the knowledge that if a Congressional caucus nomination occurred, he would be the national candidate. But more important in the reckoning for Pennsylvania, the candidacy was presented as an opportunity to strike at the arrogance of the Family party, "the Junto or rather Dynasty which appears to have the predominance in the state at present, as respects the Democratic party." The best known Crawfordites in the state were Senator Walter Lowrie and the retired Senators, Abner Lacock and Jonathan Roberts. All were aging Snyder Democrats who bitterly resented the self-serving cabal of Philadelphians. Their emotions were those of westerners against the eastern part of the state and of farmers against the city, and they were confident that "The feeling against the views of those in Phi[ladelphi]a who wish to govern every body & every thing is very general."[41]

The possibility of such a split in the Snyder Democratic party was almost as old as the party itself, for its Philadelphia wing, the New School, had always been dominated by ambitious business interests with slight sympathy for the needs of farmers. The first indication of the difference in goals had come over the banking act of 1814 framed by State Treasurer Findlay, vetoed by Governor Snyder and passed over his veto by the efforts of Findlay's friends in the legislature. No open breach occurred until after Snyder's retirement, when the easterners began to reveal the extent

---

[41]Andrew Boder to George Bryan, 6 Mar. 1823, George Bryan Papers, HSP; Walter Lowrie to Jonathan Roberts, 14 July 1822, Roberts Papers, HSP.

of their ambition, and then party loyalists like Roberts delined to take an open stand against the Findlayites because "The opposition is discredited by the heterogeneous old school cabal in Phila[,] Dauphin & else where."[42]

The declaration for rival presidential candidates in 1822 was the first public confrontation between the Clodhoppers and the Family, and this disclosure of "Schism among the active men," or regular Democrats, was baffling to outside observers. "The national politics of Pennsylvania with reference to the present administration are sound," commented John Quincy Adams. "With regard to the future I presume they are intelligible to those who manage them."[43]

An early sign of Calhoun's difficulties in Pennsylvania was the switch to Crawford by Jacob Frick, editor of the *American Sentinel*. In Philadelphia the *Sentinel* was considered second to the *Franklin Gazette* as an organ of "the great Majority of the Democratic Party." As a journalist "Sleepy Frick" was both ungifted and lazy, but he was "very anxious to be considered as the leading printer of the party," and so served as a Democratic bellwether. In 1817 he had ended his association with Binns and allied himself with the Family, but in 1822 he joined the *Democratic Press* in advocating Crawford. The westerner Walter Lowrie was delighted by the *Sentinel*'s action; support from the Philadelphia press was essential even to conduct a campaign based upon hostility to the metropolis, because only the city newspapers

---

[42]Jonathan Roberts to Matthew Roberts, 1 Jan. 1820, *ibid*.

[43]Langdon Cheves to Henry Clay, 27 July 1822, Hopkins, ed., *Clay Papers*, III, 264; J. Q. Adams to Joseph Hopkinson, 19 Nov. 1822, W. C. Ford, ed., *Writings of John Quincy Adams*, VII, 328.

circulated throughout the state. Frick claimed that he had endorsed Crawford after waiting to learn the views of the yeomanry of the country, but if he had actually hesitated in order to learn their preference, he would have declared for Andrew Jackson.[44]

IV.

The Jackson candidacy in Pennsylvania was not introduced until the spring of 1823, long after the schemes for Calhoun and Crawford, but within a year it had swept those rivals both out of contention, and at Harrisburg in March 1824 General Jackson received a unanimous nomination for President by the state of Pennsylvania. The phenomenal Jackson movement developed in three stages. In the final stage, following the ultimate capitulation to the force of Jackson by the Calhounite Family, virtually all opposition to the Hero of New Orleans had been silenced. The supporters who joined the second stage of the campaign in 1823 and helped to achieve the triumph at Harrisburg took the title of "Original Jacksonians." But the uniquely original friends of General Jackson were those who participated in the earliest phase of the movement, which reached its climax in March 1823.

The tiny band which checked the drive for Calhoun and launched the candidacy of Andrew Jackson was composed primarily of anti-caucus Democrats, formerly for Hiester and Clinton, and includ-

---

[44]Langdon Cheves to Henry Clay, 9 Nov. 1822, Hopkins, ed., Clay Papers, III, 314; John Lisle to George Bryan, 13 June 1822, George Bryan Papers, HSP; Franklin Gazette, 18, 20 July 1822; Lowrie to Jonathan Roberts, 14 July 1822, Roberts Papers, HSP. See also Jonathan Roberts to Matthew Roberts, 6 Dec. 1823, ibid.

ed the remnant of the Philadelphia Old School, led with unmatchable zeal by Stephen Simpson. In choosing to advocate the beloved Hero of New Orleans, the anti-caucus men consciously selected a man who was not tainted by association with the political Establishment. To the argument that Calhoun was more experienced in government than General Jackson, they replied that "pigmies should never be contrasted with Giants." Moreover "are we to have no school for Statesmen and Heroes, but the abominable and corrupted atmosphere of the Cabinet at Washington?"[45]

From their viewpoint, membership in the current national administration was "a decisive objection" to any candidate, "if we would keep up the appearance of Republicanism, and not go into Monarchy at once. It is idle to talk of Republicanism," wrote Hugh Hamilton, "when a new government is interested in concealing the misconduct of the one which preceded it." Hamilton, the Old School editor at Harrisburg, agreed with Duane in complaining that the Monroeites "are essentially federalists, and of the ultra stamp; that is, they pursue the measures that the republicans condemned during the Presidency of John Adams, and go beyond them." But one administration was called Federal and the other Democratic, and "you rouse a hornet's nest about your ears if you say aught against the administration of Mr. Monroe, while you may abuse the administration of Mr. Adams till your lungs or fingers are worn out in the service," Hamilton concluded, "and no one will molest you." The Jacksonians sought by means of their unorthodox nomination to

[45] Columbian Observer, 12 Sept. 1823.

achieve public rejection of the hated one party political system.[46]

The other candidates in Pennsylvania, both members of Monroe's cabinet, competed to establish their right to follow in the presidential succession. Crawford's claim was the older, because he had stepped down for Monroe in the caucus in 1816. Nonetheless Calhoun did not condemn the notion of inheritance, but sought to prove himself a legitimate and fitting heir. A new Washington newspaper established in 1822 "professes to support and defend the administration," Secretary of State Adams wrote to his wife; but the real object, already divulged, "is to identify the Secretary of War and the administration as one and the same." Adams was especially wary of the proffered aid because "the Franklin Gazette has given me a sample of the defence I am to expect in case of need from Calhounite editors. All I have to say to them is, Hands off, gentlemen; non tali auxilio."[47]

Although Crawford would probably be nominated in the event of a Congressional caucus, Calhoun did not attack the caucus in principle. He preferred to maintain the appearance of party regularity while attempting to vault over the backs of the elder leaders of the party. In Pennsylvania the Family Democrats had failed to come to terms with the popularity of the anti-caucus principle; rather than usurp the issue, they had merely postponed its effect with feeble justifications and disclaimers. The Franklin Gazette

---

[46] Harrisburg Chronicle, 21 Aug. 1821, 17 May 1819.

[47] J. Q. Adams to Louisa C. Adams, 12 Sept. 1822, W. C. Ford, ed., Writings of John Quincy Adams, VII, 304-305.

in 1822 still defended the mode of nomination by caucus; "the name, we apprehend, is more obnoxious to censure than the thing itself." The notion that the choice of candidates should be left "entirely open to the people" was a worthy sentiment, the editor acknowledged, but by what method were the people to reach a concurrence? If by "no method" then the idea was completely meaningless. There must be "a proper direction to public sentiment, without attempting to control it." Speaking for himself Norvell declared that he could not "imagine a more fair or correct mode of nomination than by the responsible representatives of the people and states in congress." The Calhoun men stubbornly continued to defend the caucus system until they were on the verge of simultaneous defeat by the Jacksonians in Pennsylvania and the Crawfordites in Congress.[48]

In March 1823 the Family leaders were supremely confident and were preparing to secure a nomination for Calhoun at the Democratic convention to choose a candidate for Governor. The expectation was destroyed by an entirely unforeseen occurrence, the introduction of a resolution from the Westmoreland county delegation "recommending General ANDREW JACKSON for the office of President of these United States." The other delegates reacted in fascination and horror, and there were numerous calls to proceed to consideration of the resolution. "But almost by common consent," according to the Franklin account, "the convention declined to have any thing to do with it. They deemed it inexpedient to perform any

---

[48]Franklin Gazette, 31 July 1822. See also ibid., 10 Oct., 12, 18, 23 Dec. 1823.

formal act upon a subject of so much delicacy and importance so early."[49]

The sequence of events which led to the resolution at Harrisburg began only two months before in the trans-Allegheny village of Greensburg. On December 28 citizens of Westmoreland county met and placed Jackson in nomination for President, the first such public declaration in Pennsylvania.[50] The _Franklin Gazette_, which denounced the meeting, revealed that the Westmorelanders in nominating Jackson had expressed a bitter judgment against the Monroe administration. General Jackson was a personal and political friend of Monroe, replied the _Franklin_, and if President he would "pursue perseveringly the policy of that very administration in opposition to which he is thus named."

The complaints which were voiced in the meeting at Greensburg chiefly reflected the continuing resentment of the panic and depression. The resolutions in support of Jackson's nomination, according to the _Franklin_, enumerated the familiar cant objections to extravagance by public officials, "_enormous importations_," and the "state of '_national embarrassment_!'" The _Franklin_ replied with impatient references to the improved financial condition. It had learned to wage the battle of economic statistics with Duane as its chief adversary. Several months earlier Congressman Ingham had sent the report that the balance of trade would be favorable for 1821, and the country was not going to ruin. "I know of no man that will be more staggered by this fact, than the Editor of the

---

[49] _Ibid._, 8 Mar. 1823. [50] Klein, _Pa. Politics_, 123.

Aurora, whose columns have long groaned under the weight of lugubrious predictions that the United States were fast sinking into poverty."

The Greensburg nominators, the hostile analysis continued, had the audacity to object to "caucusses; apparently forgetting that a caucus has already contaminated the pretensions of their candidate in Tennessee." According to the Franklin's strange definition, a caucus was any voluntary political deliberation, and "we do not presume that it can be more odious in Washington, than in Nashville or Greensburgh." In summarizing the occasion the Calhoun paper concluded that the absurd resolutions "never could have accompanied a fair, candid, and really intended exertion for general JACKSON." It speculated that they had been framed to suit "the professions of another candidate [DeWitt Clinton]: he would not go down: and the blank has been hastily filled" with a name which was unobjectionable but "like a jewel in a toad's head." The Family's undisguised assault on the original nomination was uniquely revealing comment about the first Jacksonians. The Franklin never repeated its initial candor, for soon the magic of Jackson's name made even indirect criticism impossible.[51]

Less than a week following the Greensburg meeting, Congressman Henry Baldwin of Pittsburgh, the anti-caucus leader of western Pennsylvania, wrote to General Jackson at Nashville to express "how fully the general sentiment in this part of the country coincides with mine," and to offer "my most active efforts for your success."

---

[51]Franklin Gazette, 16 Feb. 1822, 10 Jan. 1823.

May your friends "calculate on your acquiessence [*sic*] . . . and your consent?" Jackson had "hitherto avoided speaking," but now responded that it was his philosophy, "on no occasion to solicit for office; but . . . not to decline any public demand made upon my services." Soon after citizens of Dauphin county met at Harrisburg, declared for Jackson, and sent him news of the nomination. On February 23 Jackson again broke his silence and replied to their committee as he had to Baldwin that "My undeviating rule of conduct . . . has been neither to seek, or decline public invitations to office." This letter has been reported to be in the handwriting of Major William B. Lewis, Jackson's intimate friend and political adviser, sometimes described as his national campaign manager in the election of 1824. Undoubtedly the letter circulated in Harrisburg the following week, when the Westmoreland delegation placed its resolution before the state convention. The communication among the Pennsylvanians and between them and Jackson's friends in Tennessee is unknown, but the precise and effective timing of the birth of the campaign makes it impossible to doubt their coordination.[52]

The Pennsylvania Convention of March 1823 was a turning point for the candidacies of both Jackson and Calhoun. Jackson himself declared flatly that "pennsylvania has taken her course." He noted with interest that the newspapers there "stand, and disect,

---

[52] *Ibid.*, 29 Jan. 1823; Baldwin to Jackson, 1 Jan. 1823, John Spencer Bassett, ed., *Correspondence of Andrew Jackson* (*Jackson Correspondence*), 7 vols. (Washington, 1926-1935), III, 184n.; Jackson to Baldwin, 24 Jan. 1823, *ibid.*, 184; Jackson to H. W. Peterson, 23 Feb. 1823, *ibid.*, 189, 189n. See also Jackson to John Coffee, 5 Oct. 1823, *ibid.*, 210. For a discussion of Henry Baldwin's role in the campaign for Jackson see Klein, *Pa. Politics*, 121-124 and *passim*.

disapprove, and approve of the character and conduct of the different candidates at pleasure, and with great freedom." The General's unclouded optimism at the very outset of his campaign revealed his ignorance of the hazardous world of politics. A friend sought to warn him against too much reliance on the influence of newspapers. "The men most assailed and with most justice often succeed best politically."[53]

Calhoun refused to be discouraged by the setback to his plans at Harrisburg. "My friends were prepared to bring my name forward," but George Dallas explained to him that the Westmoreland nomination had created an "aversion" to the presidential question, and "they thought it prudent not to bring my name forward at all, so that even the appearance of an abortive attempt has been avoided." But "It was fully ascertained that I had 2/3 of the convention" against all other candidates, "and my friends in the state were never in better spirits." The revised strategy there would be "to bring out the next Legislature at the commencement of the session." In spite of these cheerful conclusions, the failure in 1823 was ultimately disastrous to Calhoun's ambitions. He needed an endorsement from Pennsylvania to lend support to his candidacy elsewhere. Morevoer the Family had possessed the power to command a majority of the delegates and had sacrificed an advantage. "They had the cards in their hands & have played them badly."[54]

---

[53]Jackson to John Coffee, 15 Apr. 1823, Bassett, ed., Jackson Correspondence, III, 194; Colonel James Gadsden to Jackson, 30 July 1823, ibid., 200-201.

[54]Calhoun to Virgil Maxcy, 12-13 Mar. 1823, quoted in William M. Meigs, The Life of John Caldwell Calhoun, 2 vols. (New

V.

Stephen Simpson, the principal spokesman for the remnant of Duane's Old School, had proposed the candidacy of Andrew Jackson early in 1822. In April of that year Simpson founded his own newspaper, the *Columbian Observer*, which from its outset was prepared to support the General. The first issue declared that the Hero of New Orleans would always stand with George Washington in the love and gratitude of his country. It decried the early agitation of the presidential question, advising the public to be wary of the ambitious men who sought the office. Yet because the subject had been unseasonably opened, the people would have time to speak.

On May 4 the paper announced two months before it happened that Tennessee had nominated her favorite son for the presidency. Pennsylvania, Simpson commented, should remember her debt to the Hero; for myself, "*let this be the man*." It was the first newspaper endorsement of Jackson outside Tennessee, preceding by several months any other Pennsylvania paper. Simpson had a personal reason for the extraordinary commitment, made at a time when the candidacy had scarcely gone beyond discussion among the General's intimate friends. I "had the honour and glory of serving under you," he explained to Jackson, "as a Volunteer during the Siege of N. Orleans, an event I shall ever remember with pride & exultation, both as an *American* and a *Man*."[55]

York, 1917), I, 296; Jonathan Roberts to Matthew Roberts, 12 Jan. 1824, Roberts Papers, HSP. See also J. Roberts to M. Roberts, 14 Mar. 1824, *ibid*.

[55]*Columbian Observer*, 6 Apr., 4 May 1822; Klein, *Pa. Politics*, 123; Simpson to Jackson, 5 July 1823, Andrew Jackson Papers, LC.

The *Columbian Observer* following its initial statement did not advocate Jackson directly, but began the task of deflating the pretensions of the self-declared candidates, especially John Calhoun. The paper attracted wide attention almost at once. DeWitt Clinton was an early subscriber, and by August John Quincy Adams sought to find out "who is the editor of . . . the new paper that is rising to take the place of the setting *Aurora*." In charging Adams with misanthropy, the *Observer* said "I went to church barefoot, and now says that piece of wit was *ironical*. There is no helping it," he conceded. "The donkey *will* play the lap dog." According to Jonathan Roberts, "The vulgar obscenity & grossness of that paper is hardly conceivable. It is worse than the worst specimens of Aurorian licentiousness." Simpson's own revelation that he was the author of the infamous essays of "Brutus" contributed a great deal to the notoriety and influence of his newspaper.[56]

Two weeks after Simpson announced prematurely that Jackson was nominated in Tennessee, he began to publish an "Original Biography of General Andrew Jackson," which continued in installments through the summer. It was apparently based upon the military biography of the Hero written by a Major Reid and first published by Mathew Carey, but the description of events was rewritten in Simpson's romantic style, with greater emphasis on Jackson's Irish

---

[56]J. Q. Adams to Louisa C. Adams, 23, 28 Aug. 1822, W. C. Ford, ed., *Writings of John Quincy Adams*, VII, 296, 297; J. Roberts to Matthew Roberts, 18 Jan. 1824, Roberts Papers, HSP; Simpson, *Lives of Eminent Philadelphians*, 893-894; *Franklin Gazette*, 1 Feb. 1823. The NYHS' file of the *Columbian Observer* was formerly the property of DeWitt Clinton.

birth and associations. In Nashville Jackson's friend General John Eaton, a Senator from Tennessee, was at this time expanding Reid's biography into a campaign document, but the biographical articles in the *Columbian Observer* did not follow his manuscript.

Simpson evidently established some connection with Jackson's friends in Nashville soon after founding his newspaper. In a memoir of the campaign written long after, Major William B. Lewis recalled receiving encouragement from Pennsylvania in the spring of 1822. Simpson's advocacy in Philadelphia was probably what Lewis remembered, since the preliminary efforts in the western part of the state did not begin before autumn. Jackson himself became a subscriber to the *Columbian Observer* in August, and after his Pennsylvania campaign was set in motion he apparently felt a debt of gratitude to its editor, for when Simpson wrote him, he noted that the letter "will be carefully answered--including the remark, that I am happy to be informed that I once had the honor to command a corps of which he was a member."[57]

During 1823 and 1824 Jackson's political intimates used the *Columbian Observer* as their principal organ outside Tennessee. Eaton's "Letters of Wyoming" were first published there, and Major Lewis sent long, frequent and detailed directives and commentaries on the campaign. When President Monroe and General Jackson were forced to publish their mutual correspondence from 1817, to counteract damaging rumors by the Crawfordites, they released it simultane-

---

[57]James Parton, *Life of Andrew Jackson*, 3 vols. (New York, 1860), III, 19; Simpson to Jackson, 3 Nov. 1825, Jackson Papers, LC; Simpson to Jackson, endorsement on envelope, 5 July 1823, *ibid*.

ously to the National Intelligencer and the Philadelphia Observer, and it was thereafter republished by most newspapers elsewhere. As the numbers of Jsckson partisans increased, so did complaints about Simpson's radical paper, but when requested to exercise a corrective influence on the editor, Jackson refused to interfere. A radical, trouble-making, but highly devoted Jacksonian in Pittsburgh, on the other hand, who probably had been recruited into the cause by the Philadelphian, told General Jackson that "If you had only a Stephen Simpson in every State in the union, you would be Elected President by the largest majority ever heard of in the known world."[58]

Simpson foresaw in his advocacy of Jackson the birth of a genuine national Democratic party. He stated boldly the position which Duane had stood for since 1811, that the corruption and disintegration of the Republican party was the inevitable result of its misguided moderation and the embrace of Federalism. The time had come he declared to revive the opposing parties, for the country was better off "when they flourished in their most rank luxuriance" than with the wholly selfish and unprincipled politics which had replaced them. Thomas Jefferson himself regretted the effect upon Republicanism of "the surrender of our opponents," according

---

[58]Shaw Livermore, The Twilight of Federalism: the Disintegration of the Federalist Party, 1815-1830 (Princeton, 1962), 161-162; Jackson to A. J. Donelson, 4, 16 Apr. 1824, Bassett, ed., Jackson Correspondence, III, 244, 244n., 248; William Hayden, Jr., to Jackson, 29 Mar. 1824, ibid., 242; Jackson to Hayden, 30 Mar. 1824, ibid., 243; Edward Patchell to Jackson, 7 Aug. 1824, ibid., 264. W. B. Lewis' close connection with the Columbian Observer during the campaign of 1824 may be inferred from Lewis to [Simpson], draft, 20 Sept. 1824, Jackson-Lewis Papers, NYPL.

to Simpson. "I consider the party divisions of whig and tory, the most wholesome which can exist in any government," Jefferson wrote in 1822, "and well worthy of being nourished, to keep out those of a more dangerous character." When the letter was made public three years later, it was given heavy emphasis by Simpson and like-minded Jacksonians. The editor flatly contradicted the notion held by some belated Jackson men that the Hero of New Orleans would be father to a new era of good feelings. "Such men . . . are the worst enemies of the Hero of New Orleans, who always has been, and now is a decided Party-man--a decided and uniform Democrat."[59]

The creation of a party to represent the interests of "the productive classes" had been frustrated, Simpson maintained, by the power of a few men who "assume the name of Democrats, such as the Dallas Family of this State." "The Family System of Minority Dictation has heretofore proved successful from their threatened expulsion of all from the Party who dare oppose them." Simpson was one such outcast because "we have not been baptised" at the "Family Font" by the "Holy Water of Dallas's Purity."

In Simpson's opinion, the perversion of the party name had been permitted to occur because of the prevailing influence of one-time democrats, who formerly did not consider "labour and industry a disgrace," but who rose in the world and became ashamed of their former connections. His explanation echoed Duane's analysis of the class distinction which separated the New School from the Old

---

[59] Columbian Observer, 6 Apr. 1822, 3 Apr. 1824; Jefferson to W. T. Barry, 3 July 1822, quoted in Philadelphia National Chronicle, 11 Oct. 1825.

School in Philadelphia. The successful few became contemptuous of "the _honest Democrats_, with whom they used to associate, and who, perhaps, had been the _means of making their fortunes_, through the political influence, which such a character gave them." Upon achieving personal prosperity they began to aspire "to _moderation_ in politicks; and to _refinement_ in life." But the election of Jackson would bring the overthrow of the Family system and restore the party to the people. According to the _Columbian Observer_, the city's Calhounites felt the threat, and in a letter to a New York newspaper one of them stigmatized "the _friends of Jackson_ as 'the dregs of Society.'"[60]

Simpson was especially zealous in his efforts to impede the candidacy of John Calhoun. Like Duane, he had one overriding reason for his dislike, Calhoun's association with A. J. Dallas in creating the Second Bank of the United States. "Heaven defend us, from the _authors_ of such an iniquitous scheme of plunder and oppression, for our _Presidents_, or even for our Representatives." Indeed the time has come, he believed, "when the advocates and adherents of Bank frauds, must be put down by the People, who should refuse to elect them for the most trifling office in their gift." The _Franklin Gazette_ deliberately ignored the existence of the "scurrilous newspaper," which worked so diligently to draw it into a dispute. "We cannot debase ourselves to the use of language which alone would befit a controversy with such a paper," the _Franklin_ solemnly

---

[60]_Ibid._, 10 Oct. 1825; _Columbian Observer_, 20 July 1822, 30 Oct. 1823, 23 Feb., 25, 26 Mar. 1824.

announced, breaking its rule of silence briefly to publish some extracts from "Brutus" which it hoped would be damaging.[61]

VI.

The expression of the Old School views on banking in the election of 1824 was not an isolated commitment by Simpson, but relevant to the overwhelming victory of Jackson throughout Pennsylvania. The Panic of 1819 had taught the Clodhoppers in great numbers to regard banks with as much enmity as did their urban working class brethren. Their shared feeling of antagonism toward the class of exploiters was perhaps the most profound underlying basis for their mutual support of Andrew Jackson. The reform of the state banks undertaken in 1819 had been successful in forcing them to resume and maintain specie payments. No further legislation was initiated, but the banks incorporated in 1814 were subject to renewal at the end of a decade, and there were portents of determined resistance to any extension of their charters.[62]

Presidential politics dominated the legislative session of 1824, and ironically the shortage of time for dealing with business contributed to the final decision to recharter the banks. But the extension was accomplished only after a "desperate" struggle, in spite of "the talents preponderating for the bill," and it was

---

[61] Franklin Gazette, 1 Feb. 1823; Columbian Observer, 12 Sept. 1823. See also ibid., 1, 15 June, 6 July 1822.

[62] Jonathan Roberts to Matthew Roberts, 6 Jan., 5, 7 Feb. 1824, Roberts Papers, HSP; Franklin Gazette, 16 Dec. 1822; An Act to Re-charter Certain Banks, To which are Added the Several Acts of Assembly Relative to Banks, and the By-laws of the Farmers and Mechanics Bank (Philadelphia, 1824), 13, 28, pamphlet, HSP.

granted in a form which both friends and enemies of the banks believed would lead to their eventual extinction. The leaders within the legislature of the assault upon the banks were also determined Jacksonians. Foremost among them was James S. Stevenson of Pittsburgh, a former Snyderite who had become the candidate of the anti-caucus party as well, and who was to be elected to Congress in the Jacksonian sweep of Allegheny county in the autumn of 1824. Stevenson was aided by John B. Sterigere of Montgomery county, who was to become a devoted colleague of James Buchanan, the future leader of the anti-Dallas Democrats in Pennsylvania. Another Jackson man who participated in the assembly fight against the banks was the aging Jacob Holgate of Philadelphia county, formerly a New School man but in 1824 denounced by the Calhounites "as an ignorant, low, and would-be politician, the pet of Stephen Simpson." Holgate had once been Speaker of the House at Harrisburg, but had been removed in 1816 through the aggregate of banking influence, according to Hugh Hamilton.[63]

Stevenson was the chairman of the assembly's committee on the banks, which was dominated by their enemies "by management or

---

[63] Jonathan Roberts to Matthew Roberts, 6, 12 Jan., 22, 23, 28 Feb., 21 Mar. 1824, Roberts Papers, HSP. Kehl, _Ill Feeling_, 207, declares that Stevenson, the victor in the 1824 Congressional election in Pittsburgh, was a Crawfordite, and his defeated opponent, Walter Forward, a Jacksonian. This should be reversed; Stevenson was a Jacksonian, according to the _Franklin Gazette_, 18 Dec. 1823, and Forward voted for Crawford in the rump caucus of Feb. 1824, according to Jonathan Roberts to Matthew Roberts, 28 Feb. 1824, Roberts Papers, HSP. On Sterigere see Klein, _Pa. Politics_, 164, 217. On Holgate see _ibid_., 164n.; _Columbian Observer_ 23 Feb. 1824; Hugh Hamilton to John Sergeant, 4 Jan. 1816, Sergeant Papers, HSP; Higginbotham, _Keystone_, 315-316.

by chance," and he reported "a most extraordinary" bill. "It was a common belief that his purpose was to lace them so tightly that they could not have breathed & must have expired after a short & sickly existence." Former Senator Jonathan Roberts, who had entered the assembly in an effort to help Crawford, had long been indignant at the "perverse" hostility to these "vested rights," and he at once sought action "to substitute a mere extension" of the existing charters. But he could not find a single member who was willing to take the responsibility for a resolution to withdraw Stevenson's bill, and so he assumed the leadership himself and found "the laboring oar has fallen very much on my hands." Speaking on the floor with highly unusual personal emotion, Roberts emphasized that the foreclosure of the banks at that time "would be awfully calamitous." He thought that his activity had "dispelled the vapours pretty much," and after struggling against a series of crippling amendments, he predicted that the bank bill would pass the House "not materially different" from the existing law.[64]

His sense of triumph was short-lived, for the Senate's "classification" amendment was adopted by the House. This provision placed the re-incorporated banks in three categories, based upon their fiscal soundness, and fixed their expiration dates accordingly, at eight, ten or twelve years. "The secret & open enemies of the banks have gotten what they think an assurance of suppressing these institutions by piecemeal." Roberts thought

---

[64]Jonathan Roberts to Matthew Roberts, 1 Jan. 1820, 6 Jan., 10-11, 22, 23 Feb. 1824, Roberts Papers, HSP.

there was "no likelihood that any one Class of them will be rechartered with provisions they can accept." Certainly the weak banks in the first class, after a respite of eight years, "are doomed to be exorcised by the originators of the measure[,] act as they may." The bank in Montgomery county, in which Roberts and his brother had a principal interest, was placed in the second class.

In Roberts' opinion the classification scheme revealed the blackness of human nature. "The influence of the three cities [Philadelphia, Pittsburgh and Lancaster] direct & indirect has been to destroy the banks--Such chuckling when they concurred in the classification" could be displayed only "by weak & unprincipled minds." But he took comfort in the knowledge that "I have fearlessly done my duty," and "If I had not been here it would have been much worse than it is." His attempts to stop the nomination of the detested General Jackson had been futile and increasingly bitter. But "In nothing have I been more useful than in curbing the enemies of the banks."[65]

The *Columbian Observer* declared that the recharter of the banks "commonly called the '*Litter of Forty*'" (now reduced in numbers by nearly one half) was "the most *extraordinary event* . . . that has happened in our time." Simpson was not in the slightest mollified by the classification system, although he acknowledged that the legislators had been "deprived of *free will* by the [simultaneous] mass of *Banking* influence." In justice, the Supreme Court should abolish the unconstitutional state banks. "The object of

---

[65] J. Roberts to M. Roberts, 21 Mar. 1824, *ibid*.

restraining the states from the emission of paper credits, was to confirm that power exclusively in the hands of the General Government, that the circulating medium in the country might be equalized." Yet the states in practice "do more than coin money; they charter banks, whose very existence is a perpetual and absolute edict against the coining of the metals." "In return for this indulgence, the states tolerate a Paper Usurpation in the Union."

The Family politicians in Philadelphia, like many of their fellows in the legislature, were cautiously friendly to the recharter. The objections of many to the so-called paper system "can have little or no foundation as applied to these banks," according to the Franklin Gazette. The act bound them by strict requirements for specie convertibility and, in Norvell's opinion, they were "of great benefit to the community."[66]

VII.

By January 1824 the presidential contest in Pennsylvania was approaching a decision. The Calhounites' confident plans to obtain a nomination in the legislature had collapsed by winter, because "The Jackson faction are running away with the public feeling." Although the public, "the uninformed part at least are carried away with Jackson," the Crawford and Calhoun men still hoped that "sober men will oppose the phrenzy" and not allow the state's votes to be "thrown away" on a futile candidacy.

The Jacksonian surge in 1823 had undercut the intended cam-

---

[66]Columbian Observer, 27, 29 Mar. 1824; Franklin Gazette, 31 Mar. 1824.

paign for Crawford, based upon rural resentment of the Family hub. "The Jackson men are not so corrupt as the hub," Jonathan Roberts admitted, "but they are as violent & equally disposed to extremity." But in the legislature the "good men" were silent because they feared their constituents' displeasure. Roberts, with his narrow Quaker morality, continued the struggle until he was the last Crawfordite remaining in Harrisburg. "Thee says to thee the public have been ungrateful," he replied sternly to his brother, working at home in Montgomery county; "that does not exempt thee from thy duty." Still Roberts could not refrain from expressing his pleasure that the Jacksonians had put the Family "on their backs" and that "Ingham is fast getting where he ought to be" and faced involuntary political retirement.[67]

As Calhoun's candidacy became increasingly desperate, it was said in Washington that he "appears like a stricken deer." Pennsylvania had disappointed him, and a rump caucus to nominate Crawford appeared imminent. His friends in the Pennsylvania Congressional delegation conceived a scheme which they hoped might forestall a caucus and recapture their home state--a national nominating convention. "Ingham will not yield so long as he has any hope of doing mischief." In December the Franklin Gazette first announced that a convention composed of delegates from each Congressional district "should be held at Washington on the 10th of April," and Family partisans throughout the state began to promote

---

[67]J. Roberts to M. Roberts, 26 Dec. 1823, 4, 12, 14, 18 Jan., 7, 29 Feb., 7 Mar. 1824, Roberts Papers, HSP.

the plan. They spoke and wrote of Calhoun as the "national candidate" and began to toast "Our next President: The national democrat." The Calhounites had carefully avoided appearing to criticize the Hero of New Orleans, and if Pennsylvanians could be made to believe in the alleged convention on April 10, they might be persuaded to postpone their nomination and eventually to accept Calhoun.[68]

In January the people were given the chance to decide. The legislature declared that they were to elect delegates to a convention to be held at Harrisburg on March 4. The Calhounites' hope was to send unpledged delegates, who would simply vote to send representatives to Washington the following month. But county after county elected slates which were unequivocally pledged to Andrew Jackson for President.[69]

The unexpected triumph of the Jacksonians in Philadelphia humiliated the Family party and finished the candidacy of Calhoun. The Family controlled the Democratic machinery in the city and county, but the Jacksonians cut through the official party obstacles with their overwhelming force of numbers. The Jackson men were enthusiastic and persistent, willing to come out to meetings indefinitely until they had attained their object. At the Harrisburg Convention, Roberts was to complain, half the delegates were boys, mere "giddy young men" who were there only to cheer the Hero. In Philadelphia as well an important aspect of the success was the

---

[68]J. Roberts to M. Roberts, 19, 30 Jan. 1824, ibid.; Franklin Gazette, 20, 27 Nov., 12 Dec. 1823.

[69]Klein, Pa. Politics, 160.

zeal of the young men, who were taking their first role in politics because they were enchanted with Jackson.[70]

During the hectic five weeks of the delegate elections, Stephen Simpson was almost the political master of Philadelphia. Simpson and his coterie of Old School veterans and recruits were not the exclusive members of "Hickory Club No. 1," but they formed its organizational core and provided the all-important partisan newspaper. The most dedicated aide to Simpson in writing and speaking for Jackson, "an ardent admirer of you & your deeds," was the Old Republican artist James Thackara.

Among the Original Jacksonians there were a number of men who had been New School Democrats but left the party when the Dallas family took over, and one former Quid, Chandler Price, who could not abide Simpson. The most distinguished member of the Hickory club was Thomas Leiper, "the venerable Patriarch of Democracy," perennial chairman of the general ward committee since the triumph of 1800. Leiper had been Duane's close associate until 1811 when he eschewed all factional politics in favor of the ideal of a united Republican party. The stubborn Scot had been as true and honest a Jeffersonian as any man in Pennsylvania, and he saw in Jackson the foundation for restoring those ideals. In his blunt style he wrote to Jefferson that it was said he supported Crawford but he refused to believe it. Jefferson answered him gently, "I am really done, my friend, with Politics . . . there is a time for everything, for

---

[70]J. Roberts to M. Roberts, 29 Feb., 5 Mar. 1824, Roberts Papers, HSP.

acting in this world and for getting ready to leave it. the last is now come upon me."[71]

At the outset of the campaign to elect delegates to Harrisburg, the Jacksonians confounded both John Binns and the Dallas men and boldly pirated the Democratic party machinery. According to the established procedures, the general ward committee for 1823 would announce citizens' meetings in the wards to select representatives to the new general ward committee, which would select the convention delegates. On January 9 however a special town meeting was called by a minority of Crawfordites on the committee. In order to prevent the intended proceedings in favor of a Congressional caucus, the Family also announced the meeting and urged attendance by the Democrats.

On Friday afternoon the meeting was settling into an ineffectual quarrel between Binnsites and Family speakers, on the merits of a caucus or a national convention, when "a number of the friends of General JACKSON were attracted to the meeting, and finally succeeded in breaking it up without its having been able to adopt any measure whatever." The Crawfordites had been defeated on their own ground, the Family newspaper admitted, "not by the great body of the democratic party of the city--for they would not attend the meeting--but by a part only [the Simpson wing] of the friends of JACKSON. Jonathan Roberts was irate; "The scene at the meeting in Phil[a] beggared all sufference [<u>sic</u>]. It was infinitely worse

---

[71] Simpson to Jackson, 5 July 1823, Jackson Papers, LC; <u>Columbian Observer</u>, 8 July 1824; Leiper to Jefferson, 16 Mar. 1824, TJ-LC; Jefferson to Leiper, draft, 3 Apr. 1824, TJ-LC.

says D^r [Elijah] Griffiths than Binns has described it." Roberts thought it was "how ever a good omen--Such violence & audacity is just calculated to produce the opposite effect they wish--It is the temper of Jackson & his friends every where." The Family was equally offended by the insolent citizens. "The impression now appears to be universal," according to "A Spectator," probably George Dallas, "that these town meetings have become only scenes of confusion and tumult, and ought to cease to be held."[72]

The Jacksonians used their victory at the meeting to take control of the process of electing delegates to Harrisburg. On January 9 they adjourned the proceedings until the following Saturday, when the Democrats of Philadelphia "without sectional distinction" were called to express their views on the presidential election. The Family and Binnsites disputed the authority of the call and attempted to gain a postponement, but "It seems as if the Jackson men were almost masters of the wards in Phila." They elected their slates in ten of the fourteen wards and took command of the general ward committee.[73]

Rival delegations to Harrisburg were elected in the county of Philadelphia. Exercising its control over the official district delegate system, the Family obtained an unpledged slate of convention delegates. But the Jacksonians called for open meetings by

---

[72]Franklin Gazette, 6, 7, 10 Jan. 1824; J. Roberts to M. Roberts, 14 Jan. 1824, Roberts Papers, HSP.

[74]Jackson to A. J. Donelson, 21 Jan. 1824, Bassett, ed., Jackson Correspondence, III, 225; J. Roberts to M. Roberts, 5 Feb. 1824, Roberts Papers, HSP. See also J. Roberts to M. Roberts, 7, 10-11 Feb. 1824, ibid.

the Democrats "without sectional distinction," and in the Northern Liberties, the traditional Old School stronghold, they demonstrated their force of numbers. The proceedings there were not the work of a "respectable democratic meeting," according to the Calhounites. "The well known props of democracy in the county . . . were absent to a man," they derided. "A new set, either wholly unknown, or known only for their obliquities and disaffection, supplied the places which have generally been filled by our most respected names." Yet the Jacksonian gathering in the Northern Liberties had been larger than any former meeting of its kind in the district, and "as we know of no other way of estimating the political respectability of a meeting, than by its numbers," the Columbian Observer commented, "we unhesitatingly pronounce it the largest and most respectable meeting ever held in the Northern Liberties for choice of delegates."[74]

Meanwhile the vanquished Family was privately preparing the way for an honorable capitulation to Jackson. Dallas wrote to Calhoun to warn him that it would be necessary to withdraw him from candidacy at Harrisburg, and the Franklin intimated to its partisans a forthcoming reversal. "We are happy to state," it declared on February 12, "that we have the best reason to believe that General JACKSON decidedly disapproves of the excessive violence which has been practised by some of his over-zealous friends here and elsewhere." "The truth is, according to the Franklin, "that the

---

irregular and lawless proceedings of some of the pretended friends of General JACKSON in this state are intended to injure him," by alienating the "great body of sober Pennsylvania democrats."[75]

The moment of formal triumph for Jackson in Philadelphia was on February 18 when the traditional town meeting assembled to approve the actions of the general ward committee and endorse the delegation to Harrisburg. George Dallas used the occasion to save himself from political humiliation and give the first taste of defeat to Simpson's radicals. The news of the rump caucus nomination of Crawford arrived in Philadelphia the previous day, and Dallas took that event as his justification to appear at the town meeting, tender "a sacrifice of individual predilection" and offer resolutions for united support of the Hero of New Orleans. "Dallas has struck Calhouns flag to Jackson in a manner as disgraceful to himself as his previous conduct has been contemptible," in the opinion of Roberts, who thought it undoubtedly had been done "with Inghams & Calhouns privity." But "Whether the sober men of this state are to be carried away with such a wretch as Jackson by such men as Stephen Simpson[,] G. M. Dallas & Sam. D. Ingham I cannot believe until I see it." Roberts pledged that he would disappoint the hope of "Simpson [who] talks of a unanimous vote for Jackson here on the 4th of March."[76]

Roberts was mistaken in thinking that Dallas had consulted

---

[75] Ibid., 12, 13 Feb. 1824; Meigs, Calhoun, I, 307-308.

[76] Klein, Pa. Politics, 160-161; J. Roberts to M. Roberts, 22 Feb. 1824, Roberts Papers, HSP.

Calhoun and Ingham before withdrawing Calhoun from nomination. "The movement at Philadelphia was as unexpected to me as it could have been to any of my friends," the Carolinian admitted. "It has produced the deepest excitement. . . . Tho' prepared for a defeat [at] Harrisburg, no movement in advance was anticipated." Although he felt that the action was "ill timed as it regards Dallas and our cause," he conceded that "I have no doubt the motives were pure."[77]

No one was angrier at the turn of events in Pennsylvania than Henry Clay. "I told you long ago that the friends of Mr. Calhoun were making a vain and fruitless effort," he wrote to Dallas' brother-in-law Richard Bache. Clay asserted that the state's Family-dominated Congressional delegation now regretfully agreed that they should have supported the Kentuckian. "The Pennsa. delegation are the most mortified men in the world," he reported. "They lament the course which is taking in that State for Genl. Jackson."[78]

Stephen Simpson was highly vexed by the welcome extended to the defeated enemy. In the town meeting he attempted to maintain the militant spirit of the preceding weeks, but the chairman, Thomas Leiper, was always an advocate of unity, and even "the mild young man" William John Duane "attempted to palaver about _moderation_." Because of the victory in Philadelphia, Jackson could have received an overwhelming nomination at Harrisburg without any concession

---

[77] Calhoun to Virgil Maxcy, 27 Feb. 1824, quoted in Meigs, _Calhoun_, I, 307-308.

[78] Clay to Bache, 17 Feb. 1824, Hopkins, ed., _Clay Papers_, III,645; Clay to Francis T. Brooke, 6 Mar. 1824, _ibid_., 669.

from the Calhounites, and no gratitude was due them. Simpson apparently wrote to Major Lewis to explain that Dallas had acted on his own in order to conceal the disgrace of his overthrow, because Lewis passed on to Jackson the suspicions about the matter. But Jackson replied, "On the subject of Mr Calhoun, I have no doubt myself, that his friends acted agreable [sic] to his understanding & his instructions; & that he is sincere in his wishes--some have doubted this, but I have not." The question was closed and Dallas received full credit for his high-minded declaration.[79]

VIII.

After the Harrisburg Convention placed Andrew Jackson in nomination, his candidacy nationally began to build, but in Pennsylvania the movement's vigor and spirit almost imperceptibly declined. Binns' Democratic Press, vainly seeking to lure the farmers back to Crawford, labored to disillusion them with the Family's false professions for Jackson and to convince them that "the plan of Ingham & Co.[,] the starters of Calhoun, [is] to give the vote of this State in Congress to Adams." Binns continually published reports that the Jacksonian zeal was dying and his followers beginning to fall away. The Franklin Gazette claimed this meant that one man had deserted, but "Is he not proverbial for his instability? The man alluded to is now a radical, a leveller, a would-be-

---

[79] Columbian Observer, 17, 19, 20, 21 Feb. 1824; Jackson to Lewis, 31 Mar. 1824, Jackson-Lewis Papers, NYPL. Klein, Pa. Politics, 160-161, because not aware of the Family's overthrow in the city ward meetings, states Dallas' explanation of his action in the town meeting, while rightfully expressing the suspicion that his motives were not disinterested.

destroyer of almost everything fixed, and stable, and valuable in our republican government."

Simpson however had by no means quit the cause, but was engaged in promoting the principle that the recent converts to Jackson should be excluded from the Democratic ticket in the autumn elections. The Family politicians in Philadelphia felt that they were being treated unjustly.

> *Here*, and here alone, have a few individuals, claiming to be the *original* friends of General JACKSON, when in fact they were *originally* the partisans of CLINTON, labored with might and main to *drive* the friends of CALHOUN from the support of JACKSON, denouncing them in their precious vehicle of calumny [the *Columbian Observer*], and at the corners of the streets as insincere and unprincipled, and getting up factious meetings to exclude them.

The *Franklin Gazette* urged the former Calhoun men not to be discouraged; "General JACKSON is not responsible for the black calumnies of Stephen Simpson." The plan of exclusion was not condoned by the discreet and respectable original Jacksonians in the city, the *Franklin* assured them. "It will be, above all, we have reason to *know*, distinctly disclaimed and condemned by General JACKSON himself."[80]

The general ward committee's nominations for the state and local tickets reflected the desired moderation toward all declared Jacksonians. But in the official town meeting on September 16 the Original Jackson men vanquished the Family politicians once again. "Never . . . were the proceedings and report [of] a General Ward Committee treated with so little ceremony and so much disrespect."

---

[80] *Democratic Press*, 2, 13, 21, 27, 29 Oct., 3 Nov. 1824; *Franklin Gazette*, 17 Aug. 1824.

William John Duane and others explained to the crowd that "much management had been resorted to . . . and the unanimity spoken of had been obtained by surreptitious means," and the assembled people then voted to submit the ticket to a special committee for reconsideration. When this resolution passed the Family men gave up and went home. They had anticipated the attempt to be made in cooperation with the Binnsites and had urged people to attend and defy them, but the Original Jacksonians demonstrated again their superior power to draw the people out to meetings. The Binns' faction of Crawfordites were also present but were a minority, and the Franklin Gazette acknowledged, "the friends of General JACKSON will rejoice to see the resolution so triumphantly adopted in his favor."

The committee of fourteen reported a new ticket "at a very late hour," and with one or two changes it was "agreed to by the remainder of the persons present." From the general ward committee's nominations they had replaced half the candidates for the state assembly and the common council, struck George Dallas from the select council slate and his intimate James N. Barker as the candidate for Congress. On the new ticket William John Duane was substituted for Barker, but he declined and the meeting then nominated Colonel William Duane for Congress.[81]

On Monday September 20 the town meeting was to reassemble and approve or disapprove the revised election ticket. On that evening, according to the United States Gazette, the Democrats

---

[81] Ibid., 17 Sept. 1824, quoted in National Gazette, 18 Sept. 1824; ibid.; Democratic Press, 17 Sept. 1824.

"held an _orgie_ . . . at the County Court room, and exhibited a scene that would disgrace the lowest conceptions of a Bacchanalian rout." The room was packed, "the tables, benches and railings occupied by the worshipful, the members of the party--who," the _Gazette_ reported, "shouted, bellowed, spoke, whistled, sung, hallooed, encored, vociferated, clapped, hissed and bellowed and groaned, not in reply to any notice, but in anticipation." During the early part of the evening "we learn the candles were all extinguished, and a few men of more muscles than words proceeded to the last extremity, and vented their feelings in certain sound and well placed _blows_," while the tumult continued. Finally after nine o'clock William John Duane interceded and put the motion, the only one of the evening, to adjourn until Wednesday. The meeting agreed and decided by acclamation that it was composed of "_good real Democrats_." Those were their words, said the editor.

The next day as a result of this meeting Stephen Simpson was beaten up in Chestnut street. And the county commissioners decided that the Court House in future would be available only to applicants who would take responsibility for the damage. The "furniture and fixtures of the room . . . had sustained considerable injury," it was explained, "in consequence of the frequent and indiscriminate assemblages of the citizens in town meeting."[82]

On September 22 the Philadelphians assembled again to consider the Democratic election ticket. This meeting was "more numerous and peaceable than the two preceding, and some of the Family

---

[82] _U. S. Gazette_, 22, 23 Sept. 1824; _National Gazette_, 23 Sept. 1824.

leaders reappeared to try to rectify the situation if possible. Their strongest objection was to the substitution for James Barker. "That William Duane should have been placed upon any democratic ticket . . . is most extraordinary." According to the Franklin's writer, probably Dallas himself, it was "an outrage on the feelings of the democratic party of this city." Robert Walsh's National Gazette agreed that Duane would be "especially disagreeable to most of the Federal voters," but as for the contention that Duane was "'the decided enemy of the Democratic party,'" Walsh remarked, "God save the commonwealth." The United States Gazette however thought that John Norvell explained "in a very neat and temperate manner" the "impropriety" of nominating Duane.

In the meeting Norvell described the retired editor of the Aurora as a man who "had proved a traitor to every democratic Governor and President, Jefferson excepted, that he had served under." W. J. Duane "appeared to be wonderously vexed at this attack upon his father," observed a Federalist reporter. "We had thought Mr. Duane possessed a better command of words, or a command of better words." In reply he said "that his father never left the cause of a governor, until that governor had done something worthy of censure. There was if not a want of truth," the United States Gazette commented, "at least a deficiency of ingenuousness." After "some pretty sharp shooting towards the Franklin Gazette," William John gave way to Major Francis T. Brewster, one of the earliest of the Original Jacksonians, who "talked at and to Mr. Norvell most valiantly." From the dramatic, emotional references to Duane's sufferings under the reign of terror, scoffed the Federalist paper, one would think that his son and the other orators were "not talking of some far away events."[83]

The town meeting ticket was approved and in the October election came within one hundred votes of upsetting the Federalist party, which had held control of the city for ten years. The Democratic ticket might have carried without the partial boycott by "some of the Family who would rather lose than carry the election." They allowed the Federalists to win the preliminary contests for inspectors of the general election. "Some of the most leading members of 'the Family' passed by the tavern in which the election in their ward was carrying on and would not vote." On election day itself the Democratic party officeholders abandoned the field to the would-be reformers. "There was no exertion to call the voters out, and we never saw fewer known Democrats on the ground carrying Tickets," Binns reflected. "Every vote given yesterday for the Democratic Ticket may be calculated upon as given from principle. . . . Yet, for all this, we were within a few votes of carrying the Town Meeting Ticket."[84]

Duane ran behind the ticket generally because many Family men and followers refused to vote for Congress. He could not in any case have been elected because the Philadelphia districts had been recently gerrymandered in a way which assured a Democratic

---

[83] Ibid., 23 Sept., 11 Oct. 1824; Franklin Gazette, 17 Sept. 1824, quoted in ibid., 18 Sept. 1824; U. S. Gazette, 25 Sept. 1824.

[84] Democratic Press, 2, 9, 13 Oct. 1824.

Congressman to the southern part of the county and a Federalist in the city. He was well satisfied with the honor of the nomination. Since his return from South America the sixty-four year old retired editor had sunk further financially into the approaching poverty. "Such are the strange vicissitudes of life," he wrote to Thomas Jefferson; "and it is in such circumstances that I was taken up as the Candidate of the Old Republicans in the recent Election for Members of Congress."

"It must be a consolation after nearly 30 years before the public that my son and myself should hold the place of preference among those who adhere to the principles of 1776 & 1800." Although it was true that "a great number of the leading republicans of that period have passed away," Duane thought the political events in Philadelphia showed that "the Jefferson school has had in [a] new generation successors of the same principles." The Republican ascendancy, he reflected, had caused a fundamental transformation in the political life of the country. Democratic government no longer was called jacobinism, "and those who formerly reprobated now use the language and profess the doctrine they reviled twenty four years ago." But "they do not <u>thank</u> those who aided in reforming their modes of speech; and as I was no idle spectator in the transactions which produced this <u>revolution in speech</u>," they voted against him as a candidate for Congress. Although "they profess to be all Republicans, all Federalists--they are not forgetful that I had shared in their conversion." In Philadelphia "the <u>votes</u> are given in the same way as 20 years ago," but because "the fundamental principles are no longer disputed nor reviled . . . the rising generation will receive them uncontaminated."[85]

In the November election Andrew Jackson received the greatest popular vote of the four presidential candidates and a plurality in the electoral college, but he was ultimately defeated in the House of Representatives when the Representatives from the states which had been pledged to Henry Clay cast their votes for John Quincy Adams. The reminiscence was passed on in William Duane's family, and told by his grandson to a biographer of Andrew Jackson, that "General Jackson met in one of the apartments of the presidential mansion," during Adams' inaugural celebration, "his old Philadelphia friend, Colonel Duane, of the *Aurora*, whom he had known and admired when first he represented Tennessee in Congress. 'Colonel,' said the General with emotion, 'you know how I must feel.'"[86]

---

[85] *Ibid.*, 13 Oct. 1824; Duane to Jefferson, 19 Oct. 1824, TJ-LC.

[86] Parton, *Life of Jackson*, III, 79.

CHAPTER XV

JACKSON AND THE PHILADELPHIANS

The time of Jackson's triumph and defeat was for William Duane personally the most difficult period of his life. His sufferings in India and in America in 1799 he had endured with the resilience of youth, but at sixty-five, when he was destitute and had a wife and four daughters dependent upon him, he confessed that he felt "much more disposed to go to sleep--and sleep for ever, than to dig up recollections which at every step would only bring me to compare what I have done and what I am suffering." His poor wife Margaret, accustomed to a life of plenty and educated in habits more elegant than prudent," was becoming ill from anxiety. Her fortune had been "sunk in the public cause--and she remains with four daughters a melancholy example of virtuous generosity and voluntary sacrifice." Duane's pity for his wife made his situation very much more painful. Margaret "could bear the storms of political persecution with the constancy of a Roman matron and be the consolation and the partner of her husband in danger," he said proudly, "but the adversity of need or dependance is not of that nature--and I fear that a protraction of our present condition may be fatal to her and to us all."

After the retired editor returned from South America in 1823, he had no employment and no income. His wife had received an allowance during his absence from the group of businessmen which had employed him and paid his expenses, but upon his return the "intrigue . . . of a worthless American" deprived him of his expected commission. In February 1824 Duane went to Washington to seek the help of old friends in Congress in support of a private bill to reverse the War department's judgment against him, in 1822, for his expenditures as Adjutant General. He remained in the capital four months, "settling accounts of ten years standing and rescuing myself from the opprobrium of being classed among the public defaulters." His successful appeal "relieved me from the imputation of the judgment and gave me a balance of about 2000 $ as a public creditor, restoring to me my reputation," but the money mostly went out in payment of debts and "what will remain may afford a scanty subsistence for three or four months, when no other resource appears to me at this moment open."

In these circumstances Duane again sought an appointment from the retiring President, James Monroe. A diplomatic post in Colombia or Mexico, the office of second or fourth auditor of the Treasury or assistant Postmaster General, all were spoken of for Duane by his friends while he was in Washington, and Senator Richard M. Johnson again took the lead in attempting to help him. In May he had "the satisfaction of a kind and friendly interview" with Monroe, "spoke to him unreservedly of my circumstances and desire to obtain some public employment," and from it he concluded that "I know his disposition to be good." But by autumn he realized that Monroe had no intention of appointing him to office. "It would have been more magnanimous and charitable in the President," he thought, "to have said or told some one to tell me, he set no value upon my former services--that my sacrifices were not entitled to thanks--. . . than to leave me in this state of uncertainty and wretchedness." If Duane had been less self righteous about his political principles, he would have perceived that what he asked was impossible, in spite of Monroe's inability to admit his sense of personal injury from the *Aurora*. But his hopes were raised by his anxiety, by his friends' sympathy, and above all by the knowledge that Thomas Jefferson was acting on his behalf.[1]

A friend "who chose to be anonymous" had written to Jefferson about Duane's situation and the aged ex-President responded at once, although customarily he carefully avoided using his influence upon his successors. While in Washington Duane "was surprised, and I must say gratified to learn from Col. R. M. Johnson that you had written to the President concerning me." He knew, he told Jefferson later, that "you have constantly rendered justice to me, even when you could not suspect I should ever hear of the kindness with which you spoke." In June Duane asked him to write again to Monroe, "Should it be within your ideas of propriety."

Jefferson complied and enclosed the letter from Philadelphia which he said expressed better than he could Duane's real distress. "His talents and inform[atio]n are certainly great," he commented, "and the services he rendered us when we needed them and his per-

---

[1]Duane to William Lee, 18 Nov. 1824, "Letters of Wm. Duane," *Mass. Hist. Soc. Procs.*, 2d series, XX, 384-385; Duane to Jefferson, 5 June, 8 Nov. 1824, TJ-LC.

sonal sacrifices and sufferings were signal and efficacious and left on us a moral duty not to forget him under misfortune." He reminded Monroe that "his subsequent aberrations were after we were too strong to be injured by them."

President Monroe politely refused Thomas Jefferson's request. Duane's "abuse of me for 4 or 5 years is disregarded," he insisted; "his real standing how ever in the community must be attended to, & that is such," he claimed, "as would expose me to censure if he should be placed in any trust of a marked character." He promised to keep Duane in view should a suitably minor office become available.[2]

A few weeks later Monroe rebuffed Jefferson unforgivably. The former President requested the appointment of Colonel Bernard Peyton, whom he loved as a son, as Postmaster of Richmond. For the only time during Monroe's presidency, he asked the favor as a point of friendship to himself, but Monroe coolly ignored the plea. "I had thought its success as certain as that the sun will rise tomorrow," Jefferson wrote bitterly to Peyton. As for the public, "I supposed that 60. years of faithful service would weigh with them as much as a broken leg." But for Monroe after forty-six years to grant him less consideration than "a transient acquaintance" was a source of bitterness which lasted until his death.[3]

---

[2]<u>Ibid</u>.; Jefferson to Duane, 31 May 1824, TJ-LC; Jefferson to Monroe, draft, 2 July 1824, TJ-LC; Monroe to Jefferson, 12 July 1824, TJ-LC.

[3]Jefferson to Peyton, 3 Sept. 1824, quoted in Nathan Schacner, <u>Thomas Jefferson, a Biography</u> (New York, 1951), 993.

In October the office of naval agent for the Port of Philadelphia became vacant by death. Duane immediately travelled to Washington "to solicit the station," but was faced with a painful dilemma as soon as he arrived. The previous spring he had offered "several papers containing signatures of respectable Citizens of Phil[a] and members of both chambers of Congress," but at that time "the President was so good as to say that they were not necessary." Therefore he brought none in the fall. "But the President now has said that I must obtain signatures for this special office." If petitions were to decide the appointment he was afraid other interests would prevail, yet if he returned to Philadelphia, "travelling with the utmost economy I should reach my family with not more than $3--and I should find them with not much more." He explained these things to Jefferson and implored him to act on his behalf. And after he returned to Philadelphia, almost in despair, he entreated once more. "That condition of humanity which supersedes all law is the apology which I offer for trespassing upon you again."

"Two months ago such a letter should have been complied with without a moment's delay," Jefferson replied, "but within that period the ground on which I stood has totally changed. an intervening incident forbids the possibility of my ever again asking." But "I must not explain this," he told Duane, "and must even beg of you" not to reveal any hint of the cryptic reference to Monroe's rebuff. It occurred to Jefferson however that the insulting refusal to Colonel Peyton might serve Duane in his application for the office of naval agent; "if there be any desire [in Monroe] to soothe wounded frdshp, this [avenue] will suggest itself as fav'ble." He entrusted the secret of his grievance to Duane, he explained, only because "I detest making false excuses. My best wishes will attend you," he closed, "when even worth nothing."[4]

Monroe did not appoint Duane, in spite of his promise to Jefferson to help the needy editor if an appropriate opening occurred. The disappointment reduced Duane to a state of despondency for the first time in his life. His son went to Washington to press the application, but returned "as he went--and as I anticipated--in fact I have given up all hope." "My poor Wife driven by insupportable affliction has been confined to her bed for a week--and my poor girls appear sinking" under the force of the family's distress. "This day," he wrote to an old friend in mid-November, "I endeavored to borrow some money to lengthen out this state of misery which anxiety and hopelessness barely tolerates--My son being absent in the interior . . . --I could obtain--only 3/4th of a Dollar!!" He could not send any news, he apologized, since "I have not been out of doors for the last week, but when I went out to _borrow_."[5]

The next few years were to be extremely hard for him and his family. They had a small income from his office as a city alderman and from the publication of his book on the South American trip, but his son probably contributed substantially to their sup-

---

[4]Duane to Jefferson, 19 Oct., 8 Nov. 1824, TJ-LC; Jefferson to Duane, draft, 24 Oct. 1824, TJ-LC.

[5]Duane to William Lee, 18 Nov. 1824, "Letters of Wm. Duane," _Mass. Hist. Soc. Procs._, 2d series, XX, 384-385.

port. William John, who had seven children of his own, had entered upon great prosperity as a lawyer at the same time that his father was beginning to sink. Stephen Girard, the richest man in the United States but a lifelong Republican, had employed him as his attorney about 1819; he became both legal and business consultant and was responsible for managing Girard's investments and estates. In 1821 he had moved his family to the highly fashionable Walnut street.[6]

The old Colonel and Mrs. Duane were forced in their adversity to move to a house on South Sixth at Elizabeth street. They had a corner lot but in a neighborhood "composed of poor people, who have neither property nor servants," and where a cistern when broken was left unrepaired, so that the Alderman complained, "it appears to me that the use of such water is likely to produce disease." They lived south of Spruce street in Cedar ward, a section crowded with Irish Catholic immigrants who had been arriving in large numbers since the end of the war. The principal Negro district began a bit farther south, and the mutual antagonism between these two deprived groups led to nights of bloody rioting in the summer of 1834.[7]

---

[6]Duane to Joseph Reed, 24 Aug. 1827, Pers. Papers Misc. (Duane), LC; Duane to Carey & Lea, 15 Nov. 1825, in Thompson Westcott, "Illustrated History of Philadelphia," Vol. 131, p. 2440, HSP; [Duane], _Biog. Memoir of W. J. Duane_, 14-15; Gillespie, _Book of Remembrance_, 5-7, 38; Andrew Jackson to Martin Van Buren, 25 Nov. 1832, in Van Buren, _Autobiography_, 596; Louis McLane to Van Buren, 26 Nov. 1832, _ibid_., 596-598.

[7]Duane to Mayor Joseph Watson, 24 July 1827, Pers. Papers Misc. (Duane), LC; _Franklin Gazette_, 18 Oct. 1824; G. M. Dallas to George Wolf, 17 Aug. 1834, George Wolf Papers, HSP.

The Duanes' circumstances were made somewhat easier by the marriages of three of their four daughters. In August 1827 Anastasia, twenty-one, married Richard Tilghman Lloyd of Maryland, who bore an impeccable Federalist name. In October Emma, the youngest, who was not yet sixteen, became the wife of a thirty-four year old surgeon, Edmund Louis DuBarry. Not long after Elizabeth, their eldest child and her father's favorite, married Henry S. Crabb, a Philadelphian. However, the misfortune and discomfort of the parents continued. In the spring of 1828 "the unhappy illness of my son and my wife" drove Duane anew to a "distressed state of . . . mind" which broke down his own health for several months, "such as to disable me from ordinary business."[8]

Duane received a state appointment in April 1829, as prothonotary of the Supreme Court for the eastern district of Pennsylvania, from John A. Shulze, the retiring Governor. When he was first elected in 1823, Shulze had been a compromise candidate supported by all factions of Democrats because they were preoccupied with the presidential question. At that time it was believed that he would be a tool of the Family party, but he had taken advantage of his broad support to assert his independence. The increasing enmity of the Family men would prevent his being a candidate for a third term. They had selected another favorite who again, from experience, would be supported by all the Democrats. Governor Shulze took his

---

[8]North American, 8 Dec. 1907; Duane to John Branch, Secretary of the Navy, 9 Aug. 1830, Duane Folder, Misc. Papers, NYPL; Duane to Capt. Hypolite Dumas, 29 Mar., 5 July 1828, Pers. Papers Misc. (Duane), LC.

revenge in advance by a policy which was certain to embarrass his successor, a series of removals and new appointments made during his last year in office.[9]

When his material condition became tolerable, Duane's spirit began to revive. His position as Court clerk did not pay well, for the office had no salary but was compensated on a commission basis, "like the English Custom house laws, such as I had no conception of till I came into experience of official practices." He complained that the income was too small and that the "wretched office" was "not worth the keeping to any one who has anything else," but clearly it had restored him to his old vigor. "I am revolutionizing it out of chaos and disorder & odious appurtenances" he wrote to a friend, "and whenever I leave it, shall place it on a footing such as it never possessed before, as to order, and arrangement, and security of the Records." He was to hold the office until his death.[10]

II.

Andrew Jackson became the national Democratic candidate for 1828 on the day in February 1825 that he was deprived of the presidency by the House of Representatives. In Pennsylvania the leaders of the Family party used the intervening years to fortify their claim to leadership of the Jacksonians and thereby regain the posi-

---

[9]John Hill Martin, Martin's Bench and Bar of Philadelphia (Philadelphia, 1883), 26; Klein, Pa. Politics, 136-149, 150, 188-189, 209-210, 264-265, 277.

[10]Duane to Thomas Elder, 27 Jan. 1832, Gratz Collection, HSP.

tion of political dominance in the state. They were still devoted to the interests of John Calhoun, who had become the Vice President, but they now recognized that his best hope for the top office would be as the successor to the Hero of New Orleans.

However George M. Dallas demanded the proscription of Stephen Simpson as "a previous sine qua non" to further action on Jackson's behalf. "The Columbian Observer . . . *must* be silenced--," he told Ingham, "Simpson *must* be excluded from any participation in the conduct of affairs--I say, and say again, such things *must* be." After one year of forced cooperation with the radicals, the cool patrician became frenzied by their every act. He expected Ingham in Washington to present his demand. "If the high and leading friends of the General still adhere to this fool and madman as a proper instrument and organ," he threatened, "they must not be surprized to find every thing retro grade. and every intelligent man avoid the party."

"The true men in this District, and throughout the State," Dallas believed, "will not stir a foot, as long as they are to be hazarded and betrayed by the folly and inanity of Simpson. If Jackson has not understanding enough," he sneered, "to perceive the inevitable effects of this man's interference, he ought not to support him. Let him take his choice--or rather let his friends take their choice," he instructed Ingham. "I am satisfied we cannot and will not submit to be exposed and degraded by a pet fool."[11]

Simpson was never "gagged from head-quarters" by Lewis and

---

[11]Dallas to Ingham, 16 Feb. 1825, Dallas Papers, HSP.

Eaton, but he was gradually supplanted in favor by the adroit and useful Congressman Ingham. In Pennsylvania Jackson's "original friends" of 1824 eventually yielded to the resurgent Family, the "exclusive friends" of 1829. The transition in leadership occurred in part as a result of manipulation of the "corrupt bargain" issue.

The Columbian Observer first published the charge, in January 1825, that there would be collusion between John Quincy Adams and Henry Clay to make the former President upon a pledge to appoint the latter Secretary of State. The alleged source of the information was Congressman George Kremer of Pennsylvania, a German whose devotion to Jackson was ardent but naive. Probably General Eaton wrote Kremer's letter for the Observer, but apparently Ingham controlled his conduct in the abortive inquiry in the House initiated at Clay's request. Whether or not he was guilty of wrongdoing, Adams in fact defeated Jackson by gaining the votes pledged to Clay, and in turn named him his Secretary of State.[12]

In Philadelphia when the election of Adams was announced the Jacksonians were enraged by the mockery of the people's will. The Columbian Observer immediately announced a public meeting of protest to be held in the State House yard on February 16. "The Town Meeting called by Simpson . . . was enormous," George Dallas acknowledged, "the largest I ever saw:--not less than a thousand certainly." Dallas himself refused to attend and kept others away by his influence; he would not associate with its "degenerate" organizers, and he mistrusted the excessive spontaneity. If it had

---

[12]Parton, Life of Jackson, III, 102-120.

been "delayed for a fortnight, . . . [and] summoned under the auspices of the Committee of Correspondence, . . . its resolutions," according to Dallas, "echoing from every hill and valley in the State, would have shaken "Aristocracy on his throne.'"

As it was, "No preparations were made:--everything was confided to a few heedless young men," and the result was harmful and "absolutely ludicrous." Simpson was aided in the meeting by his friend Charles I. Jack and probably by another young attorney, Zebulon Philips. He had recruited them both into the Old School party in 1820, and they had been zealous activists among the Original Jackson men. "It is mortifying and vexatious beyond bearing," said Dallas, "to see the generous and prompt and daring forwardness of more than a thousand men, prepared to constitute the basis of an overwhelming party," uselessly squandered "by the gross mismanagement and culpable carelessness of two or three contemptible boys." Because they had failed to secure a chairman in advance, the assembly could not organize, for no one who was asked would consent to take the chair. The reputation of the Original Jacksonians for tumultuous town meetings was presumably the source of these misgivings. George Dallas spied on the proceedings from a block away, and "I looked on with a feeling I cannot describe to you," he told Ingham, "almost prompted to rush in and set my life upon the cost:--the opportunity ruined so good, so inviting."

"The crowd seemed bent upon doing something, and had they been properly headed, would have done anything: They kept together for an hour and a half--in peace and good humour waiting to proceed to business." But with no chairman "and unable to get on at all," they finally "quitted the spot" reluctantly. "As they dispersed a child took the chair--then an old crazy fellow who loiters about the streets--and on the whole, the matter ended like a farce."[13]

But Samuel Ingham had his own plans to develop the corrupt bargain issue, which would not be frustrated by premature outbursts of popular feeling. His intention was not so much to help Jackson in 1828, for in Pennsylvania that victory was virtually assured, as to embarrass his rival James Buchanan. Congressman Buchanan, a former Federalist and an Original Jackson man from Lancaster county, was emerging as the statewide leader of the anti-Family or "Amalgamation" branch of the Jackson party. But allegedly he had carried an offer, identical with that to Adams, from Clay to General Jackson. He could only deny it and belie Jackson, or admit it and condemn himself. Ingham viciously exploited the dilemma, embarrassing Buchanan before the public and permanently impairing his relations with Andrew Jackson.[14]

In view of Ingham's plans, Dallas struggled to take command of the issue in Philadelphia. In June 1825 he prepared a preamble and resolutions for a proposed town meeting. "Norvell and [Chandler] Price declared them excellent &c&c. Price convoked his friends," but the _Columbian Observer_ crowd was for going much farther; "a tirade of Simpson's manufacturing was introduced--mine dished--the subject transferred to the Hickory Club," where a quarrel broke out,

---

[13]Dallas to Ingham, 16 Feb. 1825, Dallas Papers, HSP.

[14]Klein, _Pa. Politics_, 177-181, 230-239.

leaving "every thing in the wind." According to Dallas, Price needed to be soothed. "He is, at this moment, perhaps more disgusted with the Hickory Club than his prudence should permit. He talks of giving up in despair."

A year later Dallas made his first attempt to compete with Simpson's ability to appeal directly to the voters. "Our meeting was all powerful in moral and political weight--," he reported to Ingham,"but it was not as numerous as I had expected. We had not more than 400. The subordinate Jacksonmen are not yet skilled," he admitted peevishly, "in getting numbers out, at a moment's warning."[15]

The solution finally resorted to before the election of 1828 was to abolish the tradition of submitting Democratic party decisions to a town meeting for approval. Simpson did not protest the decision made by the general ward committee, because he was anxious for unity in the upcoming presidential election. After Jackson was safely elected there were expressions of resentment at the abandonment of "ancient usage" and democratic principles. One former ward delegate urged support for the newly formed Working Men's party in 1829, because "Even now, the very ticket, which is formed by the city delegates, is not to be submitted to a Town Meeting. . . . Men whose names are on that ticket," he revealed, "voted against a Town Meeting; knowing, as we do, that they would be expunged by the voice of the people."[16]

---

[15]Dallas to Ingham, 14 June 1825, 26 May 1826, Dallas Papers, HSP.

[16]Philadelphia Mechanics' Free Press, "Peter Single," 3 Oct.

There were other reasons why the Original Jacksonians declined in power. The zealous amateurs of 1824 had been effective but they lacked a base for continuing influence. The Columbian Observer stopped publication in 1825, and although Simpson founded another paper in 1827, the Philadelphia Mercury, it did not obtain the role which had been played by its predecessor.[17] In addition to his service in Jackson's cause, Simpson was trying to establish himself as a writer and literary critic and had to support his young family by working as a clerk in Girard's bank. The full time politicians and officeholders, once they had embraced Jackson, inevitably regained control of the Democratic party.

III.

The Family party's reinstatement was unfortunately confirmed in 1829 by the President-elect's appointments to office. In the formation of his administration, Jackson largely disregarded his personal preferences and acted upon the political and geographical calculations of his advisers. Ironically the two highest offices, those of Vice President and Secretary of State, were filled by men who had struggled to defeat Jackson in 1824, and the rivals Calhoun and Van Buren jealously pursued exclusive influence over the President. The second seat in the cabinet, that of Secretary of the Treasury, was reserved for the state of Pennsylvania because of its great importance in securing Jackson's victory. The President's personal

---

1829; Philadelphia Pennsylvania Inquirer, "A Ward Delegate," 25 Sept. 1829.

[17] In 1825 Simpson published a newspaper called the National Chronicle, which was essentially a continuation of the Columbian Observer.

choice was Henry Baldwin, his steadfast advocate since 1818, but through Calhoun's influence and the use of pressure by a minority of the state's Congressional delegation, the appointment was awarded to Samuel D. Ingham. "Is there no representative at Washington of the original and true friends of Genl Jackson?" demanded a friend of Baldwin, astonished at the news of "your exclusion from the Cabinet."[18]

As a cabinet officer Ingham naturally determined the pattern of the administration's relations to the Democrats of Pennsylvania. His Family friends gained complete control of the federal patronage in Philadelphia. James N. Barker was appointed Collector of the Customs and Thomas Sergeant was retained as the city Postmaster. In 1828 Sergeant, who had once left office in embarrassing circumstances himself, was allowed to take over the position and conceal the disgrace of his brother-in-law Richard Bache, through the courtesy of the Calhounite Postmaster General, John McLean, who duped President Adams.

Bache owed the government about twenty-five thousand dollars when he retired after a dozen years as Postmaster. Some of the money may have been used in 1817 to purchase the Franklin Gazette, of which he was the first editor. His brother-in-law, George Dallas, was his attorney, and none of his bondsmen--Ingham, Sergeant, Norvell, the widowed Mrs. A. J. Dallas--made good on their bonds. Once a stalwart of the Family party, Bache had aban-

---

[18]Ross Wilkins to Baldwin, 24 Feb. 1829, John Earle Reynolds Collection, Reis Library, Allegheny College, Meadville, Pennsylvania; Klein, Pa. Politics, 252-258.

doned his wife Sophia and their nine children and absconded to Texas. "There is no more direct way to my heart," George Dallas confided, "than through kindness to Mrs. Bache." When Secretary Ingham arranged the appointment of his nephew Richard as an acting midshipman, Dallas wrote, "He is enchanted--and so are his mother and all his family."[19]

One of the most seriously contested presidential appointments in the state was that of district attorney for the eastern district of Pennsylvania. The principal candidates were George Dallas and W. J. Duane. In seeking the office to which Thomas Jefferson had appointed his father, Dallas had the advantage of Secretary Ingham's support. But President Jackson was sympathetic to Duane's application, because he was an Original Jackson man, but especially because he was his father's son. Jackson was fond of recollecting "the early struggles of the old Republican party, whilst he was a Member of Congress" from the state of Tennessee. Martin Van Buren later recalled that "he had often expressed to me" his "favourable opinion . . . of the conduct, at that period, of the then redoubtable conductor of the 'Aurora'--William Duane, and the disposition . . . to befriend him whenever a suitable opportunity might offer."[20]

The district attorneyship was finally awarded to Dallas, after a period of rather ungracious waiting. He commiserated with

---

[19] _Ibid._, 203-209; Dallas to Ingham, 1 Mar., 5 June 1829, 3 Apr. 1830, Dallas Papers, HSP; Merle M. Odgers, _Alexander Dallas Bache, Scientist and Educator, 1806-1867_ (Philadelphia, 1947), 6.

[20] Dallas to Ingham, 2, 8, 9 Apr. 1829, Dallas Papers, HSP.

Ingham who was plagued with a "swarm of locusts" seeking appointment, but continually asked after the progress of his own application. His unselfconscious double standard for other office seekers and himself resembled that of his father in 1801. "I am peremptorily ordered to communicate to you the following idea," he coyly informed Ingham on April 2, "as one of those brilliant conceptions which dexterous politicians should always make the most of . . . [and] intended to fortify you in any exertion which may be made." His rivals for the position were Duane and the former Federalist, John Wurts, "and it is conceived that the President, anxious to befriend all, may be gulled by the suggestion that I already enjoy the enviable and lucrative post of Mayor." Therefore he should be told "that by our law [written to deal with the case of his father, who held three offices in 1801], the instant I accept his commission, my mayoralty terminates." If Duane and Wurts were "as they pretend, so popular and influential, one of them can be placed in the vacated chair" and the other take Dallas' job as judge of the quarter sessions. "Is not this a magnificent conception? It is somewhat beyond my humdrum notions:--and yet is so enforced and insisted upon that I was made to promise solemnly that you should have it."[21]

President Jackson wished to offer a substitute appointment to W. J. Duane, but Dallas was determined to prevent it. He and Ingham had established a position from which to dominate the administration's relationship to Pennsylvania, identical to that of the

---

[21]Dallas to Ingham, 2, 8, 9 Apr. 1829, Dallas Papers, HSP.

elder Dallas and Albert Gallatin during Jefferson's administration and used then to proscribe the senior William Duane. Eventually President Jackson was to assert his political independence from the officeholding Pennsylvanians, as Jefferson had done before him.

In 1828 the Philadelphia Jacksonians had united on local candidates and had at last carried the city. W. J. Duane, elected to the select council, was offered the position of mayor, apparently in an attempt to buy off opposition from one of the most prominent and widely respected Original Jacksonians. He had refused it and Dallas took the job. "His absolute stupidity, in declining the Mayoralty," the latter avowed, "upon pretensions which three years service in a criminal court as prosecuting attorney made glaringly hypocritical, has alienated many who before respected his supposed intelligence and candor." Dallas resolved that if Duane would not accept his charity he would receive political benefit from no one.

When someone in Washington proposed the editor's son for the directorship of the United States Mint at Philadelphia, Dallas urged the Secretary of the Treasury to prevent the appointment. "W. J. Duane is entitled to little or nothing from General Jackson. . . . He is certainly entitled to nothing but contempt," in Dallas' opinion, "from the republican party of Pennsylvania, against whose progress, harmony, and stability he has been, as long as I can remember him, an uniform, peevish, and petulant opponent." Dallas claimed that the appointment would cost the administration "ten times more" in popularity than it could gain. "Besides--he is of a peculiar character, and always ascribes an advance to him to fear rather than generosity, remaining just as jealous & inimical as before." The rebuffed ex-Mayor advised that "As to gratitude for kindness--the President may as well seek it in a lizard. He is utterly inaccessible to the feeling."[22]

Later the President nominated Duane as a government director of the Second Bank of the United States. To this "let me say that M^r. Duane is incompetent & not a stockholder," the District Attorney objected, "and that he told me he would not accept the appointment." The President nonetheless sent the nomination to the Senate and it was confirmed in February 1830, but Duane declined as Dallas predicted.[23]

IV.

In 1829, the year the Family party leaders established themselves as the exclusive friends of President Jackson, political factionalism returned in force to Philadelphia. The Working Men's party, created one year before, made enormous gains at the polls, elected several of its candidates and temporarily became the balance of power between the two major parties. The brief and enigmatic history of the Working Men's party has received more attention from historians than any other aspect of Philadelphia politics. It was however less unique than has been supposed. In spirit and in program and technique, it was a natural successor of the Old School Democrats, and it had direct links to that party through the Origi-

---

[22]Dallas to Ingham, 8 July 1829, ibid.

[23]Dallas to Ingham, n.d. [ca. Nov. 1829], ibid.; Pa. Inquirer, 13 Feb. 1830; [Duane], Biog. Memoir of W. J. Duane, 23. See also Dallas to Ingham, 24 Oct., 9 Nov. 1829, Dallas Papers, HSP.

nal Jacksonians. Like both those predecessors, its single greatest area of strength was the Northern Liberties.[24]

None of the party's specific proposals was new in the city's politics. The abolition of imprisonment for debt, for example, had been introduced into the legislature by Michael Leib about 1817. Assemblyman James Thackara in 1819 had taken an adamant stand for state elementary schools. The two great goals of the Working Men were free public education and stringent reform of paper money banking. Of these the latter was the more controversial and the more pressing. By 1830 all Democratic politicians declared their firm support of public education; the Working Men sought to goad them into faster action toward that goal. However they feared an impending setback for their hard money views and a new wave of bank incorporations, because the state was entering a period of renewed industrial prosperity. The prominence of the state banking issue is recognized by historians of Pennsylvania politics for the first time with the study of the Working Men's movement, but even here its importance has been generally underestimated.

Leaders of the Working Men gladly acknowledged their political debt to William Duane--"the able, the faithful, the independent, the patriotic Duane." The Colonel and his son were both members of

---

[24]See John R. Commons, et al., History of Labour in the United States, 4 vols. (New York, 1918-1935), I, 195-215; Joseph Dorfman, "The Jackson Wage Earner Thesis," American Historical Review, LIV (Apr. 1949), 296-306; Edward Pessen, "The Workingmen's Movement of the Jacksonian Era," Mississippi Valley Historical Review, XLIII (Dec. 1956), 428-443; Edward Pessen, "The Working Men's Party Revisited," Labor History, IV, No. 3 (fall 1963), 203-226; William A. Sullivan, "Did Labor Support Andrew Jackson?," Political Science Quarterly, LXII (Dec. 1947), 569-580.

the citizen's committee appointed by a town meeting of "Working Men and others, opposed to the chartering of any more new Banks in this Commonwealth." The committee included some hard money Federalists, notably Condy Raguet and William M. Gouge, and several Original Jacksonians, as well as the Working Men's party leaders. Its public report, which was intended to "apply to the [interests of the] capitalist as well as to the labourer," revived the dispute with the developing business system which the Old School party had begun nearly twenty years before. The report not only opposed the issuance of currency by private banks, but questioned their essential function, the dispensing of credit, and denounced the privilege of incorporation, which deprived the government and the people of their rightful control over the general welfare.[25]

The Working Men sought Duane's counsel and support on other occasions, but the old Colonel did not approve of their political party because it was deliberately class conscious. Its proposals were unobjectionable and not a sharp break from the concerns of his Old School, which for the most part had been composed of mechanics. But its encouragement to wage earners to think of themselves as an exploited class and to act in their own interests was a radical departure from Duane's philosophy. His political views and actions

---

[25]Mechanics' Free Press, 27 Sept. 1828, 21 Mar. 1829. The "Address to the Citizens of Pennsylvania," ibid., 25 Apr. 1829, is an early formal expression of what Louis Hartz has described as the "anti-charter doctrine," in Economic Policy and Democratic Thought: Pennsylvania, 1776-1860 (Cambridge, Mass., 1948). It clearly reveals the irony of the contrast between what critics of the corporate system meant by the term "free enterprise" and what it came to mean in American economic history.

had all been founded upon the premise that the Declaration of Independence implied a classless society in which all members were protected by the principle of commonweal. He cherished his eighteenth century ideals against the disillusionments of industrialism.[26]

His former colleague Stephen Simpson supported the Working Men's movement with great enthusiasm. In 1828 Simpson had attempted to discourage its organization, because he had faith that the Hero of New Orleans could perform political miracles. But after he told the President-elect and Major Lewis what he thought of the federal appointees from Pennsylvania, his relations with Jackson became somewhat strained. In 1830 he accepted the Working Men's invitation to become their Congressional candidate in the southern district of the county. The arch Original Jacksonian was the only candidate for national office ever endorsed by the short-lived labor party.[27]

Simpson's candidacy was intended solely as a gesture of protest. There could be no hope of victory because the district had been gerrymandered to serve the interests of its incumbent, Joel B. Sutherland, the demagogic colleague of George Dallas and political boss of Philadelphia county. In accepting the nomination Simpson stated his strong approval of all the goals of the Working Men's movement. "We candidly admit, that the views . . . far exceed our expectations," wrote the editor of the Mechanics Free

---

[26] Aurora, 19 July 1834.

[27] Phila. Mercury, 27 Sept., 4, 11 Oct. 1828; Simpson to Jackson, 28 Feb., 18 June 1829, Jackson Papers, LC; Jackson to Simpson, 27 June 1829, ibid.

Press, "not on the score of talent, for we always gave him due credit for possessing an uncommon share of that scar[c]e, but valuable article," but because of his former disapproval and "strong feeling of [Democratic] partizanship in his public writings."[28]

William Gouge, the Federalist Jacksonian editor, chided the candidate for his public statement that "labour is the sole source of all our wealth." He objected that the doctrine lacked "mathematical precision," according to Simpson, but the real objection was that it was too precise in stating a truth which was a call to a revolutionary spirit in the people. Admittedly he had not written a "scientific treatise" on the subject, Simpson bantered, but perhaps he would if Gouge would promise to print it in his Philadelphia Gazette. Soon after Simpson published his Working Man's Manual, which consistently asserted a labor theory of value. In a pre-Marxist assault on the sources of class division, it maintained that the amassing of capital was made possible only by withholding from labor its fair wages.[29]

Simpson received about one third of the total vote in his contest against Sutherland, in a campaign based squarely upon the policies of the Working Men's party. In the northern district of the county a more general reform movement ousted the incumbent Democratic Congressman, Daniel H. Miller. Jackson Democrats and independent working men turned out in huge numbers to vote for the Federalist candidate, John G. Watmough. As a Congressman, Watmough

---

[28]Mechanics' Free Press, 25 Sept., 2 Oct. 1830.

[29]Ibid., 6 Nov. 1830.

became a tool of Nicholas Biddle, but at the time he was elected his views were unknown and unsolicited. He owed his victory to the protest against his opponent.

Miller was a thoroughgoing sycophant of Joel Sutherland and the president of the hated new Bank of Penn Township in the district west of the Northern Liberties. The Sutherland faction had secured its charter, conspired to become its stockholders and officers, and employed its resources for political punishment and reward. The previous year the Working Men's party had defeated one of the bank's directors for state assemblyman and had nearly brought down another member of its inner circle, state Senator Jesse Burden, whom Sutherland had rescued by the utmost exertion. "Could the election have been postponed for another month," the Mechanics' Free Press asserted, "the Democrats of the county would have been precipitated on the whole [banking] question, in spite of their coward caution." The 1830 election in the third Congressional district bore out the belief that "Public opinion is materially changed on these matters."[30]

V.

President Jackson was privately delighted by the turn of events in Philadelphia. He was by this time thoroughly disillusioned with the pretended friendship of Calhoun and his associates and ready to restore to grace his Original adherents. Secretary of

---

[30] Ibid., 17 Oct., 19 Dec. 1829, 16 Oct. 1830; Pa. Inquirer, 11 Oct. 1830; American Sentinel, 4, 8, 9, 11, 12 Oct. 1830; Dallas to Ingham, 16 Aug., 1, 10 Oct., 17 Nov. 1830, Dallas Papers, HSP.

the Treasury Ingham was a particular object of his disenchantment. Jackson's response to the upset of Congressman Miller was the first hint to his intimates that Ingham was in disfavor. Andrew J. Donelson, his nephew and private secretary, was amazed to see the President's pleasure in reading the proceedings of a victory dinner for Colonel Watmough in which Simpson and Charles Jack were "the leading spirits," and in quoting aloud the toasts which denounced Ingham. The following spring the President was to reorganize his cabinet completely in order to rid it of the Secretary from Pennsylvania.[31]

As a reward to Simpson for his factious conduct in the fall elections, President Jackson decided to appoint him a commissioner under the Danish treaty, "to distribute the indemnity" for wartime damages which Denmark had agreed to pay to American claimants. He was informed that it would be necessary to resign his clerkship to Girard, who was a claimant. Simpson was very happy and very anxious about the proposed appointment. "I am now with a large family," he explained to Major Donelson, "cast like the Birds of the fields, upon the mercy & bounty of Providence--& to that Providence, & to our friend the President--do I look for provision." Major Lewis had Donelson warn him that there would be opposition in the Senate and that he should "strengthen himself" by recommendations. He was surprised by this since "I should hardly think a formidable opposition could be raised to so small a man, on so unimportant an occa-

---

[31]"Statement of A. J. Donelson," Nov. 1830, in Bassett, ed., Jackson Correspondence, IV, 202-203.

sion." But Donelson knew best, he agreed, "& acting on your hint, I have got my friends to renew their Letters,--stating the fact, that I am not a 'Highway robber,' nor 'an armed Rhinocerous'--nor 'a rugged Russian bear.'"[32]

Simpson gravely underestimated the power of the President's enemies in Congress. The Senate rejected his nomination. It was "if not the first, among the first instances of similar proceedings," aimed especially at denying office to newspaper editors. The Columbian Observer undoubtedly had been hated by many members of Congress, but Simpson himself later said that his rejection was "because of the imputed authorship of 'Brutus' in the Aurora." The President became enraged when the Secretary of the Senate informed him of the decision, and "he determined at the instant to renominate Simpson," to send the Senate his reasons and request an explanation of its objections.

That afternoon Martin Van Buren "arrived at the Executive Mansion . . . and found him in the East Room" with several other persons, "and in whose presence he spoke of the transaction with his usual unreserve and with more than usual excitement." The little magician perceived that Jackson was in danger of exposing his weakest side and increasing his reputation for arrogance. Anxious to get the angry President away from his visitors, "I raised a window opening upon the terrace and proposed a stroll," to which he agreed. "Our walk commenced in the afternoon and continued till it was dark with-

---

[32]Simpson to W. B. Lewis, 16 Dec. 1830, Andrew J. Donelson Papers, LC; Simpson to Donelson, 20 Dec. 1830, ibid.

out interruption," Van Buren recalled, "although I saw gentlemen approaching us who were turned back by the manifest earnestness of our conversation."

Van Buren could say nothing to dissuade the President from his determination to challenge the Senate. He suggested several alternate candidates, "without effect, until a chance allusion from him to our early struggles of the old Republican party" reminded Van Buren of Jackson's high opinion of the editor of the Aurora, and caused him to think of William John Duane. "The favorable impression made by the suggestion was at once apparent. There seemed to be something in the idea of sending to the federalists in the Senate the name of a son of William Duane" which greatly pleased him. It divested his acceptance of Simpson's rejection "of every appearance of yielding to their hostility." The two returned to the President's office "and prepared a new nomination to that effect." It was confirmed by the Senate and without knowing it W. J. Duane became a member of the Danish Commission. He hesitated to accept but the President "pressed . . . the trust upon me, as a duty to the public, and as a relief to himself from embarrassment."[33]

Simpson was not told the circumstances of the President's acquiescence, and later Major Lewis somewhat misrepresented the reasons why he could not be offered another appointment requiring confirmation by the Senate. Gradually he became bitterly convinced

---

[33]Simpson to James Buchanan, 1 June 1840, James Buchanan Papers, HSP; Van Buren, Autobiography, 599-600; [William J. Duane], Narrative and Correspondence concerning the Removal of the Deposites, and Occurrences Connected Therewith (Philadelphia, 1838), 1.

that Jackson had lied to him. In the presidential election of 1832 he became an advocate of the Anti-Masonic candidate and derided his former idol as "the Hypocrite of the Hermitage." "He is the only man who ever throughout a long life," Simpson averred, "acted the hypocrite so far, as to effect all the opposite virtues in their extreme degree, candour, friendship, honesty, magnanimity, . . . and wearing his heart on his sleeve," and yet be guilty of duplicity and treachery. But after the re-elected President took decisive action to annul the Second Bank of the United States, Simpson humbly apologized for his faithlessness and slanders, and the President forgave him.[34]

VI.

When Andrew Jackson was elected to a second term in the presidency, he vowed to use his remaining years before retirement in rescuing the nation's principles and morals from the "hydra of corruption," the monster Second United States Bank. The charter of the Second Bank would expire in 1836, and President Jackson had made clear since December 1829 his determination that it should not be renewed. In view of his opposition, and acting upon the political advice of Henry Clay, the Bank applied four years in advance for a renewal of the charter. In the spring of 1832 the request was approved by both houses of Congress and went to the President for his signature. Jackson vetoed the recharter act and in the

---

[34]Philadelphia Pennsylvania Whig, 31 Dec. 1831, 2 May 1832; Simpson to Jackson, 21 Oct. 1834, Jackson Papers, LC; Simpson to James Buchanan, 22 Dec. 1834, Buchanan Papers, HSP. See also Dallas to Ingham, 19, 29 May 1831, Dallas Papers, HSP.

autumn election asked the American people to grant him a vote of confidence. His victory over Henry Clay he regarded as a mandate to complete his mission to destroy the Bank.

By the autumn of 1832 President Jackson had concluded that it was imperative to check the Bank before it could fully exercise its capacity for commercial blackmail. Nicholas Biddle had amply demonstrated in the campaign for recharter and in the presidential election that he was prepared to use the Bank's powerful resources to achieve its political ends. Jackson's advisers told him that the foundation of the Bank's power was its role as fiscal agent for the government and its privilege of doing business upon the asset of the federal deposits. He accepted the recommendation that he terminate the official relationship.

The Secretary of the Treasury, according to the terms of the charter, was empowered to remove the government's deposits for cause and to state his reasons to Congress. But Jackson's Secretary, Louis McLane of Delaware, was in favor of recharter and strongly disapproved of the removals policy. Since the Secretary of State wished to retire from the cabinet, it was decided to promote McLane to that office and appoint a new head of the Treasury department. Jackson conferred with McLane and the new Vice President, Van Buren, regarding the appointment. Van Buren wanted Attorney General Roger Taney to take the office, in order to make room in the cabinet for a New Yorker, Benjamin F. Butler, but it was agreed that political priorities required the selection of a Pennsylvanian.

The President and McLane considered George Dallas, Senator William Wilkins of Pittsburgh, and James Buchanan, but to each Jackson "had what appeared to be insuperable objections, both personal and political." Then while writing to the absent Van Buren describing the qualifications he sought in a Secretary, he appended: "A happy thought has occurred: William J. Duane . . . flashed into my mind, . . . and having named him to Mr. McLane he assures me that his talents in every way, are suited to this situation." As he considered it, the President became more and more pleased at the idea of Duane, "the very person who ought to be selected."[35]

It struck Jackson as especially fitting in his struggle to restore the country to its old republican principles that he should be aided by the son of the courageous editor of the _Aurora_. "I will not conceal from you," he told the younger Duane, my satisfaction "from the reflection that it might serve to elevate" in the country's estimation "a name, which, though in an humbler sphere, had been conspicuous in the early struggles for those principles, which it has always been my desire to cherish and support." William John Duane, who was known to oppose the United States Bank and who had always acted with his father in politics, acknowledged proudly that he had been reared in the old school of democracy and "taught, with almost the rigour of Hamilcar, to entertain an hereditary dislike of all privileged classes." Those who considered his selection for the cabinet agreed that he would bring with him "a great

---

[35]McLane to Van Buren, 26 Nov. 1832, in Van Buren, _Autobiography_, 596-598; Jackson to Van Buren, 25 Nov. 1832, _ibid._, 596.

weight of moral character," for he combined the ideals of a reform Democrat with an impeccable personal reputation.[36]

A year later--after Duane had joined the cabinet, had opposed the President's policy and declined to remove the deposits, had refused to resign and forced the President to dismiss him--there were to be many questions and unspoken recriminations concerning his appointment. Van Buren and others concluded that the strange affair was the result of Secretary McLane's duplicity: that Duane was a secret friend of the Bank, and that McLane knew it and tricked the President into selecting him in order to forward his own views. These suspicions destroyed McLane's role in the cabinet and effectually forced him out of office, but they were without foundation. He was better acquainted with the new Secretary than was anyone else in the President's circle, for his father Allan McLane and Duane Senior had been friends for decades. But he did not know William John's views on the deposits question and certainly had no reason to think that they would favor the Bank. Moreover it was not he but Jackson who most strongly desired the appointment.[37]

The mystery of Duane's conduct has never been fully unravelled. His personal motivations became obscured and lost in the furor that followed the removal of the deposits. The Jacksonians

---

[36] Ibid.; Jackson to W. J. Duane, 17 July 1833, in [W. J. Duane], Narrative, 70; W. J. Duane to Jackson, unsent draft, 19 July 1833, ibid., 82.

[37] Amos Kendall, Autobiography of Amos Kendall, William Stickney, ed. (Boston, 1872), 386-387; Van Buren, Autobiography, 594.

cast him out as an enemy, and the Bank party gladly took him up, temporarily, as its first martyr. To Jackson, Van Buren tossed off the judgment: "Our quondam friend, Duane was either beyond or behind the age." He was at least several years ahead of the Democratic party. Finally, in the painful circumstances that followed the Panic of 1837, it adopted the policy which he had advocated, complete separation of the government from the banking business and currency reform by the use of the national Treasury.[38]

When he entered office on June 1, 1833, Duane was appalled to discover that he was expected by September to transfer the government deposits to state banks. Six months had elapsed from the time he was invited to become Secretary until the actual changes in the cabinet, but he had been told nothing of the fully formulated policy. He felt that he had been summoned to act as an errand boy and was "mortified at the low estimate, which had been formed of the independence of my character." His humiliation was made greater by the manner of the disclosure. Without waiting for the President to inform his new Secretary of executive policy, one of his financial advisers, Reuben Whitney, called on Duane at his lodgings and laid a full account of his duties before him.

This unfortunate beginning keenly affected the relations of President Jackson and the Secretary. It had never occurred to the President that Duane might disagree with him, but he sympathized when he saw the awkwardness of his situation and clearly regretted his failure to tell him. Jackson treated Duane with kindly courtesy

---

[38]Van Buren to Jackson, 27 Sept. 1833, <u>ibid</u>., 607.

and generosity, and their relations were cordial until a day or two before his dismissal. Although he told the Secretary that he wished to take full responsibility for the removals before Congress, he did not until the end instruct him, perhaps from a sense of delicacy, that his duty as a cabinet officer was to subordinate himself to the wishes of the President. Duane adopted and maintained the position that his role must be independent, since Congress had placed the responsibility for removals upon the Secretary of the Treasury. The Senate later agreed with him and censured the President for assuming authority not conferred by law. By his insistence, Duane sought to lend dignity to his situation and to gain time in which to influence a change of policy.[39]

In the few weeks which he was given Duane desperately sought to convince the President of the economic hazards involved in entrusting the deposits to state banks. Jackson's own statements in defense of the measure revealed that he regarded the state bank agency as experimental, but thought it could safely be replaced in the future if necessary. Duane urgently pointed out the high risk and the disastrous consequences of the experiment's failure. He fully agreed with Jackson's estimate of the United States Bank, but "Does not the President see, that, however selfish the U. S. Bank may be, the local banks have not more extended principles of action? Will not the anxiety to make money," he warned, "the ignorance, or

---

[39][W. J. Duane], _Narrative_, 6, 97, 115-116. William J. Duane, _Letters Addressed to the People of the United States, in Vindication of His Conduct_ (Philadelphia, 1834) is a less complete documentary account of the removals.

the imprudence of, particularly remote, local banks, tempt them so to extend their loans, and trade upon the public money," that they will produce financial panic?

Manifestly "the welfare of the people demands, that, instead of being a partner of either, they should be independent of both United States and local banks." In Duane's opinion the question to be considered by government was not which of "two descriptions of monopolies" was "the least pernicious," but how to rescue the people from thralldom. "Those institutions are now so powerful," he argued, "and have such a common interest; men in companies are so prone to do, what as individuals they would scarcely think of," that they would resist any efforts to reform them. Could they be affected at all if there was to be no check on their power? "Or is the evil only to be remedied, by one of those convulsions, in which, as in war, the ruin usually falls on those, who ought to escape?" A few years later, after the banks had tragically confirmed his prediction and indulged in an irresponsible expansion of paper credit and currency which sunk the country into severe depression, Duane commented that the removal of the deposits was not solely to blame for the evils. "The combustibles existed; but, instead of separating and reducing them, the Executive added to the heap and set it on fire."[40]

In stating his reasons for opposing removals, Duane also tried to alert the President to the United States Bank's continuing

---

[40] Narrative, 48, 50, 165n. See also W. J. Duane to Henry Baldwin, 20 July 1833, Reynolds Collection, Allegheny College.

power of retaliation. He disagreed that the measure would enfeeble the institution and shatter its chances for recharter. With its large capital and greatly superior specie position, it could still harasss the local banks and create confusion which would force a renewal. These fears too were borne out by experience. Even while "The gamblers are doing every thing in their power to bend M^r. Duane to their purposes," Nicholas Biddle was preparing for political contingencies by beginning curtailment. He directed the New York branch to "bring the State Banks in debt to you: and for the present it is better that you should do it--than that I should say it: for when once we begin, we shall have many things to do, which will crush the Kitchen Cabinet at once."[41]

"The struggle to be made, is not to see, which can do the other the most harm, the government or the bank," Secretary Duane pleaded. The administration should announce its desire to prepare a substitute for the expiring Bank and ask Congress to commission a general inquiry into the state of the currency. "It is not called upon to maim the bank, lest the bank should master the country." If a Treasury order removing the deposits could render the Bank harmless, he reasoned, it was a sufficient pledge for their safety. "But if it has no such power, is it discreet to commence the war?"

Duane's arguments were dismissed in spite of their cogency because they failed to offer a solution to the President's difficulties with a hostile Congress. The previous Congress had voted to

---

[41]Biddle to Robert Lenox, 30 July 1833, Reginald C. McGrane, ed., The Correspondence of Nicholas Biddle dealing with National Affairs, 1807-1844 (Boston, 1919), 212-213.

recharter the Bank and had resolved overwhelmingly that the public deposits were safe in its keeping. The President had vetoed the renewal, but if they "had remained a week longer in session, two-thirds would have been secured for the bank by corrupt means." Jackson's only chance to reverse the unfriendly attitude was to place his enormous prestige at stake in the struggle. If he took action and came under attack for it in Congress, reluctant Democrats would be forced to rally in his defense. Hence it was considered mandatory to accomplish the removals before the beginning of the next session. It was easy for Duane, as an intelligent and sensible outsider, to see that the President's advisers had devised a political stratagem and convinced themselves that it was a viable monetary policy. But unless he could suggest a politically acceptable alternative, there was no hope of changing the President's decision.[42]

Duane's chief unseen antagonist in the dispute was Amos Kendall, who had first proposed the measure and who apparently analyzed his objections and prepared the President's replies. Before coming to Washington as one of Jackson's personal advisers, Kendall had been a newspaper editor in Kentucky, the "Equal to duane in his best days." "He is a man of great power as a writer," Duane's son agreed, and "it is natural, that the President should lean upon him; and so he has a right to do." Yet William John felt that Kendall and others were making him a victim of "an under current" in Washington, "a sly, whispering, slandering system pursued, that is

---

[42]<u>Narrative</u>, 52, 9.

utterly mischievous and cruel." When Duane was appointed Secretary, Thomas Cooper had commented that he was "a man of plain practical good sense, . . . but he must of necessity in a short time adopt administration morals." Biddle however felt confident that the Philadelphian "will take a decided, firm, manly stand, and will leave his place rather than prostitute it." The kitchen cabinet was already against him, Biddle declared at the end of July, "& will endeavor to expel him," but if he resisted "he may do much to break up this nest of gamblers."[43]

Duane became ill in the anxiety of his circumstances. He had in the past been in poor health from overwork. When he reluctantly and fatalistically accepted the cabinet position, he had told a friend that if he should fail "it will be owing to the niggardliness of nature, in not endowing me with physical vigour." President Jackson returned from vacation in July and summoned the Secretary to the White House for further discussion. But when Jackson and Van Buren saw him they "were both struck with his feeble and emaciated appearance, which . . . we at once attributed to distress of mind." Van Buren could "well remember the kind manner with which the President took both his hands in his own, and gently scolding him for coming out in his actual state of health," told him to return home "and neither to think more of the deposits nor

---

[43]Richard M. Johnson to Jackson, 27 Oct. 1826, Jackson Papers, LC; W. J. Duane to unknown, 23 Aug. 1833, _Narrative_, 130; Cooper to Biddle, 12 July 1833, McGrane, ed., _Correspondence of Nicholas Biddle_, 211-212; Biddle to Cooper, 31 July 1833, _ibid_., 214. See also Biddle to Samuel Swartwout, 30 July 1833, _ibid_., 213; Biddle to Daniel Webster, 13 Aug. 1833, _ibid_., 214-215; Biddle to Cooper, 16 Aug. 1833, _ibid_., 215.

to come to him again until he was perfectly well."[44]

Duane's effort to forestall removals reached its climax in late July, when the President sent Kendall on a mission to the northern cities to inquire what arrangements might be made with the state banks for accepting the deposits. The Secretary upon request drew up instructions for the agent, but Kendall strongly objected to their tentative nature. If the bankers were invited to submit their opinions, he reasoned, they would uphold the United States Bank, but they would accept if they were merely presented with a business proposition. Jackson allowed him to modify the terms to suit himself, and Kendall set off "virtually self-instructed." The alteration of the instructions changed the mission's character from a supposed inquiry into an act putting the removals policy into operation. Duane knew this, but he deluded himself that the decision might yet be reversed. He told the President, at this point in their relations, that if he could not concur with executive policy he would resign from the cabinet. If he had done so immediately, it would have been an honorable retirement, for he had done all that he could to change the President's mind.

But Duane continued in office, and "I am just beginning to feel," he wrote in late August, "that, in this station, I might 'do the state some service.'" When Kendall returned he declared his mission a complete success, but Duane thought it "abortive, in all the particulars, which had been deemed essential." Several of "the

---

[44]W. J. Duane to James Ronaldson, 6 Feb. 1833, Narrative, 4-5; Van Buren, Autobiography, 602-603. See also W. J. Duane to Henry Baldwin, 20 July 1833, Reynolds Collection, Allegheny College.

most substantial institutions" refused to serve as fiscal agents, and some banks which agreed to act showed by their answers that "they ought not to be trusted." In all, "The banks, most ready to become depositories, showed the least ability to pay their own responsibilities in coin."[45]

As the President prepared to submit Kendall's favorable report to the cabinet, the Secretary urgently sought a postponement, in order to gain time in which to formulate a substitute bank agency. He and the President had discussed his suggestion that the federal government manage its own fiscal affairs and provide for control of the currency. But Jackson told him that he had earlier proposed such a solution himself, and the plan had been rejected because of the fears of excessive political patronage. Now time was running out, the President told him, and no further delay was possible.[46]

Duane continued to agitate the question of such an organization of the Treasury, and especially sought the ideas and counsel of his father. The President, when he passed through Philadelphia, had asked Colonel Duane to submit his opinions on the issue, and he repeated the request later. But the retired editor declined the opportunity in order to avoid hindering his son's freedom. Jackson was certain that the elder Duane would agree with him and frequently urged the Secretary to consult his father; and he told Duane of his own wish to elevate the public memory of the editor. William

---

[45]Kendall, Autobiography, 378-381; Narrative, 84-92, 96, 131.

[46]Ibid., 173. See Govan, Biddle, 122-131.

John confessed that such expressions "of all that you could have used, were most likely to lead me to the designated point--but I am not permitted to subject my judgment beneath my feelings."

Colonel Duane encouraged his son's determination to stay in office, because he believed that he was preparing a scheme for an independent treasury system, which would defeat the unrestrained issue of paper money. "Having said so much on a subject which I can never tire in execrating; I most heartily approve of your plan," he wrote in August. But William John did not really have a plan, only ideas and suggestions, and as his anxiety mounted he began to forget what had been discussed and to repeat himself. Your proposals for "local depositories" or "deputy-treasuries" have my entire confidence, his father reminded him, as William John sought new assurances. "I think if you were to make a project of this description, in some methodical form, and submit it to the President," he advised on September 3, "the effect would be good."[47]

A week later President Jackson asked the cabinet to come to a final determination. After hearing the members' views, he submitted to them on September 18 a state paper which called upon the Secretary of the Treasury to order the removal of the deposits, acting upon the responsibility of the President. Duane remained in conversation with him after the others departed, and Jackson earnestly told him, he recalled, "that, 'if I would stand by him it would be the happiest day of his life.'" The Secretary now had only a

---

[47]<u>Narrative</u>, 10n., 82, 111n.; W. J. Duane from [Duane?], 19 Aug., 3 Sept. 1833, <u>ibid</u>., 175.

few hours remaining in which to determine his final course of action. He never seriously considered carrying out the removals, but he had to decide whether he should resign voluntarily.

He thought that the events of the past two months released him from any agreement, but he felt "a lurking reluctance . . . to refuse to resign, after having said that I would." He had become a subject of newspaper speculation and attack, impugning his motives and suggesting that he was a tool of the United States Bank. Kendall, on his mission to interview the banks, had talked very freely to trusted Jacksonians, and hostile paragraphs on Duane followed in the wake of his travels. The exception was Philadelphia, where to his chagrin James Gordon Bennett of _The Pennsylvanian_ attacked Kendall instead.

If the President had requested his resignation in writing he would have complied, but he thought it perhaps too great a sacrifice to make an "unconditional surrender." Because of the gossip and political disgrace, he wanted to stand before public opinion with his position clearly defined. "My feelings were the natural effects of a deep sense of the value of reputation," he readily acknowledged. Unlike his father, he could not be consoled by self respect alone. His personality in many ways was a reaction to that of his father. Whereas Duane Senior was highly emotional, intemperate, and quick to judge, William John was mild, calm, and almost compulsively fair minded. He had been reared to set a high value on public service, but he did not have his father's love of political life. "I have through life sought the shade," he had protested when first offered the cabinet position, "and whenever I have been out of it, it has not been from choice. I have always desired to tread on the earth, lest, in ascending even a single step of the political ladder, I should be obliged to resume my former place." He admitted, "Perhaps this is morbid pride, but be it what it may, it has a powerful influence over me."

On September 18 after the cabinet meeting he returned to his lodgings and began to prepare a defensive exposition. As he wrote and pondered "I certainly looked around, and in vain, for some friendly countenance." The next morning when a messenger from the President inquired if he had come to a decision, he replied that he had "deemed it right, as I have not a friend here to advise me, to ask the counsel of my father at this crisis: I wrote to him last night, and am sure that nothing but sickness will prevent his presence to-morrow night." But later that day Major Donelson called to tell him that the President proposed to publish the decision in the *Globe* the next day. "It would seem to me but delicate," the Secretary replied, "to defer such an act, *until I shall either concur or decline*." Nonetheless the announcement appeared on Friday, September 20. "When the President took that step . . . my scruples vanished--," he recalled, "an oppressive weight was removed from my heart--and I spontaneously refused to remove the deposites, or resign."[48]

He wrote a somewhat embittered memorandum to Jackson which

---

[48] *Narrative*, 3, 98, 100, 104-112, 111n. See also Kendall, *Autobiography*, 382-383; Govan, *Biddle*, 239.

made the President angry, and for the first time their personal relations became unfriendly. "Unluckily my father did not arrive," he explained to Donelson, "until some hours, after I had gone to the President & given to him a communication written without the advice of any body." The President returned it, "as having some thing improper in it, a matter I did not intend, but excusable under the painful state in which I have been." He had sent a second letter in place of it, "but my father tells me this morning, that my course in it he in some measure disapproves, and that, without injustice to myself, I may pursue another more satisfactory to the Pres^{t}." He asked Donelson to use his good offices, "and I will make another effort to end this unhappy business less unfavourably." But Jackson was at last offended, and on September 23 he terminated their relations curtly: "I feel myself constrained to notify you that your further services as secretary of the treasury are no longer required."[49]

One of the supreme ironies of the strange affair in political history known as the Bank War was that the son of William Duane was identified as an enemy of Jackson and the son of Alexander James Dallas as his stanch friend. George Dallas, whose father was the creator of the Second Bank of the United States, in 1829 had thought that he saw in a party measure against one of the branches a "result favorable to the stability and duration of the Bank:--as it will indicate a determination to uphold the institution, provided it be properly conducted." But a month later when Jackson

---

[49] W. J. Duane to A. J. Donelson, 23 Sept. 1833, Donelson Papers, LC.

announced his opposition to recharter, Dallas quickly agreed that a national bank "as a measure of war or of extreme necessity . . . might become constitutional and expedient:--but not otherwise:--and I cannot help thinking that such was my father's view of the matter."[50]

George Dallas became a Senator from Pennsylvania in 1831, and he almost certainly intended to vote for recharter. He seemed "disposed to give all the aid he can" to the Bank's friends and promised to "help along" in influencing the Pennsylvanians in the House of Representatives. But when the Bank decided to apply for a charter in the 1832 session, during a presidential election year and in the face of a threatened veto, Dallas drew back from his position and took the path of political loyalty. Although he thought that the removal of the deposits was "ill-timed and unnecessary," and he had no general views against the Bank, he nonetheless convinced himself that the arrogance of Biddle was sufficient cause for its destruction. "I mourn over its downfall, as over the offspring of my father:--but I think I can perceive," he wrote to the wavering Pennsylvania Governor, that its directors had perverted its principles and thrown away "the very grappling irons which my father had given them to hold on to popular favor and good-will."[51]

W. J. Duane, who was ostracized by the Democrats, came far

---

[50]Govan, Biddle, 115-119; Dallas to S. D. Ingham, 9 Nov., 9 Dec. 1829, Dallas Papers, HSP.

[51]Dallas to George Wolf, 27 Feb., 2 Mar. 1834, Wolf Papers, HSP; Thomas Cadwalader to Biddle, 20 Dec. 1831, McGrane, ed., Correspondence of Nicholas Biddle, 147. See also Cadwalader to Biddle, 21, 22, 23, 24, 25, 26 Dec. 1831, ibid., 147-161.

closer to sharing and expressing the real wishes of Andrew Jackson than did countless party members who fell into line behind the President. In the long political wrangle that followed the removal of the deposits, he became a mere symbol for both sides in the Bank War, and no one was interested in knowing what his opinions had been. The loss of his perspective on the policy tended to obscure an understanding of its motives. The quarrel for a time became the national bank versus state banks and, as Duane had predicted, the United States Bank maintained that it had acted as an indispensable regulator of the currency. Duane always denied that the Bank ever served this role. In proof he cited the simple fact that in 1791 there were three banks of issue and in 1837 there were more than six hundred, and that a United States Bank had been in operation during forty of those forty-six years. Moreover the Bank "had no patriotic design as has been attributed to it," he insisted; if it excluded local paper, it was not for the public good but because its circulation "interfered with its own profits."

The two Duanes, Andrew Jackson, and countless American citizens had opposed all banks of issue and desired a return to hard money. And the shareholders of state banks, at least in the eastern cities, had generally favored the national institution. Among politicians, for example, Joel Sutherland was hated by the Working Men because he had consistently aided bank incorporations in the legislature. He also labored diligently, in cooperation with Biddle, to secure the United States Bank's recharter. Yet when he was forced to declare himself for or against Jackson, Sutherland, like

Dallas, found political loyalty advisable.

In 1837 when the Democratic administration introduced a plan for an independent treasury, a newspaper rumored that Duane had suggested it when he was Secretary. Friends of the United States Bank, who had honored him for his stand against Jackson, wrote to inquire if the story were true that he had favored separation of the government from all banks. He acknowledged it was, but said that he had not put forward a formal system. It was clear that he approved of the plan now offered. "I did not differ from the late President, on points now agitated," he emphasized. Nor should they be surprised or censorious, he chided, for "When you commended me, in 1833, what was it that you praised? Surely not abandonment, but my maintenance of the right of opinion."[52]

---

[52]W. J. Duane to unknown, 3 Nov. 1837, Narrative, 163-176. On Sutherland see Mechanics' Free Press, 15 Aug. 1829; Govan, Biddle, 150-151, 187.

CONCLUSION

On the Fourth of July 1834 the old editor William Duane took up the *Aurora* again at the age of seventy-five to uphold the President in his struggle against the Bank and to proclaim his conviction that Jackson's cause was "nothing more nor less than OLD FASHIONED JEFFERSONIAN DEMOCRACY." The talk of "*putting down*" Jackson was "but a repetition of the *old story* of 1798," and "The identity of *Federalism* and *Bankism*, becomes every day more striking." "It is not Jackson that is personally meant,--it is *Democracy*, and the Constitution, personified and slandered in him, as they were personified and slandered in JEFFERSON thirty years ago." Although "The practical *tory* professes to become a *whig*," the essential philosophy remained the same, that the propertied interests rightfully formed a privileged ruling class. In contrast Jackson avowed, as Jefferson had done before him, that "The blessings of Government, like the dews of heaven, should be dispensed alike on the rich and the poor."[1]

Duane had a uniquely "favourable position" from which to see and reveal these political parallels, and "the every-day evidence of how little the present generation knows of their own country, subsequent to the Revolution," was "Among the many incitements which led to the revival of the Aurora." He had earlier contem-

---

[1]*Aurora*, 4 Oct., 1 Aug., 27 Sept. 1834.

plated writing his "'Observations of Critical Times,'--or, 'A History of Federalism.' The purpose was not carried out," however, "because for many years the public mind has been lulled into security, almost to indifference, by the incomparable prosperity," and the tranquillity of society. But the crisis of the Bank War, in which "The issue, in a word, is SHALL THE PEOPLE RULE, OR BE RULED?" had fortunately aroused "the redeeming spirit of Democracy." Now the aging editor asked his readers again "to reflect on the enviable position we hold, as a free people, on a blessed portion of this globe." Americans possessed "more of liberty, and less of the afflictions, which too often fall to the lot of man, in society, than in any other portion of this earth. Having it, and enjoying it, we must watch over it," remembering that "vigilance is a cheap price for happiness."[2]

Jacksonian editors everywhere were delighted with the wholehearted support of the President by the famous Jeffersonian editor. The Albany *Argus*, long the public spokesman for Vice President Martin Van Buren, declared that "It dates, with great appropriateness, from the 4th of July," and that "we cannot too highly recommend the AURORA to the perusal and patronage of the Democracy of the Union." The opening address "'to the American People,' is a masterly sketch of the origin and course of political parties in this country--in which the true divisions are pointed out--the name and tendency of each illustrated, and the disguises" of Federalism exposed. "The parallel also between the 'Reign of Terror,' and the present Reign

---

[2]*Ibid.*, 6 Sept., 30, 16 Aug. 1834.

of Senatorial and Bank Corruption . . . is drawn with great force and cogency."[3]

Nothing was written in the *Aurora* or in the friendly Jacksonian press about the question that was naturally uppermost in the public mind: what were the relations between the old Colonel and William John, the disgraced Secretary of the Treasury? The editor had always cherished his closeness to his eldest son above all his family ties; yet he condemned the improper control over the federal deposits by the Treasury department as freely as if it were a mere abstract principle involving a stranger. When Duane came out of retirement, "the Whigs generally supposed that he intended to advocate the wounded honor of his house," and were shocked to discover "that he intended to 'go the entire swine' for Jackson, Kendall, [Thomas Hart] Benton, and the whole forty-thousand pampered underlings of the administration." They angrily reacted by reviving the charge that "this same 'venerable Duane' was *a reviler and slanderer of the beloved Washington!*"[4]

Duane's only response to prying newspaper comments was to deplore the intrusion by journalists into wholly private concerns. He admitted that many unworthy, "contemptible artifices" had been tried to persuade him to relinquish his plans, "among which it is painful . . . to discover the *hands of false friends*." And "Some of the Bank Directors," he reported, had "manifested . . . much

---

[3]*The* (Philadelphia) *Pennsylvanian*, 12 July 1834.

[4]Unidentified newspaper clipping, Duane folder, Misc. Papers, NYPL. See also *The Pennsylvanian*, 5 Aug. 1834.

concern" for his health. One "Director (an old acquaintance) assured one of his friends, that the editor of the Aurora was so very old, that he was feeble in body and mind--in his dotage or second childhood; and nothing to be feared from him!" Whether he "will continue of the same opinion long, we shall see," Duane promised.[5]

The personal relationship between father and son must have been strained by the public disagreement on a matter which so deeply involved William John's feelings and his reputation. Yet there is nothing to indicate that the two were estranged by the experience. William John's recollections of his father, in his published Narrative on the deposits issue, were as affectionate and respectful as if the episode had never happened. The son had returned to the practice of law after his return to Philadelphia, but for some reason, upon "the death of his father, . . . he retired to private life" and had "ever since remained secluded," until his own death in 1865.[6]

The new Aurora reviewed the editor's interests and opinions with the familiar vigor and insight. The case for hard money, of course, was argued extensively, and reinforced with articles from Frank Blair's Globe and speeches by Benton, Roger Taney, Silas Wright and others. The sad history of Irish suppression was a fre-

---

[5]Duane, "Circular," Nov. 1834, "Letters of Wm. Duane," Mass. Hist. Soc. Procs., 2d series, XX, 393; Aurora, 19 July 1834.

[6]Obituary of W. J. Duane, [New York Herald, 26 Sept. 1865], William J. Duane folder, Miscellaneous Papers, NYPL. [Duane], Biog. Memoir of W. J. Duane, 26, is wrong in the s tatement that he retired immediately upon his return to Philadelphia, judging from Franklin Bache to Albert Dabadic, draft, 24 Oct. 1835, Franklin Bache Papers, HSP.

quent topic, and Duane expressed his disdain for religious zealotry with unusual frankness and vehemence. His great curiosity about the future was undiminished. "The growth of knowledge is the most remarkable characteristic of this age," he commented. "No great public movement now affects Europe," he acknowledged, but shared the view of a distinguished Frenchman that "Europe is hastening to Democracy," for "The first paragraph of the Declaration of Independence, has become the attractive point of civilized man."[7]

Duane published his little bi-weekly journal from his house in Elizabeth street, working by himself from dawn until ten in the morning and from two o'clock until sunset. He had no advertisers and asked his subscribers to bring in their payments since he could not afford to hire a boy to make collections. Although he maintained that the subscription was "*going ahead* wonderfully," he apologetically declined the requests to exchange papers with Jacksonian editors throughout the country because "the claims of this kind, already exceed our actual subscription!" By November he still had fewer than 350 subscribers and needed at least 400 more to continue; "500 would be preferable," and "if it were 5000 I should apply it--not to my own use--for a man of 75 has few wants and no motives of ambition beyond the consolations of the past." He asked for volunteers to help him reach the sturdy Jacksonian yeomen, for "The AURORA must not depend upon a corrupt city, but upon an honest country," if his forty years of "consistency and

---

[7]*Aurora*, 19 July, 30 Aug. 1834.

rectitude" were to receive a hearing.[8]

In January he was forced by lack of funds to suspend publication, and when he resumed in March, he was able to go on for only a few weeks longer. Six months after his second retirement from the Aurora, on November 24, 1835, the seventy-six year old Revolutionary editor died at his home in Philadelphia. He was buried in Ronaldson's cemetery, later named the North Laurel Hill cemetery, in the city to which he had given distinguished public service as a journalist throughout his years in America.[9]

---

[8] Ibid., 1, 16 Aug. 1834; Duane, "Circular," Nov. 1834, "Letters of Wm. Duane," Mass. Hist. Soc. Procs., 2d series, XX, 393-394.

[9] Clark, "William Duane," Records of the Columbia Hist. Soc., IX, 61-62.

BIBLIOGRAPHY

The more important sources that contribute to Duane's biography are described briefly below. Additional sources that were of limited use are cited in the text.

MANUSCRIPTS

William Duane did not generally save his letters, except those from Thomas Jefferson, which became widely scattered after his death. Consequently there is no body of Duane papers, either in public or private possession. The small collection of family papers formerly held by Mr. Morris Duane of Philadelphia is now to be found in the library of the American Philosophical Society and in the Historical Society of Pennsylvania. The Thomas Jefferson Papers, Library of Congress, contain the largest group of letters to and from Duane, ranging in date from 1801 through 1825, and are an indispensable source for every phase of the author's career in America.

The Library of Congress also holds a random assortment of about a dozen of Duane's letters in its Personal Paper Miscellaneous, and there are several letters from him in the James Madison Papers. The David Baille Warden Papers there contain valuable correspondence from Duane concerning his relations with the Madison administration, and his personal affairs in the crisis of 1811. The New York Public Library has a small collection of Miscellaneous Papers on Duane, which is particularly useful for the sedition period. The James Monroe Papers there contain highly valuable letters from the editor. A group of Duane's letters to Caesar A. Rodnet in the General Manuscripts Collection of Columbia University is illuminating on the strife in Philadelphia with the Quid and the emerging Quadroon factions, and also useful concerning the personal affairs of the editor.

The record of Duane's conflicts with the British officials in India during his years as a journalist there was compiled in 1823 for the Court of Directors of the East India Company, for the purpose of justifying the policy of newspaper censorship in the colony which was then under attack by public opinion. It may be found in the India Office Records, Home Miscellaneous Series, Volume 537, at the Library of the India Office, Commonwealth Relations Office, London. The Francis Place Papers of the London Corresponding Society, British Museum, contain relevant material on the protest following the introduction into Parliament of the treason and sedition acts of 1795, but do not mention Duane's role in those events, nor do the extant membership lists indicate that he was a member of the society. The papers, incidentally, do contain valuable material on the political activities of John Binns until his acquittal for treason and his departure for America.

The Diary of William Wood Thackara in the Historical Society of Pennsylvania contains an important letter from Duane to James Thackara and describes Duane's situation in Philadelphia before he became editor of the *Aurora*. The British State Papers, Robert Liston Correspondence, Library of Congress, contains numerous illuminating comments by Liston to Lord Grenville on the Senate's prosecution of Duane, on the gubernatorial election of 1799 in Pennsylvania, and on the presidential election of 1800, especially as it affected the personal and political behavior of President Adams. Other collections in the Library of Congress which contain pertinent material on the Federalist party's attitudes toward Duane and the Republicans generally are the Papers of Robert Goodloe Harper, James McHenry (photostate, second series), William Plumer, and William Loughton Smith. On this subject the James A. Bayard Letter-book, New York Public Library, has some relevant material, as do the Timothy Pickering Papers and the Harrison Gray Otis Papers in the Massachusetts Historical Society.

On the relations of the Pennsylvania Republicans to the national administration, the most important sources are the Thomas Jefferson Papers, Library of Congress, and the Albert Gallatin Papers, New York Historical Society, which contain important correspondence with A. J. Dallas. James Madison did not have close ties with the state, but his correspondence with Pennsylvanians in the James Madison Papers, Library of Congress, is useful on questions of patronage and administration policy. The William C. Rives Collection of Madison Papers, Library of Congress, contains a fascinating 1801 letter from Wilson Cary Nicholas which shows the inherent moderate-radical split in Republican thinking generally, first made public in Pennsylvania. There are several pertinent items in the Thomas Jefferson Papers, Massachusetts Historical Society.

The Minutes of the Democratic Society of Pennsylvania, 1793-1794, Historical Society of Pennsylvania, are illuminating as a background for understanding the later conflicts within the party. The Society Miscellaneous Collection of Leib-Harrison Family Papers, Historical Society of Pennsylvania, contains several letters from Michael Leib to his sister Lydia, written in the 1790s, which contribute to an understanding of his personality and ambitions. The pertinent material on the Federalist party's attitudes toward Duane and the Republicans generally are the Papers of Robert Goodloe Harper, James McHenry (photostate, second series), William Plumer, and William Loughton Smith. On this subject the James A. Bayard Letter-book, New York Public Library, has some relevant material, as do the Timothy Pickering Papers and the Harrison Gray Otis Papers in the Massachusetts Historical Society.

On the relations of the Pennsylvania Republicans to the national administration, the most important sources are the Thomas Jefferson Papers, Library of Congress, and the Albert Gallatin Papers, New York Historical Society, which contain important correspondence with A. J. Dallas. James Madison did not have close ties with the state, but his correspondence with Pennsylvanians in the James Madison Papers, Library of Congress, is useful on questions of patronage and administration policy. The William C. Rives Collection of Madison Papers, Library of Congress, contains a fascinating 1801 letter from Wilson Cary Nicholas which shows the inherent moderate-radical split in Republican thinking generally, first made public in Pennsylvania. There are several pertinent items in the Thomas Jefferson Papers, Massachusetts Historical Society.

The Minutes of the Democratic Society of Pennsylvania, 1793-1794, Historical Society of Pennsylvania, are illuminating as a background for understanding the later conflicts within the party. The Society Miscellaneous Collection of Leib-Harrison Family Papers, Historical Society of Pennsylvania, contains several letters from Michael Leib to his sister Lydia, written in the 1790s, which contribute to an understanding of his personality and ambitions. The

Henley-Smith Family Papers, Library of Congress, contain some slight but inadequate leads on the well patronized Samuel Harrison Smith. The James Monroe Papers, Library of Congress, are not generally useful for this study, but do contain a number of letters from the elusive Senator Stevens Thomson Mason, which show the political intimacy of those two Virginians.

The Historical Society of Pennsylvania is a rich source of material on Republican politics, in widely scattered collections. The Society Collection, the Simon Gratz Collection, and the Ferdinand J. Dreer Collection, are the most useful of the general collections. The Lea and Febiger Papers contain some pertinent material. The Dallas Papers, which are not extensive for A. J. Dallas, the Thomas McKean Papers, and the George Logan Papers, contribute to an understanding of the Quids. The Uselma Clarke Smith Collection of William Jones Papers comprises his official correspondence largely, but includes a few letters of value on the Quid-Democratic rivalry. Some observations on the developing schism by a neutral observer are in the William Irvine Papers.

The correspondence of Duane and Leib with Caesar A. Rodney, which stopped soon after he became a member of the administration as Attorney General, is fragmentary but highly valuable for understanding the Democrats in Philadelphia. Most important for this study are the Rodney Papers in the Delaware Historical Society. The Rodney Family Papers in the Library of Congress and in the New York Public Library contain some relevant material on the Quid-Democratic split in Pennsylvania, but no Duane or Leib correspondence. The small group of Joseph Clay Papers, New York Public Library, includes letters from Duane and his son to the Congressman. The Papers of Joseph Hiester in the Gregg Collection, Library of Congress, and the Manuscripts Collection of the Library Company of Philadelphia, contain occasional items of interest.

The John Randolph-James M. Garnett Letterbook in the John Randolph Papers, Library of Congress, contains frequent comments on Duane and is especially helpful on the presidential election of 1808. It is supplemented by related material in the Joseph Nicholson Papers, Library of Congress. The Wilson Cary Nicholas Papers, Library of Congress, are primarily useful for Virginia politics, but contain pertinent material on the election of 1808. The Smiths of Maryland did not leave much evidence behind them by which to follow their factional activities. The Papers of Samuel Smith, Library of Congress, contain a few letters relative to the incipient Northern Democratic alliance against the Madison administration, but no letters from Leib and no links with Duane. Duane's friendship and later political quarrel with Secretary of War Dearborn is revealed in the Henry Dearborn Personal Papers Miscellaneous, Library of Congress, and the Henry Dearborn Papers, Massachusetts Historical Society. The correspondence of Thomas Jefferson and William Wirt in 1811 on the subject of arranging financial help for Duane in Virginia may be found in the William Wirt Papers, Maryland Historical Society. The Papers of Gideon and Francis Granger, Library of Congress, contain an important letter on Leib's appointment as Postmaster of Philadelphia in 1814.

On the differences among the Democrats of Pennsylvania, the most important sources are the Jonathan Roberts Papers and the Charles Jared Ingersoll Collection in the Historical Society of Pennsylvania. Roberts was an independent-minded Snyderite whose letters from Harrisburg documented the Leib-Boileau rivalry in the legislature. His general reflections on these events may be found in the Jonathan Roberts' Memoirs, 1799-1830, Historical Society of Pennsylvania. The extensive, often amusing correspondence of Richard Rush is a rich source of material on the New School party of Philadelphia. Most important are his letters to C. J. Ingersoll in the Ingersoll Collection. These are supplemented by his letters to his father in the Benjamin Rush Papers, Library Company of Philadelphia. The Historical Society of Pennsylvania has a small collection of Richard Rush Papers, 1812-1847, and there are a number of his letters in the Lewis Biddle Collection there. The Society also has one volume of the Correspondence of Simon Snyder, 1808-1817, consisting mostly of letters to N. B. Boileau, and there is a small group of John Binns' letters in the Jones and Clarke Papers.

For the War of 1812, there are more extant letters of William Duane than for any other period. The Allan McLane Papers, New York Historical Society, and the Daniel Parker Papers, Historical Society of Pennsylvania, contain a rich account of Duane's military ideas, his difficulties as Adjutant General, and his relations with the War department under Secretary John Armstrong. James Wilkinson's papers are widely scattered, and I have not discovered any existing correspondence between Duane and the General. However the

James Wilkinson Papers in the Chicago Historical Society and in Darlington Memorial Library, University of Pittsburgh, contain interesting material revealing Wilkinson's political connection with Samuel Smith of Maryland. There are pertinent letters of General Zebulon Pike in the Charles B. Pike Collection, Chicago Historical Society. The James Barbour Papers, New York Public Library, and the Pierpont Morgan Library, New York, contain correspondence relating to Duane's promotion of Fulton's torpedo.

The John Sergeant Papers, Historical Society of Pennsylvania, are an important source on postwar anti-caucus politics in Pennsylvania. The James Buchanan Papers there do not include much material for this early period, but contain relevant correspondence connecting anti-caucus men such as Hugh Hamilton and Stephen Simpson with Buchanan's "Amalgamation" or anti-Family wing of the Democratic party. The Henry Baldwin Papers in the Crawford County Historical Society, Meadville, Pennsylvania, are primarily for local history, but contain a few items of general interest, including an unsigned letter from William Duane. Baldwin's political correspondence may be found in the John Earle Reynolds Collection, Reis Library, Allegheny College, Meadville.

The Historical Society of Pennsylvania holds several important collections for the story of the Family party. The letters of George M. Dallas in the Dallas Papers are a rich source of detailed information for Philadelphia especially, from 1819 onwards. The Lewis S. Coryell Papers contain the correspondence of prominent Findlayites. The Mathew Carey correspondence in the Edward Carey

Gardiner Collection deals largely with tariff promotion, but includes occasional letters of wider political interest. The hostility to Governor Findlay among old Snyderites is revealed in the George Bryan Papers and the Jonathan Roberts Papers, which also contain important material on Jackson's nomination in 1824. The George Wolf Papers, including extensive correspondence from G. M. Dallas and Joel Sutherland, are an important source for Democratic politics in the late 1820s. Various clues to Nicholas Biddle's early association with the Family party may be found in the Nicholas Biddle Papers, Library of Congress, and the Nicholas Biddle Personal Letters on film at the Historical Society of Pennsylvania. There are Miscellaneous Manuscripts of Charles Jared Ingersoll in the New York Historical Society.

On Clintonian politics, the DeWitt Clinton Papers, Columbia University; the DeWitt Clinton Diary, New York Historical Society, and the small group of DeWitt Clinton Papers, New York Public Library, have provided fragmentary leads to the New Yorker's associations in Pennsylvania. The Azariah C. Flagg Papers, New York Public Library, and the rich collection of political correspondence in the John W. Taylor Papers, New York Historical Society, contain pertinent commentary on Clinton's presidential ambitions.

The Andrew Jackson Papers and the Andrew Jackson Donelson Papers, Library of Congress, include important letters from William John Duane and Stephen Simpson. The Andrew Jackson-William B. Lewis Papers, New York Public Library, contain a significant letter from Lewis to Simpson for understanding the role of the *Columbian Observer* in the election of 1824.

NEWSPAPERS

The *Aurora*, which Duane published daily for twenty years with only a brief interruption during the war, is of course the most important source for his biography. The Burney Collection, British Museum, contains incomplete files of the two newspapers which Duane worked on in London, the *General Advertiser* and the *Telegraph*. Their general editorial positions coincided with his own views in this period, but they do not disclose any link to Duane personally. The Calcutta *World* is indispensable for understanding the development of Duane's political philsophy. The Library of the India Office, Commonwealth Relations Office, London, contains a file of this paper for 1791-1793.

Philadelphia newspapers of all parties and factions are necessary for a broad understanding of Duane's role in city and state politics. Among the Federalist organs, the *Gazette of the United States* is by far the most important politically. It changed its name to the *United States Gazette* in 1804, and merged with the *True American* in 1818 to form the *Union*. Enos Bronson took over as editor in 1801 and continued as the spokesman of official Federalism for two decades. *Porcupine's Gazette* is indispensable for the early period, before William Cobbett's departure from America in 1799. It is particularly illuminating on the dissension between Hamiltonians and Adams Federalists, and on the nascent Quid-Democratic split in the Republican party. The *True American* and *Poulson's American Daily Advertiser*, both published over the whole period, are commercially oriented, but occasionally useful on politics. The National Gazette and Literary Register, established in 1820 and edited by Robert Walsh, is a second generation Federalist newspaper, the local organ of John Quincy Adams. It is a neutral and amused observer of the city's quarreling "Jacksonians" in 1824.

Several smaller, quasi-Federalist papers are illuminating on the emotional attitudes toward the Democrats. The nativist hostility to the Duane-Leib party is clearly revealed in Richard Folwell's Spirit of the Press, founded in 1805, and the Tickler, established in 1807 by George Helmbold. Both editors were keen followers of Democratic in-fighting, and provide numerous insights into the sources of New School-Old School division. During the War of 1812 a number of short-lived newspapers were founded in Philadelphia. The Corrector and American Weekly Review, of which there is only one extant copy, and the Voice of the Nation, reveal the resurgence of nativism, combining patriotism in the war effort with resentment of Irish jingoism. After the war Helmbold established a somewhat tamer journal of ridicule, the Independent Balance, 1817-1823. It was not friendly to the Old School, but its main target was the Family party and Findlayite corruption.

The Quids established the Freeman's Journal in 1804 as an attempt to counter the Aurora's influence, and it was the spokesman for McKean and the Constitution in the gubernatorial election of 1805. After that, Editor William McCorkle fell back to his pro-Federalist sympathies, which had been an embarrassment to his political sponsors. Following the War of 1812, the paper became loosely associated with the Family party, but was primarily a commercial organ. John Binns' Democratic Press, established in 1807, was the official organ of the New School Democrats until Governor Snyder's retirement; after 1817 it was hostile to Governor Findlay and the Family party. It supported Crawford in 1824, and then became allied with John Quincy Adams' administration. Binns retired during Jackson's first administration, but continued to hold Whig sympathies. The Franklin Gazette was founded in 1818 as the organ of the Family party, supporting Findlay and Schulze in the state and Calhoun in national politics, until forced to capitulate to Jackson in early 1824. John Norvell, who had succeeded Richard Bache, Jr., as editor, was driven out of business by financial troubles soon after that election. Jacob Frick's American Sentinel, which had been a second string Family paper, became the party's chief organ in the late 1820s. The Pennsylvania Inquirer in that period represented a coalition of anti-Family Jacksonians, but did not noticeably involve William John Duane or his father. The Mechanics Free Press, 1829-1831, is of great interest for its reflection of Old School issues and influences. The Pennsylvanian, established in 1833, intensely anti-Bank and pro-Jackson, honored William Duane for his stand on principle.

The Old School viewpoint was represented in several evening newspapers, supplementing the morning Aurora, during the years just before the war when Duane was not actively interested in state politics. The Pennsylvania Democrat, 1809-1810, was published by a penitent Quadroon, Joseph Lloyd, who exposed the tactics of the

Snyderites in organizing against Duane and Leib. The *Evening Star*, 1810, was founded to help the Old School in that crucial local election, and it provides valuable insights into the members' differences with the New Schoolers on economic issues. In 1812 the *Whig Chronicle* and the *Star of Liberty*, supporting DeWitt Clinton and James Madison respectively, revealed the division within the party on the presidential election. The *American Democratic Herald*, 1814-1815, published by Andrew Mitchell, had an Old School editorial position on state politics.

Stephen Simpson edited four newspapers during these years. Most important is the *Columbian Observer*, 1822-1825, which led the campaign to nominate Jackson within Pennsylvania, and was considered to be a key organ for him nationally. The *National Chronicle*, 1825, was a continuation under a different name, and concentrated heavily on the "corrupt bargain" issue. The *Philadelphia Mercury*, 1827-1829, did not attain the stature of Simpson's earlier paper, since Jackson's bandwagon was crowded by the campaign of 1828. Simpson emphasized unity and sacrifice for the candidate, even opposing the Working Men's movement, but began to express his bitterness about the Family's domination of the Jackson party soon after the election. The *Pennsylvania Whig* opposed the President for reelection in 1832, expressing Simpson's personal disillusionment with Jackson, and endorsed the Anti-Masonic ticket.

A few newspapers published elsewhere than Philadelphia have been useful. James Cheetham's *American Citizen*, New York City, had editorial views very similar to those of Duane during the first years of Jefferson's administration. Niles' Weekly Register of Baltimore furnishes a variety of useful information on national issues and politics during the Monroe administration. Hugh Hamilton's Harrisburg Chronicle is of great interest for a study of Old School principles and anti-caucus politics outside the city. The Pittsburgh Gazette, a Federalist-Hiester organ, shows a different side of the anti-caucus coalition.

PUBLISHED SOURCES

The "Letters of William Duane," Massachusetts Historical Society Proceedings, 2d series, XX (1907), 257-394, contain his letters to Thomas Jefferson, to James Madison, and his Personal Papers, Miscellaneous, in the Library of Congress. In addition to his newspaper, Duane published a number of pamphlets and books on subjects of political and intellectual interest to him. In chronological order they are: A Letter to George Washington, President of the United States: Containing Strictures on His Address of the Seventeenth of September, 1796, Notifying His Relinquishment of the Presidential Office (Philadelphia, 1796), in which Duane replied to the farewell appeal against party spirit with an eloquent defense of free speech and association as essential to the protection of civil liberty, based upon his own recent experience of suppression of dissent in England under the government of William Pitt. The history of the French Revolution which he wrote on commission after arriving in the United States was published as the fourth volume of John Gifford, The History of France, from the Earliest Times Till the Death of Louis Sixteenth . . . and Continued from the Above Period until the Conclusion of the Present War, by a Citizen of the United States (Philadelphia, 1796-1798).

Duane's account of the riot in St. Mary's churchyard and the trial following is contained in A Report of the Extraordinary Transactions which Took Place at Philadelphia in February 1799, in Consequence of a Memorial from Certain Natives of Ireland to Congress, Praying a Repeal of the Alien Bill; . . . the Assault on the Committee at St. Mary's Church . . . (Philadelphia, 1799). A record of the trial based upon Duane's pamphlet was later published in Francis Wharton, State Trials of the United States During the Administrations of Washington and Adams (Philadelphia, 1849). The anonymously published Minutes of Examination, Taken in Short Notes--on the Trial of the Rioters, for a Riot and Assault on Wm. Duane, on the 15 May, 1799--trial 28 April, 1801 (Philadelphia, 1801?), is a moving account of the beating he received from the Federalist militia officers.

An Examination of the Question, Who is the Writer of Two Forged Letters Addressed to the President of the United States? Attributed to John Rutledge, Esq., Member of Congress from South Carolina (Washington City, 1803), concludes that the Federalist Rutledge was guilty of forging two letters to Thomas Jefferson in August 1801, which were intended to mislead the President. In The Mississippi Question Fairly Stated, and the Views and Arguments of Those Who Clamor for War, Examined . . . (Philadelphia, 1803), which was published in seven articles in the Aurora in February

1803, Duane argued that the United States should not retaliate against France for its cession of Louisiana from Spain, because France had friendly intentions and because America could best protect her interests through negotiation and a policy of "magnanimous prudence."

The _Report of a Debate in the Senate of the United States, on a Resolution for Recommending to the Legislatures of the Several States, an Amendment . . ., Relative to the Mode of Electing a President and Vice President of the Said States_ ([Philadelphia], 1804), is a documentary record of the debate, without editorial comment. In his _Politics for American Farmers; Being a Series of Tracts, Exhibiting the Blessings of Free Government, as It Is Administered in the United States, Compared with the Boasted Stupendous Fabric of British Monarchy_ . . . (Washington City, 1807), published in the _Aurora_ in early 1807, Duane appealed for a foreign policy of independence from British influence, aimed at peace, neutrality and internal development.

Experience the Test of Government: In Eighteen Essays . . . (Philadelphia, 1807), originally published in the _Aurora_ in 1805 and 1806, is an appeal for reform of the Pennsylvania Constitution of 1790. It responds directly to the issues in the gubernatorial election of 1805, but it is also an important statement of Duane's political philosophy. Duane edited and published six volumes of _The Works of Dr. Benjamin Franklin, in Philosophy, Politics and Morals_ . . . (Philadelphia, 1808-1818), which have not been used in this study. _An Epitome of the Arts and Sciences, Being a Comprehen-_

sive System of the Elementary Parts of an Useful and Polite Education: Adapted to the Use of Schools in the United States . . . (Philadelphia, 1811), is a sample textbook for children, first published as a series in the Aurora, which reveals Duane's interest in educational theory and his great curiosity about natural science. On this subject see also Lowell H. Harrison, ed., "William Duane on Education: a Letter to the Kentucky Assembly, 1822," Pennsylvania Magazine of History and Biography, LXXIII (July 1949), 316-325.

In The Two Americas, Great Britain, and the Holy Alliance (Washington, 1824), Duane argued persuasively that the United States could assert her political and commercial leadership in Latin America without fear of interference from Europe, because the Holy Alliance was unable to act and Great Britain was unwilling to aid the Spanish. Duane's long, descriptive account of A Visit to Colombia, in the years 1822 & 1823, by Laguayra and Caracas, over the Cordillera to Bogota, and Thence by the Magdalena to Cartagena (Philadelphia, 1826), is an often amusing addition to the knowledge of his fascinating life. His last pamphlet, written about 1831 and attributed to "A Disciple of Franklin," is a hard money tract entitled Notes Relating to the Gold and Silver Coinage ([Philadelphia, 1831]).

Duane also published a series of military manuals, which are compilations of useful information rather than original contributions to military theory, and which are of slight interest for his biography. They are: The American Military Library; or Compendium of the Modern Tactics . . ., 2 vols. (Philadelphia, 1807-1809); A Hand Book for Infantry: Containing the First Principles of Military Discipline . . . (Philadelphia, 1813); A Hand Book for Riflemen: Containing the First Principles of Military Discipline . . . 2d ed. (Philadelphia, 1813); A Military Dictionary, or, Explanation of the Several Systems of Discipline of Different Kinds of Troops, Infantry, Artillery, and Cavalry; the Principles of Fortification, and All the Modern Improvements in the Science of Tactics . . . (Philadelphia, 1810); The System of Infantry Discipline; According to the Regulations Established for the Army of the United States (Philadelphia, 1814). The record of his negotiations with the War department after the War of 1812 concerning his expenses as Adjutant General was published by order of the Senate when Congress reversed the judgment against him: 18th Congress, 1st session, Letter from the Secretary of War, Transmitting Information Respecting . . . a Judgment Lately Obtained by the United States . . . Against Colonel William Duane . . . (Washington, 1823).

William John Duane wrote a series of Letters Addressed to the People of Pennsylvania Respecting the Internal Improvement of the Commonwealth; by Means of Roads and Canals (Philadelphia, 1811), which were published in the Aurora shortly before the election of 1810 and which expressed the Old School party's views in favor of a general, state-supported system of transportation development. After his removal as Secretary of the Treasury, William John first explained his refusal to remove the government deposits from the Second Bank of the United States and his subsequent quarrel with President Jackson in a pamphlet of Letters Addressed to the People of the United States, in Vindication of His Conduct (Philadelphia, 1834). This was superseded by the longer, more inclusive Narrative and Correspondence Concerning the Removal of the Deposites, and Occurrences Connected Therewith (Philadelphia, 1838), which includes interesting private correspondence, including fragments of letters from his father, as well as his complete correspondence with President Jackson on the subject.

William John's eldest son and his youngest daughter published volumes of family memoirs. William Duane, II, A Biographical Memoir of William J. Duane (Philadelphia, 1868), contains useful information about the life of the Aurora editor. E[lizabeth] D[uane] Gillespie, A Book of Remembrance (Philadelphia, 1901), does not mention her paternal grandfather, but includes reminiscences about her father and about the Baches, her mother's family.

The published correspondence of contemporary public figures has been useful for various aspects of Duane's biography. For the Federalist and Jeffersonian periods, the following have been helpful: Charles Francis Adams, ed., The Works of John Adams, Second President of the United States . . ., 10 vols. (Boston, 1850-1856); John C. Hamilton, ed., The Works of Alexander Hamilton . . ., 7 vols. (New York, 1850-1851); Paul Leicester Ford, ed., The Writings of Thomas Jefferson, 10 vols. (New York, 1892-1899); Worthington Chauncey Ford, ed., Thomas Jefferson and James Thomson Callender, 1798-1802 (Brooklyn, 1897); Henry Adams, ed., The Writings of Albert Gallatin, 3 vols. (Philadelphia, 1879); Philip S.

Foner, ed., The Complete Writings of Thomas Paine, 2 vols. (New York, 1945). Comments on patronage and other Administration problems during the War of 1812 are found in J. H. Powell, "Some Unpublished Correspondence of John Adams and Richard Rush, 1811-1816," Pennsylvania Magazine of History and Biography, LX, 419-454, LXI, 26-53, 137-164.

Helpful on Clintonian politics, but not directly useful for Duane, are: Everett Somerville Brown, ed., The Missouri Compromise and Presidential Politics, 1820-1825; from the Letters of William Plumer, Junior, Representative from New Hampshire (St. Louis, 1926); Charles R. King, ed., The Life and Correspondence of Rufus King . . ., 6 vols. (New York, 1900). The correspondence of three presidential candidates is illuminating on Pennsylvania's role in the election of 1824: John Spencer Bassett, ed., Correspondence of Andrew Jackson, 7 vols. (Washington, 1926-1935); James F. Hopkins, ed., The Papers of Henry Clay, series in progress, 3 vols. published (Lexington, Ky., 1959-1963); Worthington Chauncey Ford, ed., Writings of John Quincy Adams, 7 vols. (New York, 1913-1917). Interesting comments on William John Duane's troubled role as Secretary of the Treasury are contained in Reginald C. McGrane, ed., The Correspondence of Nicholas Biddle Dealing with National Affairs, 1807-1844 (Boston, 1919).

The memoirs and other writings of Duane's contemporaries are a valuable source for reconstructing the editor's life and times. George Mifflin Dallas, Life and Writings of Alexander James Dallas (Philadelphia, 1871) includes significant correspondence and is informative on many aspects of his political career. John Binns, Recollections of the Life of John Binns . . . (Philadelphia, 1854), is revealing on the personality and attitudes of the New School editor. Margaret Bayard Smith, The First Forty Years of Washington Society . . ., Gaillard Hunt, ed. (New York, 1906), contains the reminiscences of the wife of Samuel Harrison Smith, Duane's successful rival for federal patronage. The memoirs of two Philadelphia Federalists contain a few useful items: Charles Biddle, Autobiography of Charles Biddle, . . . 1745-1821 (Philadelphia, 1883); Samuel Breck, Recollections of Samuel Breck, with Passages from His Note-Books, 1771-1862 (Philadelphia, 1877). Philip S. Klein, ed., "Memoirs of a Senator from Pennsylvania: Jonathan Roberts, 1771-1854," Pennsylvania Magazine of History and Biography, LXI, 442-452, LXII, 64-97, 213-248, 361-409, 502-551, is a published edition of the memoirs contained in the Historical Society of Pennsylvania.

Charles Francis Adams, ed., Memoirs of John Quincy Adams, Comprising Portions of His Diary from 1795 to 1848, 12 vols. (Philadelphia, 1874-1877), is a richly rewarding source on the politics of the Monroe administration; it contains many unflattering comments on Duane, and records in detail his unsuccessful effort to obtain a commission to Latin America. John C. Fitzpatrick, ed., The Autobiography of Martin Van Buren, American Historical Association, Annual Report, 1918, II (Washington, 1920), is important on the relationships of William John Duane and of Stephen Simpson to the Jackson administration. Amos Kendall, Autobiography of Amos Kendall (Boston, 1872) is useful on his controversy with W. J. Duane over the removal of the deposits issue.

Several works by contemporaries influenced or reflected on Duane's thinking on the subject of banking and credit. During the debate on recharter of the first Bank of the United States, the most important of these were [Erich Bollman], Paragraphs on Banks, 2d ed., improved (Philadelphia, 1811), and two pamphlets by Mathew Carey: Desultory Reflections upon the Ruinous Consequences of a Non-Renewal of the Charter of the Bank of the United States, 2d ed. (Philadelphia, 1810); Letters to Dr. Adam Seybert, Representative in Congress for the City of Philadelphia, on the Subject of the Renewal of the Charter of the Bank of the United States, 2d ed. (Philadelphia, 1811). [Condy Raguet], An Inquiry into the Causes of the Present State of the Circulating Medium of the United States (Philadelphia, 1815), is the earliest published expression of his conservative views on paper money and credit, which he acted upon as a state senator from Philadelphia during the Panic of 1819. Stephen Simpson, The Working Man's Manual: A New Theory of Political Economy, on the Principle of Production the Source of Wealth . . .(Philadelphia, 1831), is the fullest statement of the economic views which he developed earlier as "Brutus" in the Aurora; it is indispensable for understanding the philosophy of the Old School Democratic party during the anti-caucus period.

The military situation in Philadelphia throughout the War of 1812 is well described in A Brief Sketch of the Military Operations on the Delaware during the Late War . . . (Philadelphia, 1820), written anonymously by Condy Raguet. Colonel Duane's unfortunate clash with the state militiamen encamped near Philadelphia at Marcus Hook is fully described and documented in Louis Bache, defendant, _Proceedings of a General Court Martial_ . . . _Marcus Hook_ . . . _October 1814; Whole Evidence and Documents_ (Philadelphia, 1815). A few points of interest on the local military situation are found in Charles J. Ingersoll, _Historical Sketch of the Second War Between the United States of America, and Great Britain_ . . ., 2 vols. (Philadelphia, 1849).

Other contemporary works of infrequent use are noted in the text. Some of more than routine interest should be mentioned. The anonymous _History of Two Acts, Entitled An Act for the Safety and Preservation of His Majesty's Person and Government Against Treasonable and Seditious Practices and Attempts, and an Act for the More Effectually Preventing Seditious Meetings and Assemblies_ . . . (London, 1796), is a very full account of the events surrounding the suppression of civil liberties in Britain in 1795, including a report on the London Corresponding Society's protest meeting chaired by Duane. [Jesse Higgins], _Sampson Against the Philistines, or the Reformation of Lawsuits_ . . ., 2d ed. (Philadelphia, 1805), is the most complete statement of the case for simplified local justice, which was agitated in Pennsylvania throughout Thomas McKean's administration and became the primary issue of the gubernatorial campaign of 1805. Duane published the pamphlet and supported its views, intellectually if not emotionally. [Richard Bache], _Notes on Colombia, Taken in the Years 1822-3; With an Itinerary of the Route from Caracas to Bogota_ . . . (Philadelphia, 1827), is an informative, readable supplement to Duane's narrative of the journey and includes material not contained in his step-father's book.

Pennsylvania Archives, 4th series, 12 vols. (Harrisburg, 1900-1902), comprises the "Papers of the Governors," including their annual addresses to the legislature. Pennsylvania Archives, 6th series, 15 vols. (Harrisburg, 1906-1907), contains a wide variety of useful information on the state militia.

Travel books by persons visiting Philadelphia are helpful in recreating the social structure of the city. Two accounts by Englishmen, Augustus John Foster, Jeffersonian America. Notes on the United States of America Collected in the Years 1805-6-7 and 11-12 by Sir Augustus John Foster, Bart., Richard Beale Davis, ed. (San Marino, Calif., 1954), and Charles William Janson, The Stranger in America (London, 1807), contain hostile commentaries on Duane and other Democrats. Henry Bradshaw Fearon, Sketches of America, 2d ed. (London, 1818), has revealing material on election techniques in Philadelphia. James Mease, The Picture of Philadelphia, Giving an Account of Its Origin, Increase and Improvements in Arts, Sciences, Manufactures, Commerce and Revenue . . . (Philadelphia, 1811), is an excellent introduction to the economy and to the social life and institutions of the city. The cynical humor of [Robert Waln], The Hermit in America, on a Visit to Philadelphia . . . (Philadelphia, 1819), provides numerous insights into the politics and society of Philadelphia. Thomas Brothers, The United States of North America As They Are . . . (London, 1840), which has not been directly useful for this study, contains fascinating commentaries on Joel Sutherland and on Stephen Girard.

Other travel accounts which are of some use in constructing

a picture of Philadelphia are: John Bristed, *America and Her Resources* . . . (London, 1818); William Cobbett, *A Year's Residence in the United States of America*, 3 parts (London, 1818-1819); James Flint, *Letters from America* . . ., Reuben G. Thwaites, ed., *Early Western Travels, 1748-1846*, IX (Cleveland, 1904); [Henry Cogswell Knight], *Letters from the South and West* . . . (Boston, 1824); John Palmer, *Journal of Travels in the United States of North America, and in Lower Canada Performed in the Year 1817* . . . (London, 1818); Adlard Welby, *A Visit to North America and the English Settlements in Illinois, with a Winter Residence at Philadelphia* . . ., Thwaites, ed., *Early Western Travels*, XII (Cleveland, 1905); Thomas Wilson, *Picture of Philadelphia for 1824* (Philadelphia, 1823). The Historical Society of Pennsylvania holds a complete collection of Philadelphia street directories for these years, which ordinarily include the occupations of the persons listed and which are a highly useful source of information about individuals and about local institutions.

BIOGRAPHIES

There is no biographical study of William Duane. An article by Allan C. Clark, "William Duane," *Records of the Columbia Historical Society*, IX (1906), 14-62, is a good short introduction to his life in the United States. Frank W. Leach published a genealogical article on the Duane family in the Philadelphia *North American*, 8 Dec. 1907.

A biography of outstanding usefulness for all aspects of

national politics in the Jeffersonian era is Irving Brant, James Madison, 6 vols. (Indianapolis, 1941-1961). Two biographies by Raymond Walters, Jr., Albert Gallatin: Jeffersonian Financier and Diplomat (New York, 1957), and Alexander James Dallas, Lawyer-Politician-Financier, 1759-1817 (Philadelphia, 1943), are indispensable for understanding the political role of these nationally prominent Pennsylvanians. Henry Adams, The Life of Albert Gallatin (Philadelphia, 1879), is still highly useful on political matters, especially on the feud with Duane. Adams' interpretation is intensely hostile to the editor.

The biographies of other national leaders are helpful in clarifying various issues and events which involved the editor. These include: Page Smith, John Adams, 2 vols. (Garden City, N.Y., 1962); Broadus Mitchell, Alexander Hamilton, 2 vols. (New York, 1957-1962); John C. Miller, Alexander Hamilton: Portrait in Paradox (New York, 1959); Nathan Schachner, Thomas Jefferson, a Biography (New York, 1951); Adrienne Koch, Jefferson and Madison; the Great Collaboration (New York, 1950). Alfred Owen Aldridge, Man of Reason: the Life of Thomas Paine (London, 1960), contains relevant material on his later years in America, in which he contributed essays and letters to the Aurora. Henry Adams, John Randolph (Boston, 1882) is valuable on the presidential election campaign of 1808. Charles H. Ambler, Thomas Ritchie: a Study in Virginia Politics (Richmond, 1913), provides occasional insights into the political issues of the Jefferson administration, on which Duane and the editor of the Richmond Enquirer were frequently in agreement.

There are several studies of contemporary Pennsylvanians which contribute to Duane's story. Bernard Fay, _The Two Franklins: Fathers of American Democracy_ (Boston, 1933), contains relevant information on Benjamin Franklin Bache and on his widow Margaret, Duane's second wife. Dumas Malone, _The Public Life of Thomas Cooper, 1783-1839_ (New Haven, 1926), describes Cooper's role in defending the editor against the Senate's charge of seditious libel. Some material on the Quid-Democratic rivalry in Philadelphia is found in Frederick B. Tolles, _George Logan of Philadelphia_ (New York, 1953), and in James A. Peeling, The Public Life of Thomas McKean, 1734-1817 (unpublished Ph.D. dissertation, University of Chicago, 1929), which is weak in interpretation. George Irvin Oeste, _John Randolph Clay, America's First Career Diplomat_ (Philadelphia, 1966), contains brief biographical information on Congressman Joseph Clay, his father.

There is no study of Mathew Carey which tells the story of his political activities or adequately describes his economic views before he began the promotion of the tariff. Of some use is Kenneth W. Rowe, _Mathew Carey: a Study in American Economic Development, The Johns Hopkins University Studies in Historical and Political Science_, series LI, number 4 (Baltimore, 1933). J. H. Powell, _Richard Rush: Republican Diplomat, 1780-1859_ (Philadelphia, 1942), includes material on his political apprenticeship as a Philadelphia Snyderite. Important correspondence is published in William M. Meigs, _The Life of Charles Jared Ingersoll_, 2d ed. (Philadelphia, 1900).

For the War of 1812, biographies of military figures are helpful on a number of specific questions. Of particular interest are: James Ripley Jacobs, Tarnished Warrior: Major General James Wilkinson (New York, 1938); Thomas Robson Hay, "General James Wilkinson--the Last Phase," Louisiana Historical Quarterly, XIX, No. 2 (Apr. 1936), 407-435; Freeman Cleaves, Old Tippecanoe: William Henry Harrison and His Time (New York, 1939).

The politics of the anti-caucus and Jacksonian periods are illuminated by many biographical studies. Leland Winfield Meyer, The Life and Times of Colonel Richard M. Johnson of Kentucky (New York, 1932), contains useful background information, but nothing on his friendship with Duane. Thomas P. Govan, Nicholas Biddle, Nationalist and Public Banker, 1786-1844 (Chicago, 1959), is an excellent biography, containing relevant material on his early political ambitions and his association with the Family party. Edward Pessen, "The Ideology of Stephen Simpson, Upper Class Champion of the Early Philadelphia Workingmen's Movement," Pennsylvania History, XXII (Oct. 1955), 328-340, is a good introduction to Simpson's thinking, which does not discuss his early experience as "Brutus."

There is no modern biography of DeWitt Clinton. Dorothie Bobbé, DeWitt Clinton, new edition (Port Washington, Long Island, N.Y., 1962), contains useful background information, but is severely limited on political questions. Far more informative on New York affairs and their relation to the national scene is Robert V. Remini, Martin Van Buren and the Making of the Democratic Party (New York, 1959). Useful on the presidential election of 1824 in

Pennsylvania are: J. E. D. Shipp, *Giant Days or The Life and Times of William H. Crawford* (Americus, Ga., 1909); William M. Meigs, *The Life of John Caldwell Calhoun*, 2 vols. (New York, 1917); Charles M. Wiltse, *John C. Calhoun, Nationalist, 1782-1828* (Indianapolis, 1944); James Parton, *Life of Andrew Jackson*, 3 vols. (New York, 1860).

OTHER BOOKS AND ARTICLES

Secondary sources which provide a background for understanding Duane's experience in India and in Ireland and England are cited in chapters I and II. James Morton Smith, *Freedom's Fetters: the Alien and Sedition Laws and American Civil Liberties* (Ithaca, 1956), contains an excellent, comprehensive chapter on the two attempted prosecutions of Duane for seditious libel. John C. Miller, *Crisis in Freedom: the Alien and Sedition Acts* (Boston, 1951), is a less complete but readable account. Leonard W. Levy, "Liberty and the First Amendment, 1790-1800," *American Historical Review*, LXVIII (Oct. 1962), 22-37, and *Legacy of Suppression: Freedom of Speech and Press in Early American History* (Cambridge, Mass., 1960), are valuable contributions on the complex problem of America's legal inheritance from Britain. Duane's mind was formed in the era of political thought which has been brilliantly described in Robert R. Palmer, *The Age of the Democratic Revolution: a Political History of Europe and America, 1760-1800*, 2 vols. (Princeton, 1964). Other useful studies on the 1790s are: Noble E. Cunningham, Jr., *The Jeffersonian Republicans: the Formation of Party Organization*,

1789-1801 (Chapel Hill, 1957); Harry M. Tinkcom, The Republicans and Federalists in Pennsylvania, 1790-1801: a Study in National Stimulus and Local Response (Harrisburg, 1950).

In the Jeffersonian period, the detailed state study by Sanford W. Higginbotham, The Keystone in the Democratic Arch: Pennsylvania Politics, 1800-1816 (Harrisburg, 1952), is the only scholarship on Duane's political activities after the election of 1800 and is indispensable for his biography. The Republican party's experience on such matters as federal patronage and relations with the press has been thoroughly treated for the first time in the recent study by Noble E. Cunningham, Jr., The Jeffersonian Republicans in Power: Party Operations, 1801-1809 (Chapel Hill, 1963). His article "Who Were the Quids?," Mississippi Valley Historical Review, L (Sept. 1963), 252-263, is a good introduction for students of Jeffersonian politics. Leonard W. Levy, Jefferson & Civil Liberties: the Darker Side (Cambridge, Mass., 1963), is an interesting and provocative reassessment. Although dealing with a different place and a later time, Lee Benson, The Concept of Jacksonian Democracy: New York as a Test Case (Princeton, 1961), is highly suggestive on the subject of etnnic devisions in American party politics.

Judicial reform in Pennsylvania is thoroughly treated in Higginbotham's study, but two older, uninterpretative articles are still somewhat useful: Glenn Leroy Bushey, "William Duane, Crusader for Judicial Reform," Pennsylvania History, V (July 1938), 141-156; Elizabeth K. Henderson, "The Attack on the Judiciary in Pennsylvania,

1800-1810," *Pennsylvania Magazine of History and Biography*, LXI (Apr. 1937), 113-136. Other useful studies for the Jeffersonian period are: Henry Adams, *History of the United States of America During the Administrations of Thomas Jefferson and James Madison*, 9 vols. (New York, 1889-1891); Frank L. Mott, *Jefferson and the Press* (Baton Rouge, 1943); Leonard D. White, *The Jeffersonians: a Study in Administrative History, 1801-1829* (New York, 1951).

There are many valuable studies on banking and economic policy. The comprehensive study by Bray Hammond, *Banks and Politics in America from the Revolution to the Civil War* (Princeton, 1957), is indispensable. Also helpful in answering questions about banking theory in Duane's era are two works by Fritz Redlich, *Essays in American Economic History: Eric Bollman and Studies in Banking* (New York, 1944), and *The Molding of American Banking: Men and Ideas*, 2 parts (New York, 1947). The Congressional enactment of a new national bank charter is treated in Ralph C. H. Catterall, *The Second Bank of the United States* (Chicago, 1903).

An excellent, richly detailed account of the development of banking in Pennsylvania is John Thom Holdsworth, *Financing an Empire: History of Banking in Pennsylvania*, 2 vols. (Chicago, 1928). Special studies which provide a useful background are: Anna Jacobson Schwartz, "The Beginning of Competitive Banking in Philadelphia, 1782-1809," *Journal of Political Economy*, LV (Oct. 1947), 417-431; Nicholas B. Wainwright, *History of the Philadelphia National Bank: a Century and a Half of Philadelphia Banking* (Philadelphia, 1953); Kenneth L. Brown, "Stephen Girard's Bank," *Pennsylvania Magazine of History and Biography*, LXVI (Jan. 1942), 29-55.

Louis Hartz, Economic Policy and Democratic Thought: Pennsylvania, 1776-1860 (Cambridge, Mass., 1948), which deals largely with the years after 1830, is a seminal work, the essential starting point for further scholarship. Joseph Dorfman, The Economic Mind in American Civilization, 1606-1865, 5 vols. (New York, 1946-1959), is a valuable source of reference on the thought of Duane's contemporaries. Louis M. Sears, "Philadelphia and the Embargo of 1808," American Historical Association, Annual Report, 1920 (Washington, 1925), 251-263, and Jefferson and the Embargo (Durham, 1927), describe the economic effects of the trade moratorium.

Two good studies on the economic policy of Pennsylvania are: Malcolm Rogers Eiselen, The Rise of Pennsylvania Protectionism (Philadelphia, 1932), and James Weston Livingood, The Philadelphia-Baltimore Trade Rivalry, 1780-1860 (Harrisburg, 1947). On internal improvements, Joseph A. Durrenberger, Turnpikes: a Study of the Toll Roard Movement in the Middle Atlantic States and Maryland (Valdosta, Ga., 1931), and the brief study by Wilbur C. Plummer, The Road Policy of Pennsylvania (Philadelphia, 1925), are somewhat useful. The best general study on this subject is George Rogers Taylor, The Transportation Revolution, 1815-1860 (New York, 1951).

Among the many helpful books on the War of 1812, a few are particularly valuable for Duane's biography. Roger H. Brown, The Republic in Peril: 1812 (New York, 1964), is an outstanding work of political history, on the internal division in the United States over the decision for war against Britain. Bradford Perkins, Prologue to War: England and the United States, 1805-1812 (Berkeley,

1961), makes extensive use of the Aurora to illustrate its theme that irrational Anglophobia was an important cause of the war. The sources of Duane's military ideas are illuminated by two histories of European military theory, Basil H. Liddell Hart, The Ghost of Napoleon (London, 1933), and Robert S. Quimby, The Background of Napoleonic Warfare: the Theory of Military Tactics in Eighteenth-Century France (New York, 1957).

On American relations with Latin America, the best general study is Samuel Flagg Bemis, John Quincy Adams and the Foundations of American Foreign Policy (New York, 1949). Joseph Byrne Lockey, Pan Americanism: Its Beginnings (New York, 1920), contains an excellent account of the Amelia island incident, which preoccupied the Aurora in early 1818. Hyman German, "The Philadelphia 'Aurora' on Latin American Affairs," Pennsylvania History, VIII (Apr. 1941), 110-130, surveys the paper's views on the subject between 1817 and 1820. Sanford W. Higginbotham has published an article on "Philadelphia Commerce with Latin America, 1820-1830," ibid., IX (Oct. 1942), 252-266.

There are several important studies of postwar politics. On the conflicts within the amorphous state Democratic party during the 1820s, Philip S. Klein, Pennsylvania Politics, 1817-1832: a Game Without Rules (Philadelphia, 1940), is authoritative and indispensable. There is no adequate study of state politics in the anti-caucus period. James A. Kehl, Ill Feeling in the Era of Good Feeling: Western Pennsylvania Political Battles, 1815-1825 (Pittsburgh, 1956), which follows Klein in political interpretation, provides valuable social and economic information for the counties west of the Allegheny mountains. Murray N. Rothbard, The Panic of 1819, Reactions and Policies (New York, 1962), which has an anti-hard money bias, is an informative account of emergency legislation and reform proposals throughout the country. Northern public opinion on slavery restriction is thoroughly treated in Glover Moore, The Missouri Controversy, 1819-1821 (Lexington, Ky., 1953). Other useful studies are: George Dangerfield, The Era of Good Feelings (New York, 1952); Russell J. Ferguson, Early Western Pennsylvania Politics (Pittsburgh, 1938); Shaw Livermore, The Twilight of Federalism; the Disintegration of the Federalist Party, 1815-1830 (Princeton, 1962).

Clintonian politics is a murky subject, suffering from the lack of a scholarly biography of DeWitt Clinton. The best study is still Jabez D. Hammond, The History of Political Parties in the State of New York, from the Ratification of the Federal Constitution to December 1840, 2 vols. (Albany, 1842). Dixon Ryan Fox, The Decline of Aristocracy in the Politics of New York (New York, 1918), is still useful despite its simplistic, pro-Bucktail interpretation. The revisionist study by Alvin Kass, Politics in New York State, 1800-1830 (Syracuse, 1965), is weak in analysis, but contributes new information on the Clintonians. Other useful studies are: Gustavus Myers, The History of Tammany Hall (New York, 1917); Robert V. Remini, "New York and the Presidential Election of 1816," New York History, XXXI (July 1950), 308-324; Edward K. Spann, "The Souring of Good Feelings: John W. Taylor and the Speakership Election of 1821," ibid., XLI (Oct. 1960), 379-399.

Histories of the city of Philadelphia and its inhabitants are highly useful. On political matters, the most helpful study is John Thomas Scharf and Thompson Westcott, History of Philadelphia, 1609-1884, 3 vols. (Philadelphia, 1884). John F. Watson, Watson's Annals of Philadelphia, and Pennsylvania, in the Olden Time, 3 vols. (Philadelphia, 1887), which was completed in 1842, is rich in local information. Nathaniel Burt, The Perennial Philadelphians: the Anatomy of an American Aristocracy (Boston, 1963), is a scholarly and enjoyable social history of the elite. Henry Simpson, The Lives of Eminent Philadelphians, Now Deceased, Collected from Original and Authentic Sources (Philadelphia, 1859), includes a short biography of Stephen Simpson. A valuable reference work on federal patronage appointments is John Hill Martin, Martin's Bench and Bar of Philadelphia (Philadelphia, 1883).

Other city histories which are occasionally useful are: Edward P. Allinson and Boies Penrose, Philadelphia, 1681-1887: A History of Municipal Development (Philadelphia, 1887); Horace K. Lippincott, Early Philadelphia: Its People, Life and Progress (Philadelphia, 1917). Works which are helpful in identifying persons and places in Philadelphia include: John H. Campbell, History of the Friendly Sons of St. Patrick and of the Hibernian Society for the Relief of Emigrants from Ireland, 1771-1892 (Philadelphia, 1892); William Bucke Campbell, Old Towns and Districts of Philadelphia: an Address Delivered before the City History Society of Philadelphia, Feb. 26, 1941 (Philadelphia, 1942), HSP; Joseph Jackson, America's Most Historic Highway, Market Street, Philadelphia

(Philadelphia, 1926); Abraham Ritter, *Philadelphia and Her Merchants, as Constituted Fifty & Seventy Years Ago* . . . (Philadelphia, 1860).